WADSWORTH
CENGAGE Learning

The River Reader, Eleventh Edition

Joseph F. Trimmer

Publisher: Monica Eckman

Acquisitions Editor: Kate Derrick

Development Editor: Kathy Sands-Boehmer

Assistant Editor: Danielle Warchol

Editorial Assistant: Marjorie Cross

Media Editor: Janine Tangney

Marketing Manager: Melissa Holt

Marketing Coordinator: Brittany Blais

Marketing Communications Manager: Linda Yip

Content Project Manager: Aimee Chevrette Bear

Art Director: Marissa Falco

Print Buyer: Betsy Donaghey

Rights Acquisition Specialist: Alexandra Ricciardi

VP, Director, Advanced and Elective Products Program: Alison Zetterquist

Editorial Coordinator, Advanced and Elective Products Program: Jean Woy

Production Service: MPS Limited

Cover Designer: Gary Ragaglia

Cover Image: iStockphoto/Doxa

Compositor: MPS Limited

For product information and technology assistance, contact us at
**Cengage Learning Customer & Sales Support,
1-800-354-9706**

For permission to use material from this text or product, submit all requests online at
www.cengage.com/permissions.
Further permissions questions can be emailed to **permissionrequest@cengage.com.**

Library of Congress Control Number: 2012938711

ISBN-13: 978-1-285-17060-2
ISBN-10: 1-285-17060-1

Wadsworth
20 Channel Center Street
Boston, MA 02210
USA

Cengage Learning is a leading provider of customized learning solutions with office locations around the globe, including Singapore, the United Kingdom, Australia, Mexico, Brazil, and Japan. Locate your local office at **international.cengage.com/region**

Cengage Learning products are represented in Canada by Nelson Education, Ltd.

For your course and learning solutions, visit
www.cengage.com

Cengage Learning products are represented in high schools by Holt McDougal, a division of Houghton Mifflin Harcourt.

* "Advanced Placement" and "AP" are registered trademarks of the College Board, which was not involved in the production of, and does not endorse, this product.

Printed in the United States of America
1 2 3 4 5 6 7 16 15 14 13 12

The RIVER READER

ELEVENTH EDITION

Joseph F. Trimmer

Ball State University

WADSWORTH
CENGAGE Learning·

Australia • Brazil • Japan • Korea • Mexico • Singapore • Spain • United Kingdom •
United States

CONTENTS

One of the twentieth century's most famous novelists creates a
fantasy of seventeenth-century life to dramatize the obstacles faced
by talented women of that time.

Visual Strategies: A Visual Essay

CHAPTER 1

NARRATION AND DESCRIPTION 35

CHAPTER 2

PROCESS ANALYSIS   99

CHAPTER 3

COMPARISON AND CONTRAST   149

CHAPTER 4
DIVISION AND CLASSIFICATION   199

CHAPTER 5

DEFINITION   277

CHAPTER 6

CAUSE AND EFFECT   327

CHAPTER 7

PERSUASION AND ARGUMENT   389

A Debate About Racism

In this landmark speech rich with metaphor and allusion, the most
famous civil rights leader of the 1960s urges his listeners to share his
vision of freedom and equality.

An Ivy League graduate whose parents were poor Chinese immigrants defines the American Dream not as achieving material wealth
but as offering freedom, opportunity, and responsibility.

A Debate About Animal Rights

A British animal-rights activist draws an analogy between animals
and slaves to support her contention that "the relationship between
humans to other animals is one of unremitting exploitation."

A professional dog trainer argues that many animal-rights activists
are sentimentalists who have only a shallow conception of animals'
real needs and satisfactions.

A Debate About the Death Penalty

A journalist and critic known for his outrageous commentary and
irreverent opinions claims that the only valid objection to capital
punishment is that we can't carry it out quickly enough.

CHAPTER 8

RESOURCES FOR WRITING THE FAMILY: A CASEBOOK 463

CHAPTER 9

USING AND DOCUMENTING
SOURCES   569

THEMATIC TABLE OF CONTENTS

Women

Work

PREFACE

For almost three decades, *The River Reader* has set the standard for rhetorical readers. Its explanations of purpose, audience, and strategies have enabled a generation of students to read prose models effectively and to write their own essays successfully. Indeed, its thorough coverage and thoughtful advice about many issues and problems embedded in the reading and writing processes have established this book as one of the core texts in the college composition curriculum.

The eleventh edition of *The River Reader*, like its predecessors, presents essays by acknowledged masters of prose style, including George Orwell, Flannery O'Connor, and Alice Walker, along with many new voices, such as Brian Doyle, Terry Tempest Williams, and Scott Russell Sanders. Almost one-third of the selections are new to this edition. As always, introductions, readings, study questions, and writing assignments are clear, creative, and cogent.

THE PURPOSE OF *THE RIVER READER*

The first seven chapters in this reader are arranged in a sequence familiar to most writing teachers. Beginning with narration and description, moving through the five expository patterns, and ending with persuasion and argument, these chapters group readings according to traditional writing strategies.

The readings within each chapter have been chosen to illustrate what the chapter introductions say they illustrate: there are no strange hybrids or confusing models. Within each chapter, the selections are arranged in an ascending order of complexity. The ultimate purpose of *The River Reader* is to produce good writing. For that reason, the writing assignments in this book are presented after each selection. The four assignments after each selection prompt students to analyze, practice, argue, and synthesize both the rhetorical strategies and the content of the selection.

THE ENDURING FEATURES OF *THE RIVER READER*

At the core of *The River Reader* is the desire to assist students with their reading and writing by helping them see the interaction between the two processes.

- The **connection between the reading and writing process** is highlighted in the Introduction. The familiar terminology of *purpose, audience,* and *strategies* provide a framework for the Introduction and for subsequent study questions and writing assignments.
- **Guidelines for Reading an Essay** is paired with **Guidelines for Determining Your Purpose, Guidelines for Analyzing Your Audience**, and **Guidelines for Selecting Your Strategy** to enhance and advance the students' understanding of the reading/writing connection.
- An **annotated essay** by Virginia Woolf, "Shakespeare's Sister," demonstrates how one reader responds to reading by writing.
- A **student essay**, Kristie Ferguson's "The Scenic Route," is illustrated in its various stages of development. The essay, which focuses on one student's early experiences as a writer, is followed by commentary on what the student discovered about her writing.

- To demonstrate the increasing importance of visual literacy in our culture, each chapter features a **visual text**—such as a cartoon, picture, or advertisement. Each of these texts is followed by an assignment that encourages students to look more closely at the image, discuss its significance to the chapter's rhetorical strategy, and write about what they have discovered.

- In addition, the Introduction includes a four-page color insert that illustrates the kind of **visual graphics** students are likely to encounter in their reading and might decide to use to enrich the information they are presenting in their writing.

- An **extended Introduction** now provides more in-depth discussions of the reading and writing processes, including additional coverage of *purpose, audience,* and *strategies.*

- *New!* Each chapter has been enriched by at least one **new** selection.

- A **Points to Remember** list concludes each chapter introduction and provides a convenient summary of the essential tasks and techniques of each strategy.

- A **short story** concludes each chapter to provide an interesting perspective on a particular writing strategy and to give students opportunities to broaden their reading skills. *New* to this edition are Paule Marshall's "To Da-du, in Memoriam" and Ursula K. Le Guin's "Those Who Walk Away from Omelas."

- The chapter introductions to **Cause and Effect** and **Persuasion and Argument** have been substantially rewritten.

- **Study questions and writing assignments** have been thoroughly revised throughout the text.

- Selections in the **Persuasion and Argument** chapter are paired to present different perspectives on issues such as race, animal rights, and capital punishment.

- *New!* **A new case study, "The Family,"** presents variations on the theme of the family. The eight essays and one short story, which are arranged to repeat the patterns presented in the seven rhetorical chapters, illustrate how such strategies enable a writer to investigate a theme from a variety of perspectives.

- *New!* An eight-page **color photographic essay,** "Images of the Family," emphasizes the power of images to evoke ideas and insights. Each image is followed by a writing assignment that encourages students to connect what they see with what they read and plan to write.
- A **Thematic Table of Contents** is provided for teachers who wish to organize their course by themes or issues.
- Chapter 9, **"Using and Documenting Sources,"** provides expanded instruction on using and documenting sources in the format of the latest Modern Language Association (MLA) style. Special attention is given to the problem of plagiarism and the citation of electronic sources.
- *New!* Chapter 9 concludes with an **Annotated Student Research Paper,** Tricia Johnson's "Pixels or Pages: The Textbook Debate," which uses both print and electronic sources.
- This edition includes a compact **Rhetorical Glossary** that defines the key terms used throughout the rhetorical information provided in the text.

SUPPLEMENTS FOR *THE RIVER READER*

The River Reader eleventh edition Online Instructor's Resource Manual is designed to give instructors maximum flexibility in planning and customizing their courses and provides an abundance of materials. This manual helps instructors prepare for class more quickly and effectively with such resources as discussion suggestions and suggested answers for questions on the text readings. The IRM can be found on the password-protected instructor's Companion Website.

The River Reader complimentary-access Companion Website contains an extensive library of interactive exercises and animations that cover grammar, mechanics, and punctuation. It also includes a complete library of student papers and a section on avoiding plagiarism.

xxii PREFACE

ACKNOWLEDGMENTS

I am grateful to the following writing instructors who have provided extensive commentary on *The River Reader* for this edition: Jeffrey Canino, SUNY–New Paltz; Sharynn Owens Etheridge-Logan, Claflin University; Hanke Galmish, Green River Community College; Mike Hampton, University of Cincinnati; Fred Kille, Western Nevada College; John Peruggia, University of Delaware; Patricia Rudden, New York City College of Technology; Mitali Wong, Claflin University; and numerous other reviewers from earlier editions.

I am grateful to my students, Kristie Ferguson and Tricia Johnson, for allowing me to reprint their work.

A special thanks to my acquisitions editor, Kate Derrick, and my developmental editor, Kathy Sands-Boehmer. And, of course, my debt to all my students is ongoing.

INTRODUCTION

People who do well in college are nearly always good readers and good writers. They have to read well to absorb and
evaluate the wealth of information they encounter online and
in articles and books, and they have to write well to show that
they are thinking and learning. In this book, we try to help
you connect your reading and writing and become skillful at
both crafts, for they are complementary skills, and you can
master both of them through practice.

THE ACTIVE READING PROCESS

Although you have already discovered ways of reading that no
doubt work for you, there is a big difference between being
a passive reader—a reader who simply consumes, uncriti-
cally, another's writing—and an active reader—a reader who
questions, challenges, and reflects on the way another writer

1

addresses a subject and develops its interlocking topics. By practicing the following steps in the reading process, you will learn to interact effectively with a text.

- *Step 1.* When you are reading a piece of writing you need to master, go over it quickly at first to get the main idea and the flavor of the piece. Just enjoy it for what you are learning. Unless you get lost or confused, don't go back to reread or stop to analyze the writer's argument.
- *Step 2.* Now slow down. If you are reading from a book or magazine you don't own, photocopy the text. If you are reading on the Internet, print the document. Go back over your paper copy, this time underlining or highlighting key points and jotting notes in the margins. You may want to develop a scheme for such annotations, such as the one illustrated in the sample annotated analysis of Virginia Woolf's essay "Shakespeare's Sister" on pages 7 to 10, where summaries of the main points are written in the *left* margin, and questions or objections are written in the *right* margin.
- *Step 3.* On a separate piece of paper or in a separate file, jot down your responses to the reading. What appeals to you about the writer's ideas? What puzzles you? What elements in the piece remind you of some of your own experiences? How does this text relate to other texts you have read? Remember there's not necessarily one "right" reaction to what you are reading. Each reader brings different experiences to reading a piece of writing. So every response will be individual, and each reader will have a slightly different perspective. The notes you take on your reading will help you if you go on to write about the piece or discuss it in class.

READING TO BECOME A BETTER WRITER

Many people have learned to improve their performance in a sport or activity by watching a professional at work and then patterning their activity on that of the professional.

In the same way, you can sharpen your reading and writing skills by paying attention to how professional writers practice their craft. This book is organized around that assumption. Thus you will find tips about what strategies to look for as you read these authors and questions that give you insight into their writing process. Here are three things to look for:

- *What is the writer's purpose?* What does he or she want to accomplish? How does the writer communicate that purpose? For instance, in "Shakespeare's Sister," Woolf's purpose is to challenge the age-old claim that women must be, inherently, less creative than men because there have been so few famous women writers, painters, or musicians.
- *Who is the writer's audience?* What assumptions does the writer make about what the audience knows or needs to know? Woolf's immediate audience—those who first read *A Room of One's Own* (1929)—were people interested in the arts and familiar with Shakespeare's plays and poems. Certainly Woolf assumed that many of her readers were women who did not need to be convinced about the significance of her argument.
- *What are the writer's strategies?* How does the writer organize his or her information? Does he or she tell stories, give examples, analyze evidence, or assert claims? Woolf creates a narrative to dramatize her points, knowing that she will arouse sympathy for her imaginary character, Judith Shakespeare. She also uses other strategies, such as comparison and contrast and cause and effect, to advance her argument.

When you get in the habit of asking questions about a writer's purpose, audience, and strategies, you will begin to understand how writers work and begin to master some elements of their craft for your own writing.

READING *THE RIVER READER*

Before you begin to read essays from a chapter of *The River Reader*, look over the introduction to that section to get a feel for what to expect. The introduction will explain the purpose, audience, and strategies employed in a particular writing pattern. It will also suggest how you might incorporate these strategies into your own writing. Each introduction concludes with a boxed list of Points to Remember.

Before each essay is a biographical headnote that explains the author's background and work. Following each essay is a set of questions to help you analyze the writer's *purpose, audience,* and *strategies.* After this set of questions are four kinds of writing assignments:

1. *Analysis:* This assignment asks you to analyze how the writer exploits the features of a particular writing pattern.
2. *Practice:* This assignment encourages you to use the strategies you have studied to write a similar kind of essay.
3. *Argument:* This assignment invites you to extend or contest the argument embedded in the essay.
4. *Synthesis:* This assignment urges you to research additional sources on the theme explored in the essay and then use them to advance your own thesis about that theme.

Each chapter concludes with a short story that evokes the writing strategy illustrated in the essays. After each story, a Comment discusses some of its main features.

Finally, at the end of the introduction each chapter, you will find a *visual text* and a series of questions and writing assignments that will enable you to see how a particular writing pattern can be represented in graphic form.

On pages 5 to 6, we provide you with Guidelines for Reading an Essay, and after those guidelines you will find Woolf's "Shakespeare's Sister," complete with one reader's annotations and response, a set of questions For Study and Discussion, and four assignments For Writing and Research.

Guidelines for Reading an Essay

I. READ THE ESSAY THROUGH CAREFULLY

a. Consider the title and what expectations it raises.
b. Note when the essay was written and where it was first published.
c. Look at the author information in the headnote, and consider what important leads that information gives you about what to expect from the essay.
d. Now go back over the essay, underlining or highlighting key ideas and jotting down any questions you have.

II. THINK ABOUT YOUR RESPONSE TO THE ESSAY

a. Note what you liked and/or disliked about it, and analyze why you had that reaction.
b. Decide what questions you have after reading the essay.
c. Think about the issues the essay raises for you.
d. What else have you read that suggests or refutes the issues in the essay?

III. WRITE A BRIEF STATEMENT OF WHAT SEEMS TO BE THE AUTHOR'S PURPOSE

a. Consider how the information about the author's life and experience may account for that purpose.
b. Decide to what extent you think the author achieved his or her purpose.

IV. AS FAR AS YOU CAN, IDENTIFY THE AUTHOR'S ORIGINAL AUDIENCE

a. Make a guess about what those readers' interests are.
b. Compare your interests and experiences to those of the readers the author had in mind when writing the essay, and decide how similar or different they are.

V. LOOK AT THE STRATEGIES THE WRITER USES TO ENGAGE AND HOLD THE READER'S INTEREST

a. Look at the lead the author uses to engage the reader.
b. Identify the main pattern the writer uses in the essay, and consider how that pattern helps to develop his or her main idea.
c. Pick out the descriptions, events, or anecdotes that make a particular impression, and consider why they're effective.
d. Identify passages or images that you find especially powerful, or that reveal that the author is using strategies from other patterns.

VI. REFLECT ON THE ESSAY, AND TRY TO STATE ITS CONTENT AND MAIN ARGUMENT IN TWO OR THREE SENTENCES

VIRGINIA WOOLF

Virginia Woolf (1882–1941) was born in London, England, the daughter of Victorian critic and philosopher Leslie Stephen. She educated herself in her father's magnificent library and, after his death, lived with her sister and two brothers in Bloomsbury, a district of London that later became identified with her and the group of writers and artists she entertained. In 1912, she married journalist Leonard Woolf and together they founded the Hogarth Press, which published the work of the Bloomsbury group, including Woolf's own novels. Woolf's adult life was tormented by intermittent periods of nervous depression; finally, she drowned herself in the river near her home at Rodmell. Her novels include *Mrs. Dalloway* (1925), *To the Lighthouse* (1927), and *Orlando* (1928). Woolf's essays and reviews are collected in books such as *The*

Common Reader (1925). One of Woolf's most
popular works is *A Room of One's Own* (1929),
an extended analysis of the subject of women
and creativity. In this selection, taken from that
volume, Woolf creates a hypothetical argument
to demonstrate the limitations encountered by
women in Shakespeare's time.

Shakespeare's Sister[1]

States problem   It is a perennial puzzle why no woman wrote a word of that   1
extraordinary [Elizabethan] literature when every other man,
it seemed, was capable of song or sonnet. What were the   Why didn't women write?
conditions in which women lived, I asked myself; for fiction,
imaginative work that is, is not dropped like a pebble upon
cription: ompares nce and fiction   the ground, as science may be; fiction is like a spider's web,
attached ever so lightly perhaps, but still attached to life at
all four corners. Often the attachment is scarcely percep-
tible; Shakespeare's plays, for instance, seem to hang there
complete by themselves. But when the web is pulled askew,
hooked up at the edge, torn in the middle, one remembers
that these webs are not spun in mid-air by incorporeal creatures, but are the work of suffering human beings, and are
attached to grossly material things, like health and money
and the house we live in.

But what I find . . . is that nothing is known about   2
women before the eighteenth century. I have no model in
ooks for vidence   my mind to turn about this way and that. Here am I asking why women did not write poetry in the Elizabethan
age, and I am not sure how they were educated; whether   Why has no one researched these questions before?
they were taught to write; whether they had sitting-rooms
to themselves; how many women had children before they
were twenty-one; what, in short, they did from eight in the

---

[1] Virginia Woolf, "Shakespear's Sister" *from A Room of One's Own* by
Virginia Woolf, copyright 1929 by Harcourt, Inc. and renewed 1957
by Leonard Woolf, reprinted by permission of the publisher.

morning till eight at night. They had no money evidently;

according to Professor Trevelyan they were married whether they liked it or not before they were out of the nursery, at fifteen or sixteen very likely. It would have been extremely odd, even upon this showing, had one of them suddenly written the plays of Shakespeare, I concluded, and I thought of that old gentleman, who is dead now, but was a bishop, I think, who declared that it was impossible for any woman, past,

present, or to come, to have the genius of Shakespeare. He wrote to the papers about it. He also told a lady who applied to him for information that cats do not as a matter of fact go to heaven, though they have, he added, souls of a sort. How much thinking those old gentlemen used to save one! How the borders of ignorance shrank back at their approach! Cats do not go to heaven. Women cannot write the plays of Shakespeare.

Be that as it may, I could not help thinking, as I looked 3 at the works of Shakespeare on the shelf, that the bishop was right at least in this; it would have been impossible completely and entirely, for any woman to have written the plays

of Shakespeare in the age of Shakespeare. Let me imagine, since facts are so hard to come by, what would have hap-

pened had Shakespeare had a wonderfully gifted sister, called Judith, let us say. Shakespeare himself went, very probably— his mother was an heiress—to the grammar school, where he may have learnt Latin—Ovid, Virgil and Horace—and the elements of grammar and logic. He was, it is well known, a wild boy who poached rabbits, perhaps shot a deer, and had, rather sooner than he should have done, to marry a woman in the neighbourhood, who bore him a child rather quicker than was right. That escapade sent him to seek his fortune in London. He had, it seemed, a taste for the theatre; he began by holding horses at the stage door. Very soon he got work in the theatre, became a successful actor, and lived at the hub of the universe, meeting everybody, knowing everybody, practising his art on the boards, exercising his wits in the streets, and even getting access to the palace of the

queen. Meanwhile his extraordinarily gifted sister, let us suppose, remained at home. She was as adventurous, as imaginative, as agog to see the world as he was. But she was not sent
to school. She had no chance of learning grammar and logic,
let alone of reading Horace and Virgil. She picked up a book
now and then, one of her brother's perhaps, and read a few
pages. But then her parents came in and told her to mend the
stockings or mind the stew and not moon about with books
and papers. They would have spoken sharply but kindly,
for they were substantial people who knew the conditions
of life for a woman and loved their daughter—indeed, more
likely than not she was the apple of her father's eye. Perhaps
she scribbled some pages up in an apple loft on the sly, but
was careful to hide them or set fire to them. Soon, however,
before she was out of her teens, she was to be betrothed to
the son of a neighbouring wool-stapler. She cried out that
marriage was hateful to her, and for that she was severely
beaten by her father. Then he ceased to scold her. He begged
her instead not to hurt him, not to shame him in this matter
of her marriage. He would give her a chain of beads or a
fine petticoat, he said; and there were tears in his eyes. How
could she disobey him? How could she break his heart?
The force of her own gift alone drove her to it. She made
up a small parcel of her belongings, let herself down by a
rope one summer's night and took the road to London.
She was not seventeen. The birds that sang in the hedge
were not more musical than she was. She had the quickest
fancy, a gift like her brother's, for the tune of words. Like
him, she had a taste for the theatre. She stood at the stage
door; she wanted to act, she said. Men laughed in her face.
The manager—a fat, loose-lipped man—guffawed. He bellowed something about poodles dancing and women acting—no woman, he said, could possibly be an actress. He
hinted—you can imagine what. She could get no training
in her craft. Could she even seek her dinner in a tavern or
roam the streets at midnight? Yet her genius was for fiction
and lusted to feed abundantly upon the lives of men and

B. Shakespeare's sister

Why wasn't she given a chance?

Is this why she left?

Compares Shakespeare and sister

women and the study of their ways. At last—for she was
very young, oddly like Shakespeare the poet in her face, with
the same grey eyes and rounded brows—at last Nick Greene *Why?*
the actor-manager took pity on her; she found herself with
child by that gentleman and so—who shall measure the heat
and violence of the poet's heart when caught and tangled in
a woman's body?—killed herself one winter's night and lies
buried at some cross-roads where the omnibuses now stop
outside the Elephant and Castle.

 That, more or less, is how the story would run, I think, if 4
Moves from a woman in Shakespeare's day had had Shakespeare's genius.
narrative to But for my part, I agree with the deceased bishop, if such
argument he was—it is unthinkable that any woman in Shakespeare's
day should have had Shakespeare's genius. For genius like
Shakespeare's is not born among labouring, uneducated,
servile people. It was not born in England among the Sax-
ons and the Britons. It is not born today among the working
classes. How, then, could it have been born among women
whose work began, according to Professor Trevelyan, almost
Have laws and before they were out of the nursery, who were forced to it
customs changed by their parents and held to it by all the power of law and
that much? custom?

Reader's Response

Woolf paints a realistic picture. That's a shame because in
her time, Shakespeare's sister would have been treated just as
she was presented—as inconsequential. It makes me wonder
why women weren't given the option to read and write when
the head of state, Queen Elizabeth, was more capable and
dynamic than most of the men of the time.

 What's puzzling is why women accepted gender inequity.
I know quite a few outstanding and confident women who
would never have accepted that tradition.

 Watching Judith's struggle to be accepted in a man's
world reminds me of my own struggle to be accepted. Often-
times I have felt small in comparison to my world, but there
always seems to be a path available to me to fit into the world.

VISUAL
STRATEGIES
A VISUAL ESSAY

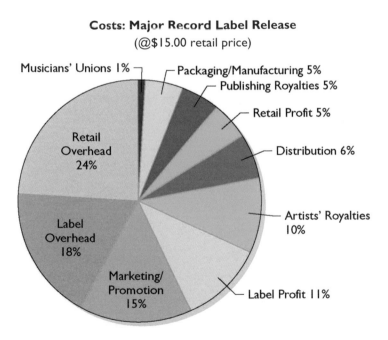

Costs: Major Record Label Release
(@$15.00 retail price)

Musicians' Unions 1%
Packaging/Manufacturing 5%
Publishing Royalties 5%
Retail Profit 5%
Retail Overhead 24%
Distribution 6%
Label Overhead 18%
Artists' Royalties 10%
Label Profit 11%
Marketing/Promotion 15%

Figure 1.1: Pie Chart
A pie chart is an effective way to classify *the various* subdivisions *of a subject. This pie chart subdivides the total cost of a major record label into various segments.*

Will the Candy Float or Sink?

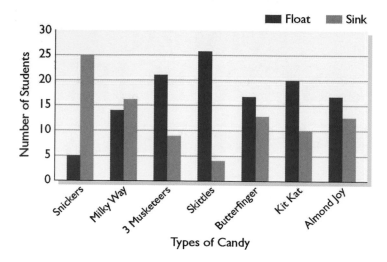

Figure 1.2: Bar Graph
A bar graph is a useful device for comparing *and* contrasting *information. This bar graph compares student opinion on whether particular candy bars will float of sink.*

Prevalence of Overweight and Obesity Among Adults by Sex and Education, 1997 (Age-adjusted)

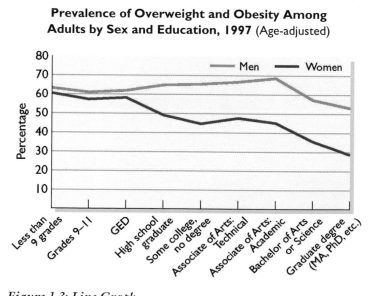

Figure 1.3: Line Graph
A line graph helps compare causes *and* effects. *This line graph documents how sex and education can be seen as contributing causes of obesity and overweight.*

Domino Unified Communications

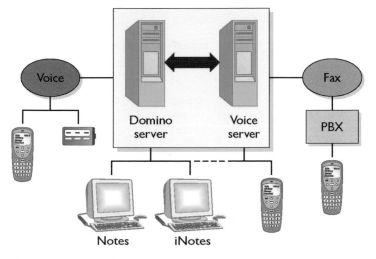

Figure 1.4: Flow Chart
A flow chart illustrates parts of a structure or steps in a process. This flow chart displays how a communication system is connected and routed through various technological devices.

The Human Heart

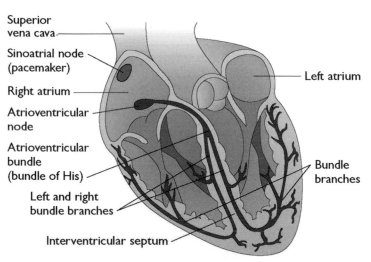

Figure 1.5: Diagram
A diagram—like a flow chart—defines the parts of a structure. This diagram identifies the chambers and arteries of the heart.

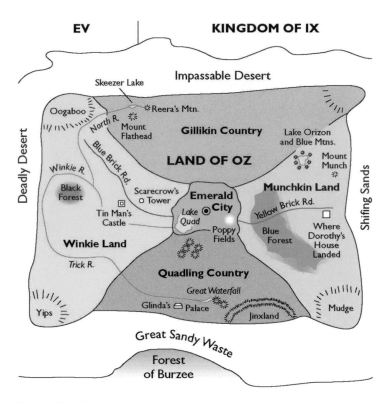

Figure 1.6: Map
A map represents the form, size and sections of an area. This map represents the various settings described *in the* narrative *of Oz.*

Apparently the women of a few centuries ago could not find such a path.

For Study and Discussion

QUESTIONS ABOUT PURPOSE

1. What is the perennial question about women and creativity that Woolf tries to answer in this essay?
2. What connection does she seek to establish between the conditions under which a person lives and what that person can accomplish?

QUESTIONS ABOUT AUDIENCE

1. What assumptions does Woolf make about the cultural knowledge of her readers?
2. Do you think men or women would be most interested in Woolf's argument? Why?

QUESTIONS ABOUT STRATEGIES

1. To what extent does Woolf's speculative narrative about Judith Shakespeare seem constructed from verifiable evidence?
2. What is the argument that Woolf establishes in paragraph 4? Is it convincing? Why or why not?

For Writing and Research

1. *Analyze* the way Woolf mixes strategies—narrative, comparison and contrast, cause and effect—to construct her argument.
2. *Practice* Woolf's strategies by composing a speculative narrative about an imaginary author who reveals the experience that helped him or her to write a particular kind of book—for example, a cookbook, a children's book, or a romance novel.

3. *Argue* that in many ways today's laws and customs still discourage women from pursuing an active creative life.
4. *Synthesize* several sources that comment on how changes in laws and customs have made it possible for women to become the preeminent creative writers in our time.

THE WRITING PROCESS

If you are like most people, you find writing hard work. But writing is also an opportunity. It allows you to express something about yourself, to explore and explain ideas, and to assess the claims of other people. At times the tasks may seem overwhelming, but the rewards make the hard work worthwhile. By working through the four stages of the writing process, you will develop the confidence you need to become an effective writer.

- *Stage 1: Planning.* Planning enables you to find and formulate information in writing. When you begin a writing project, you need to make a list to explore a variety of subjects, to experiment with alternative ways to think about a subject, and to construct a rough outline to see how to develop your information.
- *Stage 2: Drafting.* Drafting enables you to organize and develop a sustained piece of writing. Once planning has helped you to identify several subjects and to gather information on those subjects from different perspectives, you need to select one subject, organize your information into meaningful clusters, and then discover links that connect those clusters.
- *Stage 3: Revising.* Revising enables you to reexamine and reevaluate the choices that have created a piece of writing. After you have completed a preliminary draft, you need to stand back from your text and decide whether to embark on *global revision*—a complete re-creation of the world of your writing—or begin *local revision*—a concentrated effort to perfect the smaller elements of your writing.

- *Stage 4: Editing.* Editing enables you to correct spelling, mechanics, and usage. After you have revised your text, you should proofread it carefully to make sure you have not inadvertently misspelled words, mangled sentences, or created typographical errors.

WRITING WITHIN THE PROCESS

The division of the writing process into four stages is deceptive because it suggests that *planning, drafting, revising,* and *editing* proceed in a linear sequence. According to this logic, you would have to complete all the activities in one stage before you could move on to the next. But writing is a complex mental activity that usually unfolds as a more flexible and recursive sequence of tasks. You may have to repeat the activities in one stage several times before you are ready to move on to the next, or you may have to loop back to an earlier stage before you can move forward again.

Experienced writers seem to perform within the process in different ways. Some spend an enormous amount of time planning every detail before they write; others prefer to dispense with planning and discover their direction in drafting or revising. The American humorist James Thurber once acknowledged that he and one of his collaborators worked quite differently when writing a play:

> Eliot Nugent . . . is a careful constructor. When we were working on *The Male Animal* together, he was constantly concerned with plotting the play. He could plot the thing from back to front— what was going to happen here, what sort of situation would end the first-act curtain and so forth. I can't work that way. Nugent would say, "Well, Thurber, we've got our problem, we've got all these people in the living room. Now what are we going to do with them?" I'd say that I didn't know and couldn't tell him until I'd sat down at

my typewriter and found out. I don't believe the
writer should know too much where he's going.

(James Thurber, *Writers at Work: The Paris
Review Interviews*)[2]

Even experienced writers with established routines for
producing a particular kind of work admit that each project
inevitably presents new problems. Woolf planned, drafted, and
revised some of her novels with great speed, but she was bewildered by her inability to repeat the process with other novels:

> . . . blundering on at *The Waves*. I write two pages
> of arrant nonsense, after straining; I write variations of every sentence; compromises; bad shots;
> possibilities; till my writing book is like a lunatic's
> dream. Then I trust to inspiration on re-reading;
> and pencil them into some sense. Still I am not
> satisfied . . . I press to my centre. I don't care if it
> all is scratched out . . . and then, if nothing comes
> of it—anyhow I have examined the possibilities.

(Virginia Woolf, "Boxing Day 1929,"
A Writer's Diary)[3]

Writers often discover a whole set of new problems when
they are asked to write in a different context. Those writers
who feel comfortable telling stories about their personal experience, for example, may encounter unexpected twists and
turns in their writing process when they are asked to describe
the lives of other people, explain a historical event, or analyze
the arguments in an intellectual controversy. Each context
requires them to make adjustments in the way they typically
uncover, assess, and assert information. Calvin Trillin, an
especially versatile writer, admits that he changes his writing
process dramatically when he shifts from writing investigative
reports to writing humorous essays or weekly columns.

---

[2] James Thurber, The Art of Fiction No. 10. Interviewed by George Plimpton & Max Steele, *Writers at Work: The Paris Review Interviews*.
[3] Virginia Woolf, "Boxing Day 1929," *A Writer's Diary*.

In my reporting pieces, I worry a lot about structure. Everything is there—in interviews, clippings, documents—but I don't know how to get it all in. I think that's why I do what we call around the house the vomit-out. I just start writing—to see how much I've got, how it might unfold, and what I've got to do to get through to the end. In my columns and humor pieces, I usually don't know the end or even the middle. I might start with a joke, but I don't know where it's going, so I fiddle along, polishing each paragraph, hoping something will tell me what to write next. (Personal interview)[4]

This range of responses suggests that what appears to be a simple four-stage procedure may at times be a disorderly, contradictory process. But experienced writers know that disorder and contradiction are inevitable—although temporary—disturbances in the composition of most pieces of writing. Confusion occurs when you know too little about your writing project; contradiction occurs when you think too little about what you know. The secret to moving through such temporary impasses is to keep your eye on the constants in every writing situation.

MAKING DECISIONS IN THE WRITING PROCESS

As you write, you discover that you are constantly making decisions. Some of these decisions are complex, as when you are trying to shape ideas. Others are simple, as when you are trying to select words. But each decision, large or small, affects every other decision you make so that you are constantly adjusting and readjusting your writing to make sure it is consistent, coherent, and clear. You can test the effectiveness of your decisions by measuring them against this dictum: in every writing situation a writer is trying to communicate a *purpose* to an *audience* by manipulating *strategies*.

---

[4] Personal Interview with Calvin Trillin—Reprinted with permission of the author and Lescher & Lescher, Ltd. All rights reserved.

Initially, think of these three elements as *prompts*, ways to consider what you want to write and how you want to write about it. Later, as you move through planning and drafting to revising and editing, think of them as *touchstones*, ways to assess what you set out to accomplish. But mainly think of them as *guidelines*, ways to control every decision you make throughout the writing process, from formulating ideas to reformatting sentences.

DETERMINING YOUR PURPOSE

Writers write most effectively when they write with a purpose. Inexperienced writers occasionally have difficulty writing with a purpose because they see many purposes: to complete the assignment, to earn a grade, to publish their writing. These "purposes" lie *outside* the writing situation, but they certainly influence the way you think about your purpose. If you want a good grade, you will define your purpose in terms of your teacher's writing assignment. If you want to publish your essay, you will define your purpose in terms of a given publisher's statement about its editorial policies.

When *purpose* is considered as an element *inside* the writing situation, the term has a specific meaning: *purpose is the overall design that governs what writers do in their writing.* Writers who have determined their purpose know what kind of information they need, how they want to organize and develop it, and why they think it's important. In effect, purpose directs and controls all the decisions writers make. It is both the *what* and the *how* of that process—that is, the specific subject the writer selects *and* the strategies the writer uses to communicate the subject most effectively.

Forming a Working Purpose: The Hypothesis

A *hypothesis* is a provisional conjecture that serves as a guide to an investigation. Forming a hypothesis is a major step in determining your purpose. Sometimes you come to your writing certain of your hypothesis: you know from the outset what you want to prove and how you need to prove it. More often, you need to consider various possibilities. To convey something meaningful in your writing, something that bears your own mark, you need to keep an open mind and explore your options fully. Eventually, however, you must choose one hypothesis that you think most accurately says what you want to say about your subject and how you want to say it.

How do you know which hypothesis to choose? There is no easy answer to this question. The answer ultimately emerges from your temperament, experiences, and interests, and also from the requirements of the context—whether you are writing for yourself or as an assignment. Sometimes you can make the choice intuitively as you proceed. In thinking about your subject and audience, you see at once the perspective you want to adopt and how it will direct your writing. At other times you may find it helpful to write out various hypotheses and then consider their relative effectiveness. Which will be the most interesting to write about? Which expresses your way of looking at things? With which can you make the strongest case or most compelling assertions?

Testing Your Hypothesis: The Discovery Draft

After you have chosen your hypothesis, you need to determine whether this preliminary statement of purpose provides the direction and control you need to produce an effective piece of writing. You can test your hypothesis by writing a first, or *discovery*, draft. Sometimes your discovery draft demonstrates that your hypothesis works. More often, however, as you continue the writing process, you discover new information or unforeseen complications that cause you to modify your original hypothesis. In other cases, you discover you simply cannot prove what your hypothesis suggested you might be able to prove.

Whatever you discover about your hypothesis, you must proceed in writing. If your discovery draft reveals that your hypothesis represents what you want to prove and needs only slight modification, then change your perspective somewhat or find additional information so that you can modify it. If, on the other hand, your discovery draft demonstrates that your hypothesis lacks conviction or that you do not have (and suspect you cannot get) the information you need to make your case, then choose another hypothesis that reflects your intentions more accurately.

Purpose and Thesis

Whether you proceed with your original hypothesis, modify it, or choose another, you must eventually arrive at a final decision about your purpose. You make that decision during revision, when you know what you want to do and how you want to do it. Once you have established your purpose, you can make or refine other decisions—about your organization, examples, and style. One way to express your purpose is to state your thesis. A *thesis* is a sentence that usually appears in the first paragraph of your essay and states the main idea you are going to develop. Although the thesis is often called a purpose statement, thesis and purpose are not precisely the same thing. Your purpose is both contained in and larger than your thesis: it consists of all the strategies you will use to demonstrate your thesis in a sustained and successful piece of writing.

Your thesis makes a *restricted, unified,* and *precise* assertion about your subject—an assertion that can be developed in the amount of space you have, that treats only one idea, and that is open to only one interpretation.

In many ways, the difference between a hypothesis (a working purpose) and a thesis (a final assertion) explains why you can speculate about your purpose *before* you write but can specify your purpose only *after* you have written. This connection between your writing process and your writing purpose requires you to pause frequently to consult the criteria set forth in the following guidelines.

Guidelines for Determining Your Purpose

I. WHAT ARE THE REQUIREMENTS OF YOUR WRITING PROJECT?

a. If you are writing to fulfill an assignment, do you understand the assignment?

b. If you are writing on your own, do you have definite expectations of what you want to accomplish?

II. AS YOU PROCEED IN THIS PROJECT, WHAT DO YOU NEED TO KNOW?

a. Do you have a good understanding of your subject, or do you need more information?

b. Have you considered the possible audiences who might read your writing?

III. WHAT HYPOTHESIS CAN YOU USE AS A WORKING PURPOSE?

a. How many different hypotheses can you formulate about your subject?

b. Which of them seems to direct and control your information in the most effective manner?

IV. WHAT PURPOSE HAVE YOU DISCOVERED FOR THIS WRITING PROJECT?

a. Has your purpose changed as you have learned more about your subject and audience?

b. Have you discovered, by working with a hypothesis or hypotheses, what you want to do in your writing?

V. WHAT IS YOUR THESIS?

a. How can you state your main idea in a thesis sentence?

b. Does your thesis limit the scope of your writing to what you can demonstrate in the available space?

c. Does it focus your writing on one specific assertion?
d. Does it make an exact statement about what your writing intends to do?

ANALYZING YOUR AUDIENCE

Most inexperienced writers assume that their audience is their writing teacher. But writing teachers, like writing assignments, often vary in what they teach, what they assume, and what they expect. Such variation has often prompted inexperienced writers to define their writing tasks as "trying to figure out what the teacher wants." This definition is naïve and smart at the same time. Superficially, it suggests that the sole purpose of any writing assignment is to satisfy another person's whims. On a deeper level, it suggests that when writers analyze the knowledge, assumptions, and expectations of their readers, they develop a clearer perception of their purpose and strategies. To make this analysis truly effective, though, writers must remember that they are writing for multiple audiences, not for a single person.

The most immediate audience is *you*. You write not only to convey your ideas to others but also to clarify them for yourself. To think of yourself as an audience, however, you must stop thinking like a writer and begin thinking like a reader. This change in perspective offers advantages, for you are the reader you know best. You are also a fairly representative reader because you share broad concerns and interests with other people. If you feel your writing is clear, lively, and informed, other readers will probably feel that way, too. If you sense that your text is confused or incomplete, the rest of your audience is likely to be disappointed, too.

The main drawback to considering yourself as audience is your inclination to deceive yourself. You want every sentence and paragraph to be perfect, but you know how much time and energy you invested in composing them, and that effort may blur your judgment. You may accept bad writing from yourself even though you wouldn't accept it from someone else. For that reason you need a second audience.

These readers—usually, friends, classmates, and teachers—are your most attentive audience. They help you choose your subject, coach you through various stages of the writing process, and counsel you about how to improve your sentences and paragraphs. As you write, you must certainly anticipate detailed advice from these readers. But you must remember that writing teachers and even peers are essentially collaborators and thus not your ultimate audience. They know what you have considered, cut, and corrected. The more they help you, the more eager they are to commend your writing as it approaches their standards of acceptability.

Your most significant audience consists of readers who neither know how much time and energy you invested in your writing nor care about the many choices you considered and rejected. These readers want writing that tells them something interesting or important, and they are put off by writing that is tedious or trivial. It is this wider audience that you (and your collaborators) must consider as you work through the writing process.

At times this audience may seem like a nebulous creature, and you may wonder how you can direct your writing to it if you do not know any of its distinguishing features. In those cases, it may be helpful to imagine a single significant reader—an attentive, sensible, reasonably informed person who will give you a sympathetic reading as long as you do not waste his or her time. Imagine an important person whom you respect and whose respect you want. This reader—specifically imagined, though often termed the "general reader," the "universal reader," or the "common reader"—is essentially a fiction, but a helpful fiction. Your writing will benefit from the objectivity and sincerity with which you address this reader.

Many times, however, especially as you learn more about your subject, you discover a real-world audience for your writing. More precisely, as you consider your subject in a specific context, you may identify a number of audiences, in which case you will ultimately have to choose among them. Suppose, for example, you want to write about your evolution as a writer—an essay such as the student essay on pages 30–33. After some deliberation you see that you have three possible audiences: (1) those who love to talk about their development as writers, (2) those who refuse even to discuss an activity they despise, and (3) those who have not thought too much about how writers work.

Now that you have identified these three audiences, analyze the distinctive features of each group. What do they know? What do they think they know? What do they need to know? The more you know about each group, the more you will be able to direct your writing to their assumptions and expectations. If you have spent a lot of time discussing the challenges of writing, you will have little difficulty analyzing the devotees and detesters of the composing process. You have heard the devotees explain how they have discovered strategies for becoming successful writers. Similarly, you have heard the detesters complain that their failures have convinced them that they never want to think about writing again.

At first you may have difficulty with the third group because these readers have not developed any preconceptions about learning how to write. In some ways, readers in the third group are like the "general reader"—thoughtful, discerning people who are willing to read about the writing process if you can convince them that the subject is worth their attention.

Although this sort of audience analysis helps you to visualize a group of readers, it does not help you decide which group is most suitable for your essay. If you target one group, you may fall into the trap of allowing its preferences to determine the direction of your writing. If you try to accommodate all three groups, you may waiver indecisively among them so that your writing never finds any direction. Your decision about audience, like your decision about purpose, has to be made in the context of the complete writing situation. For that reason, look at the guidelines for analyzing your audience.

Guidelines for Analyzing Your Audience

I. WHO ARE THE READERS WHO WILL BE MOST INTERESTED IN YOUR WRITING?

a. What are their probable age, gender, education, economic status, and social position?
b. What values, assumptions, and prejudices characterize their general attitude toward life?

II. WHAT DO YOUR READERS KNOW OR THINK THEY KNOW ABOUT YOUR SUBJECT?

a. What is the probable source of their knowledge—direct experience, observation, reading, rumor?
b. Will your readers react positively or negatively toward your subject?

III. WHY WILL YOUR READERS READ YOUR WRITING?

a. If they know a great deal about your subject, what will they expect to learn from reading your writing?
b. If they know only a few things about your subject, what will they expect to be told about it?
c. Will they expect to be entertained, informed, or persuaded?

IV. HOW CAN YOU INTEREST YOUR READERS IN YOUR SUBJECT?

a. If they are hostile toward it, how can you convince them to give your writing a fair reading?
b. If they are sympathetic, how can you fulfill and enhance their expectations?
c. If they are neutral, how can you catch and hold their attention?

V. HOW CAN YOU HELP YOUR READERS
READ YOUR WRITING?

a. What kind of organizational pattern will help them see its purpose?
b. What kind of strategies and transitional markers will they need to follow this pattern?
c. What (and how many) examples will they need to understand your general statements?

SELECTING YOUR STRATEGY

As you work your way through the writing process, you will uncover various patterns for developing your ideas. In *planning*, these patterns often emerge as answers to the basic questions you might ask about any body of information: *What is it? How does it work? Why does it matter?* These questions are like the different lenses you attach to your camera: each lens gives you a different picture of your subject.

Suppose you want to write an essay on the subject of women and science. You might begin by asking why so few women are ranked among the world's great scientists. You might continue asking questions. What historical forces have discouraged women from becoming scientists? How do women scientists define problems, analyze evidence, and formulate conclusions; and do they go about these processes differently than men do? If women scientists look at the world differently than men do, does this difference have an effect on the established notions of inquiry? As you can see, each question not only shifts your perspective on your subject but also suggests a different method for developing your information about it.

If planning gives you the opportunity to envision your subject from a variety of perspectives, then *drafting* encourages you to develop the pattern (or patterns) that appear to you most effective for demonstrating your purpose. In some writing projects, a pattern may seem to emerge naturally from your planning. If you decide to write about your observation of a game of lacrosse, your choice seems obvious: to tell what happened. In attempting this, however, you may need to answer other questions about this unfamiliar sport: What do the field and equipment look like? What rules govern the way the game is played? How is it similar to or different from other sports? Developing this new information may complicate your original purpose.

You can solve this problem most effectively during *revision*. As you look over your draft, you will need to make two decisions. First, you must decide whether individual segments or patterns of information develop or distort your purpose. The history of lacrosse—its creation by Iroquois Indians, its discovery by French explorers, and its development by Canadians—is an interesting body of information; but it may need to be reshaped, relocated, or even eliminated to preserve your original purpose—to tell what happened. Second, you must decide whether your original design, a design that often mirrors the process by which you uncovered your information, is still the best method for presenting your information to your audience. Instead of telling "what happened," you may decide that you can best express your ideas by choosing a more formal structure—comparing lacrosse to games with which your readers are more familiar, such as soccer or hockey.

Whatever you decide, you need to understand the purpose, audience, and strategies of each pattern if you are going to use it successfully to develop a paragraph, a section of your essay, or your whole essay. For that reason, *The River Reader* is organized to demonstrate the most common patterns and questions encountered in the writing process:

> Narration and Description: What happened? What did it look like?
> Process Analysis: How do you do it?
> Comparison and Contrast: How is it similar or different?
> Division and Classification: What kind of subdivisions does it contain?
> Definition: How would you characterize it?
> Cause and Effect: Why did it happen? What happened next?
> Persuasion and Argument: How can you prove it?

The introductions to the chapters that feature each of these patterns of development explain its purpose, audience, and strategies. The essays in each chapter are arranged in an ascending order of complexity and are followed by questions that call your attention to how the writer has asserted his or her purpose, addressed his or her audience, and used the various techniques of each strategy to develop his or her essay. If you study these essays and answer these questions, you will see how you can adapt these common writing patterns to your writing.

By analyzing these strategies in action, you will also learn two important lessons. First, you will understand what you are expected to write when you encounter words such as *describe, compare,* and *define* in a writing assignment. Second, you will discover that you do not have to limit yourself to a single pattern for an entire piece of writing. Writers may structure their essay around one dominant strategy but use other strategies to enrich or advance their purpose.

The following guidelines will help you in selecting an appropriate strategy.

Guidelines for Selecting Your Strategy

I. WHAT STRATEGY DOES YOUR WRITING ASSIGNMENT REQUIRE?

a. What words—such as *define* or *defend*—are embedded in your writing assignment?

b. What assumptions and expectations do these words evoke?

II. WHAT STRATEGY EMERGES AS YOU PLAN YOUR ESSAY?

a. What questions naturally occur to you as you study a particular subject?

b. What patterns of development do these questions suggest?

III. WHAT OTHER STRATEGIES EMERGE AS YOU DRAFT YOUR ESSAY?

a. What new questions emerge as you draft your writing?
b. What kind of information do you need to answer these questions?

IV. HOW CAN YOU REVISE YOUR ESSAY TO INCLUDE THIS NEW INFORMATION?

a. Does this new information distort or develop your purpose?
b. Will it require you to impose a new strategy on your information to clarify your purpose to your readers?

V. HOW CAN YOU MIX STRATEGIES TO ENRICH YOUR ESSAY?

a. How does mixing strategies supplement your purpose?
b. How might such mixing confuse your readers?

Student Essay

Student Writer in Progress

Kristie Ferguson, "The Scenic Route"[5]

The following material illustrates how one student, Kristie Ferguson, responded to a writing assignment by working her way through the writing process.

Writing Assignment: Read Woolf's "Shakespeare's Sister." Then compose a narrative that describes the experiences that contributed to (or prevented) your development as a writer.

Planning (Journal Entry)

I am not sure I ever <u>developed</u> as a writer. My teachers all seemed to want different things.

> Never made Mrs. Scott's bulletin board
> Mrs. Pageant and those dumb squirrels
> Logan and that contest

I could never figure out what they wanted. I suppose they wanted to teach me. But I always felt lost.

Possible Hypothesis: I should probably describe what I didn't learn. How my confusion prevented me from becoming a good writer. But then how do you explain that contest?

Drafting (Discovery Draft)

What's Wrong with This Picture?

On one of those days that convinces you certain things don't belong together, like sunshine and first grade or hot flashes in Alaska, another writing period was about to begin. At the grand old age of six, I was certain that I would never learn to write. After all I had never made the list. In the corner

---

[5] "The Scenic Route"—© Cengage Learning

of our room, Mrs. Scott kept a bulletin board commending those in the class who had neat handwriting and no spelling errors. I was cursed on both counts. My handwriting looked like hieroglyphics, and my spelling always made people ask, "What's wrong with this picture."

That day Mrs. Scott surprised us. "Class, I'm cutting writing period in half so that you can go to the auditorium to see a movie." Freedom! Relief! I started to clap my hands. But wait! Something was wrong with this picture. "I am going to ask you to write a brief theme," Mrs. Scott continued. "When you are done you can go to the auditorium." I knew there must be a catch. Still, it was only a brief theme and afterward there was a movie. I grabbed my Number 2 and thumbed through my notebook looking for a clean page. "One more thing," she announced. "You must spell all words neatly and correctly. No erasers or dictionaries. I may ask for do-over's." No eraser? No dictionary? Why not cut off both my arms?

How was I ever going to make it to the auditorium? I started slowly, reminding myself to make each letter and word carefully. When I finished, I went to Mrs. Scott's desk. "Too sloppy. Misspelled words." I retreated to my desk for another try. This time she smiled. "Misspelled word. Do it over." I slumped back to my desk. The next time I looked up the room was empty. Desperate, I narrowed the culprit to one of those "ie" words. I rubbed out the letters, reprinted them, and placed a dot more or less between them. I handed my paper to Mrs. Scott. "You erased," she hissed. She was such a treasure. "No ma'am." She eyed the paper and me again, and then, finally, let me go. At last—the movie.

Collapsing near my best friend Karla, I arrived in time to watch the end of a promotion film for dental hygiene. Teeth! All that for teeth!

Revision (Revision Agenda)

1. *What is my purpose?*

Tell a story about my early failures as a writer. Most of my grade school teachers emphasized handwriting and spelling and I was terrible at both.

2. *Who is my audience?*

Everyone who has gone to school. They have all had a Mrs. Scott. Most remember that in school good writing meant good handwriting and no mistakes.

3. *What strategies do I use?*

I focused on my attempt to complete one writing assignment so I could go to a movie. I slowed the pace down and described the details of my writing process. I also used dialogue to dramatize Mrs. Scott.

4. *What revisions do I want to make in my next draft?*
    a. Include other writing experiences—fourth grade, high school.
    b. Rework introduction—state thesis—to explain why I am telling these stories.

New Hypothesis: I like the story because it tells how I tricked Mrs. Scott—and then myself. All that work for teeth. But I take too long getting there. Is learning how to write simply learning a trick? Maybe it's more like taking a trip.

Second Draft

The Scenic Route

As a writer, I always seem to take the scenic route. I don't plan it that way. My teachers provide detailed maps pointing me down the most direct road, but somehow I miss a turn or make a wrong turn and there I am—standing at some unmarked crossroads, head pounding, stomach churning, hopelessly lost. On such occasions, I used to curse my teachers, my maps, and myself. But recently, I have come to expect, even enjoy, in a perverse way, the confusion and panic of being lost. Left to my own devices, I have learned to discover my own way to my destination. And afterwards, I have a story to tell.

I did not learn this all at once. In the beginning I was confused about where I was going. One day in first grade, Mrs. Scott told us that if we wrote a brief theme we could go to a movie. I grabbed my Number 2 and listened for directions. "No erasers. No dictionaries. I may ask for do-over's."

Lost! I was the worst speller in the class. My first draft was "Too sloppy. Do it over." My second, "Misspelled word. Do it over." Now I was really lost. One misspelled word. They all looked right—and then they all looked wrong. Blind luck led me to one of those "ie" words. I rubbed out the letters, reprinted them, and placed the dot between them. "Kristie, you erased," she hissed. "No ma'am." She eyed my paper and then me again, and with a sigh waved me toward the auditorium. Collapsing next to my best friend, Karla, I arrived in time to watch a film about dental hygiene. Teeth! All that for teeth!

My next problem was trying to figure out why I was going. Mrs. Pageant, my fifth-grade teacher, was the source of my confusion. Seemingly unaware of my errors, she wrote enthusiastic notes on all my essays, suggesting on one, "Kristie, you're so creative. Why don't you write a book?" Why indeed? Why should the first-grade dummy begin such a perilous journey? "You should, Kristie. You really should. You could even write a fantasy book like the one we read today." Luckily fantasy was my forte. I used to make up stories about the family of squirrels in my backyard. And so I wrote *Squirrel Family Starts a Grocery Store,* in which, after the hoopla on page one, the squirrels run out of food on page three and close their store on page four.

As she read my book to the class, Mrs. Pageant could hardly contain herself. "What a delightful story, Kristie. You must write another immediately." My head pounded. My stomach churned. I had stumbled onto one story, but why keep going? Because Mrs. Pageant "just loved" those dumb squirrels. So there was *Squirrel Family Starts a Bank,* in which the squirrels run out of money, and *Squirrel Family Starts a Newspaper,* in which they run out of stories. By then I was looking for the nearest off-ramp. I couldn't think of another squirrel story, and Karla told me that if she had to listen to one more, she would throw up.

When I got to the eleventh grade, I knew for the first time where I was going and why. The poster on Mr. Logan's bulletin board announced a writing contest: "Threats to the

Free Enterprise System." Sponsored by the Blair County
Board of Realtors. First prize $200. Now my problem was
how to get there. Mr. Logan took us to the school library and
mapped out the first half of his strategy. Look up sources in
the database. Take notes. Organize notes into an outline for
first draft. It seemed like a sensible plan, but, as usual, I got
lost at the first turn. I pulled a few books off the shelf, but it
was pointless. I couldn't find anything on free enterprise or
anybody who was threatening it.

As the deadline for the first draft approached, I was so
desperate I asked my parents for directions. "Ask some local
business people what they think." Not bad for parents. I borrowed my father's tape recorder and made the rounds—the
grocery store, the pizza parlor, the newspaper. Most of the
people seemed a lot like me—lost. They talked a lot, but they
didn't focus on the question. Maybe I was asking the wrong
question. I listened to the tape a couple of times and picked
out some common themes. Then I rewrote my questions:
"How do taxes, government regulation and foreign competition threaten your business?" The next time around people
seemed to know what they were talking about. I organized
their answers under my three categories, wrote out my draft,
and made the deadline.

In class, Mr. Logan announced the second half of his
strategy. Read draft. Listen to student and teacher responses.
Revise draft. Mail essay. Karla went first. She quoted every
book in the school library. Looking down at my paper, I saw
myself stranded again. After a few more papers I felt better.
All the papers sounded alike. I knew my quotes would be
different—the guy at the pizza parlor, the newspaper editor.
"You didn't do any research," Karla complained. "I bet you
didn't read one article." A chorus of "yes's" came from the
guys in the back row. Mr. Logan didn't say anything for a
while. Then, smiling, he looked at Karla. "What is research?"
Now Karla looked lost. The guys looked in their notebooks.
Silence. Finally, the bell. What's the answer? What am I supposed to do? Mr. Logan never said. I thought about what I

had done, considered my options, and, with a sigh, mailed my essay.

A few weeks later, I was standing not at some unmarked crossroads but in the center of town—behind the lectern in front of a room full of people. A man from the Blair County Board of Realtors handed me a trophy and an envelope and asked me to tell how I wrote the paper. I started to panic and then smiled. "Well . . . ." I caught Mr. Logan's eye. "I asked a lot of people what they thought. At first they didn't know what I was talking about. Neither did I. Then I fixed my question and they helped me figure out what to say." I looked at Mr. Logan again. He just smiled. I looked at my trophy and wondered what to say next. Finally, I said "Well . . . I guess I did research."

Revision (Revision Agenda)

1. *What is my purpose?*

   Describe how I learned to trust my own judgment about writing.

2. *Who is my audience?*

   Again, anyone who has gone to school. Everybody has had to write silly stories and research papers. I'll bet they all tried to write something for some dumb contest. I suppose another audience might be those guys at the Blair County Board of Realtors.

3. *What strategies do I use?*

   I use brief narratives that I try to connect with my title—"The Scenic Route." I keep Karla in each episode as a kind of commentator. I also use dialogue to dramatize Mrs. Scott, Mrs. Pageant, and Mr. Logan. I try to slow the pace down at important moments—like when I read my research paper for the first time or when I was accepting my trophy.

4. *What revisions do I want to make in my next draft?*

   Rework introduction so I can get right to my thesis—"trust your own judgment."

   Do Mrs. Scott and Mrs. Pageant fit the thesis? If I cut them, I'll lose my funniest stuff. If I use them, I'll have to figure out a new way.

This draft seems more organized, but I force my material into the structure—*where* I was going, *why* I was going, *how* I got there. Maybe the scenic route metaphor gets in the way.

Work more with contest. It's the one story that makes my point.

Figure out "what's wrong with this picture?" This essay seems to be getting better and worse at the same time.

Comment. This essay takes readers on a tour of Kristie's development as a writer and highlights three memorable experiences along the way. Although the narrative focuses on her personal experiences, it conjures up memories for many fledgling writers: first, the autocratic teacher from first grade who demands perfection and loves to punish mistakes; then the sweetie-pie teacher from fifth grade who gushes and lavishes praise on stuff the writer knows is junk; finally, the practical and organized eleventh-grade teacher who outlines a writing process and guides the students through it for a real-world audience.

CHAPTER 1

NARRATION
AND
DESCRIPTION

The writer who *narrates* tells a story to make a point. The writer who *describes* evokes the senses to create a picture. Although you can use either strategy by itself, you will probably discover that they work best in combination if you want to write a detailed account of some memorable experience— your first trip alone, a last-minute political victory, a picnic in some special place. When you want to explain what happened, you will need to tell the story in some kind of chronological order, putting the most important events—I took the wrong turn, she made the right speech, we picked the perfect spot—in the most prominent position. When you want to give the texture of the experience, you will need to select words and images that help your readers see, hear, and feel what happened—the road snaked to a dead end, the crowd thundered into applause, the sunshine softened our scowls. When you show and tell in this way, you can help your readers see the meaning of the experience you want to convey.

PURPOSE

You can use narration and description for three purposes. Most simply, you can use them to introduce or illustrate a complicated subject. You might begin an analysis of the energy crisis, for example, by telling a personal anecdote that dramatizes wastefulness. Or you might conclude an argument for gun control by giving a graphic description of a shooting incident. In each case, you are using a few sentences or a detailed description to support some other strategy, such as causal analysis or argument.

Writers use narration and description most often not as isolated examples but as their primary method when they are analyzing an issue or theme. For example, you might spend a whole essay telling how you came to a new awareness of patriotism because of your experience in a foreign country. Even though your personal experience would be the center of the essay, your narrative purpose (what happened) and your descriptive purpose (what it felt like) might be linked to other purposes. You might want to *explain* what caused your new awareness (why it happened) or to *argue* that everyone needs such awareness (why everyone should reach the same conclusion you did).

The writers who use narration and description most often are those who write autobiography, history, and fiction. If you choose to write in any of these forms, your purpose will be not so much to introduce an example or tell about an experience to throw light on your subject. You may explain why events happened as they did or argue that such events should never happen again, but you may choose to suggest your ideas subtly through telling a story or giving a description rather than stating them as direct assertions. Your primary purpose is to report the actions and describe the feelings of people entangled in the complex web of circumstance.

AUDIENCE

As you think about writing an essay using narration and description, consider how much you will need to tell your readers and how much you will need to show them. If you are writing from personal experience, few readers will know the story before you tell it. They may know similar stories or have had similar experiences, but they do not know your story. Because you can tell your story in so many different ways—adding or deleting material to fit the occasion—you need to decide how much information your readers will need. Do they need to know every detail of your story, only brief summaries of certain parts, or some mixture of detail and summary?

To decide what details you should provide, you need to think about how much your readers know and what they are going to expect. If your subject is unusual (a trip to see an erupting volcano), your readers will need a lot of information, much of it technical, to understand the novel experience you are going to describe. They not only will expect an efficient, matter-of-fact description of volcanoes but also want you to give them some sense of how it feels to see one erupting. If your subject is familiar to most people (your experience with lawn sprinklers), your readers will need few technical details to understand your subject. But they will expect you to give them new images and insights that create a fresh vision of your subject—for example, portraying lawn sprinklers as the languid pulse of summer.

STRATEGIES

The writers in this section demonstrate that you need to use certain strategies to write a successful narrative and descriptive essay. For openers, you must recognize that an experience and an essay about that experience are not the same thing. When you have any experience, no matter how long it lasts, your memory of that experience is going to be disorganized and poorly defined, but the essay you write about that experience must have a purpose and be sharply focused. When you want to transform your experience into an essay, start by locating the central **conflict.** It may be (1) between the writer and himself or herself, as when George

Orwell finds himself in a quandary about whether to shoot the elephant; (2) between the writer and others, as when Maya Angelou responds to Mrs. Cullinan and her friends; or (3) between the writer and the environment, as when Judith Ortiz Cofer tries to explain the difference between *individuals* and *social stereotypes.*

Once you have identified the conflict, arrange the action so that your readers know how the conflict started, how it developed, and how it was resolved. This coherent sequence of events is called a **plot.** Sometimes you may want to create a plot that sticks to a simple chronological pattern. In "My Name Is Margaret," Maya Angelou begins her account of events at the beginning and describes them as they occur. At other times you may want to start your essay in the middle or even near the end of the events you are describing. In "Digging," Andre Dubus concludes his narrative by speculating about a different "middle." The authors choose a pattern according to their purpose: Angelou wants to describe the evolution of events leading up to the broken china; Dubus wants to describe why coming home for lunch would have changed the whole story.

When you figure out what the beginning, middle, and end of your plot should be, you can establish how each event in those sections should be paced. **Pace** is the speed at which the writer recounts events. Sometimes you can narrate events quickly by omitting details, compressing time, and summarizing experience. For example, Cofer summarizes several episodes that reveal her contact with a stereotype. At other times you may want to pace events more slowly and carefully because they are vital to your purpose. You will need to include every detail, expand on time, and present the situation as a fully realized scene rather than in summary form. Dubus creates such a scene when he describes his first morning of "digging."

You can make your scenes and summaries effective by your careful **selection of details.** Just adding more details doesn't satisfy this requirement. You must select those special details that satisfy the needs of your readers and further your purpose in the essay. For example, sometimes you will need to give *objective* or *technical* details to help your readers understand your subject. Cofer provides this kind of detail when she describes the cultural customs of Puerto Rico. At other times you will want to give *subjective* or *impressionistic* details to appeal to your readers' senses. Orwell provides much of this kind of detail as he tries to re-create his physical and psychological response to shooting an elephant. Finally, you may want to present your details so they form a *figurative image* or create a *dominant impression*. Williams uses both of these strategies: the first when she describes the "Wolf Pole," the second when she describes the impact of her Uncle's seizures.

To identify the conflict, organize the plot, vary the pace, and select details for your essay, you need to determine your **point of view:** the person and position of the narrator (*point*) and the attitude toward the experience being presented (*view*). You choose your *person* by deciding whether you want to tell your story as "I" saw it (as Angelou does in her story about her confrontation with Mrs. Cullinan) or as "he" or "she" saw it (as Dubus does when he describes his father's life).

You choose your *position* by deciding how close you want to be to the action in time and space. You may be involved in the action or view it from the position of an observer, or you may tell about the events as they are happening or many years after they have taken place. For example, Orwell, the young police officer, is the chief actor in his narrative, but Orwell, the author, still wonders, years after the event, why he shot the elephant. You create your attitude—how you view the events you intend to present and interpret—by the person and position you choose for writing your essay. The attitudes of the narrators in the following essays might be characterized as angry (Angelou), reverent (Williams), perplexed (Cofer), reticent (Dubus), and ambivalent (Orwell).

NARRATION AND DESCRIPTION

Points to Remember

1. Focus your narrative on the "story" in your story—that is, focus on the conflict that defines the plot.
2. Vary the pace of your narrative so that you can summarize some events quickly and render others as fully realized scenes.
3. Supply evocative details to help your readers experience the dramatic development of your narrative.
4. Establish a consistent point of view so that your readers know how you have positioned yourself in your story.
5. Represent the events in your narrative so that your story makes its point.

In this excerpt from her graphic novel Persepolis: The Story of a Childhood *(2003), Marjane Satrapi recounts the reaction of young schoolgirls to the law requiring them to wear "the veil." Some argue that the veil debases and even erases female identity. Others argue that it provides women with safety and secret power. How do the characters in Satrapi's narrative feel about this regulation? Write a narrative describing your own reactions to some obligatory dress code.*

MAYA ANGELOU

Maya Angelou (given name, Marguerite Johnson) was born in St. Louis, Missouri, in 1928 and spent her early years in California and Arkansas. A woman of varied accomplishments, she is a novelist, poet, playwright, stage and screen performer, composer, and singer. She is perhaps best known for her autobiographical novels: *I Know Why the Caged Bird Sings* (1970), *Gather Together in My Name* (1974), *Oh Pray My Wings Are Gonna Fit Me Well* (1975), *Singin' and Swingin' and Gettin' Merry Like Christmas* (1976), *The Heart of a Woman* (1981), *All God's Children Need Traveling Shoes* (1986), *Wouldn't Take Nothing for My Journey Now* (1993), *A Brave and Startling Truth* (1995), *A Song Flung Up to Heaven* (2002), and *Letter to My Daughter* (2008). Angelou's poetry is equally well respected and is published in her *Complete Collected Poems* (1994). President Obama presented Angelou with the Presidential Medal of Freedom in 2011. In the following selection from *I Know Why the Caged Bird Sings*, Angelou recounts how she maintained her identity in a world of prejudice.

My Name Is Margaret[1]

RECENTLY A WHITE woman from Texas, who would 1 quickly describe herself as a liberal, asked me about my hometown. When I told her that in Stamps my grandmother had owned the only Negro general merchandise store since

---

[1] Maya Angelou, "My Name Is Margaret," copyright © 1969 and renewed 1997 by Maya Angelou, from *I Know Why the Caged Bird Sings* by Maya Angelou. Used by permission of Random House, Inc.

the turn of the century, she exclaimed, "Why, you were a debutante." Ridiculous and even ludicrous. But Negro girls in small Southern towns, whether poverty-stricken or just munching along on a few of life's necessities, were given as extensive and irrelevant preparations for adulthood as rich white girls shown in magazines. Admittedly the training was not the same. While white girls learned to waltz and sit gracefully with a tea cup balanced on their knees, we were lagging behind, learning the mid-Victorian values with very little money to indulge them. (Come and see Edna Lomax spending the money she made picking cotton on five balls of ecru tatting thread. Her fingers are bound to snag the work and she'll have to repeat the stitches time and time again. But she knows that when she buys the thread.)

We were required to embroider and I had trunkfuls of colorful dishtowels, pillowcases, runners and handkerchiefs to my credit. I mastered the art of crocheting and tatting, and there was a lifetime's supply of dainty doilies that would never be used in sacheted dresser drawers. It went without saying that all girls could iron and wash, but the finer touches around the home, like setting a table with real silver, baking roasts and cooking vegetables without meat, had to be learned elsewhere. Usually at the source of those habits. During my tenth year, a white woman's kitchen became my finishing school.

Mrs. Viola Cullinan was a plump woman who lived in a three-bedroom house somewhere behind the post office. She was singularly unattractive until she smiled, and then the lines around her eyes and mouth which made her look perpetually dirty disappeared, and her face looked like the mask of an impish elf. She usually rested her smile until late afternoon when her women friends dropped in and Miss Glory, the cook, served them cold drinks on the closed-in porch.

During my tenth year, a white woman's kitchen became my finishing school.

The exactness of her house was inhuman. This glass went   4
here and only here. That cup had its place and it was an act
of impudent rebellion to place it anywhere else. At twelve
o'clock the table was set. At 12:15 Mrs. Cullinan sat down to
dinner (whether her husband had arrived or not). At 12:16
Miss Glory brought out the food.

It took me a week to learn the difference between a salad   5
plate, a bread plate and a dessert plate.

Mrs. Cullinan kept up the tradition of her wealthy parents.   6
She was from Virginia. Miss Glory, who was a descendant of
slaves that had worked for the Cullinans, told me her history.
She had married beneath her (according to Miss Glory). Her
husband's family hadn't had their money very long and what
they had "didn't 'mount to much."

As ugly as she was, I thought privately, she was lucky to   7
get a husband above or beneath her station. But Miss Glory
wouldn't let me say a thing against her mistress. She was
very patient with me, however, over the housework. She
explained the dishware, silverware and servants' bells. The
large round bowl in which soup was served wasn't a soup
bowl, it was a tureen. There were goblets, sherbet glasses,
ice-cream glasses, wine glasses, green glass coffee cups with
matching saucers, and water glasses. I had a glass to drink
from, and it sat with Miss Glory's on a separate shelf from the
others. Soup spoons, gravy boat, butter knives, salad forks
and carving platter were additions to my vocabulary and in
fact almost represented a new language. I was fascinated with
the novelty, with the fluttering Mrs. Cullinan and her Alice-
in-Wonderland house.

Her husband remains, in my memory, undefined. I lumped   8
him with all the other white men that I had ever seen and
tried not to see.

On our way home one evening, Miss Glory told me that   9
Mrs. Cullinan couldn't have children. She said that she was
too delicate-boned. It was hard to imagine bones at all under
those layers of fat. Miss Glory went on to say that the doctor had taken out all her lady organs. I reasoned that a pig's
organs included the lungs, heart and liver, so if Mrs. Cullinan

was walking around without those essentials, it explained why she drank alcohol out of unmarked bottles. She was keeping herself embalmed.

When I spoke to Bailey about it, he agreed that I was right, 10 but he also informed me that Mr. Cullinan had two daughters by a colored lady and that I knew them very well. He added that the girls were the spitting image of their father. I was unable to remember what he looked like, although I had just left him a few hours before, but I thought of the Coleman girls. They were very light-skinned and certainly didn't look very much like their mother (no one ever mentioned Mr. Coleman).

My pity for Mrs. Cullinan preceded me the next morn- 11 ing like the Cheshire cat's smile. Those girls, who could have been her daughters, were beautiful. They didn't have to straighten their hair. Even when they were caught in the rain, their braids still hung down straight like tamed snakes. Their mouths were pouty little cupid's bows. Mrs. Cullinan didn't know what she missed. Or maybe she did. Poor Mrs. Cullinan.

For weeks after, I arrived early, left late and tried very hard 12 to make up for her barrenness. If she had had her own children, she wouldn't have had to ask me to run a thousand errands from her back door to the back door of her friends. Poor old Mrs. Cullinan.

Then one evening Miss Glory told me to serve the ladies 13 on the porch. After I set the tray down and turned toward the kitchen, one of the women asked, "What's your name, girl?" It was the speckled-faced one. Mrs. Cullinan said, "She doesn't talk much. Her name's Margaret."

"Is she dumb?"   14

"No. As I understand it, she can talk when she wants to but 15 she's usually quiet as a little mouse. Aren't you, Margaret?"

I smiled at her. Poor thing. No organs and couldn't even 16 pronounce my name correctly.

"She's a sweet little thing, though."   17

"Well, that may be, but the name's too long. I'd never 18 bother myself. I'd call her Mary if I was you."

I fumed into the kitchen. That horrible woman would 19
never have the chance to call me Mary because if I was starving I'd never work for her. I decided I wouldn't pee on her
if her heart was on fire. Giggles drifted in off the porch and
into Miss Glory's pots. I wondered what they could be laughing about.

Whitefolks were so strange. Could they be talking about 20
me? Everybody knew that they stuck together better than the
Negroes did. It was possible that Mrs. Cullinan had friends in
St. Louis who heard about a girl from Stamps being in court
and wrote to tell her. Maybe she knew about Mr. Freeman.

My lunch was in my mouth a second time and I went out- 21
side and relieved myself on the bed of four-o'clocks. Miss
Glory thought I might be coming down with something and
told me to go on home, that Momma would give me some
herb tea, and she'd explain to her mistress.

I realized how foolish I was being before I reached the 22
pond. Of course Mrs. Cullinan didn't know. Otherwise she
wouldn't have given me two nice dresses that Momma cut
down, and she certainly wouldn't have called me a "sweet
little thing." My stomach felt fine, and I didn't mention anything to Momma.

That evening I decided to write a poem on being white, 23
fat, old and without children. It was going to be a tragic
ballad. I would have to watch her carefully to capture the
essence of her loneliness and pain.

The very next day, she called me by the wrong name. Miss 24
Glory and I were washing up the lunch dishes when Mrs.
Cullinan came to the doorway. "Mary?"

Miss Glory asked, "Who?" 25

Mrs. Cullinan, sagging a little, knew and I knew. "I want 26
Mary to go down to Mrs. Randall's and take her some soup.
She's not been feeling well for a few days."

Miss Glory's face was a wonder to see. "You mean Marga- 27
ret, ma'am. Her name's Margaret."

"That's too long. She's Mary from now on. Heat that 28
soup from last night and put it in the china tureen and, Mary,
I want you to carry it carefully."

Every person I knew had a hellish horror of being "called   29
out of his name." It was a dangerous practice to call a Negro
anything that could be loosely construed as insulting because
of the centuries of their having been called niggers, jigs,
dinges, blackbirds, crows, boots and spooks.

Miss Glory had a fleeting second of feeling sorry for me.   30
Then as she handed me the hot tureen she said, "Don't
mind, don't pay that no mind. Sticks and stones may break
your bones, but words . . . You know, I been working for her
for twenty years."

She held the back door open for me. "Twenty years. I   31
wasn't much older than you. My name used to be Hallelujah.
That's what Ma named me, but my mistress give me 'Glory,'
and it stuck. I likes it better too."

I was in the little path that ran behind the houses when   32
Miss Glory shouted, "It's shorter too."

For a few seconds it was a tossup over whether I would   33
laugh (imagine being named Hallelujah) or cry (imagine
letting some white woman rename you for her convenience).
My anger saved me from either outburst. I had to quit the
job, but the problem was going to be how to do it. Momma
wouldn't allow me to quit for just any reason.

"She's a peach. That woman is a real peach." Mrs. Randall's   34
maid was talking as she took the soup from me, and I wondered
what her name used to be and what she answered to now.

For a week I looked into Mrs. Cullinan's face as she called   35
me Mary. She ignored my coming late and leaving early. Miss
Glory was a little annoyed because I had begun to leave egg
yolk on the dishes and wasn't putting much heart in polishing the silver. I hoped that she would complain to our boss,
but she didn't.

Then Bailey solved my dilemma. He had me describe   36
the contents of the cupboard and the particular plates she
liked best. Her favorite piece was a casserole shaped like a
fish and the green glass coffee cups. I kept his instructions in
mind, so on the next day when Miss Glory was hanging out
clothes and I had again been told to serve the old biddies on
the porch, I dropped the empty serving tray. When I heard

Mrs. Cullinan scream, "Mary!" I picked up the casserole and two of the green glass cups in readiness. As she rounded the kitchen door I let them fall on the tiled floor.

I could never absolutely describe to Bailey what hap- 37 pened next, because each time I got to the part where she fell on the floor and screwed up her ugly face to cry, we burst out laughing. She actually wobbled around on the floor and picked up shards of the cups and cried, "Oh, Momma. Oh, dear Gawd. It's Momma's china from Virginia. Oh, Momma, I sorry."

Miss Glory came running in from the yard and the women 38 from the porch crowded around. Miss Glory was almost as broken up as her mistress. "You mean to say she broke our Virginia dishes? What we gone do?"

Mrs. Cullinan cried louder, "That clumsy nigger. Clumsy 39 little black nigger."

Old speckled-face leaned down and asked, "Who did it, 40 Viola? Was it Mary? Who did it?"

Everything was happening so fast I can't remember 41 whether her action preceded her words, but I know that Mrs. Cullinan said, "Her name's Margaret, goddamn it, her name's Margaret." And she threw a wedge of the broken plate at me. It could have been the hysteria which put her aim off, but the flying crockery caught Miss Glory right over the ear and she started screaming.

I left the front door wide open so all the neighbors could 42 hear.

Mrs. Cullinan was right about one thing. My name wasn't 43 Mary.

For Study and Discussion

QUESTIONS ABOUT PURPOSE

1. In what sense does Mrs. Cullinan's kitchen serve as Angelou's "finishing school"? What is she supposed to learn there? What does she learn?

2. How does Angelou's description of Mrs. Cullinan's house as *exact* and *inhuman* support her purpose in recounting the events that take place there?

QUESTIONS ABOUT AUDIENCE

1. How does Angelou's comment about the liberal woman from Texas identify the immediate audience for her essay?
2. What assumptions does Angelou make about her other readers when she comments on the laughter of the white women on the porch?

QUESTIONS ABOUT STRATEGIES

1. How does Angelou use the three discussions of her name to organize her narrative? How does she pace the third discussion to provide an effective resolution for her essay?
2. How does Angelou's intention to write a poem about Mrs. Cullinan establish her initial attitude toward her employer? What changes her attitude toward Mrs. Cullinan's "loneliness and pain"?

For Writing and Research

1. *Analyze* the strategies Angelou uses to reveal her changing attitude toward Mrs. Cullinan.
2. *Practice* by enacting an experience in which someone mispronounces or forgets your name.
3. *Argue* Glory's versus Bailey's position about the destruction of the fish-shaped casserole.
4. *Synthesize* the advice given to girls in popular magazines. Then use this evidence to argue that such advice is an irrelevant preparation for adulthood.

Terry Tempest Williams was born in 1955 in
the Salt Valley of Utah and was educated at the
University of Utah. She has taught on a Navajo
reservation and in the women's studies program
at the University of Utah. She currently serves
as the curator of education and naturalist-in-
residence at the Utah Museum of Natural
History in Salt Lake City. Williams has written
children's books with nature themes, including
The Secret Language of Snow (1984); a collection of
short stories set in Utah, *Coyote's Canyon* (1989);
four works of nonfiction that blend natural
history and personal experience: *Pieces of White
Shell: A Journey to Navajo-Land* (1984), *Refuge: An Unnatural History of Family and Place*
(1991), *An Unspoken Hunger: Stories from the
Field* (1994), and *Red: Passion and Patience in
the Desert* (2001); as well as *Finding Beauty in
a Broken World* (2008) and *The Open Space of
Democracy* (2010). In "The Village Watchman,"
reprinted from *An Unspoken Hunger,* Williams
describes the remarkable lessons she learned
from her Uncle Alan.

The Village Watchman[2]

S TORIES CARVED IN cedar rise from the deep woods of Sitka.   1
These totem poles are foreign to me, this vertical lineage
of clans; Eagle, Raven, Wolf, and Salmon. The Tlingit crafts-
men create a genealogy of the earth, a reminder of mentors,

[2] Terry Tempest Williams, "The Village Watchman" from *An Unspoken Hunger*
by Terry Tempest Williams, copyright © 1994 by Terry Tempest Williams.
Used by permission of Pantheon Books, a division of Random House, Inc.

that we come into this world in need of proper instruction. I sit on the soft floor of this Alaskan forest and feel the presence of Other.

The totem before me is called "Wolf Pole" by locals. The Village Watchman sits on top of Wolf's head with his knees drawn to his chest, his hands holding them tight against his body. He wears a red-and-black-striped hat. His eyes are direct, deep-set, painted blue. The expression on his face reminds me of a man I loved, a man who was born into this world feet first.

"Breech—" my mother told me of her brother's birth. "Alan was born feet first. As a result, his brain was denied oxygen. He is special."

As a child, this information impressed me. I remember thinking fish live underwater. Maybe Alan had gills, maybe he didn't need a face-first gulp of air like the rest of us. His sweet breath of initiation came in time, slowly moving up through the soles of his tiny webbed feet. The amniotic sea he had

---

Alan was wild, like a mustang in the desert and, like most wild horses, he was eventually rounded up.

---

floated in for nine months delivered him with a fluid memory. He knew something. Other.

Wolf, who resides in the center of this totem, holds the tail of Salmon with his feet. The tongue of Wolf hangs down, blood-red, as do his front paws, black. Salmon, a sockeye, is poised downriver—a swish of a tail and he could be gone, but the clasp of Wolf is strong.

There is a story of a boy who was kidnapped from his village by the Salmon People. He was taken from his family to learn the ways of water. When he returned many years later to his home, he was recognized by his own as a Holy Man privy to the mysteries of the unseen world. Twenty years after my uncle's death, I wonder if Alan could have been that boy.

But our culture tells a different story, more alien than those 7
of Tlingit or Haida. My culture calls people of sole-births
retarded, handicapped, mentally disabled or challenged. We
see them for who they are not, rather than for who they are.

My grandmother, Lettie Romney Dixon, wrote in her 8
journal, "It wasn't until Alan was sixteen months old that a
busy doctor cruelly broke the news to us. Others may have
suspected our son's limitations but to those of us who loved
him so unquestionably, lightning struck without warning.
I hugged my sorrow to myself. I felt abandoned and lost. I
wouldn't accept the verdict. Then we started the trips to a
multitude of doctors. Most of them were kind and explained
that our child was like a car without brakes, like an electric wire
without insulation. They gave us no hope for a normal life."

Normal. Latin: *normalis; norma,* a rule; conforming with 9
or constituting an accepted standard, model, or pattern, especially corresponding to the median or average of a large group
in type, appearance, achievement, function, or development.

Alan was not normal. He was unique; one and only; sin- 10
gle; sole; unusual; extraordinary; rare. His emotions were not
measured, his curiosity not bridled. In a sense, he was wild
like a mustang in the desert and, like most wild horses, he was
eventually rounded up.

He was unpredictable. He created his own rules and they 11
changed from moment to moment. Alan was twelve years
old, hyperactive, mischievous, easily frustrated, and unable to
learn in traditional ways. The situation was intensified by his
seizures. Suddenly, without warning, he would stiffen like a
rake, fall forward and crash to the ground, hitting his head.
My grandparents could not keep him home any longer. They
needed professional guidance and help. In 1957 they reluctantly placed their youngest child in an institution for handicapped children called the American Fork Training School.
My grandmother's heart broke for the second time.

Once again, from her journal: "Many a night my pillow is wet 12
from tears of sorrow and senseless dreamings of 'if things had
only been different,' or wondering if he is tucked in snug and
warm, if he is well and happy, if the wind still bothers him. . . ."

The wind may have continued to bother Alan, certainly 13
the conditions he was living under were less than ideal, but as
a family there was much about his private life we never knew.
What we did know was that Alan had an enormous capacity
for adaptation. We had no choice but to follow him.

I followed him for years. 14

Alan was ten years my senior. In my mind, growing up, he 15
was mythic. Everything I was taught not to do, Alan did. We
were taught to be polite, to not express displeasure or anger in
public. Alan was sheer, physical expression. Whatever was on
his mind was vocalized and usually punctuated with colorful
speech. We would go bowling as a family on Sundays. Each of
us would take our turn, hold the black ball to our chest, take
a few steps, swing our arm back, forward, glide, and release—
the ball would roll down the alley, hit a few pins, we would
wait for the ball to return, and then take our second run.
Little emotion was shown. When it was Alan's turn, it was an
event. Nothing subtle. His style was Herculean. Big man. Big
ball. Big roll. Big bang. Whether it was a strike or a gutter,
he clapped his hands, spun around in the floor, slapped his
thighs and cried, "God-damn! Did you see that one? Send me
another ball, sweet Jesus" And the ball was always returned.

I could always count on my uncle for a straight answer. He 16
was my mentor in understanding that one of the remarkable
aspects of being human was to hold opposing views in our
mind at once.

"How are you doing?" I would ask. 17

"Ask me how I am feeling?" he answered. 18

"Okay, how are you feeling?" 19

"Today? Right now?" 20

"Yes." 21

"I am very happy and very sad." 22

"How can you be both at the same time?" I asked in all 23
seriousness, a girl of nine or ten.

"Because both require each other's company. They live in 24
the same house. Didn't you know?"

We would laugh and then go on to another topic. Talk- 25
ing to my uncle was always like entering a maze of riddles.

Ask a question. Answer with a question and see where it leads you.

My younger brother Steve and I spent a lot of time with   26
Alan. He offered us shelter from the conventionality of a Mormon family. At our home during Christmas, he would direct us in his own nativity plays. "More"—he would say to us, making wide gestures with his hands. "Give me more of yourself." He was not like anyone we knew. In a culture where we were taught socially to be seen not heard, Alan was our mirror. We could be different too. His unquestioning belief in us as children, as human beings, was in startling contrast to the way we saw the public react to him. It hurt us. What we could never tell was if it hurt him.

Each week, Steve and I would accompany our grandpar-   27
ents south to visit Alan. It was an hour's drive to the training school from Salt Lake City, mostly through farmlands.

We would enter the grounds, pull into the parking lot of   28
the institution where a playground filled with huge papier-mâché storybook figures stood (a twenty-foot pied piper, a pumpkin carriage with Cinderella inside, the old woman who lived in a shoe), and nine out of ten times, Alan would be standing outside his dormitory waiting for us. We would get out of the car and he would run toward us, throwing his powerful arms around us. His hugs cracked my back and at times I had to fight for my breath. My grandfather would calm him down by simply saying, "We're here, son. You can relax now."

Alan was a formidable man, now in his early twenties,   29
stocky and strong. His head was large with a protruding forehead that bore many scars, a line-by-line history of seizures. He always had on someone else's clothes—a tweed jacket too small, brown pants too big, a striped golf shirt that didn't match. He showed us appearances didn't matter, personality did. If you didn't know him, he could look frightening. It was an unspoken rule in our family that the character of others was gauged in how they treated him. The only thing consistent about his attire was that he always wore a silver football helmet from Olympus High School where my grandfather was coach. It was a loving, practical solution to protect Alan

when he fell. Quite simply, the helmet cradled his head and absorbed the shock of the seizures.

"Part of the team," my grandfather Sanky would say as he 30 slapped him affectionately on the back. "You're a Titan, son, and I love you—you're a real player on our team."

The windows to the dormitory were dark, reflecting 31 Mount Timpanogos to the east. It was hard to see inside, but I knew what the interior held. It looked like an abandoned gymnasium without bleachers, filled with hospital beds. The stained white walls and yellow-waxed floors offered no warmth to its residents. The stench was nauseating, sweat and urine trapped in the oppression of stale air. I recall the dirty sheets, the lack of privacy, and the almond-eyed children who never rose from their beds. And then I would turn around and face Alan's cheerfulness, the open and loving manner in which he would introduce me to his friends, the pride he exhibited as he showed me around his home. I kept thinking, Doesn't he see how bad this is, how poorly they are being treated? His words would return to me, "I am very happy and I am very sad."

For my brother and me, Alan was our guide, our elder. He 32 was fearless. But neither one of us will ever be able to escape the image of Alan kissing his parents good-bye after an afternoon with family and slowly walking back to his dormitory. Before we drove away, he would turn toward us, take off his silver helmet, and wave. The look on his face haunts me still. Alan walked point for all of us.

Alan liked to talk about God. Perhaps it was in these pri- 33 vate conversations that our real friendship was forged.

"I know Him," he would say when all the adults were 34 gone.

"You do?" I asked.   35

"I talk to Him every day."   36

"How so?"   37

"I talk to Him in my prayers. I listen and then I hear His 38 voice."

"What does He tell you?"   39

"He tells me to be patient. He tells me to be kind. He tells 40 me that He loves me."

In Mormon culture, children are baptized a member of   41
the Church of Jesus Christ of Latter-Day Saints when they
turn eight years old. Alan had never been baptized because
my grandparents believed it should be his choice, not something simply taken for granted. When he turned twenty-two,
he expressed a sincere desire to join the Church. A date was
set immediately.

The entire Dixon clan convened in the Lehi Chapel, a few   42
miles north of the group home where Alan was now living.
We were there to support and witness his conversion. As we
walked toward the meetinghouse where this sacred rite was
to be performed, Alan had a violent seizure. My grandfather
and Uncle Don, Alan's elder brother, dropped down with
him, holding his head and body as every muscle thrashed on
the pavement like a school of netted fish brought on deck.
I didn't want to look, but to walk away would have been
worse. We stayed with him, all of us.

"Talk to God," I heard myself saying under my breath. "I   43
love you, Alan."

"Can you hear me, darling?" It was my grandmother's   44
voice, her hand holding her son's hand.

By now, many of us were gathered on our knees around   45
him, our trembling hands on his rigid body.

> *And we, who have always thought*
> *Of happiness as rising, would feel,*
> *The emotion that almost overwhelms us*
> *Whenever a happy thing falls.*
> *—Rainer Maria Rilke*

Alan opened his eyes. "I want to be baptized," he said.   46
The men helped him to his feet. The gash on his left temple was deep. Blood dripped down the side of his face. He
would forgo stitches once again. My mother had her arm
around my grandmother's waist. Shaken, we all followed
him inside.

Alan's father and brother ministered to him, stopped the   47
bleeding and bandaged the pressure wound, then helped

him change into the designated white garments for baptism. He entered the room with great dignity and sat on the front pew with a dozen or more eight-year-old children seated on either side. Row after row of family sat behind him.

"Alan Romney Dixon." His name was called by the presiding bishop. Alan rose from the pew and met his brother Don, also dressed in white, who took his hand and led him down the blue-tiled stairs into the baptismal font filled with water. They faced the congregation. Don raised his right arm to the square in the gesture of a holy oath as Alan placed his hands on his brother's left forearm. The sacred prayer was offered in the name of the Father, the Son, and the Holy Ghost, after which my uncle put his right hand behind Alan's shoulder and gently lowered him into the water for a complete baptism by immersion. 48

Alan emerged from the holy waters like an angel. 49

> *The breaking away of childhood*
> *Left you intact. In a moment,*
> *You stood there, as if completed*
> *In a miracle, all at once.*
>   *—Rainer Maria Rilke*

Six years later, I found myself sitting in a chair across from my uncle at the University Hospital, where he was being treated for a severe ear infection. I was eighteen. He was twenty-eight. 50

"Alan," I asked. "What is it really like to be inside your body?" 51

He crossed his legs and placed both hands on the arms of the chair. His brown eyes were piercing. 52

"I can't tell you what it's like except to say I feel pain for not being seen as the person I am." 53

A few days later, Alan died alone; unique; one and only; single; in American Fork, Utah. 54

The Village Watchman sits on top of his totem with Wolf and Salmon—it is beginning to rain in the forest. I find it curious 55 that this spot in southeast Alaska has brought me back into relation with my uncle, this man of sole-birth who came into the world feet first. He reminds me of what it means to live and love with a broken heart; how nothing is sacred, how everything is sacred. He was a weather vane—a storm and a clearing at once.

Shortly after his death, Alan appeared to me in a dream.   56
We were standing in my grandmother's kitchen. He was leaning against the white stove with his arms folded.

"Look at me, now, Terry," he said smiling. "I'm normal—   57
perfectly normal." And then he laughed. We both laughed.

He handed me his silver football helmet that was resting   58
on the counter, kissed me, and opened the back door.

"Do you recognize who I am?"   59

On this day in Sitka, I remember.   60

For Study and Discussion

QUESTIONS ABOUT PURPOSE

1. How does Williams's title suggest the purpose of her description of her Uncle Alan's life?
2. How does Williams's description of the Wolf Pole present the purpose of her narrative?

QUESTIONS ABOUT AUDIENCE

1. How does Williams's use of the pronoun *our* in the following phrase identify her audience: "our culture tells a different story, more alien"?
2. How does the following sentence separate Williams's family from her audience: "His unquestioning belief in us . . . was in startling contrast to the way we saw the public react to him"?

QUESTIONS ABOUT STRATEGIES

1. How does Williams use the quotation from Rilke's poetry to interpret Alan's baptism?
2. How does she use the visits at the school, and particularly her last visit to the hospital, to slow the pace of her narrative?

For Writing and Research

1. *Analyze* the strategies Williams uses to correct or enrich your understanding of "special" people.
2. *Practice* by enacting your reactions and reflections on your encounter with a "special" person.
3. *Argue* that the words *normal* and *special* are used or misused in our culture.
4. *Synthesize*: Research the way the media (television, movies) portray "special" people. Then use this evidence to demonstrate that such people are denigrated or celebrated.

JUDITH ORTIZ COFER

Judith Ortiz Cofer was born in Hormigueros, Puerto Rico, in 1952. She emigrated to the United States in 1956 and was educated at Augusta College, Florida Atlantic University, and Oxford University. She has taught in the public schools of Palm Beach County, Florida, as well as at several universities, such as Miami University and the University of Georgia. Her poetry is collected in *Reaching for the Mainland* (1987) and *Terms of Survival* (1987); and her first novel, *The Line of the Sun* (1989), was nominated for the Pulitzer Prize. Her books include *The Latin Deli: Prose and Poetry* (1993), *An Island Like You: Stories of the Barrio* (1995), *The Meaning of Consuelo* (2003), and *A Love Story Beginning in Spanish: Poems* (2005). In "The Myth of the Latin Woman: I Just Met a Girl Named María," reprinted from *The Latin Deli*, Cofer describes several experiences that taught her about the pervasive stereotypes of Latin women.

The Myth of the Latin Woman[3]
I Just Met a Girl Named María

O N A BUS trip to London from Oxford University where   1
I was earning some graduate credits one summer, a young man, obviously fresh from a pub, spotted me and as if struck by inspiration went down on his knees in the aisle. With both hands over his heart he broke into an Irish tenor's rendition of "María" from *West Side Story*. My politely

---

[3]Judith Ortiz Cofer, "The Myth of the Latin Woman: I Just Met a Girl Named Maria" from *The Latin Deli Prose and Poetry*, © 1993 by Judith Oritz Cofer. Reprinted by permission of the University of Georgia Press.

amused fellow passengers gave his lovely voice the round of gentle applause it deserved. Though I was not quite as amused, I managed my version of an English smile: no show of teeth, no extreme contortions of the facial muscles—I was at this time of my life practicing reserve and cool. Oh, that British control, how I coveted it. But María had followed me to London, reminding me of a prime fact of my life: you can leave the Island, master the English language, and travel as far as you can, but if you are a Latina, especially one like me who so obviously belongs to Rita Moreno's gene pool, the Island travels with you.

---

*When a Puerto Rican girl dressed in her idea of what is attractive meets a man from the mainstream culture who has been trained to react to certain types of clothing as **a sexual signal**, a clash is likely to take place.*

This is sometimes a very good thing—it may win you that   2
extra minute of someone's attention. But with some people, the same things can make *you* an island—not so much a tropical paradise as an Alcatraz, a place nobody wants to visit. As a Puerto Rican girl growing up in the United States and wanting like most children to "belong," I resented the stereotype that my Hispanic appearance called forth from many people I met.

Our family lived in a large urban center in New Jersey dur-   3
ing the sixties, where life was designed as a microcosm of my parents' casas on the island. We spoke in Spanish, we ate Puerto Rican food bought at the bodega, and we practiced strict Catholicism complete with Saturday confession and Sunday mass at a church where our parents were accommodated into a one-hour Spanish mass slot, performed by a Chinese priest trained as a missionary for Latin America.

As a girl I was kept under strict surveillance, since virtue   4
and modesty were, by cultural equation, the same as family
honor. As a teenager I was instructed on how to behave as
a proper señorita. But it was a conflicting message girls got,
since the Puerto Rican mothers also encouraged their daughters to look and act like women and to dress in clothes our
Anglo friends and their mothers found too "mature" for our
age. It was, and is, cultural, yet I often felt humiliated when
I appeared at an American friend's party wearing a dress more
suitable to a semiformal than to a playroom birthday celebration. At Puerto Rican festivities, neither the music nor the
colors we wore could be too loud. I still experience a vague
sense of letdown when I'm invited to a "party" and it turns
out to be a marathon conversation in hushed tones rather
than a fiesta with salsa, laughter, and dancing—the kind of
celebration I remember from my childhood.

I remember Career Day in our high school, when teach-   5
ers told us to come dressed as if for a job interview. It quickly
became obvious that to the barrio girls, "dressing up" sometimes meant wearing ornate jewelry and clothing that would
be more appropriate (by mainstream standards) for the company Christmas party than as daily office attire. That morning I had agonized in front of my closet, trying to figure out
what a "career girl" would wear because, essentially, except
for Marlo Thomas on TV, I had no models on which to base
my decision. I knew how to dress for school: at the Catholic
school I attended we all wore uniforms; I knew how to dress
for Sunday mass, and I knew what dresses to wear for parties
at my relatives' homes. Though I do not recall the precise
details of my Career Day outfit, it must have been a composite
of the above choices. But I remember a comment my friend
(an Italian-American) made in later years that coalesced my
impressions of that day. She said that at the business school
she was attending the Puerto Rican girls always stood out
for wearing "everything at once." She meant, of course, too
much jewelry, too many accessories. On that day at school, we
were simply made the negative models by the nuns who were
themselves not credible fashion experts to any of us. But it was

painfully obvious to me that to the others, in their tailored skirts and silk blouses, we must have seemed "hopeless" and "vulgar." Though I now know that most adolescents feel out of step much of the time, I also know that for the Puerto Rican girls of my generation that sense was intensified. The way our teachers and classmates looked at us that day in school was just a taste of the culture clash that awaited us in the real world, where prospective employers and men on the street would often misinterpret our tight skirts and jingling bracelets as a come-on.

Mixed cultural signals have perpetuated certain stereotypes— for example, that of the Hispanic woman as the "Hot Tamale" or sexual firebrand. It is a one-dimensional view that the media have found easy to promote. In their special vocabulary, advertisers have designated "sizzling" and "smoldering" as the adjectives of choice for describing not only the foods but also the women of Latin America. From conversations in my house I recall hearing about the harassment that Puerto Rican women endured in factories where the "boss men" talked to them as if sexual innuendo was all they understood and, worse, often gave them the choice of submitting to advances or being fired.   6

It is custom, however, not chromosomes, that leads us to choose scarlet over pale pink. As young girls, we were influenced in our decisions about clothes and colors by the women—older sisters and mothers who had grown up on a tropical island where the natural environment was a riot of primary colors, where showing your skin was one way to keep cool as well as to look sexy. Most important of all, on the island, women perhaps felt freer to dress and move more provocatively, since, in most cases, they were protected by the traditions, mores, and laws of a Spanish/Catholic system of morality and machismo whose main rule was: *You may look at my sister, but if you touch her I will kill you.* The extended family and church structure could provide a young woman with a circle of safety in her small pueblo on the island; if a man "wronged" a girl, everyone would close in to save her family honor.   7

This is what I have gleaned from my discussions as an adult   8
with older Puerto Rican women. They have told me about
dressing in their best party clothes on Saturday nights and
going to the town's plaza to promenade with their girlfriends
in front of the boys they liked. The males were thus given
an opportunity to admire the women and to express their
admiration in the form of *piropos:* erotically charged street
poems they composed on the spot. I have been subjected to
a few piropos while visiting the Island, and they can be outrageous, although custom dictates that they must never cross
into obscenity. This ritual, as I understand it, also entails a
show of studied indifference on the woman's part; if she is
"decent," she must not acknowledge the man's impassioned
words. So I do understand how things can be lost in translation. When a Puerto Rican girl dressed in her idea of what is
attractive meets a man from the mainstream culture who has
been trained to react to certain types of clothing as a sexual
signal, a clash is likely to take place. The line I first heard based
on this aspect of the myth happened when the boy who took
me to my first formal dance leaned over to plant a sloppy over-
eager kiss painfully on my mouth, and when I didn't respond
with sufficient passion said in a resentful tone: "I thought you
Latin girls were supposed to mature early"—my first instance
of being thought of as a fruit or vegetable—I was supposed to
ripen, not just grow into womanhood like other girls.

It is surprising to some of my professional friends that some   9
people, including those who should know better, still put others "in their place." Though rarer, these incidents are still commonplace in my life. It happened to me most recently during a
stay at a very classy metropolitan hotel favored by young professional couples for their weddings. Late one evening after the
theater, as I walked toward my room with my new colleague
(a woman with whom I was coordinating an arts program), a
middle-aged man in a tuxedo, a young girl in satin and lace on
his arm, stepped directly into our path. With his champagne
glass extended toward me, he exclaimed, "Evita!"

Our way blocked, my companion and I listened as the man   10
half-recited, half-bellowed "Don't Cry for Me, Argentina."

When he finished, the young girl said: "How about a round of applause for my daddy?" We complied, hoping this would bring the silly spectacle to a close. I was becoming aware that our little group was attracting the attention of the other guests. "Daddy" must have perceived this too, and he once more barred the way as we tried to walk past him. He began to shout-sing a ditty to the tune of "La Bamba"—except the lyrics were about a girl named María whose exploits all rhymed with her name and gonorrhea. The girl kept saying "Oh, Daddy" and looking at me with pleading eyes. She wanted me to laugh along with the others. My companion and I stood silently waiting for the man to end his offensive song. When he finished, I looked not at him but at his daughter. I advised her calmly never to ask her father what he had done in the army. Then I walked between them and to my room. My friend complimented me on my cool handling of the situation. I confessed to her that I really had wanted to push the jerk into the swimming pool. I knew that this same man—probably a corporate executive, well educated, even worldly by most standards—would not have been likely to regale a white woman with a dirty song in public. He would perhaps have checked his impulse by assuming that she could be somebody's wife or mother, or at least *somebody* who might take offense. But to him, I was just an Evita or a María: merely a character in his cartoon-populated universe.

Because of my education and my proficiency with the 11 English language, I have acquired many mechanisms for dealing with the anger I experience. This was not true for my parents, nor is it true for the many Latin women working at menial jobs who must put up with stereotypes about our ethnic group such as: "They make good domestics." This is another facet of the myth of the Latin woman in the United States. Its origin is simple to deduce. Work as domestics, waitressing, and factory jobs are all that's available to women with little English and few skills. The myth of the Hispanic menial has been sustained by the same media phenomenon that made "Mammy" from *Gone with the Wind* America's idea of the black woman for generations; María, the housemaid or counter girl, is now indelibly etched into the national psyche. The big and the little screens have presented us with the picture of the funny Hispanic maid, mispronouncing words and cooking up a spicy storm in a shiny California kitchen.

This media-engendered image of the Latina in the United States has been documented by feminist Hispanic scholars, who claim that such portrayals are partially responsible for the denial of opportunities for upward mobility among Latinas in the professions. I have a Chicana friend working on a Ph.D. in philosophy at a major university. She says her doctor still shakes his head in puzzled amazement at all the "big words" she uses. Since I do not wear my diplomas around my neck for all to see, I too have on occasion been sent to that "kitchen," where some think I obviously belong. 12

One such incident that has stayed with me, though I recognize it as a minor offense, happened on the day of my first public poetry reading. It took place in Miami in a boat-restaurant where we were having lunch before the event. I was nervous and excited as I walked in with my notebook in my hand. An older woman motioned me to her table. Thinking (foolish me) that she wanted me to autograph a copy of my brand new slender volume of verse, I went over. She ordered a cup of coffee from me, assuming that I was the waitress. Easy enough to mistake my poems for menus, I suppose. I know that it wasn't an intentional act of cruelty, yet of all the good things that happened that day, I remember that scene most clearly, because it reminded me of what I had to overcome before anyone would take me seriously. In retrospect I understand that my anger gave my reading fire, that I have almost always taken doubts in my abilities as a challenge—and that the result is, most times, a feeling of satisfaction at having won a convert when I see the cold, appraising eyes warm to my words, the body language change, the smile that indicates that I have opened some avenue for communication. That day I read to that woman and her lowered eyes told me that she was embarrassed at her little faux pas, and when I willed her to look up at me, it was my victory, and she graciously allowed me to punish her with my full attention. We shook hands at the end of the reading, 13 and I never saw her again. She has probably forgotten the whole thing but maybe not.

Yet I am one of the lucky ones. My parents made it pos- 14
sible for me to acquire a stronger footing in the mainstream culture by giving me the chance at an education. And books and art have saved me from the harsher forms of ethnic and racial prejudice that many of my Hispanic *compañeras* have had to endure. I travel a lot around the United States, reading from my books of poetry and my novel, and the reception I most often receive is one of positive interest by people who want to know more about my culture. There are, however, thousands of Latinas without the privilege of an education or the entrée into society that I have. For them life is a struggle against the misconceptions perpetuated by the myth of the Latina as whore, domestic or criminal. We cannot change this by legislating the way people look at us. The transformation, as I see it, has to occur at a much more individual level. My personal goal in my public life is to try to replace the old pervasive stereotypes and myths about Latinas with a much more interesting set of realities. Every time I give a reading, I hope the stories I tell, the dreams and fears I examine in my work, can achieve some universal truth which will get my audience past the particulars of my skin color, my accent, or my clothes.

I once wrote a poem in which I called us Latinas "God's 15
brown daughters." This poem is really a prayer of sorts, offered upward, but also, through the human-to-human channel of art, outward. It is a prayer for communication, and for respect. In it, Latin women pray "in Spanish to an Anglo God/with a Jewish heritage," and they are "fervently hoping/that if not omnipotent,/at least He be bilingual."

For Study and Discussion

QUESTIONS ABOUT PURPOSE

1. Why does Cofer introduce the conflict between *custom* and *chromosomes*? How does this conflict help explain the concept of *stereotype*?

2. How does this narrative help accomplish Cofer's "personal goal in her public life"?

QUESTIONS ABOUT AUDIENCE

1. In what ways does Cofer use the references to *María* and *Evita* to identify her audience?
2. How does she use the example of the *piropos* to educate her audience?

QUESTIONS ABOUT STRATEGIES

1. How does Cofer use the details of Career Day to explain how a cultural stereotype is perpetuated?
2. How does she manipulate point of view at her "first public poetry reading" to illustrate how she intends to change that stereotype?

For Writing and Research

1. *Analyze* the way Cofer uses *Gone with the Wind* to illustrate how the media create stereotypes.
2. *Practice* by enacting an experience in which people have misread your behavior by focusing on your clothes, your language, or your looks.
3. *Argue* that stereotypes are the result of custom or caricature.
4. *Synthesize:* Research how people respond to stereotyping. Then use this evidence to argue for the most effective way to eliminate stereotyping.

Andre Dubus (1936–1999) was born in Lake Charles, Louisiana, and educated at McNeese State College and the University of Iowa. He taught writing at universities such as the University of Alabama and Boston University. His work includes novels such as *The Lieutenant* (1967), *Voices from the Moon* (1984), and several collections of short stories, including *Finding a Girl in America* (1980) and *Dancing After Hours* (1996). In 1986, he barely survived a devastating traffic accident that cost him his leg. He writes about confronting his disability in a series of essays, *Meditations from a Moveable Chair* (1998). In "Digging," reprinted from that collection, Dubus remembers the lessons he learned from physical labor.

Digging[4]

THAT HOT JUNE in Lafayette, Louisiana, I was sixteen, I would be seventeen in August, I weighed 105 pounds, and my ruddy, broad-chested father wanted me to have a summer job. I only wanted the dollar allowance he gave me each week, and the dollar and a quarter I earned caddying for him on weekend and Wednesday afternoons. With a quarter I could go to a movie, or buy a bottle of beer, or a pack of cigarettes to smoke secretly. I did not have a girlfriend, so I did not have to buy drinks or food or movie tickets for anyone else. I did not want to work. I wanted to drive around with my friends, or walk with them downtown, to stand in

1

---

front of the department store, comb our ducktails, talk, look at girls.

My father was a civil engineer, and the district manager for the Gulf States Utilities Company. He had been working for them since he left college, beginning as a surveyor, wearing boots and khakis and, in a holster on his belt, a twenty-two caliber pistol for cottonmouths. At home he was quiet; in the evenings he sat in his easy chair, and smoked, and read: *Time, The Saturday Evening Post, Collier's, The Reader's Digest,* detective novels, books about golf, and Book-of-the-Month Club novels. He loved to talk, and he did this at parties I listened to from my bedroom, and with his friends on the golf course, and drinking in the clubhouse after playing eighteen holes. I listened to more of my father's conversations about politics and golf and his life and the world than I ever engaged in, during the nearly twenty-two years I lived with him. I was afraid of angering him, seeing his blue eyes, and reddening face, hearing the words he would use to rebuke me; but what I feared most was his voice, suddenly and harshly rising. He never yelled for long, only a few sentences, but they emptied me, as if his voice had pulled my soul from my body. His voice seemed to empty the house, too, and, when he stopped yelling, the house filled with silence. He did not yell often. That sound was not part of our family life. The fear of it was part of my love for him.

---

*It is time to thank my father for wanting
me to work and telling me I had to work . . .
and buying me lunch and a pith
helmet instead of taking me home to
my mother and sister.*

I was shy with him. Since my forties I have believed that he was shy with me too, and I hope it was not as painful for him as it was for me. I think my shyness had very little to do with my fear. Other boys had fathers who yelled longer and more often, fathers who spanked them or, when they were in their teens, slapped or punched them. My father spanked me only three times, probably because he did not know of most of my transgressions. My friends with harsher fathers were neither afraid nor shy; they quarreled with their fathers, provoked them. My father sired a sensitive boy, easily hurt or frightened, and he worried about me; I knew he did when I was a boy, and he told me this on his deathbed, when I was a Marine captain.

My imagination gave me a dual life: I lived in my body, 4 and at the same time lived a life no one could see. All my life I have told myself stories, and have talked in my mind to friends. Imagine my father sitting at supper with my mother and two older sisters and me: I am ten and small and appear distracted. Every year at school there is a bully, sometimes a new one, sometimes the one from the year before. I draw bullies to me, not because I am small, but because they know I will neither fight nor inform on them. I will take their pushes or pinches or punches, and try not to cry, and I will pretend I am not hurt. My father does not know this. He only sees me at supper, and I am not there. I am riding a horse and shooting bad men. My father eats, glances at me. I know he is trying to see who I am, who I will be.

Before my teens, he took me to professional wrestling 5 matches because I wanted to go; he told me they were fake, and I did not believe him. We listened to championship boxing matches on the radio. When I was not old enough to fire a shotgun he took me dove hunting with his friends: we crouched in a ditch facing a field, and I watched the doves fly toward us and my father rising to shoot, then I ran to fetch the warm, dead and delicious birds. In summer he took me fishing with his friends; we walked in woods to creeks and bayous and fished with bamboo poles. When I was ten he learned to play golf and stopped hunting and fishing, and on weekends I was his caddy. I did not want to be, I wanted to play with my friends, but when I became a man and left home, I was grateful that I had spent those afternoons watching him, listening to him. A minor league baseball team made our town its home, and my father took me to games, usually with my mother. When I was twelve or so, he taught me to play golf, and sometimes I played nine holes with him; more often and more comfortably, I played with other boys.

If my father and I were not watching or listening to some- 6 thing and responding to it, or were not doing something, but were simply alone together, I could not talk, and he did not, and I felt that I should, and I was ashamed. That June of my seventeenth year, I could not tell him that I did not want a job. He talked to a friend of his, a building contractor, who hired me as a carpenter's helper; my pay was seventy-five cents an hour.

On a Monday morning my father drove me to work. I 7 would ride the bus home and, next day, would start riding the bus to work. Probably my father drove me that morning because it was my first day; when I was twelve he had taken me to a store to buy my first pair of long pants; we boys wore shorts and, in fall and winter, knickers and long socks till we were twelve; and he had taken me to a barber for my first haircut. In the car I sat frightened, sadly resigned, and feeling absolutely incompetent. I had the lunch my mother had put in a brown paper bag, along with a mason jar with sugar and squeezed lemons in it, so I could make lemonade with water from the cooler. We drove to a street with houses and small stores and parked at a corner where, on a flat piece of land, men were busy. They were building a liquor store, and I assumed I would spend my summer handing things to a carpenter. I hoped he would be patient and kind.

As a boy in Louisiana's benevolent winters and hot sum- 8 mers I had played outdoors with friends: we built a clubhouse, chased each other on bicycles, shot air rifles at birds, tin cans, bottles, trees; in fall and winter, wearing shoulder pads and helmets, we played football on someone's very large side lawn; and in summer we played baseball in a field that a father mowed for us; he also built us a backstop of wood and chicken wire. None of us played well enough to be on a varsity team; but I wanted that gift, not knowing that it was a gift, and I felt ashamed that I did not have it. Now we drove cars, smoked, drank in nightclubs. This was French Catholic country; we could always buy drinks. Sometimes we went on dates with girls, but more often looked at them and talked about them; or visited them, when several girls were gathered at the home of a girl whose parents were out for the evening. I had never done physical work except caddying, pushing a lawn mower, and raking leaves, and I was walking from the car with my father toward working men. My father wore his straw hat and seersucker suit. He introduced me to the foreman and said: "Make a man of him."

Then he left. The foreman wore a straw hat and looked old; everyone looked old; the foreman was probably thirty-five. I stood mutely, waiting for him to assign me to some good-hearted Cajun carpenter. He assigned me a pickaxe and a shovel and told me to get into the trench and go to work. In all four sides of the trench were files of black men, swinging picks, and shoveling. The trench was about three feet deep and it would be the building's foundation; I went to where the foreman pointed, and laid my tools on the ground; two black men made a space for me, and I jumped between them. They smiled and we greeted each other. I would learn days later that they earned a dollar an hour. They were men with families and I knew this was unjust, as everything else was for black people. But on that first morning I did not know what they were being paid, I did not know their names, only that one was working behind me and one in front, and they were good to me and stronger than I could ever be. All I really knew in those first hours under the hot sun was raising the pickaxe and swinging it down, raising it and swinging, again and again till the earth was loose; then putting the pick on the ground beside me and taking the shovel and plunging it into dirt that I lifted and tossed beside the trench.

I did not have the strength for this: not in my back, my legs, my arms, my shoulders. Certainly not in my soul. I only wanted it to end. The air was very humid, and sweat dripped on my face and arms, soaked my shirts and jeans. My hands gripping the pick or shovel were sore, my palms burned, the muscles in my arms ached, and my breath was quick.

Sometimes I saw tiny black spots before my eyes. Weakly I raised the pick, straightening my back, then swung it down, bending my body with it, and it felt heavier than I was, more durable, this thing of wood and steel that was melting me. I laid it on the ground and picked up the shovel and pushed it into the dirt, lifted it, grunted, and emptied it beside the trench. The sun, always my friend till now, burned me, and my mouth and throat were dry, and often I climbed out of the trench and went to the large tin water cooler with a block of ice in it and water from a hose. At the cooler were paper cups and salt tablets, and I swallowed salt and drank and drank, and poured water onto my head and face; then I went back to the trench, the shovel, the pick.

Nausea came in the third or fourth hour. I kept swinging   11
the pick, pushing and lifting the shovel. I became my sick and hot and tired and hurting flesh. Or it became me; so, for an hour or more, I tasted a very small piece of despair. At noon in Lafayette a loud whistle blew, and in the cathedral the bell rang. I could not hear the bell where we worked, but I heard the whistle, and lowered the shovel and looked around. I was dizzy and sick. All the men had stopped working and were walking toward shade. One of the men with me said it was time to eat, and I climbed out of the trench and walked with black men to the shade of the tool shed. The white men went to another shaded place; I do not remember what work they had been doing that morning, but it was not with picks and shovels in the trench. Everyone looked hot but comfortable. The black men sat talking and began to eat and drink. My bag of lunch and jar with lemons and sugar were on the ground in the shade. Still I stood, gripped by nausea. I looked at the black men and at my lunch bag. Then my stomach tightened and everything in it rose, and I went around the corner of the shed where no one could see me and, bending over, I vomited and moaned and heaved until it ended. I went to the water cooler and rinsed my mouth and spat, and then I took another paper cup and drank. I walked back to the shade and lay on my back, tasting vomit. One of the black men said: "You got to eat."

"I threw up," I said, and closed my eyes and slept for the 12
rest of the hour that everyone—students and workers—had
for the noon meal. At home my nineteen-year-old sister and
my mother and father were eating dinner, meat and rice and
gravy, vegetables and salad and iced tea with a leaf of mint;
and an oscillating fan cooled them. My twenty-two-year-old
sister was married. At one o'clock the whistle blew, and I
woke up and stood and one of the black men said: "Are you
all right?"

I nodded. If I had spoken, I may have wept. When I was 13
a boy I could not tell a man what I felt, if I believed what I
felt was unmanly. We went back to the trench, down into it,
and I picked up the shovel I had left there at noon, and shov-
eled out all the loose earth between me and the man in front
of me, then put the shovel beside the trench, lifted the pick,
raised it over my shoulder, and swung it down into the dirt.
I was dizzy and weak and hot; I worked for forty minutes or
so; then, above me, I heard my father's voice, speaking my
name. I looked up at him; he was here to take me home, to
forgive my failure, and in my great relief I could not know
that I would not be able to forgive it. I was going home. But
he said: "Let's go buy you a hat."

Every man there wore a hat, most of them straw, the oth- 14
ers baseball caps. I said nothing. I climbed out of the trench,
and went with my father. In the car, in a voice softened with
pride, he said: "The foreman called me. He said the Nigras
told him you threw up, and didn't eat, and you didn't tell
him."

"That's right," I said, and shamefully watched the road, 15
and cars with people who seemed free of all torment, and
let my father believe I was brave, because I was afraid to tell
him that I was afraid to tell the foreman. Quietly we drove
to town and he parked and took me first to a drugstore with
air-conditioning and a lunch counter, and bought me a 7-Up
for my stomach, and told me to order a sandwich. Sweet-
smelling women at the counter were smoking. The men in
the trench had smoked while they worked, but my body's
only desire had been to stop shoveling and swinging the pick,

to be with no transition at all in the shower at home, then to lie on my bed, feeling the soft breath of the fan on my damp skin. I would not have smoked at work anyway, with men. Now I wanted a cigarette. My father smoked, and I ate a bacon and lettuce and tomato sandwich.

Then we walked outside, into humidity and the heat and glare of the sun. We crossed the street to the department store where, in the work clothes section, my father chose a pith helmet. I did not want to wear a pith helmet. I would happily wear one in Africa, hunting lions and rhinoceroses. But I did not want to wear such a thing in Lafayette. I said nothing; there was no hat I wanted to wear. I carried the helmet in its bag out of the store and, in the car, laid it beside me. At that place where sweating men worked, I put it on; a thin leather strap looped around the back of my head. I went to my two comrades in the trench. One of them said: "That's a good hat." 16

I jumped in. 17

The man behind me said: "You going to be all right now." 18

I was; and I still do not know why. A sandwich and a soft drink had not given me any more strength than the breakfast I had vomited. An hour's respite in the car and the cool drugstore and buying the helmet that now was keeping my wet head cool certainly helped. But I had the same soft arms and legs, the same back and shoulders I had demanded so little of in my nearly seventeen years of stewardship. Yet all I remember of that afternoon is the absence of nausea. 19

At five o'clock the whistle blew downtown and we climbed out of the trench and washed our tools with the hose, then put them in the shed. Dirt was on my arms and hands, my face and neck and clothes. I could have wrung sweat from my shirt and jeans. I got my lunch from the shade. My two comrades said, See you tomorrow. I said I would see them. I went to the bus stop at the corner and sat on the bench. My wet clothes cooled my skin. I looked down at my dirty tennis shoes; my socks and feet were wet. I watched people in passing cars. In one were teenaged boys, and they laughed and shouted something about my helmet. I watched the car 20 till it was blocks away, then took off the helmet and held it on my lap. I carried it aboard the bus; yet all summer I wore it at work, maybe because my father bought it for me and I did not want to hurt him, maybe because it was a wonderful helmet for hard work outdoors in Louisiana.

My father got home before I did and told my mother 21 and sister the story, the only one he knew, or the only one I assumed he knew. The women proudly greeted me when I walked into the house. They were also worried. They wanted to know how I felt. They wore dresses, they smelled of perfume or cologne, they were drinking bourbon and water, and my sister and father were smoking cigarettes. Standing in the living room, holding my lunch and helmet, I said I was fine. I could not tell the truth to these women who loved me, even if my father were not there. I could not say that I was not strong enough and that I could not bear going back to work tomorrow, and all summer, any more than I could tell them I did not believe I was as good at being a boy as other boys were: not at sports, or with girls; and now not with a man's work. I was home, where vases held flowers, and things were clean, and our manners were good.

Next morning, carrying my helmet and lunch, I rode the 22 bus to work and joined the two black men in the trench. I felt that we were friends. Soon I felt this about all the black men at work. We were digging the foundation; we were the men and the boy with picks and shovels in the trench. One day the foundation was done. I use the passive voice, because this was a square or rectangular trench, men were working at each of its sides. I had been working with my comrades on the same side for weeks, moving not forward but down. Then it was done. Someone told us. Maybe the contractor was there, with the foreman. Who dug out that last bit of dirt? I only knew that I had worked as hard as I could, I was part of the trench, it was part of me, and it was finished; it was there in the earth to receive concrete and probably never to be seen again. Someone should have blown a bugle, we should have climbed exultant from the trench, gathered to wipe sweat from our brows, drink water, shake hands, then walk together to each of the four sides and marvel at what we had made.

On that second morning of work I was not sick, and at   23
noon I ate lunch with the blacks in the shade, then we all slept on the grass till one o'clock. We worked till five, said goodbye to each other, and they went to the colored section of town, and I rode the bus home. When I walked into the living room, into cocktail hour, and my family asked me about my day, I said it was fine. I may have learned something if I had told them the truth: the work was too hard, but after the first morning I could bear it. And all summer it would be hard; after we finished the foundation, I would be transferred to another crew. We would build a mess hall at a Boy Scout camp and, with a black man, I would dig a septic tank in clay so hard that the foreman kept hosing water into it as we dug; black men and I would push wheelbarrows of mixed cement; on my shoulder I would carry eighty-pound bags of dry cement, twenty-five pounds less than my own weight; and at the summer's end my body would be twenty pounds heavier. If I had told these three people who loved me that I did not understand my weak body's stamina, they may have taught me why something terrible had so quickly changed to something arduous.

It is time to thank my father for wanting me to work and   24
telling me I had to work and getting the job for me and buying me lunch and a pith helmet instead of taking me home to my mother and sister. He may have wanted to take me home. But he knew he must not, and he came tenderly to me. My mother would have been at home that afternoon; if he had taken me to her she would have given me iced tea and, after my shower, a hot dinner. When my sister came home from work, she would have understood, and told me not to despise myself because I could not work with a pickaxe and a shovel. And I would have spent the summer at home, nestled in the love of the two women, peering at my father's face, and yearning to be someone I respected, a varsity second baseman, a halfback, someone cheerleaders and drum majorettes and pretty scholars loved; yearning to be a

man among men, and that is where my father sent me with a helmet on my head.

For Study and Discussion

QUESTIONS ABOUT PURPOSE

1. How do Dubus's father's instructions to the foreman—"Make a man of him"—reveal the narrator's purpose?
2. How is the narrator's admission that he lived a "dual life" revealed in his story?

QUESTIONS ABOUT AUDIENCE

1. How does Dubus's characterization of himself as sensitive and shy help establish his connection with his readers?
2. How does his friendship with black workmen help him teach his audience something about justice?

QUESTIONS ABOUT STRATEGIES

1. How does Dubus pace his first day at work to reveal the intensity of his efforts?
2. How do his speculations about what would have happened if he had gone home to lunch help clarify the purpose of his narrative?

For Writing and Research

1. *Analyze* how Dubus develops the plot of his narrative to reveal what he learned from physical labor.
2. *Practice* by narrating your own story about a job that required you to develop new skills.
3. *Argue* that it is (or is not) difficult to tell the truth to family and friends.
4. *Synthesize:* Research the way the "work ethic" is passed on in families from generation to generation. Then use this information to demonstrate how fathers or mothers pass this ethic on to their children.

GEORGE ORWELL

George Orwell, the pen name for Eric Blair (1903–1950), was born in Motihari, Bengal, where his father was employed with the Bengal civil service. He was brought to England at an early age for schooling (Eton), but rather than completing his education, he served with the Indian imperial police in Burma (1922–1927). Later he returned to Europe and worked at various jobs (described in *Down and Out in Paris and London,* 1933) before fighting on the Republican side in the Spanish Civil War. (See *Homage to Catalonia,* 1938.) Orwell's attitudes toward war and government are reflected in his most famous books: *Animal Farm* (1945), *1984* (1949), and *Shooting an Elephant and Other Essays* (1950). In the title essay from the last volume, Orwell reports a "tiny incident" that gave him deeper insight into his own fears and "the real motives for which despotic governments act."

Shooting an Elephant[5]

I N MOULMEIN, in lower Burma, I was hated by large numbers of people—the only time in my life that I have been important enough for this to happen to me. I was subdivisional police officer of the town, and in an aimless, petty kind of way anti-European feeling was very bitter. No one

1

---

[5] George Orwell, "Shooting an Elephant" from *Shooting an Elephant and other Essays* by George Orwell, copyright 1950 by Sonia Brownell Orwell and renewed 1978 by Sonia Pitt-Rivers, reprinted by permission of Houghton Mifflin Harcourt Publishing Company and Bill Hamilton as the Literary Executor of the Estate of the Late Sonia Brownell Orwell and Secker & Warburg Ltd. All rights reserved.

had the guts to raise a riot, but if a European woman went through the bazaars alone somebody would probably spit betel juice over her dress. As a police officer I was an obvious target and was baited whenever it seemed safe to do so. When a nimble Burman tripped me up on the football field and the referee (another Burman) looked the other way, the crowd yelled with hideous laughter. This happened more than once. In the end the sneering yellow faces of young men that met me everywhere, the insults hooted after me when I was at a safe distance, got badly on my nerves. The young Buddhist priests were the worst of all. There were several thousands of them in the town and none of them seemed to have anything to do except stand on street corners and jeer at Europeans.

As soon as I saw the elephant I knew with perfect certainty that I ought not to shoot him.

All this was perplexing and upsetting. For at that time I 2 had already made up my mind that imperialism was an evil thing and the sooner I chucked up my job and got out of it the better. Theoretically—and secretly, of course—I was all for the Burmese and all against their oppressors, the British. As for the job I was doing, I hated it more bitterly than I can perhaps make clear. In a job like that you see the dirty work of Empire at close quarters. The wretched prisoners huddling in the stinking cages of the lock-ups, the gray, cowed faces of the long-term convicts, the scarred buttocks of the men who had been flogged with bamboos—all these oppressed me with an intolerable sense of guilt. But I could get nothing into perspective. I was young and ill educated and I had had to think out my problems in the utter silence that is imposed on every Englishman in the East. I did not even know that the British Empire is dying, still less did I know that it is a great deal better than the younger empires that are going

to supplant it. All I knew was that I was stuck between my
hatred of the empire I served and my rage against the evil-
spirited little beasts who tried to make my job impossible.
With one part of my mind I thought of the British Raj as an
unbreakable tyranny, as something clamped down, in *saecula
saeculorum,* upon the will of prostrate peoples; with another
part I thought that the greatest joy in the world would be
to drive a bayonet into a Buddhist priest's guts. Feelings like
these are the normal by-products of imperialism; ask any
Anglo-Indian official, if you can catch him off duty.

   One day something happened which in a roundabout way   3
was enlightening. It was a tiny incident in itself; but it gave
me a better glimpse than I had had before of the real nature
of imperialism—the real motives for which despotic governments act. Early one morning the sub-inspector at a police
station the other end of town rang me up on the 'phone
and said that an elephant was ravaging the bazaar. Would
I please come and do something about it? I did not know
what I could do, but I wanted to see what was happening
and I got on to a pony and started out. I took my rifle, an
old .44 Winchester and much too small to kill an elephant,
but I thought the noise might be useful *in terrorem.* Various
Burmans stopped me on the way and told me about the elephant's doings. It was not, of course, a wild elephant, but a
tame one which had gone "must." It had been chained up, as
tame elephants always are when their attack of "must" is due,
but on the previous night it had broken its chain and escaped.
Its mahout, the only person who could manage it when it
was in that state, had set out in pursuit, but had taken the
wrong direction and was now twelve hours' journey away,
and in the morning the elephant had suddenly reappeared
in the town. The Burmese population had no weapons and
were quite helpless against it. It had already destroyed somebody's bamboo hut, killed a cow and raided some fruitstalls
and devoured the stock; also it had met the municipal rubbish van and, when the driver jumped out and took to his
heels, had turned the van over and inflicted violences upon it.

The Burmese sub-inspector and some Indian constables 4
were waiting for me in the quarter where the elephant had
been seen. It was a very poor quarter, a labyrinth of squalid
bamboo huts, thatched with palm-leaf, winding all over a
steep hillside. I remember that it was a cloudy, stuffy morning at the beginning of the rains. We began questioning the
people as to where the elephant had gone and, as usual, failed
to get any definite information. That is invariably the case in
the East; a story always sounds clear enough at a distance,
but the nearer you get to the scene of events the vaguer it
becomes. Some of the people said that the elephant had gone
in one direction, some said that he had gone in another,
some professed not even to have heard of any elephant. I
had almost made up my mind that the whole story was a
pack of lies, when we heard yells a little distance away. There
was a loud, scandalized cry of "Go away, child! Go away this
instant!" and an old woman with a switch in her hand came
round the corner of a hut, violently shooing away a crowd of
naked children. Some more women followed, clicking their
tongues and exclaiming; evidently there was something that
the children ought not to have seen. I rounded the hut and
saw a man's dead body sprawling in the mud. He was an
Indian, a black Dravidian coolie, almost naked, and he could
not have been dead many minutes. The people said that the
elephant had come suddenly upon him round the corner of
the hut, caught him with its trunk, put its foot on his back
and ground him into the earth. This was the rainy season and
the ground was soft, and his face had scored a trench a foot
deep and a couple of yards long. He was lying on his belly
with arms crucified and head sharply twisted to one side.
His face was coated with mud, the eyes wide open, the teeth
bared and grinning with an expression of unendurable agony.
(Never tell me, by the way, that the dead look peaceful. Most
of the corpses I have seen looked devilish.) The friction of the
great beast's foot had stripped the skin from his back as neatly
as one skins a rabbit. As soon as I saw the dead man I sent an
orderly to a friend's house nearby to borrow an elephant rifle.

I had already sent back the pony, not wanting it to go mad with fright and throw me if it smelt the elephant.

The orderly came back in a few minutes with a rifle and 5 five cartridges, and meanwhile some Burmans had arrived and told us that the elephant was in the paddy fields below, only a few hundred yards away. As I started forward practically the whole population of the quarter flocked out of the houses and followed me. They had seen the rifle and were all shouting excitedly that I was going to shoot the elephant. They had not shown much interest in the elephant when he was merely ravaging their homes, but it was different now that he was going to be shot. It was a bit of fun to them, and it would be to an English crowd; besides they wanted the meat. It made me vaguely uneasy. I had no intention of shooting the elephant—I had merely sent for the rifle to defend myself if necessary—and it is always unnerving to have a crowd following you. I marched down the hill, looking and feeling a fool, with the rifle over my shoulder and an ever-growing army of people jostling at my heels. At the bottom, when you got away from the huts, there was a metalled road and beyond that a miry waste of paddy fields a thousand yards across, not yet ploughed but soggy from the first rains and dotted with coarse grass. The elephant was standing eight yards from the road, his left side toward us. He took not the slightest notice of the crowd's approach. He was tearing up bunches of grass, beating them against his knees to clean them, and stuffing them into his mouth.

I had halted on the road. As soon as I saw the elephant I 6 knew with perfect certainty that I ought not to shoot him. It is a serious matter to shoot a working elephant—it is comparable to destroying a huge and costly piece of machinery— and obviously one ought not to do it if it can possibly be avoided. And at that distance, peacefully eating, the elephant looked no more dangerous than a cow. I thought then and I think now that his attack of "must" was already passing off; in which case he would merely wander harmlessly about until the mahout came back and caught him. Moreover, I did not in the least want to shoot him. I decided that I would watch him for a little while to make sure that he did not turn savage again, and then go home.

But at that moment I glanced round at the crowd that 7 had followed me. It was an immense crowd, two thousand at the least and growing every minute. It blocked the road for a long distance on either side. I looked at the sea of yellow faces above the garish clothes—faces all happy and excited over this bit of fun, all certain that the elephant was going to be shot. They were watching me as they would watch a con- jurer about to perform a trick. They did not like me, but with the magical rifle in my hands I was momentarily worth watch- ing. And suddenly I realized that I should have to shoot the elephant after all. The people expected it of me and I had got to do it; I could feel their two thousand wills pressing me for- ward, irresistibly. And it was at this moment, as I stood there with the rifle in my hands, that I first grasped the hollowness, the futility of the white man's dominion in the East. Here was I, the white man with his gun, standing in front of the unarmed native crowd—seemingly the leading actor of the piece; but in reality I was only an absurd puppet pushed to and fro by the will of those yellow faces behind. I perceived in this moment that when the white man turns tyrant it is his own freedom that he destroys. He becomes a sort of hollow, posing dummy, the conventionalized figure of a sahib. For it is the condition of his rule that he shall spend his life in try- ing to impress the "natives," and so in every crisis he has got to do what the "natives" expect of him. He wears a mask, and his face grows to fit it. I had got to shoot the elephant. I had committed myself to doing it when I sent for the rifle. A sahib has got to act like a sahib; he has got to appear reso- lute, to know his own mind and do definite things. To come all that way, rifle in hand, with two thousand people march- ing at my heels, and then to trail feebly away, having done nothing—no, that was impossible. The crowd would laugh at me. And my whole life, every white man's life in the East, was one long struggle not to be laughed at.

But I did not want to shoot the elephant. I watched 8 him beating his bunch of grass against his knees with that preoccupied grandmotherly air that elephants have. It seemed to me that it would be murder to shoot him. At that age I was not squeamish about killing animals, but I had never shot an elephant and never wanted to. (Somehow it always seems worse to kill a *large* animal.) Besides, there was the beast's owner to be considered. Alive, the elephant was worth at least a hundred pounds; dead, he would only be worth the value of his tusks, five pounds, possibly. But I had got to act quickly. I turned to some experienced-looking Burmans who had been there when we arrived, and asked them how the elephant had been behaving. They all said the same thing: he took no notice of you if you left him alone, but he might charge if you went too close to him.

It was perfectly clear to me what I ought to do. I ought 9 to walk up to within, say, twenty-five yards of the elephant and test his behavior. If he charged, I could shoot; if he took no notice of me, it would be safe to leave him until the mahout came back. But also I knew that I was going to do no such thing. I was a poor shot with a rifle and the ground was soft mud into which one would sink at every step. If the elephant charged and I missed him, I should have about as much chance as a toad under a steam-roller. But even then I was not thinking particularly of my own skin, only of the watchful yellow faces behind. For at that moment, with the crowd watching me, I was not afraid in the ordinary sense, as I would have been if I had been alone. A white man mustn't be frightened in front of "natives"; and so, in general, he isn't frightened. The sole thought in my mind was that if anything went wrong those two thousand Burmans would see me pursued, caught, trampled on, and reduced to a grinning corpse like that Indian up the hill. And if that happened it was quite probable that some of them would laugh. That would never do. There was only one alternative. I shoved the cartridges into the magazine and lay down on the road to get a better aim.

The crowd grew very still, and a deep, low, happy sigh, as 10 of people who see the theater curtain go up at last, breathed from innumerable throats. They were going to have their bit of fun after all. The rifle was a beautiful German thing with cross-hair sights. I did not then know that in shooting an elephant one would shoot to cut an imaginary bar running from ear-hole to ear-hole. I ought, therefore, as the elephant was sideways on, to have aimed straight at his ear-hole; actually I aimed several inches in front of this, thinking the brain would be further forward.

When I pulled the trigger I did not hear the bang or feel the 11
kick—one never does when a shot goes home—but I heard the devilish roar of glee that went up from the crowd. In that instant, in too short a time, one would have thought, even for the bullet to get there, a mysterious, terrible change had come over the elephant. He neither stirred, nor fell, but every line of his body had altered. He looked suddenly stricken, shrunken, immensely old, as though the frightful impact of the bullet had paralyzed him without knocking him down. At last, after what seemed a long time—it might have been five seconds, I dare say—he sagged flabbily to his knees. His mouth slobbered. An enormous senility seemed to have settled upon him. One could have imagined him thousands of years old. I fired again into the same spot. At the second shot he did not collapse but climbed with desperate slowness to his feet and stood weakly upright, with legs sagging and head drooping. I fired a third time. That was the shot that did for him. You could see the agony of it jolt his whole body and knock the last remnant of strength from his legs. But in falling he seemed for a moment to rise, for as his hind legs collapsed beneath him he seemed to tower upward like a huge rock toppling, his trunk reaching skyward like a tree. He trumpeted, for the first and only time. And then down he came, his belly toward me, with a crash that seemed to shake the ground even where I lay.

I got up. The Burmans were already racing past me across 12
the mud. It was obvious that the elephant would never rise again, but he was not dead. He was breathing very rhythmically with long rattling gasps, his great mound of a side painfully rising and falling. His mouth was wide open—I could see far down into caverns of pale pink throat. I waited a long time for him to die, but his breathing did not weaken. Finally

I fired my two remaining shots into the spot where I thought his heart must be. The thick blood welled out of him like red velvet, but still he did not die. His body did not even jerk when the shots hit him, the tortured breathing continued without a pause. He was dying, very slowly and in great agony, but in some world remote from me where not even a bullet could damage him further. I felt that I had got to put an end to that dreadful noise. It seemed dreadful to see the great beast lying there, powerless to move and yet powerless to die, and not even to be able to finish him. I sent back for my small rifle and poured shot after shot into his heart and down his throat. They seemed to make no impression. The tortured gasps continued as steadily as the ticking of a clock.

In the end I could not stand it any longer and went away. I heard later that it took him half an hour to die. Burmans were bringing dash and baskets even before I left, and I was told they had stripped his body almost to the bones by the afternoon.   13

Afterward, of course, there were endless discussions about the shooting of the elephant. The owner was furious, but he was only an Indian and could do nothing. Besides, legally I had done the right thing, for a mad elephant has to be killed, like a mad dog, if its owner fails to control it. Among the Europeans opinion was divided. The older men said I was right, the younger men said it was a damn shame to shoot an elephant for killing a coolie, because an elephant was worth more than any damn Coringhee coolie. And afterward I was very glad that the coolie had been killed; it put me legally in the right and it gave me a sufficient pretext for shooting the elephant. I often wondered whether any of the others grasped that I had done it solely to avoid looking a fool.   14

For Study and Discussion

QUESTIONS ABOUT PURPOSE

1. What thesis about "the real nature of imperialism" does Orwell prove by narrating this "tiny incident"?

2. What are the reasons Orwell considers when he tries to decide whether to shoot the elephant?

QUESTIONS ABOUT AUDIENCE

1. How does Orwell present himself to his audience in paragraphs 6 through 9?
2. Which of the three positions stated in the final paragraph does Orwell expect his readers to agree with?

QUESTIONS ABOUT STRATEGIES

1. Although Orwell begins narrating the incident in paragraph 3, he does not describe the elephant until the end of paragraph 5. What details does he use to intensify the dramatic conflict?
2. How does Orwell pace the shooting of the elephant in paragraphs 11 and 12?

For Writing and Research

1. *Analyze* how Orwell's description of the elephant's slow death affects his point of view toward what he has done.
2. *Practice* by narrating an incident in which you committed an act to avoid looking like a fool.
3. *Argue* that Orwell's plight is similar to the plight of the young American soldiers who are serving in Afghanistan.
4. *Synthesize:* Research the words *imperialism* and *despotism.* Then construct an essay in which you explain how the recent actions of a foreign or domestic government could be perceived as *imperialistic* or *despotic.*

W. D. WETHERELL

Walter David Wetherell was born in 1948 in Mineola, New York, and educated at Hofstra University. After working at a variety of odd jobs—movie extra, tour guide, and freelance journalist—he taught creative writing at the University of Vermont. He published his short fiction in magazines such as *Virginia Quarterly Review, Adventure,* and *New England Quarterly.* His novels include *Souvenirs* (1981), *Chekhov's Sister* (1990), *Morning* (2001), and *A Century of November* (2004). His other works include several collections of essays such as *Vermont River* (1984), *Upland Stream: Notes on the Fishing Passion* (1991), *One River More* (1998) *Soccer Dad: A Father, a Son, and a Magic* Season (2008), *Hills Like White Hills* (2009), and *On Admiration* (2010). "The Bass, the River, and Sheila Mant," reprinted from the collection of stories, *The Man Who Loved Levittown* (1985), recalls the comic twists in a romantic summer fantasy.

The Bass, the River,
and Sheila Mant[6]

THERE was a summer in my life when the only creature   1
that seemed lovelier to me than a largemouth bass was Sheila Mant. I was fourteen. The Mants had rented the cottage next to ours on the river; with their parties, their frantic games of softball, their constant comings and goings, they appeared to me denizens of a brilliant existence. "Too noisy

---

[6]W. D. Wetherell, "The Bass, the River and Sheila Mant" by W. D. Wetherell, from *The Man Who Loved Levittown* by W. D. Wetherell, © 1985. Reprinted by permission of the University of Pittsburgh Press.

by half," my mother quickly decided, but I would have given anything to be invited to one of their parties, and when my parents went to bed I would sneak through the woods to their hedge and stare enchanted at the candlelit swirl of white dresses and bright, paisley skirts.

Sheila was the middle daughter—at seventeen, all but out 2 of reach. She would spend her days sunbathing on a float my Uncle Sierbert had moored in their cove, and before July was over I had learned all her moods. If she lay flat on the diving board with her hand trailing idly in the water, she was pensive, not to be disturbed. On her side, her head propped up by her arm, she was observant, considering those around her with a look that seemed queenly and severe. Sitting up, arms tucked around her long, suntanned legs, she was approachable, but barely, and it was only in those glorious moments when she stretched herself prior to entering the water that her various suitors found the courage to come near.

These were many. The Dartmouth heavyweight crew 3 would scull by her house on their way upriver, and I think all eight of them must have been in love with her at various times during the summer; the coxswain would curse at them through his megaphone, but without effect—there was always a pause in their pace when they passed Sheila's float. I suppose to these jaded twenty-year-olds she seemed the incarnation of innocence and youth, while to me she appeared unutterably suave, the epitome of sophistication. I was on the swim team at school, and to win her attention would do endless laps between my house and the Vermont shore, hoping she would notice the beauty of my flutter kick, the power of my crawl. Finishing, I would boost myself up onto our dock and glance casually over toward her, but she was never watching, and the miraculous day she was, I immediately climbed the diving board and did my best tuck and a half for her, and continued diving until she had left and the sun went down and my longing was like a madness and I couldn't stop.

It was late August by the time I got up the nerve to ask her 4 out. The tortured will-I's, won't-I's, the agonized indecision

over what to say, the false starts toward her house and embarrassed retreats—the details of these have been seared from
my memory, and the only part I remember clearly is emerging from the woods toward dusk while they were playing
softball on their lawn, as bashful and frightened as a unicorn.

Sheila was stationed halfway between first and second, well   5
outside the infield. She didn't seem surprised to see me—as a
matter of fact, she didn't seem to see me at all.

"If you're playing second base, you should move closer,"   6
I said.

She turned—I took the full brunt of her long red hair and   7
well-spaced freckles.

"I'm playing outfield," she said, "I don't like the respon-   8
sibility of having a base."

"Yeah, I can understand that," I said, though I couldn't.   9
"There's a band in Dixford tomorrow night at nine. Want
to go?"

One of her brothers sent the ball sailing over the left-   10
fielder's head; she stood and watched it disappear toward the
river.

"You have a car?" she said, without looking up.   11

I played my master stroke. "We'll go by canoe."   12

I spent all of the following day polishing it. I turned it   13
upside down on our lawn and rubbed every inch with Brillo,
hosing off the dirt, wiping it with chamois until it gleamed
as bright as aluminum ever gleamed. About five, I slid it into
the water, arranging cushions near the bow so Sheila could
lean on them if she was in one of her pensive moods, prop-
ping up my father's transistor radio by the middle thwart so
we could have music when we came back. Automatically,
without thinking about it, I mounted my Mitchell reel on
my Pfleuger spinning rod and stuck it in the stern.

I say automatically, because I never went anywhere that   14
summer without a fishing rod. When I wasn't swimming laps
to impress Sheila, I was back in our driveway practicing casts,
and when I wasn't practicing casts, I was tying the line to
Tosca, our springer spaniel, to test the reel's drag, and when
I wasn't doing any of those things, I was fishing the river for
bass.

Too nervous to sit at home, I got in the canoe early and   15
started paddling in a huge circle that would get me to Sheila's
dock around eight. As automatically as I brought along my
rod, I tied on a big Rapala plug, let it down into the water, let
out some line and immediately forgot all about it.

It was already dark by the time I glided up to the Mants'   16
dock. Even by day the river was quiet, most of the summer
people preferring Sunapee or one of the other nearby lakes,
and at night it was a solitude difficult to believe, a corridor
of hidden life that ran between banks like a tunnel. Even the
stars were part of it. They weren't as sharp anywhere else;
they seemed to have chosen the river as a guide on their slow
wheel toward morning, and in the course of the summer's
fishing, I had learned all their names.

I was there ten minutes before Sheila appeared. I heard the   17
slam of their screen door first, then saw her in the spotlight
as she came slowly down the path. As beautiful as she was on
the float, she was even lovelier now—her white dress went
perfectly with her hair, and complimented her figure even
more than her swimsuit.

It was her face that bothered me. It had on its delightful   18
fullness a very dubious expression.

"Look," she said. "I can get Dad's car."   19

"It's faster this way," I lied. "Parking's tense up there.   20
Hey, it's safe. I won't tip it or anything."

She let herself down reluctantly into the bow. I was glad   21
she wasn't facing me. When her eyes were on me, I felt like
diving in the river again from agony and joy.

I pried the canoe away from the dock and started paddling   22
upstream. There was an extra paddle in the bow, but Sheila
made no move to pick it up. She took her shoes off, and
dangled her feet over the side.

Ten minutes went by.   23

"What kind of band?" she said.   24

"It's sort of like folk music. You'll like it."   25

"Eric Caswell's going to be there. He strokes number   26
four."

"No kidding?" I said. I had no idea who she meant.   27

"What's that sound?" she said, pointing toward shore.   28

"Bass. That splashing sound?"   29

"Over there."   30

"Yeah, bass. They come into the shallows at night to chase   31
frogs and moths and things. Big largemouths. *Micropetrus
salmonides*," I added, showing off.

"I think fishing's dumb," she said, making a face. "I mean,   32
it's boring and all. Definitely dumb."

Now I have spent a great deal of time in the years since   33
wondering why Sheila Mant should come down so hard on
fishing. Was her father a fisherman? Her antipathy toward
fishing nothing more than normal filial rebellion? Had she
tried it once? A messy encounter with worms? It doesn't matter. What does, is that at that fragile moment in time I would
have given anything not to appear dumb in Sheila's severe
and unforgiving eyes.

She hadn't seen my equipment yet. What I *should* have   34
done, of course, was push the canoe in closer to shore and
carefully slide the rod into some branches where I could pick
it up again in the morning. Failing that, I could have sur-
reptitiously dumped the whole outfit overboard, written off
the forty or so dollars as love's tribute. What I actually *did* do
was gently lean forward, and slowly, ever so slowly, push the
rod back through my legs toward the stern where it would be
less conspicuous.

It must have been just exactly what the bass was waiting   35
for. Fish will trail a lure sometimes, trying to make up their
mind whether or not to attack, and the slight pause in the
plug's speed caused by my adjustment was tantalizing enough
to overcome the bass's inhibitions. My rod, safely out of sight
at last, bent double. The line, tightly coiled, peeled off the
spool with the shrill, tearing zip of a high-speed drill.

Four things occurred to me at once. One, that it was a   36
bass. Two, that it was a big bass. Three, that it was the biggest bass I had ever hooked. Four, that Sheila Mant must not
know.

"What was that?" she said, turning half around.   37

"Uh, what was what?"   38

"That buzzing noise."   39

"Bats." 40

She shuddered, quickly drew her feet back into the canoe. 41
Every instinct I had told me to pick up the rod and strike
back at the bass, but there was no need to—it was already
solidly hooked. Downstream, an awesome distance downstream, it jumped clear of the water, landing with a concus-
sion heavy enough to ripple the entire river. For a moment, I
thought it was gone, but then the rod was bending again, the
tip dancing into the water. Slowly, not making any motion
that might alert Sheila, I reached down to tighten the drag.

While all this was going on, Sheila had begun talking and 42
it was a few minutes before I was able to catch up with her
train of thought.

"I went to a party there. These fraternity men. Katherine 43
says I could get in there if I wanted. I'm thinking more of
UVM or Bennington. Somewhere I can ski."

The bass was slanting toward the rocks on the New 44
Hampshire side by the ruins of Donaldson's boathouse. It
had to be an old bass—a young one probably wouldn't have
known the rocks were there. I brought the canoe back out
into the middle of the river, hoping to head it off.

"That's neat," I mumbled. "Skiing. Yeah, I can see that." 45

"Eric said I have the figure to model, but I thought I 46
should get an education first. I mean, it might be a while
before I get started and all. I was thinking of getting my hair
styled, more swept back? I mean, Ann-Margret? Like hers,
only shorter."

She hesitated. "Are we going backwards?" 47

We were. I had managed to keep the bass in the middle 48
of the river away from the rocks, but it had plenty of room
there, and for the first time a chance to exert its full strength. I
quickly computed the weight necessary to draw a fully loaded
canoe backwards—the thought of it made me feel faint.

"It's just the current," I said hoarsely. "No sweat or any- 49
thing."

I dug in deeper with my paddle. Reassured, Sheila began 50
talking about something else, but all my attention was taken
up now with the fish. I could feel its desperation as the water

grew shallower. I could sense the extra strain on the line, the frantic way it cut back and forth in the water. I could visualize what it looked like—the gape of its mouth, the flared gills and thick, vertical tail. The bass couldn't have encountered many forces in its long life that it wasn't capable of handling, and the unrelenting tug at its mouth must have been a source of great puzzlement and mounting panic.

Me, I had problems of my own. To get to Dixford, I had to   51
paddle up a sluggish stream that came into the river beneath a covered bridge. There was a shallow sandbar at the mouth of this stream—weeds on one side, rocks on the other. Without doubt, this is where I would lose the fish.

"I have to be careful with my complexion. I tan, but in   52
segments. I can't figure out if it's even worth it. I wouldn't even do it probably. I saw Jackie Kennedy in Boston and she wasn't tan at all."

Taking a deep breath, I paddled as hard as I could for   53
the middle, deepest part of the bar. I could have threaded the eye of a needle with the canoe, but the pull on the stern threw me off and I overcompensated—the canoe veered left and scraped bottom. I pushed the paddle down and shoved. A moment of hesitation . . . a moment more. . . . The canoe shot clear into the deeper water of the stream. I immediately looked down at the rod. It was bent in the same, tight arc— miraculously, the bass was still on.

The moon was out now. It was low and full enough that   54
its beam shone directly on Sheila there ahead of me in the canoe, washing her in a creamy, luminous glow. I could see the lithe, easy shape of her figure. I could see the way her hair curled down off her shoulders, the proud, alert tilt of her head, and all these things were as a tug on my heart. Not just Sheila, but the aura she carried about her of parties and casual touchings and grace. Behind me, I could feel the strain of the bass, steadier now, growing weaker, and this was another tug on my heart, not just the bass but the beat of the river and the slant of the stars and the smell of the night, until finally it seemed I would be torn apart between longings, split in half. Twenty yards ahead of us was the road, and

once I pulled the canoe up on shore, the bass would be gone, irretrievably gone. If instead I stood up, grabbed the rod and started pumping, I would have it—as tired as the bass was, there was no chance it could get away. I reached down for the rod, hesitated, looked up to where Sheila was stretching herself lazily toward the sky, her small breasts rising beneath the soft fabric of her dress, and the tug was too much for me, and quicker than it takes to write down, I pulled a penknife from my pocket and cut the line in half.

With a sick, nauseous feeling in my stomach, I saw the rod 55 unbend.

"My legs are sore," Sheila whined. "Are we there yet?" 56

Through a superhuman effort of self-control, I was able 57 to beach the canoe and help Sheila off. The rest of the night is much foggier. We walked to the fair—there was the smell of popcorn, the sound of guitars. I may have danced once or twice with her, but all I really remember is her coming over to me once the music was done to explain that she would be going home in Eric Caswell's Corvette.

"Okay," I mumbled. 58

For the first time that night she looked at me, really 59 looked at me.

"You're a funny kid, you know that?" 60

Funny. Different. Dreamy. Odd. How many times was I 61 to hear that in the years to come, all spoken with the same quizzical, half-accusatory tone Sheila used then. Poor Sheila! Before the month was over, the spell she cast over me was gone, but the memory of that lost bass haunted me all summer and haunts me still. There would be other Sheila Mants in my life, other fish, and though I came close once or twice, it was these secret, hidden tuggings in the night that claimed me, and I never made the same mistake again.

COMMENT ON "THE BASS, THE RIVER, AND SHEILA MANT"

"The Bass, the River, and Sheila Mant" is an excellent illustration of how narration and description are used in short fiction.

Although the plot seems arranged in a simple chronological pattern, the narrator indicates that the events took place when he was younger (age fourteen) and that they continue to haunt him. The story is paced at two speeds: the opening is slow and languid as the young boy describes the enchanting moods of Sheila Mant; the action speeds up once they are in the canoe and he accidentally hooks the biggest bass he has ever seen. The complicated situation creates a clear choice—Sheila or the fish. Beguiled by her sensual beauty—even though he suspects it is superficial—the narrator chooses Sheila. Older, wiser, he concludes that he will never make that mistake again.

CHAPTER 2

PROCESS ANALYSIS

A **process** is an operation that moves through a series of steps to bring about a desired result. You can call almost any procedure a process, whether it is getting out of bed in the morning or completing a transaction on the stock exchange. A useful way to identify a particular kind of process is by its principal function. A process can be *natural* (the birth of a baby), *mechanical* (starting a car engine), *physical* (dancing), or *mental* (reading).

Analysis is an operation that divides something into its parts in order to understand the whole more clearly. For example, poetry readers analyze the lines of a poem to find meaning. Doctors analyze a patient's symptoms to prescribe treatment. Politicians analyze the opinions of individual voters and groups of voters to plan campaigns.

If you want to write a process-analysis essay, you need to go through three steps: (1) divide the process you are going to explain into its individual steps; (2) show the movement of the process, step by step, from beginning to end; and

(3) explain how each step works, how it relates to other steps in the sequence, and how it brings about the desired result.

PURPOSE

Usually you will write a process analysis to accomplish two purposes: *to give directions* and *to provide information*. Sometimes you might find it difficult to separate the two purposes. After all, when you give directions about how to do something (hit a baseball), you also have to provide information on how the whole process works (rules of the game—strike zone, walks, hits, base running, outs, scoring). But usually you can separate the two because you're trying to accomplish different goals. When you give directions, you want to help your readers do something (change a tire). When you give information, you want to satisfy your readers' curiosity about some process they'd like to know about but are unlikely to perform (pilot a space shuttle).

You might also write a process analysis to demonstrate that (1) a task that looks difficult is really easy or (2) a task that looks easy is really quite complex. For instance, you might want to show that selecting a specific tool can simplify a complex process (using a microwave oven to cook a six-course dinner). You might also want to show why it's important to have a prearranged plan to make a process seem simple (explaining the preparations for an informal television interview).

AUDIENCE

When you write a process-analysis essay, you must think carefully about who your audience will be. First, you need to decide whether you're writing *to* an audience (giving directions) or writing *for* an audience (providing information). If you are writing *to* an audience, you can address directly readers who are already interested in your subject: "If you want to plant a successful garden, you must follow these seven steps." If you are writing *for* an audience, you can write from a more detached point of view, but you have to find a way to catch the interest of more casual readers: "Although many Americans say they are concerned about nuclear power, few understand how a nuclear power plant works."

Second, you have to determine how wide the knowledge gap is between you and your readers. Writing about a process suggests you are something of an expert in that area. If you can be sure your readers are also experts, you can make certain assumptions as you write your analysis. For instance, if you're outlining courtroom procedure to a group of fellow law students, you can assume you don't have to define the special meaning of the word *brief*.

On the other hand, if you feel sure your intended audience knows almost nothing about a process (or has only general knowledge), you can take nothing for granted. If you are explaining how to operate a BlackBerry to readers who have never used one, you will have to define special terms and explain all procedures. If you assume your readers are experts when they are not, you will confuse or annoy them. If you assume they need to be told everything when they don't, you will bore or antagonize them. And, finally, remember that to analyze a process effectively, you must either research it carefully or have firsthand knowledge of its operation. It's risky to try to explain something you don't really understand.

STRATEGIES

The best way to write a process analysis is to organize your essay according to five parts:

> Overview
> Special terms
> Sequence of steps
> Examples
> Results

The first two parts help your readers understand the process, the next two show the process in action, and the last one evaluates the worth of the completed process.

Begin your analysis with an *overview* of the whole process. To make such an overview, you take these four steps:

1. Define the objective of the process.
2. Identify (and number) the steps in the sequence.
3. Group some small steps into larger units.
4. Call attention to the most important steps or units.

For example, P. J. O'Rourke begins by explaining the purpose of the process he is about to explain. Nikki Giovanni makes her recommendations for black students in sequence and then goes on to illustrate some of the common problems that occur with each recommendation.

Each process has its own *special terms* to describe tools, tasks, and methods, and you will have to define those terms for your readers. You can define them at the beginning so your readers will understand the terms when you use them, but often you do better to define them as you use them. Your readers may have trouble remembering specialized language out of context, so it's often practical to define your terms throughout the course of the essay, pausing to explain their special meaning or use the first time you introduce them. Ernest Hemingway combines these strategies by listing several kinds of cooking gear and then illustrating their use later when he prepares a meal.

When you write a process-analysis essay, you must present the *sequence of steps* clearly and carefully. As you do so, give the reason for each step and, where appropriate, provide these reminders:

1. *Do not omit any steps.* A sequence is a sequence because all steps depend on one another. Giovanni explains the importance of going to class to establish "a consistent presence in the classroom."
2. *Do not reverse steps.* A sequence is a sequence because each step must be performed according to a necessary and logical pattern. If Hemingway's fisherman wants to avoid mosquito bites, he must apply the protective ointment on his neck, forehead, and wrist before he starts fishing.

3. *Suspend certain steps.* Occasionally, a whole series of steps must be suspended and another process completed before the sequence can resume. O'Rourke suggests that a whole sequence of steps can be avoided if you suspend the sequence and give everybody "big wads of money."

4. *Do not overlook steps within steps.* Each sequence is likely to have a series of smaller steps buried within each step. Lars Eighner reminds his readers that if they start eating something before they have inspected it, they are likely to discover moldy bread or sour milk after they have put it in their mouths.

5. *Avoid certain steps.* It is often tempting to insert steps that are not recommended but that appear "logical." Ann Zwinger warns her readers that beginning a drawing with an outline can keep you in a corner.

You may want to use several kinds of *examples* to explain the steps in a sequence.

1. *Pictures.* You can use graphs, charts, and diagrams to illustrate the operation of the process. Although none of the writers in this section uses pictures, Zwinger's purpose is to demonstrate what you can learn from drawing them.

2. *Anecdotes.* Because you're claiming some level of expertise by writing a process analysis, you can clarify your explanation by using examples from your own experience. O'Rourke uses this method—for comic effect—when he describes roadblocks and animals in the right of way.

3. *Variants.* You can mention alternative steps to show that the process may not be as rigid or simplistic as it often appears. Giovanni uses sample questions and answers to illustrate different ways to participate in class.

4. *Comparisons.* You can use comparisons to help your readers see that a complex process is similar to a process they already know. O'Rourke uses this strategy when he compares Third World and American driving habits.

Although you focus on the movement of the process when you write a process-analysis essay, you should also try to evaluate the *results* of that process. You can move to this last part by asking two questions: How do you know it's done? How do you know it's good? Sometimes the answer is simple: the car starts; the meal turns out well. At other times, the answer is not so clear: racial situations are not always easy to understand; eating food from a dumpster may cause dysentery.

PROCESS ANALYSIS

Points to Remember

1. Arrange the steps in your process in an orderly sequence.
2. Identify and explain the purpose of each of the steps in the process.
3. Describe the special tools, terms, and tasks needed to complete the process.
4. Provide warnings, where appropriate, about the consequences of omitting, reversing, or overlooking certain steps.
5. Supply illustrations and personal anecdotes to help clarify aspects of the process.

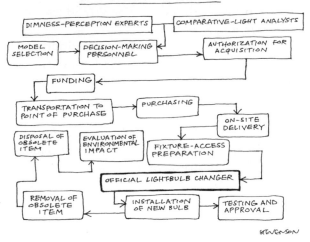

HOW MANY IT TAKES

*In this comic drawing, James Stevenson offers yet another variation
of the old joke "How many [fill in the blank] does it take to change
a light bulb?" Trace the various steps in this overwrought flow chart.
Has Stevenson missed a step or placed steps out of sequence? Construct
your own flow chart for a simple process such as making an ATM
transaction or hitting a golf ball. Then write an analysis of your chart
demonstrating why this simple process contains hidden steps or must be
explained in a larger context.*

ANN ZWINGER

Ann Zwinger was born in Muncie, Indiana, in 1925, and was educated at Wellesley College and Indiana University. She has taught art at Smith College and the University of Arizona, and served as naturalist-in-residence at Carleton College. She is best known for books she has written and illustrated about the environment, such as *Beyond the Aspen Grove* (1970); *Run, River Run: A Naturalist's Journey Down One of the Great Rivers of the West* (1975); *The Mysterious Lands: The Four Deserts of the United States* (1989); *Shaped by Wind and Water: Reflections of a Naturalist* (2000), and *Grand Canyon: Little Things in a Big Place* (2006). Her artwork has been exhibited throughout the country and in her hometown, Colorado Springs, and she has published (with her daughter) a book of writings and photographs, *Women in the Wilderness* (1995). In "Drawing on Experience," reprinted from a collection of essays on nature and culture from *Orion* magazine, *Finding Home* (1992), Zwinger explains the "simple act of pencil rotating softly on paper."

Drawing on Experience[1]

I T REALLY DOESN'T matter whether you can draw or not— just the time taken to examine in detail, to turn a flower or a shell over in your fingers, opens doors and windows. The time spent observing pays, and you can better observe 1

---

[1]Ann Zwinger, Drawing An Experience From Finding Home. This article originally appeared in the Winter 1987 issue of Orion Magazine, 197 Main Street, Great Barrington, MA 01230. Reprinted with permission from the author.

with a hand lens than without one. A hand lens is a joy and a delight, an entrée to another world just below your normal vision. Alice in Wonderland never had it so good—no mysterious potions are needed, just a ten- or fifteen-power hand lens hung around your neck. There's a kind of magic in seeing stellate hairs on a mustard stem, in seeing the retrorsely barbed margin of a nettle spine—there all the time but never visible without enhancement.

But to take the next step—to draw these in the margin 2 of your notebook, on the back of an envelope, in a sketch pad, or even in the sand—establishes a connection between hand and eye that reinforces the connection between eye and memory. Drawing fastens the plant in memory.

I speak of plants because they are what I enjoy drawing. 3 I find small plants easier to translate to paper than a minute ant's antennae or a full-blown, horizon-to-horizon landscape. Landscapes are beautiful for what you leave out; the most magnificent landscapes I know are those Rembrandt did with a wash from a couple of brush strokes enlivened with a crisp pen. But that took years of practice and a large dose of genius, which are not the point here—I speak of the enjoyment of learning from precise observation.

I think of drawing not as an end in itself but as a learning process, of doing research with a hand lens and pencil instead of a book and note cards.

With a plant, I start with a small detail and build up 4 because it's easier to extend outward into the infinite space of the page than to be caught in the finite space of an outline. If you begin with the big outline and fill in, and if you have any of the proportion problems I do, you often draw yourself into a corner. I begin with the stigma and stamens, or perhaps a petal, or perhaps the part that's closest, and work outward, relating each part to what's been put down before rather than blocking in a general outer shape and working down to detail.

When I begin in the center, as it were, and move outward, I build up a reality in which each detail relates to the one before. I wonder if this is also a way of apprehending a world, of composing it from many observations, a detail here, a detail there, creating an infinitely expandable universe. I always thought I worked this way because I was myopic, but maybe it's deeper than that and has to do with judgments, perceived realities, and whether there are five or six stamens.

Small things, large enough to see easily, but small enough to hold in the hand or put on the table in front of you, small enough to translate more or less one-to-one, seem to me the easiest subjects for the neophyte illustrator. Why deal with complex proportions if you don't have to? Forget the tea rose and the peony. Forgo the darlings of the garden that have been bred into complex, complicated flowers with multiple petals and fancy shapes. Try instead an interesting leaf, noting how the veining webs, or the edges curl or notch. Or try a simple flower—a phlox or lily-of-the-valley or an open, five-petaled wild rose.

Pale-colored plants are easier to draw: dark or brilliant colors often obscure the shape and character of the flower. Seedheads, summer's skeletons, are often felicitous subjects. So are cow parsnip's umbrella ribs or pennycress's orbicular pods, shepherd's purse or lily pods, which likewise give a sense of seasons past and springs to come.

Plants are nice because they stay still. I draw insects but only deceased ones, collected, pinned, and dried. Trying to portray a moving bug is a ridiculous task ending only in frustration.

Quick sketches of larger moving animals are difficult but greatly rewarding. If you are a birdwatcher and have the patience, drawing is a good way to learn how birds move, orient and tilt their bodies, and to pick up a lot on animal behavior because the observation is focused. (I happen to find birds hard to draw but suspect it's because I don't practice.) An afternoon sketching at the zoo with pencil and pad will astound anyone who's never tried it before. Pick out the movement, never mind the details, and by the end of the afternoon the improvement, both in drawing and observation, is measurable.

Shells, beach debris, offer endless possibilities. Think of   10
what you are doing as doodling, not immortalizing a shell for posterity. Play with different points of view and different scales. Find out how a snail builds its shell by the Fibonacci numbers, how the inside of an oyster shell reveals in color and pattern where the oyster was attached and how it lived.

Or go to your local natural history museum and draw   11
stuffed animals, although a weasel in the bush is worth two in the display. I remember wanting to draw a pocket gopher, and the sole specimen easily available was in a natural history museum. Only the front part was visible, the rest of the specimen having presumably been blown to bits on capture. It was not a successful drawing, and I never used it.

Drawing is like practicing the piano: you have to do it on   12
a fairly regular basis to keep your hand in.

I have no patience with the "Oh,-if-I-could-only-draw!"   13
school. Drawing is a state of mind—how much you want to do it, how much time you're willing to practice. It is, after all, simply a neural connection between eye and mind and hand, and the more that connection is reinforced, the more satisfying the result is going to be. I knew an art teacher who required students in his class to draw their own hand, once a week. His theory was that the subject was always on the premises, had infinite possibilities of outline and pose and was not very easy to draw. The difference between the first hand drawn and the last was remarkable, a real confidence builder.

I'm also impatient with those who say "It doesn't *look* like   14
what I wanted it to look like!" So what? Don't demand of yourself what you're not able to do at the time. Enjoy the feel of pencil on paper without imposing goals you can't meet.

I don't know why this setting of impossible goals happens more with drawing than with other creative endeavors. People who accept that they can't sit down and write a   15 symphony in a week expect to produce a skilled drawing the first time out. Potters spend hours learning how to center on the wheel; violinists practice scales all their lives. Drawing is in the same category: it takes time to develop the basic skills. And patience. When you hit a wrong note on the piano it fades off into the air before you play the correct one. If you make a wrong line, you can erase it. Or start over.

There are some wonderful books on drawing—Frederick   16 Franck's *The Zen of Drawing* and, best of all, *Drawing on the Right Side of the Brain* by Betty Edwards. The exercises she suggests, along with her practical how-tos, open a whole new way of looking and seeing.

A drawing class can also be useful, but it's not necessary.   17 What *is* necessary is to toss out some preconceived notions, and to accept and appreciate your fallibility and then forget it. Masterpieces of self-expression are not devoutly to be wished. Drawing is an experience of the facts and figures of a visual world that you can learn about in no other way.

Fancy tools aren't necessary either. Although I used to   18 carry a full complement of pencils, I now carry a single automatic one with a .5 mm lead that I buy at the supermarket. I prefer a spiral sketch pad because the papers remain anchored better, and I like one with little "tooth," as smooth as will comfortably take pencil. And if there's space in your pack or purse, carry a can of workable spray fixative. It's dismaying in the extreme to see a labored-over drawing reduced to a smear, and know that it can't be restored.

Colored pencils are a delight to use, but there's a great deal   19 to be said for learning with black pencil on white paper. The analogy of black-and-white and color photography comes to mind: color is lively, but color obfuscates. I don't learn as much about a plant when I draw with color. The structure and the detail are clearer in black and white.

When I am drawing I am usually very content in the plea-   20 sures of focusing outward. I think of drawing not as an end in itself but as a learning process, of doing research with a hand lens and pencil instead of a book and note cards. I think of it as seeing what I did not see before, of discovering, of walking around in the stamens and the pistil, of pacing off the petals, of touching the plant and knowing who it is.

In touch, you are given knowledge in an immediate and 21 practical way. You find out quickly that a cholla spine stings, that a blue spruce stabs, that a juniper prickles, that a mullein leaf is soft. There is also a communication established, an intimacy between mind and plant.

I remember a morning an April ago. I had been out in the 22 desert for three days and had an ice chest full of plants. No matter how hard I worked in the evening, I couldn't catch up with all there was to draw, so I took that morning just to draw. And I'm not sure but what it isn't a good time for drawing—your mind is yet uncluttered, energy is high, the capacity for concentration undiluted. The light tends to be bright and cool and better for drawing than the artificial light needed at night.

Two days prior a kindly hostess had said, "Let me get you 23 a glass to put the lily in so you don't have to hold it in your hand." I had replied without thinking, "No thank you—I need to see what's on the other side." I thought of that that morning as I drew the lily, which had been carefully cossetted in the ice chest since.

When I had acquired the lily, it had five buds. That morn- 24 ing only one remained closed, two were open, and two were spent. It was a delicate, difficult flower, spreading its sepals and petals into a six-pointed star, stretching out gold-powdered sepals that would attract no pollinator, extending a white, three-partite stigma beyond where it could catch its own pollen, a stigma that now, in the end, would catch none. But even as I had plucked the stalk (there was no time to draw it on site) I knew the bulb would endure, to produce another stalk of flowers next year, nourished by the ruffled leaves that spread across the dry, hard ground.

I propped the lily up in the folds of the bedspread, arranged 25 it so that the two open flowers gave different aspects of the same reality, arranged it so it said not only *Hemerocallis* but *undulata* and Sonoran Desert at ten o'clock on an April morning. A light breeze came in the window at my right shoulder and the perfect light, bright but soft, illuminated the ruffled edges of the petals, revealing a trace of where they had overlapped in the bud.

The quintessential lily, based on a trinity of shapes: I drew 26 three lines, enough to put a turned-back sepal on paper, layered pencil lines to limn the greenish stripe down the middle, checked the proportions, width against length, ruffle against sweep of edge. And picked it up. Unconsciously. Turned it over, looked it round, set it back, realized that knowing what was on the other side mattered a great deal. How do you know where you're going if you don't know where you've been?

The appearance of the lily on the page is the future, but 27 I've already seen it in my mind's eye, turned it in my hand, seen all lilies in this lily, known dryness in my roots, spreading in my leaves, sunshine polishing my stalk. Because of this lily, which I never saw until a few days ago, I know all about waiting for enough warmth, all about cool dawns and wilting noons. Because of this lily I know about desert heat and winter sleep and what the desert demands.

This lily is fixed in my mind's memory, on the page and 28 blowing in a desert spring. No matter what the season, this lily blooms as part of experience, part of understanding, a deep part of knowledge beyond words. Words, visual images, straight memory—none bring that lily to flower in the mind like the notation of its curve and the line of its flare, a memory of the eye and the hand inscribed in the simple act of pencil rotating softly on paper.

For Study and Discussion

QUESTIONS ABOUT PURPOSE

1. According to Zwinger, what is the purpose of drawing?
2. Why does she encourage her readers to enjoy "the feel of pencil on paper without imposing goals you can't meet"?

QUESTIONS ABOUT AUDIENCE

1. How does Zwinger address her readers who belong to the "Oh,-if-I-could-only-draw!" school?
2. How does she respond to those readers who say, "It doesn't *look* like what I wanted it to look like"?

QUESTIONS ABOUT STRATEGIES

1. How does Zwinger recommend drawing small things? Why does she begin at the center?
2. What sort of tools and techniques does she recommend? Why is black and white more effective than color?

For Writing and Research

1. *Analyze* how Zwinger uses the example of the lily to illustrate how "drawing is an experience of the facts and figures of a visual world you can learn about in no other way."
2. *Practice* by analyzing the process you used the last time you tried to draw a picture.
3. *Argue* that drawing is the result of natural talent, or the result of extensive practice.
4. *Synthesize:* Research how several painters from different historical periods learned to draw. Use this information to explain the evolution of a particular painting style—for example, abstract expressionism.

LARS EIGHNER

Lars Eighner was born in 1948 in Corpus Christi, Texas, and attended the University of Texas at Austin. He held a series of jobs, including work as an attendant at the state mental hospital in Austin, before he became homeless. For five years he drifted between Austin and Hollywood, living on the streets and in abandoned buildings. Then he began to contribute essays to the *Threepenny Review;* these writings are collected in his memoir, *Travels with Lizabeth* (1993). His other writing includes a collection of short stories, *Bayou Boy and Other Stories* (1993), and a novel, *Pawn to Queen Four* (1995). In "My Daily Dives in the Dumpster," reprinted from *The Threepenny Review* (Fall 1988), Eighner analyzes the "predictable series of stages that a person goes through in learning to scavenge."

My Daily Dives in the Dumpster[2]

I BEGAN DUMPSTER diving about a year before I became 1
homeless.

I prefer the term "scavenging" and use the word "scroung- 2
ing" when I mean to be obscure. I have heard people, evidently meaning to be polite, use the word "foraging," but I prefer to reserve that word for gathering nuts and berries and such which I do also, according to the season and opportunity.

---

[2]Lars Eighner, "My Daily Dives into the Dumpster" from *Travels with Lizbeth: Three Years on the Road and on the Streets,* by Lars Eighner, © 1993 by the author and reprinted by permission of St. Martin's Press, LLC.

I like the frankness of the word "scavenging." I live from 3 the refuse of others. I am a scavenger. I think it a sound and honorable niche, although if I could I would naturally prefer to live the comfortable consumer life, perhaps—and only perhaps—as a slightly less wasteful consumer owing to what I have learned as a scavenger.

Except for jeans, all my clothes come from Dumpsters. 4 Boom boxes, candles, bedding, toilet paper, medicine, books, a typewriter, a virgin male love doll, change sometimes amounting to many dollars: All came from Dumpsters. And, yes, I eat from Dumpsters too.

There are a predictable series of stages that a person goes 5 through in learning to scavenge. At first the new scavenger is filled with disgust and self-loathing. He is ashamed of being seen and may lurk around trying to duck behind things, or he may try to dive at night. (In fact, this is unnecessary, since most people instinctively look away from scavengers.)

Scavenging, more than most other pursuits, tends to yield returns in some proportion to the effort and the intelligence brought to bear.

Every grain of rice seems to be a maggot. Everything 6 seems to stink. The scavenger can wipe the egg yolk off the found can, but he cannot erase the stigma of eating garbage from his mind.

This stage passes with experience. The scavenger finds a 7 pair of running shoes that fit and look and smell brand-new. He finds a pocket calculator in perfect working order. He finds pristine ice cream, still frozen, more than he can eat or keep. He begins to understand: People do throw away perfectly good stuff, a lot of perfectly good stuff.

At this stage he may become lost and never recover. All the 8 Dumpster divers I have known come to the point of trying to acquire everything they touch. Why not take it, they reason, it is all free. This is, of course, hopeless, and most divers come to realize that they must restrict themselves to items of relatively immediate utility.

The finding of objects is becoming something of an urban   9 art. Even respectable, employed people will sometimes find something tempting sticking out of a Dumpster or standing beside one. Quite a number of people, not all of them of the bohemian type, are willing to brag that they found this or that piece in the trash.

But eating from Dumpsters is the thing that separates the   10 dilettanti from the professionals. Eating safely involves three principles: using the senses and common sense to evaluate the condition of the found materials; knowing the Dumpsters of a given area and checking them regularly; and seeking always to answer the question, Why was this discarded?

Perhaps everyone who has a kitchen and a regular supply   11 of groceries has, at one time or another, eaten half a sandwich before discovering mold on the bread, or has gotten a mouthful of milk before realizing the milk had turned. Nothing of the sort is likely to happen to a Dumpster driver because he is constantly reminded that most food is discarded for a reason.

Yet perfectly good food can be found in Dumpsters. Canned   12 goods, for example, turn up fairly often in the Dumpsters I frequent. All except the most phobic people would be willing to eat from a can even if it came from a Dumpster. I have few qualms about dry foods such as crackers, cookies, cereal, chips and pasta if they are free of visible contaminants and still dry and crisp. Raw fruits and vegetables with intact skins seem perfectly safe to me, excluding, of course, the obviously rotten. Many are discarded for minor imperfections that can be pared away. Chocolate is often discarded only because it has become discolored as the cocoa butter de-emulsified.

I began scavenging by pulling pizzas out of the Dumpster   13 behind a pizza delivery shop. In general, prepared food requires caution, but in this case I knew what time the shop closed and went to the Dumpster as soon as the last of the help left.

Because the workers at these places are usually inexperi-   14 enced, pizzas are often made with the wrong topping, baked incorrectly, or refused on delivery for being cold. The products to be discarded are boxed up because inventory is kept by counting boxes: A boxed pizza can be written off; an unboxed pizza does not exist. So I had a steady supply of fresh, sometimes warm pizza.

The area I frequent is inhabited by many affluent college students. I am not here by chance; the Dumpsters are very rich. Students throw out many good things, including food, particularly at the end of the semester and before and after breaks. I find it advantageous to keep an eye on the academic calendar. 15

A typical discard is a half jar of peanut butter—though non-organic peanut butter does not require refrigeration and is unlikely to spoil in any reasonable time. Occasionally I find a cheese with a spot of mold, which, of course, I just pare off, and because it is obvious why the cheese was discarded, I treat it with less suspicion than an apparently perfect cheese found in similar circumstances. One of my favorite finds is yogurt—often discarded, still sealed, when the expiration date has passed—because it will keep for several days, even in warm weather. 16

I avoid ethnic foods I am unfamiliar with. If I do not know what it is supposed to look or smell like when it is good, I cannot be certain I will be able to tell if it is bad. 17

No matter how careful I am I still get dysentery at least once a month, oftener in warm weather. I do not want to paint too romantic a picture. Dumpster diving has serious drawbacks as a way of life. 18

Though I have a proprietary feeling about my Dumpsters, I don't mind my direct competitors, other scavengers, as much as I hate the soda-can scroungers. 19

I have tried scrounging aluminum cans with an able-bodied companion, and afoot we could make no more than a few dollars a day. I can extract the necessities of life from the Dumpsters directly with far less effort than would be required to accumulate the equivalent value in aluminum. Can scroungers, then, are people who *must* have small amounts of cash—mostly drug addicts and winos. 20

I do not begrudge them the cans, but can scroungers tend to tear up the Dumpsters, littering the area and mixing the 21 contents. There are precious few courtesies among scavengers, but it is a common practice to set aside surplus items: pairs of shoes, clothing, canned goods, and such. A true scavenger hates to see good stuff go to waste, and what he cannot use he leaves in good condition in plain sight. Can scroungers lay waste to everything in their path and will stir one of a pair of good shoes to the bottom of a Dumpster to be lost or ruined in the muck. They become so specialized that they can see only cans and earn my contempt by passing up change, canned goods, and readily hockable items.

Can scroungers will even go through individual garbage   22
cans, something I have never seen a scavenger do. Going through individual garbage cans without spreading litter is almost impossible, and litter is likely to reduce the public's tolerance of scavenging. But my strongest reservation about going through individual garbage cans is that this seems to me a very personal kind of invasion, one to which I would object if I were a homeowner.

Though Dumpsters seem somehow less personal than   23
garbage cans, they still contain bank statements, bills, correspondence, pill bottles, and other sensitive information. I avoid trying to draw conclusions about the people who dump in the Dumpsters I frequent. I think it would be unethical to do so, although I know many people will find the idea of scavenger ethics too funny for words.

Occasionally a find tells a story. I once found a small paper   24
bag containing some unused condoms, several partial tubes of flavored sexual lubricant, a partially used compact of birth control pills, and the torn pieces of a picture of a young man. Clearly, the woman was through with him and planning to give up sex altogether.

Dumpster things are often sad—abandoned teddy bears,   25
shredded wedding albums, despaired-of sales kits. I find diaries and journals. College students also discard their papers; I am horrified to discover the kind of paper that now merits an A in an undergraduate course.

Dumpster diving is outdoor work, often surprisingly pleas-   26
ant. It is not entirely predictable; things of interest turn up

every day, and some days there are finds of great value. I am always very pleased when I can turn up exactly the thing I most wanted to find. Yet in spite of the element of chance, scavenging, more than most other pursuits, tends to yield returns in some proportion to the effort and intelligence brought to bear.

I think of scavenging as a modern form of self-reliance. 27 After ten years of government service, where everything is geared to the lowest common denominator, I find work that rewards initiative and effort refreshing. Certainly I would be happy to have a sinecure again, but I am not heartbroken to be without one.

I find from the experience of scavenging two rather deep 28 lessons. The first is to take what I can use and let the rest go. I have come to think that there is no value in the abstract. A thing I cannot use or make useful, perhaps by trading, has no value, however fine or rare it may be. (I mean useful in the broad sense   some art, for example, I would think valuable.)

The second lesson is the transience of material being. I do 29 not suppose that ideas are immortal, but certainly they are longer-lived than material objects.

The things I find in Dumpsters, the love letters and rag 30 dolls of so many lives, remind me of this lesson. Many times in my travels I have lost everything but the clothes on my back. Now I hardly pick up a thing without envisioning the time I will cast it away. This, I think, is a healthy state of mind. Almost everything I have now has already been cast out at least once, proving that what I own is valueless to someone.

I find that my desire to grab for the gaudy bauble has been 31 largely sated. I think this is an attitude I share with the very wealthy—we both know there is plenty more where whatever we have came from. Between us are the rat-race millions who have confounded their selves with the objects they grasp and who nightly scavenge the cable channels looking for they know not what.

I am sorry for them. 32

For Study and Discussion

QUESTIONS ABOUT PURPOSE

1. Why does Eighner prefer the term *scavenging* to *scrounging* or *foraging* to characterize the process he analyzes?
2. In what ways does he demonstrate that Dumpster diving is a "sound and honorable niche"?

QUESTIONS ABOUT AUDIENCE

1. How does Eighner anticipate his audience's reaction to his subject by presenting the "predictable stages that a person goes through in learning to scavenge"?
2. How do his "scavenger ethics" enhance his standing with his readers?

QUESTIONS ABOUT STRATEGIES

1. How does Eighner use the example of pizza to illustrate the three principles of eating from a Dumpster?
2. How does his analysis of the process of "soda-can scrounging" help distinguish that process from the process of "scavenging"?

For Writing and Research

1. *Analyze* how Eighner uses anecdotes to illustrate the various steps in learning to scavenge.
2. *Practice* by listing the steps by which your readers can become conscientious consumers.
3. *Argue* that Eighner's attitudes toward consumption and waste are similar to those of the wealthy.
4. *Synthesize:* Research the current solutions to homelessness. Then construct an argument for the most effective solution to the problem.

ERNEST HEMINGWAY

Ernest Hemingway (1899–1961) was born and raised in Oak Park, Illinois (a suburb of Chicago), but he spent his summers hunting and fishing at his father's summer home in Upper Michigan. After high school he worked as a reporter for the *Kansas City Star*, where he learned to compose those vigorous sentences that would become the hallmark of his distinctive style. In the 1920s he moved to Paris and began writing short stories and novels that eventually earned him the legendary place in American letters suggested succinctly by his nickname, Papa. His novels include *The Sun Also Rises* (1926), *A Farewell to Arms* (1929), *For Whom the Bell Tolls* (1940), and *The Old Man and the Sea* (1953). He won both the Pulitzer Prize and the Nobel Prize for Literature. Hemingway used his favorite shotgun to take his own life on July 2, 1961. Hemingway's favorite subjects were war and sport, those activities that placed people in crisis situations. The Hemingway code argued that one became courageous by performing gracefully under the pressure of such crises—by doing it right and without complaint. Although he wrote this essay on camping for the *Toronto Star* before he became a famous novelist, he adheres to his code by arguing that any process must be performed according to the correct procedures.

When You Camp Out,
Do It Right[3]

T HOUSANDS OF PEOPLE will go into the bush this summer   1
to cut the high cost of living. A man who gets his two
weeks' salary while he is on vacation should be able to put
those two weeks in fishing and camping and be able to save
one week's salary clear. He ought to be able to sleep comfortably every night, to eat well every day and to return to the
city rested and in good condition.

But if he goes into the woods with a frying pan, an ignorance   2
of black flies and mosquitoes, and a great and abiding lack of
knowledge about cookery the chances are that his return will
be very different. He will come back with enough mosquito
bites to make the back of his neck look like a relief map of the
Caucasus. His digestion will be wrecked after a valiant battle to
assimilate half-cooked or charred grub. And he won't have had
a decent night's sleep while he has been gone.

He will solemnly raise his right hand and inform you that   3
he has joined the grand army of never-agains. The call of the
wild may be all right, but it's a dog's life. He's heard the call
of the tame with both ears. Waiter, bring him an order of
milk toast.

In the first place he overlooked the insects. Black flies,   4
no-see-ums, deer flies, gnats and mosquitoes were instituted
by the devil to force people to live in cities where he could
get at them better. If it weren't for them everybody would
live in the bush and he would be out of work. It was a rather
successful invention.

But there are lots of dopes that will counteract the pests.   5
The simplest perhaps is oil of citronella. Two bits' worth of
this purchased at any pharmacist's will be enough to last for
two weeks in the worst fly and mosquito-ridden country.

---

[3] Ernest Hemingway, Reprinted with the permission of Scribner, a division
of Simon & Schuster, Inc., from ERNEST HEMINGWAY: DATELINE:
TORONTO by William White, editor. Copyright © 1985 by Mary Hemingway, John Hemingway, Patrick Hemingway, and Gregory Hemingway. All
rights reserved.

Rub a little on the back of your neck, your forehead and your wrists before you start fishing, and the blacks and skeeters will shun you. The odor of citronella is not offensive to people. It smells like gun oil. But the bugs do hate it. 6

Oil of pennyroyal and eucalyptol are also much hated by mosquitoes, and with citronella they form the basis for many proprietary preparations. But it is cheaper and better to buy the straight citronella. Put a little on the mosquito netting that covers the front of your pup tent or canoe tent at night, and you won't be bothered. 7

To be really rested and get any benefit out of a vacation a man must get a good night's sleep every night. The first requisite for this is to have plenty of cover. It is twice as cold as you expect it will be in the bush, four nights out of five, and a good plan is to take just double the bedding that you think you will need. An old quilt that you can wrap up in is as warm as two blankets. 8

Nearly all outdoor writers rhapsodize over the browse bed. It is all right for the man who knows how to make one and has plenty of time. But in a succession of one-night camps on a canoe trip all you need is level ground for your tent floor and you will sleep all right if you have plenty of covers under you. Take twice as much cover as you think that you will need, and then put two-thirds of it under you. You will sleep warm and get your rest. 9

When it is clear weather you don't need to pitch your tent if you are only stopping for the night. Drive four stakes at the head of your made-up bed and drape your mosquito bar over that, then you can sleep like a log and laugh at the mosquitoes. 10

Outside of insects and bum sleeping the rock that wrecks most camping trips is cooking. The average tyro's idea of cooking is to fry everything and fry it good and plenty. Now, a frying pan is a most necessary thing to any trip, but you also need the old stew kettle and the folding reflector baker. 11

A pan of fried trout can't be bettered and they don't cost any more than ever. But there is a good and bad way of frying them. 12

The beginner puts his trout and his bacon in and over a brightly burning fire the bacon curls up and dries into a dry 13 tasteless cinder and the trout is burned outside while it is still raw inside. He eats them and it is all right if he is only out for the day and going home to a good meal at night. But if he is going to face more trout and bacon the next morning and other equally well-cooked dishes for the remainder of two weeks he is on the pathway to nervous dyspepsia.

The proper way is to cook over coals. Have several cans of   14 Crisco or Cotosuet or one of the vegetable shortenings along that are as good as lard and excellent for all kinds of shortening. Put the bacon in and when it is about half cooked lay the trout in the hot grease, dipping them in corn meal first. Then put the bacon on top of the trout and it will baste them as it slowly cooks.

The coffee can be boiling at the same time and in a smaller   15 skillet pancakes being made that are satisfying the other campers while they are waiting for the trout.

With the prepared pancake flours you take a cupful of pan-   16 cake flour and add a cup of water. Mix the water and flour and as soon as the lumps are out it is ready for cooking. Have the skillet hot and keep it well greased. Drop the batter in and as soon as it is done on one side loosen it in the skillet and flip it over. Apple butter, syrup or cinnamon and sugar go well with the cakes.

While the crowd have taken the edge from their appetites   17 with flapjacks the trout have been cooked and they and the bacon are ready to serve. The trout are crisp outside and firm and pink inside and the bacon is well done—but not too done. If there is anything better than that combination the writer has yet to taste it in a lifetime devoted largely and studiously to eating.

The stew kettle will cook your dried apricots when they   18 have resumed their predried plumpness after a night of soaking, it will serve to concoct a mulligan in, and it will cook macaroni. When you are not using it, it should be boiling water for the dishes.

In the baker, mere man comes into his own, for he can   19 make a pie that to his bush appetite will have it all over the product that mother used to make, like a tent. Men have always believed that there was something mysterious and difficult about making a pie. Here is a great secret. There is nothing to it. We've been kidded for years. Any man of average office intelligence can make at least as good a pie as his wife.

All there is to a pie is a cup and a half of flour, one-half 20
teaspoonful of salt, one-half cup of lard and cold water. That will make pie crust that will bring tears of joy into your camping partner's eyes.

Mix the salt with the flour, work the lard into the flour, 21
make it up into a good workmanlike dough with cold water. Spread some flour on the back of a box or something flat, and pat the dough around a while. Then roll it out with whatever kind of round bottle you prefer. Put a little more lard on the surface of the sheet of dough and then slosh a little flour on and roll it up and then roll it out again with the bottle.

Cut out a piece of the rolled out dough big enough to 22
line a pie tin. I like the kind with holes in the bottom. Then put in your dried apples that have soaked all night and been sweetened, or your apricots, or your blueberries, and then take another sheet of the dough and drape it gracefully over the top, soldering it down at the edges with your fingers. Cut a couple of slits in the top dough sheet and prick it a few times with a fork in an artistic manner.

Put it in the baker with a good slow fire for forty-five min- 23
utes and then take it out and if your pals are Frenchmen they will kiss you. The penalty for knowing how to cook is that the others will make you do all the cooking.

It is all right to talk about roughing it in the woods. But 24
the real woodsman is the man who can be really comfortable in the bush.

A man who gets two weeks' salary while he is
on vacation should be able to put those two
weeks in fishing and camping and be able to
save one week's salary clear.

For Study and Discussion

QUESTIONS ABOUT PURPOSE

1. In what ways does Hemingway establish the purpose of his essay in the first paragraph? Does he suggest that he will be giving directions or providing information?
2. According to Hemingway, what purposes do people expect to achieve by camping? Why do most people fail to achieve those purposes?

QUESTIONS ABOUT AUDIENCE

1. Although this essay appeared in a mass circulation newspaper, it is directed at a specific group of readers. Who are they, and why does Hemingway assume that they are *his* audience?
2. What group of readers does he exclude from his analysis? Why does he assume they have no interest in camping?

QUESTIONS ABOUT STRATEGIES

1. How many processes does Hemingway analyze in this essay?
2. He devotes most of his essay to explaining how to cook a meal. What steps must be suspended while others are completed? What steps should be avoided? What small steps are buried within larger steps?

For Research and Writing

1. *Analyze* the "insider's advice" that Hemingway provides for getting a good night's sleep.
2. *Practice* by providing your own "insider's advice" on how to prepare for a trip to the woods.
3. *Argue* that camping is simply a cheap way to take a vacation.
4. *Synthesize:* Research the various tips travel agents provide for people taking a vacation to another country. Then use this information to define the purpose of a vacation.

Nikki Giovanni was born in 1943 in Knoxville, Tennessee, and was educated at Fisk University, the University of Pennsylvania, and Columbia University. She has taught creative writing at Rutgers University and Virginia Tech and worked for the Ohio Humanities Council and the Appalachian Community Fund. Her poems have appeared in the collections *My House* (1972), *The Women and the Men* (1975), *Those Who Ride the Night Winds* (1983), *The Collected Poetry of Nikki Giovanni: 1968–1998* (2003), and *Bicycles: Love Poems* (2009) Her other work appears in books such as *Gemini: An Extended Autobiographical Statement on My First Twenty-five Years Being a Black Poet* (1971), *Sacred Cows . . . and Other Edibles* (1988), *Racism 101* (1994), and *Prosaic Soul of Nikki Giovanni* (2003), In "Campus Racism 101," reprinted from *Racism 101,* Giovanni tells black students how to succeed at predominantly white colleges.

Campus Racism 101[4]

THERE IS A bumper sticker that reads: TOO BAD IGNORANCE ISN'T PAINFUL. I like that. But ignorance is. We just seldom attribute the pain to it or even recognize it when we see it. Like the postcard on my corkboard. It shows a young man in a very hip jacket smoking a cigarette. In the background is a high school with the American flag waving. The caption says: "Too cool for school. Yet too stupid for the real world."

---

[4]Nikki Giovanni, "Campus Racism 101" from *Racism* 101 by Nikki Giovanni. Copyright © 1994 by Nikki Giovanni. Reprinted by permission of HarperCollins Publishers, Inc.

Out of the mouth of the young man is a bubble enclosing the words "Maybe I'll start a band." There could be a postcard showing a jock in a uniform saying, "I don't need school. I'm going to the NFL or NBA." Or one showing a young man or woman studying and a group of young people saying, "So you want to be white." Or something equally demeaning. We need to quit it.

I am a professor of English at Virginia Tech. I've been   2
here for four years, though for only two years with academic rank. I am tenured, which means I have a teaching position for life, a rarity on a predominantly white campus. Whether from malice or ignorance, people who think I should be at a predominantly Black institution will ask, "Why are you at Tech?" Because it's here. And so are Black students. But even if Black students weren't here, it's painfully obvious that this nation and this world cannot allow white students to go through higher education without interacting with Blacks in authoritative positions. It is equally clear that predominantly

---

Your job is not to educate white people; it is to obtain an education.

Black colleges cannot accommodate the numbers of Black students who want and need an education.

Is it difficult to attend a predominantly white college?   3
Compared with what? Being passed over for promotion because you lack credentials? Being turned down for jobs because you are not college-educated? Joining the armed forces or going to jail because you cannot find an alternative to the streets? Let's have a little perspective here. Where can you go and what can you do that frees you from interacting with the white American mentality? You're going to interact; the only question is, will you be in some control of yourself and your actions, or will you be controlled by others? I'm going to recommend self-control.

What's the difference between prison and college? They 4
both prescribe your behavior for a given period of time. They
both allow you to read books and develop your writing.
They both give you time alone to think and time with your
peers to talk about issues. But four years of prison doesn't
give you a passport to greater opportunities. Most likely that
time only gives you greater knowledge of how to get back in.
Four years of college gives you an opportunity not only to
lift yourself but to serve your people effectively. What's the
difference when you are called nigger in college from when
you are called nigger in prison? In college you can, though I
admit with effort, follow procedures to have those students
who called you nigger kicked out or suspended. You can
bring issues to public attention without risking your life. But
mostly, college is and always has been the future. We, neither
less nor more than other people, need knowledge. There are
discomforts attached to attending predominantly white colleges, though no more so than living in a racist world. Here
are some rules to follow that may help:

Go to class. No matter how you feel. No matter how you 5
think the professor feels about you. It's important to have
a consistent presence in the classroom. If nothing else, the
professor will know you care enough and are serious enough
to be there.

Meet your professors. Extend your hand (give a firm hand- 6
shake) and tell them your name. Ask them what you need to
do to make an A. You may never make an A, but you have put
them on notice that you are serious about getting good grades.

Do assignments on time. Typed or computer-generated. 7
You have the syllabus. Follow it, and turn those papers in. If
for some reason you can't complete an assignment on time,
let your professor know before it is due and work out a new
due date—then meet it.

Go back to see your professor. Tell him or her your name 8
again. If an assignment received less than an A, ask why, and
find out what you need to do to improve the next assignment.

Yes, your professor is busy. So are you. So are your parents 9
who are working to pay or help with your tuition. Ask early

what you need to do if you feel you are starting to get into academic trouble. Do not wait until you are failing.

Understand that there will be professors who do not like you; 10 there may even be professors who are racist or sexist or both. You must discriminate among your professors to see who will give you the help you need. You may not simply say, "They are all against me." They aren't. They mostly don't care. Since you are the one who wants to be educated, find the people who want to help.

Don't defeat yourself. Cultivate your friends. Know your 11 enemies. You cannot undo hundreds of years of prejudicial thinking. Think for yourself and speak up. Raise your hand in class. Say what you believe no matter how awkward you may think it sounds. You will improve in your articulation and confidence.

Participate in some campus activity. Join the newspaper 12 staff. Run for office. Join a dorm council. Do something that involves you on campus. You are going to be there for four years, so let your presence be known, if not felt.

You will inevitably run into some white classmates who 13 are troubling because they often say stupid things, ask stupid questions—and expect an answer. Here are some comebacks to some of the most common inquiries and comments:

Q: What's it like to grow up in a ghetto? 14
A: I don't know. 15
Q: (from the teacher): Can you give us the Black perspec- 16 tive on Toni Morrison, Huck Finn, slavery, Martin Luther King, Jr., and others?
A: I can give you *my* perspective. (Do not take the burden 17 of 22 million people on your shoulders. Remind everyone that you are an individual, and don't speak for the race or any other individual within it.)
Q: Why do all the Black people sit together in the dining 18 hall?
A: Why do all the white students sit together? 19
Q: Why should there be an African-American studies course? 20
A: Because white Americans have not adequately studied 21 the contributions of Africans and African-Americans. Both

Black and white students need to know our total common history.

Q: Why are there so many scholarships for "minority" 22 students?

A: Because they wouldn't give my great-grandparents 23 their forty acres and the mule.

Q: How can whites understand Black history, culture, 24 literature, and so forth?

A: The same way we understand white history, culture, 25 literature, and so forth. That is why we're in school: to learn.

Q: Should whites take African-American studies courses? 26

A: Of course. We take white-studies courses, though the 27 universities don't call them that.

Comment: When I see groups of Black people on campus, 28 it's really intimidating.

Comeback: I understand what you mean. I'm frightened 29 when I see white students congregating.

Comment: It's not fair. It's easier for you guys to get into 30 college than for other people.

Comeback: If it's so easy, why aren't there more of us? 31

Comment: It's not our fault that America is the way it is. 32

Comeback: It's not our fault, either, but both of us have 33 a responsibility to make changes.

It's really very simple. Educational progress is a national con- 34 cern; education is a private one. Your job is not to educate white people; it is to obtain an education. If you take the racial world on your shoulders, you will not get the job done. Deal with yourself as an individual worthy of respect, and make everyone else deal with you the same way. College is a little like playing grown-up. Practice what you want to be. You have been telling your parents you are grown. Now is your chance to act like it.

For Study and Discussion

QUESTIONS ABOUT PURPOSE

1. How does Giovanni explain her reasons for teaching at a predominantly white school?

2. In what ways does the issue of control, particularly self-control, explain the purpose of her advice?

QUESTIONS ABOUT AUDIENCE

1. How do the examples in the first paragraph and the advice in the last paragraph identify Giovanni's primary audience?
2. How does Giovanni's status as professor at a predominantly white college establish her authority to address her audience on "Racism 101"?

QUESTIONS ABOUT STRATEGIES

1. How does Giovanni arrange her advice? Why is her first suggestion—"Go to class"—her *first* suggestion? Why is her last suggestion—"Participate in some campus activity"—her *last* suggestion?
2. How does she use sample questions and answers to illustrate the experience of learning on a white campus?

For Writing and Research

1. *Analyze* how Giovanni uses comparisons—for example, college and prison—to explain the process of acquiring an education.
2. *Practice* by analyzing the process by which students can respond to teachers who do not "like" them.
3. *Argue* that, in a way, it is the job of black students to educate white people.
4. *Synthesize* the current research on America's educational progress. Then analyze the process by which the country can improve its status.

P. J. O'ROURKE

Patrick Jake O'Rourke was born in 1947 in Toledo, Ohio, and was educated at Miami University and Johns Hopkins University. He began his writing career working for underground newspapers such as *Harry* in Baltimore before landing jobs as a feature editor and freelance writer for the *New York Herald*, executive editor for *National Lampoon*, and correspondent for *Rolling Stone* and *Atlantic Monthly*. His humorous style is showcased in *The 1964 High School Yearbook Parody* (1974), *Modern Manners: An Etiquette Book for Rude People* (1983), *The Bachelor's Home Companion: A Practical Guide to Keeping House Like a Pig* (1987), and *Holidays in Hell* (1988). O'Rourke's humor always has a political edge, evident in books such as *Republican Party Reptile: Essays and Outrages* (1987), *Give War a Chance: Eyewitness Accounts of Mankind's Struggle Against Tyranny, Injustice and Alcohol-Free Beer* (1992), *The CEO of the Sofa* (2001), *Peace Kills: America's Fun New Imperialism* (2004), *Driving Like Crazy* (2009), and *Don't Vote—It Just Encourages the Bastards* (2010). In "Third World Driving Hints and Tips," reprinted from *Holidays in Hell*, O'Rourke analyzes the rules of the road for driving in a different country.

Third World Driving Hints and Tips[5]

D URING THE PAST couple of years I've had to do my share 1
of driving in the Third World—in Mexico, Lebanon, the Philippines, Cyprus, El Salvador, Africa and Italy. (Italy is

---

not technically part of the Third World, but no one has told the Italians.) I don't pretend to be an expert, but I have been making notes. Maybe these notes will be useful to readers who are planning to do something really stupid with their Hertz #1 Club cards.

ROAD HAZARDS

What would be a road hazard anywhere else, in the Third World is probably the road. There are two techniques for coping with this. One is to drive very fast so your wheels "get on top" of the ruts and your car sails over the ditches and gullies. Predictably, this will result in disaster. The other technique is to drive very slowly. This will also result in disaster. No matter how slowly you drive into a ten-foot hole, you're still going to get hurt. You'll find the locals themselves can't make up their minds. Either they drive at 2 m.p.h.—which they do every time there's absolutely no way to get around them. Or else they drive at 100 m.p.h.—which they do coming right at you when you finally get a chance to pass the guy going 2 m.p.h.

Never look where you're going— you'll only scare yourself.

BASIC INFORMATION

It's important to have your facts straight before you begin piloting a car around an underdeveloped country. For instance, which side of the road do they drive on? This is easy. They drive on your side. That is, you can depend on it, any oncoming traffic will be on your side of the road. Also, how do you translate kilometres into miles? Most people don't know this, but one kilometre = ten miles, exactly. True, a kilometre is only 62 per cent of a mile, but if something is one hundred kilometres away, read that as one thousand miles because the roads are 620 percent worse than anything you've ever seen. And when you see a 50-k.p.h. speed limit, you might as well figure that means 500 *m.p.h.* because nobody cares. The Third World does not have Broderick Crawford and the Highway Patrol. Outside the cities, it doesn't have many police at all. Law enforcement is in the hands of the army. And soldiers, if they feel like it, will shoot you no matter what speed you're going.

TRAFFIC SIGNS AND SIGNALS

Most developing nations use international traffic symbols. 4 Americans may find themselves perplexed by road signs that look like Boy Scout merit badges and by such things as an iguana silhouette with a red diagonal bar across it. Don't worry, the natives don't know what they mean, either. The natives do, however, have an elaborate set of signals used to convey information to the traffic around them. For example, if you're trying to pass someone and he blinks his left turn signal, it means go ahead. Either that or it means a large truck is coming around the bend, and you'll get killed if you try. You'll find out in a moment.

Signalling is further complicated by festive decorations 5 found on many vehicles. It can be hard to tell a hazard flasher from a string of Christmas-tree lights wrapped around the bumper, and brake lights can easily be confused with the dozen red Jesus statuettes and the ten stuffed animals with blinking eyes on the package shelf.

DANGEROUS CURVES

Dangerous curves are marked, at least in Christian lands, by 6 white wooden crosses positioned to make the curves even more dangerous. These crosses are memorials to people who've died in traffic accidents, and they give a rough statistical indication of how much trouble you're likely to have at that spot in the road. Thus, when you come through a curve in a full-power slide and are suddenly confronted with a veritable forest of crucifixes, you know you're dead.

LEARNING TO DRIVE LIKE A NATIVE

It's important to understand that in the Third World most ⁊ driving is done with the horn, or "Egyptian Brake Pedal," as it is known. There is a precise and complicated etiquette of horn use. Honk your horn only under the following circumstances:

1. When anything blocks the road.
2. When anything doesn't.
3. When anything might.
4. At red lights.
5. At green lights.
6. At all other times.

ROAD-BLOCKS

One thing you can count on in Third World countries is ₈ trouble. There's always some uprising, coup or Marxist insurrection going on, and this means military road-blocks. There are two kinds of military road-block, the kind where you slow down so they can look you over, and the kind where you come to a full stop so they can steal your luggage. The important thing is that you must *never* stop at the slow-down kind of road-block. If you stop, they'll think you're a terrorist about to attack them, and they'll shoot you. And you must *always* stop at the full-stop kind of road-block. If you just slow down, they'll think you're a terrorist about to attack them, and they'll shoot you. How do you tell the difference between the two kinds of road-block? Here's the fun part: you can't!

(The terrorists, of course, have road-blocks of their own. ₉ They always make you stop. Sometimes with land mines.)

ANIMALS IN THE RIGHT OF WAY

As a rule of thumb, you should slow down for donkeys, speed ₁₀ up for goats and stop for cows. Donkeys will get out of your way eventually, and so will pedestrians. But never actually stop for either of them or they'll take advantage, especially the pedestrians. If you stop in the middle of a crowd of Third

World pedestrians, you'll be there buying Chiclets and bogus antiquities for days.

Drive like hell through the goats. It's almost impossible to 11 hit a goat. On the other hand, it's almost impossible *not* to hit a cow. Cows are immune to horn-honking, shouting, swats with sticks and taps on the hind quarters with the bumper. The only thing you can do to make a cow move is swerve to avoid it, which will make the cow move in front of you with lightning speed.

Actually, the most dangerous animals are the chickens. In 12 the United States, when you see a ball roll into the street, you hit your brakes because you know the next thing you'll see is a kid chasing it. In the Third World, it's not balls the kids are chasing, but chickens. Are they practising punt returns with a leghorn? Dribbling it? Playing stick-hen? I don't know. But Third Worlders are remarkably fond of their chickens and, also, their children (population problems not withstanding). If you hit one or both, they may survive. But you will not.

ACCIDENTS

Never look where you're going—you'll only scare yourself. 13 Nonetheless, try to avoid collisions. There are bound to be more people in that bus, truck or even on that moped than there are in your car. At best you'll be screamed deaf. And if the police do happen to be around, standard procedure is to throw everyone in jail regardless of fault. This is done to forestall blood feuds, which are a popular hobby in many of these places. Remember the American consul is very busy fretting about that Marxist insurrection, and it may be months before he comes to visit.

If you do have an accident, the only thing to do is go on 14 the offensive. Throw big wads of American money at everyone, and hope for the best.

SAFETY TIPS

One nice thing about the Third World, you don't have to 15 fasten your safety belt. (Or stop smoking. Or cut down on saturated fats.) It takes a lot off your mind when average life expectancy is forty-five minutes.

For Study and Discussion

QUESTIONS ABOUT PURPOSE

1. How do O'Rourke's travels establish his credentials to provide advice to drivers?
2. At what point in the essay do you realize that his purpose is to entertain rather than inform?

QUESTIONS ABOUT AUDIENCE

1. How does O'Rourke identify his readers when he refers to "Hertz #1 Club cards" and "big wads of American money"?
2. How might the "natives" referred to in this essay respond to his characterization of their driving habits?

QUESTIONS ABOUT STRATEGIES

1. How does O'Rourke's analysis of the "Egyptian Brake Pedal" reveal that his hints are not really meant to inform?
2. How does his discussion of "animals in the right of way" and children complicate his analysis?

For Writing and Research

1. *Analyze* how O'Rourke arranges the sequence of his "driving hints and tips."
2. *Practice* by analyzing the process by which you learned to drive.
3. *Argue* that O'Rourke's use of the words *Third World* and *underdeveloped* suggests an attitude of smug cultural superiority.
4. *Synthesize:* Interview driving instructors and police officers in your hometown. Then use this information to analyze the driving habits they have encountered.

ELIZABETH WINTHROP

Elizabeth Winthrop was born in 1948 in Washington, D.C., and educated at Sarah Lawrence College. She worked for Harper and Row editing Harper Junior Books before she began her own career as author of books for children. She has written more than thirty such books, including *Bunk Beds* (1972), *Potbellied Possums* (1977), *In My Mother's House* (1988), *The Battle for the Castle* (1993), and *As the Crow Flies* (1998). Her latest novel is *Counting on Grace* (2006) that focuses on the problem of child labor in the early years of the twentieth century. Winthrop has twice won the PEN Syndicated Fiction Contest, once in 1985 with her story "Bad News" and again in 1990 with "The Golden Darters." In the latter story, reprinted from *American Short Fiction,* a young girl betrays her father by using their creation for the wrong purpose.

The Golden Darters[6]

I WAS TWELVE years old when my father started tying flies. It was an odd habit for a man who had just undergone a serious operation on his upper back, but, as he remarked to my mother one night, at least it gave him a world over which he had some control.   1

The family grew used to seeing him hunched down close to his tying vise, hackle pliers in one hand, thread bobbin in the other. We began to bandy about strange phrases—foxy   2

---

[6] Elizabeth Winthrop, "The Golden Darters." First published in *Best American Short Stories,* p. 339 Copyright © 1991 by Elizabeth Winthrop. Reprinted by permission of the author.

quills, bodkins, peacock hurl. Father's corner of the living room was off limits to the maid with the voracious and destructive vacuum cleaner. Who knew what precious bit of calf's tail or rabbit fur would be sucked away never to be seen again?

Because of my father's illness, we had gone up to our summer cottage on the lake in New Hampshire a month early. None of my gang of friends ever came till the end of July, so in the beginning of that summer I hung around home watching my father as he fussed with the flies. I was the only child he allowed to stand near him while he worked. "Your brothers bounce," he muttered one day as he clamped the vise onto the curve of a model-perfect hook. "You can stay and watch if you don't bounce." 3

So I took great care not to bounce or lean or even breathe too noisily on him while he performed his delicate maneuvers, holding back hackle with one hand as he pulled off the final flourish of a whip finish with the other. I had never been so close to my father for so long before, and while he studied his tiny creations, I studied him. I stared at the large pores of his skin, the sleek black hair brushed straight back from the soft dip of his temples, the jaw muscles tightening and slackening. Something in my father seemed always to be ticking. He did not take well to sickness and enforced confinement. 4

When he leaned over his work, his shirt collar slipped down to reveal the recent scar, a jagged trail of disrupted tissue. The tender pink skin gradually paled and then toughened during those weeks when he took his prescribed afternoon nap, lying on his stomach on our little patch of front lawn. Our house was one of the closest to the lake and it seemed to embarrass my mother to have him stretch himself out on the grass for all the swimmers and boaters to see. 5

"At least sleep on the porch," she would say. "That's why we set the hammock up there." 6

"Why shouldn't a man sleep on his own front lawn if he so chooses?" he would reply. "I have to mow the bloody thing. I might as well put it to some use." 7

And my mother would shrug and give up. 8

At the table when he was absorbed, he lost all sense of any- 9
thing but the magnified insect under the light. Often when
he pushed his chair back and announced the completion of
his latest project to the family, there would be a bit of down
or a tuft of dubbing stuck to the edge of his lip. I did not
tell him about it but stared, fascinated, wondering how long
it would take to blow away. Sometimes it never did, and I
imagine he discovered the fluff in the bathroom mirror when
he went upstairs to bed. Or maybe my mother plucked it off
with one of those proprietary gestures of hers that irritated
my brothers so much.

In the beginning, Father wasn't very good at the fly-tying. 10
He was a large, thick-boned man with sweeping gestures, a
robust laugh, and a sudden terrifying temper. If he had not
loved fishing so much, I doubt he would have persevered
with the fussy business of the flies. After all, the job required
tools normally associated with woman's work. Thread and
bobbins, soft slippery feathers, a magnifying glass, and an
instruction manual that read like a cookbook. It said things
like, "Cut off a bunch of yellowtail. Hold the tip end with the
left hand and stroke out the short hairs."

But Father must have had a goal in mind. You tie flies 11
because one day, in the not-too-distant future, you will attach
them to a tippet, wade into a stream, and lure a rainbow trout
out of his quiet pool.

There was something endearing, almost childish, about 12
his stubborn nightly ritual at the corner table. His head
bent under the standing lamp, his fingers trembling slightly,
he would whisper encouragement to himself, talk his way
through some particularly delicate operation. Once or twice
I caught my mother gazing silently across my brothers' heads
at him. When our eyes met, she would turn away and busy
herself in the kitchen.

Finally, one night, after weeks of allowing me to watch, he 13
told me to take his seat. "Why, Father?"

"Because it's time for you to try one."   14

"That's all right. I like to watch."   15

"Nonsense, Emily. You'll do just fine."   16

He had stood up. The chair was waiting. Across the room, ₁₇
my mother put down her knitting. Even the boys, embroiled
in a noisy game of double solitaire, stopped their wrangling for
a moment. They were all waiting to see what I would do. It
was my fear of failing him that made me hesitate. I knew that
my father put his trust in results, not in the learning process.

"Sit down, Emily."   ₁₈

I obeyed, my heart pounding. I was a cautious, secre- ₁₉
tive child, and I could not bear to have people watch me
doing things. My piano lesson was the hardest hour in the
week. The teacher would sit with a resigned look on her face
while my fingers groped across the keys, muddling through
a sonata that I had played perfectly just an hour before. The
difference was that then nobody had been watching.

"—so we'll start you off with a big hook." He had been ₂₀
talking for some time. How much had I missed already?

"Ready?" he asked.   ₂₁

I nodded.   ₂₂

"All right then, clamp this hook into the vise. You'll be ₂₃
making the golden darter, a streamer. A big flashy fly, the
kind that imitates a small fish as it moves underwater."

Across the room, my brothers had returned to their game, ₂₄
but their voices were subdued. I imagined they wanted to hear
what was happening to me. My mother had left the room.

"Tilt the magnifying glass so you have a good view of the ₂₅
hook. Right. Now tie on with the bobbin thread."

It took me three tries to line the thread up properly on the ₂₆
hook, each silken line nesting next to its neighbor. "We're
going to do it right, Emily, no matter how long it takes."

"It's hard," I said quietly.   ₂₇

Slowly I grew used to the tiny tools, to the oddly enlarged ₂₈
view of my fingers through the magnifying glass. They looked
as if they didn't belong to me anymore. The feeling in their
tips was too small for their large, clumsy movements. Despite
my father's repeated warnings, I nicked the floss once against
the barbed hook. Luckily it did not give way.

"It's Emily's bedtime," my mother called from the kitchen. ₂₉

"Hush, she's tying in the throat. Don't bother us now." ₃₀

I could feel his breath on my neck. The mallard barbules 31
were stubborn, curling into the hook in the wrong direction.
Behind me, I sensed my father's fingers twisting in imitation
of my own.

"You've almost got it," he whispered, his lips barely mov- 32
ing. "That's right. Keep the thread slack until you're all the
way around."

I must have tightened it too quickly. I lost control of the 33
feathers in my left hand, the clumsier one. First the gold
mylar came unwound and then the yellow floss.

"Damn it all, now look what you've done," he roared, and 34
for a second I wondered whether he was talking to me. He
sounded as if he were talking to a grown-up. He sounded
the way he had just the night before when an antique teacup
had slipped through my mother's soapy fingers and shattered
against the hard surface of the sink. I sat back slowly, resting
my aching spine against the chair for the first time since we'd
begun.

"Leave it for now, Gerald," my mother said tentatively 35
from the kitchen. Out of the corner of my eye, I could see
her sponging the kitchen counter with small, defiant sweeps
of her hand. "She can try again tomorrow."

"What happened?" called a brother. They both started 36
across the room toward us but stopped at a look from my
father.

"We'll start again," he said, his voice once more under 37
control. "Best way to learn. Get back on the horse."

With a flick of his hand, he loosened the vise, removed my 38
hook, and threw it into the wastepaper basket.

"From the beginning?" I whispered. 39

"Of course," he replied. "There's no way to rescue a mess 40
like that."

My mess had taken almost an hour to create. 41

"Gerald," my mother said again. "Don't you think—" 42

"How can we possibly work with all these interruptions?" 43
he thundered. I flinched as if he had hit me. "Go on upstairs,
all of you. Emily and I will be up when we're done. Go on,
for God's sake. Stop staring at us."

At a signal from my mother, the boys backed slowly away   44
and crept up to their room. She followed them. I felt all
alone, as trapped under my father's piercing gaze as the hook
in the grip of its vise.

We started again. This time my fingers were trembling so   45
much that I ruined three badger hackle feathers, stripping off
the useless webbing at the tip. My father did not lose his temper again. His voice dropped to an even, controlled mono-
tone that scared me more than his shouting. After an hour of
painstaking labor, we reached the same point with the stubborn mallard feathers curling into the hook. Once, twice, I
repinched them under the throat, but each time they slipped
away from me. Without a word, my father stood up and leaned
over me. With his cheek pressed against my hair, he reached
both hands around and took my fingers in his. I longed to
surrender the tools to him and slide away off the chair, but we
were so close to the end. He captured the curling stem with
the thread and trapped it in place with three quick wraps.

"Take your hands away carefully," he said. "I'll do the   46
whip finish. We don't want to risk losing it now."

I did as I was told, sat motionless with his arms around   47
me, my head tilted slightly to the side so he could have the
clear view through the magnifying glass. He cemented the
head, wiped the excess glue from the eye with a waste feather,
and hung my golden darter on the tackle box handle to dry.
When at last he pulled away, I breathlessly slid my body back
against the chair. I was still conscious of the havoc my clumsy
hands or an unexpected sneeze could wreak on the table,
which was cluttered with feathers and bits of fur.

"Now, that's the fly you tied, Emily. Isn't it beautiful?"   48
I nodded. "Yes, Father."   49
"Tomorrow, we'll do another one. An olive grouse.   50
Smaller hook but much less complicated body. Look. I'll
show you in the book."

As I waited to be released from the chair, I didn't think   51
he meant it. He was just trying to apologize for having lost
his temper, I told myself, just trying to pretend that our time
together had been wonderful. But the next morning when

I came down, late for breakfast, he was waiting for me with the materials for the olive grouse already assembled. He was ready to start in again, to take charge of my clumsy fingers with his voice and talk them through the steps.

That first time was the worst, but I never felt comfortable 52 at the fly-tying table with Father's breath tickling the hair on my neck. I completed the olive grouse, another golden darter to match the first, two muddler minnows, and some others. I don't remember all the names anymore.

Once I hid upstairs, pretending to be immersed in my 53 summer reading books, but he came looking for me.

"Emily," he called. "Come on down. Today we'll start the 54 lead-winged coachman. I've got everything set up for you."

I lay very still and did not answer. 55

"Gerald," I heard my mother say. "Leave the child alone. 56 You're driving her crazy with those flies."

"Nonsense," he said, and started up the dark, wooden 57 stairs, one heavy step at a time.

I put my book down and rolled slowly off the bed so that 58 by the time he reached the door of my room, I was on my feet, ready to be led back downstairs to the table.

Although we never spoke about it, my mother became 59 oddly insistent that I join her on trips to the library or the general store.

"Are you going out again, Emily?" my father would call 60 after me. "I was hoping we'd get some work done on this minnow."

"I'll be back soon, Father," I'd say. "I promise." 61

"Be sure you do," he said. 62

And for a while I did. 63

Then at the end of July, my old crowd of friends from across 64 the lake began to gather and I slipped away to join them early in the morning before my father got up.

The girls were a gang. When we were all younger, we'd 65 held bicycle relay races on the ring road and played down at the lakeside together under the watchful eyes of our mothers. Every July, we threw ourselves joyfully back into each other's lives. That summer we talked about boys and smoked illicit cigarettes in Randy Kidd's basement and held leg-shaving parties in her bedroom behind a safely locked door. Randy was the ringleader. She was the one who suggested we pierce our ears.

"My parents would die," I said. "They told me I'm not allowed to pierce my ears until I'm seventeen." 66

"Your hair's so long, they won't even notice," Randy said. "My sister will do it for us. She pierces all her friends' ears at college." 67

In the end, only one girl pulled out. The rest of us sat in a row with the obligatory ice cubes held to our ears, waiting for the painful stab of the sterilized needle. 68

Randy was right. At first my parents didn't notice. Even when my ears became infected, I didn't tell them. All alone in my room, I went through the painful procedure of twisting the gold studs and swabbing the recent wounds with alcohol. Then on the night of the club dance, when I had changed my clothes three times and played with my hair in front of the mirror for hours, I came across the small plastic box with dividers in my top bureau drawer. My father had given it to me so that I could keep my flies in separate compartments, untangled from one another. I poked my finger in and slid one of the golden darters up along its plastic wall. When I held it up, the mylar thread sparkled in the light like a jewel. I took out the other darter, hammered down the barbs of the two hooks, and slipped them into the raw holes in my earlobes. 69

Someone's mother drove us all to the dance, and Randy and I pushed through the side door into the ladies' room. I put my hair up in a ponytail so the feathered flies could twist and dangle above my shoulders. I liked the way they made me look—free and different and dangerous, even. And they made Randy notice. 70

"I've never seen earrings like that," Randy said. "Where did you get them?" 71

"I made them with my father. They're flies. You know, for fishing." 72

"They're great. Can you make me some?" 73

I hesitated. "I have some others at home I can give you," 74
I said at last. "They're in a box in my bureau."

"Can you give them to me tomorrow?" she asked. 75

"Sure," I said with a smile. Randy had never noticed any- 76
thing I'd worn before. I went out to the dance floor, swinging my ponytail in time to the music.

My mother noticed the earrings as soon as I got home. 77

"What has gotten into you, Emily? You know you were 78
forbidden to pierce your ears until you were in college. This
is appalling."

I didn't answer. My father was sitting in his chair behind 79
the fly-tying table. His back was better by that time, but he
still spent most of his waking hours in that chair. It was as if
he didn't like to be too far away from his flies, as if something
might blow away if he weren't keeping watch.

I saw him look up when my mother started in with me. 80
His hands drifted ever so slowly down to the surface of the
table as I came across the room toward him. I leaned over so
that he could see my earrings better in the light.

"Everybody loved them, Father. Randy says she wants a 81
pair, too. I'm going to give her the muddler minnows."

"I can't believe you did this, Emily," my mother said in a 82
loud, nervous voice. "It makes you look so cheap."

"They don't make me look cheap, do they, Father?" I 83
swung my head so he could see how they bounced, and my
hip accidentally brushed the table. A bit of rabbit fur floated
up from its pile and hung in the air for a moment before it
settled down on top of the foxy quills.

"For God's sake, Gerald, speak to her," my mother said 84
from her corner.

He stared at me for a long moment as if he didn't know 85
who I was anymore, as if I were a trusted associate who had
committed some treacherous and unspeakable act. "That
is not the purpose for which the flies were intended," he
said.

"Oh, I know that," I said quickly. "But they look good 86
this way, don't they?"

He stood up and considered me in silence for a long time   87
across the top of the table lamp.

"No, they don't," he finally said. "They're hanging upside   88
down."

Then he turned off the light and I couldn't see his face   89
anymore.

COMMENT ON "THE GOLDEN DARTERS"

"The Golden Darters" questions the purpose of learning a
particular process. Emily's father decides to tie fishing flies
to help him recuperate from back surgery. Although he is
clumsy at first, he masters the tools, the procedure, and the
artistry of tying. He has a goal in mind—to "attach [the flies]
to a tippet, wade into a stream, and lure a rainbow trout out
of his quiet pool." Emily's father decides to teach her what
he has learned, even though his presence makes her nervous
and her mistakes complicate the work process. Emily eventually escapes his obsession and joins her girlfriends to learn
other procedures—smoking, leg shaving, ear piercing. The
last procedure enables Emily to experiment—to wear two
yellow darters as earrings to the club dance. Although she
dazzles her friends, she disappoints her father, who sees her
experiment as a betrayal.

CHAPTER 3

COMPARISON AND CONTRAST

Technically speaking, when you **compare** two or more things, you're looking for similarities; when you **contrast** them, you're looking for differences. In practice, of course, the operations are opposite sides of the same coin, and one implies the other. When you look for what's similar, you will also notice what is different. You can compare things at all levels, from the trivial (plaid shoelaces and plain ones) to the really serious (the differences between a career in medicine and one in advertising). Often when you compare things at a serious level, you do so to make a choice. That's why it's helpful to know how to organize your thinking so that you can analyze similarities and differences in a systematic, useful way that brings out significant differences. It's particularly helpful to have such a system when you are going to write a comparison-and-contrast essay.

PURPOSE

You can take two approaches to writing comparison-and-contrast essays; each has a different purpose. You can make a *strict* comparison, exploring the relationship between things in the same class, or you can do a *fanciful* comparison, looking at the relationship among things from different classes.

When you write a *strict* comparison, you compare only things that are truly alike—actors with actors, musicians with musicians, but *not* actors with musicians. You're trying to find similar information about both your subjects. For instance, what are the characteristics of actors, whether they are movie or stage actors? How are jazz musicians and classical musicians alike, even if their music is quite different? In a strict comparison, you probably also want to show how two things in the same class are different in important ways. Often when you focus your comparison on differences, you do so in order to make a judgment and, finally, a choice. That's one of the main reasons people make comparisons, whether they're shopping or writing.

When you write a *fanciful* comparison, you try to set up an imaginative, illuminating comparison between two things that don't seem at all alike, and you do it for a definite reason: to help explain and clarify a complex idea. For instance, the human heart is often compared to a pump—a fanciful and useful comparison that enables one to envision the heart at work. You can use similar fanciful comparisons to help your readers see new dimensions to events. For instance, you can compare the astronauts landing on the moon to Columbus discovering the New World, or you can compare the increased drug use among young people to an epidemic spreading through part of our culture.

You may find it difficult to construct an entire essay around a fanciful comparison—such attempts tax the most creative energy and can quickly break down. Probably you can use this method of comparison most effectively as a device for enlivening your writing and highlighting dramatic similarities. When you're drawing fanciful comparisons, you're not very likely to be comparing to make judgments or recommend choices.

Instead, your purpose in writing a fanciful comparison is to catch your readers' attention and show new connections between unlike things.

AUDIENCE

As you plan a comparison-and-contrast essay, think ahead about what your readers already know and what they're going to expect. First, ask yourself what they know about the items or ideas you're going to compare. Do they know a good deal about both—for instance, two popular television programs? Do they know very little about either item—for instance, Buddhism and Shintoism? Or do they know quite a bit about one but little about the other—for instance, football and rugby?

If you're confident that your readers know a lot about both items (the television programs), you can spend a little time pointing out similarities and concentrate on your reasons for making the comparison. When readers know little about either (Eastern religions), you'll have to define each, using concepts they are familiar with, before you can point out important contrasts. If readers know only one item in a pair (football and rugby), then use the known to explain the unknown. Emphasize what is familiar to them about football, and explain how rugby is like it but also how it is different.

As you think about what your readers need, remember that they want your essay to be fairly balanced, not 90 percent about Buddhism and 10 percent about Shintoism, or two paragraphs about football and nine or ten about rugby. When your focus seems so unevenly divided, you appear to be using one element in the comparison only as a springboard to talk about the other. Such an imbalance can disappoint your readers, who expect to learn about both.

STRATEGIES

You can use two basic strategies for organizing a comparison-and-contrast essay. The first is the *divided,* or *subject-by-subject,* pattern. The second is the *alternating,* or *point-by-point,* pattern.

When you use the *divided* pattern, you present all your information on one topic before you bring in information on the other topic. Mark Twain uses this method in "Two Views of the River." First he gives an apprentice's poetic view, emphasizing the beauty of the river; then he gives the pilot's practical view, emphasizing the technical problems the river poses.

When you use the *alternating* pattern, you work your way through the comparison point by point, giving information first on one aspect of the topic, then on the other. If Twain had used an alternating pattern, he would have given the apprentice's poetic view of a particular feature of the river, then the pilot's pragmatic view of that same feature. He would have followed that pattern throughout, commenting on each feature—the wind, the surface of the river, the sunset, the color of the water—by alternating between the apprentice's and the pilot's points of view.

Although both methods are useful, you'll find that each has benefits and drawbacks. The divided pattern lets you present each part of your essay as a satisfying whole. It works especially well in short essays, such as Twain's, where you're presenting only two facets of a topic and your reader can easily keep track of the points you want to make. Its drawback is that sometimes you slip into writing what seems like two separate essays. When you're writing a long comparison essay about a complex topic, you may have trouble organizing your material clearly enough to keep your readers on track.

The alternating pattern works well when you want to show the two subjects you're comparing side by side, emphasizing the points you're comparing. You'll find it particularly good for longer essays, such as David Sedaris's "Remembering My Childhood," when you show many complex points of comparison and need to help your readers see how those points match up. The drawback of the alternating pattern is that you may reduce your analysis to an exercise. If you use it for making only a few points of comparison in a short essay on a simple topic, your essay sounds choppy and disconnected, like a simple list.

Often you can make the best of both worlds by *combining strategies*. For example, you can start out using a divided pattern to give an overall, unified view of the topics you're going to compare. Then you can shift to an alternating pattern to show how many points of comparison you've found between your subjects. Bruce Catton uses a version of this strategy in "Grant and Lee: A Study in Contrasts" when he presents biographical sketches of Lee and then Grant before he combines his analysis of both men.

When you want to write a good comparison-and-contrast analysis, keep three guidelines in mind: (1) *balance parts*, (2) *include reminders*, and (3) *supply reasons*. Look, for example, at how Sarah Vowell balances the American and Canadian approaches to frontier law. Catton uses a similar strategy when he contrasts the lives of Robert E. Lee and Ulysses S. Grant. And Brian Doyle uses his concluding paragraphs to provide the reasons he had for making his initial comparison between the hummingbird and the blue whale.

COMPARISON AND CONTRAST

Points to Remember

1. Decide whether you want the pattern of your comparison to focus on complete units (*divided*) or specific features (*alternating*).
2. Consider the possibility of combining the two patterns.
3. Determine which subject should be placed in the first position and why.
4. Arrange the points of your comparison in a logical, balanced, and dramatic sequence.
5. Make sure you introduce and clarify the reasons for making your comparison.

Donna Barstow

In this cartoon, Donna Barstow uses the image of a duel to compare exercise and diet. The men are moving in opposite directions, but the eventual shootout will not be pretty. One of the men will probably survive the duel, but since we don't know which one, one could argue that neither diet nor exercise will solve the problem. However, notice that the exercise man is a bit taller than the diet man. Also, notice that one man is right-handed and the other left-handed. Write an essay explaining why exercising or dieting is the best way to lose weight. Or write an essay analyzing the difference between left-handed and right-handed people.

MARK TWAIN

Mark Twain (the pen name of Samuel Clemens, 1835–1910) was born in Florida, Missouri, and grew up in the river town of Hannibal, Missouri, where he watched the comings and goings of the steamboats he would eventually pilot. Twain spent his young adult life working as a printer, a pilot on the Mississippi, and a frontier journalist. After the Civil War, he began a career as a humorist and storyteller, writing such classics as *The Adventures of Tom Sawyer* (1876), *Life on the Mississippi* (1883), *The Adventures of Huckleberry Finn* (1884), and *A Connecticut Yankee in King Arthur's Court* (1889). His place in American writing was best characterized by editor William Dean Howells, who called Twain the "Lincoln of our literature." In "Two Views of the River," taken from *Life on the Mississippi,* Twain compares the way he saw the river as an innocent apprentice to the way he saw it as an experienced pilot.

Two Views of the River[1]

NOW WHEN I had mastered the language of this water, and had come to know every trifling feature that bordered the great river as familiarly as I knew the letters of the alphabet, I had made a valuable acquisition. But I had lost something, too. I had lost something which could never be restored to me while I lived. All the grace, the beauty, the poetry, had gone out of the majestic river! I still keep in mind a certain wonderful sunset which I witnessed when steamboating was new to me. A broad expanse of the river was

[1] Mark Twain, "Two Views of the River" by Mark Twain.

turned to blood; in the middle distance the red hue bright-
ened into gold, through which a solitary log came floating
black and conspicuous; in one place a long, slanting mark
lay sparkling upon the water; in another the surface was broken by boiling, tumbling rings that were as many-tinted as
an opal; where the ruddy flush was faintest, was a smooth
spot that was covered with graceful circles and radiating lines,
ever so delicately traced; the shore on our left was densely
wooded, and the somber shadow that fell from this forest
was broken in one place by a long, ruffled trail that shone like
silver; and high above the forest wall a clean-stemmed dead
tree waved a single leafy bough that glowed like a flame in the
unobstructed splendor that was flowing from the sun. There
were graceful curves, reflected images, woody heights, soft
distances; and over the whole scene, far and near, the dissolving lights drifted steadily, enriching it every passing moment
with new marvels of coloring.

*When I mastered the language of this
water, . . . I had made a valuable
acquisition. But I had lost something too.*

I stood like one bewitched. I drank it in, in a speechless   2
rapture. The world was new to me, and I had never seen anything like this at home. But as I have said, a day came when I
began to cease from noting the glories and the charms which
the moon and the sun and the twilight wrought upon the
river's face; another day came when I ceased altogether to
note them. Then, if that sunset scene had been repeated,
I should have looked upon it without rapture, and should
have commented upon it, inwardly, after this fashion: "This
sun means that we are going to have wind tomorrow; that
floating log means that the river is rising, small thanks to it;
that slanting mark on the water refers to a bluff reef which

is going to kill somebody's steamboat one of these nights, if it keeps on stretching out like that; those tumbling 'boils' show a dissolving bar and a changing channel there; the lines and circles in the slick water over yonder are a warning that that troublesome place is shoaling up dangerously; that silver streak in the shadow of the forest is the 'break' from a new snag, and he has located himself in the very best place he could have found to fish for steamboats; that tall dead tree, with a single living branch, is not going to last long, and then how is a body ever going to get through this blind place at night without the friendly old landmark?"

No, the romance and beauty were all gone from the river. 3 All the value any feature of it had for me now was the amount of usefulness it could furnish toward compassing the safe piloting of a steamboat. Since those days, I have pitied doctors from my heart. What does the lovely flush in a beauty's cheek mean to a doctor but a "break" that ripples above some deadly disease? Are not all her visible charms sown thick with what are to him the signs and symbols of hidden decay? Does he ever see her beauty at all, or doesn't he simply view her professionally, and comment upon her unwholesome condition all to himself? And doesn't he sometimes wonder whether he has gained most or lost most by learning his trade?

For Study and Discussion

QUESTIONS ABOUT PURPOSE

1. What does Twain think he has gained and lost by learning the river?
2. What does Twain accomplish by *dividing* the two views of the river rather than *alternating* them beneath several headings?

QUESTIONS ABOUT AUDIENCE

1. Which attitude—poetic or pragmatic—does Twain anticipate his readers have toward the river? Explain your answer.
2. How does he expect his readers to answer the questions he raises in paragraph 3?

QUESTIONS ABOUT STRATEGIES

1. What sequence does Twain use to arrange the points of his comparison?
2. Where does Twain use transitional phrases and sentences to match up the parts of his comparison?

For Writing and Research

1. *Analyze* the strategies Twain uses to compose and contrast his two views of the river.
2. *Practice* by describing your reactions to a special place in your childhood and then comparing the way you respond to it now.
3. *Argue* that learning too much about the technical details of a process—such as painting or singing—destroys one's ability to appreciate its beauty.
4. *Synthesize* your knowledge of Twain's life and writing. Then use this evidence to argue that creative achievement depends on the willingness to take risks.

BRIAN DOYLE

Brian Doyle was born in 1956 in New York City and educated at Notre Dame University. An award-winning essayist and the editor of *Portland,* a magazine noted for publishing the work of fine writers, Doyle has published his own work in the *Atlantic Monthly, Orion, Harper's,* and the *Best American Essay Anthologies.* His collections of creative nonfiction include *Saints Passionate and Peculiar* (2002) and *Mink River* (2010). His first collection of poems, *Epiphanies and Elegies: Very Short Stories,* was published in 2007. In "Joyas Voladoras," reprinted from *The American Scholar,* Doyle compares the pencil-eraser-size heart of a hummingbird with the "house of a heart" in a blue whale.

Joyas Voladoras[2]

Consider the hummingbird for a long moment. A hummingbird's heart beats ten times a second. A hummingbird's heart is the size of a pencil eraser. A hummingbird's heart is a lot of the hummingbird. *Joyas voladoras,* flying jewels, the first white explorers in the Americas called them, and the white men had never seen such creatures, for hummingbirds came into the world only in the Americas, nowhere else in the universe, more than three hundred species of them whirring and zooming and nectaring in hummer time zones nine times removed from ours, their hearts hammering faster than we could clearly hear if we pressed our elephantine ears to their infinitesimal chests.

---

[2] Brian Doyle, "Joyas Valadoras" first appeared in *The American Scholar,* included in *Best American Essays 2005,* p. 28. Reprinted by permission of the author.

Each one visits a thousand flowers a day. They can dive at   2
sixty miles an hour. They can fly backward. They can fly more
than five hundred miles without pausing to rest. But when
they rest they come close to death: on frigid nights, or when
they are starving, they retreat into torpor, their metabolic rate
slowing to a fifteenth of their normal sleep rate, their hearts
sludging nearly to a halt, barely beating, and if they are not
soon warmed, if they do not soon find that which is sweet,
their hearts grow cold, and they cease to be. Consider for a
moment those hummingbirds who did not open their eyes
again today, this very day, in the Americas: bearded helmet-
crests and booted racket-tails, violet-tailed sylphs and violet-
capped woodnymphs, crimson topazes and purple-crowned
fairies, red-tailed comets and amethyst woodstars, rainbow-
bearded thornbills and glittering-bellied emeralds, velvet-
purple coronets and golden-bellied star-frontlets, fiery-tailed
awlbills and Andean hillstars, spatuletails and pufflegs, each
the most amazing thing you have never seen, each thunderous wild heart the size of an infant's fingernail, each mad
heart silent, a brilliant music stilled.

Hummingbirds, like all flying birds but more so, have   3
incredible enormous immense ferocious metabolisms. To
drive those metabolisms they have racecar hearts that eat
oxygen at an eye-popping rate. Their hearts are built of thinner, leaner fibers than ours. Their arteries are stiffer and more
taut. They have more mitochondria in their heart muscles—
anything to gulp more oxygen. Their hearts are stripped to
the skin for the war against gravity and inertia, the mad search
for food, the insane idea of flight. The price of their ambition is a life closer to death; they suffer more heart attacks
and aneurysms and ruptures than any other living creature.
It's expensive to fly. You burn out. You fry the machine. You
melt the engine. Every creature on earth has approximately
two billion heartbeats to spend in a lifetime. You can spend
them slowly, like a tortoise, and live to be two hundred years
old, or you can spend them fast, like a hummingbird, and live
to be two years old.

The biggest heart in the world is inside the blue whale.   4
It weighs more than seven tons. It's as big as a room. It is
a room, with four chambers. A child could walk around in
it, head high, bending only to step through the valves. The
valves are as big as the swinging doors in a saloon. This house
of a heart drives a creature a hundred feet long. When this
creature is born it is twenty feet long and weighs four tons.
It is waaaaay bigger than your car. It drinks a hundred gal-
lons of milk from its mama every day and gains two hundred pounds a day, and when it is seven or eight years old
it endures an unimaginable puberty and then it essentially
disappears from human ken, for next to nothing is known of
the mating habits, travel patterns, diet, social life, language,
social structure, diseases, spirituality, wars, stories, despairs,
and arts of the blue whale. There are perhaps ten thousand
blue whales in the world, living in every ocean on earth, and
of the largest mammal who ever lived we know nearly nothing. But we know this: the animals with the largest hearts
in the world generally travel in pairs, and their penetrating
moaning cries, their piercing yearning tongue, can be heard
underwater for miles and miles.

*Every creature on earth has approximately
two billion heartbeats to spend in a lifetime.*

Mammals and birds have hearts with four chambers. Rep-   5
tiles and turtles have hearts with three chambers. Fish have
hearts with two chambers. Insects and mollusks have hearts
with one chamber. Worms have hearts with one chamber,
although they may have as many as eleven single-chambered
hearts. Unicellular bacteria have no hearts at all; but even
they have fluid eternally in motion, washing from one side of
the cell to the other, swirling and whirling. No living being is
without interior liquid motion. We all churn inside.

So much held in a heart in a lifetime. So much held in 6
a heart in a day, an hour, a moment. We are utterly open
with no one, in the end—not mother and father, not wife or
husband, not lover, not child, not friend. We open windows
to each but we live alone in the house of the heart. Perhaps
we must. Perhaps we could not bear to be so naked, for fear
of a constantly harrowed heart. When young we think there
will come one person who will savor and sustain us always;
when we are older we know this is the dream of a child, that
all hearts finally are bruised and scarred, scored and torn,
repaired by time and will, patched by force of character, yet
fragile and rickety forevermore, no matter how ferocious the
defense and how many bricks you bring to the wall. You can
brick up your heart as stout and tight and hard and cold and
impregnable as you possibly can and down it comes in an
instant, felled by a woman's second glance, a child's apple
breath, the shatter of glass in the road, the words "I have
something to tell you," a cat with a broken spine dragging
itself into the forest to die, the brush of your mother's papery
ancient hand in the thicket of your hair, the memory of your
father's voice early in the morning echoing from the kitchen
where he is making pancakes for his children.

For Study and Discussion

QUESTIONS ABOUT PURPOSE

1. Why does Doyle use other comparisons to compare the hearts of
   a hummingbird and the blue whale?
2. How does his comparison enable him to establish a link to the
   sentence "Every creature on earth has approximately two billion
   heartbeats to spend in a lifetime"?

QUESTIONS ABOUT AUDIENCE

1. What assumptions does Doyle make about his readers' knowledge of the hummingbird and the blue whale?
2. How does he use the following sentence to establish a connection with his readers: "We all churn inside"?

1. Why does Doyle describe the hummingbird first in the divided pattern in his essay?
2. How does he use the concluding paragraph of his essay to expand the meaning of the initial comparison in his essay?

For Writing and Research

1. *Analyze* the points of comparison that Doyle creates between the hummingbird and the blue whale.
2. *Practice* by describing an incident that bruised your heart.
3. *Argue* that you can/cannot establish emotional defenses to protect your heart.
4. *Synthesize:* Research the recent medical innovations that have sustained the health of the human heart. Then use this information to argue that such innovations perpetuate our illusions of longevity.

Sarah Vowell was born in 1969, raised in rural Oklahoma, and educated at Montana State University and the School of the Art Institute in Chicago. She started contributing her witty essays to the radio program *This American Life* (Public Radio International) and the Internet magazine *Salon.com*. Her experience with radio is documented in *Radio On: A Listener's Diary* (1997). Her other essays are collected in *Take the Cannoli: Stories from the New World* (2000), *The Partly Cloudy Patriot* (2002), *Assassination Vacation* (2005), *The Wordy Shipmates* (2008), and *Unfamiliar Fishes* (2011). In "Cowboys v. Mounties," reprinted from *The Partly Cloudy Patriot,* Vowell compares the American and Canadian frontier experience.

Cowboys v. Mounties[3]

CANADA HAUNTS ME. The United States' neighbor to the   1
north first caught my fancy a few years back when I started listening to the CBC. I came for the long-form radio documentaries; I stayed for the dispatches from the Maritimes and Guelph. On the CBC, all these nice people, seemingly normal but for the hockey obsession, had a likable knack for loving their country in public without resorting to swagger or hate.

A person keen on all things French is called a Francophile.   2
One who has a thing for England is called an Anglophile. An admirer of Germany in the 1930s and '40s is called Pat

---

Buchanan. But no word has been coined to describe Americans obsessed with Canada, not that dictionary publishers have been swamped with requests. The comedian Jon Stewart used to do a bit in which a Canadian woman asked him to come clean with what Americans *really* think of Canada. "We don't," he said.

Keeping track of Canadians is like watching a horror 3
movie. It's *Invasion of the Body Snatchers* in slow-mo. They look like us, but there's something slightly, eerily off. Why is that? The question has nagged me for years. Asking why they are the way they are begs the follow-up query about how we ended up this way too.

There's a sad sack quality to the Canadian chronology 4
I find entirely endearing. I once asked the CBC radio host Ian Brown how on earth one could teach Canadian schoolchildren their history in a way that could be remotely inspiring, and he answered, "It isn't inspiring."

---

*Everyone knows what the individualistic
American cowboy fetish gets us: shot.*

Achieving its independence from Britain gradually and 5
cordially, through polite meetings taking place in nice rooms, Canada took a path to sovereignty that is one of the most hilariously boring stories in the world. One Canadian history textbook I have describes it thus, "British North Americans moved through the 1850s and early sixties towards a modestly spectacular resolution of their various ambitions and problems." Modestly spectacular. Isn't that adorable?

One day, while nonchalantly perusing the annals of Canadian 6
history, I came across mention of the founding of the Mounties. The Royal Canadian Mounted Police, called the North-West Mounted Police at its inception, was created, I read, to establish law and order on the Canadian frontier in anticipation of settlement and the Canadian Pacific Railroad. In 1873, Canada's first prime minister, John Macdonald, saw what was happening in

the American Wild West and organized a police force to make sure Canada steered clear of America's bloodbath.

That's it. Or, as they might say in Quebec, voilà! That 7 explains how the Canadians are different from Americans. No cowboys for Canada. Canada got Mounties instead—Dudley Do-Right, not John Wayne. It's a mind-set of "Here I come to save the day" versus "Yippee-ki-yay, motherfucker." Or maybe it's chicken and egg: The very idea that the Canadian head of state would come to the conclusion that establishing law and order *before* large numbers of people migrated west, to have rules and procedures and authorities waiting for them, is anathema to the American way.

Not only did the Mounties aim to avoid the problems 8 we had faced on our western frontier, especially the violent, costly Indian wars, they had to clean up after our spillover mess. In a nineteenth-century version of that drug-war movie *Traffic,* evil American whiskey traders were gouging and poisoning Canadian Indian populations. Based in Fort Benton, Montana, they sneaked across the border to peddle their rotgut liquor, establishing illegal trading posts, including the infamous Fort Whoop-up, in what is now Alberta. You can't throw a dart at a map of the American West without hitting some mass grave or battleground—Sand Creek, Little Bighorn, Wounded Knee—but it's fitting that the most famous such Canadian travesty, the Cypress Hills Massacre, happened because American whiskey and fur traders were exacting revenge on a few Indians believed to have stolen their horses. The Americans slaughtered between one and two hundred Assiniboine men, women, and children. Never mind that the horse thieves had been Cree. That was 1873. The Mounties were under formation, but they hadn't yet marched west.

The most remarkable thing about the Mounties was their 9 mandate: one law. One law for everyone, Indian or white. The United States makes a big to-do about all men being created equal, but we're still working out the kinks of turning that idea into actual policy. Reporting to the force's commissioner in 1877, one Mountie wrote of Americans in his jurisdiction, "These men always look upon the Indians as their natural enemies, and it is their rule to shoot at them if they approach after being warned off. I was actually asked the other day by an American who has settled here, if we had the same law here as on the other side, and if he was justified in shooting any Indian who approached his camp after being warned not to in advance."

Word of the Canadians' fairness got around. Some north- 10
western tribes referred to the border between the United States and Canada as the "medicine line." Robert Higheagle, a Lakota Sioux from Sitting Bull's band, recalled, "They told us this line was considered holy. They called that a holy trail. They believe things are different when you cross from one side to another. You are altogether different. On one side you are perfectly free to do as you please. On the other you are in danger."

To Canada's dismay, the northern side of the medicine 11
line became an attractive destination for American Indians, including the most famous, most difficult one of all, Sitting Bull. On the run after Little Bighorn, Sitting Bull and entourage settled near Canada's Fort Walsh, under the command of Major James Walsh. Walsh and, as he called him, Bull became such great friends that the Canadian government had Walsh transferred to another post to separate him from Sitting Bull. Sitting Bull was an American problem and the Canadian government wanted to boot him south. Walsh even defied orders and went to Chicago to lobby on Sitting Bull's behalf, but to no avail, ensuring that Sitting Bull would die south of the medicine line.

All the Sitting Bull complications make Walsh my favorite 12
Mountie. But he's a very American choice—he bucked the system, he played favorites for a friend, he defied policy, he stuck out. (Apparently, even having a favorite Mountie is an American trait. When I asked the twentieth commissioner of Mounties, Giuliano "Zach" Zaccardelli, who was his favorite RCMP commissioner in history, he answered Canadianly, "Every one of them has contributed tremendously to the legacy of the RCMP, and I hope that during my tenure I will be

able to add some value to the legacy that those nineteen who came before me left for this organization.") When Walsh heard that Sitting Bull had been fatally shot in Minnesota, he wrote, "Bull's ambition is I am afraid too great to let him settle down and be content with an uninteresting life." This strikes me as almost treasonously individualistic, with American shades of "pursuit of happiness" and "liberty or death."

Everyone knows what the individualistic American cow-   13
boy fetish gets us: shot. It all comes down to guns. The population of the United States is ten times that of Canada, but we have about thirty times more firearms. Two-thirds of our homicides are committed with firearms, compared with one-third of theirs. (Which begs the question, just what are Canadian killers using, hair dryers tossed into bathtubs?)

The famous (well, in Canada) historian Pierre Berton, in   14
his surprisingly out-of-print book *Why We Act Like Canadians*, informs an American friend that it has to do with weather. Having been to Edmonton in January, I cede his point. He wrote,

> *Hot weather and passion, gunfights and race riots go together. Your mythic encounters seem to have taken place at high noon, the sun beating down on a dusty Arizona street. I find it difficult to contemplate a similar gunfight in Moose Jaw, in the winter, the bitter rivals struggling vainly to shed two pairs of mitts and reach under several layers of parka for weapons so cold that the slightest touch of flesh on steel would take the skin off their thumbs.*

Most of the time, I feel Canadian. I live a quiet life. I own   15
no firearms (though, as a gunsmith's daughter, I stand to inherit a freaking arsenal). I revere the Bill of Rights, but at the same time I believe that anyone who's using three or more of them at a time is hogging them too much. I'm a newspaper-reading, French-speaking, radio-documentary-loving square. A lot of my favorite comedians, such as Martin Short, Eugene Levy, the Kids in the Hall, are Canadian. I like that self-

deprecating Charlie Brown sense of humor. As Canadian-born *Saturday Night Live* producer Lorne Michaels once put it in a panel discussion devoted to the question of why Canadians are so funny at the Ninety-second Street Y, a Canadian would never have made a film called *It's a Wonderful Life* because "that would be bragging." The Canadian version, he said, would have been titled "It's an All Right Life."

So I mostly walk the Canadian walk, but the thing about a lot of Canadian talk is that it sounds bad. When I went to Ottawa, the "Washington of the North," to see the RCMP's Musical Ride, which is sort of like synchronized swimming on horseback, I was telling a constable in the Mounties about a new U.S. Army recruiting ad. The slogan was "an army of one." It aimed to reassure American kids that they wouldn't be nameless, faceless nobodies, that they could join the army and still do their own thing. 16

The Mountie was horrified. He said, "I think we have to try and work as a team and work together. If you start to be an individualist, then everybody's going their own way. One person might be doing something and the other person might be doing something else and everybody wants to put their word in and thinks, I'm better than him or My idea's better than his. You need conformity. You need everybody to stick together and work as a team." 17

It hurt my ears when he said "you need conformity." I know he's probably right, and what organization more than a military one requires lockstep uniformity so that fewer people get killed? But still. No true American would ever talk up the virtue of conformity. Intellectually, I roll my eyes at the cowboy outlaw ethic, but in my heart I know I buy into it a little, that it's a deep part of my identity. Once, when I was living in Holland, I went to the movies, and when a Marlboro Man ad came on the screen, I started bawling with homesickness. I may be the only person who cried all the way through *Don't Tell Mom the Babysitter's Dead*. 18

The Mounties on the Musical Ride dress in the old-fashioned red serge suits and Stetson hats, like Dudley Do-Right. Seeing them on their black horses, riding in time to 19

music, was entirely lovable, yet lacking any sort of, for lack
of a better word, edge. I tried to ask some of them about it.

I say, "In the States, the Mountie is a squeaky-clean icon.   20
Does that ever bother you that the Mountie is not 'cool'?"

He stares back blankly. I ask him, "You know what I   21
mean?"

"No, I don't."   22

"There's no dark side," I tell him. "The Mounties have no   23
dark side."

He laughs. "That might be one of the things that upset   24
the Americans, because we're just that much better." Then
he feels so bad about this little put-down that he repents,
backtracking about how "there's good and bad in everybody," that Americans and Canadians "just have different
views," and that "Canadians are no better than anyone else."

Another constable, overhearing, says, "Our country is far   25
younger than the United States, but at the same time, the
United States is a young country when you compare it to the
countries of Europe."

"Yeah," I answer, "but you're a very well-behaved young   26
country."

"Well"—he smiles—"that's just the way my mum raised   27
me."

For Study and Discussion

QUESTIONS ABOUT PURPOSE

1. In what ways does Vowell's characterization of Canadian history
   help her reinterpret American history?
2. How does Vowell reverse her friend's assertion that Canadian
   history "isn't inspiring"?

QUESTIONS ABOUT AUDIENCE

1. How does Vowell anticipate her readers' reactions when she
   quotes an American as saying he doesn't think about Canada?

2. What does Vowell mean when she says she feels Canadian? Is she trying to connect with Canadian readers or help her American readers understand the appeal of Canadian values?

QUESTIONS ABOUT STRATEGIES

1. How does Vowell use the "medicine line" to distinguish between American and Canadian culture?
2. How does Pierre Berton use weather to explain the difference between Americans and Canadians?

For Writing and Research

1. *Analyze* how Vowell illustrates the difference between being "cool" and being "well-behaved."
2. *Practice* by comparing movies that have shaped your perception of "cowboys" and "Mounties."
3. *Argue* by defending the cultural values embedded in the U.S. recruiting ad.
4. *Synthesize:* Research the participation of Canada's army in the wars in Iraq and Afghanistan. Then use this information to demonstrate that Canadian and American values are not that different.

David Sedaris was born in New York State; raised
in Raleigh, North Carolina; and educated at Kent
State University and the School of the Art Institute
of Chicago. He has presented his humorous autobiographical essays on National Public Radio on
This American Life. His essay collections include
Barrel Fever (1994), *Naked* (1997), *Dress Your
Family in Corduroy and Denim* (2004), and *Squirrel Seeks Chipmunk: A Modest Bestiary* (2010). In
2001, he won the Thurber Prize for American
Humor and was named "Humorist of the Year"
by *Time* magazine. In "Remembering My Childhood on the Continent of Africa," reprinted from
Me Talk Pretty One Day (2000), Sedaris compares
his unremarkable childhood with the exotic childhood of his partner, Hugh Hamrick.

Remembering My Childhood
on the Continent of Africa [4]

WHEN HUGH WAS IN THE FIFTH GRADE, his class took a   1
field trip to an Ethiopian slaughterhouse. He was living in Addis Ababa at the time, and the slaughterhouse was
chosen because, he says, "it was convenient."

This was a school system in which the matter of proximity   2
outweighed such petty concerns as what may or may not be
appropriate for a busload of eleven-year-olds. "What?" I asked.
"Were there no autopsies scheduled at the local morgue? Was
the federal prison just a bit too far out of the way?"

---

[4] David Sedaris, from *Me Talk Pretty One Day* by David Sedaris. Copyright ©
2000 by David Sedaris. By permission of Little, Brown and Company. All
rights reserved.

Hugh defends his former school, saying, "Well, isn't that the whole point of a field trip? To see something new?" 3

"Technically yes, but . . ." 4

"All right then," he says. "So we saw some new things." 5

One of his field trips was literally a trip to a field where the class watched a wrinkled man fill his mouth with rotten goat meat and feed it to a pack of waiting hyenas. On another occasion they were taken to examine the bloodied bedroom curtains hanging in the palace of the former dictator. There were tamer trips, to textile factories and sugar refineries, but my favorite is always the slaughterhouse. It wasn't a big company, just a small rural enterprise run by a couple of brothers operating out of a low-ceilinged concrete building. Following a brief lecture on the importance of proper sanitation, a small white piglet was herded into the room, its dainty hooves clicking against the concrete floor. The class gathered in a circle to get a better look at the animal, who seemed delighted with the attention he was getting. He turned from face to face and was looking up at Hugh when one of the brothers drew a pistol from his back pocket, held it against the animal's temple, and shot the piglet, execution-style. Blood spattered, frightened children wept, and the man with the gun offered the teacher and bus driver some meat from a freshly slaughtered goat. 6

When I'm told such stories, it's all I can do to hold back my feelings of jealousy. An Ethiopian slaughterhouse. Some people have all the luck. When I was in elementary school, the best we ever got was a trip to Old Salem or Colonial Williamsburg, one of those preserved brick villages where time supposedly stands still and someone earns his living as a town crier. There was always a blacksmith, a group of wandering patriots, and a collection of bonneted women hawking corn bread or gingersnaps made "the ol'-fashioned way." Every now and then you might come across a doer of bad deeds serving time in the stocks, but that was generally as exciting as it got. 7

Certain events are parallel, but compared with Hugh's, my childhood was unspeakably dull. When I was seven years 8 old, my family moved to North Carolina. When he was seven years old, Hugh's family moved to the Congo. We had a collie and a house cat. They had a monkey and two horses named Charlie Brown and Satan. I threw stones at stop signs. Hugh threw stones at crocodiles. The verbs are the same, but he definitely wins the prize when it comes to nouns and objects. An eventful day for my mother might have involved a trip to the dry cleaner or a conversation with the potato-chip deliveryman. Asked one ordinary Congo afternoon what she'd done with her day, Hugh's mother answered that she and a fellow member of the Ladies' Club had visited a leper colony on the outskirts of Kinshasa. No reason was given for the expedition, though chances are she was staking it out for a future field trip.

Certain events are parallel, but compared with Hugh's, my childhood was unspeakably dull.

Due to his upbringing, Hugh sits through inane movies never realizing that they're often based on inane television shows. There were no poker-faced sitcom martians in his part of Africa, no oil-rich hillbillies or aproned brides trying to wean themselves from the practice of witchcraft. From time to time a movie would arrive packed in a dented canister, the film scratched and faded from its slow trip around the world. The theater consisted of a few dozen folding chairs arranged before a bedsheet or the blank wall of a vacant hangar out near the airstrip. Occasionally a man would sell warm soft drinks out of a cardboard box, but that was it in terms of concessions.   9

When I was young, I went to the theater at the nearby shopping center and watched a movie about a talking Volkswagen. I believe the little car had a taste for mischief but I can't be certain, as both the movie and the afternoon proved unremarkable and have faded from my memory. Hugh saw   10 the same movie a few years after it was released. His family had left the Congo by this time and were living in Ethiopia. Like me, Hugh saw the movie by himself on a weekend afternoon. Unlike me, he left the theater two hours later, to find a dead man hanging from a telephone pole at the far end of the unpaved parking lot. None of the people who'd seen the movie seemed to care about the dead man. They stared at him for a moment or two and then headed home, saying they'd never seen anything as crazy as that talking Volkswagen. His father was late picking him up, so Hugh just stood there for an hour, watching the dead man dangle and turn in the breeze. The death was not reported in the newspaper, and when Hugh related the story to his friends, they said, "You saw the movie about the talking car?"

I could have done without the flies and the primitive the- 11 aters, but I wouldn't have minded growing up with a houseful of servants. In North Carolina it wasn't unusual to have a once-a-week maid, but Hugh's family had houseboys, a word that never fails to charge my imagination. They had cooks and drivers, and guards who occupied a gatehouse, armed with machetes. Seeing as I had regularly petitioned my parents for an electric fence, the business with the guards strikes me as the last word in quiet sophistication. Having protection suggests that you are important. Having that protection paid for by the government is even better, as it suggests your safety is of interest to someone other than yourself.

Hugh's father was a career officer with the U.S. State 12 Department, and every morning a black sedan carried him off to the embassy. I'm told it's not as glamorous as it sounds, but in terms of fun for the entire family, I'm fairly confident that it beats the sack race at the annual IBM picnic. By the age of three, Hugh was already carrying a diplomatic passport. The rules that applied to others did not apply to him. No tickets, no arrests, no luggage search: he was officially licensed to act like a brat. Being an American, it was expected of him, and who was he to deny the world an occasional tantrum?

They weren't rich, but what Hugh's family lacked finan- 13 cially they more than made up for with the sort of exoticism that works wonders at cocktail parties, leading always to the remark "That sounds fascinating." It's a compliment one rarely receives when describing an adolescence spent drinking Icees at the North Hills Mall. No fifteen-foot python ever wandered onto my school's basketball court. I begged, I prayed nightly, but it just never happened. Neither did I get to witness a military coup in which forces sympathetic to the colonel arrived late at night to assassinate my next-door neighbor. Hugh had been at the Addis Ababa teen club when the electricity was cut off and soldiers arrived to evacuate the building. He and his friends had to hide in the back of a jeep and cover themselves with blankets during the ride home. It's something that sticks in his mind for one reason or another.

Among my personal highlights is the memory of having   14
my picture taken with Uncle Paul, the legally blind host of a Raleigh children's television show. Among Hugh's is the memory of having his picture taken with Buzz Aldrin on the last leg of the astronaut's world tour. The man who had walked on the moon placed his hand on Hugh's shoulder and offered to sign his autograph book. The man who led Wake County schoolchildren in afternoon song turned at the sound of my voice and asked, "So what's your name, princess?"

When I was fourteen years old, I was sent to spend ten   15
days with my maternal grandmother in western New York State. She was a small and private woman named Billie, and though she never came right out and asked, I had the distinct impression she had no idea who I was. It was the way she looked at me, squinting through her glasses while chewing on her lower lip. That, coupled with the fact that she never once called me by name. "Oh," she'd say, "are you still here?" She was just beginning her long struggle with Alzheimer's disease, and each time I entered the room, I felt the need to reintroduce myself and set her at ease. "Hi, it's me. Sharon's boy, David. I was just in the kitchen admiring your collection of ceramic toads." Aside from a few trips to summer camp, this was the longest I'd

ever been away from home, and I like to think I was toughened by the experience.

About the same time I was frightening my grandmother,   16
Hugh and his family were packing their belongings for a
move to Somalia. There were no English-speaking schools
in Mogadishu, so, after a few months spent lying around
the family compound with his pet monkey, Hugh was sent
back to Ethiopia to live with a beer enthusiast his father had
met at a cocktail party. Mr. Hoyt installed security systems
in foreign embassies. He and his family gave Hugh a room.
They invited him to join them at the table, but that was
as far as they extended themselves. No one ever asked him
when his birthday was, so when the day came, he kept it to
himself. There was no telephone service between Ethiopia
and Somalia, and letters to his parents were sent to Washington and then forwarded on to Mogadishu, meaning that
his news was more than a month old by the time they got it.
I suppose it wasn't much different than living as a foreign-
exchange student. Young people do it all the time, but to
me it sounds awful. The Hoyts had two sons about Hugh's
age who were always saying things like "Hey that's our sofa
you're sitting on" and "Hands off that ornamental stein. It
doesn't belong to you."

He'd been living with these people for a year when he   17
overheard Mr. Hoyt tell a friend that he and his family would
soon be moving to Munich, Germany, the beer capital of the
world.

"And that worried me," Hugh said, "because it meant I'd   18
have to find some other place to live."

Where I come from, finding shelter is a problem the aver-   19
age teenager might confidently leave to his parents. It was
just something that came with having a mom and a dad.
Worried that he might be sent to live with his grandparents in
Kentucky, Hugh turned to the school's guidance counselor,
who knew of a family whose son had recently left for college.
And so he spent another year living with strangers and not
mentioning his birthday. While I wouldn't have wanted to
do it myself, I can't help but envy the sense of fortitude he

gained from the experience. After graduating from college, he moved to France knowing only the phrase "Do you speak French?"—a question guaranteed to get you nowhere unless you also speak the language.

While living in Africa, Hugh and his family took frequent   20 vacations, often in the company of their monkey. The Nairobi Hilton, some suite of high-ceilinged rooms in Cairo or Khartoum: these are the places his people recall when gathered at a common table. "Was that the summer we spent in Beirut or, no, I'm thinking of the time we sailed from Cyprus and took the *Orient Express* to Istanbul."

Theirs was the life I dreamt about during my vacations in   21 eastern North Carolina. Hugh's family was hobnobbing with chiefs and sultans while I ate hush puppies at the Sanitary Fish Market in Morehead City, a beach towel wrapped like a hijab around my head. Someone unknown to me was very likely standing in a muddy ditch and dreaming of an evening spent sitting in a clean family restaurant, drinking iced tea and working his way through an extra-large seaman's platter, but that did not concern me, as it meant I should have been happy with what I had. Rather than surrender to my bitterness, I have learned to take satisfaction in the life that Hugh has led. His stories have, over time, become my own. I say this with no trace of a kumbaya. There is no spiritual symbiosis; I'm just a petty thief who lifts his memories the same way I'll take a handful of change left on his dresser. When my own experiences fall short of the mark, I just go out and spend some of his. It is with pleasure that I sometimes recall the dead man's purpled face or the report of the handgun ringing in my ears as I studied the blood pooling beneath the dead white piglet. On the way back from the slaughterhouse, we stopped for Cokes in the village of Mojo, where the gas-station owner had arranged a few tables and chairs beneath a dying canopy of vines. It was late afternoon by the time we returned to school, where a second bus carried me to the foot of Coffeeboard Road. Once there, I walked through a grove of eucalyptus trees and alongside a bald pasture of starving cattle, past the guard napping in his gatehouse, and into the waiting arms of my monkey.

For Study and Discussion

QUESTIONS ABOUT PURPOSE

1. What is Sedaris's purpose in this essay: to demonstrate differences or to find similarities between his childhood and Hugh's?
2. What does he mean when he says, Hugh's "stories have, over time, become my own"?

QUESTIONS ABOUT AUDIENCE

1. How does Sedaris demonstrate to his readers that he has not surrendered to "bitterness"?
2. Whose experience—Hugh's or his own—does Sedaris usually present first? What expectations does this pattern—or its reversal—create for his readers?

QUESTIONS ABOUT STRATEGIES

1. What are the categories—field trips, movies, and so on—Sedaris uses to establish his points of comparison?
2. How does Sedaris compress the alternating pattern in paragraph 8?

For Writing and Research

1. *Analyze* what Sedaris means when he says, "The verbs are the same, but he definitely wins the prize when it comes to nouns and objects."
2. *Practice* by comparing your childhood memories with those of someone who was brought up in a different culture.
3. *Argue* that the "grass is always greener" by constructing how Hugh might argue that Sedaris had lived a more interesting childhood.
4. *Synthesize:* Read some of Sedaris's other essays that include references to his partner, Hugh Hamrick. Then use this information to explain the satisfaction and loose change Sedaris has learned to "take" from Hugh.

Bruce Catton (1899–1978) was born in Petosky, Michigan, and attended Oberlin College. After a career as a reporter for newspapers in Boston and Cleveland, he served as a director of information for various government agencies in Washington, D.C., before accepting the position of editor of *American Heritage* magazine. His fourth book, *A Stillness at Appomattox* (1953), earned him the Pulitzer Prize, the National Book Award, and the unofficial title of America's most popular historian of the Civil War. In addition to his many books on that subject—such as *Mr. Lincoln's Army* (1951), *The Coming Fury* (1961), and *Grant Takes Command* (1964)—Catton wrote a memorable account of his own boyhood in Michigan, *Waiting for the Morning Train: An American Boyhood* (1974). "Grant and Lee: A Study in Contrasts" first appeared in *The American Story* (1956), a collection of essays by eminent historians, and has been cited often as one of the classic examples of the comparison-and-contrast essay. In his analysis, Catton considers both the differences in background and similarities in character in these two great Civil War generals.

Grant and Lee: A Study in Contrasts[5]

WHEN ULYSSES S. GRANT and Robert E. Lee met in the parlor of a modest house at Appomattox Court House, Virginia, on April 9, 1865, to work out the terms for

[5]Bruce Catton—Catton, Bruce "Grant and Lee: A Study in Contrasts" Reprinted from *The American Story*, edited by Earl Schenk Miers. Copyright © 1956. Reprinted by permission of the United States Capitol Historical Society.

the surrender of Lee's Army of Northern Virginia, a great chapter in American life came to a close, and a great new chapter began.

These men were bringing the Civil War to its virtual finish. To be sure, other armies had yet to surrender, and for a few days the fugitive Confederate government would struggle desperately and vainly, trying to find some way to go on living now that its chief support was gone. But in effect it was all over when Grant and Lee signed the papers. And the little room where they wrote out the terms was the scene of one of the poignant, dramatic contrasts in American history. 2

They were two strong men, these oddly different generals, and they represented the strengths of two conflicting currents that, through them, had come into final collision. 3

Back of Robert E. Lee was the notion that the old aristocratic concept might somehow survive and be dominant in American life. 4

Lee was tidewater Virginia, and in his background were family, culture, and tradition . . . the age of chivalry transplanted to a New World which was making its own legends and its own myths. He embodied a way of life that had come down through the age of knighthood and the English country squire. America was a land that was beginning all over again, dedicated to nothing much more complicated than the rather hazy belief that all men had equal rights, and should have an equal chance in the world. In such a land Lee stood for the feeling that it was somehow of advantage to human society to have a pronounced inequality in the social structure. There should be a leisure class, backed by ownership of land; in turn, society itself should be keyed to the land as the chief source of wealth and influence. It would bring forth (according to this ideal) a class of men with a strong sense of obligation to the community; men who lived not to gain advantage for themselves, but to meet the solemn obligations which had been laid on them by the very fact that they were privileged. From them the country would get its leadership; to them it could look for the higher values—of thought, of conduct, of personal deportment—to give it strength and virtue. 5

Lee embodied the noblest elements of this aristocratic   6
ideal. Through him, the landed nobility justified itself. For
four years, the Southern states had fought a desperate war to
uphold the ideals for which Lee stood. In the end, it almost
seemed as if the Confederacy fought for Lee; as if he himself
was the Confederacy . . . the best thing that the way of life
for which the Confederacy stood could ever have to offer.
He had passed into legend before Appomattox. Thousands
of tired, underfed, poorly clothed Confederate soldiers, long
since past the simple enthusiasm of the early days of the
struggle, somehow considered Lee the symbol of everything
for which they had been willing to die. But they could not
quite put this feeling into words. If the Lost Cause, sanctified
by so much heroism and so many deaths, had a living justification, its justification was General Lee.

Grant, the son of a tanner on the Western frontier, was   7
everything Lee was not. He had come up the hard way, and
embodied nothing in particular except the eternal toughness
and sinewy fiber of the men who grew up beyond the mountains. He was one of a body of men who owed reverence and
obeisance to no one, who were self-reliant to a fault, who
cared hardly anything for the past but who had a sharp eye
for the future.

These frontier men were the precise opposites of the tide-   8
water aristocrats. Back of them, in the great surge that had
taken people over the Alleghenies and into the opening Western country, there was a deep, implicit dissatisfaction with a
past that had settled into grooves. They stood for democracy,
not from any reasoned conclusion about the proper ordering
of human society, but simply because they had grown up in
the middle of democracy and knew how it worked. Their society might have privileges, but they would be privileges each
man had won for himself. Forms and patterns meant nothing.
No man was born to anything, except perhaps to a chance to
show how far he could rise. Life was competition.

Yet along with this feeling had come a deep sense of   9
belonging to a national community. The Westerner who
developed a farm, opened a shop or set up in business as a

trader, could hope to prosper only as his own community prospered—and his community ran from the Atlantic to the Pacific and from Canada down to Mexico. If the land was settled, with towns and highways and accessible markets, he could better himself. He saw his fate in terms of the nation's own destiny. As its horizons expanded, so did his. He had, in other words, an acute dollars-and-cents stake in the continued growth and development of his country.

And that, perhaps, is where the contrast between Grant and Lee becomes most striking. The Virginia aristocrat, inevitably, saw himself in relation to his own region. He lived in a static society which could endure almost anything except change. Instinctively, his first loyalty would go to the locality in which that society existed. He would fight to the limit of endurance to defend it, because in defending it he was defending everything that gave his own life its deepest meaning. 10

The Westerner, on the other hand, would fight with an equal tenacity for the broader concept of society. He fought so because everything he lived by was tied to growth, expansion, and a constantly widening horizon. What he lived by would survive or fall with the nation itself. He could not possibly stand by unmoved in the face of an attempt to destroy the Union. He would combat it with everything he had, because he could only see it as an effort to cut the ground out from under his feet. 11

So Grant and Lee were in complete contrast, representing two diametrically opposed elements in American life. Grant was the modern man emerging; beyond him, ready to come on the stage, was the great age of steel and machinery, of crowded cities and a restless, burgeoning vitality. Lee might have ridden down from the old age of chivalry, lance in hand, silken banner fluttering over his head. Each man was the perfect champion of his cause, drawing both his strengths and his weaknesses from the people he led. 12

Yet it was not all contrast, after all. Different as they were— in background, in personality, in underlying aspiration—these two great soldiers had much in common. Under everything 13 else, they were marvelous fighters. Furthermore, their fighting qualities were really very much alike.

Each man had, to begin with, the great virtue of utter 14 tenacity and fidelity. Grant fought his way down the Mississippi Valley in spite of acute personal discouragement and profound military handicaps. Lee hung on in the trenches at Petersburg after hope itself had died. In each man there was an indomitable quality . . . the born fighter's refusal to give us as long as he can still remain on his feet and lift his two fists.

Daring and resourcefulness they had, too; the ability to 15 think faster and move faster than the enemy. These were the qualities which gave Lee the dazzling campaigns of Second Manassas and Chancellorsville and won Vicksburg for Grant.

Lastly, and perhaps greatest of all, there was the ability, at 16 the end, to turn quickly from war to peace once the fighting was over. Out of the way these two men behaved at Appomattox came the possibility of a peace of reconciliation. It was a possibility not wholly realized, in the years to come, but which did, in the end, help the two sections to become one nation again . . . after a war whose bitterness might have seemed to make such a reunion wholly impossible. No part of either man's life became him more than the part he played in their brief meeting in the McLean house at Appomattox. Their behavior there put all succeeding generations of Americans in their debt. Two great Americans, Grant and Lee—very different, yet under everything very much alike. Their encounter at Appomattox was one of the great moments of American history.

For Study and Discussion

QUESTIONS ABOUT PURPOSE

1. Catton's title identifies his essay as a strict comparison of two men—opposing military generals in the same war. What is his primary purpose in comparing them—to compare their biographies, their values, their military abilities, or their causes?

2. Catton's subtitle suggests that his purpose is to study contrasts. Does his analysis suggest that one man was superior to the other? Explain your answer.

QUESTIONS ABOUT AUDIENCE

1. How much knowledge does Catton assume his readers have about the Civil War? Do they need to know the specific details of the battles of Second Manassas, Chancellorville, and Vicksburg to understand this essay? Explain your answer.
2. Although Catton's title is "Grant and Lee," he presents Lee first and Grant second. Why? Does he assume his readers know more about Lee, are more fascinated by Lee, or prefer to read about the loser first and the winner second?

QUESTIONS ABOUT STRATEGIES

1. How does Catton arrange the points of his contrast? To what extent does he provide equal treatment of each point?
2. One strategy Catton uses to characterize his two subjects is to compare their values to the values of people in other times and places. If Lee embodies the values of chivalry, knighthood, and aristocracy, what values does Grant embody?

For Writing and Research

1. *Analyze* the strategies Catton uses to illustrate how Grant was a good winner and Lee was a good loser.
2. *Practice* by comparing two people who share many experiences and characteristics. Consider such points as dress, behavior, education, work, and style as you try to contrast the values each character embodies.
3. *Argue* that in the final analysis military leaders show more similarities than differences.
4. *Synthesize* the research on Grant and Lee's attitudes toward slavery. Then use this evidence to explain their position on what most historians consider the major cause of the Civil War.

PAULE MARSHALL

Paule Marshall was born in 1929 in Brooklyn, New York, the daughter of Immigrants from Barbados. With degrees from Brooklyn College and Hunter College, Marshall became a writer for the magazine *Our World* while she wrote her first novel, *Brown Girl, Brownstones* (1959). She has taught creative writing at Oxford University, Yale University, Cornell University, and Virginia Commonwealth University. Marshall's fiction— *Soul Clap Hands and Sing* (1961), *The Chosen Place, the Timeless People* (1969), *Praisesong for the Widow* (1983), *Reena and Other Stories* (1983), *The Fisher King* (2001), and *Triangular Road* (2009)—is distinguished by its inclusion of the variety of voices from her cross-cultural heritage. "To Da-duh, In Memoriam," reprinted from *Reena and Other Stories,* contrasts the experience and values of Da-duh, an old woman who has lived her life in the natural beauty of Barbados, with those of her granddaughter, who has grown up amid the urban splendor of New York City.

To Da-duh, In Memoriam[6]

". . . Oh Nana! all of you is not involved in this evil business 1
Death,
Nor all of us in life."
—From "At My Grandmother's Grave," by Lebert Bethune

I did not see her at first I remember. For not only was it 2
dark inside the crowded disembarkation shed in spite of the

[6] Paule Marshall, "To Da-duh, In Memoriam" copyright © 1967, 1983 by Paule Marshall. From the book *Reena and Other Stories.* Published by The Feminist Press at the City University of New York. All rights reserved.

daylight flooding in from outside, but standing there waiting for her with my mother and sister I was still somewhat
blinded from the sheen of tropical sunlight on the water of
the bay which we had just crossed in the landing boat, leaving
behind us the ship that had brought us from New York lying
in the offing. Besides, being only nine years of age at the time
and knowing nothing of islands I was busy attending to the
alien sights and sounds of Barbados, the unfamiliar smells.

I did not see her, but I was alerted to her approach by my   3
mother's hand which suddenly tightened around mine, and
looking up I traced her gaze through the gloom in the shed
until I finally made out the small, purposeful, painfully erect
figure of the old woman headed our way.

Her face was drowned in the shadow of an ugly rolled-   4
brim brown felt hat, but the details of her slight body and
of the struggle taking place within it were clear enough—an
intense, unrelenting struggle between her back which was
beginning to bend ever so slightly under the weight of her
eighty-odd years and the rest of her which sought to deny
those years and hold that back straight, keep it in line. Moving swiftly toward us (so swiftly it seemed she did not intend
stopping when she reached us but would sweep past us out
the doorway which opened onto the sea and like Christ walk
upon the water!), she was caught between the sunlight at
her end of the building and the darkness inside—and for a
moment she appeared to contain them both: the light in
the long severe old-fashioned white dress she wore which
brought the sense of a past that was still alive into our bustling present and in the snatch of white at her eye; the darkness in her black high-top shoes and in her face which was
visible now that she was closer.

It was as stark and fleshless as a death mask, that face. The   5
maggots might have already done their work, leaving only
the framework of bone beneath the ruined skin and deep
wells at the temple and jaw. But her eyes were alive, unnerv-
ingly so for one so old, with a sharp light that flicked out of
the dim clouded depths like a lizard's tongue to snap up all
in her view. Those eyes betrayed a child's curiosity about the

world, and I wondered vaguely seeing them, and seeing the way the bodice of her ancient dress had collapsed in on her flat chest (what had happened to her breasts?), whether she might not be some kind of child at the same time that she was a woman, with fourteen children, my mother included, to prove it. Perhaps she was both, both child and woman, darkness and light, past and present, life and death—all the opposites contained and reconciled in her.

"My Da-duh," my mother said formally and stepped forward. The name sounded like thunder fading softly in the distance. 6

"Child," Da-duh said, and her tone, her quick scrutiny of my mother, the brief embrace in which they appeared to shy from each other rather than touch, wiped out the fifteen years my mother had been away and restored the old relationship. My mother, who was such a formidable figure in my eyes, had suddenly with a word been reduced to my status. 7

"Yes, God is good," Da-duh said with a nod that was like a tic. "He has spared me to see my child again." 8

We were led forward then, apologetically because not only did Da-duh prefer boys but she also liked her grandchildren to be "white," that is, fair-skinned; and we had, I was to discover, a number of cousins, the outside children of white estate managers and the like, who qualified. We, though, were as black as she. 9

My sister being the oldest was presented first. "This one takes after the father," my mother said and waited to be reproved. 10

Frowning, Da-duh tilted my sister's face toward the light. But her frown soon gave way to a grudging smile, for my sister with her large mild eyes and little broad winged nose, with our father's high-cheeked Barbadian cast to her face, was pretty. 11

"She's goin' be lucky," Da-duh said and patted her once on the cheek. "Any girl child that takes after the father does be lucky." 12

She turned then to me. But oddly enough she did not   13
touch me. Instead leaning close, she peered hard at me, and
then quickly drew back. I thought I saw her hand start up
as though to shield her eyes. It was almost as if she saw not
only me, a thin truculent child who it was said took after no
one but myself, but something in me which for some reason
she found disturbing, even threatening. We looked silently at
each other for a long time there in the noisy shed, our gaze
locked. She was the first to look away.

"But Adry," she said to my mother and her laugh was   14
cracked, thin, apprehensive. "Where did you get this one
here with this fierce look?"

"We don't know where she came out of, my Da-duh," my   15
mother said, laughing also. Even I smiled to myself. After all
I had won the encounter. Da-duh had recognized my small
strength—and this was all I ever asked of the adults in my life
then.

"Come, soul," Da-duh said and took my hand. "You must   16
be one of those New York terrors you hear so much about."

She led us, me at her side and my sister and mother behind,   17
out of the shed into the sunlight that was like a bright driving
summer rail and over to a group of people clustered beside
a decrepit lorry. They were our relatives, most of them from
St. Andrews although Da-duh herself lived in St. Thomas,
the women wearing bright print dresses, the colors vivid
against their darkness, the men rusty black suits that encased
them like straitjackets. Da-duh, holding fast to my hand,
became my anchor as they circled round us like a nervous sea,
exclaiming, touching us with their calloused hands, embracing us shyly. They laughed in awed bursts: "But look Adry
got big-big children!"/"And see the nice things they wearing, wrist watch and all!"/"I tell you, Adry has done all right
for sheself in New York. . . ."

Da-duh, ashamed at their wonder, embarrassed for them,   18
admonished them the while. "But oh Christ," she said, "why
you all got to get on like you never saw people from 'Away'
before? You would think New York is the only place in the

world to hear wunna. That's why I don't like to go anyplace with you St. Andrews people, you know. You all ain't been colonized."

We were in the back of the lorry finally, packed in among   19
the barrels of ham, flour, cornmeal and rice and the trunks of clothes that my mother had brought as gifts. We made our way slowly through Bridgetown's clogged streets, part of a funereal procession of cars and open-sided buses, bicycles and donkey carts. The dim little limestone shops and offices along the way marched with us, at the same mournful pace, toward the same grave ceremony—as did the people, the women balancing huge baskets on top their heads as if they were no more than hats they wore to shade them from the sun. Looking over the edge of the lorry I watched as their feet slurred the dust. I listened, and their voices, raw and loud and dissonant in the heat, seemed to be grappling with each other high overhead.

Da-duh sat on a trunk in our midst, a monarch amid her   20
court. She still held my hand, but it was different now. I had suddenly become her anchor, for I felt her fear of the lorry with its asthmatic motor (a fear and distrust, I later learned, she held of all machines) beating like a pulse in her rough palm.

As soon as we left Bridgetown behind though, she relaxed,   21
and while the others around us talked she gazed at the canes standing tall on either side of the winding marl road. "C'dear," she said softly to herself after a time. "The canes this side are pretty enough."

They were too much for me. I thought of them as giant   22
weeds that had overrun the island, leaving scarcely any room for the small tottering houses of sunbleached pine we passed or the people, dark streaks as our lorry hurtled by. I suddenly feared that we were journeying, unaware that we were, toward some dangerous place where the canes, grown as high and thick as a forest, would close in on us and run us through with their stiletto blades. I longed then for the familiar: for the street in Brooklyn where I lived, for my father who had refused to accompany us ("Blowing out good money on

foolishness," he had said of the trip), for a game of tag with my friends under the chestnut tree outside our aging brownstone house.

"Yes, but wait till you see St. Thomas canes," Da-duh was saying to me. "They's canes father, bo," she gave a proud arrogant nod. "Tomorrow, God willing, I goin' take you out in the ground and show them to you." 23

True to her word Da-duh took me with her the following day out into the ground. It was a fairly large plot adjoining her weathered board and shingle house and consisting of a small orchard, a good-sized canepiece and behind the canes, where the land sloped abruptly down, a gully. She had purchased it with Panama money sent her by her eldest son, my uncle Joseph, who had died working on the canal. We entered the ground along a trail no wider than her body and as devious and complex as her reasons for showing me her land. Da-duh strode briskly ahead, her slight form filled out this morning by the layers of sacking petticoats she wore under her working dress to protect her against the damp. A fresh white cloth, elaborately arranged around her head, added to her height, and lent her a vain, almost roguish air. 24

Her pace slowed once we reached the orchard, and glancing back at me occasionally over her shoulder, she pointed out the various trees. 25

"This is a breadfruit," she said. "That one yonder is a papaw. Here's a guava. This is a mango. I know you don't have anything like these in New York. Here's a sugar apple." (The fruit looked more like artichokes than apples to me.) "This one bears limes. . . ." She went on for some time, intoning the names of the trees as though they were those of her gods. Finally, turning to me, she said, "I know you don't have anything this nice where you come from." Then, as I hesitated: "I said I know you don't have anything this nice where you come from. . . ." 26

"No," I said and my world did seem suddenly lacking. 27

Da-duh nodded and passed on. The orchard ended and we were on the narrow cart road that led through the canepiece, the canes clashing like swords above my cowering 28

head. Again she turned and her thin muscular arms spread
wide, her dim gaze embracing the small field of canes, she
said—and her voice almost broke under the weight of her
pride, "Tell me, have you got anything like these in that place
where you were born?"

"No."   29

"I din' think so. I bet you don't even know that these   30
canes here and the sugar you eat is one and the same thing.
That they does throw the canes into some damn machine
at the factory and squeeze out all the little life in them to
make sugar for you all so in New York to eat. I bet you don't
know that."

"I've got two cavities and I'm not allowed to eat a lot of   31
sugar."

But Da-duh didn't hear me. She had turned with an   32
inexplicably angry motion and was making her way rapidly
out of the canes and down the slope at the edge of the field
which led to the gully below. Following her apprehensively
down the incline amid a stand of banana plants whose leaves
flapped like elephants' ears in the wind, I found myself in the
middle of a small tropical wood—a place dense and damp
and gloomy and tremulous with the fitful play of light and
shadow as the leaves high above moved against the sun that
was almost hidden from view. It was a violent place, the
tangled foliage fighting each other for a chance at the sunlight, the branches of the trees locked in what seemed an
immemorial struggle, one both necessary and inevitable.
But despite the violence, it was pleasant, almost peaceful
in the gully, and beneath the thick undergrowth the earth
smelled like spring.

This time Da-duh didn't even bother to ask her usual   33
question, but simply turned and waited for me to speak.

"No," I said, my head bowed. "We don't have anything   34
like this in New York."

"Ah," she cried her triumph complete. "I din' think so.   35
Why, I've heard that's a place where you can walk till you
near drop and never see a tree."

"We've got a chestnut tree in front of our house," I said.   36

"Does it bear?" She waited. "I ask you, does it bear?"   37

"Not anymore," I muttered. "It used to, but not any-   38
more."

She gave the nod that was like a nervous twitch. "You see,"   39
she said. "Nothing can bear there." Then, secure behind her
scorn, she added, "But tell me, what's this snow like that you
hear so much about?"

Looking up, I studied her closely, sensing my chance, and   40
then I told her, describing at length and with as much drama
as I could summon not only what snow in the city was like,
but what it would be like here, in her perennial summer
kingdom.

". . . And you see all these trees you got here," I said.   41
"Well, they'd be bare. No leaves, no fruit, nothing. They'd
be covered in snow. You see your canes. They'd be buried
under tons of snow. The snow would be higher than your
head, higher than your house, and you wouldn't be able to
come down into this here gully because it would be snowed
under. . . ."

She searched my face for the lie, still scornful but intrigued.   42
"What a thing, huh?" she said finally, whispering it softly to
herself.

"And when it snows you couldn't dress like you are now,"   43
I said. "Oh no, you'd freeze to death. You'd have to wear
a hat and gloves and galoshes and ear muffs so your ears
wouldn't freeze and drop off, and a heavy coat. I've got a
Shirley Temple coat with fur on the collar. I can dance. You
wanna see?"

Before she could answer I began, with a dance called the   44
Truck which was popular back then in the 1930s. My right
forefinger waving, I trucked around the nearby trees and
around Da-duh's awed and rigid form. After the Truck I did
the Suzy-Q, my lean hips swishing, my sneakers sidling zig-
zag over the ground. "I can sing," I said and did so, starting with "I'm Gonna Sit Right Down and Write Myself a
Letter," then without pausing, "Tea for Two," and ending
with "I Found a Million Dollar Baby in a Five and Ten Cent
Store."

For long moments afterwards Da-duh stared at me as if   45
I were a creature from Mars, an emissary from some world
she did not know but which intrigued her and whose power
she both felt and feared. Yet something about my performance must have pleased her, because bending down she
slowly lifted her long skirt and then, one by one, the layers
of petticoats until she came to a drawstring purse dangling at
the end of a long strip of cloth tied round her waist. Opening the purse she handed me a penny. "Here," she said half-
smiling against her will. "Take this to buy yourself a sweet
at the shop up the road. There's nothing to be done with
you, soul."

From then on, whenever I wasn't taken to visit relatives,   46
I accompanied Da-duh out into the ground, and alone with
her amid the canes or down in the gully I told her about
New York. It always began with some slighting remark on
her part: "I know they don't have anything this nice where
you come from," or "Tell me, I hear those foolish people in
New York does do such and such. . . ." But as I answered,
re-creating my towering world of steel and concrete and
machines for her, building the city out of words, I would
feel her give way. I came to know the signs of her surrender:
the total stillness that would come over her little hard dry
form, the probing gaze that like a surgeon's knife sought to
cut through my skull to get at the images there, to see if I
were lying; above all, her fear, a fear nameless and profound,
the same one I had felt beating in the palm of her hand that
day in the lorry.

Over the weeks I told her about refrigerators, radios, gas   47
stoves, elevators, trolley cars, wringer washing machines,
movies, airplanes, the cyclone at Coney Island, subways,
toasters, electric lights: "At night, see, all you have to do is
flip this little switch on the wall and all the lights in the house
go on. Just like that. Like magic. It's like turning on the sun
at night."

"But tell me," she said to me once with a faint mocking   48
smile, "do the white people have all these things too or it's
only the people looking like us?"

I laughed. "What d'ya mean," I said. 'The white people   49
have even better." Then: "I beat up a white girl in my class
last term."

"Beating up white people!" Her tone was incredulous.   50

"How you mean!" I said, using an expression of hers. "She   51
called me a name."

For some reason Da-duh could not quite get over this and   52
repeated in the same hushed, shocked voice, "Beating up
white people now! Oh, the lord, the world's changing up so
I can scarce recognize it anymore."

One morning toward the end of our stay, Da-duh led me   53
into a part of the gully that we had never visited before, an
area darker and more thickly overgrown than the rest, almost
impenetrable. There in a small clearing amid the dense bush,
she stopped before an incredibly tall royal palm which rose
cleanly out of the ground, and drawing the eye up with it,
soared high above the trees around it into the sky. It appeared
to be touching the blue dome of sky, to be flaunting its dark
crown of fronds right in the blinding white face of the late
morning sun.

Da-duh watched me a long time before she spoke, and   54
then she said very quietly, "All right, now, tell me if you've
got anything this tall in that place you're from."

I almost wished, seeing her face, that I could have said no.   55
"Yes," I said. "We've got buildings hundreds of times this tall
in New York. There's one called the Empire State Building
that's the tallest in the world. My class visited it last year and
I went all the way to the top. It's got over a hundred floors. I
can't describe how tall it is. Wait a minute. What's the name
of that hill I went to visit the other day, where they have the
police station?"

"You mean Bissex?"   56

"Yes, Bissex. Well, the Empire State Building is way taller   57
than that."

"You're lying now!" she shouted, trembling with rage.   58
Her hand lifted to strike me.

"No, I'm not," I said. "It really is, if you don't believe   59
me I'll send you a picture postcard of it soon as I get back

home so you can see for yourself. But it's way taller than Bissex."

All the fight went out of her at that. The hand poised to 60 strike me fell limp to her side, and as she stared at me, seeing not me but the building that was taller than the highest hill she knew, the small stubborn light in her eyes (it was the same amber as the flame in the kerosene lamp she lit at dusk) began to fail. Finally, with a vague gesture that even in the midst of her defeat still tried to dismiss me and my world, she turned and started back through the gully, walking slowly, her steps groping and uncertain, as if she were suddenly no longer sure of the way, while I followed triumphant yet strangely saddened behind.

The next morning I found her dressed for our morning 61 walk but stretched out on the Berbice chair in the tiny drawing room where she sometimes napped during the afternoon heat, her face turned to the window beside her. She appeared thinner and suddenly indescribably old.

"My Da-duh," I said.   62

"Yes, nuh," she said. Her voice was listless and the face she 63 slowly turned my way was, now that I think back on it, like a Benin mask, the features drawn and almost distorted by an ancient abstract sorrow.

"Don't you feel well?" I asked.   64

"Girl, I don't know."   65

"My Da-duh, I goin' boil you some bush tea," my aunt, 66 Da-duh's youngest child, who lived with her, called from the shed roof kitchen.

"Who tell you I need bush tea?" she cried, her voice 67 assuming for a moment its old authority. "You can't even rest nowadays without some malicious person looking for you to be dead. Come girl," she motioned me to a place beside her on the old-fashioned lounge chair, "give us a tune."

I sang for her until breakfast at eleven, all my brash irrever- 68 ent Tin Pan Alley songs, and then just before noon we went out into the ground. But it was a short, dispirited walk. Da-duh didn't even notice that the mangoes were beginning to ripen and would have to be picked before the village boys got to them. And when she paused occasionally and looked out across the canes or up at her trees it wasn't as if she were seeing them but something else. Some huge, monolithic shape had imposed itself, it seemed, between her and the land, obstructing her vision. Returning to the house she slept the entire afternoon on the Berbice chair.

She remained like this until we left, languishing away the   69
mornings on the chair at the window gazing out at the land as if it were already doomed; then, at noon, taking the brief stroll with me through the ground during which she seldom spoke, and afterwards returning home to sleep till almost dusk sometimes.

On the day of our departure she put on the austere, ankle-   70
length white dress, the black shoes and brown felt hat (her town clothes she called them), but she did not go with us to town. She saw us off on the road outside her house and in the midst of my mother's tearful protracted farewell, she leaned down and whispered in my ear, "Girl, you're not to forget now to send me the picture of that building, you hear."

By the time I mailed her the large colored picture postcard   71
of the Empire State Building she was dead. She died during the famous '37 strike which began shortly after we left. On the day of her death England sent planes flying low over the island in a show of force—so low, according to my aunt's letter, that the downdraft from them shook the ripened mangoes from the trees in Da-duh's orchard. Frightened, everyone in the village fled into the canes. Except Da-duh. She remained in the house at the window so my aunt said, watching as the planes came swooping and screaming like monstrous birds down over the village, over her house, rattling her trees and flattening the young canes in her field. It must have seemed to her lying there that they did not intend pulling out of their dive, but like the hard-back beetles which hurled themselves with suicidal force against the walls of the house at night, those menacing silver shapes would hurl themselves in an ecstasy of self-immolation onto the land, destroying it utterly.

When the planes finally left and the villagers returned they 72
found her dead on the Berbice chair at the window.

She died and I lived, but always, to this day even, within 73
the shadow of her death. For a brief period after I was grown
I went to live alone, like one doing penance, in a loft above a
noisy factory in downtown New York and there painted seas of
sugar-cane and huge swirling Van Gogh suns and palm trees
striding like brightly-plumed Tutsi warriors across a tropical
landscape, while the thunderous tread of the machines downstairs jarred the floor beneath my easel, mocking my efforts.

COMMENT ON "TO DA-DUH, IN MEMORIAM"

Paule Marshall's "To Da-duh, In Memoriam" sets up a
comparison between the natural world of Da-duh and the
urban world of the young narrator. For Da-duh, Barbados
is a magnificent, magical place that she is eager to show her
visiting granddaughter. As they walk between the canes or
among the banana plants, she wants to know whether her
companion has "anything this nice where you come from."
The narrator says no to most of these questions but eventually begins "describing at length and with as much drama as
I could summon" all the marvels of New York—from snow
to electrical appliances to the Empire State Building. The
once proud Da-duh learns a lesson, slowly surrendering to
the new world where trees do not bear fruit, black people
beat up white people, and a building is "taller than the highest hill she knew." The story concludes as she dies trying to
face down the English airplanes that invade her world. But
the last lesson is reserved for the narrator, who, when she is
grown, moves into a noisy loft in downtown New York to
paint Da-duh's world: "seas of sugar-cane and high swirling
Van Gogh suns and palm trees striding like brightly-plumed
Tutsi warriors across a tropical landscape."

CHAPTER 4

DIVISION AND CLASSIFICATION

Division and **classification** are mental processes that often work together. When you *divide,* you separate something (a college, a city) into sections (departments, neighborhoods). When you *classify,* you place examples of something (restaurants, jobs) into categories or classes (restaurants: moderately expensive, expensive, very expensive; jobs: unskilled, semi-skilled, and skilled).

When you divide, you move downward from a concept to the subunits of that concept. When you classify, you move upward from specific examples to classes or categories that share a common characteristic. For example, you could *divide* a television news program into subunits such as news, features, editorials, sports, and weather. And you could *classify* some element of that program—such as the editorial commentator on the six o'clock news—according to his or her style, knowledge, and trustworthiness. You

199

can use either division or classification singly, depending on your purpose, but most of the time you will probably use them together when you are writing a classification essay. First you might identify the subunits of a college sports program—football, basketball, hockey, volleyball, tennis; then you could classify them according to their budgets—most money budgeted for football, the least budgeted for volleyball.

PURPOSE

When you write a classification essay, your chief purpose is to *explain*. You might want to explain an established method for organizing information, such as the Library of Congress system, or a new plan for arranging data, such as the Internal Revenue Service's latest schedule for itemizing tax deductions. On one level, your purpose in such an essay is simply to show how the system works. At a deeper level, your purpose is to define, analyze, and justify the organizing principle that underlies the system.

You can also write a classification essay to *entertain* or to *persuade*. If you classify to entertain, you have an opportunity to be clever and witty. If you classify to persuade, you have a chance to be cogent and forceful. If you want to entertain, you might concoct an elaborate scheme for classifying fools, pointing out the distinguishing features of each category and giving particularly striking examples of each type. But if you want to persuade, you could explain how some new or controversial plan, such as the metric system or congressional redistricting, is organized, pointing out how the schemes use new principles to identify and organize information. Again, although you may give your readers a great deal of information in such an essay, your main purpose is to persuade them that the new plan is better than the old one.

AUDIENCE

As with any writing assignment, when you write a classification essay, you need to think carefully about what your readers already know and what they need to learn from your writing. If you're writing on a new topic (social patterns in a primitive society) or if you're explaining a specialized system of classification (the botanist's procedure for identifying plants), your readers need precise definitions and plenty of illustrations for each subcategory. If your readers already know about your subject and the system it uses for classification (the movies' G, PG, PG-13, R, and NC-17 rating codes), then you don't need to give them an extensive demonstration. In that kind of writing situation, you might want to sketch the system briefly to refresh your readers' memories but then move on, using examples of specific movies to analyze whether the system really works.

You also need to think about how your readers might use the classification system that you explain in your essay. If you're classifying rock musicians, your readers are probably going to regard the system you create as something self-enclosed—interesting and amusing, perhaps something to quibble about, but not something they're likely to use in their everyday lives. In contrast, if you write an essay classifying digital video equipment, your readers may want to use your system when they shop. For the first audience, you can use an informal approach to classification, dividing your subject into interesting subcategories and illustrating them with vivid examples. For the other audience, you need to be careful and strict in your approach, making sure you divide your topic into all its possible classes and illustrating each class with concrete examples.

STRATEGIES

When you write a classification essay, your basic strategy for organization should be to *divide your subject* into major categories that exhibit a common trait, then subdivide those categories into smaller units. Next, *arrange your categories* into a sequence that shows a logical or a dramatic progression. Finally, *define each of your categories.* Show how each category is different from the others; then discuss its most vivid examples.

To make this strategy succeed, you must be sure that your classification system is *consistent, complete, emphatic,* and *significant.* Here is a method for achieving this goal. First, when you divide your subject into categories, *apply the same principle of selection to each class.* You may find this hard to do if you're trying to explain a system that someone else has already established but that is actually inconsistent. You have undoubtedly discovered that record stores use overlapping and inconsistent categories. CDs by Norah Jones, for example, may be found in sections labeled *jazz, pop,* and *female vocal.* You can avoid such tangles if you create and control your own classification system.

For instance, Judith Viorst classifies four types of lies, Lewis Thomas classifies different kinds of medical technology, Louis Kronenberger classifies different kinds of nonconformists, and David Cole classifies different myths about immigration.

After you have divided your subject into separate and consistent categories, *make sure your division is complete.* The simplest kind of division separates a subject into two categories: A and Not-A (for example, conformists and nonconformists). This kind of division, however, is rarely encouraged. It allows you to tell your readers about category A (conformists), but you won't tell them much about category Not-A (nonconformists). For this reason, you should try to exhaust your subject by finding at least three separate categories and by acknowledging any examples that don't fit into the system. When authors write a formal classification essay, such as Cole's "Five Myths About Immigration," they try to be definitive—to include everything significant. Even when writers are writing less formal classification essays, such as Viorst's "The Truth About Lying," they try to set up a reasonably complete system.

Once you have completed your process of division, *arrange your categories and examples in an emphatic order*. Thomas arranges his classification of medical technology from least to most effective. The authors in this chapter reveal the principal purpose underlying their classification schemes: to show variety in similarity, to challenge the arbitrariness of an established system, and to point out how concepts change.

Finally, you need to *show the significance of your system of classification*. The strength of the classification process is that you can use it to analyze a subject in any number of ways. Its weakness is that you can use it to subdivide a subject into all kinds of trivial or pointless categories. You can classify people by their educational backgrounds, their work experience, or their significant achievements. You can also classify them by their shoe size, the kind of socks they wear, or their tastes in ice cream. Notice that Malcolm Gladwell devotes his essay to pointing out the defects in several classification systems, including the system that ranks the educational quality of America's colleges and universities.

DIVISION AND CLASSIFICATION

Points to Remember

1. Determine whether you want to (a) explain an existing system of classification or (b) create your own system.
2. Divide your subject into smaller categories by applying the same principle of selection to each category.
3. Make sure that your division is complete by establishing separate and consistent types of categories.
4. Arrange your categories (and the examples you use to illustrate each category) in a logical and emphatic sequence.
5. Demonstrate the significance of your system by calling your readers' attention to its significance.

In this quirky cartoon, Roz Chast classifies the different kinds of clouds one can see in the sky. Examine the various categories in her "Cloud Chart." Reflect on your own experiences watching clouds. What categories has she omitted or mislabeled? Write an essay that explains how meteorologists classify clouds or, alternatively, how clouds figure metaphorically in expressions ("his face clouded over"), literature (including song lyrics), or art.

JUDITH VIORST

Judith Viorst was born in 1931 in Newark, New Jersey, and educated at Rutgers University and Washington Psychoanalytic Institute. She began her career by writing a science book about NASA's space program, *Projects: Space* (1962). Viorst then turned to poetry, *The Village Square* (1965), and eventually children's literature, *Sunday Morning* (1968). In her distinguished career as a poet, fiction writer, and children's author, she has blended her wry humor with critical analysis. Her more recent books include *Super-Completely and Totally the Messiest* (2000), *Suddenly Sixty and Other Shocks of Later Life* (2000), and *I'm Too Young to Be Seventy* (2005). She received the Foremother Award for lifetime achievements from the National Research Center for Women & Families in 2011. In "The Truth About Lying," reprinted from *Redbook,* Viorst classifies lying in terms of "a series of moral puzzles."

The Truth About Lying[1]

I 'VE BEEN WANTING to write on a subject that intrigues and   1
challenges me: the subject of lying. I've found it very difficult to do. Everyone I've talked to has a quite intense and personal but often rather intolerant point of view about what we can—and can never *never*—tell lies about. I've finally reached the conclusion that I can't present any ultimate conclusions, for too many people would promptly disagree. Instead, I'd like to present a series of moral puzzles, all

[1] "The Truth About Lying" by Judith Viorst. Copyright © 1981 by Judith Viorst. Originally appeared in *Redbook*. Used by permission of The Choate Agency, LLC. All rights reserved.

205

concerned with lying. I'll tell you what I think about them.
Do you agree?

SOCIAL LIES

Most of the people I've talked with say that they find social   2
lying acceptable and necessary. They think it's the civilized
way for folks to behave. Without these little white lies, they
say, our relationships would be short and brutish and nasty.
It's arrogant, they say, to insist on being so incorruptible and
so brave that you cause other people unnecessary embarrass-
ment or pain by compulsively assailing them with your honesty. I basically agree. What about you?

Will you say to people, when it simply isn't true, "I like   3
your new hairdo," "You're looking much better," "It's so
nice to see you," "I had a wonderful time"?

Will you praise hideous presents and homely kids?   4

Will you decline invitations with "We're busy that night—   5
so sorry we can't come," when the truth is you'd rather stay
home than dine with the So-and-sos?

And even though, as I do, you may prefer the polite eva-   6
sion of "You really cooked up a storm" instead of "The
soup"—which tastes like warmed-over coffee—"is wonderful," will you, if you must, proclaim it wonderful?

---

*Everyone I've talked to has a quite intense
and personal but often rather intolerant
view about what we can—and can never
never—tell lies about.*

There's one man I know who absolutely refuses to tell   7
social lies. "I can't play that game," he says; "I'm simply not
made that way." And his answer to the argument that saying nice things to someone doesn't cost anything is, "Yes, it
does—it destroys your credibility." Now, he won't, unsolic-
ited, offer his views on the painting you just bought, but you
don't ask his frank opinion unless you want *frank*, and his

silence at those moments when the rest of us liars are muttering, "Isn't it lovely?" is, for the most part, eloquent enough. My friend does not indulge in what he calls "flattery, false praise and mellifluous comments." When others tell fibs he will not go along. He says that social lying is lying, that little white lies are still lies. And he feels that telling lies is morally wrong. What about you?

PEACE-KEEPING LIES

Many people tell peace-keeping lies; lies designed to avoid   8
irritation or argument; lies designed to shelter the liar from possible blame or pain; lies (or so it is rationalized) designed to keep trouble at bay without hurting anyone.

I tell these lies at times, and yet I always feel they're wrong.   9
I understand why we tell them, but still they feel wrong. And whenever I lie so that someone won't disapprove of me or think less of me or holler at me, I feel I'm a bit of a coward, I feel I'm dodging responsibility, I feel . . . guilty. What about you?

Do you, when you're late for a date because you overslept,   10
say that you're late because you got caught in a traffic jam?

Do you, when you forget to call a friend, say that you   11
called several times but the line was busy?

Do you, when you didn't remember that it was your father's   12
birthday, say that his present must be delayed in the mail?

And when you're planning a weekend in New York City   13
and you're not in the mood to visit your mother, who lives there, do you conceal—with a lie, if you must—the fact that you'll be in New York? Or do you have the courage—or is it the cruelty?—to say, "I'll be in New York, but sorry—I don't plan on seeing you"?

(Dave and his wife Elaine have two quite different points   14
of view on this very subject. He calls her a coward. She says she's being wise. He says she must assert her right to visit New York sometimes and not see her mother. To which she always patiently replies: "Why should we have useless fights? My mother's too old to change. We get along much better when I lie to her.")

Finally, do you keep the peace by telling your husband lies 15
on the subject of money? Do you reduce what you really paid
for your shoes? And in general do you find yourself ready,
willing and able to lie to him when you make absurd mistakes
or lose or break things?

"I used to have a romantic idea that part of intimacy was 16
confessing every dumb thing that you did to your husband.
But after a couple of years of that," says Laura, "have I
changed my mind!"

And having changed her mind, she finds herself telling 17
peace-keeping lies. And yes, I tell them too. What about you?

PROTECTIVE LIES

Protective lies are lies folks tell—often quite serious lies— 18
because they're convinced that the truth would be too damaging. They lie because they feel there are certain human
values that supersede the wrong of having lied. They lie, not
for personal gain, but because they believe it's for the good
of the person they're lying to. They lie to those they love, to
those who trust them most of all, on the grounds that breaking this trust is justified.

They may lie to their children on money or marital 19
matters.

They may lie to the dying about the state of their health.   20

They may lie about adultery, and not—so they insist—to 21
save their own hide, but to save the heart and the pride of the
men they are married to.

They may lie to their closest friend because the truth about 22
her talents or son or psyche would be—or so they insist—
utterly devastating.

I sometimes tell such lies, but I'm aware that it's quite pre- 23
sumptuous to claim I know what's best for others to know.
That's called playing God. That's called manipulation and
control. And we never can be sure, once we start to juggle
lies, just where they'll land, exactly where they'll roll.

And furthermore, we may find ourselves lying in order to 24
back up the lies that are backing up the lie we initially told.

And furthermore—let's be honest—if conditions were 25
reversed, we certainly wouldn't want anyone lying to us.

Yet, having said all that, I still believe that there are times 26
when protective lies must nonetheless be told. What about
you?

If your Dad had a very bad heart and you had to tell him 27
some bad family news, which would you choose: to tell him
the truth or lie?

If your former husband failed to send his monthly child- 28
support check and in other ways behaved like a total rat,
would you allow your children—who believed he was simply
wonderful—to continue to believe that he was wonderful?

If your dearly beloved brother selected a wife whom you 29
deeply disliked, would you reveal your feelings or would you
fake it?

And if you were asked, after making love, "And how was 30
that for you?" would you reply, if it wasn't too good, "Not
too good"?

Now, some would call a sex lie unimportant, little more 31
than social lying, a simple act of courtesy that makes all
human intercourse run smoothly. And some would say all
sex lies are bad news and unacceptably protective. Because,
says Ruth, "a man with an ego that fragile doesn't need your
lies—he needs a psychiatrist." Still others feel that sex lies are
indeed protective lies, more serious than simple social lying,
and yet at times they tell them on the grounds that when it
comes to matters sexual, everybody's ego is somewhat fragile.

"If most of the time things go well in sex," says Sue, "I 32
think you're allowed to dissemble when they don't. I can't
believe it's good to say, 'Last night was four stars, darling,
but tonight's performance rates only a half.'"

I'm inclined to agree with Sue. What about you?   33

TRUST-KEEPING LIES

Another group of lies are trust-keeping lies, lies that involve 34
triangulation, with *A* (that's you) telling lies to *B* on behalf
of *C* (whose trust you'd promised to keep). Most people

concede that once you've agreed not to betray a friend's con-fidence, you can't betray it, even if you must lie. But I've talked with people who don't want you telling them anything that they might be called on to lie about.

"I don't tell lies for myself," says Fran, "and I don't want 35 to have to tell them for other people." Which means, she agrees, that if her best friend is having an affair, she absolutely doesn't want to know about it.

"Are you saying," her best friend asks, "that if I went off 36 with a lover and I asked you to tell my husband I'd been with you, that you wouldn't lie for me, that you'd betray me?"

Fran is very pained but very adamant. "I wouldn't want to 37 betray you, so . . . don't ask me."

Fran's best friend is shocked. What about you?   38

Do you believe you can have close friends if you're not 39 prepared to receive their deepest secrets?

Do you believe you must always lie for your friends?   40

Do you believe, if your friend tells a secret that turns out 41 to be quite immoral or illegal, that once you've promised to keep it, you must keep it?

And what if your friend were your boss—if you were per- 42 haps one of the President's men—would you betray or lie for him over, say, Watergate?

As you can see, these issues get terribly sticky.   43

It's my belief that once we've promised to keep a trust, 44 we must tell lies to keep it. I also believe that we can't tell Watergate lies. And if these two statements strike you as quite contradictory, you're right—they're quite contradictory. But for now they're the best I can do. What about you?

Some say that truth will out and thus you might as well tell 45 the truth. Some say you can't regain the trust that lies lose. Some say that even though the truth may never be revealed, our lies pervert and damage our relationships. Some say . . . well, here's what some of them have to say.

"I'm a coward," says Grace, "about telling close people 46 important, difficult truths. I find that I'm unable to carry it off. And so if something is bothering me, it keeps building up inside till I end up just not seeing them anymore."

"I lie to my husband on sexual things, but I'm furious," 47
says Joyce, "that he's too insensitive to know I'm lying."

"I suffer most from the misconception that children can't 48
take the truth," says Emily. "But I'm starting to see that
what's harder and more damaging for them is being told lies,
is *not* being told the truth."

"I'm afraid," says Joan, "that we often wind up feeling a 49
bit of contempt for the people we lie to."

And then there are those who have no talent for lying. 50

"Over the years, I tried to lie," a friend of mine explained, 51
"but I always got found out and I always got punished. I
guess I gave myself away because I feel guilty about any kind
of lying. It looks as if I'm stuck with telling the truth."

For those of us, however, who are good at telling lies, for 52
those of us who lie and don't get caught, the question of
whether or not to lie can be a hard and serious moral problem.
I liked the remark of a friend of mine who said, "I'm willing to
lie. But just as a last resort—the truth's always better."

"Because," he explained, "though others may completely 53
accept the lie I'm telling, I don't."

I tend to feel that way too. 54

What about you? 55

For Study and Discussion

QUESTIONS ABOUT PURPOSE

1. How does Viorst's confession that she finds the subject of lying
   intriguing, challenging, and difficult establish the purpose of her
   essay?
2. How does her inability to "present any ultimate conclusions"
   explain the design of her essay?

QUESTIONS ABOUT AUDIENCE

1. What assumptions does Viorst make about her readers' interest
   in and familiarity with her subject?
2. How does she use the pronoun *you* to establish a connection
   with her readers?

1. Into what main categories does Viorst divide the subject of lying? Can you think of other categories she might have included?
2. What inconsistencies does she admit she has created in some of her categories?

For Writing and Research

1. *Analyze* how Viorst classifies the people who tell lies and the people who are lied to.
2. *Practice* by classifying the situations in which it is acceptable and appropriate to lie.
3. *Argue* that telling one lie requires telling many additional lies.
4. *Synthesize:* Research the definitions of *integrity*. Then use this information to support Viorst's suggestions about the relationship between telling the truth and maintaining trust.

Lewis Thomas (1913–1993) was born in Flushing, New York, and was educated at Princeton University and Harvard University Medical School. He held appointments at numerous research hospitals and medical schools before assuming the position of president of the Sloan-Kettering Cancer Center in New York City. In 1974, his collection of essays, *The Lives of a Cell: Notes of a Biology Watcher*, won the National Book Award for Arts and Letters. His other books include *The Medusa and the Snail: More Notes of a Biology Watcher* (1979), *The Youngest Science* (1983), *Late Night Thoughts on Listening to Mahler's Ninth Symphony* (1983), and *The Fragile Species* (1992). In "The Technology of Medicine," from *The Lives of a Cell,* Thomas classifies "three quite different levels of technology in medicine."

The Technology of Medicine[2]

T ECHNOLOGY ASSESSMENT HAS become a routine exercise for the scientific enterprises on which the country is obliged to spend vast sums for its needs. Brainy committees are continually evaluating the effectiveness and cost of doing various things in space, defense, energy, transportation, and the like, to give advice about prudent investments for the future. 1

Somehow medicine, for all the $80-odd billion that it is said to cost the nation, has not yet come in for much of this analytical treatment. It seems taken for granted that the technology of medicine simply exists, take it or leave it, and 2

[2]Lewis Thomas, "The Technology of Medicine," copyright © 1971 by The Massachusetts Medical Society, from *The Lives Of A Cell* by Lewis Thomas. Used by permission of Viking Penguin, a division of Penguin Group (USA), Inc.

the only major technologic problem which policy-makers are interested in is how to deliver today's kind of health care, with equity, to all the people.

When, as is bound to happen sooner or later, the analysts   3
get around to the technology of medicine itself, they will have to face the problem of measuring the relative cost and effectiveness of all the things that are done in the management of disease. They make their living at this kind of thing, and I wish them well, but I imagine they will have a bewildering time. For one thing, our methods of managing disease are constantly changing—partly under the influence of new bits of information brought in from all corners of biologic science. At the same time, a great many things are done that are not so closely related to science, some not related at all.

There are three quite different levels of technology in medicine, so unlike each other as to seem altogether different undertakings.

In fact, there are three quite different levels of technology   4
in medicine, so unlike each other as to seem altogether different undertakings. Practitioners of medicine and the analysts will be in trouble if they are not kept separate.

1. First of all, there is a large body of what might be termed   5
"nontechnology," impossible to measure in terms of its capacity to alter either the natural course of disease or its eventual outcome. A great deal of money is spent on this. It is valued highly by the professionals as well as the patients. It consists of what is sometimes called "supportive therapy." It tides patients over through diseases that are not, by and large, understood. It is what is meant by the phrases "caring for" and "standing by." It is indispensable. It is not, however, a technology in any real sense, since it does not involve measures directed at the underlying mechanism of disease.

It includes the large part of any good doctor's time that   6
is taken up with simply providing reassurance, explaining to

patients who fear that they have contracted one or another lethal disease that they are, in fact, quite healthy.

It is what physicians used to be engaged in at the bedside 7 of patients with diphtheria, meningitis, poliomyelitis, lobar pneumonia, and all the rest of the infectious diseases that have since come under control.

It is what physicians must now do for patients with intrac- 8 table cancer, severe rheumatoid arthritis, multiple sclerosis, stroke, and advanced cirrhosis. One can think of at least twenty major diseases that require this kind of supportive medical care because of the absence of an effective technology. I would include a large amount of what is called mental disease, and most varieties of cancer, in this category.

The cost of this nontechnology is very high, and getting 9 higher all the time. It requires not only a great deal of time but also very hard effort and skill on the part of physicians; only the very best of doctors are good at coping with this kind of defeat. It also involves long periods of hospitalization, lots of nursing, lots of involvement of nonmedical professionals in and out of the hospital. It represents, in short, a substantial segment of today's expenditures for health.

2. At the next level up is a kind of technology best termed 10 "halfway technology." This represents the kinds of things that must be done after the fact, in efforts to compensate for the incapacitating effects of certain diseases whose course one is unable to do very much about. It is a technology designed to make up for disease, or to postpone death.

The outstanding examples in recent years are the trans- 11 plantations of hearts, kidneys, livers, and other organs, and the equally spectacular inventions of artificial organs. In the public mind, this kind of technology has come to seem like the equivalent of the high technologies of the physical sciences. The media tend to present each new procedure as though it represented a breakthrough and therapeutic triumph, instead of the makeshift that it really is.

In fact, this level of technology is, by its nature, at the 12 same time highly sophisticated and profoundly primitive. It is the kind of thing that one must continue to do until there is a genuine understanding of the mechanisms involved in disease. In chronic glomerulonephritis, for example, a much clearer insight will be needed into the events leading to the destruction of glomeruli by the immunologic reactants that now appear to govern this disease, before one will know how to intervene intelligently to prevent the process, or turn it around. But when this level of understanding has been reached, the technology of kidney replacement will not be much needed and should no longer pose the huge problems of logistics, cost, and ethics that it poses today.

An extremely complex and costly technology for the man-   13
agement of coronary heart disease has evolved—involving specialized ambulances and hospital units, all kinds of electronic gadgetry, and whole platoons of new professional personnel—to deal with the end results of coronary thrombosis. Almost everything offered today for the treatment of heart disease is at this level of technology, with the transplanted and artificial hearts as ultimate examples. When enough has been learned to know what really goes wrong in heart disease, one ought to be in a position to figure out ways to prevent or reverse the process, and when this happens the current elaborate technology will probably be set to one side.

Much of what is done in the treatment of cancer, by sur-   14
gery, irradiation, and chemotherapy, represents halfway technology, in the sense that these measures are directed at the existence of already established cancer cells, but not at the mechanisms by which cells become neoplastic.

It is a characteristic of this kind of technology that it costs an   15
enormous amount of money and requires a continuing expansion of hospital facilities. There is no end to the need for new, highly trained people to run the enterprise. And there is really no way out of this, at the present state of knowledge. If the installation of specialized coronary-care units can result in the extension of life for only a few patients with coronary disease (and there is no question that this technology is effective in a few cases), it seems to me an inevitable fact of life that as many of these as can be will be put together, and as much money as can be found will be spent. I do not see that anyone has much choice in this. The only thing that can move medicine away

from this level of technology is new information, and the only imaginable source of this information is research.

3. The third type of technology is the kind that is so effec- 16 tive that it seems to attract the least public notice; it has come to be taken for granted. This is the genuinely decisive technology of modern medicine, exemplified best by modern methods for immunization against diphtheria, pertussis, and the childhood virus diseases, and the contemporary use of antibiotics and chemotherapy for bacterial infections. The capacity to deal effectively with syphilis and tuberculosis represents a milestone in human endeavor, even though full use of this potential has not yet been made. And there are, of course, other examples: the treatment of endocrinologic disorders with appropriate hormones, the prevention of hemolytic disease of the newborn, the treatment and prevention of various nutritional disorders, and perhaps just around the corner the management of Parkinsonism and sickle-cell anemia. There are other examples, and everyone will have his favorite candidates for the list, but the truth is that there are nothing like as many as the public has been led to believe.

The point to be made about this kind of technology— 17 the real high technology of medicine—is that it comes as the result of a genuine understanding of disease mechanisms, and when it becomes available, it is relatively inexpensive, and relatively easy to deliver.

Offhand, I cannot think of any important human disease 18 for which medicine possesses the outright capacity to prevent or cure where the cost of the technology is itself a major problem. The price is never as high as the cost of managing the same diseases during the earlier stages of nontechnology or halfway technology. If a case of typhoid fever had to be managed today by the best methods of 1935, it would run to a staggering expense. At, say, around fifty days of hospitalization, requiring the most demanding kind of nursing care, with the obsessive concern for details of diet that characterized the therapy of that time, with daily laboratory monitoring, and, on occasion, surgical intervention for abdominal catastrophe, I should think $10,000 would be a conservative estimate for the illness, as contrasted with today's cost of a bottle of chloramphenicol and a day or two of fever. The halfway technology that was evolving for poliomyelitis in the early 1950s, just before the emergence of the basic research that made the vaccine possible, provides another illustration of the point. Do you remember Sister Kenny, and the cost of those institutes for rehabilitation, with all those ceremonially applied hot fomentations, and the debates about whether the affected limbs should be totally immobilized or kept in passive motion as frequently as possible, and the masses of statistically tormented data mobilized to support one view or the other? It is the cost of that kind of technology, and its relative effectiveness, that must be compared with the cost and effectiveness of the vaccine.

Pulmonary tuberculosis had similar episodes in its history. 19 There was a sudden enthusiasm for the surgical removal of infected lung tissue in the early 1950s, and elaborate plans were being made for new and expensive installations for major pulmonary surgery in tuberculosis hospitals, and then INH and streptomycin came along and the hospitals themselves were closed up.

It is when physicians are bogged down by their incomplete 20 technologies, by the innumerable things they are obliged to do in medicine when they lack a clear understanding of disease mechanisms, that the deficiencies of the health-care system are most conspicuous. If I were a policy-maker, interested in saving money for health care over the long haul, I would regard it as an act of high prudence to give high priority to a lot more basic research in biologic science. This is the only way to get the full mileage that biology owes to the science of medicine, even though it seems, as used to be said in the days when the phrase still had some meaning, like asking for the moon.

For Study and Discussion

QUESTIONS ABOUT PURPOSE

1. Is Thomas's primary purpose to explain the various kinds of medical technology or to argue that certain technologies are more useful than others? Explain your answer.

2. What does Thomas demonstrate about the relationship between cost-effective technology and a genuine understanding of the disease mechanism?

QUESTIONS ABOUT AUDIENCE

1. How does Thomas's assertion that policy makers are interested in "how to deliver today's kind of health care, with equity, to all the people," suggest that he is aware of his readers' interest in the issue he will discuss?
2. To what extent does Thomas assume that his readers are familiar with the diseases he uses to illustrate each category? How does he provide assistance to his readers when the disease may be unfamiliar? See, for example, his discussion of typhoid fever in paragraph 18.

QUESTIONS ABOUT STRATEGIES

1. How does Thomas's definition of his three categories— nontechnology, halfway technology, and effective technology— clarify the single principle he has used to establish his classification system?
2. How does Thomas's discussion of specific diseases demonstrate that his divisions are complete? What aspect of his system enables him to discuss cancer as an illustration in two categories?

For Writing and Research

1. *Analyze* how Thomas uses the word *technology* to classify various medical treatments.
2. *Practice* by classifying the emotional reactions you have felt when you have had various kinds of medical tests.
3. *Argue* that the best solution to the problem of illness is wellness—that is, eating carefully, exercising regularly, and avoiding dangerous addictions such as smoking.
4. *Synthesize* the research on diseases Thomas does not mention, diseases such as AIDS or SARS. Explain where such a disease would fit into his classification system.

LOUIS KRONENBERGER

Louis Kronenberger (1904–1980) was born in Cincinnati, Ohio, and attended the University of Cincinnati. He started working as a book editor for Boni & Liveright publishers, transferred to a similar position at Alfred A. Knopf, and then began a career as an editor for magazines such as *Fortune* and *Time*. For intermittent periods, he accepted appointments as a visiting professor of English at the following distinguished universities: Columbia, Brandeis, Oxford, Harvard, Princeton, and Stanford. Kronenberger used his editorial skills to compile numerous anthologies, including *An Anthology of Light Verse* (1935), *The Portable Johnson and Boswell* (1947), and *Novelists on Novelists* (1962). His own writing is highlighted by books such as *The Thread of Laughter* (1952), *A Month of Sundays* (1961), and *Extraordinary Mr. Wilkes: His Life and Times* (1975). In "Cranks, Eccentrics, and Individuals," excerpted from one of his best-known collections of essays, *Company Manners* (1954), Kronenberger divides a familiar American type— the nonconformist—into three distinct categories.

Cranks, Eccentrics, and Individuals[3]

I SUSPECT . . . that the American distaste for individualism is partly due to our past forms of moral nonconformity, to our early crop of militant puritans and cranks. In pioneer days

1

---

it must have often seemed as though cantankerousness were next to godliness. Our fetish of the good guy may well owe something to our inherited fear of the Puritan; the backslapper may well be a retort upon the bluenose; it has perhaps required all of the American dream to blot out the Early American nightmare. And once dissent has become associated with disapproval of all normal pleasures, clearly the inducements of a conformist society will prove very great; and the accompanying good-guy psychology will in time prove quite decisive. Even now, to be sure, a sense of guilt pervades the professional classes, the intellectual and quasi-intellectual world, though this is a sense of guilt derived from Freud rather than Jonathan Edwards. Something remains, of course, of the old New England conscience—and with it, quite admirably, something of the old New England character. But in general we are today a people who much less fear God than hate themselves. Moreover, where our current guilts aren't Freudian, they seem rather Catholic than Protestant—rather the Catholic puritanism of Ireland than the Congregationalist puritanism of New England. What dominates, in any case, is much less guilt than self-righteousness, much less breast-beating than backslapping. Even the clergyman—whether priest, minister or rabbi—does well to prove a good mixer, the church or synagogue to stress its clubroom and recreation hall. America possesses a few, but only a few, truly august figures, whether real or symbolic; the others best flourish by blending authority with affability. In all of this there is a sound desire to avoid the pompous: nothing delights us more than to find that the President of our country, or of our college, or of our corporation, is really one of the boys. This seems to me a valuable trait, a real safeguard against Communist or Fascist blandishments; we want our leaders to display the human touch.

Our well-founded distaste for cranks has, however, rather blurred our ability to tell a crank from a mere eccentric, or even an eccentric from an individual. On a very rough-and-ready basis we might define an eccentric as a man who is a law unto himself, and crank as one who, having determined what

the law is, insists on laying it down to others. An eccentric*
puts ice cream on steak simply because he likes it; should a
crank do so, he would endow the act with moral grandeur
and straightway denounce as sinners (or reactionaries) all who
failed to follow suit. The crank, however, seldom deals in anything so agreeable as steak or ice cream; the crank prefers the
glories of health bread or the splendors of soybeans. Cranks,
at their most familiar, are a sort of peevish prophets, and it's
not enough that they should be in the right; others must also
be in the wrong. They are by definition obsessed, and, by connotation, obsessed with something odd. They mistake the part
for the whole, the props for the play, the inconvenience for the
efficacy; they are spoilsport humanitarians, full of the sour milk
of human kindness.†

The crank is for several reasons a fairly common figure in   3
American life. To begin with, our reaction against cranks has
helped breed more of them. A society that worships good-
guyism brands the mere dissenter a misfit, and people who
are shunned as square pegs will soon find something deeply
immoral about round holes. A society, again, that runs to
fads and crazes, that has a natural turn for the ingenious and
inventive, will encourage some of its members to be cranks
and will doom others. There must be, so to speak, lots of
factory-damaged human products that, from being looked
upon as rejects, come to crankhood rather than true creativity. Careerwise, there is frequently a missed-the-boat quality
in cranks, a psychological origin for their moral obsessive-
ness; and their "flourishing" off failure is tied up with their

---

*Many "eccentrics" are, of course, mere poseurs and publicity seekers. But
many are real, and I speak here only of such.

†They can be useful, at moments even invaluable, goads; but they fail of love
no less than of humor, and seem most ready to plow the earth where they
can spoil the lawn. John the Baptist *requires* the wilderness, and even a man
of the critical excellence of Mr. F. R. Leavis evokes the workhouse. After
all the gush of the Janeites, Mr. and Mrs. Leavis are well worth hearing on
Jane Austen; but they, in the end, misrepresent her no less. They are the
sort of people who, in assessing champagne, would give no consideration
to the fizz.

having failed at the outset. The crank not only increasingly harangues his audience, but the audience increasingly yawns at, and even walks out on, the crank.*

Where a crank is either a moral crusader by nature or a man at war with his surroundings, an eccentric is neither given to crusading nor oppressed by the world. Perhaps a certain amount of enjoyment is essential to the eccentric—his life is satisfactory *because* it is pleasant—as a certain lack of enjoyment is essential to the crank. The great blessing of eccentricity is that, since it is a law unto itself, one isn't constantly torn between what is expedient on the one side and what is personally desirable on the other. Something of an anarchist (as your crank is something of a bigot), the eccentric will often display very unsound, or unsocial, habits and beliefs. But there is nothing self-righteous about his wrongheadedness; he doesn't drag God into keeping a pet leopard in his back yard, or Americanism into going in for rifle practice at 2:00 A.M.

True eccentrics, I would think, are fairly rare, for they must not only differ from other people but be quite indifferent to other peoples' ways: they must, in other words, be as well adjusted as they are odd. So soon as maladjustment enters in, they cease to be characters and turn into cases. On the other hand, many people who with a little encouragement might emerge as eccentrics are, from childhood on, judged— and hence turned into—misfits. Where their peculiarities are mocked, and certainly where they are penalized, the results can be very unhappy. In America, where even the slightest individualist must resist great pressure, the true eccentric is never free from it. In England there is a proud tradition of eccentricity: the English are far more given than we are to

---

*Just as many eccentrics are poseurs, so many cranks are charlatans. The charlatan shrewdly exploits human weakness where the true crank rails against it; the charlatan, preaching some form of nudism or trial marriage, some "holy" brand of licentiousness or God-sent type of laxative, may end up a millionaire. But the true crank has only a chip on his shoulder or bee in his bonnet, not a card up his sleeve.

keeping strange pets, collecting strange objects, pursuing strange hobbies, adopting strange careers; even where they most conform, as in their club life, they will behave toward one another with what, to other races, seems a wild and splendid strangeness. This is so true that England's—and sometimes New England's—eccentrics have often a great air about them, possess style rather than mere singularity. Consider how Julia Margaret Cameron would walk the two miles from her house to the railway station stirring a cup of tea as she went. In England and New England on the one hand, and in most of America on the other, there may be a quite opposite basis for eccentricity: in the one case, the law unto oneself born of social privilege; in the other, the self-made world born of being left out of things. The English eccentric suggests a grande dame, the American a spinster.

The individualist is by no means an eccentric. He is for one thing aware of alternatives; he chooses—for the most part consciously—between the expedient and the self-satisfying; he refuses to play ball rather than doesn't know a game is in progress; and he will seldom seem freakish or even picturesque. Yet, more and more, the individualist is being looked on as an eccentric and perhaps even a crank: though this attitude is scarcely deliberate on the public's part, it yet subconsciously—or by force of repetition—constitutes a gimmick, a pressure to make people conform. The other method of diminishing individualism in America has been to foster and develop "personality." Though the difference between "personality" and individuality is vast, there exists a strong, however thoughtless, tendency to identify the one with the other. So greatly has conformity triumphed that, no matter how orthodox a man's opinions or conventional his behavior, if he happens to express or conduct himself with the slightest vividness or briskness, he is rated and touted a "person"—what might be supposed an individual! Actually, he may not even have an iota of real personality, may just possess a breezy, adaptable, quick-on-the-trigger manner that enables him to be the life of the party or the spark plug of the conference. In the same way, a woman with a gift for dinner-party chatter and a feminine, discreetly flirtatious air will be thought to have enormous personality.

And though such mere types must be written off, there 7 yet *are* a great many Americans with true personality—with an easy charm, a distinctive way of doing and saying things, a regional tang, a surviving girlishness or small-boy quality. They have the appeal, at the very least, of not being like everyone else. But that, in the cliché sense, they are "real persons" is to be doubted. One may go a year without hearing them utter an original, not to say controversial, remark, or seeing them perform a striking, not to say truly unorthodox, act. The centrifugal and extrovert charm of personality is in many ways hostile to individualism, which more naturally manifests itself in withdrawal than in contact, in quiet dissent than in eager acquiescence. Personality and individuality are by no means mutually exclusive, nor is genuine personality necessarily engaging nor genuine individuality necessarily difficult. But the fact remains that we regard personality as a decided blessing, as something a man can't have too much of, and individuality as, oftener than not, a handicap. Individuality is almost by definition antisocial; and the sound "social" maneuver—or it were perhaps better called instinct—is to discredit individuality and eventually outlaw it through enabling people to live *colorfully* alike. As for "personality," it has passed from having great social to acquiring great economic importance: it is the prime mark, and prize asset, of the salesman. And ours is the country where, in order to sell your product, you don't so much point out its merits as you first work like hell to sell yourself.

For Study and Discussion

QUESTIONS ABOUT PURPOSE

1. Why does Kronenberger begin his essay by tracing "the American distaste for individualism"?
2. Why does he object to the "good guy psychology"?

1. What prejudices does Kronenberger suspect his readers have about cranks, eccentrics, and individuals?
2. What preferences does he assume his readers have about those who "display the human touch"?

1. How does Kronenberger use concrete examples to classify his various types?
2. How many subcategories (poseur, charlatan, personality) does he introduce into his analysis? How does he include or exclude them from his three principal categories?

For Writing and Research

1. *Analyze* the way Kronenberger explains the similarities and difference between *individuality* and *personality.*
2. *Practice* by classifying and illustrating various subcategories of "good guys."
3. *Argue* that America also has a "proud tradition" of *eccentricity.*
4. *Synthesize:* Make a list of contemporary public figures who fit into Kronenberger's categories. Research their biographies for details that will help you write an essay that supports his argument.

David Cole was born in 1958 and educated at Yale University. He has worked as an attorney for the Center for Constitutional Rights, taught at Georgetown Law School, and served as legal correspondent for *The Nation* and legal commentator on *All Things Considered* on National Public Radio. His books include *No Equal Justice: Race and Class in the American Criminal Justice System* (1999), *Enemy Aliens: Double Standards and Constitutional Freedoms in the War on Terrorism* (2003), and (with Jules Lobel) *Less Safe, Less Free: Why America Is Losing the War on Terror* (2007). In "Five Myths About Immigration," reprinted from *The Nation*, Cole classifies the myths that "distort public debate and government policy relating to immigrants."

Five Myths About Immigration[4]

F OR A BRIEF PERIOD in the mid-nineteenth century, a new political movement captured the passions of the American public. Fittingly labeled the "Know-Nothings," their unifying theme was nativism. They liked to call themselves "Native Americans," although they had no sympathy for people we call Native Americans today. And they pinned every problem in American society on immigrants. As one Know-Nothing wrote in 1856: "Four-fifths of the beggary and three-fifths of the crime spring from our foreign population; more than half the public charities, more than half the prisons and almshouses, more than half the police and the cost of administering criminal justice are for foreigners."

---

[4]David Cole, "Five Myths About Immigration," reprinted with permission from the October 17, 1994, issue of *The Nation*. For subscription information, call 1-800-333-8536. Portions of each week's *Nation* magazine can be accessed at http://www.thenation.com.

227

At the time, the greatest influx of immigrants was from   2
Ireland, where the potato famine had struck, and Germany,
which was in political and economic turmoil. Anti-alien and
anti-Catholic sentiments were the order of the day, especially
in New York and Massachusetts, which received the brunt of
the wave of immigrants, many of whom were dirt-poor and
uneducated. Politicians were quick to exploit the sentiment:
There's nothing like a scapegoat to forge an alliance.

I am especially sensitive to this history: My forebears were   3
among those dirt-poor Irish Catholics who arrived in the
1860s. Fortunately for them, and me, the Know-Nothing
movement fizzled within fifteen years. But its pilot light kept
burning, and is turned up whenever the American public
begins to feel vulnerable and in need of an enemy.

Although they go by different names today, the Know-   4
Nothings have returned. As in the 1850s, the movement is
strongest where immigrants are most concentrated: California and Florida. The objects of prejudice are of course no longer Irish Catholics and Germans; 140 years later, "they" have
become "us." The new "they"—because it seems "we" must
always have a "they"—are Latin Americans (most recently,
Cubans), Haitians, and Arab-Americans, among others.

But just as in the 1850s, passion, misinformation and   5
shortsighted fear often substitute for reason, fairness, and
human dignity in today's immigration debates. In the interest of advancing beyond know-nothingism, let's look at five
current myths that distort public debate and government
policy relating to immigrants.

[P]assion, misinformation and shortsighted
fear often substitute for reason, fairness
and human dignity in today's
immigration debates.

America is being overrun with immigrants. In one sense,   6
of course, this is true, but in that sense it has been true since
Christopher Columbus arrived. Except for the real Native
Americans, we are a nation of immigrants.

It is not true, however, that the first-generation immigrant 7
share of our population is growing. As of 1990, foreign-born
people made up only 8 percent of the population, as compared with a figure of about 15 percent from 1870 to 1920.
Between 70 and 80 percent of those who immigrate every
year are refugees or immediate relatives of U.S. citizens.

Much of the anti-immigrant fervor is directed against the 8
undocumented, but they make up only 13 percent of all
immigrants residing in the United States, and only 1 percent
of the American population. Contrary to popular belief, most
such aliens do not cross the border illegally but enter legally
and remain after their student or visitor visa expires. Thus,
building a wall at the border, no matter how high, will not
solve the problem.

Immigrants take jobs from U.S. citizens. There is virtually no 9
evidence to support this view, probably the most widespread
misunderstanding about immigrants. As documented by a
1994 A.C.L.U. Immigrants' Rights Project report, numerous
studies have found that immigrants actually *create* more jobs
than they fill. The jobs immigrants take are of course easier to
see, but immigrants are often highly productive, run their own
businesses, and employ both immigrants and citizens. One
study found that Mexican immigration to Los Angeles County
between 1970 and 1980 was responsible for 78,000 new jobs.
Governor Mario Cuomo reports that immigrants own more
than 40,000 companies in New York, which provide thousands
of jobs and $3.5 billion to the state's economy every year.

Immigrants are a drain on society's resources. This claim 10
fuels many of the recent efforts to cut off government benefits to immigrants. However, most studies have found that
immigrants are a net benefit to the economy because, as a
1994 Urban Institute report concludes, "immigrants generate significantly more in taxes paid than they cost in services
received." The Council of Economic Advisers similarly found
in 1986 that "immigrants have a favorable effect on the overall standard of living."

Anti-immigrant advocates often cite studies purportedly 11
showing the contrary, but these generally focus only on taxes
and services at the local or state level. What they fail to explain

is that because most taxes go to the federal government, such studies would also show a net loss when applied to U.S. citizens. At most, such figures suggest that some redistribution of federal and state monies may be appropriate; they say nothing unique about the costs of immigrants.

Some subgroups of immigrants plainly impose a net cost in 12 the short run, principally those who have most recently arrived and have not yet "made it." California, for example, bears substantial costs for its disproportionately large undocumented population, largely because it has on average the poorest and least educated immigrants. But that has been true of every wave of immigrants that has ever reached our shores; it was as true of the Irish in the 1850s, for example, as it is of Salvadorans today. From a long-term perspective, the economic advantages of immigration are undeniable.

Some have suggested that we might save money and 13 diminish incentives to immigrate illegally if we denied undocumented aliens public services. In fact, undocumented immigrants are already ineligible for most social programs, with the exception of education for schoolchildren, which is constitutionally required, and benefits directly related to health and safety, such as emergency medical care and nutritional assistance to poor women, infants, and children. To deny such basic care to people in need, apart from being inhumanly callous, would probably cost us more in the long run by exacerbating health problems that we would eventually have to address.

Aliens refuse to assimilate, and are depriving us of our cul- 14 *tural and political unity.* This claim has been made about every new group of immigrants to arrive on U.S. shores. Supreme Court Justice Stephen Field wrote in 1884 that the Chinese "have remained among us a separate people, retaining their original peculiarities of dress, manners, habits, and modes of living, which are as marked as their complexion and language." Five years later, he upheld the racially based exclusion of Chinese immigrants. Similar claims have been made over different periods of our history about Catholics, Jews, Italians, Eastern Europeans, and Latin Americans.

In most instances, such claims are simply not true; "Ameri- 15
can culture" has been created, defined, and revised by persons
who for the most part are descended from immigrants once
seen as anti-assimilationist. Descendants of the Irish Catholics,
for example, a group once decried as separatist and alien, have
become Presidents, senators, and representatives (and all of these
in one family, in the case of the Kennedys). Our society exerts
tremendous pressure to conform, and cultural separatism rarely
survives a generation. But more important, even if this claim
were true, is this a legitimate rationale for limiting immigration
in a society built on the values of pluralism and tolerance?

Noncitizen immigrants are not entitled to constitutional 16
rights. Our government has long declined to treat immigrants as full human beings, and nowhere is that more clear
than in the realm of constitutional rights. Although the Constitution literally extends the fundamental protections in the
Bill of Rights to all people, limiting to citizens only the right
to vote and run for federal office, the federal government acts
as if this were not the case.

In 1893 the executive branch successfully defended a stat- 17
ute that required Chinese laborers to establish their prior residence here by the testimony of "at least one credible white
witness." The Supreme Court ruled that this law was constitutional because it was reasonable for Congress to presume
that non-white witnesses could not be trusted.

The federal government is not much more enlightened 18
today. In a pending case I'm handling in the Court of
Appeals for the Ninth Circuit, the Clinton Administration
has argued that permanent resident aliens lawfully living here
should be extended no more First Amendment rights than
aliens applying for first-time admission from abroad—that is,
none. Under this view, students at a public university who
are citizens may express themselves freely, but students who
are not citizens can be deported for saying exactly what their
classmates are constitutionally entitled to say.

Growing up, I was always taught that we will be judged by 19
how we treat others. If we are collectively judged by how we
have treated immigrants—those who would appear today to

be "other" but will in a generation be "us"—we are not in very good shape.

For Study and Discussion

QUESTIONS ABOUT PURPOSE

1. Why does Cole begin his essay with a discussion of the "Know-Nothing" political movement?
2. Why does he describe his categories as *myths* rather than errors or mistakes?

QUESTIONS ABOUT AUDIENCE

1. How does Cole use his own family history to establish a connection with his readers?
2. How does he address his readers who may favor the anti-immigrant position?

QUESTIONS ABOUT STRATEGIES

1. What kind of evidence does Cole use to dispute each of the five myths?
2. How does he use his last paragraph to bring his analysis to an appropriate conclusion?

For Writing and Research

1. *Analyze* the evidence Cole uses to assert the long-term economic advantages of immigration.
2. *Practice* by classifying several *myths* about a specific group of immigrants in your community.
3. *Argue* that there is some justification for the assertion that immigrants resist—or at least have great difficulty—assimilating into American culture.
4. *Synthesize:* Research the immigration history of your family. Then use this information to help explain why certain generations of your family seemed to support or refute one of Cole's myths.

MALCOLM GLADWELL

Malcolm Gladwell was born in 1963 in England, grew up in Canada, and graduated with a degree in history from the University of Toronto. He has worked at the *Washington Post,* first as a science writer and then as New York City bureau chief. He is currently a staff writer for the *New Yorker,* where he has written on a range of issues concerning media, education and business. His books include *The Tipping Point: How Little Things Make a Big Difference* (2000), *Blink* (2005), *Outliers* (2008), and *What the Dog Saw* (2009). In "The Order of Things," reprinted from the *New Yorker,* Gladwell points out the defects in several famous ranking systems.

The Order of Things[5]
What college ranking really tell us

L AST SUMMER, the editors of *Car and Driver* conducted   1
a comparison test of three sports cars, the Lotus Evora, the Chevrolet Corvette Grand Sport, and the Porsche Cayman S. The cars were taken on an extended run through mountain passes in Southern California, and from there to a race track north of Los Angeles, for precise measurements of performance and handling. The results of the road tests were then tabulated according to a twenty-one-variable, two-hundred-and-thirty-five-point rating system, based on four categories: vehicle (driver comfort, styling, fit and finish, etc.); power train (transmission, engine, and fuel economy); chassis (steering, brakes, ride, and handling); and "fun to drive." The magazine concluded, "The range of these three

---

[5] Malcolm Gladwell, "The Order of Things" *The New Yorker*, February 14 & 21, 2011, pp. 68–75. Reprinted with permission.

cars' driving personalities is as various as the pajama sizes of Papa Bear, Mama Bear, and Baby Bear, but a clear winner emerged nonetheless." This was the final tally:

1. Porsche Cayman 193
2. Chevrolet Corvette 186
3. Lotus Evora 182

Car and Driver is one of the most influential editorial 2 voices in the automotive world. When it says that it likes one car better than another, consumers and carmakers take notice. Yet when you inspect the magazine's tabulations it is hard to figure out why *Car and Driver* was so sure that the Cayman is better than the Corvette and the Evora. The trouble starts with the fact that the ranking methodology *Car and Driver* used was essentially the same one it uses for all the vehicles it tests—from S.U.V.s to economy sedans. It's not set up for sports cars. Exterior styling, for example, counts for four per cent of the total score. Has anyone buying a sports car ever placed so little value on how it looks? Similarly, the categories of "fun to drive" and "chassis"—which cover the subjective experience of driving the car—count for only eighty-five points out of the total of two hundred and thirty-five. That may make sense for S.U.V. buyers. But, for people interested in Porsches and Corvettes and Lotuses, the subjective experience of driving is surely what matters most. In other words, in trying to come up with a ranking that is heterogeneous—a methodology that is broad enough to cover *all* vehicles— *Car and Driver* ended up with a system that is absurdly ill-suited to some vehicles.

Suppose that *Car and Driver* decided to tailor its grad- 3 ing system just to sports cars. Clearly, styling and the driving experience ought to count for much more. So let's make exterior styling worth twenty-five per cent, the driving experience worth fifty per cent, and the balance of the criteria worth twenty-five per cent. The final tally now looks like this:

1. Lotus Evora 205
2. Porsche Cayman 198
3. Chevrolet Corvette 192

There's another thing funny about the *Car and Driver* 4
system. Price counts only for twenty points, less than ten per cent
of the total. There's no secret why: *Car and Driver* is edited
by auto enthusiasts. To them, the choice of a car is as important as the choice of a home or a spouse, and only a philistine
would let a few dollars stand between him and the car he
wants. (They leave penny-pinching to their frumpy counter-
parts at *Consumer Reports.*) But for most of us price matters,
especially in a case like this, where the Corvette, as tested,
costs $67,565—thirteen thousand dollars less than the
Porsche, and eighteen thousand dollars less than the Lotus.
Even to a car nut, that's a lot of money. So let's imagine
that *Car and Driver* revised its ranking system again, giving a
third of the weight to price, a third to the driving experience,
and a third split equally between exterior styling and vehicle
characteristics. The tally would now be:

1. Chevrolet Corvette 205
2. Lotus Evora 195
3. Porsche Cayman 195

So which is the best car?

Car and Driver's ambition to grade every car in the world 5
according to the same methodology would be fine if it limited itself to a single dimension. A heterogeneous ranking
system works if it focusses just on, say, how much fun a car
is to drive, or how good-looking it is, or how beautifully it
handles. The magazine's ambition to create a comprehensive
ranking system—one that considered cars along twenty-one
variables, each weighted according to a secret sauce cooked
up by the editors—would also be fine, as long as the cars
being compared were truly similar. It's only when one car is
thirteen thousand dollars more than another that juggling
twenty-one variables starts to break down, because you're
faced with the impossible task of deciding how much a difference of that degree ought to matter. A ranking can be
heterogeneous, in other words, as long as it doesn't try to be
too comprehensive. And it can be comprehensive as long as

it doesn't try to measure things that are heterogeneous. But it's an act of real audacity when a ranking system tries to be comprehensive *and* heterogeneous—which is the first thing to keep in mind in any consideration of *U.S. News & World Report's* annual "Best Colleges" guide.

The *U.S. News* rankings are run by Robert Morse, whose   6
six-person team operates out of a small red brick office building in the Georgetown neighborhood of Washington, D.C. Morse is a middle-aged man with gray hair who looks like the prototypical Beltway wonk: rumpled, self-effacing, mildly preppy and sensibly shoed. His office is piled high with the statistical detritus of more than two decades of data collection. When he took on his current job, in the mid-nineteen-eighties, the college guide was little more than an item of service journalism tucked away inside *U.S. News* magazine. Now the weekly print magazine is defunct, but the rankings have taken on a life of their own. In the month that the 2011 rankings came out, the *U.S. News* Web site recorded more than ten million visitors. *U.S. News* has added rankings of graduate programs, law schools, business schools, medical schools, and hospitals—and Morse has become the dean of a burgeoning international rankings industry.

"In the early years, the thing that's happening now would   7
not have been imaginable," Morse says. "This idea of using the rankings as a benchmark, college presidents setting a goal of 'We're going to rise in the *U.S. News* ranking,' as proof of their management, or as proof that they're a better school, that they're a good president. That wasn't on anybody's radar. It was just for consumers."

Over the years, Morse's methodology has steadily evolved.   8
In its current form, it relies on seven weighted variables:

1. Undergraduate academic reputation, 22.5 per cent
2. Graduation and freshman retention rates, 20 per cent
3. Faculty resources, 20 per cent
4. Student selectivity, 15 per cent
5. Financial resources, 10 per cent
6. Graduation rate performance, 7.5 per cent
7. Alumni giving, 5 per cent

From these variables, *U.S. News* generates a score for each 9
institution on a scale of 1 to 100, where Harvard is a 100 and
the University of North Carolina-Greensboro is a 22. Here
is a list of the schools that finished in positions forty-one
through fifty in the 2011 "National University" category:

41. Case Western Reserve, 60
41. Rensselaer Polytechnic Institute, 60
41. University of California-Irvine, 60
41. University of Washington, 60
45. University of Texas-Austin, 59
45. University of Wisconsin-Madison, 59
47. Penn State University-University Park, 58
47. University of Illinois, Urbana-Champaign, 58
47. University of Miami, 58
50. Yeshiva University, 57

This ranking system looks a great deal like the *Car and* 10
Driver methodology. It is heterogeneous. It doesn't just
compare U.C. Irvine, the University of Washington, the
University of Texas-Austin, the University of Wisconsin-
Madison, Penn State, and the University of Illinois, Urbana-
Champaign—all public institutions of roughly the same
size. It aims to compare Penn State—a very large, public,
land-grant university with a low tuition and an economically
diverse student body, set in a rural valley in central Pennsylvania and famous for its football team—with Yeshiva University, a small, expensive, private Jewish university whose
undergraduate program is set on two campuses in Manhattan
(one in mid-town, for the women, and one far uptown, for
the men) and is definitely *not* famous for its football team.

The system is also comprehensive. It doesn't simply com- 11
pare schools along one dimension—the test scores of incoming freshmen, say, or academic reputation. An algorithm
takes a slate of statistics on each college and transforms them
into a single score: it tells us that Penn State is a better school
than Yeshiva by one point. It is easy to see why the *U.S. News*
rankings are so popular. A single score allows us to judge
between entities (like Yeshiva and Penn State) that otherwise
would be impossible to compare. At no point, however, do

the college guides acknowledge the extraordinary difficulty of the task they have set themselves. A comprehensive, heterogeneous ranking system was a stretch for *Car and Driver*— and all it did was rank inanimate objects operated by a single person. The Penn State campus at University Park is a complex institution with dozens of schools and departments, four thousand faculty members, and forty-five thousand students. How on earth does anyone propose to assign a number to something like that?

The first difficulty with rankings is that it can be surprisingly hard to measure the variable you want to rank—even in cases where that variable seems perfectly objective. Consider an extreme example: suicide. Here is a ranking of suicides per hundred thousand people, by country: 12

 1. Belarus, 35.1
 2. Lithuania, 31.5
 3. South Korea, 31.0
 4. Kazakhstan, 26.9
 5. Russia, 26.5
 6. Japan, 24.4
 7. Guyana, 22.9
 8. Ukraine, 22.6
 9. Hungary, 21.8
10. Sri Lanka, 21.6

This list looks straightforward. Yet no self-respecting epidemiologist would look at it and conclude that Belarus has the worst suicide rate in the world, and that Hungary belongs in the top ten. Measuring suicide is just too tricky. It requires someone to make a surmise about the intentions of the deceased at the time of death. In some cases, that's easy. Maybe the victim jumped off the Golden Gate Bridge, or left a note. In most cases, though, there's ambiguity, and different coroners and different cultures vary widely in the way they choose to interpret that ambiguity. In certain places, cause of death is determined by the police, who some believe are more likely to call an ambiguous suicide an accident. In other places, the decision is made by a physician, who may be less likely to do so. In some cultures, suicide is considered 13 so shameful that coroners shy away from that determination, even when it's obvious. A suicide might be called a suicide, a homicide, an accident, or left undetermined. David Phillips, a sociologist at the University of California-San Diego, has argued persuasively that a significant percentage of single-car crashes are probably suicides, and criminologists suggest that a good percentage of civilians killed by police officers are actually cases of "suicide by cop"—instances where someone deliberately provoked deadly force. The reported suicide rate, then, is almost certainly less than the actual suicide rate. But no one knows whether the relationship between those two numbers is the same in every country. And no one knows whether the proxies that we use to estimate the real suicide rate are any good.

"Many, many people who commit suicide by poison 14 have something else wrong with them—let's say the person has cancer—and the death of this person might be listed as primarily associated with cancer, rather than with deliberate poisoning," Phillips says. "Any suicides in that category would be undetectable. Or it is frequently noted that Orthodox Jews have a low recorded suicide rate, as do Catholics. Well, it could be because they have this very solid community and proscriptions against suicide, or because they are unusually embarrassed by suicide and more willing to hide it. The simple answer is nobody knows whether suicide rankings are real."

The *U.S. News* rankings suffer from a serious case of the 15 suicide problem. There's no direct way to measure the quality of an institution—how well a college manages to inform, inspire, and challenge its students. So the *U.S. News* algorithm relies instead on proxies for quality—and the proxies for educational quality turn out to be flimsy at best.

Take the category of "faculty resources," which counts for 16 twenty per cent of an institution's score. "Research shows that the more satisfied students are about their contact with professors," the College Guide's explanation of the category begins, "the more they will learn and the more likely it is they will graduate." That's true. According to educational researchers, arguably the most important variable in a successful college education is a vague but crucial concept called student "engagement"—that is, the extent to which students immerse themselves in the intellectual and social life of their college—and a major component of engagement is the quality of a student's contacts with faculty. As with suicide, the disagreement isn't about *what* we want to measure. So what proxies does *U.S. News* use to measure this elusive dimension of engagement? The explanation goes on:

> We use six factors from the 2009–10 academic year to assess a school's commitment to instruction. Class size has two components, the proportion of classes with fewer than 20 students (30 percent of the faculty resources score) and the proportion with 50 or more students (10 percent of the score). Faculty salary (35 percent) is the average faculty pay, plus benefits, during the 2008–09 and 2009–10 academic years, adjusted for regional differences in the cost of living. . . . We also weigh the proportion of professors with the highest degree in their fields (15 percent), the student-faculty ratio (5 percent), and the proportion of faculty who are full time (5 percent).

This is a puzzling list. Do professors who get paid more 17 money really take their teaching roles more seriously? And why does it matter whether a professor has the highest degree in his or her field? Salaries and degree attainment are known to be predictors of research productivity. But studies show that being oriented toward research has very little to do with being good at teaching. Almost none of the *U.S. News* variables, in fact, seem to be particularly effective proxies for engagement. As the educational researchers Patrick Terenzini and Ernest Pascarella concluded after analyzing twenty-six hundred reports on the effects of college on students:

> After taking into account the characteristics, abilities, and backgrounds students bring with them to

college, we found that how much students grow or change has only inconsistent and, perhaps in a practical sense, trivial relationships with such traditional measures of institutional "quality" as educational expenditures per student, student/faculty ratios, faculty salaries, percentage of faculty with the highest degree in their field, faculty research productivity, size of the library, [or] admissions selectivity.

The reputation score that serves as the most important 18 variable in the *U.S. News* methodology—accounting for 22.5 per cent of a college's final score—isn't any better. Every year, the magazine sends a survey to the country's university and college presidents, provosts, and admissions deans (along with a sampling of high-school guidance counsellors) asking them to grade all the schools in their category on a scale of one to five. Those at national universities, for example, are asked to rank all two hundred and sixty-one other national universities—and Morse says that the typical respondent grades about half of the schools in his or her category. But it's far from clear how any one individual could have insight into that many institutions. In an article published recently in the *Annals of Internal Medicine*, Ashwini Sehgal analyzed *U.S. News's* "Best Hospitals" rankings, which also rely heavily on reputation ratings generated by professional peers. Sehgal put together a list of objective criteria of performance—such as a hospital's mortality rates for various surgical procedures, patient-safety rates, nursing-staffing levels, and key technologies. Then he checked to see how well those measures of performance matched each hospital's reputation rating. The answer, he discovered, was that they didn't. Having good outcomes doesn't translate into being admired by other doctors. Why, after all, should a gastroenterologist at the Ochsner Medical Center, in New Orleans, have any specific insight into the performance of the gastroenterology department at Mass General, in Boston, or even, for that matter, have anything more than an anecdotal impression of the gastroenterology department down the road at some hospital in Baton Rouge?

Some years ago, similarly, a former chief justice of the 19 Michigan supreme court, Thomas Brennan, sent a question-naire to a hundred or so of his fellow-lawyers, asking them to rank a list of ten law schools in order of quality. "They included a good sample of the big names. Harvard. Yale. University of Michigan. And some lesser-known schools. John Marshall. Thomas Cooley," Brennan wrote. "As I recall, they ranked Penn State's law school right about in the middle of the pack. Maybe fifth among the ten schools listed. Of course, Penn State doesn't have a law school."

Those lawyers put Penn State in the middle of the pack, 20 even though every fact they thought they knew about Penn State's law school was an illusion, because in their minds Penn State is a middle-of-the-pack brand. (Penn State does have a law school today, by the way.) Sound judgments of educa-tional quality have to be based on specific, hard-to-observe features. But reputational ratings are simply inferences from broad, readily observable features of an institution's identity, such as its history, its prominence in the media, or the ele-gance of its architecture. They are prejudices.

And where do these kinds of reputational prejudices come 21 from? According to Michael Bastedo, an educational sociolo-gist at the University of Michigan who has published widely on the *U.S. News* methodology, "rankings drive reputation." In other words, when *U.S. News* asks a university president to perform the impossible task of assessing the relative merits of dozens of institutions he knows nothing about, he relies on the only source of detailed information at his disposal that assesses the relative merits of dozens of institutions he knows nothing about: *U.S. News.* A school like Penn State, then, can do little to improve its position. To go higher than forty-seventh, it needs a better reputation score, and to get a bet-ter reputation score it needs to be higher than forty-seventh. The *U.S. News* ratings are a self-fulfilling prophecy.

Bastedo, incidentally, says that reputation ratings can 22 sometimes work very well. It makes sense, for example, to ask professors within a field to rate others in their field: they read one another's work, attend the same conferences, and hire one another's graduate students, so they have real knowledge on which to base an opinion. Reputation scores can work for one-dimensional rankings, created by people with specialized knowledge. For instance, the *Wall Street Journal* has ranked colleges according to the opinions of corporate recruiters. Those opinions are more than a proxy. To the extent that people chose one college over another to enhance their prospects in the corporate job markets, the reputation rankings of corporate recruiters are of direct relevance. The No. 1 school in the *Wall Street Journal's* corporate recruiter's ranking, by the way, is Penn State.

For several years, Jeffrey Stake, a professor at the Indiana   23 University law school, has run a Web site called the Ranking Game. It contains a spreadsheet loaded with statistics on every law school in the country, and allows users to pick their own criteria, assign their own weights, and construct any ranking system they want.

Stake's intention is to demonstrate just how subjective   24 rankings are, to show how determinations of "quality" turn on relatively arbitrary judgments about how much different variables should be weighted. For example, his site makes it easy to mimic the *U.S. News* rankings. All you have to do is give equal weight to "academic reputation," "LSAT scores at the 75th percentile," "student-faculty ratio," and "faculty law-review publishing," and you get a list of élite schools which looks similar to the *U.S. News* law-school rankings:

1. University of Chicago
2. Yale University
3. Harvard University
4. Stanford University
5. Columbia University
6. Northwestern University
7. Cornell University
8. University of Pennsylvania
9. New York University
10. University of California, Berkeley

There's something missing from that list of variables, of 25
course: it doesn't include price. That is one of the most distinctive features of the *U.S. News* methodology. Both its college rankings and its law-school rankings reward schools for
devoting lots of financial resources to educating their students, but not for being affordable. Why? Morse admitted
that there was no formal reason for that position. It was just a
feeling. "We're not saying that we're measuring educational
outcomes," he explained. "We're not saying we're social scientists, or we're subjecting our rankings to some peer-review
process. We're just saying we've made this judgment. We're
saying we've interviewed a lot of experts, we've developed
these academic indicators, and we think these measures measure quality schools."

As answers go, that's up there with the parental "Because 26
I said so." But Morse is simply being honest. If we don't
understand what the right proxies for college quality are,
let alone how to represent those proxies in a comprehensive, heterogeneous grading system, then our rankings are
inherently arbitrary. All Morse was saying was that, on the
question of price, he comes down on the *Car and Driver*
side of things, not on the *Consumer Reports* side. *U.S. News*
thinks that schools that spend a lot of money on their students are nicer than those that don't, and that this niceness
ought to be factored into the equation of desirability. Plenty
of Americans agree: the campus of Vanderbilt University
or Williams College is filled with students whose families
are largely indifferent to the price their school charges but
keenly interested in the flower beds and the spacious suites
and the architecturally distinguished lecture halls those high
prices make possible.

Of course, given that the rising cost of college has become 27
a significant social problem in the United States in recent
years, you can make a strong case that a school ought to
be rewarded for being affordable. So suppose we go back
to Stake's ranking game, and re-rank law schools based on
student-faculty ratio, L.S.A.T. scores at the seventy-fifth

percentile, faculty publishing, and price, all weighted equally. The list now looks like this:

1. University of Chicago
2. Yale University
3. Harvard University
4. Stanford University
5. Northwestern University
6. Brigham Young University
7. Cornell University
8. University of Colorado
9. University of Pennsylvania
10. Columbia University

The revised ranking tells us that there are schools—like 28 B.Y.U. and Colorado—that provide a good legal education at a decent price, and that, by choosing not to include tuition as a variable, *U.S. News* has effectively penalized those schools for trying to provide value for the tuition dollar. But that's a very subtle tweak. Let's say that value for the dollar is something we really care about. And so what we want is a three-factor ranking, counting value for the dollar at forty per cent, L.S.A.T. scores at forty per cent of the total, and faculty publishing at twenty per cent. Look at how the top ten changes:

1. University of Chicago
2. Brigham Young University
3. Harvard University
4. Yale University
5. University of Texas
6. University of Virginia
7. University of Colorado
8. University of Alabama
9. Stanford University
10. University of Pennsylvania

Welcome to the big time, Alabama!

The *U.S. News* rankings turn out to be full of these kinds 29 of implicit ideological choices. One common statistic used to evaluate colleges, for example, is called "graduation rate performance," which compares a school's actual graduation rate with its predicted graduation rate given the socioeconomic status and the test scores of its incoming freshman class. It is a measure of the school's efficacy: it quantifies the impact of a school's culture and teachers and institutional support mechanisms. Tulane, given the qualifications of the students that it admits, ought to have a graduation rate of eighty-seven per cent; its actual 2009 graduation rate was seventy-three per cent. That shortfall suggests that something is amiss at Tulane.

Another common statistic for measuring college quality   30
is "student selectivity." This reflects variables such as how many of a college's freshmen were in the top ten per cent of their high-school class, how high their S.A.T. scores were, and what percentage of applicants a college admits. Selectivity quantifies how accomplished students are when they first arrive on campus.

Each of these statistics matters, but for very different rea-   31
sons. As a society, we probably care more about efficacy: America's future depends on colleges that make sure the students they admit leave with an education and a degree. If you are a bright high-school senior and you're thinking about your own future, though, you may well care more about selectivity, because that relates to the prestige of your degree.

But no institution can excel at both. The national univer-   32
sity that ranks No. 1 in selectivity is Yale. A crucial part of what it considers its educational function is to assemble the most gifted group of freshmen it can. Because it maximizes selectivity, though, Yale will never do well on an efficacy scale. Its freshmen are so accomplished that they have a predicted graduation rate of ninety-six per cent: the highest Yale's efficacy score could be is plus four. (It's actually plus two.) Of the top fifty national universities in the "Best Colleges" ranking, the least selective school is Penn State. Penn State sees its educational function as serving a wide range of students. That gives it the opportunity to excel at efficacy—and it does so brilliantly. Penn State's freshmen have an expected graduation rate of seventy-three per cent and an actual graduation rate of eighty-five per cent, for a score of plus twelve: no other school in the *U.S. News* top fifty comes close.

There is no *right* answer to how much weight a ranking   33
system should give to these two competing values. It's a matter of which educational model you value more—and here,
once again, *U.S. News* makes its position clear. It gives twice
as much weight to selectivity as it does to efficacy. It favors
the Yale model over the Penn State model, which means that
the Yales of the world will always succeed at the *U.S. News*
rankings because the *U.S. News* system is designed to reward
Yale-ness. By contrast, to the extent that Penn State succeeds
at doing a better job of being Penn State—of attracting a
diverse group of students and educating them capably—it
will only do worse. Rankings are not benign. They enshrine
very particular ideologies, and, at a time when American
higher education is facing a crisis of accessibility and afford-
ability, we have adopted a de-facto standard of college quality that is uninterested in both of those factors. And why?
Because a group of magazine analysts in an office building in
Washington, D.C., decided twenty years ago to value selectivity over efficacy, to use proxies that scarcely relate to what
they're meant to be proxies for, and to pretend that they
can compare a large, diverse, low-cost land-grant university
in rural Pennsylvania with a small, expensive, private Jewish
university on two campuses in Manhattan.

"If you look at the top twenty schools every year, forever,   34
they are all wealthy private universities," Graham Spanier,
the president of Penn State, told me. "Do you mean that
even the most prestigious public universities in the United
States, and you can take your pick of what you think they
are—Berkeley, U.C.L.A., University of Michigan, University
of Wisconsin, Illinois, Penn State, U.N.C.—do you mean to
say that not one of those is in the top tier of institutions? It
doesn't really make sense, until you drill down into the rankings, and what do you find? What I find more than anything
else is a measure of wealth: institutional wealth, how big is
your endowment, what percentage of alumni are donating
each year, what are your faculty salaries, how much are you
spending per student. Penn State may very well be the most
popular university in America—we get a hundred and fifteen

thousand applications a year for admission. We serve a lot of people. Nearly a third of them are the first people in their entire family network to come to college. We have seventy-six per cent of our students receiving financial aid. There is no possibility that we could do anything here at this university to get ourselves into the top ten or twenty or thirty—except if some donor gave us billions of dollars."

In the fall of 1913, the prominent American geographer   35
Ellsworth Huntington sent a letter to two hundred and thir-teen scholars from twenty-seven countries. "May I ask your cooperation in the preparation of a map showing the distri-bution of the higher elements of civilization throughout the world?" Huntington began, and he continued:

> My purpose is to prepare a map which shall show
> the distribution of those characteristics which are
> generally recognized as of the highest value. I
> mean by this the power of initiative, the capacity
> for formulating new ideas and for carrying them
> into effect, the power of self-control, high stan-
> dards of honesty and morality, the power to lead
> and to control other races, the capacity for dis-
> seminating ideas, and other similar qualities which
> will readily suggest themselves.

Each contributor was given a list of a hundred and eighty-   36
five of the world's regions—ranging from the Amur district of Siberia to the Kalahari Desert—with instructions to give each region a score of one to ten. The scores would then be summed and converted to a scale of one to a hundred. The rules were strict. The past could not be considered: Greece could not be given credit for its ancient glories. "If two races inhabit a given region," Huntington specified further, both must be considered, and the rank of the region must depend upon the average of the two." The reputation of immigrants could be used toward the score of their country of origin, but only those of the first generation. And size and commer-cial significance should be held constant: the Scots should not suffer relative to, say, the English, just because they were less

populous. Huntington's respondents took on the task with the utmost seriousness. "One appreciates what a big world this is and how little one knows about it when he attempts such a task as you have set," a respondent wrote back to Huntington. "It is a most excellent means of taking the conceit out of one." England and Wales and the North Atlantic states of America scored a perfect hundred, with central and northwestern Germany and New England coming in at ninety-nine.

Huntington then requested from the twenty-five of his correspondents who were Americans an in-depth ranking of the constituent regions of the United States. This time, he proposed a six-point scale. Southern Alaska, in this second reckoning, was last, at 1.5, followed by Arizona and New Mexico, at 1.6. The winners: Massachusetts, at 6.0, followed by Connecticut, Rhode Island, and New York, at 5.8. The citadel of American civilization was New England and New York, Huntington concluded, in his magisterial 1915 work "Civilization and Climate." [37]

In case you are wondering, Ellsworth Huntington was a professor of geography at Yale, in New Haven, Connecticut. "Civilization and Climate" was published by Yale University Press, and the book's appendix contains a list of Huntington's American correspondents, of which the following bear special mention: [38]

J. Barrell, geologist, New Haven, Conn.
P. Bigelow, traveler and author, Malden, N.Y.
I. Bowman, geographer, New York City
W. M. Brown, geographer, Providence, R.I.
A. C. Coolidge, historian, Cambridge, Mass.
S. W. Cushing, geographer, Salem, Mass.
L. Farrand, anthropologist, New York City
C. W. Furlong, traveler and author, Boston, Mass.
E. W. Griffis, traveler and author, Ithaca, N.Y.
A. G. Keller, anthropologist, New Haven, Conn.
E. F. Merriam, editor, Boston, Mass.
J. R. Smith, economic geographer, Philadelphia, Pa.
Anonymous, New York City

"In spite of several attempts I was unable to obtain any   39
contributor in the states west of Minnesota or south of the
Ohio River," Huntington explains, as if it were a side issue.
It isn't, of course—not then and not now. Who comes out
on top, in any ranking system, is really about who is doing
the ranking.

---

*Who comes out on top, in any ranking
system, is really about who is doing
the ranking.*

For Study and Discussion

QUESTIONS ABOUT PURPOSE

1. Why does Gladwell think *Car and Driver*'s testing system is
   defective?
2. Why does he think the system *U.S. News* uses to rank colleges is
   inconsistent?

QUESTIONS ABOUT AUDIENCE

1. How does Gladwell use suicide rates to help his readers understand the difficulty of using one variable to classify information
   in one category?
2. How does he use the example of law schools to help his readers
   understand the problem of reputation?

QUESTIONS ABOUT STRATEGIES

1. How does Gladwell illustrate the "self-fulfilling prophecy" of
   reputation and ranking?
2. How does he use the Yale model and the Penn State model to
   illustrate the problem of classifying the quality of an education?

For Writing and Research

1. *Analyze* the division and classification defects Gladwell explains in one of the ranking systems he describes.
2. *Practice* by classifying and ranking various brands of a consumer product with which you are familiar—such as cell phones or electronic readers.
3. *Argue* that a major ranking system—such as the system that ranks college football teams—has serious flaws. Then suggest a more efficient alternative ranking system.
4. *Synthesize:* Research the names, positions, and other relevant information about the rankers who have been asked to participate in a system that ranks people, college, companies, and so forth. Then use this information to prove or disprove Gladwell's conclusion: "Who comes out on top, in any ranking system, is really about who is doing the ranking."

Flannery O'Connor (1925–1964) was born in
Savannah, Georgia, and was educated at the
Women's College of Georgia and the University of Iowa. She returned to her mother's farm
near Milledgeville, Georgia, when she discovered
that she had contracted lupus erythematosus, the
systemic disease that had killed her father and of
which she herself was to die. For the last fourteen years of her life, she lived a quiet, productive life on the farm—raising peacocks, painting,
and writing the extraordinary stories and novels
that won her worldwide acclaim. Her novels,
Wise Blood (1952), which was adapted for film in
1979, and *The Violent Bear It Away* (1960), deal
with fanatical preachers. Her thirty-one carefully
crafted stories, combining grotesque comedy and
violent tragedy, appear in *A Good Man Is Hard
to Find* (1955), *Everything That Rises Must Con-
verge* (1965), and *The Complete Stories* (1971),
which won the National Book Award. "Revelation," reprinted from *The Complete Stories,* dramatizes the ironic discoveries a woman makes about
how different classes of people fit into the order
of things.

Revelation[6]

THE DOCTOR'S WAITING room, which was very small, was   1
almost full when the Turpins entered and Mrs. Turpin,
who was very large, made it look even smaller by her presence. She stood looming at the head of the magazine table

[6]Flannery O'Connor, "Revelation" from *The Complete Stories* by Flannery
O'Connor. Copyright © 1971 by the Estate of Mary Flannery O'Connor.
Reprinted by permission of Farrar, Straus and Giroux, LLC.

set in the center of it, a living demonstration that the room was inadequate and ridiculous. Her little bright black eyes took in all the patients as she sized up the seating situation. There was one vacant chair and a place on the sofa occupied by a blond child in a dirty blue romper who should have been told to move over and make room for the lady. He was five or six, but Mrs. Turpin saw at once that no one was going to tell him to move over. He was slumped down in the seat, his arms idle at his sides and his eyes idle in his head; his nose ran unchecked.

Mrs. Turpin put a firm hand on Claud's shoulder and said 2
in a voice that included anyone who wanted to listen, "Claud, you sit in that chair there," and gave him a push down into the vacant one. Claud was florid and bald and sturdy, somewhat shorter than Mrs. Turpin, but he sat down as if he were accustomed to doing what she told him to.

Mrs. Turpin remained standing. The only man in the 3
room besides Claud was a lean stringy old fellow with a rusty hand spread out on each knee, whose eyes were closed as if he were asleep or dead or pretending to be so as not to get up and offer her his seat. Her gaze settled agreeably on a well-dressed gray-haired lady whose eyes met hers and whose expression said: if that child belonged to me, he would have some manners and move over—there's plenty of room there for you and him too.

Claud looked up with a sigh and made as if to rise. 4

"Sit down," Mrs. Turpin said. "You know you're not sup- 5
posed to stand on that leg. He has an ulcer on his leg," she explained.

Claud lifted his foot onto the magazine table and rolled 6
his trouser leg up to reveal a purple swelling on a plump marble-white calf.

"My!" the pleasant lady said. "How did you do that?" 7

"A cow kicked him," Mrs. Turpin said. 8

"Goodness!" said the lady. 9

Claud rolled his trouser leg down. 10

"Maybe the little boy would move over," the lady sug- 11
gested, but the child did not stir.

"Somebody will be leaving in a minute," Mrs. Turpin   12
said. She could not understand why a doctor—with as much
money as they made charging five dollars a day to just stick
their head in the hospital door and look at you—couldn't
afford a decent-sized waiting room. This one was hardly bigger than a garage. The table was cluttered with limp-looking
magazines and at one end of it there was a big green glass
ash tray full of cigarette butts and cotton wads with little
blood spots on them. If she had had anything to do with the
running of the place, that would have been emptied every so
often. There were no chairs against the wall at the head of the
room. It had a rectangular-shaped panel in it that permitted
a view of the office where the nurse came and went and the
secretary listened to the radio. A plastic fern in a gold pot
sat in the opening and trailed its fronds down almost to the
floor. The radio was softly playing gospel music.

Just then the inner door opened and a nurse with the high-   13
est stack of yellow hair Mrs. Turpin had ever seen put her
face in the crack and called for the next patient. The woman
sitting beside Claud grasped the two arms of her chair and
hoisted herself up; she pulled her dress free from her legs and
lumbered through the door where the nurse had disappeared.

Mrs. Turpin eased into the vacant chair, which held her   14
tight as a corset. "I wish I could reduce," she said, and rolled
her eyes and gave a comic sigh.

"Oh, *you* aren't fat," the stylish lady said.   15

"Ooooo I am too," Mrs. Turpin said. "Claud he eats all   16
he wants to and never weighs over one hundred and seventy-
five pounds, but me I just look at something good to eat
and I gain some weight," and her stomach and shoulders
shook with laughter. "You can eat all you want to, can't you,
Claud?" she asked, turning to him.

Claud only grinned.   17

"Well, as long as you have such a good disposition," the   18
stylish lady said, "I don't think it makes a bit of difference
what size you are. You just can't beat a good disposition."

Next to her was a fat girl of eighteen or nineteen, scowling   19
into a thick blue book which Mrs. Turpin saw was entitled

Human Development. The girl raised her head and directed her scowl at Mrs. Turpin as if she did not like her looks. She appeared annoyed that anyone should speak while she tried to read. The poor girl's face was blue with acne and Mrs. Turpin thought how pitiful it was to have a face like that at that age. She gave the girl a friendly smile but the girl only scowled the harder. Mrs. Turpin herself was fat but she had always had good skin, and, though she was forty-seven years old, there was not a wrinkle in her face except around her eyes from laughing too much.

Next to the ugly girl was the child, still in exactly the same position, and next to him was a thin leathery old woman in a cotton print dress. She and Claud had three sacks of chicken feed in their pump house that was in the same print. She had seen from the first that the child belonged with the old woman. She could tell by the way they sat—kind of vacant and white-trashy, as if they would sit there until Doomsday if nobody called and told them to get up. And at right angles but next to the well-dressed pleasant lady was a lank-faced woman who was certainly the child's mother. She had on a yellow sweat shirt and wine-colored slacks, both gritty-looking, and the rims of her lips were stained with snuff. Her dirty yellow hair was tied behind with a little piece of red paper ribbon. Worse than niggers any day, Mrs. Turpin thought.

The gospel hymn playing was, "When I looked up and He looked down," and Mrs. Turpin, who knew it, supplied the last line mentally, "And wona these days I know I'll wear a crown."

Without appearing to, Mrs. Turpin always noticed people's feet. The well-dressed lady had on red and gray suede shoes to match her dress. Mrs. Turpin had on her good black patent leather pumps. The ugly girl had on Girl Scout shoes and heavy socks. The old woman had on tennis shoes and the white-trashy mother had on what appeared to be bedroom slippers, black straw with gold braid threaded through them—exactly what you would have expected her to have on.

Sometimes at night when she couldn't go to sleep, Mrs. 23
Turpin would occupy herself with the question of who she
would have chosen to be if she couldn't have been herself. If
Jesus had said to her before he made her, "There's only two
places available for you. You can either be a nigger or white-
trash," what would she have said? "Please, Jesus, please," she
would have said, "just let me wait until there's another place
available," and he would have said, "No, you have to go
right now and I have only those two places so make up your
mind." She would have wiggled and squirmed and begged
and pleaded but it would have been no use and finally she
would have said, "All right, make me a nigger then—but that
don't mean a trashy one." And he would have made her a
neat clean respectable Negro woman, herself but black.

Next to the child's mother was a red-headed youngish 24
woman, reading one of the magazines and working a piece
of chewing gum, hell for leather, as Claud would say. Mrs.
Turpin could not see the woman's feet. She was not white-
trash, just common. Sometimes Mrs. Turpin occupied herself at night naming the classes of people. On the bottom
of the heap were most colored people, not the kind she
would have been if she had been one, but most of them; then
next to them—not above, just away from—were the white-
trash; then above them were the home-owners, and above
them the home-and-land-owners, to which she and Claud
belonged. Above she and Claud were people with a lot of
money and much bigger houses and much more land. But
here the complexity of it would begin to bear in on her, for
some of the people with a lot of money were common and
ought to be below she and Claud and some of the people
who had good blood had lost their money and had to rent
and then there were colored people who owned their homes
and land as well. There was a colored dentist in town who
had two red Lincolns and a swimming pool and a farm with
registered white-face cattle on it. Usually by the time she had
fallen asleep all the classes of people were moiling and roil-
ing around in her head, and she would dream they were all

crammed in together in a box car, being ridden off to be put in a gas oven.

"That's a beautiful clock," she said and nodded to her 25 right. It was a big wall clock, the face encased in a brass sunburst.

"Yes, it's very pretty," the stylish lady said agreeably. "And 26 right on the dot too," she added, glancing at her watch.

The ugly girl beside her cast an eye upward at the clock, 27 smirked, then looked directly at Mrs. Turpin and smirked again. Then she returned her eyes to her book. She was obviously the lady's daughter because, although they didn't look anything alike as to disposition, they both had the same shape of face and the same blue eyes. On the lady they sparkled pleasantly but in the girl's seared face they appeared alternately to smolder and to blaze.

What if Jesus had said, "All right, you can be white-trash 28 or a nigger or ugly"!

Mrs. Turpin felt an awful pity for the girl, though she 29 thought it was one thing to be ugly and another to act ugly.

The woman with the snuff-stained lips turned around in 30 her chair and looked up at the clock. Then she turned back and appeared to look a little to the side of Mrs. Turpin. There was a cast in one of her eyes. "You want to know wher you can get you one of themther clocks?" she asked in a loud voice.

"No, I already have a nice clock," Mrs. Turpin said. Once 31 somebody like her got a leg in the conversation, she would be all over it.

"You can get you one with green stamps," the woman said. 32 "That's most likely wher he got hisn. Save you up enough, you can get you most anythang. I got me some joo'ry."

Ought to have got you a wash rag and some soap, Mrs. 33 Turpin thought.

"I get contour sheets with mine," the pleasant lady said. 34

The daughter slammed her book shut. She looked straight 35 in front of her, directly through Mrs. Turpin and on through the yellow curtain and the plate glass window which made the wall behind her. The girl's eyes seemed lit all of a sudden with a peculiar light, an unnatural light like night road signs give. Mrs. Turpin turned her head to see if there was anything going on outside that she should see, but she could not see anything. Figures passing cast only a pale shadow through the curtain. There was no reason the girl should single her out for her ugly looks.

"Miss Finley," the nurse said, cracking the door. The 36 gum-chewing woman got up and passed in front of her and Claud and went into the office. She had on red high-heeled shoes.

Directly across the table, the ugly girl's eyes were fixed on 37 Mrs. Turpin as if she had some very special reason for disliking her.

"This is wonderful weather, isn't it?" the girl's mother 38 said.

"It's good weather for cotton if you can get the niggers to 39 pick it," Mrs. Turpin said, "but niggers don't want to pick cotton any more. You can't get the white folks to pick it and now you can't get the niggers—because they got to be right up there with the white folks."

"They gonna *try* anyways," the white-trash woman said, 40 leaning forward.

"Do you have one of the cotton-picking machines?" the 41 pleasant lady asked.

"No," Mrs. Turpin said, "they leave half the cotton in the 42 field. We don't have much cotton anyway. If you want to make it farming now, you have to have a little of everything. We got a couple of acres of cotton and a few hogs and chickens and just enough white-face that Claud can look after them himself."

"One thang I don't want," the white-trash woman said, 43 wiping her mouth with the back of her hand. "Hogs. Nasty stinking things, a-gruntin and a-rootin all over the place."

Mrs. Turpin gave her the merest edge of her attention. 44 "Our hogs are not dirty and they don't stink," she said. "They're cleaner than some children I've seen. Their feet never touch the ground. We have a pig-parlor—that's where you raise them on concrete," she explained to the pleasant lady, "and Claud scoots them down with the hose every afternoon and washes off the floor." Cleaner by far than that child right there, she thought. Poor nasty little thing. He had not moved except to put the thumb of his dirty hand into his mouth.

The woman turned her face away from Mrs. Turpin. "I know I wouldn't scoot down no hog with no hose," she said to the wall.   45

You wouldn't have no hog to scoot down, Mrs. Turpin said to herself.   46

"A-gruntin and a-rootin and a-groanin," the woman muttered.   47

"We got a little of everything," Mrs. Turpin said to the pleasant lady. "It's no use in having more than you can handle yourself with help like it is. We found enough niggers to pick our cotton this year but Claud he has to go after them and take them home again in the evening. They can't walk that half a mile. No they can't. I tell you," she said and laughed merrily, "I sure am tired of buttering up niggers, but you got to love em if you want em to work for you. When they come in the morning, I run out and I say, 'Hi yawl this morning?' and when Claud drives them off to the field I just wave to beat the band and they just wave back." And she waved her hand rapidly to illustrate.   48

"Like you read out of the same book," the lady said, showing she understood perfectly.   49

"Child, yes," Mrs. Turpin said. "And when they come in from the field, I run out with a bucket of icewater. That's the way it's going to be from now on," she said. "You may as well face it."   50

"One thang I know," the white-trash woman said. "Two thangs I ain't going to do: love no niggers or scoot down no hog with no hose." And she let out a bark of contempt.   51

The look that Mrs. Turpin and the pleasant lady exchanged indicated they both understood that you had to *have* certain things before you could *know* certain things. But every time Mrs. Turpin exchanged a look with the lady, she was aware   52 that the ugly girl's peculiar eyes were still on her, and she had trouble bringing her attention back to the conversation.

"When you got something," she said, "you got to look after 53 it." And when you ain't got a thing but breath and britches, she added to herself, you can afford to come to town every morning and just sit on the Court House coping and spit.

A grotesque revolving shadow passed across the curtain 54 behind her and was thrown palely on the opposite wall. Then a bicycle clattered down against the outside of the building. The door opened and a colored boy glided in with a tray from the drugstore. It had two large red and white paper cups on it with tops on them. He was a tall, very black boy in discolored white pants and a green nylon shirt. He was chewing gum slowly, as if to music. He set the tray down in the office opening next to the fern and stuck his head through to look for the secretary. She was not in there. He rested his arms on the ledge and waited, his narrow bottom stuck out, swaying to the left and right. He raised a hand over his head and scratched the base of his skull.

"You see that button there, boy?" Mrs. Turpin said. "You 55 can punch that and she'll come. She's probably in the back somewhere."

"Is thas right?" the boy said agreeably, as if he had never 56 seen the button before. He leaned to the right and put his finger on it. "She sometime out," he said and twisted around to face his audience, his elbows behind him on the counter. The nurse appeared and he twisted back again. She handed him a dollar and he rooted in his pocket and made the change and counted it out to her. She gave him fifteen cents for a tip and he went out with the empty tray. The heavy door swung too slowly and closed at length with the sound of suction. For a moment no one spoke.

"They ought to send all them niggers back to Africa," the 57 white-trash woman said. "That's wher they come from in the first place."

"Oh, I couldn't do without my good colored friends," the 58 pleasant lady said.

"There's a heap of things worse than a nigger," Mrs. Tur- 59
pin agreed. "It's all kinds of them just like it's all kinds of us."

"Yes, and it takes all kinds to make the world go round," 60
the lady said in her musical voice.

As she said it, the raw-complexioned girl snapped her teeth 61
together. Her lower lip turned downwards and inside out,
revealing the pale pink inside of her mouth. After a second it
rolled back up. It was the ugliest face Mrs. Turpin had ever
seen anyone make and for a moment she was certain that the
girl had made it at her. She was looking at her as if she had
known and disliked her all her life—all of Mrs. Turpin's life, it
seemed too, not just all the girl's life. Why, girl, I don't even
know you, Mrs. Turpin said silently.

She forced her attention back to the discussion. "It 62
wouldn't be practical to send them back to Africa," she said.
"They wouldn't want to go. They got it too good here."

"Wouldn't be what they wanted—if I had anythang to do 63
with it," the woman said.

"It wouldn't be a way in the world you could get all the 64
niggers back over there," Mrs. Turpin said. "They'd be hid-
ing out and lying down and turning sick on you and wailing
and hollering and raring and pitching. It wouldn't be a way
in the world to get them over there."

"They got over here," the trashy woman said. "Get back 65
like they got over."

"It wasn't so many of them then," Mrs. Turpin explained. 66

The woman looked at Mrs. Turpin as if here was an idiot 67
indeed but Mrs. Turpin was not bothered by the look, considering where it came from.

"Nooo," she said, "they're going to stay here where they 68
can go to New York and marry white folks and improve their
color. That's what they all want to do, every one of them,
improve their color."

"You know what comes of that, don't you?" Claud asked. 69

"No, Claud, what?" Mrs. Turpin said. 70

Claud's eyes twinkled. "White-faced niggers," he said with 71
never a smile.

Everybody in the office laughed except the white-trash and   72
the ugly girl. The girl gripped the book in her lap with white
fingers. The trashy woman looked around her from face to
face as if she thought they were all idiots. The old woman in
the feed sack dress continued to gaze expressionless across
the floor at the high-top shoes of the man opposite her, the
one who had been pretending to be asleep when the Turpins
came in. He was laughing heartily, his hands still spread out
on his knees. The child had fallen to the side and was lying
now almost face down in the old woman's lap.

While they recovered from their laughter, the nasal chorus   73
on the radio kept the room from silence.

> *You go to blank blank*
> *And I'll go to mine*
> *But we'll all blank along*
> *To-geth-ther,*
> *And all along the blank*
> *We'll hep each other out*
> *Smile-ling in any kind of*
> *Weath-ther!*

Mrs. Turpin didn't catch every word but she caught   74
enough to agree with the spirit of the song and it turned her
thoughts sober. To help anybody out that needed it was her
philosophy of life. She never spared herself when she found
somebody in need, whether they were white or black, trash
or decent. And of all she had to be thankful for, she was
most thankful that this was so. If Jesus had said, "You can
be high society and have all the money you want and be thin
and svelte-like, but you can't be a good woman with it,"
she would have had to say, "Well don't make me that then.
Make me a good woman and it don't matter what else, how
fat or how ugly or how poor!" Her heart rose. He had not
made her a nigger or white-trash or ugly! He had made her
herself and given her a little of everything. Jesus, thank you!
she said. Thank you thank you thank you! Whenever she
counted her blessings she felt as buoyant as if she weighed

one hundred and twenty-five pounds instead of one hundred and eighty.

"What's wrong with your little boy?" the pleasant lady   75
asked the white-trashy woman.

"He has a ulcer," the woman said proudly. "He ain't give   76
me a minute's peace since he was born. Him and her are just alike," she said, nodding at the old woman, who was running her leathery fingers through the child's pale hair. "Look like I can't get nothing down them two but Co' Cola and candy."

That's all you try to get down em, Mrs. Turpin said to   77
herself. Too lazy to light the fire. There was nothing you could tell her about people like them that she didn't know already. And it was not just that they didn't have anything. Because if you gave them everything, in two weeks it would all be broken or filthy or they would have chopped it up for lightwood. She knew all this from her own experience. Help them you must, but help them you couldn't.

All at once the ugly girl turned her lips inside out again.   78
Her eyes fixed like two drills on Mrs. Turpin. This time there was no mistaking that there was something urgent behind them.

Girl, Mrs. Turpin exclaimed silently, I haven't done a thing   79
to you! The girl might be confusing her with somebody else. There was no need to sit by and let herself be intimidated. "You must be in college," she said boldly, looking directly at the girl. "I see you reading a book there."

The girl continued to stare and pointedly did not answer.   80

Her mother blushed at this rudeness. "The lady asked you   81
a question, Mary Grace," she said under her breath.

"I have ears," Mary Grace said.   82

The poor mother blushed again. "Mary Grace goes to   83
Wellesley College," she explained. She twisted one of the buttons on her dress. "In Massachusetts," she added with a grimace. "And in the summer she just keeps right on studying. Just reads all the time, a real book worm. She's done real well at Wellesley; she's taking English and Math and History and Psychology and Social Studies," she rattled on, "and I

think it's too much. I think she ought to get out and have fun."

The girl looked as if she would like to hurl them all through   84
the plate glass window.

"Way up north," Mrs. Turpin murmured and thought,   85
well, it hasn't done much for her manners.

"I'd almost rather to have him sick," the white-trash   86
woman said, wrenching the attention back to herself. "He's
so mean when he ain't. Look like some children just take
natural to meanness. It's some gets bad when they get sick
but he was the opposite. Took sick and turned good. He
don't give me no trouble now. It's me waitin to see the doctor," she said.

If I was going to send anybody back to Africa, Mrs. Turpin   87
thought, it would be your kind, woman. "Yes, indeed," she
said aloud, but looking up at the ceiling, "it's a heap of things
worse than a nigger." And dirtier than a hog, she added to
herself.

"I think people with bad dispositions are more to be pitied   88
than anyone on earth," the pleasant lady said in a voice that
was decidedly thin.

"I thank the Lord he has blessed me with a good one,"   89
Mrs. Turpin said. "The day has never dawned that I couldn't
find something to laugh at."

"Not since she married me anyways," Claud said with a   90
comical straight face.

Everybody laughed except the girl and the white-trash.   91

Mrs. Turpin's stomach shook. "He's such a caution," she   92
said, "that I can't help but laugh at him."

The girl made a loud ugly noise through her teeth.   93

Her mother's mouth grew thin and tight. "I think the   94
worst thing in the world," she said, "is an ungrateful person.
To have everything and not appreciate it. I know a girl," she
said, "who has parents who would give her anything, a little
brother who loves her dearly, who is getting a good education, who wears the best clothes, but who can never say a
kind word to anyone, who never smiles, who just criticizes
and complains all day long."

"Is she too old to paddle?" Claud asked.   95

The girl's face was almost purple.   96

"Yes," the lady said, "I'm afraid there's nothing to do but   97
leave her to her folly. Some day she'll wake up and it'll be
too late."

"It never hurt anyone to smile," Mrs. Turpin said. "It just   98
makes you feel better all over."

"Of course," the lady said sadly, "but there are just some   99
people you can't tell anything to. They can't take criticism."

"If it's one thing I am," Mrs. Turpin said with feeling,   100
"it's grateful. When I think who all I could have been besides
myself and what all I got, a little of everything, and a good disposition besides, I just feel like shouting, 'Thank you, Jesus,
for making everything the way it is!' It could have been different!" For one thing, somebody else could have got Claud.
At the thought of this, she was flooded with gratitude and a
terrible pang of joy ran through her. "Oh thank you, Jesus,
Jesus, thank you!" she cried aloud.

The book struck her directly over her left eye. It struck   101
almost at the same instant that she realized the girl was about
to hurl it. Before she could utter a sound, the raw face came
crashing across the table toward her, howling. The girl's fingers sank like clamps into the soft flesh of her neck. She heard
the mother cry out and Claud shout, "Whoa!" There was an
instant when she was certain that she was about to be in an
earthquake.

All at once her vision narrowed and she saw everything   102
as if it were happening in a small room far away, or as if she
were looking at it through the wrong end of a telescope.
Claud's face crumpled and fell out of sight. The nurse ran
in, then out, then in again. Then the gangling figure of the
doctor rushed out of the inner door. Magazines flew this way
and that as the table turned over. The girl fell with a thud
and Mrs. Turpin's vision suddenly reversed itself and she
saw everything large instead of small. The eyes of the white-
trashy woman were staring hugely at the floor. There the girl,
held down on one side by the nurse and on the other by
her mother, was wrenching and turning in their grasp. The

doctor was kneeling astride her, trying to hold her arm down. He managed after a second to sink a long needle into it.

Mrs. Turpin felt entirely hollow except for her heart which 103 swung from side to side as if it were agitated in a great empty drum of flesh.

"Somebody that's not busy call for the ambulance," the 104 doctor said in the off-hand voice young doctors adopt for terrible occasions.

Mrs. Turpin could not have moved a finger. The old man 105 who had been sitting next to her skipped nimbly into the office and made the call, for the secretary still seemed to be gone.

"Claud!" Mrs. Turpin called.   106

He was not in his chair. She knew she must jump up and 107 find him but she felt like some one trying to catch a train in a dream, when everything moves in slow motion and the faster you try to run the slower you go.

"Here I am," a suffocated voice, very unlike Claud's, said. 108

He was doubled up in the corner on the floor, pale as 109 paper, holding his leg. She wanted to get up and go to him but she could not move. Instead, her gaze was drawn slowly downward to the churning face on the floor, which she could see over the doctor's shoulder.

The girl's eyes stopped rolling and focused on her. They 110 seemed a much lighter blue than before, as if a door that had been tightly closed behind them was now open to admit light and air.

Mrs. Turpin's head cleared and her power of motion 111 returned. She leaned forward until she has looking directly into the fierce brilliant eyes. There was no doubt in her mind that the girl did know her, knew her in some intense and personal way, beyond time and place and condition. "What you got to say to me?" she asked hoarsely and held her breath, waiting, as for a revelation.

The girl raised her head. Her gaze locked with Mrs. Turpin's. 112 "Go back to hell where you came from, you old wart hog," she whispered. Her voice was low but clear. Her eyes burned for a moment as if she saw with pleasure that her message had struck its target.

Mrs. Turpin sank back in her chair. 113

After a moment the girl's eyes closed and she turned her 114 head wearily to the side.

The doctor rose and handed the nurse the empty syringe. 115 He leaned over and put both hands for a moment on the mother's shoulders, which were shaking. She was sitting on the floor, her lips pressed together, holding Mary Grace's hand in her lap. The girl's fingers were gripped like a baby's around her thumb. "Go on to the hospital," he said. "I'll call and make the arrangements."

"Now let's see that neck," he said in a jovial voice to Mrs. 116 Turpin. He began to inspect her neck with his first two fingers. Two little moon-shaped lines like pink fish bones were indented over her windpipe. There was the beginning of an angry red swelling above her eye. His fingers passed over this also.

"Lea' me be," she said thickly and shook him off. "See 117 about Claud. She kicked him."

"I'll see about him in a minute," he said and felt her pulse. 118 He was a thin gray-haired man, given to pleasantries. "Go home and have yourself a vacation the rest of the day," he said and patted her on the shoulder.

Quit your pattin me, Mrs. Turpin growled to herself. 119

"And put an ice pack over that eye," he said. Then he went 120 and squatted down beside Claud and looked at his leg. After a moment he pulled him up and Claud limped after him into the office.

Until the ambulance came, the only sounds in the room 121 were the tremulous moans of the girl's mother, who continued to sit on the floor. The white-trash woman did not take her eyes off the girl. Mrs. Turpin looked straight ahead at nothing. Presently the ambulance drew up, a long dark shadow, behind the curtain. The attendants came in and set the stretcher down beside the girl and lifted her expertly onto it and carried her out. The nurse helped the mother gather up her things. The shadow of the ambulance moved silently away and the nurse came back in the office.

"That ther girl is going to be a lunatic, ain't she?" the 122 white-trash woman asked the nurse, but the nurse kept on to the back and never answered her.

"Yes, she's going to be a lunatic," the white-trash woman 123 said to the rest of them.

"Po' critter," the old woman murmured. The child's face 124 was still in her lap. His eyes looked idly out over her knees. He had not moved during the disturbance except to draw one leg up under him.

"I thank Gawd," the white-trash woman said fervently, "I 125 ain't a lunatic."

Claud came limping out and the Turpins went home.   126

As their pick-up truck turned into their own dirt road and 127 made the crest of the hill, Mrs. Turpin gripped the window ledge and looked out suspiciously. The land sloped gracefully down through a field dotted with lavender weeds and at the start of the rise their small yellow frame house, with its little flower beds spread out around it like a fancy apron, sat primly in its accustomed place between two giant hickory trees. She would not have been startled to see a burnt wound between two blackened chimneys.

Neither of them felt like eating so they put on their house 128 clothes and lowered the shade in the bedroom and lay down, Claud with his leg on a pillow and herself with a damp wash-cloth over her eye. The instant she was flat on her back, the image of a razor-backed hog with warts on its face and horns coming out behind its ears snorted into her head. She moaned, a low quiet moan.

"I am not," she said tearfully, "a wart hog. From hell." 129 But the denial had no force. The girl's eyes and her words, even the tone of her voice, low but clear, directed only to her, brooked no repudiation. She had been singled out for the message, though there was trash in the room to whom it might justly have been applied. The full force of this fact struck her only now. There was a woman there who was neglecting her own child but she had been overlooked. The message had been given to Ruby Turpin, a respectable, hard-working, church-going woman. The tears dried. Her eyes began to burn instead with wrath.

She rose on her elbow and the washcloth fell into her 130 hand. Claud was lying on his back, snoring. She wanted to tell him what the girl had said. At the same time, she did not wish to put the image of herself as a wart hog from hell into his mind.

"Hey, Claud," she muttered and pushed his shoulder. 131

Claud opened one pale baby blue eye. 132

She looked into it warily. He did not think about any 133 thing. He just went his way.

"Wha, whasit?" he said and closed the eye again. 134

"Nothing," she said. "Does your leg pain you?" 135

"Hurts like hell," Claud said. 136

"It'll quit terreckly," she said and lay back down. In a 137 moment Claud was snoring again. For the rest of the afternoon they lay there. Claud slept. She scowled at the ceiling. Occasionally she raised her fist and made a small stabbing motion over her chest as if she was defending her innocence to invisible guests who were like the comforters of Job, reasonable-seeming but wrong.

About five-thirty Claud stirred. "Got to go after those nig- 138 gers," he sighed, not moving.

She was looking straight up as if there were unintelligible 139 handwriting on the ceiling. The protuberance over her eye had turned a greenish-blue. "Listen here," she said.

"What?" 140

"Kiss me." 141

Claud leaned over and kissed her loudly on the mouth. 142 He pinched her side and their hands interlocked. Her expression of ferocious concentration did not change. Claud got up, groaning and growling, and limped off. She continued to study the ceiling.

She did not get up until she heard the pick-up truck com- 143 ing back with the Negroes. Then she rose and thrust her feet in her brown oxfords, which she did not bother to lace, and stumped out onto the back porch and got her red plastic bucket. She emptied a tray of ice cubes into it and filled it half full of water and went out into the back yard. Every afternoon after Claud brought the hands in, one of the boys helped him put out hay and the rest waited in the back of the truck until he was ready to take them home. The truck was parked in the shade under one of the hickory trees.

"Hi yawl this evening?" Mrs. Turpin asked grimly, appear- 144 ing with the bucket and the dipper. There were three women and a boy in the truck.

"Us doin nicely," the oldest woman said. "Hi you doin?" 145 and her gaze stuck immediately on the dark lump on Mrs. Turpin's forehead. "You done fell down, ain't you?" she asked in a solicitous voice. The old woman was dark and almost toothless. She had on an old felt hat of Claud's set back on her head. The other two women were younger and lighter and they both had new bright green sunhats. One of them had hers on her head; the other had taken hers off and the boy was grinning beneath it.

Mrs. Turpin set the bucket down on the floor of the truck. 146 "Yawl hep yourselves," she said. She looked around to make sure Claud had gone. "No, I didn't fall down," she said, fold-ing her arms. "It was something worse than that."

"Ain't nothing bad happen to you!" the old woman said. 147 She said it as if they all knew that Mrs. Turpin was protected in some special way by Divine Providence. "You just had you a little fall."

"We were in town at the doctor's office for where the cow 148 kicked Mr. Turpin," Mrs. Turpin said in a flat tone that indi-cated they could leave off their foolishness. "And there was this girl there. A big fat girl with her face all broke out. I could look at that girl and tell she was peculiar but I couldn't tell how. And me and her mama was just talking and going along and all of a sudden WHAM! She throws this big book she was reading at me and..."

"Naw!" the old woman cried out. 149

"And then she jumps over the table and commences to 150 choke me."

"Naw!" they all exclaimed, "naw!" 151

"Hi come she do that?" the old woman asked. "What ail 152
her?"

Mrs. Turpin only glared in front of her. 153

"Somethin ail her," the old woman said. 154

"They carried her off in an ambulance," Mrs. Turpin con- 155
tinued, "but before she went she was rolling on the floor and
they were trying to hold her down to give her a shot and she
said something to me." She paused. "You know what she
said to me?"

"What she say?" they asked. 156

"She said," Mrs. Turpin began, and stopped, her face 157
very dark and heavy. The sun was getting whiter and whiter,
blanching the sky overhead so that the leaves of the hickory
tree were black in the face of it. She could not bring forth the
words. "Something real ugly," she muttered.

"She sho shouldn't said nothin ugly to you," the old 158
woman said. "You so sweet. You the sweetest lady I know."

"She pretty too," the one with the hat on said. 159

"And stout," the other one said. "I never knowed no 160
sweeter white lady."

"That's the truth befo' Jesus," the old woman said. 161
"Amen! You des as sweet and pretty as you can be."

Mrs. Turpin knew exactly how much Negro flattery was 162
worth and it added to her rage. "She said," she began again
and finished this time with a fierce rush of breath, "that I was
an old wart hog from hell."

There was an astounded silence. 163

"Where she at?" the youngest woman cried in a piercing 164
voice.

"Lemme see her. I'll kill her!" 165

"I'll kill her with you!" the other one cried. 166

"She b'long in the sylum," the old woman said emphati- 167
cally. "You the sweetest white lady I know."

"She pretty too," the other two said. "Stout as she can be 168
and sweet. Jesus satisfied with her!"

"Deed he is," the old woman declared. 169

Idiots! Mrs. Turpin growled to herself. You could never 170
say anything intelligent to a nigger. You could talk at them

but not with them. "Yawl ain't drunk your water," she said shortly. "Leave the bucket in the truck when you're finished with it. I got more to do than just stand around and pass the time of day," and she moved off and into the house.

She stood for a moment in the middle of the kitchen. The 171 dark protuberance over her eye looked like a miniature tornado cloud which might any moment sweep across the horizon of her brow. Her lower lip protruded dangerously. She squared her massive shoulders. Then she marched into the front of the house and out the side door and started down the road to the pig parlor. She had the look of a woman going single-handed, weaponless, into battle.

The sun was a deep yellow now like a harvest moon and 172 was riding westward very fast over the far tree line as if it meant to reach the hogs before she did. The road was rutted and she kicked several good-sized stones out of her path as she strode along. The pig parlor was on a little knoll at the end of a lane that ran off from the side of the barn. It was a square of concrete as large as a small room, with a board fence about four feet high around it. The concrete floor sloped slightly so that the hog wash could drain off into a trench where it was carried to the field for fertilizer. Claud was standing on the outside, on the edge of the concrete, hanging onto the top board, hosing down the floor inside. The hose was connected to the faucet of a water trough nearby.

Mrs. Turpin climbed up beside him and glowered down 173 at the hogs inside. There were seven long-snouted bristly shoats in it—tan with liver-colored spots—and an old sow a few weeks off from farrowing. She was lying on her side grunting. The shoats were running about shaking themselves like idiot children, their little slit pig eyes searching the floor for anything left. She had read that pigs were the most intelligent animal. She doubted it. They were supposed to be smarter than dogs. There had even been a pig astronaut. He had performed his assignment perfectly but died of a heart attack afterwards because they left him in his electric suit, sitting upright throughout his examination when naturally a hog should be on all fours.

A-gruntin and a-rootin and a-groanin.   174

"Gimme that hose," she said, yanking it away from Claud. 175 "Go on and carry them niggers home and then get off that leg."

"You look like you might have swallowed a mad dog," 176 Claud observed, but he got down and limped off. He paid no attention to her humors.

Until he was out of earshot, Mrs. Turpin stood on the side 177 of the pen, holding the hose and pointing the stream of water at the hind quarters of any shoat that looked as if it might try to lie down. When he had had time to get over the hill, she turned her head slightly and her wrathful eyes scanned the path. He was nowhere in sight. She turned back again and seemed to gather herself up. Her shoulders rose and she drew in her breath.

"What do you send me a message like that for?" she said in 178 a low fierce voice, barely above a whisper but with the force of a shout in its concentrated fury. "How am I a hog and me both? How am I saved and from hell too?" Her free fist was knotted and with the other she gripped the hose, blindly pointing the stream of water in and out of the eye of the old sow whose outraged squeal she did not hear.

The pig parlor commanded a view of the back pasture 179 where their twenty beef cows were gathered around the hay-bales Claud and the boy had put out. The freshly cut pasture sloped down to the highway. Across it was their cotton field and beyond that a dark green dusty wood which they owned as well. The sun was behind the wood, very red, looking over the paling of trees like a farmer inspecting his own hogs.

"Why me?" she rumbled. "It's no trash around here, black 180 or white, that I haven't given to. And break my back to the bone every day working. And do for the church."

She appeared to be the right size woman to command 181 the arena before her. "How am I a hog?" she demanded. "Exactly how am I like them?" and she jabbed the stream of water at the shoats. "There was plenty of trash there. It didn't have to be me.

"If you like trash better, go get yourself some trash then," 182 she railed. "You could have made me trash. Or a nigger. If

trash is what you wanted why didn't you make me trash?"
She shook her fist with the hose in it and a watery snake
appeared momentarily in the air. "I could quit working and
take it easy and be filthy," she growled. "Lounge about the
sidewalks all day drinking root beer. Dip snuff and spit in
every puddle and have it all over my face. I could be nasty.

"Or you could have made me a nigger. It's too late for me   183
to be a nigger," she said with deep sarcasm, "but I could act
like one. Lay down in the middle of the road and stop traffic.
Roll on the ground."

In the deepening light everything was taking on a mysteri-   184
ous hue. The pasture was growing a peculiar glassy green and
the streak of highway had turned lavender. She braced herself
for a final assault and this time her voice rolled out over the
pasture. "Go on," she yelled, "call me a hog! Call me a hog
again. From hell. Call me a wart hog from hell. Put that bottom rail on top. There'll still be a top and bottom!"

A garbled echo returned to her.   185

A final surge of fury shook her and she roared, "Who do   186
you think you are?"

The color of everything, field and crimson sky, burned for   187
a moment with a transparent intensity. The question carried
over the pasture and across the highway and the cotton field
and returned to her clearly like an answer from beyond the
wood.

She opened her mouth but no sound came out of it.   188

A tiny truck, Claud's, appeared on the highway, heading   189
rapidly out of sight. Its gears scraped thinly. It looked like
a child's toy. At any moment a bigger truck might smash
into it and scatter Claud's and the niggers' brains all over the
road.

Mrs. Turpin stood there, her gaze fixed on the highway, all   190
her muscles rigid, until in five or six minutes the truck reappeared, returning. She waited until it had had time to turn
into their own road. Then like a monumental statue coming
to life, she bent her head slowly and gazed, as if through
the very heart of mystery, down into the pig parlor at the
hogs. They had settled all in one corner around the old sow

who was grunting softly. A red glow suffused them. They appeared to pant with a secret life.

Until the sun slipped finally behind the tree line, Mrs. Turpin 191 remained there with her gaze bent to them as if she were absorbing some abysmal life-giving knowledge. At last she lifted her head. There was only a purple streak in the sky, cutting through a field of crimson and leading, like an extension of the highway, into the descending dusk. She raised her hands from the side of the pen in a gesture hieratic and profound. A visionary light settled in her eyes. She saw the streak as a vast swinging bridge extending upward from the earth through a field of living fire. Upon it a vast horde of souls were rumbling toward heaven. There were whole companies of white-trash, clean for the first time in their lives, and bands of black niggers in white robes, and battalions of freaks and lunatics shouting and clapping and leaping like frogs. And bringing up the end of the procession was a tribe of people whom she recognized at once as those who, like herself and Claud, had always had a little of everything and the God-given wit to use it right. She leaned forward to observe them closer. They were marching behind the others with great dignity, accountable as they had always been for good order and common sense and respectable behavior. They alone were on key. Yet she could see by their shocked and altered faces that even their virtues were being burned away. She lowered her hands and gripped the rail of the hog pen, her eyes small but fixed unblinkingly on what lay ahead. In a moment the vision faded but she remained where she was, immobile.

At length she got down and turned off the faucet and made 192 her slow way on the darkening path to the house. In the woods around her the invisible cricket choruses had struck up, but what she heard were the voices of the souls climbing upward into the starry field and shouting hallelujah.

COMMENT ON "REVELATION"

Ruby Turpin, the central character in O'Connor's "Revelation," is obsessed with the classification process. At night she occupies herself "naming the classes of people": most "colored people" are on the bottom; "next to them—not above, just away from—are the white trash"; and so on. Mrs. Turpin puzzles about the exceptions to her system—the black dentist who owns property and the decent white folks who have lost their money—but for the most part, she is certain about her system and her place in it. In the doctor's waiting room, she sizes up the other patients, placing them in their appropriate classes. But her internal and external dialogue reveals the ironies and inconsistencies in her rigid system. Self-satisfied, pleased that Jesus is on her side, she is not prepared for the book on human development that is thrown at her or the events that follow—the transparent flattery of the black workers, her cleaning of the pig parlor, and, finally, her vision of the highway to heaven that reveals her real place in God's hierarchy.

CHAPTER 5

DEFINITION

As a writer, both in and out of college, you're likely to spend a good deal of time writing definitions. In an astronomy class, you may be asked to explain what the Doppler effect is or what a white dwarf star is. In a literature class, you may be asked to define a sonnet and identify its different forms. If you become an engineer, you may write to define problems your company proposes to solve or to define a new product your company has developed. If you become a business executive, you may have to write a brochure to describe a new service your company offers or to draft a letter that defines the company's policy on credit applications.

Writers use definitions to establish boundaries, to show the essential nature of something, and to explain the special qualities that identify a purpose, place, object, or concept and distinguish it from others similar to it. Writers often write extended definitions—definitions that go beyond the one-sentence or one-paragraph explanations that you find in a dictionary or encyclopedia—to expand on and examine the essential qualities of a policy, an event, a group, or a trend. Sometimes an extended definition becomes an entire book. Some books are written to define the good life; others are written to define the ideal university or the best kind of government. In fact, many of the books on any current nonfiction best-seller list are primarily definitions. The essays in this chapter of *The River Reader* are all extended definitions.

PURPOSE

When you write, you can use definitions in several ways. For instance, you can define to *point out the special nature* of something. You may want to show the special flavor of San Francisco that makes it different from other major cities in the world, or you may want to describe the unique features that make the Macintosh computer different from other personal computers.

You can also define to *explain*. In an essay about cross-country skiing, you might want to show your readers what the sport is like and point out why it's less hazardous and less expensive than downhill skiing but better exercise. You might also define to *entertain*—to describe the essence of what it means to be a "good old boy," for instance. Often you define to *inform;* that is what you are doing in college papers when you write about West Virginia folk art or postmodern architecture. Often you write to *establish a standard,* perhaps for a good exercise program, a workable environmental policy, or even the ideal pair of running shoes. Notice that when you define to set a standard, you may also be defining to *persuade,* to convince your reader to accept the ideal you describe. Many definitions are essentially arguments.

Sometimes you may even write to *define yourself.* That is what you are doing when you write an autobiographical statement for a college admissions officer or a scholarship committee, or when you write a job application letter. You hope to give your readers the special information that will distinguish you from all other candidates. When that is your task, you'll profit by knowing the common strategies for defining and by recognizing how other writers have used them.

AUDIENCE

When you're going to use definition in your writing, you can benefit by thinking ahead of time about what your readers expect from you. Why are they reading, and what questions will they want you to answer? You can't anticipate all their questions, but you should plan on responding to at least two kinds of queries.

First, your readers are likely to ask, "What distinguishes what you're writing about? What's typical or different about it? How do I know when I see one?" For example, if you were writing about the Olympic Games, your readers would perhaps want to know the difference between today's Olympic Games and the original games in ancient Greece. With a little research, you could tell them about several major differences.

Second, for more complex topics you should expect that your readers will also ask, "What is the basic character or the essential nature of what you're writing about? What do you mean when you say 'alternative medicine,' 'Marxist theory,' or 'white-collar crime'?" Answering questions such as these is more difficult; but if you're going to use terms like these in an essay, you have an obligation to define them, using as many strategies as you need to clarify your terms. To define white-collar crime, for instance, you could specify that it is nonviolent, is likely to happen within businesses, and involves illegal manipulation of funds or privileged information. You should also strengthen your definition by giving examples that your readers might be familiar with.

STRATEGIES

You can choose from several strategies for defining, using them singly or in combination. A favorite strategy we all use is *giving examples,* something we do naturally when we point to a special automobile we like or show a child a picture of a raccoon in a picture book. Writers use the same method when they describe a scene, create a visual image, or cite a specific instance of something.

Every author in this chapter uses an abundance of examples. Kathleen Norris relies on examples to illustrate what she means by "gossip." Diane Ackerman introduces a wealth of examples from several societies to make her point that to some extent the way people experience pain is cultural.

You can define by *analyzing qualities* to emphasize what specific traits distinguish the person or thing you're defining. When you use this strategy for people, you focus on certain qualities or behaviors that reveal that individual's personality and character. James Gleick uses this strategy to illustrate how people try to complete multiple tasks in smaller and smaller periods of time. In the opening paragraph of "Pain," Ackerman shows what she calls T. E. Lawrence's "quintessential machismo" by describing him holding his hand in a candle flame.

A similar strategy is *attributing characteristics.* Kathleen Norris uses this strategy when she says that telling stories is characteristic of small towns.

Another strategy is *defining negatively.* In "A Word's Meaning Can Often Depend on Who Says It," Gloria Naylor explains how the black community has transformed a negative word into a complex word that signifies a variety of meanings.

Another way to define is by *using analogies.* Joan Didion uses the "wagon-train morality" to create an analogy to illustrate what she means by the basic social code.

You can also define by *showing function.* Often the most important feature about an object, agency, or institution is what it does. The element of function figures centrally in Toni Cade Bambara's story as Miss Moore tries to teach her students the meaning of the word *cost.*

COMBINING STRATEGIES

Even when you're writing an essay that is primarily an exercise in definition, you may want to do as professional writers often do and bring in other strategies, perhaps narration or argument or process analysis. For instance, in "Stone Soup" (pages 453 to 462), Barbara Kingsolver provides a definition of family and then argues that we need an expanded definition.

Some writers also combine definition with narration and description. In "The Myth of the Latin Woman: I Just Met a Girl Named María" (pages 60 to 67), Judith Ortiz Cofer challenges stereotypes to define the true character of Hispanic women. In "Stone Soup" (pages 453 to 462), Barbara Kingsolver uses stories about children as a way of defining a strong family. So you can mix and mingle strategies even though one may dominate. As you read essays in this chapter, and especially as you reread them, try to be conscious of the strategies authors are using. You may find that you can incorporate some of them into your own writing.

DEFINITION

Points to Remember

1. Remember that you are obligated to define key terms that you use in your writing (such as *Marxism, alternative medicine,* or *nontraditional student*).
2. Understand your purpose in defining: to explain, to entertain, to persuade, to set boundaries, or to establish a standard.
3. Understand how writers construct an argument from a definition. For example, by defining the good life or good government, they argue for that kind of life or government.
4. Know the several ways of defining: giving examples, analyzing qualities, attributing characteristics, defining negatively, using analogies, and showing function.
5. Learn to use definition in combination with other strategies, as a basis on which to build an argument, or as supporting evidence.

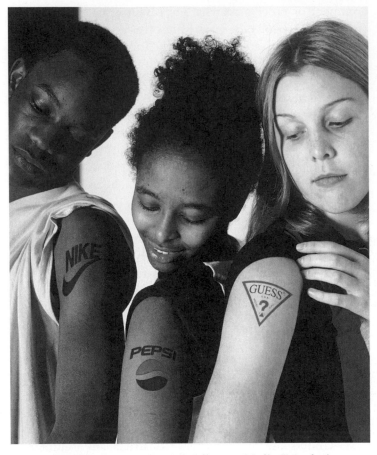

© *Courtesy Shannon Mendes and Adbusters Media Foundation.*

In this photograph, reprinted from an early issue of the anticommer-
cial, anticonsumption magazine Adbusters, *Shannon Mendes cap-*
tures three high school students showing off their tattoos. In what ways
do these tattoos define these students? In what ways are some of the
tattoos dated? Write an essay in which you explain how your choice of
some product—beverage, clothes, car—defines you.

GLORIA NAYLOR

Gloria Naylor was born in 1950 in New York City and was educated at Brooklyn College and Yale University. For several years she worked as a missionary for the Jehovah's Witnesses, working "for better world conditions." While teaching at several universities, such as George Washington and Princeton, Naylor published numerous stories and essays and interconnected novels: *The Women of Brewster Place* (1982), *Linden Hills* (1985), *Mamma Day* (1988), *Bailey's Café* (1992), *The Men of Brewster Place* (1998), and *1996* (2005). *The Women of Brewster Place,* which won the National Book Award for best first novel, was adapted as a television miniseries. Naylor is also the recipient of Guggenheim and National Endowment for the Arts fellowships for her novels and the New York Foundation for the Arts Fellowship for screenwriting. In "A Word's Meaning Can Often Depend on Who Says It," first published in the *New York Times* (1986), Naylor explains that the meaning of a word depends on social context and community consensus.

A Word's Meaning Can Often Depend on Who Says It[1]

L ANGUAGE IS THE subject. It is the written form with which I've managed to keep the wolf away from the door and, in diaries, to keep my sanity. In spite of this, I consider the written word inferior to the spoken, and much of the frustration experienced by novelists is the awareness that

---

[1] Gloria Naylor, Reprinted by permission of SLL/Sterling Lord Literistic, Inc. Copyright by Gloria Naylor. The author wants it understood that the use of the word "nigger" is reprehensible in today's society. This essay speaks to a specific time and place when that word was utilized to empower African Americans; today it is used to degrade them even if spoken from their own mouths.

283

whatever we manage to capture in even the most transcendent passages falls far short of the richness of life. Dialogue achieves its power in the dynamics of a fleeting moment of sight, sound, smell, and touch.

I'm not going to enter the debate here about whether it   2
is language that shapes reality or vice versa. That battle is doomed to be waged whenever we seek intermittent reprieve from the chicken and egg dispute. I will simply take the position that the spoken word, like the written word, amounts to a nonsensical arrangement of sounds or letters without a consensus that assigns "meaning." And building from the meanings of what we hear, we order reality. Words themselves are innocuous; it is the consensus that gives them true power.

I remember the first time I heard the word *nigger*. In my   3
third-grade class, our math tests were being passed down the rows, and as I handed the papers to a little boy in back of me, I remarked that once again he had received a much lower mark than I did. He snatched his test from me and spit out that word. Had he called me a nymphomaniac or a necrophiliac, I couldn't have been more puzzled. I didn't know what a nigger was, but I knew that whatever it meant, it was something he shouldn't have called me. This was verified when I raised my hand, and in a loud voice repeated what he had said and watched the teacher scold him for using a "bad" word. I was later to go home and ask the inevitable question that every black parent must face—"Mommy, what does *nigger* mean?"

[T]he spoken word, like the written word, amounts to a nonsensical arrangement of sounds and letter without a consensus that assigns meaning.

And what exactly did it mean? Thinking back, I realize   4
that this could not have been the first time the word was used in my presence. I was part of a large extended family that had migrated from the rural South after World War II and formed a close-knit network that gravitated around my

maternal grandparents. Their ground-floor apartment in one of the buildings they owned in Harlem was a weekend mecca for my immediate family, along with countless aunts, uncles, and cousins who brought along assorted friends. It was a bustling and open house with assorted neighbors and tenants popping in and out to exchange bits of gossip, pick up an old quarrel, or referee the ongoing checkers game in which my grandmother cheated shamelessly. They were all there to let down their hair and put up their feet after a week of labor in the factories, laundries, and shipyards of New York.

Amid the clamor, which could reach deafening proportions— 5 two or three conversations going on simultaneously, punctuated by the sound of a baby's crying somewhere in the back rooms or out on the street—there was still a rigid set of rules about what was said and how. Older children were sent out of the living room when it was time to get into the juicy details about "you-know-who" up on the third floor who had gone and gotten herself "p-r-e-g-n-a-n-t!" But my parents, knowing that I could spell well beyond my years, always demanded that I follow the others out to play. Beyond sexual misconduct and death, everything else was considered harmless for our young ears. And so among the anecdotes of the triumphs and disappointments in the various workings of their lives, the word *nigger* was used in my presence, but it was set within contexts and inflections that caused it to register in my mind as something else.

In the singular, the word was always applied to a man who 6 had distinguished himself in some situation that brought their approval for his strength, intelligence, or drive:

"Did Johnny *really* do that?" 7

"I'm telling you, that nigger pulled in $6,000 of over- 8 time last year. Said he got enough for a down payment on a house."

When used with a possessive adjective by a woman—"my 9 nigger"—it became a term of endearment for her husband or boyfriend. But it could be more than just a term applied to a man. In their mouths it became the pure essence of manhood—a disembodied force that channeled their past history of struggle and present survival against the odds into

a victorious statement of being: "Yeah, that old foreman
found out quick enough—you don't mess with a nigger."

In the plural, it became a description of some group within   10
the community that had overstepped the bounds of decency
as my family defined it. Parents who neglected their children,
a drunken couple who fought in public, people who simply
refused to look for work, those with excessively dirty mouths
or unkempt households were all "trifling niggers." This particular circle could forgive hard times, unemployment, the occasional bout of depression—they had gone through all of that
themselves—but the unforgivable sin was a lack of self-respect.

A woman could never be a "nigger" in the singular, with   11
its connotation of confirming worth. The noun *girl* was its
closest equivalent in that sense, but only when used in direct
address and regardless of the gender doing the addressing.
Girl was a token of respect for a woman. The one-syllable
word was drawn out to sound like three in recognition of
the extra ounce of wit, nerve, or daring that the woman had
shown in the situation under discussion.

"G-i-r-l, stop. You mean you said that to his face?"   12

But if the word was used in a third-person reference or   13
shortened so that it almost snapped out of the mouth, it
always involved some element of communal disapproval. And
age became an important factor in these exchanges. It was
only between individuals of the same generation, or from any
older person to a younger (but never the other way around),
that *girl* would be considered a compliment.

I don't agree with the argument that use of the word   14
nigger at this social stratum of the black community was
an internalization of racism. The dynamics were the exact
opposite: The people in my grandmother's living room took
a word that whites used to signify worthlessness or degra-
dation and rendered it impotent. Gathering there together,
they transformed *nigger* to signify the varied and complex
human beings they knew themselves to be. If the word was
to disappear totally from the mouths of even the most liberal
of white society, no one in that room was naive enough to
believe it would disappear from white minds. Meeting the
word head-on, they proved it had absolutely nothing to do
with the way they were determined to live their lives.

So there must have been dozens of times that *nigger* was 15
spoken in front of me before I reached the third grade. But
I didn't "hear" it until it was said by a small pair of lips that
had already learned it could be a way to humiliate me. That
was the word I went home and asked my mother about. And
since she knew that I had to grow up in America, she took me
in her lap and explained.

For Study and Discussion

QUESTIONS ABOUT PURPOSE

1. Why does Naylor think that written language is inferior to spoken language?
2. How does she use the word *nigger* to support her assertion?

QUESTIONS ABOUT AUDIENCE

1. What does Naylor assume about the racial identity of most of her
   readers?
2. What does she assume her readers think about the word *nigger*?

QUESTIONS ABOUT STRATEGIES

1. How does Naylor illustrate the difference between the way the
   white community and the black community use the word *nigger*?
2. How does she explain why the word could never be applied to a
   woman?

For Writing and Research

1. *Analyze* how Naylor illustrates the various ways the black
   community uses the word *nigger*.
2. *Practice* by defining a word that has special, perhaps even
   an opposite, meaning when it is used in your social group.
3. *Argue* that the way a word is spoken—by particular people
   in a particular context—gives it its true meanings.
4. *Synthesize* the explanations of the way the black community
   uses the word *girl*. See paragraphs 11 through 13 in Naylor's
   essay. Then use this information to explain how the word is
   used among contemporary women, as in "You go, girl!"

KATHLEEN NORRIS

Kathleen Norris was born in 1947 in Washington, D.C., and educated at Bennington College. She worked for a brief period as program secretary for the Academy of American Poets in New York before moving to South Dakota, where she became affiliated with Leaves of Grass, Inc. She has contributed poems and essays to *Dragonfly, Sumac,* and *Tennessee Poetry Journal;* published two collections of poetry, *Falling Off* (1971) and *Middle of the World* (1981), and five works of nonfiction, *Dakota: A Spiritual Geography* (1993), *The Cloister Walk* (1996), *Amazing Grace* (1998), *The Virgin of Bennington* (2000), *Acedia and Me: A Marriage, Monks and a Writer's Life* (2003). In "The Holy Use of Gossip," reprinted from *Dakota,* Norris defines the various uses of gossip in a small town.

The Holy Use of Gossip[2]

It is the responsibility of writers to listen to gossip and pass it on. It is the way all storytellers learn about life.
— GRACE PALEY

If there's anything worth calling theology, it is listening to people's stories, listening to them and cherishing them.
— MARY PELLAUER

I ONCE SCANDALIZED a group of North Dakota teenagers   1
who had been determined to scandalize me. Working as an artist-in-residence in their school for three weeks, I happened

---

to hit prom weekend. Never much for proms in high school, I helped decorate, cutting swans out of posterboard and sprinkling them with purple glitter as the school gym was festooned with lavender and silver crepe paper streamers. On Monday morning a group of the school outlaws was gossiping in the library, just loud enough for me to hear, about the drunken exploits that had taken place at a prairie party in the wee hours after the dance: kids meeting in some remote spot, drinking beer and listening to car stereos turned up loud, then, near dawn, going to one girl's house for breakfast. I finally spoke up and said, "See, it's like I told you: the party's not over until you've told the stories. That's where all writing starts." They looked up at me, pretending that it bothered them that I'd heard.

"And," I couldn't resist adding, "everyone knows you 2 don't get piss-drunk and then eat scrambled eggs. If you didn't know it before, you know it now." "You're not going to write about that, are you?" one girl said, her eyes wide. "I don't know," I replied, "I might. It's all grist for the mill."

At its deepest level, small-town gossip is about how we face matters of life and death.

When my husband and I first moved to Dakota, people 3 were quick to tell us about an eccentric young man who came from back East and gradually lost his grip on reality. He shared a house with his sheep until relatives came and took him away. "He was a college graduate," someone would always add, looking warily at us as if to say, we know what can happen to Easterners who are too well educated. This was one of the first tales to go into my West River treasure-house of stories. It was soon joined by the story of the man who shot himself to see what it felt like. He hit his lower leg and later said that while he didn't feel anything for a few seconds, after that it hurt like hell.

There was Rattlesnake Bill, a cowboy who used to carry   4
rattlers in a paper sack in his pickup truck. If you didn't
believe him, he'd put his hand in without looking and take
one out to show you. One night Bill limped into a downtown
bar on crutches. A horse he was breaking dragged him for
about a mile, and he was probably lucky to be alive. He'd
been knocked out, he didn't know for how long, and when
he regained consciousness he had crawled to his house and
changed clothes to come to town. Now Bill thought he'd
drink a little whiskey for the pain. "Have you been to a doctor?" friends asked. "Nah, whiskey'll do."

Later that night at the steak house I managed to get Bill   5
to eat something, most of my steak, as it turned out, but he
needed it more than I. The steak was rare, and that didn't sit
well with Bill. A real man eats his steak well done. But when
I said, "What's the matter, are you too chicken to eat rare
meat?" he gobbled it down. He slept in his pickup that night,
and someone managed to get him to a doctor the next day.
He had a broken pelvis.

There was another cowboy who had been mauled by a   6
bobcat in a remote horse barn by the Grand River. The animal had leapt from a hayloft as he tied up a horse, and he
had managed to grab a rifle and shoot her. He felt terrible
afterwards, saying, "I should have realized the only reason
she'd have attacked like that was because she was protecting
young." He found her two young cubs, still blind, in the loft.
In a desperate attempt to save them he called several veterinarians in the hope that they might know of a lactating cat
who had aborted. Such a cat was found, but the cubs lived
just a few more days.

There was the woman who nursed her husband through a   7
long illness. A dutiful farm daughter and ranch wife, she had
never experienced life on her own. When she was widowed,
all the town spoke softly about "poor Ida." But when "poor
Ida" kicked up her heels and, entering a delayed adolescence
in her fifties, dyed her hair, dressed provocatively, and went
dancing more than once a week at the steak house, the sympathetic cooing of the gossips turned to outrage. The woman

at the center of the storm hadn't changed; she was still an innocent, bewildered by the calumny now directed at her. She lived it down and got herself a steady boyfriend, but she still dyes her hair and dresses flashy. I'm grateful for the color she adds to the town.

Sometimes it seems as if the whole world is fueled by gossip. 8 Much of what passes for hard news today is the Hollywood fluff that was relegated to pulp movie magazines when I was a girl. From the Central Intelligence Agency to *Entertainment Tonight*, gossip is big business. But in small towns, gossip is still small-time. And as bad as it can be—venal, petty, mean— in the small town it also stays closer to the roots of the word. If you look up gossip in the *Oxford English Dictionary* you find that it is derived from the words for God and sibling, and originally meant "akin to God." It was used to describe one who has contracted spiritual kinship by acting as a sponsor at baptism; one who helps "give a name to." Eric Partridge's *Origins*, a dictionary of etymology, tells you simply to "see God," and there you find that the word's antecedents include gospel, godspell, *sippe* (or consanguinity) and "*sabha*, a village community—notoriously interrelated."

We are interrelated in a small town, whether or not we're 9 related by blood. We know without thinking about it who owns what car; inhabitants of a town as small as a monastery learn to recognize each other's footsteps in the hall. Story is a safety valve for people who live as intimately as that; and I would argue that gossip done well can be a holy thing. It can strengthen communal bonds.

Gossip provides comic relief for people under tension. 10 Candidates at one monastery are told of a novice in the past who had such a hot temper that the others loved to bait him. Once when they were studying he closed a window and the other monks opened it; once, twice. When he got up to close the window for the third time, he yelled at them, "Why are you making me sin with this window?"

Gossip can help us give a name to ourselves. The most 11 revealing section of the weekly *Lemmon Leader* is the personal column in the classified ads, where people express thanks to

those who helped with the bloodmobile, a 4-H booth at the
county fair, a Future Homemakers of America fashion show,
a benefit for a family beset by huge medical bills. If you've
been in the hospital or have suffered a death in the family,
you take out an ad thanking the doctor, ambulance crew,
and wellwishers who visited, sent cards, offered prayers, or
brought gifts of food.

Often these ads are quite moving, written from the heart. 12
The parents of a small boy recently thanked those who had
remembered their son with

> prayers, cards, balloons, and gifts, and gave moral
> support to the rest of the family when Ty under-
> went surgery. . . . It's great to be home again in
> this caring community, and our biggest task now
> is to get Ty to eat more often and larger amounts.
> Where else but Lemmon would we find people
> who would stop by and have a bedtime snack and
> milk with Ty or provide good snacks just to help
> increase his caloric intake, or a school system with
> staff that take the time to make sure he eats his
> extra snacks. May God Bless all of you for caring
> about our "special little" boy—who is going to
> gain weight!

No doubt it is the vast land surrounding us, brooding on 13
the edge of our consciousness that makes it necessary for us
to call such attention to human activity. Publicly asserting,
as do many of these ads, that we live in a caring community
helps us keep our hopes up in a hard climate or hand times,
and gives us a sense of identity. Privacy takes on another
meaning in such an environment, where you are asked to
share your life, humbling yourself before the common wisdom, such as it is. Like everyone else, you become public
property and come to accept things that city people would
consider rude. A young woman using the pay phone in a
West River Cafe is scrutinized by several older women who
finally ask her, "Who are you, anyway?" On discovering that
she is from a ranch some sixty miles south, they question her

until, learning her mother's maiden name, they are satisfied. They know her grandparents by reputation: good ranchers, good people.

The *Leader* has correspondents in rural areas within some   14
fifty miles of Lemmon—Bison, Chance, Duck Creek, Howe, Morristown, Rosebud (on the Grand River), Shadehill, Spring Butte, Thunder Hawk, White Butte—as well as at the local nursing home and in the town of Lemmon itself, who report on "doings." If you volunteer at the nursing home's weekly popcorn party and sing-along, your name appears. If you host a card party at your home, this is printed, along with the names of your guests. If you have guests from out of town, their names appear. Many notices would baffle an outsider, as they require an intimate knowledge of family relationships to decipher. One recent column from White Butte, headed "Neighbors Take Advantage of Mild Winter Weather to Visit Each Other," read in part: "Helen Johanssen spent several afternoons with Gaylene Francke; Mavis Merdahl was a Wednesday overnight guest at the Alvera Ellis home."

Allowing yourself to be a subject of gossip is one of the   15
sacrifices you make, living in a small town. And the pain caused by the loose talk of ignorant people is undeniable. One couple I know, having lost their only child to a virulent pneumonia (a robust thirty-five years old, he was dead in a matter of days) had to endure rumors that he had died of suicide, AIDS, and even anthrax. But it's also true that the gossips don't know all that they think they know, and often misread things in a comical way. My husband was once told that he was having an affair with a woman he hadn't met, and I still treasure the day I was encountered by three people who said, "Have you sold your house yet?" "When's the baby due?" and, "I'm sorry to hear your mother died."

I could trade the sources of the first two rumors: we'd   16
helped a friend move into a rented house, and I'd bought baby clothes downtown when I learned that I would soon become an aunt. The third rumor was easy enough to check; I called my mother on the phone. The flip side, the saving grace, is that despite the most diligent attentions of the diehard gossips, it is possible to have secrets. Of course the

most important things can't be hidden: birth, sickness, death, divorce. But gossip is essentially democratic. It may be the plumber and his wife who had a screaming argument in a bar, or it could be the bank president's wife who moved out and rented a room in the motel; every one is fair game. And although there are always those who take delight in the misfortunes of others, and relish a juicy story at the expense of truth and others' feelings, this may be the exception rather than the rule. Surprisingly often, gossip is the way small-town people express solidarity.

I recall a marriage that was on the rocks. The couple had   17
split up, and gossip ran wild. Much sympathy was expressed for the children, and one friend of the couple said to me, "The worst thing she could do is to take him back too soon. This will take time." Those were healing words, a kind of prayer. And when the family did reunite, the town breathed a collective sigh of relief.

My own parents' marriage was of great interest in   18
Lemmon back in the 1930s. My mother, the town doctor's only child, eloped with another Northwestern University student; a musician, of all things. A poor preacher's kid. "This will bear watching," one matriarch said. My parents fooled her. As time went on, the watching grew dull. Now going on fifty-five years, their marriage has outlasted all the gossip.

Like the desert tales that monks have used for centuries   19
as a basis for a theology and way of life, the tales of small-town gossip are often morally instructive, illustrating the ways ordinary people survive the worst that happens to them; or, conversely, the ways in which self-pity, anger, and despair can overwhelm and destroy them. Gossip is theology translated into experience. In it we hear great stories of conversion, like the drunk who turns his or her life around, as well as stories of failure. We can see that pride really does go before a fall, and that hope is essential. We watch closely those who retire, or who lose a spouse, lest they lose interest in living. When we gossip we are also praying, not only for them but for ourselves.

At its deepest level, small-town gossip is about how we   20
face matters of life and death. We see the gossip of earlier

times, the story immortalized in ballads such as "Barbara Allen," lived out before our eyes as a young man obsessively in love with a vain young woman nearly self-destructs. We also see how people heal themselves. One of the bravest people I know is a young mother who sewed and embroidered exquisite baptismal clothes for her church with the memorial money she received when her first baby died. When she gave birth to a healthy girl a few years later, the whole town rejoiced.

My favorite gossip takes note of the worst and the best that 21
is in us. Two women I know were diagnosed with terminal cancer. One said, "If I ever get out of this hospital, I'm going to look out for Number One." And that's exactly what she did. Against overwhelming odds, she survived, and it made her mean. The other woman spoke about the blessings of a life that had taken some hard blows: her mother had killed herself when she was a girl, her husband had died young. I happened to visit her just after she'd been told that she had less than a year to live. She was dry-eyed, and had been reading the Psalms. She was entirely realistic about her illness and said to me, "The one thing that scares me is the pain. I hope I die before I turn into an old bitch." I told her family that story after the funeral, and they loved it; they could hear in it their mother's voice, the way she really was.

For Study and Discussion

QUESTIONS ABOUT PURPOSE

1. What common attitude about gossip does Norris hope to counteract?
2. What kind of picture of a small town does Norris create? What common beliefs about small towns does she seek to overcome?

QUESTIONS ABOUT AUDIENCE

1. What assumptions does Norris make about the way most people react to stories?

2. Although today relatively few people live in small towns, why does Norris suggest that her readers should see that her generalizations apply to larger communities?

QUESTIONS ABOUT STRATEGIES

1. How does Norris expand the definition of *gossip* into something that goes beyond the ordinary use of the term?
2. How does she demonstrate that everyone is "fair game" for gossip?

For Writing and Research

1. *Analyze* how the tales Norris tells are "morally instructive."
2. *Practice* by describing some negative effects of gossip that you have witnessed.
3. *Argue* that there are significant reasons for not passing on gossip.
4. *Synthesize:* Read several "gossip" magazines about a celebrity or political figure. Then define the effect on privacy of creating such gossip.

DIANE ACKERMAN

Diane Ackerman was born in 1948 in Waukegan, Illinois, and was educated at Boston University, Pennsylvania State University, and Cornell University. After jobs as a researcher and editorial assistant, Ackerman began teaching writing at such schools as the University of Pittsburgh; Washington University, St. Louis; and Cornell University. Her own writing includes several collections of poems (*The Planets: A Cosmic Pastoral,* 1976; and *The Senses of Animals,* 2000), a play (*Reverse Thunder: A Dramatic Poem,* 1988), two television documentaries (*Ideas,* 1990; and *The Senses,* 1995), and numerous works of nonfiction (*A Natural History of the Senses,* 1990; *A Natural History of Love,* 1994; *A Natural History of My Garden,* 2001; *An Alchemy of Mind: The Marvel and Mystery of the Brain,* 2004; *The Zookeeper's Wife,* 2008; and *One Hundred Names for Love: A Stroke, a Marriage, and the Language of Healing,* 2011). In "Pain," reprinted from *A Natural History of the Senses,* Ackerman examines the difficulty of defining pain.

Pain[3]

IN THE SAND-SWEPT sprawl of the panoramic film *Lawrence of Arabia* a scene of quintessential machismo stands out: T. E. Lawrence holding his hand over a candle flame until the flesh starts to sizzle. When his companion tries the same thing, he recoils in pain, crying "Doesn't that hurt you?" as

1

---

he nurses his burned hand. "Yes," Lawrence replies coolly. "Then what is the trick?" the companion asks. "The trick," Lawrence answers, "is not to mind."

One of the great riddles of biology is why the experi-   2 ence of pain is so subjective. Being able to withstand pain depends to a considerable extent on culture and tradition. Many soldiers have denied pain despite appalling wounds, not even requesting morphine, although in peacetime they would have demanded it. Most people going into the hospital for an operation focus completely on their pain and suffering, whereas soldiers or saints and other martyrs can think about something nobler and more important to them, and this clouds their sense of pain. Religions have always encouraged their martyrs to experience pain in order to purify the spirit. We come into this world with only the slender word "I," and giving it up in a sacred delirium is the painful ecstasy religions demand. When a fakir runs across hot coals, his skin does begin to singe—you can smell burning flesh; he just doesn't feel it. In Bali a few years ago, my mother saw men go into trances and pick up red-hot cannonballs from an open fire, then carry them down the road. As meditation techniques and biofeedback have shown, the mind can learn to conquer pain. This is particularly true in moments of crisis or exaltation, when concentrating on something outside oneself seems to distract the mind from the body, and the body from suffering and time. Of course, there are those who welcome pain in order to surmount it. In 1989, I read about a new craze in California: well-to-do business people taking weekend classes in hot-coal-walking. Pushing the body to or beyond its limits has always appealed to human beings. There is a part of our psyche that is pure timekeeper and weather watcher. Not only do we long to know how fast we can run, how high we can jump, how long we can hold our breath under water—we also like to keep checking these limits regularly to see if they've changed. Why? What difference does it make? The human body is miraculous and beautiful, whether it can "clean and jerk" three hundred pounds, swim the English Channel, or survive a year riding the subway.

In anthropological terms, we've come to be who we are by evolving sharper ways to adapt to the environment, and, from the outset, what has guided us has been an elaborate system of rewards. Small wonder we're addicted to quiz shows and lotteries, paychecks and bonuses. We've always explored our mental limits, too, and pushed them without letup. In the early eighties, I spent a year as a soccer journalist, following the dazzling legwork of Pelé, Franz Beckenbauer, and virtually every other legendary international star the New York Cosmos had signed up for equally legendary sums of American cash. Choose your favorite sport; now imagine seeing all the world's best players on one team. I was interested in the ceremonial violence of sports, the psychology of games, the charmed circle of the field, the breezy rhetoric of the legs, the anthropological spectacle of watching twenty-two barely clad men run on grass in the sunlight, hazing the quarry of a ball toward the net. The fluency and grace of soccer appealed for a number of reasons, and I wanted to absorb some of its atmosphere for a novel I was writing. I was amazed to discover that the players frequently realized only at halftime or after a match that they'd hurt themselves badly and were indeed in wicked pain. During the match, there hadn't been the rumor of pain, but once the match was over and they could afford the luxury of suffering, pain screamed like a noon factory whistle.

Being able to withstand pain depends to a considerable extent on culture and tradition.

Often our fear of pain contributes to it. Our culture 3 expects childbirth to be a deeply painful event, and so, for us, it is. Women from other cultures stop their work in the fields to give birth, returning to the fields immediately afterward. Initiation and adolescence rites around the world often involve penetrating pain, which initiates must endure to prove themselves worthy. In the sun dance of the Sioux, for instance, a young warrior would allow the skin of his chest to be pierced by iron rods; then he was hung from a stanchion. When I was in Istanbul in the 1970s, I saw teenage boys dressed in shiny silk fezzes and silk suits decorated with glitter. They were preparing for circumcision, a festive event in the life of a Turk, which occurs at around the age of fifteen. No anesthetic is used; instead, a boy is given a jelly candy to chew. Sir Richard Burton's writings abound with descriptions of tribal mutilation and torture rituals, including one in which a shaman removes an apron of flesh from the front of a boy, cutting all the way from the stomach to the thighs, producing a huge white scar.

Women in some cultures go through many painful initiation rites, often including circumcision, which removes or destroys the clitoris. Being able to endure the pain of childbirth is expected of women, but there are also disguised rites of pain, pain that is endured for the sake of health or beauty. Women have their legs waxed as a matter of fashion, and have done so throughout the ages. When mine were waxed at a Manhattan beauty salon recently, the pain, which began like 10,000 bees stinging me simultaneously, was excruciating. Change the woman from a Rumanian cosmetician to a German Gestapo agent. Change the room from a cubicle in a beauty emporium to a prison cell. Keep the level of pain exactly the same, and it easily qualifies as torture. We tend to think of torture in the name of beauty as an aberration of the ancients, but there are modern scourging parlors. People have always mutilated their skins, often enduring pain to be beautiful, as if the pain chastened the beauty, gave it the special veneer of sacrifice. Many women experience extreme pain during their periods each month, but they accept the pain because they understand that it's not caused by someone else, it's not malicious, and it doesn't surprise them; and this makes all the difference.

There are also illusions of pain as vivid as optical illusions, times when the sufferer imagines he or she feels pain that cannot possibly exist. In some cultures, the father experiences a false pregnancy—*couvade* as it's called—and takes to bed with childbirth pains, going through his own arduous experience of having a baby. The internal organs don't have many pain receptors (the skin is supposed to be the guard post), so people often feel "referred pain" when one of their organs is in trouble. Heart attacks frequently produce a pain in the stomach, the left arm, or the shoulder. When this happens, the brain can't figure out exactly where the message is coming from. In the classic phenomenon of phantom-limb pain, the brain gets faulty signals and continues to feel pain in a limb that has been amputated; such pain can be torturous, perverse, and maddening, since there is nothing physically present to hurt.

Pain has plagued us throughout the history of our species. 6 We spend our lives trying to avoid it, and, from one point of view, what we call "happiness" may be just the absence of pain. Yet it is difficult to define pain, which may be sharp, dull, shooting, throbbing, imaginary, or referred. We have many pains that surge from within as cramps and aches. And we also talk about emotional distress as pain. Pains are often combined, the emotional with the physical, and the physical with the physical. When you burn yourself, the skin swells and blisters, and when the blister breaks, the skin hurts in yet another way. A wound may become infected. Then histamine and serotonin are released, which dilate the blood vessels and trigger a pain response. Not all internal injuries can be felt (it's possible to do brain surgery under a local anesthetic), but illnesses that constrict blood flow often are: Angina pectoris, for example, which occurs when the coronary arteries shrink too tight for blood to comfortably pass. Even intense pain often eludes accurate description, as Virginia Woolf reminds us in her essay "On Being Ill": "English, which can express the thoughts of Hamlet and the tragedy of Lear, has no words for the shiver and the headache . . . let a sufferer try to describe a pain in his head to a doctor and language at once runs dry."

For Study and Discussion

QUESTIONS ABOUT PURPOSE

1. How does Ackerman's opening paragraph introduce the main purpose of her essay?
2. What assumptions about pain do you think she is challenging?

QUESTIONS ABOUT AUDIENCE

1. How does Ackerman's discussion of the ways different people deal with pain suggest that her readers should rethink their conventional wisdom about the sensation?
2. How does Ackerman's use of the phrase "our culture" help her identify her readers?

QUESTIONS ABOUT STRATEGIES

1. How does Ackerman illustrate "why the experience of pain is so subjective"?
2. How does she explain the illusion of pain?

For Writing and Research

1. *Analyze* the range of examples that support Ackerman's assertion that pain depends on "culture and tradition."
2. *Practice* by describing your attempt to define a strange pain to a doctor.
3. *Argue* that advertising encourages the illusion that most pain can be averted by taking some magic potion.
4. *Synthesize:* Research the pain management business in our culture. Then use this information to argue that this business is (1) a valuable medical technology or (2) a hoax.

JAMES GLEICK

James Gleick was born in 1954 in New York City and began his career as a copyeditor for the *New York Times*. He began writing articles on science for the *Times*, eventually publishing a series of widely acclaimed books, such as *Chaos: Making a New Science* (1987), *Year of Genius: The Life and Science of Richard Feynman* (1992), and *Faster: The Acceleration of Just About Everything* (1999). In his more recent books, *What Just Happened: A Chronicle from the Information Frontier* (2002) *Isaac Newton* (2003), and *The Information: A History, a Theory, a Flood* (2011). In "Attention! Multitaskers," reprinted from *Faster: The Acceleration of Just About Everything,* Gleick defines the origin and significance of the word that describes the "simultaneous fragmentation and overloading of human attention."

Attention! Multitaskers[4]

THE FINAL, FATAL flaw in the time-use pie chart is that we are multitasking creatures. It is possible, after all, to tie shoes and watch television, to eat and read, to shave and talk with the children. These days it is possible to drive, eat, listen to a book, and talk on the phone, all at once, if you dare. No segment of time—not a day, not a second—can really be a zero-sum game. 1

"Attention! Multitaskers," says an advertisement for an AT&T wireless telephone service. "Demo all these exciting features"—namely E-mail, voice telephone, and pocket 2

---

[4]James Gleick, From *Faster* by James Gleick, copyright © 1999 by James Gleick. Used by permission of Pantheon Books, a division of Random House, Inc.

303

organizer. Pay attention if you can. We have always multi-tasked—inability to walk and chew gum is a time-honored cause for derision—but never so intensely or so self-consciously as now. If haste is the gas pedal, multitasking is overdrive. We are multitasking connoisseurs—experts in crowding, pressing, packing, and overlapping distinct activities in our all-too-finite moments. Some reports from the front lines:

David Feldman, in New York, schedules his tooth-flossing 3 to coincide with his regular browsing of on-line discussion groups (the latest in food, the latest in Brian Wilson). He has learned to hit Page Down with his pinky. Mark Maxham of California admits to even more embarrassing arrangements of tasks. "I find myself doing strange little optimizations," he says, "like life is a set of computer code and I'm a compiler." Similarly, by the time Michael Hartl heads for the bathroom in his California Institute of Technology digs each morning, he has already got his computer starting its progress through the Windows boot sequence, and then, as he runs to breakfast, he hits Control-Shift-D to dial into the campus computer network, and then he gets his Web browser started, downloading graphics, so he can check the news while he eats. "I figure I save at least two or three minutes a day this way," he says. "Don't laugh." Then there's the subroutine he thinks of as "the mouthwash gambit," where he swigs a mouthful on one pass by the sink, swishes it around in his mouth as he gets his bicycle, and spits out as he heads back in the other direction, toward a class in general relativity.

> *If haste is the gas pedal, multitasking is overdrive.*

The word *multitasking* came from computer scientists 4 of the 1960s. They arranged to let a single computer serve multiple users on a network. When a computer multitasks, it usually just alternates tasks, but on the finest of time scales. It slices time and interleaves its tasks. Unless, that is, it has more than one processor running, in which case multitasking can be truly parallel processing. Either way, society grabbed the term as fast as it did *Type A*. We apply it to our own flesh-and-blood CPUs. Not only do we multitask, but, with computers as our guides, we multitask self-consciously.

Multitasking begins in the service of efficiency. Working at   5
a computer terminal in the London newsroom of Bloomberg News, Douglas McGill carried on a long telephone conversation with a colleague in New York. His moment of realization came when, still talking on the phone, he sent off an E-mail message to another colleague in Connecticut and immediately received her reply. "It squeezes more information than was previously squeezable into a given amount of time," he says. "I wonder if this contributes to that speeding-up sensation we all feel?" Clearly it does.

Is there any limit? A few people claim to be able to listen to   6
two different pieces of music at once. Many more learn to take advantage of the brain's apparent ability to process spoken and written text in separate channels. Mike Holderness, in London, watches television with closed captioning so that he can keep the sound off and listen to the unrelated music of his choice. Or he writes several letters at once—"in the sense that I have processes open and waiting." None of this is enough for a cerebral cortex conditioned to the pace of life on-line, he realizes:

> *Ten years ago, I was delighted and enthralled that I could get a telegram-like E-mail from Philadelphia to London in only fifteen minutes. Three years ago, I was delighted and enthralled that I could fetch an entire thesis from Texas to London in only five minutes. Now, I drum my fingers on the desk when a hundred-kilobyte file takes more than twenty seconds to arrive . . . damn, it's coming from New Zealand . . .*

It seems natural to recoil from this simultaneous fragmen-   7
tation and overloading of human attention. How well can

people really accomplish their multitasks? "It's hard to get around the forebrain bottleneck," said Earl Hunt, a professor of psychology and computer science at the University of Washington. "Our brains function the same way the Cro-Magnon brains did, so technology isn't going to change that." But for many—humans, not computers—a sense of satisfaction and well-being comes with this saturation of parallel pathways in the brain. We divide ourselves into parts, perhaps, each receiving sensations, sending messages, or manipulating the environment in some way. We train ourselves as Samuel Renshaw would have trained us. Or, then again, we slice time just as a computer does, feeding each task a bit of our attention in turn. Perhaps the young have an advantage because of the cultural conditioning they received from early exposure to computers and fast entertainment media. Corporate managers think so. Marc Prensky, a Bankers Trust vice president, had to learn to overcome instinctive annoyance when a young subordinate began reading E-mail during a face-to-face conversation; the subordinate explained: "I'm still listening; I'm parallel processing." This whole generation of workers, Prensky decided, weaned on video games, operates at *twitch speed*—"your thumbs going a million miles a minute," and a good thing, if managers can take advantage of it.

At least one computer manufacturer, Gateway, applies 8 multitasking to technical support. Customers call in for help, wait on hold, and then hear voices. "Hello," they are told. "You are on a conference call." William Slaughter, a lawyer calling from Philadelphia, slowly realizes that he has joined a tech-support group therapy session. He listens to Brian helping Vince. Next, Vince listens to Brian helping William. It's like a chess master playing a simultaneous exhibition, William thinks, though Brian seems a bit frazzled. Somehow the callers cope with their resentment at not being deemed worthy of Brian's undivided attention. Why should he sit daydreaming while they scurry to reboot? "Hello, Vicky," they hear him say. "You are on a conference call."

There is ample evidence that many of us choose this style   9
of living. We're willing to pay for the privilege. An entire class
of technologies is dedicated to the furthering of multitasking.
Waterproof shower radios and, now, telephones. Car phones,
of course. Objects as innocent-seeming as trays for magazines
on exercise machines are tools for multitasking (and surely
television sets are playing in the foreground, too). Picture-
in-picture display on your television set. (Gregory Stevens, in
Massachusetts: "PIP allows me to watch PBS/C-Span or the
like, and keep the ball game on or an old movie. Of course,
it is impossible for anyone else to enjoy this, with me changing the pictures and audio feed every few seconds. When the
computer and the phone are available in a multiwindow form
on the television, things are going to be very different.")
Even without picture-in-picture, the remote control enables
a time-slicing variation on the same theme. Marc Weiden-
baum, in San Francisco, has a shorthand for describing an
evening's activities to his girlfriend: "Got home. Ate some
soup. Watched twenty or thirty shows." He means this more
or less literally:

> *I'll watch two sitcoms and a* Star Trek: Voyager *epi-*
> *sode and routinely check MTV (didn't they used to*
> *run music videos?) and CNN (didn't they used to*
> *run news?) in a single hour.*
> *And really not feel like I'm missing out on*
> *anything.*

Nothing could be more revealing of the transformation   10
of human sensibility over the past century than this widespread unwillingness to settle for soaking up, in single-task
fashion, the dynamic flow of sound and picture coming from
a television screen. Is any one channel, in itself, monotonous? Marshall McLuhan failed to predict this: the medium
of television seemed *cool* and all-absorbing to him, so different from the experience available to us a generation later.
For the McLuhan who announced that the medium was the

message, television was a black-and-white, unitary stream. McLuhan did not surf with remote control. Sets were tiny and the resolution poor—"visually low in data," he wrote in 1964, "a ceaselessly forming contour of things limned by the scanning finger." People were seen mostly in close-up, perforce. Thus he asserted: "TV will not work as background. It engages you. You have to be *with* it."

No longer. Paradoxically, perhaps, as television has gained   11 in vividness and clarity, it has lost its command of our foreground. For some people television has been bumped off its pedestal by the cool, fast, fluid, indigenously multitasking activity of browsing the Internet. Thus anyone—say, Steven Leibel of California—can counter McLuhan definitively (typing in one window while reading a World Wide Web page in another): "The Web and TV complement each other perfectly. TV doesn't require much attention from the viewer. It fits perfectly into the spaces created by downloading Web pages." If he really needs to concentrate, he turns down the sound momentarily. Not everyone bothers concentrating. Eight million American households report television sets and personal computers running, together in the same room, "often" or "always."

Not long ago, listening to the simpler audio stream of   12 broadcast radio was a single-task activity for most people. The radio reached into homes and grabbed listeners by the lapel. It could dominate their time and attention—for a few decades. "A child might sit," Robinson and Godbey recall sentimentally, "staring through the window at the darkening trees, hearing only the Lone Ranger's voice and the hooves of horses in the canyon." Now it is rare for a person to listen to the radio *and do nothing else.* Programmers structure radio's content with the knowledge that they can count on only a portion of the listener's attention, and only for intermittent intervals. And rarely with full attention. Much of the radio audience at any given moment has its senses locked up in a more demanding activity—probably driving. Or showering, or cooking, or jogging. Radio has become a secondary task in a multitasking world.

For Study and Discussion

QUESTIONS ABOUT PURPOSE

1. How does the title of Gleick's book, *Faster: The Acceleration of Just About Everything*, help explain the purpose of this essay?
2. What is he attempting to prove about the relationship between time and productivity?

QUESTIONS ABOUT AUDIENCE

1. What assumptions does Gleick make about his readers' attitude toward the effective use of time?
2. How does he identify generational differences in his readers' attitude toward multitasking?

QUESTIONS ABOUT STRATEGIES

1. How does Gleick explain the origin of the word *multitasking*?
2. How does he use the routines of people such as David Feldman, Mark Maxham, and Michael Hartl to illustrate the word?

For Writing and Research

1. *Analyze* how Gleick uses television to help define *multitasking*.
2. *Practice* by describing a typical day when you have found yourself multitasking.
3. *Argue* that multitasking creates inefficiency rather than productivity.
4. *Synthesize:* Research the impact of emerging technologies such as computers, BlackBerry handheld devices, and iPhones. Then use this information to explain how multitasking has created a demand for these gadgets.

JOAN DIDION

Joan Didion was born in Sacramento, California, in 1934, and educated at the University of California at Berkeley. She worked as a feature editor at *Vogue* and later as a contributing editor at *National Review* and *Esquire*. She has written five novels: *Run River* (1963), *Play It As It Lays* (1970), *A Book of Common Prayer* (1976), *Democracy* (1984), and *The Last Thing He Wants* (1996). But Didion is perhaps best known for her meticulously crafted nonfiction, articulating her personal vision of events public and private. *Slouching Toward Bethlehem* (1968), often described as a classic, describes the cultural turmoil of the 1960s. Her other work includes *The White Album* (1983) and books about the death of her husband, *The Year of Magical Thinking* (2006), and her daughter, *Blue Nights* (2011). In "On Morality," excerpted from *Slouching Toward Bethlehem,* Didion explains the difficulty of defining an abstract word such as *morality.*

On Morality[5]

A S IT HAPPENS I am in Death Valley, in a room at the Enterprise Motel and Trailer Park, and it is July, and it is hot. In fact it is 119°. I cannot seem to make the air conditioner work, but there is a small refrigerator, and I can wrap ice cubes in a towel and hold them against the small of my back. With the help of the ice cubes I have been trying

---

[5] Joan Didion, "On Morality" from *Slouching Towards Bethlehem* by Joan Didion. Copyright © 1966, 1968 renewed 1996 by Joan Didion. Reprinted by permission of Farrar, Straus and Giroux, LLC.

to think, because *The American Scholar* asked me to write, in some abstract way, about "morality," a word I distrust more every day, but my mind veers inflexibly toward the particular.

Here are some particulars. At midnight last night, on the road in from Las Vegas to Death Valley Junction, a car hit a shoulder and turned over. The driver, very young and apparently drunk, was killed instantly. His girl was found alive but bleeding internally, deep in shock. I talked this afternoon to the nurse who had driven the girl to the nearest doctor, 185 miles across the floor of the Valley and three ranges of lethal mountain road. The nurse explained that her husband, a talc miner, had stayed on the highway with the boy's body until the coroner could get over the mountains from Bishop, at dawn today. "You can't just leave a body on the highway," she said. "It's immoral."

It was one instance in which I did not distrust the word, because she meant something quite specific. She meant that if a body is left alone for even a few minutes on the desert, the coyotes close in and eat the flesh. Whether or not a corpse is torn apart by coyotes may seem only a sentimental consideration, but of course it is more: one of the promises we make to one another is that we will try to retrieve our casualties, try not to abandon our dead to the coyotes. If we have been taught to keep our promises—if, in the simplest terms, our upbringing is good enough—we stay with the body, or have bad dreams.

I am talking, of course, about the kind of social code that is sometimes called, usually pejoratively, "wagon-train morality." In fact that is precisely what it is. For better or worse, we are what we learned as children: my own childhood was illuminated by graphic litanies of the grief awaiting those who failed in their loyalties to each other. The Donner-Reed Party, starving in the Sierra snows, all the ephemera of civilization gone save that one vestigial taboo, the provision that no one should eat his own blood kin. The Jayhawkers, who quarreled and separated not far from where I am tonight. Some of them died in the Funerals and some of them died down near Badwater and most of the rest of them died in the Panamints. A woman who got through gave the Valley its name. Some might say that the Jayhawkers were killed by the desert summer, and the Donner Party by the mountain winter, by circumstances beyond control; we were taught instead that they had somewhere abdicated their responsibilities, somehow breached their primary loyalties, or they would not have found themselves helpless in the mountain winter or the desert summer, would not have given way to acrimony, would not have deserted one another, would not have *failed*. In brief, we heard such stories as cautionary tales, and they still suggest the only kind of "morality" that seems to me to have any but the most potentially mendacious meaning.

You are quite possibly impatient with me by now; I am   5 talking, you want to say, about a "morality" so primitive that it scarcely deserves the name, a code that has as its point only survival, not the attainment of the ideal good. Exactly. Particularly out here tonight, in this country so ominous and terrible that to live in it is to live with antimatter, it is difficult to believe that "the good" is a knowable quantity. Let me tell you what it is like out here tonight. Stories travel at night on the desert. Someone gets in his pickup and drives a couple of hundred miles for a beer, and he carries news of what is happening, back wherever he came from. Then he drives another hundred miles for another beer, and passes along stories from the last place as well as from the one before; it is a network kept alive by people whose instincts tell them that if they do not keep moving at night on the desert they will lose all reason. Here is a story that is going around the desert tonight: over across the Nevada line, sheriff's deputies are diving in some underground pools, trying to retrieve a couple of bodies known to be in the hole. The widow of one of the drowned boys is over there; she is eighteen, and pregnant and is said not to leave the hole. The divers go down and come up, and she just stands there and stares into the water. They have been diving for ten days but have found no bottom to the caves, no bodies and no trace of them, only the black 90° water going down and down and down, and a single translucent fish, not classified. The story tonight is

that one of the divers has been hauled up incoherent, out
of his head, shouting—until they got him out of there so
that the widow could not hear—about water that got hotter instead of cooler as he went down, about light flickering through the water, about magma, about underground
nuclear testing.

That is the tone stories take out here, and there are quite 6
a few of them tonight. And it is more than the stories alone.
Across the road at the Faith Community Church a couple of
dozen old people, come here to live in trailers and die in the
sun, are holding a prayer sing. I cannot hear them and do not
want to. What I can hear are occasional coyotes and a constant chorus of "Baby the Rain Must Fall" from the jukebox
in the Snake Room next door, and if I were also to hear those
dying voices, those Midwestern voices drawn to this lunar
country for some unimaginable atavistic rites, *rock of ages cleft
for me,* I think I would lose my own reason. Every now and
then I imagine I hear a rattlesnake, but my husband says that
it is a faucet, a paper rustling, the wind. Then he stands by
a window, and plays a flashlight over the dry wash outside.

What does it mean? It means nothing manageable. There 7
is some sinister hysteria in the air out here tonight, some
hint of the monstrous perversion to which any human idea
can come. "I followed my own conscience." "I did what I
thought was right." How many madmen have said it and
meant it? How many murderers? Klaus Fuchs said it, and the
men who committed the Mountain Meadows Massacre said
it, and Alfred Rosenberg said it. And, as we are rotely and
rather presumptuously reminded by those who would say it
now, Jesus said it. Maybe we have all said it, and maybe we
have been wrong. Except on that most primitive level—our
loyalties to those we love—what could be more arrogant than
to claim the primacy of personal conscience? ("Tell me," a
rabbi asked Daniel Bell when he said, as a child, that he did
not believe in God. "Do you think God cares?") At least
some of the time, the world appears to me as a painting by
Hieronymous Bosch; were I to follow my conscience then, it
would lead me out onto the desert with Marion Faye, out to

where he stood in *The Deer Park* looking east to Los Alamos and praying, as if for rain, that it would happen: "*. . . let it come and clear the rot and the stench and the stink, let it come for all of everywhere, just so it comes and the world stands clear in the white dead dawn.*"

Of course you will say that I do not have the right, even 8 if I had the power, to inflict that unreasonable conscience upon you; nor do I want you to inflict your conscience, however reasonable, however enlightened, upon me. ("We must be aware of the dangers which lie in our most generous wishes," Lionel Trilling once wrote. "Some paradox of our nature leads us, when once we have made our fellow men the objects of our enlightened interest, to go on to make them the objects of our pity, then of our wisdom, ultimately of our coercion.") That the ethic of conscience is intrinsically insidious seems scarcely a revelatory point, but it is one raised with increasing infrequency; even those who do raise it tend to *segue* with troubling readiness into the quite contradictory position that the ethic of conscience is dangerous when it is "wrong," and admirable when it is "right."

You see, I want to be quite obstinate about insisting that 9 we have no way of knowing—beyond that fundamental loyalty to the social code—what is "right" and what is "wrong," what is "good" and what "evil." I dwell so upon this because the most disturbing aspect of "morality" seems to me to be the frequency with which the word now appears; in the press, on television, in the most perfunctory kinds of conversation. Questions of straightforward power (or survival) politics, questions of quite indifferent public policy, questions of almost anything: they are all assigned these factious moral burdens. There is something facile going on, some self-indulgence at work. Of course we would all like to "believe" in something, like to assuage our private guilts in public causes, like to lose our tiresome selves; like, perhaps, to transform the white flag of defeat at home into the brave white banner of battle away from home. And of course it is all right to do that; that is how, immemorially, things have gotten done. But I think it is all right only so long as we do not delude ourselves about what we are doing, and why. It is all right only so long as we remember that all the ad hoc committees, all the picket lines, all the brave signatures in the *New York Times*, all the tools of agitprop straight across the spectrum, do not confer upon anyone any ipso facto virtue. It is all right only so long as we recognize that the end may or may not be expedient, may or may not be a good idea, but in any case has nothing to do with "morality." Because when we start deceiving ourselves into thinking not that we want something or need something, not that it is a pragmatic necessity for us to have it, but that it is a moral imperative that we have it, then is when we join the fashionable madmen, and then is when the thin whine of hysteria is heard in the land, and then is when we are in bad trouble. And I suspect we are already there.

For Study and Discussion

QUESTIONS ABOUT PURPOSE

1. Why does Didion admit that she distrusts definitions of *morality*?
2. Why does she caution her readers about the delusions of using the word?

QUESTIONS ABOUT AUDIENCE

1. How does Didion's reference to *The American Scholar* identify the kind of readers she is supposed to be addressing in her essay?
2. What does she accomplish when she addresses her readers directly?

QUESTONS ABOUT STRATEGIES

1. How does Didion use the particulars of the highway accident to illustrate the basic social code?
2. How does she use the phrase "I did what I thought was right" to illustrate the difficulty of defining *morality*?

For Writing and Research

1. *Analyze* how Didion uses "particulars" to illustrate the problems of defining an "abstract" word such as *morality*.
2. *Practice* by describing an experience that you would characterize as "immoral" or "moral"
3. *Argue* that Didion is right or wrong to say that it is arrogant "to claim the primacy of personal conscience."
4. *Synthesize:* Research some of Didion's examples—the Donner Party, the Mountain Meadows Massacre, Klaus Fuchs, Alfred Rosenberg—and then use them to support Didion's argument in more detail.

TONI CADE BAMBARA

Toni Cade Bambara (1939–1995) was born in New York City and educated at Queens College, the University of Florence, the Ecole de Mme. Etienne Decroux in Paris, and the City College of the City University of New York. Her work experience was extremely varied: a social investigator for the New York State Department of Welfare, a director of recreation in the psychiatry department of New York's Metropolitan Hospital, a visiting professor of Afro-American studies (Stephens College in Columbia, Missouri), a consultant on women's studies (Emory University in Atlanta), and a writer-in-residence at Spelman College in Atlanta. She contributed stories and essays to magazines as diverse as *Negro Digest, Prairie Schooner,* and *Redbook.* Her two collections of short stories, *Gorilla, My Love* (1972) and *The Sea Birds Are Still Alive: Collected Stories* (1977), deal with the emerging sense of self of black women. Her novels include *The Salt Eaters* (1980) and *Those Bones Are Not My Child* (1999). "The Lesson," reprinted from *Gorilla, My Love,* focuses on the experiences of several black children who learn how much things "cost."

The Lesson[6]

BACK IN THE days when everyone was old and stupid or   1
young and foolish and me and Sugar were the only ones just right, this lady moved on our block with nappy hair

---

[6]Toni Cade Bambara, "The Lesson," copyright © 1972 by Toni Cade Bambara, from *Gorilla, My Love* by Toni Cade Bambara. Used by permission of Random House, Inc.

and proper speech and no makeup. And quite naturally we laughed at her, laughed the way we did at the junk man who went about his business like he was some big-time president and his sorry-ass horse his secretary. And we kinda hated her too, hated the way we did the winos who cluttered up our parks and pissed on our handball walls and stank up our hallways and stairs so you couldn't halfway play hide-and-seek without a goddamn gas mask. Miss Moore was her name. The only woman on the block with no first name. And she was black as hell, cept for her feet, which were fish-white and spooky. And she was always planning these boring-ass things for us to do, us being my cousin, mostly, who lived on the block cause we all moved North the same time and to the same apartment then spread out gradual to breathe. And our parents would yank our heads into some kinda shape and crisp up our clothes so we'd be presentable for travel with Miss Moore, who always looked like she was going to church, though she never did. Which is just one of the things the grownups talked about when they talked behind her back like a dog. But when she came calling with some sachet she'd sewed up or some gingerbread she'd made or some book, why then they'd all be too embarrassed to turn her down and we'd get handed over all spruced up. She'd been to college and said it was only right that she should take responsibility for the young ones' education, and she not even related by marriage or blood. So they'd go for it. Specially Aunt Gretchen. She was the main gofer in the family. You got some ole dumb shit foolishness you want somebody to go for, you send for Aunt Gretchen. She been screwed into the go-along for so long, it's a blood-deep natural thing with her. Which is how she got saddled with me and Sugar and Junior in the first place while our mothers were in a la-de-da apartment up the block having a good ole time.

So this one day Miss Moore rounds us all up at the mail-   2
box and it's puredee hot and she's knockin herself out about arithmetic. And school suppose to let up in summer I heard, but she don't never let up. And the starch in my pinafore scratching the shit outta me and I'm really hating

this nappy-head bitch and her goddamn college degree. I'd much rather go to the pool or to the show where it's cool. So me and Sugar leaning on the mailbox being surly, which is a Miss Moore word. And Flyboy checking out what everybody brought for lunch. And Fat Butt already wasting his peanut-butter-and-jelly sandwich like the pig he is. And Junebug punchin on Q. T.'s arm for potato chips. And Rosie Giraffe shifting from one hip to the other waiting for somebody to step on her foot or ask her if she from Georgia so she can kick ass, preferably Mercedes'. And Miss Moore asking us do we know what money is, like we a bunch of retards. I mean real money, she say, like it's only poker chips or monopoly papers we lay on the grocer. So right away I'm tired of this and say so. And would much rather snatch Sugar and go to the Sunset and terrorize the West Indian kids and take their hair ribbons and their money too. And Miss Moore files that remark away for next week's lesson on brotherhood, I can tell. And finally I say we oughta get to the subway cause it's cooler and besides we might meet some cute boys. Sugar done swiped her mama's lipstick, so we ready.

So we heading down the street and she's boring us silly 3 about what things cost and what our parents make and how much goes for rent and how money ain't divided up right in this country. And then she gets to the part about we all poor and live in the slums, which I don't feature. And I'm ready to speak on that, but she steps out in the street and hails two cabs just like that. Then she hustles half the crew in with her and hands me a five-dollar bill and tells me to calculate 10 percent tip for the driver. And we're off. Me and Sugar and Junebug and Flyboy hangin out the window and hollering to everybody, putting lipstick on each other cause Flyboy a faggot anyway, and making farts with our sweaty armpits. But I'm mostly trying to figure how to spend this money. But they all fascinated with the meter ticking and Junebug starts laying bets as to how much it'll read when Flyboy can't hold his breath no more. Then Sugar lays bets as to how much it'll be when we get there. So I'm stuck. Don't nobody want to go for my plan, which is to jump out at the next light and run

off to the first bar-b-que we can find. Then the driver tells
us to get the hell out cause we there already. And the meter
reads eighty-five cents. And I'm stalling to figure out the tip
and Sugar say give him a dime. And I decide he don't need
it bad as I do, so later for him. But then he tries to take off
with Junebug foot still in the door so we talk about his mama
something ferocious. Then we check out that we on Fifth
Avenue and everybody dressed up in stockings. One lady in a
fur coat, hot as it is. White folks crazy.

"This is the place," Miss Moore say, presenting it to us in   4
the voice she uses at the museum. "Let's look in the windows
before we go in."

"Can we steal?" Sugar asks very serious like she's getting the   5
ground rules squared away before she plays. "I beg your par-
don," say Miss Moore, and we fall out. So she leads us around
the windows of the toy store and me and Sugar screamin,
"This is mine, that's mine, I gotta have that, that was made for
me, I was born for that," till Big Butt drowns us out.

"Hey, I'm goin to buy that there."   6
"That there? You don't even know what it is, stupid."   7
"I do so," he say punchin on Rosie Giraffe. "It's a micro-   8
scope."
"Whatcha gonna do with a microscope, fool?"   9
"Look at things."   10
"Like what, Ronald?" ask Miss Moore. And Big Butt ain't   11
got the first notion. So here go Miss Moore gabbing about
the thousands of bacteria in a drop of water and the somethin-
orother in a speck of blood and the million and one living
things in the air around us is invisible to the naked eye. And
what she say that for? Junebug go to town on that "naked"
and we rolling. Then Miss Moore ask what it cost. So we all
jam into the window smudgin it up and the price tag say $300.
So then she ask how long'd take for Big Butt and Junebug
to save up their allowances. "Too long," I say. "Yeh," adds
Sugar, "outgrown it by that time." And Miss Moore say no,
you never outgrow learning instruments. "Why, even medical students and interns and," blah, blah, blah. And we ready
to choke Big Butt for bringing it up in the first damn place.

"This here costs four hundred eighty dollars," say Rosie 12
Giraffe. So we pile up all over her to see what she pointin out.
My eyes tell me it's a chunk of glass cracked with something
heavy, and different-color inks dripped into the splits, then
the whole thing put into a oven or something. But for $480
it don't make sense.

"That's a paperweight made of semi-precious stones fused 13
together under tremendous pressure," she explains slowly,
with her hands doing the mining and all the factory work.

"So what's a paperweight?" asks Rosie Giraffe. 14

"To weigh paper with, dumbbell," say Flyboy, the wise 15
man from the East.

"Not exactly," say Miss Moore, which is what she say 16
when you warm or way off too. "It's to weigh paper down so
it won't scatter and make your desk untidy." So right away
me and Sugar curtsy to each other and then to Mercedes who
is more the tidy type.

"We don't keep paper on top of the desk in my class," say 17
Junebug, figuring Miss Moore crazy or lyin one.

"At home, then," she say. "Don't you have a calendar 18
and a pencil case and a blotter and a letter-opener on your
desk at home where you do your homework?" And she know
damn well what our homes look like cause she nosys around
in them every chance she gets.

"I don't even have a desk," say Junebug. "Do we?" 19

"No. And I don't get no homework neither," says Big 20
Butt.

"And I don't even have a home," say Flyboy like he do at 21
school to keep the white folks off his back and sorry for him.
Send this poor kid to camp posters, is his specialty.

"I do," says Mercedes. "I have a box of stationery on my 22
desk and a picture of my cat. My godmother bought the stationery and the desk. There's a big rose on each sheet and the
envelopes smell like roses."

"Who wants to know about your smelly-ass stationery," 23
say Rosie Giraffe fore I can get my two cents in.

"It's important to have a work area all your own so 24
that . . ."

"Will you look at this sailboat, please," say Flyboy, cuttin 25
her off and pointin to the thing like it was his. So once again
we tumble all over each other to gaze at this magnificent
thing in the toy store which is just big enough to maybe sail
two kittens across the pond if you strap them to the posts
tight. We all start reciting the price tag like we in assembly.
"Handcrafted sailboat of fiberglass at one thousand one hundred ninety-five dollars."

"Unbelievable," I hear myself say and am really stunned. 26
I read it again for myself just in case the group recitation put
me in a trance. Same thing. For some reason this pisses me
off. We look at Miss Moore and she lookin at us, waiting for
I dunno what.

"Who'd pay all that when you can buy a sailboat set for 27
a quarter at Pop's, a tube of glue for a dime, and a ball of
string for eight cents? It must have a motor and a whole lot
else besides," I say. "My sailboat cost me about fifty cents."

"But will it take water?" say Mercedes with her smart ass. 28

"Took mine to Alley Pond Park once," say Flyboy. "String 29
broke. Lost it. Pity."

"Sailed mine in Central Park and it keeled over and sank. 30
Had to ask my father for another dollar."

"And you got the strap," laugh Big Butt. "The jerk didn't 31
even have a string on it. My old man wailed on his behind."

Little Q. T. was staring hard at the sailboat and you could 32
see he wanted it bad. But he too little and somebody'd just
take it from him. So what the hell. "This boat for kids, Miss
Moore?"

"Parents silly to buy something like that just to get all 33
broke up," say Rosie Giraffe.

"That much money it should last forever," I figure. 34

"My father'd buy it for me if I wanted it." 35

"Your father, my ass," say Rosie Giraffe getting a chance 36
to finally push Mercedes.

"Must be rich people shop here," say Q. T. 37

"You are a very bright boy," say Flyboy. "What was your 38
first clue?" And he rap him on the head with the back of his
knuckles, since Q. T. the only one he could get away with.

Though Q. T. liable to come up behind you years later and get his licks in when you half expect it.

"What I want to know is," I says to Miss Moore though I 39 never talk to her, I wouldn't give the bitch that satisfaction, "is how much a real boat costs? I figure a thousand'd get you a yacht any day."

"Why don't you check that out," she says, "and report 40 back to the group?" Which really pains my ass. If you gonna mess up a perfectly good swim day least you could do is have some answers. "Let's go in," she say like she got something up her sleeve. Only she don't lead the way. So me and Sugar turn the corner to where the entrance is, but when we get there I kinda hang back. Not that I'm scared, what's there to be afraid of, just a toy store. But I feel funny, shame. But what I got to be shamed about? Got as much right to go in as anybody. But somehow I can't seem to get hold of the door, so I step away from Sugar to lead. But she hangs back too. And I look at her and she looks at me and this is ridiculous. I mean, damn, I have never ever been shy about doing nothing or going nowhere. But then Mercedes steps up and then Rosie Giraffe and Big Butt crowd in behind and shove, and next thing we all stuffed into the doorway with only Mercedes squeezing past us, smoothing out her jumper and walking right down the aisle. Then the rest of us tumble in like a glued-together jigsaw done all wrong. And people lookin at us. And it's like the time me and Sugar crashed into the Catholic church on a dare. But once we got in there and everything so hushed and holy and the candles and the bowin and the handkerchiefs on all the drooping heads, I just couldn't go through with the plan. Which was for me to run up to the altar and do a tap dance while Sugar played the nose flute and messed around in the holy water. And Sugar kept givin me the elbow. Then later teased me so bad I tied her up in the shower and turned it on and locked her in. And she'd be there till this day if Aunt Gretchen hadn't finally figured I was lyin about the boarder takin a shower.

Same thing in the store. We all walkin on tiptoe and hardly 41 touchin the games and puzzles and things. And I watched

Miss Moore who is steady watchin us like she waitin for a sign. Like Mama Drewery watches the sky and sniffs the air and takes note of just how much slant is in the bird formation. Then me and Sugar bump smack into each other, so busy gazing at the toys, 'specially the sailboat. But we don't laugh and go into our fat-lady bump-stomach routine. We just stare at that price tag. Then Sugar run a finger over the whole boat. And I'm jealous and want to hit her. Maybe not her, but I sure want to punch somebody in the mouth.

"Watcha bring us here for, Miss Moore?"   42

"You sound angry, Sylvia. Are you mad about some-   43
thing?" Givin me one of them grins like she tellin a grown-up joke that never turns out to be funny. And she's lookin very closely at me like maybe she plannin to do my portrait from memory. I'm mad, but I won't give her that satisfaction. So I slouch around the store bein very bored and say, "Let's go."

Me and Sugar at the back of the train watchin the tracks   44
whizzin by large then small then gettin gobbled up in the dark. I'm thinking about this tricky toy I saw in the store. A clown that somersaults on a bar then does chin-ups just cause you yank lightly at his leg. Cost $35. I could see me askin my mother for a $35 birthday clown. "You wanna who that costs what?" she'd say, cocking her head to the side to get a better view of the hole in my head. Thirty-five dollars could buy new bunk beds for Junior and Gretchen's boy. Thirty five dollars and the whole household could go visit Granddaddy Nelson in the country. Thirty-five dollars would pay for the rent and the piano bill too. Who are these people that spend that much for performing clowns and $1000 for toy sailboats? What kinda work they do and how they live and how come we ain't in on it? Where we are is who we are, Miss Moore always pointin out. But it don't necessarily have to be that way, she always adds then waits for somebody to say that poor people have to wake up and demand their share of the pie and don't none of us know what kind of pie she talking about in the first damn place. But she ain't so smart cause I still got her four dollars from the taxi and she sure ain't gettin it. Messin up my day with this shit. Sugar nudges me in my pocket and winks.

Miss Moore lines us up in front of the mailbox where we 45
started from, seem like years ago, and I got a headache for
thinkin so hard. And we lean all over each other so we can
hold up under the draggy-ass lecture she always finishes us off
with at the end before we thank her for borin us to tears. But
she just looks at us like she readin tea leaves. Finally she say,
"Well, what did you think of F.A.O. Schwarz?"

Rosie Giraffe mumbles, "White folks crazy."   46

"I'd like to go there again when I get my birthday money," 47
says Mercedes, and we shove her out the pack so she has to
lean on the mailbox by herself.

"I'd like a shower. Tiring day," say Flyboy.   48

Then Sugar surprises me by sayin, "You know, Miss Moore, 49
I don't think all of us here put together eat in a year what
that sailboat costs." And Miss Moore lights up like somebody goosed her. "And?" she say, urging Sugar on. Only I'm
standin on her foot so she don't continue.

"Imagine for a minute what kind of society it is in which 50
some people can spend on a toy what it would cost to feed a
family of six or seven. What do you think?"

"I think," say Sugar pushing me off her feet like she never 51
done before, cause I whip her ass in a minute, "that this is
not much of a democracy if you ask me. Equal chance to
pursue happiness means an equal crack at the dough, don't
it?" Miss Moore is besides herself and I am disgusted with
Sugar's treachery. So I stand on her foot one more time to
see if she'll shove me. She shuts up, and Miss Moore looks at
me, sorrowfully I'm thinkin. And somethin weird is goin on,
I can feel it in my chest.

"Anybody else learn anything today?" lookin dead at me. 52
I walk away and Sugar has to run to catch up and don't even
seem to notice when I shrug her arm off my shoulder.

"Well, we got four dollars anyway," she says.   53

"Uh hunh."   54

"We could go to Hascombs and get half a chocolate layer 55
and then go to the Sunset and still have plenty money for
potato chips and ice cream sodas."

"Uh hunh."   56

"Race you to Hascombs," she say.   57

We start down the block and she gets ahead which is O.K. 58
by me cause I'm going to the West End and then over to
the Drive to think this day through. She can run if she want
to and even run faster. But ain't nobody gonna beat me at
nuthin.

COMMENT ON "THE LESSON"

"The Lesson" is an excellent illustration of how narration
and description are used in short fiction to create a definition
of the word *cost*. Although the plot seems arranged in a simple chronology, the narrator, Sylvia, suggests that the events
took place "Back in the days when everyone was old and stupid or young and foolish and me and Sugar were the only
ones just right." Sylvia's tough talk is directed at an audience she presumes will understand why she sees Miss Moore
and her activities as "boring-ass." But as Sylvia describes the
various toys at F.A.O. Schwarz, she reveals that her point of
view is defensive. She is stunned by what things cost, embarrassed by her ignorance, and confused by her anger and Sugar's treachery. She will not acknowledge publicly that she has
learned Miss Moore's lesson about the inequities in society,
but privately she concludes that "ain't nobody gonna beat
me at nuthin."

CHAPTER 6

CAUSE AND EFFECT

If you are like most people, you're just naturally curious: you look at the world around you and wonder why things happen. But you're also curious because you want some control over your life and over your environment, and you can't have that control unless you can understand **causes.** That's why so much writing is cause-and-effect writing, writing that seeks to explain the causes of change and new developments. In almost every profession you will be asked to do writing that analyzes causes; that's why such writing has an important place in college composition courses.

You also want to understand **effects.** If A happens, will B be the effect? You want to try to predict the consequences of putting some plan into effect or look at some effect and explain what brought it about. Or you want to set a goal (the effect) and plan a strategy for reaching it. This kind of writing also prepares you for writing you're likely to do later in your career.

PURPOSE

When you write cause-and-effect essays, you're likely to have one of three purposes. Sometimes you want to *explain* why something happened or what might be likely to happen under certain circumstances. Daniel Goleman is writing that kind of essay in "Peak Performance: Why Records Fall" when he explains how new knowledge about training practices and about human mental capacities have led to athletic feats that seemed impossible only a few decades ago. At other times, you might write a cause-and-effect paper to *speculate* about an interesting topic—for instance, to speculate why a new computer game has become so popular or what the effects of a new kind of body suit will be for competitive swimmers.

Writers often use a cause-and-effect essay to *argue,* or prove a point. In "Comforting Thoughts," Calvin Trillin argues that a strange chain of causes and effects allows him to feel "much better." In "How Flowers Changed the World," Loren Eiseley argues that flowers helped create and sustain life on earth.

AUDIENCE

When you begin to analyze your audience for a cause-and-effect argument, it helps to think of them as jurors to whom you are going to present a case. You can make up a list of questions just as a lawyer would to help him or her formulate an argument. For example:

- How should I prepare my readers for my argument? What background information do they need?
- What kind of evidence are they likely to want? Factual, statistical, anecdotal?
- How much do I have to explain? Will they have enough context to understand my points and make connections without my spelling them out?

Like a trial lawyer, you're trying to establish a chain of cause and effect. Perhaps you can't establish absolute proof, but you can show probability. The format for such arguments can be as follows:

- State your claim early, usually in the first paragraph.
- Show the connection you want to establish.
- Present your supporting evidence.
- Repeat your claim in your conclusion.

STRATEGIES

Writers may choose among a number of strategies when they write about cause and effect. The simplest one is to describe an action or event and then show what its consequences were. People who write case studies in psychology or social work use this strategy. Trillin creates a humorous version of this strategy in "Comforting Thoughts" when he traces the consequences of his reading two scientific studies.

Another favorite strategy is to describe an event or circumstance that seems significant and then examine the probable reasons for it. Eiseley does this in his essay "How Flowers Changed the World" when he speculates about how flowers' seeds became airborne.

Conversely, a writer sometimes begins a cause-and-effect essay by isolating an effect and then looking for plausible explanations of what caused it. Goleman follows this strategy when he tries to explain why there are so many peak performances in athletics. In writing this kind of essay you must be careful to distinguish between the **direct** or **simple cause** and the **indirect** or **complex cause.** Terry McMillan attempts to make such distinctions in "The Movie That Changed My Life" when she writes about the changes she noticed in herself after she first saw *The Wizard of Oz*.

Another way to approach cause-and-effect writing is to focus on two apparently related phenomena and speculate whether there may be a cause-and-effect connection between them. Such speculation is risky, and you must be prepared to back up your assertions with strong evidence. Nevertheless, this kind of hypothesizing can be fruitful and enlightening;

it is essentially what Lucy Kavaler is doing in "Of Riot, Murder and the Heat of Passion" when she speculates about the effect of heat on human behavior.

There are still other ways to write about cause and effect; the ones given here are by no means the only strategies writers use. In order to be effective and responsible, however, all strategies should meet the following criteria.

1. *Do not overstate your case.* When you write about complex situations, particularly those that involve people, you do best to say, "X will *probably* cause Y" or "A *seems* to be the effect of B," rather than insist that there must be a necessary and direct causal connection between two events. Many plausible cause-and-effect relationships are difficult to prove conclusively, and your readers will trust your analysis when you do not claim too much.

2. *Do not oversimplify cause-and-effect relationships.* Seldom does an important effect result from a simple and direct cause. For instance, if 15 percent fewer people died of heart attacks in 2012 than in 2011, a researcher should assume that many factors contributed to the decline— not one element. Furthermore, most happenings of any significance have more than one effect, and any cause and effect may be only one link in a long chain of causes and effects. For that reason, qualify your assertions with phrases such as "a major cause," "one result," and "an immediate effect."

3. *Do not mistake coincidence or simple sequence for a necessary cause-and-effect relationship.* The fact that the crime rate in a state rose the year after the legal drinking age was lowered to eighteen does not mean that there is a direct connection between the two occurrences. If you jump to conclusions about cause and effect too quickly, you will be committing a fallacy known as *post hoc, ergo propter hoc* (Latin for "after this, therefore because of this").

These cautions do not, however, mean that you should refrain from drawing conclusions about cause and effect until you are absolutely certain of your conclusion. It is not always possible or wise to wait for complete certainty before analyzing what happened or forecasting what may happen. The best you can do is observe carefully and speculate intelligently.

CAUSE AND EFFECT

Points to Remember

1. Remember that, in human events, you can almost never prove direct, simple cause-and-effect relationships. Qualify your claims.

2. Be careful not to oversimplify your cause-and-effect statements; be cautious about saying that a cause always produces a certain effect or that a remedy never succeeds.

3. Avoid confusing coincidence or simple sequence with cause and effect; because B follows A doesn't mean that A caused B.

4. Build your cause-and-effect argument as a trial lawyer would. Present as much evidence as you can, and argue for your hypothesis.

© *Underwood & Underwood /Corbis*

In this documentary photograph, Frank Hurley chronicles a dramatic moment during Sir Ernest Shackleton's journey across the Antarctic (1914–1916). Research the Shackleton expedition. What prompted them to go? What caused their ship, Endurance, *to be trapped in the ice? What happened to the expedition? Write an essay analyzing the causes and effects of this legendary voyage.*

CALVIN TRILLIN

Calvin Trillin was born in Kansas City, Missouri, in 1935 and educated at Yale University. He began his career by working as a reporter for *Time* magazine and then as a columnist for *The New Yorker*. In recent years, he has written a national newspaper column and staged a one-man show off-Broadway. His writing includes three novels, *Runestruck* (1977), *Floater* (1980), and *Tepper Isn't Going Out* (2001); books of poetry, including *Deadline Poet; or, My Life as a Doggerelist* (1994) and *Obliviously on He Sails: The Bush Administration in Rhyme* (2004); collections of reporting, including *U.S. Journal* (1971), *Killings* (1984), and *American Stories* (1991); a best-selling memoir, *Remembering Denny* (1993); numerous books of humor, such as *Family Man* (1998); and a portrait of his late wife, *About Alice* (2006). In "Comforting Thoughts," Trillin speculates on several procedures that are supposed to make him feel more comfortable.

Comforting Thoughts[1]

February 29, 1988

FIRST I READ about a study in Meriden, Connecticut, which indicated that talking to yourself is a perfectly legitimate way of getting comfort during a difficult time. Then I saw an item about research at Yale demonstrating that stress seems to be reduced in some people by exposing them to the aromas of certain desserts. Then I started talking to myself about desserts with aromas I find soothing. Then I felt a lot better. Isn't science grand?

I didn't feel perfect. One thing that was bothering me— 2 this is what I decided after I was asked by myself, "Well, what seems to be the trouble, guy?"—was that the ten most popular methods of comforting yourself listed in the Meriden study didn't mention sniffing desserts, even though Yale, where all the sniffing research was going on, is only about twenty miles down the road. Does this mean that some of these scientists are so busy talking to themselves that they don't talk to each other? It got me so upset that I went to the back door of a baker in our neighborhood to sniff the aroma of chocolate chip cookies. I was talking to myself the whole time, of course.

Isn't science grand?

"What the Yale people think," I said to myself, "is that a 3 person's soothed by the smell of, say, chocolate chip cookies because it brings back pleasant memories, like the memory of his mother baking chocolate chip cookies."

"What if his mother always burned the chocolate chip 4 cookies?" I replied.

"Are you talking about my mother?"   5

"Whose mother do you think I'm talking about?" I said. 6 "We're the only one here."

"Were those cookies burnt?"   7

"What do you think all that black stuff was?"   8

"I thought that was the chocolate chips."   9

"No, she always forgot the chocolate chips."   10

I wasn't finding the conversation very comforting at all. I 11 don't like to hear anyone make light of my mother's chocolate chip cookies, even me. I must have raised my voice, because the next thing I knew, the baker had come out to see what was going on.

Even though the Meriden study had shown that being 12 with someone else was the most comforting thing of all— it finished ahead of listening to music and even watching

TV—I saw right away that being with the baker wasn't going
to be much more comforting than talking to myself. He said,
"What are you, some kind of nut case, or what?"

I told him that I was engaging in two therapies that had   13
been scientifically proven effective: sniffing chocolate chip
cookies and talking to myself. He told me that I owed him
two dollars and fifty cents. "For sniffing, we charge a buck
and a quarter a dozen," he explained.

"How do you know I sniffed two dozen?" I asked.   14

"We got ways," he said.   15

I told him that according to the research done at Yale, 16
certain odors caused the brain to produce alpha waves, which
are associated with relaxation. I told him that in my case the
odor of chocolate chip cookies—particularly slightly burnt
chocolate chip cookies—was such an odor. I told him that he
ought to be proud to confirm the scientific research done at
one of the great universities of the English-speaking world.
That alone, I told him, ought to be payment enough for
whatever small part of the aroma of his chocolate chip cookies I had used up with my sniffing.

He thought about it for a moment. Then he said, "Take   17
a walk, buddy."

I was happy to. As it happens, going for a walk finished 18
tenth in the Meriden study, just behind recalling pleasant
memories. Naturally, I talked to myself on the way.

"Maybe I can find someplace to smell what the Yale peo- 19
ple call 'spiced apple,'" I said to myself. "They found that the
smell of spiced apple is so effective that with some people it
can stop panic attacks."

"But I don't know what spiced apple smells like," I replied. 20
"Spiced with what?"

That was bothering me enough that my walk wasn't actu- 21
ally very soothing. I thought about bolstering it with some
of the other activities on the list, but reading or watching TV
seemed impractical. Prayer was also on the list, but praying
for the aroma of spiced apple seemed frivolous.

I walked faster and faster. It occurred to me that I might 22
be getting a panic attack. Desperately I tried to recall some
pleasant memories. I recalled the time before I knew about

the Meriden list, when I talked to myself only in private. I recalled the time before I knew about the Yale research and didn't have to worry about finding any spiced apple. Then I felt a lot better. I didn't feel perfect, but you can't always feel perfect.

For Study and Discussion

QUESTIONS ABOUT PURPOSE

1. What does Trillin's essay attempt to demonstrate about scientific studies?
2. How does he use his first paragraph to reveal that his purpose is to entertain?

QUESTIONS ABOUT AUDIENCE

1. How does Trillin use dialogue—"talking to himself"—to engage his readers?
2. How does the baker's response (paragraph 17) anticipate the possible reaction of Trillin's readers to his speculations?

QUESTIONS ABOUT STRATEGIES

1. How many of the "ten most popular methods for comforting yourself" does Trillin mention?
2. In paragraph 22, what causes Trillin to feel "a lot better"?

For Writing and Research

1. *Analyze* the probable cause of Trillin's conclusion that you "can't always feel perfect."
2. *Practice* by describing a method you have developed for comforting yourself during times of stress.
3. *Argue* that the conclusions of a particular "pop scientific study" are based on faulty causal analysis.
4. *Synthesize:* Research scientific studies on one of the "ten most popular methods" Trillin mentions—such as walking. Then use this information to demonstrate that it can cause multiple positive effects.

DANIEL GOLEMAN

Daniel Goleman was born in 1946 in Stockton, California, and was educated at Amherst College and Harvard University. After working for several years as a professor of psychology, he began his career as an editor for *Psychology Today*. He has contributed more than fifty articles to psychology journals and has written a dozen books, including *The Meditative Mind* (1988); *The Creative Spirit* (1992); *Mind Body Medicine: How to Use Your Mind for Better Health* (1993); *Emotional Intelligence* (1995); *Working with Emotional Intelligence* (1998); *Social Intelligence* (2006); and *Ecological Intelligence* (2009). In "Peak Performance: Why Records Fall," reprinted from a 1994 *New York Times* article, Goleman analyzes how dedication to practice contributes to peak performances.

Peak Performance[2]
Why Records Fall

THE OLD JOKE—How do you get to Carnegie Hall? Practice, practice, practice—is getting a scientific spin. Researchers are finding an unexpected potency from deliberate practice in world-class competitions of all kinds, including chess matches, musical recitals and sporting events.

Studies of chess masters, virtuoso musicians and star athletes show that the relentless training routines of those at the top allow them to break through ordinary limits in memory

---

[2] Daniel Goleman, From *The New York Times*, October 11, 1994, © 1994 The New York Times. All rights reserved. Used by permission and protected by the Copyright Laws of the United States. The printing, copying, redistribution, or retransmission of this Content without express written permission is prohibited.

and physiology, and so perform at levels that had been thought impossible.

World records have been falling inexorably over the last 3 century. For example, the marathon gold medalist's time in the 1896 Olympics Games was, by 1990, only about as good as the qualifying time for the Boston Marathon.

"Over the last century Olympics have become more and 4 more competitive, and so athletes steadily have had to put in more total lifetime hours of practice," said Dr. Michael Mahoney, a psychologist at the University of North Texas in Denton, who helps train the United States Olympic weight-lifting team. "These days you have to live your sport."

That total dedication is in contrast to the relatively lei- 5 surely attitude taken at the turn of the century, when even world-class athletes would train arduously for only a few months before their competition.

"As competition got greater, training extended to a whole 6 season," said Dr. Anders Ericsson, a psychologist at Florida State University in Tallahassee who wrote an article on the role of deliberate practice for star performance recently in the journal *American Psychologist*. "Then it extended through the year, and then for several years. Now the elite performers start their training in childhood. There is a historical trend toward younger starting ages, which makes possible a greater and greater total number of hours of practice time."

Through their hours of practice, elite performers of all kinds master shortcuts that give them an edge.

To be sure, there are other factors at work: coaching 7 methods have become more sophisticated, equipment has improved and the pool of people competing has grown. But new studies are beginning to reveal the sheer power of training itself.

Perhaps the most surprising data show that extensive 8 practice can break through barriers in mental capacities, particularly short-term memory. In short-term memory, information is stored for the few seconds that it is used and then fades, as in hearing a phone number which one forgets as soon as it is dialed.

The standard view, repeated in almost every psychology 9 textbook, is that the ordinary limit on short-term memory is for seven or so bits of information—the length of a phone number. More than that typically cannot be retained in short-term memory with reliability unless the separate units are "chunked," as when the numbers in a telephone prefix are remembered as a single unit.

But, in a stunning demonstration of the power of sheer 10 practice to break barriers in the mind's ability to handle information, Dr. Ericsson and associates at Carnegie-Mellon University have taught college students to listen to a list of as many as 102 random digits and then recite it correctly. After 50 hours of practice with differing sets of random digits, four students were able to remember up to 20 digits after a single hearing. One student, a business major not especially talented in mathematics, was able to remember 102 digits. The feat took him more than 400 hours of practice.

The ability to increase memory in a particular domain 11 is at the heart of a wide range high-level performance, said Dr. Herbert Simon, professor of computer science and psychology at Carnegie-Mellon University and a Nobel laureate. Dr. Ericsson was part of a team studying expertise led by Dr. Simon.

"Every expert has acquired something like this memory ability" in his or her area of expertise, said Dr. Simon. 12 "Memory is like an index; experts have approximately 50,000 chunks of familiar units of information they recognize. For a physician, many of those chunks are symptoms."

A similar memory training effect, Dr. Simon said, seems 13 to occur with many chess masters. The key skill chess players rehearse in practicing is, of course, selecting the best move. They do so by studying games between two chess masters and guessing the next move from their own study of the board as the game progresses.

Repeated practice results in a prodigious memory for chess positions. The ability of some chess masters to play blind-folded, while simply told what moves their opponents make, has long been known; in the 1940s Adrian DeGroot, himself a Dutch grandmaster, showed that many chess masters are able to look at a chess board in midgame for as little as five seconds and then repeat the position of every piece on the board.   14

Later systematic studies by Dr. Simon's group showed that the chess masters' memory feat was limited to boards used in actual games; they had no such memory for randomly placed pieces. "They would see a board and think, that reminds me of Spassky versus Lasker," said Dr. Simon.   15

This feat of memory was duplicated by a college student who knew little about chess, but was given 50 hours of train-ing in remembering chess positions by Dr. Ericsson in a 1990 study.   16

Through their hours of practice, elite performers of all kinds master shortcuts that give them an edge. Dr. Bruce Abernathy, a researcher at the University of Queensland in Australia, has found that the most experienced players in racquet sports like squash and tennis are able to predict where a serve will land by cues in the server's posture before the ball is hit.   17

A 1992 study of baseball greats like Hank Aaron and Rod Carew by Thomas Hanson, then a graduate student at the University of Virginia in Charlottesville, found that the all-time best hitters typically started preparing for games by study-ing films of the pitchers they would face, to spot cues that would tip off what pitch was about to be thrown. Using such fleeting cues demands rehearsing so well that the response to them is automatic, cognitive scientists have found.   18

The maxim that practice makes perfect has been borne out through research on the training of star athletes and art-ists. Dr. Anthony Kalinowski, a researcher at the University of Chicago, found that swimmers who achieved the level of national champion started their training at an average age of 10, while those who were good enough to make the United   19

States Olympic teams started on average at 7. This is the same age difference found for national and international chess champions in a 1987 study.

Similarly, the best violinists of the 20th century, all with international careers as soloists for more than 30 years, were found to have begun practicing their instrument at an average age of 5, while violinists of only national prominence, those affiliated with the top music academy in Berlin, started at 8, Dr. Ericsson found in research reported last year in *The Psychological Review.* 20

Because of limits on physical endurance and mental alertness, world-class competitors—whether violinists or weight lifters—typically seem to practice arduously no more than four hours a day, Dr. Ericsson has found from studying a wide variety of training regimens. 21

"When we train Olympic weight lifters, we find we often have to throttle back the total time they work out," said Dr. Mahoney. "Otherwise you find a tremendous drop in mood, and a jump in irritability, fatigue and apathy." 22

Because their intense practice regimen puts them at risk for burnout or strain injuries, most elite competitors also make rest part of their training routine, sleeping a full eight hours and often napping a half-hour a day, Dr. Ericsson found. 23

Effective practice focuses not just on the key skills involved, but also systematically stretches the person's limits. "You have to tweak the system by pushing, allowing for more errors at first as you increase your limits," said Dr. Ericsson. "You don't get benefits from mechanical repetition, but by adjusting your execution over and over to get closer to your goal." 24

Violin virtuosos illustrate the importance of starting early in life. In his 1993 study Dr. Ericsson found that by age 20 top-level violinists in music academies had practiced a lifetime total of about 10,000 hours, while those who were slightly less accomplished had practiced an average of about 7,500 hours. 25

A study of Chinese Olympic divers, done by Dr. John Shea of Florida State University, found that some 11-year-old divers had spent as many hours in training as had 21-year-old American divers. The Chinese divers started training at age 4. 26

"It can take 10 years of extensive practice to excel in any- 27 thing," said Dr. Simon. "Mozart was 4 when he started compos- ing, but his world-class music started when he was about 17."

Total hours of practice may be more important than time 28 spent in competition, according to findings not yet published by Dr. Neil Charness, a colleague of Dr. Ericsson at Florida State University. Dr. Charness, comparing the rankings of 107 competitors in the 1993 Berlin City Tournament, found that the more time they spent practicing alone, the higher their ranking as chess players. But there was no relationship between the chess players' rankings and the time they spent playing others.

As has long been known, the extensive training of an elite 29 athlete molds the body to fit the demands of a given sport. What has been less obvious is the extent of these changes.

"The sizes of hearts and lungs, joint flexibility and bone 30 strength all increase directly with hours of training," said Dr. Ericsson. "The number of capillaries that supply blood to trained muscles increases."

And the muscles themselves change, Dr. Ericsson said. 31 Until very recently, researchers believed that the percent- age of muscle fiber types was more than 90 percent deter- mined by heredity. Fast-twitch muscles, which allow short bursts of intense effort, are crucial in sports like weight lift- ing and sprinting, while slow-twitch muscles, richer in red blood cells, are essential for endurance sports like marathons. "Muscle fibers in those muscles can change from fast twitch to slow twitch, as the sport demands," said Dr. Ericsson.

Longitudinal studies show that years of endurance training 32 at champion levels leads athletes' hearts to increase in size well beyond the normal range for people their age.

Such physiological changes are magnified when train- 33 ing occurs during childhood, puberty and adolescence. Dr. Ericsson thinks this may be one reason virtually all top ath- letes today began serious practice as children or young ado- lescents, though some events, like weight training, may be exceptions because muscles need to fully form before intense lifting begins.

The most contentious claim made by Dr. Ericsson is that 34 practice alone, not natural talent, makes for a record-breaking performance. "Innate capacities have very little to do with becoming a champion," said his colleague, Dr. Charness. "What's key is motivation and temperament, not a skill specific to performance. It's unlikely you can get just any child to apply themselves this rigorously for so long."

But many psychologists argue that the emphasis on prac- 35 tice alone ignores the place of talent in superb performance. "You can't assume that random people who practice a lot will rise to the top," said Dr. Howard Gardner, a psychologist at Harvard University. Dr. Ericsson's theories "leave out the question of who selects themselves—or are selected—for intensive training," adding, "It also leaves out what we most value in star performance, like innovative genius in a chess player or emotional expressiveness in a concert musician."

Dr. Gardner said: "I taught piano for many years, and 36 there's an enormous difference between those who practice dutifully and get a little better every week, and those students who break away from the pack. There's plenty of room for innate talent to make a difference over and above practice time. Mozart was not like you and me."

For Study and Discussion

QUESTIONS ABOUT PURPOSE

1. What message do you think the experts quoted in this essay are giving to young people who want to excel in something? What do you see as the impact of that message?
2. What role do you think science plays in sports these days? What is your feeling about that role?

QUESTIONS ABOUT AUDIENCE

1. What groups of readers do you see as people who would particularly benefit from learning about the research reported here? In what way would they benefit?

2. How would the value system of a reader—that is, the complex of things that the reader thinks is important—affect the way he or she responds to this essay?

QUESTIONS ABOUT STRATEGIES

1. What is the impact of Goleman's pointing out that the marathon runner who won an Olympic gold medal a hundred years ago could barely qualify for the Boston Marathon today?
2. How does Goleman's use of diverse authorities strengthen his essay?

For Writing and Research

1. *Analyze* the factors in a competitor's performance that Goleman fails to mention.
2. *Practice* by analyzing the effects that attempting to be a top performer have had on your friends and family.
3. *Argue* that talent rather than training explains "peak performances."
4. *Synthesize:* Research the lives of some top performers who started very young—for instance, violinist Midori, chess prodigy Bobby Fischer, or tennis player Jennifer Capriati. Then use this information to support Goldman's argument.

LUCY KAVALER

Lucy Kavaler (1930–2010) was born in New York City and was educated at Oberlin College. She worked as the senior editor of medical publications for a publishing company and as the executive editor of *The Female Patient.* She has contributed articles to periodicals such as *National History, Smithsonian,* and *Redbook.* Her other publications include books on science for children—*The Wonder of Algae* (1961), *Dangerous Air* (1967), *The Dangers of Noise* (1978)—books on social history—*The Private World of High Society* (1960) and *The Astors: A Family Chronicle* (1966)—and several books on public issues—*Noise: The New Menace* (1975) and *A Matter of Degree: Heat, Life, and Death* (1981). In "Of Riot, Murder, and the Heat of Passion," reprinted from *A Matter of Degree,* Kavaler demonstrates how temperature, especially excessive heat, affects human behavior.

Of Riot, Murder, and the Heat of Passion[3]

O N A JUNE Sunday in 1967, three young men broke into   1
a photographic supply warehouse in Tampa, Florida. The temperature was in the mid-90s and the humidity was high; nonetheless, both citizens and police gave chase. One of the robbers, stripped to the waist to better endure the heat, was stopped in his run by a high cyclone fence, and there he was shot by a policeman. As the bullet struck, the

---

young man reached up, grabbed at the fence, and hung on. He was in this position, with his hands over his head, when other pursuers rushed up. The scene was prolonged, because the ambulance called by a bystander was lost on its way. The young man was black and the policeman was white. All the criteria for a riot were present. And by nightfall, despite police guarantees of an investigation of the shooting, crowds had gathered and police cars were being stoned, stores looted, and power lines knocked down.

Similar scenes of violence took place that year in Newark, 2 Cincinnati, Atlanta, and many other cities. By the end of September, 164 riots had broken out in 128 cities, five of them in New York and four in Chicago. The largest number took place in July, the National Advisory Commission on Civil Disorders learned, after studying the records month by month. There had been just one minor disorder in January, none in February.

The temperature records of the cities in which riots 3 occurred gave high readings for the day preceding the incident that precipitated the violence. It was 90 degrees Fahrenheit or higher in Atlanta, Newark, Cincinnati, Phoenix, Tucson, Dayton, Paterson, Cambridge, and Tampa and was in the 80s before riots in Rockford, Illinois; Detroit and Grand Rapids, Michigan; and Elizabeth, Englewood, New Brunswick, and Jersey City, New Jersey. And so it has become customary to blame the long hot summer for riots.

Heat alone, to be sure, does not bring on a riot; poverty, 4 unemployment, economic and social injustices, and real or fancied antagonisms are basic causes. But summertime temperatures make the lives of the city poor increasingly miserable. Brick and concrete retain much more heat than do soil and grass; even after sundown the buildings and streets remain hotter than the air, while grass by then is cooler. Winds that might bring relief are blocked by buildings. At night the inner city is an island of heat.

The discomfort of their crowded airless rooms drives city 5 residents out onto the streets in the evenings in numbers sufficient to be dangerous should a provocative incident occur. Most riots begin between 7 P.M. and 1:30 A.M., before exhaustion sends people back inside to bed.

New York City has had two major power blackouts, one 6 on a November night and the other in July. There was little looting in November. During the July blackout, stores were emptied to the bare walls, and furniture, television sets, large appliances and small, clothing, and anything else that could be carried away was taken. Estimated losses of storekeepers ranged from $150 to $300 million, and 3,076 people were arrested.

When the lights came on again, the November blackout 7 was recalled. A comparison between the two is not truly valid, because the July blackout lasted much longer; however, it seems logical to attribute some of the lawlessness to the high summer temperatures. Many New Yorkers, weary after a day of readings over 90 degrees, were out on the streets. A city plunged in darkness was provocation for plunder, and it was warm enough for looters to stay outside and go from one store to another, taking more each time.

Tempers explode when it is hot. In cool weather, discon 8 tent may be expressed with less violence. Astronomers of an earlier day used to say that inhabitants of Mercury had to be very hot-tempered, because that is the planet closest to the sun. At the end of a ten-day heat wave, a newspaper reported that a knife fight broke out when one man asked another, "Hot enough for you?"

On the night of August 4, 1892, murder took place in the 9 town of Fall River, Massachusetts, and Lizzie Borden was accused of having hacked her father and stepmother to death with an ax. Although she was acquitted after a sensational trial, many went on believing in her guilt.

Few of the hundreds of thousands of words that have been 10 written about the murder mentioned the great heat wave in Fall River that August. But all those living in the Borden house must have been at a high level of irritability because of the heat. Was Lizzie the most affected, or might it have been the maid in her stifling attic room? Some witnesses did later claim to have seen the maid commit the act, but their words were discounted.

What really happened in Fall River long ago may never be known, but deaths by violence are indeed a feature of heat waves. Both New York and St. Louis sweltered in July 1966. Thirty-one homicides and 23 suicides took place that month, compared to 13 homicides and 38 suicides during a period of moderate temperatures.

The New York City Police Department Crime Comparison Reports reveal that 157 murders and non-negligent manslaughters occurred in July of 1977, compared to 117 in May. The total of felonies known to have been committed in July of the previous year amounted to 42,734, against 38,516 that May. August is a bad month too. In the summers of 1979 and 1980, the New York police department transferred men from headquarters duty and ordered overtime to increase the number of officers patrolling the streets. During the prolonged 1980 heat wave, the Texas Department of Human Resources found the number of cases of child abuse to be markedly higher than in previous summers, when heat was less intense.

To study the effects of heat on human behavior, a test was carried out at the Kansas Institute for Environmental Research in which high school dropouts, juvenile delinquents, and parolee volunteers were packed in a small, hot room. Arguments and fistfights broke out, and one young man threatened another with a knife. When the same volunteers were placed in less crowded conditions in a cooler room, nobody became aggressive.

Even normally calm people tend to become tense, irritable, and unreasonable, given to snapping over trivia at spouses, children, lovers, relatives, friends, and colleagues, when it is hot. Students crowded in a 90-degree room were hostile to a speaker, while those in a cooler room were prepared to give him a chance. The discomfort of heat could affect a personnel manager deciding whether to hire an applicant, a couple deciding whether to separate.

When heat is accompanied by humidity, irritability reaches 15 a peak. In a study, "The Child and the Weather," reported in the *Pedagogical Seminary* in 1898, Edwin G. Dexter, a Denver teacher, related the frequency of corporal punishment in the schools to the weather. After analyzing 606 instances occurring from 1883 to 1897, he claimed that humidities of 80 to 90 percent, rare in Denver, were linked to an increase of 100 percent in disciplinary problems, compared to the days of low humidity. (Little attention was paid to the fact that the decision as to whether behavior deserved punishment was made by adults, equally irritable in the humidity.)

When heat is accompanied by hot winds, the effect is even 16 more unsettling, particularly to the emotionally unstable. And some winds, like the chinook from the Rockies, can raise the temperature 40 degrees within hours. It has often been said that Italian judges are lenient about crimes of passion committed when the hot, dust-bearing sirocco blows up from the Sahara. "A society's treatment of crime may also be indicative of its emotional attitude—in Latin countries, for example, the law of murder differs considerably from that prevailing among the Teutonic people, and more allowance is made for the state of mind of the murderer." This statement from the *Encyclopaedia Britannica* (1957 edition) presents a stereotype that probably does not stand careful scrutiny. But many Americans share the implied view that a person who commits a crime of passion in certain foreign countries will be acquitted or given a mild sentence. And it happens often enough to keep the stereotype alive.

Such a case began on a March day in 1972 when Ginette 17 Vidal, a forty-one-year-old French medical secretary, and her handsome twenty-nine-year-old lover, Gerard Osselin, drew up a contract swearing to be faithful for life and stating that if either of them broke the contract, the other could kill the faithless one. Both lovers were married, but even sexual relations with spouses was considered breaking the contract. The lovers lived together, but Gerard, lonely for his wife, slipped away to see her every so often. One day Ginette came home when her lover was sleeping, went through his pockets, and found a shopping list in his wife's handwriting. Considering this sufficient proof of infidelity, she shot him where he lay.

At her trial, she cited the contract, surprised to learn it 18 was not legal. Her defense attorney pleaded, "It is hard at this woman's age when you have heard the bells of perfect love ringing, suddenly to see all this taken away from you." The jury found her guilty, but the sentence was for only ten years. The emotion that had caused her to kill was taken as an extenuating circumstance. Although many criminals motivated by jealousy do not get off as lightly as Mme. Vidal, some sympathy is felt for them, and the "crime of passion" is seen as quite different from a murder in cold blood.

Our vocabulary reveals how, misery, riot, and murder not 19 withstanding, we are prejudiced in favor of heat and against cold. To be hot-blooded is to be human. Our deepest feelings are linked with heat, and even negative emotions are viewed as better than none at all. We burn with passion, or with rage or lust. We are consumed in the flame of love or, less happily, in the green flame of envy. Being human means being able to catch fire with excitement. Hot-tempered, we take action in the heat of anger, carry on heated arguments, and get hot under the collar. We may send a scorching letter without waiting to cool off. We glow, simmer, seethe, and boil. And when the passion of love or anger is spent, it leaves us burned out. We breathe fire when aroused and see fire in the eye of an angry opponent. Burned up, worked up to a white heat, we may be incited by the inflammatory words of a fiery speaker or firebrand, even a hothead. We may go into a red-hot or white-hot rage. Wishing to succeed, we become fired with ambition. We fall into a hotbed of iniquity, never a cold one. Many of us have a low boiling point. Those who are likable are warmhearted and warm in their manner.

Dogs, cats, and other animals who are given human attri 20 butes are warm-blooded. In contrast, cold-blooded creatures such as snakes or lizards are commonly viewed as emotionless.

To be a lukewarm lover is not good enough. We do not 21 like the cold person, the cold-blooded, or the one whose heart is like ice while planning things coolly. A lack of sexual and/or emotional response is known as being frigid. We are repelled by anyone who is icy, glacial, chilly, chilling, frosty, frostbitten, or wintry in manner; who freezes us out or gives us the cold shoulder. The old slang expression for jail was the "cooler," where those who were hot-tempered were sent to cool off.

The practice of combining words involving heat with words connoting deep feeling has a kind of logic, based on the fact that the body's reactions to the sudden onset of rage, fear, lust, or intense anxiety are remarkably similar to those induced by sudden exposure to extreme heat. The heart beats faster in response both to emotion and to external heat, and breathing quickens. The blood vessels in the skin dilate, and there is an increase in blood flow, making the skin flush. If the blood vessels remain dilated for long, some liquid leaks into the tissues and the face looks swollen. This is the face we associate both with sexual passion and with rage. There is not much difference between the facial expressions for each of these very different emotions. The endocrine glands are activated by heat and hormone secretion is increased. There is a heightened feeling of excitement. Sweating is not only a response to heat but also to nervousness; it begins instantly when one is trapped in an elevator, threatened by a menacing person, or interviewed for a job. 22

While excessive heat produces many unpleasant results, warmth is the state that humans prefer to all others. Cold is dreaded and the feeling of being chilled detested. Despair is associated with low temperatures, and the negativism of coldness adds a nuance to F. Scott Fitzgerald's "In a real dark night of the soul, it is always three o'clock in the morning" ("The Crackup" [1936], *Esquire*). Three o'clock in the morning, standing for the low point of the day and of life, happens to be the time when body temperature drops to its lowest level, some 3 degrees below its daytime peak. Metabolism is slowed, and it is harder to take action. 23

When we remember childhood, it is always high noon in summer, the sun is shining with a golden light, and one clear 24 beautiful warm day follows another. The Arctic and Antarctic are described as unfriendly and hostile, while the tropics are viewed as having a friendly warmth.

It is only when pleasing warmth turns into unpleasant 25 hotness that negative emotional and physical characteristics appear. Some people are stimulated by the heat to perform at their peak. Well-motivated individuals compensate for their discomfort by trying harder and keep the quality of their endeavors high by more intense concentration. However, a drop in efficiency, accuracy, and judgment is so common that before air conditioning came into general use, many offices closed early on hot days.

The extent of the decline was investigated by the U.S. 26 Army Research Institute of Environmental Medicine in order to determine how soldiers would perform in hot climates, but the results apply to civilians as well. Soldiers were required to exercise in heat of 103 degrees at high humidity, which caused a rise in body temperature. They were allowed to rest for a while and then, still overheated, were asked to detect light signals flashed in a random manner. A second group of men exercised at 75 degrees. More light flashes were reported by the men who were hotter, which at first seemed to indicate that this state increased their alertness and competence. But when their detection reports were compared with the true number of signals, it was found that the increase was in false reports. Their judgment was not as sound as that of cooler men. They had become more willing to take a risk and insist that they saw a signal when in fact there was none.

Purdue University students participating in a psychologi- 27 cal test carried out in an oppressively hot room gave what they believed were electric shocks to a stranger who had written nasty things about them. However, another group of students, deliberately made angry *before* entering the overheated room, gave fewer shocks. When questioned by psychologists Robert A. Baron and Paul A. Bell, one spoke for all: "The only thing I thought about was getting the hell out of there." The less they reacted to the stranger and the fewer shocks they gave, the sooner they could leave the room. Similarly, outside of the psychology laboratory on many occasions a hot, angry person decides not to stay and argue or commit violence but simply to go home.

Have these reactions anything to do with riot behavior? 28 Dwellers in the crowded, foul-smelling, noisy slums face the heat after having in all probability been angered by employers, shopkeepers, bus drivers, policemen, and members of their families. On very hot days, says Baron, they, like the college students, would probably prefer to escape, but they have no place to go, so they commit violent acts. While riot control depends in the long run on amelioration of basic economic and social problems, Baron sees the establishment of small neighborhood parks, swimming pools, baseball fields, basketball and handball courts, and air-conditioned community centers as a way of helping people cool off physically and emotionally.

The temperature that induces excitement, argument, riots, 29 and aggression is very high, but there is an upper limit. Once heat goes beyond that, it is less rather than more stimulating. Studying mice so as to better understand human aggression, Kansas State University researcher Gary Greenberg conducted temperature experiments. To a point, the hotter it got, the more the mice bit one another. But when the temperature reached 95 degrees, the biting declined and the animals became placid, moved about slowly, trying to keep cool, and were indifferent to the other mice.

Animal bites of humans occur much more frequently in 30 summer than the rest of the year, notes the New York City Department of Health, but this biting cannot just be blamed on heat-induced irritability. It is rather more in line with Noel Coward's old song about mad dogs and Englishmen going out in the midday sun. Pleasant summer weather brings dogs (mad and otherwise) and children out of doors in great numbers. Children between the ages of five and nine are the most often bitten. Once it gets really hot, stray dogs become less and less active and do less and less biting.

For people, too, when high temperatures are prolonged, no 31 effort, no emotional upset, no physical activity is undertaken that will add to the burden of heat the body is enduring. A great indifference to other people and to situations that would normally be exciting or troublesome takes over. "Some loss in initiative is probably the most important single direct result of exposure to a hot environment," states Douglas H. K. Lee, formerly Associate Director of the National Institute of Environmental Health Sciences and an expert on adaptations to desert conditions.

"Who cares about the troop withdrawal? It's too hot to   32 care about anything" was the frequent comment by inhabitants of Seoul, South Korea, when American troop cutbacks were being discussed in August of 1977. In temperatures of 95 to 100 degrees, the air over Seoul was a thick, brown smaze.

Similarly, the French Foreign Legionnaires, waiting to go   33 home in 1977 from newly independent Djibouti in Africa, became lethargic. Until then they had recognized the importance of carrying out their duties in the strategic Red Sea port, even though they considered it a desolate hotbox. Motivation must be high if individuals are to overcome their inclination to heat-induced lassitude. Once that motivation was lost, groups of Legionnaires spent the afternoons in the stifling Café de Paris beneath ceiling fans circulating hot air. The ice in the whiskey melted so fast that the drinks were warm before they could be swallowed. Hour after hour the men sat without speaking. They were too enervated to do more than swat the flies. And so passed one long hot afternoon after another.

Whenever, as in cases like these, northerners in hot regions   34 become inactive or are unable to function effectively in their jobs, it is taken as confirmation of a popular belief, nurtured by fiction: Americans and Europeans transported to the tropics, it is said, go to seed, failing in their efforts to run the rubber plantation or hold the job in the foreign department of the bank or export-import firm, often drinking too much. As alcohol makes the body hotter, they become even more uncomfortable and incapable of effective action. Scorpions run through their houses, wives return home or take lovers, servants cheat them, meals are inedible, and sleep impossible. In fact, however, far from going to seed, most immigrants do become acclimatized and manage to run the plantation and do their work in the office. But this does not make so good a story.

The stereotype of the native of Africa and the Far East is also that of a lazy person, lying in the shade and refusing to do a good day's work. The custom of the siesta seems to provide additional proof of local lassitude; surely only children and old people take naps in the daytime. Northern tourists are frustrated at finding themselves with no place to go during what they view as the peak hours of the day. The hours from 12 to 3 P.M., even in a capital city such as Asunción, Paraguay, are quiet, with shops and business offices closed and everyone gone home.

It is often suggested that civilizations in the tropics have lagged behind those of temperate zones in terms of scientific, industrial, literary, and artistic development, because the high temperatures make people lethargic. There is some truth in this, but not in the way it is commonly meant. Heat of itself does not prevent a high level of intellectual achievement. The great early civilizations arose in tropical and subtropical regions. High temperatures did not impede the ancient Egyptians and Babylonians. The massive temples and pyramids of Luxor, the great palace of Ashurbanipal in Assyria, are clearly the creations of highly civilized and striving peoples, not savages relaxing all day under a tree. Complex philosophies and sophisticated art forms have been developed by the hot-climate Indians and Chinese. The magnificent temple cities of Chichén Itzá and Uxmal in the torrid Yucatán survive as evidence of an extremely advanced culture in the American tropics.

Even today, with these great civilizations long gone, many people, both native and foreign, are active and successful in tropical regions. The natives are physiologically well-adapted to their environment, and a good number vigorously exploit their opportunities in agriculture, industry, and government. They behave in ways that seem slow to northerners but that are appropriate to the tropics. The high-powered individual who works at top speed is the most likely to fall victim to heat exhaustion. Those who do best in the heat yield to it to some degree. The scorned siesta is not childlike or lazy; it is advisable to work early and late in the day and avoid exertion during the hottest hours.

Still, there is no denying that progress toward industrial 38 development is exceedingly slow in many countries of the tropics, especially where there seems little reason to achieve complex agricultural and manufacturing systems. To take the most extreme example, in some remote tropical jungles people can live off the land well enough to remain at a Stone Age stage of development to this day. The Tasadays discovered only recently in the Philippines were so primitive as to be ignorant of the fact that any humans other than their small tribe existed in the world; exploration was not necessary when sufficient food was available in the area they inhabited.

But tribes able to survive in this way are increasingly rare. 39 Gradually, population pressures in hot regions have been becoming so great as to demand a real effort to fulfill basic needs. But even this has not led to rapid industrialization. The failure can be attributed largely to indirect, rather than direct, effects of heat. The natives of the tropics and deserts of the world are often weakened by famines resulting from drought, flood, or civil war and, even in better times, by a low-protein diet. Illness is rampant, causing millions upon millions to drag out their days. Thus heat contributes to a low standard of living among those best equipped by nature to endure it.

One might think that heat could not both quench ambi- 40 tion and stimulate passion, but it is so. Excitement and anger, lassitude and indolence are but a few of the many human responses to excessive heat.

At night the inner city is an island of heat.

For Study and Discussion

QUESTIONS ABOUT PURPOSE

1. How does Kavaler avoid overstating her claim that heat causes summer lawlessness?
2. How does she expand her argument to make claims about industrial development?

QUESTIONS ABOUT AUDIENCE

1. How does Kavaler use the first person plural pronoun, as in "we are prejudiced in favor of hot and against cold," to connect with her readers?
2. Why does her description of people who are overheated suggest to her readers that she is making a balanced argument?

QUESTIONS ABOUT STRATEGIES

1. How does Kavaler use various research studies to illustrate the difference between direct and complex causes?
2. How does she use phrases such as "crime of passion" and "in cold blood" to illustrate our attitudes toward heat?

For Writing and Research

1. *Analyze* how the effect of Kavaler's analysis of words with warm and cold connotations.
2. *Practice* by analyzing the factors that usually cause you to lose your temper.
3. *Argue* that the language of cultural stereotyping misrepresents the characters in a crime.
4. *Synthesize:* Examine the experiments Kalaver cites. Then analyze whether their procedures cause them to simplify or overstate their conclusions.

LOREN EISELEY

Loren Eiseley (1907–1979) was born in Lincoln, Nebraska, and was educated at the University of Nebraska and the University of Pennsylvania. He held faculty positions at the University of Kansas, Oberlin College, and the University of Pennsylvania, where he was Franklin Professor of Anthropology and History of Science. He contributed articles to scientific journals, such as *American Anthropologist* and *Scientific Monthly,* and popular magazines, such as *Holiday* and *Ladies' Home Journal.* His books include *The Immense Journey* (1957), *Darwin's Century* (1958), *The Mind as Nature* (1962), *Francis Bacon and the Modern Dilemma* (1963), and *The Unexpected Universe* (1969). In "How Flowers Changed the World," reprinted from *The Immense Journey,* Eiseley explains the sequence of events that caused a change in the Earth's environment and made possible the development of humankind.

How Flowers Changed the World[4]

I F IT HAD been possible to observe the Earth from the far   1
side of the solar system over the long course of geological epochs, the watchers might have been able to discern a subtle change in the light emanating from our planet. That world of long ago would, like the red deserts of Mars, have reflected light from vast drifts of stone and gravel, the sands of wandering wastes, the blackness of naked basalt, the yellow dust

---

[4]Loren Eiseley, "How Flowers Changed the World" from *The Immense Journey* by Loren Eiseley, copyright 1946, 1950, 1951, 1953, 1955, 1956, 1957 by Loren Eiseley. Used by permission of Random House, Inc.

of endlessly moving storms. Only the ceaseless marching of the clouds and the intermittent flashes from the restless surface of the sea would have told a different story, but still essentially a barren one. Then, as the millennia rolled away and age followed age, a new and greener light would, by degrees, have come to twinkle across those endless miles.

This is the only difference those far watchers, by the use of 2 subtle instruments, might have perceived in the whole history of the planet Earth. Yet that slowly growing green twinkle would have contained the epic march of life from the tidal oozes upward across the raw and unclothed continents. Out of the vast chemical bath of the sea—not from the deeps, but from the element-rich, light-exposed platforms of the continental shelves—wandering fingers of green had crept upward along the meanderings of river systems and fringed the gravels of forgotten lakes.

Once upon a time there were no flowers at all.

In those first ages plants clung of necessity to swamps and 3 watercourses. Their reproductive processes demanded direct access to water. Beyond the primitive ferns and mosses that enclosed the borders of swamps and streams the rocks still lay vast and bare, the winds still swirled the dust of a naked planet. The grass cover that holds our world secure in place was still millions of years in the future. The green marchers had gained a soggy foothold upon the land, but that was all. They did not reproduce by seeds but by microscopic swimming sperm that had to wriggle their way through water to fertilize the female cell. Such plants in their higher forms had clever adaptations for the use of rain water in their sexual phases, and survived with increasing success in a wet land environment. They now seem part of man's normal environment. The truth is, however, that there is nothing very "normal" about nature. Once upon a time there were no flowers at all.

A little while ago—about one hundred million years, as   4
the geologist estimates time in the history of our four-billion-
year-old planet—flowers were not to be found anywhere on
the five continents. Wherever one might have looked, from
the poles to the equator, one would have seen only the cold
dark monotonous green of a world whose plant life possessed
no other color.

Somewhere, just a short time before the close of the Age   5
of Reptiles, there occurred a soundless, violent explosion. It
lasted millions of years, but it was an explosion, nevertheless.
It marked the emergence of the angiosperms—the flowering
plants. Even the great evolutionist, Charles Darwin, called
them "an abominable mystery," because they appeared so
suddenly and spread so fast.

Flowers changed the face of the planet. Without them,   6
the world we know—even man himself—would never have
existed. Francis Thompson, the English poet, once wrote
that one could not pluck a flower without troubling a star.
Intuitively he had sensed like a naturalist the enormous inter-
linked complexity of life. Today we know that the appearance
of the flowers contained also the equally mystifying emergence of man.

If we were to go back into the Age of Reptiles, its drowned   7
swamps and birdless forest would reveal to us a warmer but,
on the whole, a sleepier world than that of today. Here and
there, it is true, the serpent heads of bottom-feeding dino-
saurs might be upreared in suspicion of their huge flesh-eat-
ing compatriots. Tyrannosaurs, enormous bipedal caricatures
of men, would stalk mindlessly across the sites of future cities
and go their slow way down into the dark of geologic time.

In all that world of living things nothing saw save with   8
the intense concentration of the hunt, nothing moved except
with the grave sleepwalking intentness of the instinct-driven
brain. Judged by modern standards, it was a world in slow
motion, a cold-blooded world whose occupants were most
active at noonday but torpid on chill nights, their brains
damped by a slower metabolism than any known to even the
most primitive of warm-blooded animals today.

A high metabolic rate and the maintenance of a constant 9
body temperature are supreme achievements in the evolution
of life. They enable an animal to escape, within broad limits,
from the overheating or the chilling of its immediate surroundings, and at the same time to maintain a peak mental
efficiency. Creatures without a high metabolic rate are slaves
to weather. Insects in the first frosts of autumn all run down
like little clocks. Yet if you pick one up and breathe warmly
upon it, it will begin to move about once more.

In a sheltered spot such creatures may sleep away the 10
winter, but they are hopelessly immobilized. Though a few
warm-blooded mammals, such as the woodchuck of our day,
have evolved a way of reducing their metabolic rate in order
to undergo winter hibernation, it is a survival mechanism
with drawbacks, for it leaves the animal helplessly exposed
if enemies discover him during his period of suspended ani-
mation. Thus bear or woodchuck, big animal or small, must
seek, in this time of descending sleep, a safe refuge in some
hidden den or burrow. Hibernation is, therefore, primarily a
winter refuge of small, easily concealed animals rather than
of large ones.

A high metabolic rate, however, means a heavy intake of 11
energy in order to sustain body warmth and efficiency. It is
for this reason that even some of these later warm-blooded
mammals existing in our day have learned to descend into a
slower, unconscious rate of living during the winter months
when food may be difficult to obtain. On a slightly higher
plane they are following the procedure of the cold-blooded
frog sleeping in the mud at the bottom of a frozen pond.

The agile brain of the warm-blooded birds and mammals 12
demands a high oxygen consumption and food in concentrated forms, or the creatures cannot long sustain themselves. It was the rise of the flowering plants that provided
that energy and changed the nature of the living world. Their
appearance parallels in a quite surprising manner the rise of
the birds and mammals.

Slowly, toward the dawn of the Age of Reptiles, some- 13
thing over two hundred and fifty million years ago, the little

naked sperm cells wriggling their way through dew and rain-
drops had given way to a kind of pollen carried by the wind.
Our present-day pine forests represent plants of a pollen-
disseminating variety. Once fertilization was no longer dependent on exterior water, the march over drier regions could be
extended. Instead of spores simple primitive seeds carrying
some nourishment for the young plant had developed, but
true flowers were still scores of millions of years away. After a
long period of hesitant evolutionary groping, they exploded
upon the world with truly revolutionary violence.

The event occurred in Cretaceous times in the close of 14
the Age of Reptiles. Before the coming of the flowering
plants our own ancestral stock, the warm-blooded mammals,
consisted of a few mousy little creatures hidden in trees and
underbrush. A few lizard-like birds with carnivorous teeth
flapped awkwardly on ill-aimed flights among archaic shrub-
bery. None of these insignificant creatures gave evidence of
any remarkable talents. The mammals in particular had been
around for some millions of years, but had remained well
lost in the shadow of the mighty reptiles. Truth to tell, man
was still, like the genie in the bottle, encased in the body of a
creature about the size of a rat.

As for the birds, their reptilian cousins the Pterodactyls, 15
flew farther and better. There was just one thing about the
birds that paralleled the physiology of the mammals. They,
too, had evolved warm blood and its accompanying temperature control. Nevertheless, if one had been seen stripped of
his feathers, he would still have seemed a slightly uncanny
and unsightly lizard.

Neither the birds nor the mammals, however, were quite 16
what they seemed. They were waiting for the Age of Flowers. They were waiting for what flowers, and with them the
true encased seed, would bring. Fish-eating, gigantic leather-
winged reptiles, twenty-eight feet from wing tip to wing tip,
hovered over the coasts that one day would be swarming
with gulls.

Inland the monotonous green of the pine and spruce for- 17
ests with their primitive wooden cone flowers stretched everywhere. No grass hindered the fall of the naked seeds to earth.

Great sequoias towered to the skies. The world of that time has a certain appeal but it is a giant's world, a world moving slowly like the reptiles who stalked magnificently among the boles of its trees.

The trees themselves are ancient, slow-growing and 18 immense, like the redwood groves that have survived to our day on the California coast. All is stiff, formal, upright and green, monotonously green. There is no grass as yet; there are no wide plains rolling in the sun, no tiny daisies dotting the meadows underfoot. There is little versatility about this scene; it is, in truth, a giant's world.

A few nights ago it was brought home vividly to me that 19 the world has changed since that far epoch. I was awakened out of sleep by an unknown sound in my living room. Not a small sound—not a creaking timber or a mouse's scurry— but a sharp, rending explosion as though an unwary foot had been put down upon a wine glass. I had come instantly out of sleep and lay tense, unbreathing. I listened for another step. There was none.

Unable to stand the suspense any longer, I turned on 20 the light and passed from room to room glancing uneasily behind chairs and into closets. Nothing seemed disturbed, and I stood puzzled in the center of the living room floor. Then a small button-shaped object upon the rug caught my eye. It was hard and polished and glistening. Scattered over the length of the room were several more shining up at me like wary little eyes. A pine cone that had been lying in a dish had been blown the length of the coffee table. The dish itself could hardly have been the source of the explosion. Beside it I found two ribbonlike strips of a velvety-green. I tried to place the two strips together to make a pod. They twisted resolutely away from each other and would no longer fit.

I relaxed in a chair, then, for I had reached a solution of 21 the midnight disturbance. The twisted strips were wistaria pods that I had brought in a day or two previously and placed in the dish. They had chosen midnight to explode and distribute their multiplying fund of life down the length of the room. A plant, a fixed, rooted thing, immobilized in a single spot, had devised a way of propelling its offspring across open space. Immediately there passed before my eyes the million airy troopers of the milkweed pod and the clutching hooks of the sandburs. Seeds on the coyote's tail, seeds on the hunter's coat, thistledown mounting on the winds—all were somehow triumphing over life's limitations. Yet the ability to do this had not been with them at the beginning. It was the product of endless effort and experiment.

The seeds on my carpet were not going to lie stiffly where   22
they had dropped like their antiquated cousins, the naked seeds on the pine-cone scales. They were travelers. Struck by the thought, I went out next day and collected several other varieties. I line them up now in a row on my desk—so many little capsules of life, winged, hooked or spiked. Every one is an angiosperm, a product of the true flowering plants. Contained in these little boxes is the secret of that far-off Cretaceous explosion of a hundred million years ago that changed the face of the planet. And somewhere in here, I think, as I poke seriously at one particularly resistant seedcase of a wild grass, was once man himself.

For Study and Discussion

QUESTIONS ABOUT PURPOSE

1. What are the key events in the chain of cause and effect that, as Eiseley shows, culminated in the development of warm-blooded mammals?
2. What is Eiseley suggesting about the process of scientific discovery when he recounts the incident of the seed pod exploding in his kitchen (paragraphs 19 through 22)?

QUESTIONS ABOUT AUDIENCE

1. How much geology and biology does Eiseley assume his readers know?
2. What kind of language and writing style do most readers expect to encounter in books and articles about science? Does this essay confirm that expectation?

QUESTIONS ABOUT STRATEGIES

1. How does Eiseley use narrative strategies to develop his explanation about evolutionary cause and effect?
2. Why does Eiseley use the pronouns *we* and *you* in this essay and end his account with a narrative told in the first person?

For Writing and Research

1. *Analyze* the basic information about evolutionary theory Eiseley is trying to communicate to his readers.
2. *Practice* by speculating about how certain natural events might *cause* other natural events.
3. *Argue* that the destruction of trees, bushes, and flowers for commercial purposes has caused global warming.
4. *Synthesize* some of the research on the prehistoric world. Then use this evidence to support Eiseley's description of what life was like in those times.

TERRY McMILLAN

Terry McMillan was born in 1951 in Port Huron, Michigan, and was educated at the University of California at Berkeley and Columbia University. She taught at the University of Wyoming and the University of Arizona before the critical success of her first novel, *Mama* (1987), and the controversy surrounding her second novel, *Disappearing Acts* (1989), encouraged her to devote her full attention to writing. Her third novel, *Waiting to Exhale* (1992), a story of the romantic complications besetting four contemporary African American women friends, was adapted into an extremely popular film. Her most recent work includes *How Stella Got Her Groove Back* (1996), *The Interruption of Everything* (2005), and *Getting to Happy* (2010). In "The Movie That Changed My Life," reprinted from *The Movie That Changed My Life* (1991), McMillan analyzes her positive and negative reactions to watching *The Wizard of Oz*.

The Movie That Changed My Life[5]

I GREW UP in a small industrial town in the thumb of 1 Michigan: Port Huron. We had barely gotten used to the idea of color TV. I can guess how old I was when I first saw *The Wizard of Oz* on TV because I remember the house we lived in when I was still in elementary school. It was a huge, drafty house that had a fireplace we never once lit. We lived on two acres of land, and at the edge of the back yard

---

[5]Terry McMillan, "The Movie That Changed My Life" from *The Movie That Changed My Life*, edited by David Rosenberg, 1991. Penguin Putnam. Reprinted by permission of The Friedrich Agency.

was the woods, which I always thought of as a forest. We had weeping willow trees, plum and pear trees, and blackberry bushes. We could not see into our neighbors' homes. Railroad tracks were part of our front yard, and the house shook when a train passed—twice, sometimes three times a day. You couldn't hear the TV at all when it zoomed by, and I was often afraid that if it ever flew off the tracks, it would land on the sun porch, where we all watched TV. I often left the room during this time, but my younger sisters and brother thought I was just scared. I think I was in the third grade around this time.

It was a raggedy house which really should've been condemned, but we fixed it up and kept it clean. We had our German shepherd, Prince, who slept under the rickety steps to the side porch that were on the verge of collapsing but never did. I remember performing a ritual whenever *Oz* was coming on. I either baked cookies or cinnamon rolls or popped popcorn while all five of us waited for Dorothy to spin from black and white on that dreary farm in Kansas to the luminous land of color of Oz.

> *The movie* [The Wizard of Oz] *taught me that it's okay to be an idealist, that you have to imagine something better and go for it.*

My house was chaotic, especially with four sisters and brothers and a mother who worked at a factory, and if I'm remembering correctly, my father was there for the first few years of the *Oz* (until he got tuberculosis and had to live in a sanitarium for a year). I do recall the noise and the fighting of my parents (not to mention my other relatives and neighbors). Violence was plentiful, and I wanted to go wherever Dorothy was going where she would not find trouble. To put it bluntly, I wanted to escape because I needed an escape.

I didn't know any happy people. Everyone I knew was either angry or not satisfied. The only time they seemed to laugh was when they were drunk, and even that was short-lived. Most of the grown-ups I was in contact with lived their lives as if it had all been a mistake, an accident, and they were paying dearly for it. It seemed as if they were always at someone else's mercy—women at the mercy of men (this prevailed in my hometown) and children at the mercy of frustrated parents. All I knew was that most of the grown-ups felt trapped, as if they were stuck in this town and no road would lead out. So many of them felt a sense of accomplishment just getting up in the morning and making it through another day. I overheard many a grown-up conversation, and they were never life-affirming: "Chile, if the Lord'll just give me the strength to make it through another week . . ."; "I just don't know how I'ma handle this, I can't take no more. . . ." I rarely knew what they were talking about, but even a fool could hear that it was some kind of drudgery. When I was a child, it became apparent to me that these grown-ups had no power over their lives, or, if they did, they were always at a loss as to how to exercise it. I did not want to grow up and have to depend on someone else for my happiness or be miserable or have to settle for whatever I was dished out—if I could help it. That much I knew already.

I remember being confused a lot. I could never understand 5 why no one had any energy to do anything that would make them feel good, besides drinking. Being happy was a transient and very temporary thing which was almost always offset by some kind of bullshit. I would, of course, learn much later in my own adult life that these things are called obstacles, barriers—or again, bullshit. When I started writing, I began referring to them as "knots." But life wasn't one long knot. It seemed to me it just required stamina and common sense and the wherewithal to know when a knot was before you and you had to dig deeper than you had in order to figure out how to untie it. It could be hard, but it was simple.

The initial thing I remember striking me about *Oz* was 6 how nasty Dorothy's Auntie Em talked to her and everybody on the farm. I was used to that authoritative tone of voice, because my mother talked to us the same way. She never asked you to do anything; she gave you a command and never said "please," and, once you finished it, rarely said "thank you." The tone of her voice was always hostile, and Auntie Em sounded just like my mother—bossy and domineering. They both ran the show, it seemed, and I think that because my mother was raising five children almost single-handedly, I must have had some inkling that being a woman didn't mean you had to be helpless. Auntie Em's husband was a wimp, and for once the tables were turned: he took orders from her! My mother and Auntie Em were proof to me that if you wanted to get things done you had to delegate authority and keep everyone apprised of the rules of the game as well as the consequences. In my house it was punishment—you were severely grounded. What little freedom we had was snatched away: As a child, I often felt helpless, powerless, because I had no control over my situation and couldn't tell my mother when I thought (or knew) she was wrong or being totally unfair, or when her behavior was inappropriate. I hated this feeling to no end, but what was worse was not being able to do anything about it except keep my mouth shut.

So I completely identified when no one had time to listen 7 to Dorothy. That dog's safety was important to her, but no one seemed to think that what Dorothy was saying could possibly be as urgent as the situation at hand. The bottom line was, it was urgent to her. When I was younger, I rarely had the opportunity to finish a sentence before my mother would cut me off or complete it for me, or, worse, give me something to do. She used to piss me off, and nowadays I catch myself—stop myself—from doing the same thing to my seven-year-old. Back then, it was as if what I had to say wasn't important or didn't warrant her undivided attention. So when Dorothy's Auntie Em dismisses her and tells her to find somewhere where she'll stay out of trouble, and little Dorothy starts thinking about if there in fact is such a place— one that is trouble free—I was right there with her, because I wanted to know, too.

I also didn't know or care that Judy Garland was supposed 8 to have been a child star, but when she sang "Somewhere

Over the Rainbow," I *was* impressed. Impressed more by the song than by who was singing it. I mean, she wasn't exactly Aretha Franklin or the Marvelettes or the Supremes, which was the only vocal music I was used to. As kids, we often laughed at white people singing on TV because their songs were always so corny and they just didn't sound anything like the soulful music we had in our house. Sometimes we would mimic people like Doris Day and Fred Astaire and laugh like crazy because they were always so damn happy while they sang and danced. We would also watch square-dancing when we wanted a real laugh and try to look under the women's dresses. What I hated more than anything was when in the middle of a movie the white people always had to start singing and dancing to get their point across. Later, I would hate it when black people would do the same thing—even though it was obvious to us that at least they had more rhythm and, most of the time, more range vocally.

We did skip through the house singing "We're off to see 9 the Wizard," but other than that, most of the songs in this movie are a blank, probably because I blanked them out. Where I lived, when you had something to say to someone, you didn't sing it, you told them, so the cumulative effect of the songs wore thin.

I was afraid for Dorothy when she decided to run away, but 10 at the same time I was glad. I couldn't much blame her—I mean, what kind of life did she have, from what I'd seen so far? She lived on an ugly farm out in the middle of nowhere with all these old people who did nothing but chores, chores, and more chores. Who did she have to play with besides that dog? And even though I lived in a house full of people, I knew how lonely Dorothy felt, or at least how isolated she must have felt. First of all, I was the oldest, and my sisters and brothers were ignorant and silly creatures who often bored me because they couldn't hold a decent conversation. I couldn't ask them questions, like: Why are we living in this dump? When is Mama going to get some more money? Why can't we go on vacations like other people? Like white people? Why does our car always break down? Why are we poor?

Why doesn't Mama ever laugh? Why do we have to live in
Port Huron? Isn't there someplace better than this we can go
live? I remember thinking this kind of stuff in kindergarten,
to be honest, because times were hard, but I'd saved twenty-
five cents in my piggy bank for hotdog-and-chocolate-milk
day at school, and on the morning I went to get it, my piggy
bank was empty. My mother gave me some lame excuse as
to why she had to spend it, but all I was thinking was that I
would have to sit there (again) and watch the other children
slurp their chocolate milk, and I could see the ketchup and
mustard oozing out of the hot-dog bun that I wouldn't get
to taste. I walked to school, and with the exception of walking to my father's funeral when I was sixteen, this was the
longest walk of my entire life. My plaid dress was starched
and my socks were white, my hair was braided and not a
strand out of place; but I wanted to know why I had to feel
this kind of humiliation when in fact I had saved the money
for this very purpose. Why? By the time I got to school, I'd
wiped my nose and dried my eyes and vowed not to let anyone know that I was even moved by this. It was no one's
business why I couldn't eat my hot dog and chocolate milk,
but the irony of it was that my teacher, Mrs. Johnson, must
have sensed what had happened, and she bought my hot dog
and chocolate milk for me that day. I can still remember feeling how unfair things can be, but how they somehow always
turn out good. I guess seeing so much negativity had already
started to turn me into an optimist.

I was a very busy child, because I was the oldest and had   11
to see to it that my sisters and brother had their baths and
did their homework; I combed my sisters' hair, and by fourth
grade I had cooked my first Thanksgiving dinner. It was my
responsibility to keep the house spotless so that when my
mother came home from work it would pass her inspection,
so I spent many an afternoon and Saturday morning mop-
ping and waxing floors, cleaning ovens and refrigerators, grocery shopping, and by the time I was thirteen, I was paying
bills for my mother and felt like an adult. I was also tired of
it, sick of all the responsibility. So yes, I rooted for Dorothy

when she and Toto were vamoosing, only I wanted to know: Where in the hell was she going? Where would I go if I were to run away? I had no idea because there was nowhere to go. What I did know was that one day I would go somewhere— which is why I think I watched so much TV. I was always on the lookout for Paradise, and I think I found it a few years later on "Adventures in Paradise," with Gardner McKay, and on "77 Sunset Strip." Palm trees and blue water and islands made quite an impression on a little girl from a flat, dull little depressing town in Michigan.

Professor Marvel really pissed me off, and I didn't believe   12
for a minute that that crystal ball was real, even before he started asking Dorothy all those questions, but I knew this man was going to be important, and I just couldn't figure out how. Dorothy was so gullible, I thought, and I knew this word because my mother used to always drill it in us that you should "never believe everything somebody tells you." So after Professor Marvel convinced Dorothy that her Auntie Em might be in trouble, and Dorothy scoops up Toto and runs back home, I was totally disappointed, because now I wasn't going to have an adventure. I was thinking I might actually learn how to escape drudgery by watching Dorothy do it successfully, but before she even gave herself the chance to discover for herself that she could make it, she was on her way back home. "Dummy" we all yelled on the sun porch. "Dodo brain!"

The storm. The tornado. Of course, now the entire set of   13
this film looks so phony it's ridiculous, but back then I knew the wind was a tornado because in Michigan we had the same kind of trapdoor underground shelter that Auntie Em had on the farm. I knew Dorothy was going to be locked out once Auntie Em and the workers locked the door, and I also knew she wasn't going to be heard when she knocked on it. This was drama at its best, even though I didn't know what drama was at the time.

In the house she goes, and I was frightened for her. I knew   14
that house was going to blow away, so when little Dorothy gets banged in the head by a window that flew out of its

casement, I remember all of us screaming. We watched everybody fly by the window, including the wicked neighbor who
turns out to be the Wicked Witch of the West, and I'm sure
I probably substituted my mother for Auntie Em and fan-
tasized that all of my siblings would fly away, too. They all
got on my nerves because I could never find a quiet place in
my house—no such thing as peace—and I was always being
disturbed.

It wasn't so much that I had so much I wanted to do by   15
myself, but I already knew that silence was a rare commodity,
and when I managed to snatch a few minutes of it, I could
daydream, pretend to be someone else somewhere else—and
this was fun. But I couldn't do it if someone was bugging me.
On days when my mother was at work, I would often send
the kids outside to play and lock them out, just so I could
have the house to myself for at least fifteen minutes. I loved
pretending that none of them existed for a while, although
after I finished with my fantasy world, it was reassuring to see
them all there. I think I was grounded.

When Dorothy's house began to spin and spin and spin,   16
I was curious as to where it was going to land. And to be
honest, I didn't know little Dorothy was actually dreaming
until she woke up and opened the door and everything was in
color! It looked like Paradise to me. The foliage was almost
an iridescent green, the water bluer than I'd ever seen in any
of the lakes in Michigan. Of course, once I realized she was
in fact dreaming, it occurred to me that this very well might
be the only way to escape. To dream up another world. Create your own.

I had no clue that Dorothy was going to find trouble,   17
though, even in her dreams. Hell, if I had dreamed up
something like another world, it would've been a perfect
one. I wouldn't have put myself in such a precarious situation. I'd have been able to go straight to the Wizard, no
strings attached. First of all, that she walked was stupid to
me; I would've asked one of those Munchkins for a ride.
And I never bought into the idea of those slippers, but once
I bought the whole idea, I accepted the fact that the girl was

definitely lost and just wanted to get home. Personally, all I kept thinking was, if she could get rid of that Wicked Witch of the West, the Land of Oz wasn't such a bad place to be stuck in. It beat the farm in Kansas.

At the time, I truly wished I could spin away from my fam- 18 ily and home and land someplace as beautiful and surreal as Oz—if only for a little while. All I wanted was to get a chance to see another side of the world, to be able to make compari- sons, and then decide if it was worth coming back home.

What was really strange to me, after the Good Witch of 19 the North tells Dorothy to just stay on the Yellow Brick Road to get to the Emerald City and find the Wizard so she can get home, was when Dorothy meets the Scarecrow, the Tin Man, and the Lion—all of whom were missing something I'd never even given any thought to. A brain? What did having one really mean? What would not having one mean? I had one, didn't I, because I did well in school. But because the Scarecrow couldn't make up his mind, thought of himself as a failure, it dawned on me that having a brain meant you had choices, you could make decisions and, as a result, make things happen. Yes, I thought, I had one, and I was going to use it. One day. And the Tin Man, who didn't have a heart. Not having one meant you were literally dead to me, and I never once thought of it as being the house of emo- tions (didn't know what emotions were), where feelings of jealousy, devotion, and sentiment lived. I'd never thought of what else a heart was good for except keeping you alive. But I did have feelings, because they were often hurt, and I was envious of the white girls at my school who wore mohair sweaters and box-pleat skirts, who went skiing and tobog- ganing and yachting and spent summers in Quebec. Why didn't white girls have to straighten their hair? Why didn't their parents beat each other up? Why were they always so goddamn happy?

And courage. Oh, that was a big one. What did having 20 it and not having it mean? I found out that it meant hav- ing guts and being afraid but doing whatever it was you set out to do anyway. Without courage, you couldn't do much of anything. I liked courage and assumed I would acquire it somehow. As a matter of fact, one day my mother *told* me to get her a cup of coffee, and even though my heart was pounding and I was afraid, I said to her pointblank, "Could you please say please?" She looked up at me out of the corner of her eye and said, "What?" So I repeated myself, feeling more powerful because she hadn't slapped me across the room already, and then something came over her and she looked at me and said, "Please." I smiled all the way to the kitchen, and from that point forward, I managed to get away with this kind of behavior until I left home when I was seventeen. My sisters and brother—to this day—don't know how I stand up to my mother, but I know. I decided not to be afraid or intimidated by her, and I wanted her to treat me like a friend, like a human being, instead of her slave.

I do believe that Oz also taught me much about friendship. I mean, the Tin Man, the Lion, and the Scarecrow hung in there for Dorothy, stuck their "necks" out and made sure she was protected, even risked their own "lives" for her. They told each other the truth. They trusted each other. All four of them had each other's best interests in mind. I believe it may have been a while before I actually felt this kind of sincerity in a friend, but really good friends aren't easy to come by, and when you find one, you hold on to them.

Okay. So Dorothy goes through hell before she gets back to Kansas. But the bottom line was, she made it. And what I remember feeling when she clicked those heels was that you have to have faith and be a believer, for real, or nothing will ever materialize. Simple as that. And not only in life but even in your dreams there's always going to be adversity, obstacles, knots, or some kind of bullshit you're going to have to deal with in order to get on with your life. Dorothy had a good heart and it was in the right place, which is why I suppose she won out over the evil witch. I've learned that one, too. That good *always* overcomes evil; maybe not immediately, but in the long run, it does. So I think I vowed when I was little to try to be a good person. An honest person. To care about others and not just myself. Not to be a selfish person, because my heart would be of no service if I used it only for myself. And I had to have the courage to see other people and myself as not being perfect (yes, I had a heart and a brain, but some other things would turn up missing, later), and I would have to learn to untie every knot that I encountered—some self-imposed, some not—in my life, and to believe that if I did the right things, I would never stray too far from my Yellow Brick Road.

I'm almost certain that I saw *Oz* annually for at least five   23 or six years, but I don't remember how old I was when I stopped watching it. I do know that by the time my parents were divorced (I was thirteen), I couldn't sit through it again. I was a mature teen-ager and had finally reached the point where Dorothy got on my nerves. Singing, dancing, and skipping damn near everywhere was so corny and utterly sentimental that even the Yellow Brick Road became sickening. I already knew what she was in for, and sometimes I rewrote the story in my head. I kept asking myself, what if she had just run away and kept going, maybe she would've ended up in Los Angeles with a promising singing career. What if it had turned out that she hadn't been dreaming, and the Wizard had given her an offer she couldn't refuse—say, for instance, he had asked her to stay on in the Emerald City, that she could visit the farm whenever she wanted to, but, get a clue, Dorothy, the Emerald City is what's happening; she could make new city friends and get a hobby and a boyfriend and free rent and never have to do chores. . . .

I had to watch *The Wizard of Oz* again in order to write   24 this, and my six-and-a-half-year-old son, Solomon, joined me. At first he kept asking me if something was wrong with the TV because it wasn't in color, but as he watched, he became mesmerized by the story. He usually squirms or slides to the floor and under a table or just leaves the room if something on TV bores him, which it usually does, except if he's watching Nickelodeon, a high-quality cable kiddie channel. His favorite shows, which he watches with real consistency, and, I think, actually goes through withdrawal if he can't get them for whatever reason, are "Inspector Gadget," "Looney

Tunes," and "Mr. Ed." "Make the Grade," which is sort of a junior-high version of "Jeopardy," gives him some kind of thrill, even though he rarely knows any of the answers. And "Garfield" is a must on Saturday morning. There is hardly anything on TV that he watches that has any real, or at least plausible, drama to it, but you can't miss what you've never had.

The Wicked Witch intimidated the boy no end, and he was 25 afraid of her. The Wizard was also a problem. So I explained— no, I just told him pointblank—"Don't worry, she'll get it in the end, Solomon, because she's bad. And the Wizard's a fake, and he's trying to sound like a tough guy, but he's a wus." That offered him some consolation, and even when the Witch melted he kind of looked at me with those *Home Alone* eyes and asked "But where did she go, Mommy?" "She's history," I said. "Melted. Gone. Into the ground. Remember, this is pretend. It's not real. Real people don't melt. This is only TV," I said. And then he got that look in his eyes as if he'd remembered something.

Of course he had a nightmare that night and of course 26 there was a witch in it, because I had actually left the sofa a few times during this last viewing to smoke a few cigarettes (the memory bank is a powerful place—I still remembered many details), put the dishes in the dishwasher, make a few phone calls, water the plants. Solomon sang "We're off to see the Wizard" for the next few days because he said that was his favorite part, next to the Munchkins (who also showed up in his nightmare).

So, to tell the truth, I really didn't watch the whole movie 27 again. I just couldn't. Probably because about thirty or so years ago little Dorothy had made a lasting impression on me, and this viewing felt like overkill. You only have to tell me, show me, once in order for me to get it. But even still, the movie itself taught me a few things that I still find challenging. That it's okay to be an idealist, that you have to imagine something better and go for it. That you have to believe in *something,* and it's best to start with yourself and take it from there. At least give it a try. As corny as it may sound, sometimes I am afraid of what's around the corner, or what's not around the corner. But I look anyway. I believe that writing is one of my "corners"—an intersection, really; and when I'm confused or reluctant to look back, deeper, or ahead, I create my own Emerald Cities and force myself to take longer looks, because it is one sure way that I'm able to see.

Of course, I've fallen, tumbled, and been thrown over all   28
kinds of bumps on my road, but it still looks yellow, although every once in a while there's still a loose brick. For the most part, though, it seems paved. Perhaps because that's the way I want to see it.

For Study and Discussion

QUESTIONS ABOUT PURPOSE

1. In the process of showing why the movie was significant for her, what does McMillan reveal about herself?
2. What advantages does McMillan suggest that fantasy has for children? What effects might fantasies other than *The Wizard of Oz* have, perhaps books like C. S. Lewis's Narnia series or a movie like *Star Trek?*

QUESTIONS ABOUT AUDIENCE

1. How justified do you think McMillan is in assuming that her readers are very familiar with the movie *The Wizard of Oz?* What would be the effect if they're not familiar with the movie?
2. What personality traits and outlook on life do you think readers are likely to have who like this essay and find it persuasive? To what extent do you think you and your friends share those traits?

QUESTIONS ABOUT STRATEGIES

1. How does McMillan tie the attraction that the Oz movie has for her to conditions in her own life? How well does that strategy work?
2. How does McMillan fill in details of the movie for readers who may have forgotten or didn't know the story of *The Wizard of Oz?* How good a job does she do?

For Writing and Research

1. *Analyze* the strategies McMillan uses to connect the story of her own life with the story of *The Wizard of Oz*.
2. *Practice* by analyzing the effect a contemporary movie or television show has had on you and your circle of friends.
3. *Argue* that the "philosophy" of *The Wizard of Oz* has shaped the central values of American culture.
4. *Synthesize* information from the books about Oz by L. Frank Baum and Gregory Maguire and the Broadway musical *Wicked*. Then use this evidence to speculate on the effect of Dorothy's departure on Oz.

Ursula K. Le Guin was born in 1929 in Berkeley, California, and was educated at Radcliffe College and Columbia University. In 1952, she obtained a Fulbright Fellowship to study in Paris, where she met her husband, historian Charles A. Le Guin. In the mid-1950s, she worked as a part-time writing instructor at Mercer University and the University of Idaho before moving to Portland, Oregon, where she was able to pursue a full-time career as a writer. She published her first novel, *Rocannon's World,* in 1964 and established herself as a leading writer of science fiction and fantasy. Le Guin has contributed short stories, essays, and reviews to numerous science fiction, scholarly, and popular journals, such as *Fantastic, Western Humanities Review,* and *The New Yorker.* Her novels include *The Left Hand of Darkness* (1969), *The Lathe of Heaven* (1970), and her Earthsea trilogy: *A Wizard of Earthsea* (1968), *The Tombs of Atuan* (1971), and *The Farthest Shore* (1972). The last volume was selected for a National Book Award. Le Guin's short fiction, which has won numerous prizes, is collected in *The Wind's Twelve Quarters* (1975) and *Orsinian Tales* (1976). Her more recent work includes *The Beginning Place* (1980), *Hard Words and Other Poems* (1981), *Always Coming Home* (1985), *Tehanu* (1990), and *Unlocking the Air and Other Stories* (1996). "The Ones Who Walk Away from Omelas," reprinted from *The Wind's Twelve Quarters,* depicts an idyllic community where the conditions for happiness are "strict and absolute."

The Ones Who Walk Away from Omelas[6]

Wᴵᴛʜ ᴀ ᴄʟᴀᴍᴏʀ of bells that set the swallows soaring,   1
the Festival of Summer came to the city Omelas,
bright-towered by the sea. The rigging of the boats in harbor
sparkled with flags. In the streets between houses with red
roofs and painted walls, between old moss-grown gardens
and under avenues of trees, past great parks and public buildings, processions moved. Some were decorous: old people in
long stiff robes of mauve and gray, grave master workmen,
quiet, merry women carrying their babies and chatting as
they walked. In other streets the music beat faster, a shim-
mering of gong and tambourine, and the people went dancing, the procession was a dance. Children dodged in and out,
their high calls rising like the swallows' crossing flights over
the music and the singing. All the processions wound towards
the north side of the city, where on the great water-meadow
called the Green Fields boys and girls, naked in the bright air,
with mud-stained feet and ankles and long, lithe arms, exercised their restive horses before the race. The horses wore no
gear at all but a halter without bit. Their manes were braided
with streamers of silver, gold, and green. They flared their
nostrils and pranced and boasted to one another; they were
vastly excited, the horse being the only animal who has
adopted our ceremonies as his own. Far off to the north and
west the mountains stood up half encircling Omelas on her
bay. The air of morning was so clear that the snow still crown-
ing the Eighteen Peaks burned with white-gold fire across
the miles of sunlit air, under the dark blue of the sky. There
was just enough wind to make the banners that marked the
racecourse snap and flutter now and then. In the silence of
the broad green meadows one could hear the music winding

throughout the city streets, farther and nearer and ever approaching, a cheerful faint sweetness of the air from time to time trembled and gathered together and broke out into the great joyous clanging of the bells.

Joyous! How is one to tell about joy? How describe the cit- 2 izens of Omelas? They were not simple folk, you see, though they were happy. But we do not say the words of cheer much anymore. All smiles have become archaic. Given a description such as this one tends to make certain assumptions. Given a description such as this one tends to look next for the King, mounted on a splendid stallion and surrounded by his noble knights, or perhaps in a golden litter borne by great-muscled slaves. But there was no king. They did not use swords, or keep slaves. They were not barbarians. I do not know the rules and laws of their society, but I suspect that they were singularly few. As they did without monarchy and slavery, so they also got on without the stock exchange, the advertisement, the secret police, and the bomb. Yet I repeat that these were not simple folk, not dulcet shepherds, noble savages, bland utopians. There were not less complex than us.

The trouble is that we have a bad habit, encouraged by 3 pedants and sophisticates, of considering happiness as something rather stupid. Only pain is intellectual, only evil interesting. This is the treason of the artist: a refusal to admit the banality of evil and the terrible boredom of pain. If you can't lick 'em, join 'em. If it hurts, repeat it. But to praise despair is to condemn delight, to embrace violence is to lose hold of everything else. We have almost lost hold; we can no longer describe happy man, nor make any celebration of joy. How can I tell you about the people of Omelas? They were not naïve and happy children—though their children were, in fact, happy. They were mature, intelligent, passionate adults whose lives were not wretched. O miracle! But I wish I could describe it better. I wish I could convince you. Omelas sounds in my words like a city in a fairy tale, long ago and far away, once upon a time. Perhaps it would be best if you imagined it as your own fancy bids, assuming it will rise to the occasion, for certainly I cannot suit you all. For instance, how about technology? I think that there would be no cars or helicopters in and above the streets; this follows from the fact that the people of Omelas are happy people. Happiness is based on a just discrimination of what is necessary, what is neither necessary nor destructive, and what is destructive. In the middle category, however—that of the unnecessary but undestructive, that of comfort, luxury, exuberance, etc.—they could perfectly well have central heating, subway trains, washing machines, and all kinds of marvelous devices not yet invented here, floating light-sources, fuelless power, a cure for the common cold. Or they could have none of that: it doesn't matter. As you like it. I incline to think that people from towns up and down the coast have been coming to Omelas during the last days before the Festival on very fast little trains and double-decked trams, and that the train station of Omelas is actually the handsomest building in town, though plainer than the magnificent Farmers' Market. But even granted trains, I fear that Omelas so far strikes some of you as goody-goody. Smiles, bells, parades, horses, bleh. If so, please add an orgy. If an orgy would help, don't hesitate. Let us not, however, have temples from which issue beautiful nude priests and priestesses already half in ecstasy and ready to copulate with any man or woman, lover or stranger, who desires union with the deep godhead of the blood, although that was my first idea. But really it would be better not to have any temples in Omelas—at least, not manned temples. Religion yes, clergy no. Surely the beautiful nudes can just wander about, offering themselves like divine soufflés to the hunger of the needy and the rapture of the flesh. Let them join the processions. Let tambourines be struck above the copulations, and the glory of desire be proclaimed upon the gongs, and (a not unimportant point) let the offspring of these delightful rituals be beloved and looked after by all. One thing I know there is none of in Omelas is guilt. But what else should there be? I thought at first there were no drugs, but that is puritanical. For those who like it, the faint insistent sweetness of *drooz* may perfume the ways of the city, *drooz* which first brings a great lightness and brilliance to the mind and limbs, and then after some hours a dreamy languor, and wonderful visions at last of the very arcane and inmost secrets of the Universe, as well as exciting the pleasure of sex beyond all belief; and it is not habit-forming. For more modest tastes I think there ought to be beer. What else, what else belongs in the joyous city? The sense of victory, surely, the celebration of courage. But as we did without clergy, let us do without soldiers. The joy built upon successful slaughter is not the right kind of joy; it will not do; it is fearful and it is trivial. A boundless and generous contentment, a magnanimous triumph felt not against some outer enemy but in communion with the finest and fairest in the souls of all men everywhere and the splendor of the world's summer: This is what swells the hearts of the people of Omelas, and the victory they celebrate is that of life. I don't think many of them need to take *drooz*.

Most of the processions have reached the Green Fields by now. A marvelous smell of cooking goes forth from the red and blue tents of the provisioners. The faces of small children are amiably sticky; in the benign gray beard of a man a couple of crumbs of rich pastry are entangled. The youths and girls have mounted their horses and are beginning to group around the starting line of the course. An old woman, small, fat, and laughing, is passing out flowers from a basket, and tall young men wear her flowers in their shining hair. A child of nine or ten sits at the edge of the crowd alone, playing on a wooden flute. People pause to listen, and they smile, but they do not speak to him, for he never ceases playing and never sees them, his dark eyes wholly rapt in the sweet, thin magic of the tune.

He finishes, and slowly lowers his hands holding the wooden flute.

As if that little private silence were the signal, all at once a trumpet sounds from the pavilion near the starting line: imperious, melancholy, piercing. The horses rear on their slender legs, and some of them neigh in answer. Sober-faced, the young riders stroke the horses' necks and soothe them, whispering. "Quiet, quiet, there my beauty, my hope. . . ."

They begin to form in rank along the starting line. The crowds along the racecourse are like a field of grass and flowers in the wind. The Festival of Summer has begun.

Do you believe? Do you accept the festival, the city, the   7
joy? No? Then let me describe one more thing.

In a basement under one of the beautiful public buildings   8
of Omelas, or perhaps in the cellar of one of its spacious private homes, there is a room. It has one locked door, and no window. A little light seeps in dustily between cracks in the boards, secondhand from a cobwebbed window somewhere across the cellar. In one corner of the little room a couple of mops, with stiff, clotted, foul-smelling heads, stand near a rusty bucket. The floor is dirt, a little damp to the touch, as cellar dirt usually is. The room is about three paces long and two wide: a mere broom closet or disused tool room. In the room, a child is sitting. It could be a boy or a girl. It looks about six, but actually is nearly ten. It is feeble-minded. Perhaps it was born defective, or perhaps it has become imbecile through fear, malnutrition, and neglect. It picks its nose and occasionally fumbles vaguely with its toes or genitals, as it sits hunched in the corner farthest from the bucket and the two mops. It is afraid of the mops. It finds them horrible. It shuts its eyes, but it knows the mops are still standing there; and the door is locked; and nobody will come. The door is always locked; and nobody ever comes, except that sometimes—the child has no understanding of time or interval—sometimes the door rattles terribly and opens, and a person, or several people, are there. One of them may come in and kick the child to make it stand up. The others never come close, but peer in at it with frightened, disgusted eyes. The food bowl and the water jug are hastily filled, the door is locked; the eyes disappear. The people at the door never say anything, but the child, who has not always lived in the tool room, and can remember sunlight and its mother's voice, sometimes speaks. "I will be good," it says. "Please let me out. I will be good!" They never answer. The child used to scream for help at night, and cry a good deal, but now it only makes a kind of whining, "eh-haa, eh-haa," and it speaks less and less often.

It is so thin there are no calves to its legs; its belly protrudes; it lives on a half-bowl of corn meal and grease a day. It is naked. Its buttocks and thighs are a mass of festered sores, as it sits in its own excrement continually.

They all know it is there, all the people of Omelas. Some of them have come to see it, others are content merely to know it is there. They all know that it has to be there. Some of them understand why, and some do not, but they all understand that their happiness, the beauty of their city, the tenderness of their friendships, the health of their children, the wisdom of their scholars, the skill of their makers, even the abundance of their harvest and the kindly weathers of their skies, depend wholly on this child's abominable misery. 9

This is usually explained to children when they are between eight and twelve, whenever they seem capable of understanding; and most of those who come to see the child are young people, though often enough an adult comes, or comes back, to see the child. No matter how well the matter has been explained to them, these young spectators are always shocked and sickened at the sight. They feel disgust, which they had thought themselves superior to. They feel anger, outrage, impotence, despite all the explanations. They would like to do something for the child. But there is nothing they can do. If the child were brought up into the sunlight out of that vile place, if it were cleaned and fed and comforted, that would be a good thing, indeed; but if it were done, in that day and hour all the prosperity and beauty and delight of Omelas would wither and be destroyed. Those are the terms. To exchange all the goodness and grace of every life in Omelas for that single, small improvement: to throw away the happiness of thousands for the chance of happiness of one: that would be to let guilt within the walls indeed. 10

The terms are strict and absolute; there may not even be a kind word spoken to the child. 11

Often the young people go home in tears, or in a tearless rage, when they have seen the child and faced this terrible paradox. They may brood over it for weeks or years. But as time goes on they begin to realize that even if the child could 12 be released, it would not get much good of its freedom: a little vague pleasure of warmth and food, no real doubt, but little more. It is too degraded and imbecile to know any real joy. It has been afraid too long ever to be free of fear. Its habits are too uncouth for it to respond to humane treatment. Indeed, after so long it would probably be wretched without walls about it to protect it, and darkness for its eyes, and its own excrement to sit in. Their tears at the bitter injustice dry when they begin to perceive the terrible justice of reality, and to accept it. Yet it is their tears and anger, the trying of their generosity and the acceptance of their helplessness, which are perhaps the true source of the splendor of their lives. Theirs is no vapid, irresponsible happiness. They know that they, like the child, are not free. They know compassion. It is the existence of the child, and their knowledge of its existence, that makes possible the nobility of their architecture, the poignancy of their music, the profundity of their science. It is because of the child that they are so gentle with children. They know that if the wretched one were not there sniveling in the dark, the other one, the flute-player, could make no joyful music as the young riders line up in their beauty for the race in the sunlight of the first morning of summer.

Now do you believe them? Are they not more credible? But 13 there is one more thing to tell, and this is quite incredible.

At times one of the adolescent girls or boys who go see the 14 child does not go home to weep or rage, does not, in fact, go home at all. Sometimes also a man or a woman much older falls silent for a day or two, then leaves home. These people go out into the street, and walk down the street alone. They keep walking, and walk straight out of the city of Omelas, through the beautiful gates. They keep walking across the farmlands of Omelas. Each one goes alone, youth or girl, man or woman. Night falls; the traveler must pass down village streets, between the houses with yellow-lit windows, and on out into the darkness of the fields. Each alone, they go west or north, towards the mountains. They go on. They leave Omelas, they walk ahead into the darkness, and they do not come back. The place they go towards is a place even less imaginable to most of us than the city of happiness. I cannot describe it at all. It is possible that it does not exist. But they seem to know where they are going, the ones who walk away from Omelas.

COMMENT ON "THE ONES WHO WALK AWAY FROM OMELAS"

Le Guin is clearly a moralist as demonstrated by this story of a utopia with a twist. The overriding joy of the town of Omelas depends on the suffering of one child, one youngster whose misery somehow causes restitution for thousands of other citizens and ensures their happiness. Only those with the moral integrity to reject this unusual setup "walk away" from this "paradise." The effect of their decision, the story suggests, will mean that their lives will be no longer happy or easy. Nevertheless, they have made an admirable, enviable moral choice.

CHAPTER 7

PERSUASION AND ARGUMENT

Readers encounter persuasion and argument every day as writers try to persuade them to spend money, take action, support a cause, accept an opinion, or consider an idea. The starting point for persuasion and argument is an assertion, a statement of belief or a claim that the writer undertakes to explain and support. At one extreme, both the statement and the support may be highly emotional, depending heavily on biased language and strong appeals to feelings and instincts; this kind of writing is classified as **persuasion.** At the other extreme, the assertion and support may be strictly rational, depending on logical explanations and appeals to intelligence; this kind of writing is classified as **argument.** Advertising and political writing cluster toward the persuasion end of the continuum, whereas scientific writing and grant proposals cluster toward the argument end.

Seldom, however, does persuasive writing appeal only to emotions, and seldom does argument rely entirely on reason. Rather, when people write to convince, they appeal to both emotions and intelligence, but they vary the balance of emotion and reason according to their audience and purpose.

Writing that is primarily rational is not necessarily better than writing that is primarily emotional. Some occasions call for appeals to pride and patriotism, for vivid metaphors that reach the senses, and for strong language that arouses the passions. This kind of writing is called **ceremonial discourse.** The audience already knows and probably agrees with what the writer (or speaker) is going to say, and expects not intellectual stimulation but emotional satisfaction and inspiration. Inaugural speeches, graduation addresses, and political speeches usually fit into this emotional category and are often successful precisely because they are emotional.

Most arguments, however, must be fairly rational if they are to convince critical readers, and those readers are justified in expecting writers to support major assertions with evidence and logic. Generally speaking, people who write effective arguments do what a good trial lawyer does: they present a case persuasively but give strong reasons to support their assertions. In the final analysis, the quality of any argument must be judged not by some absolute standard of rationality, but by how well it has accomplished its intended purpose with its intended audience.

PURPOSE

Although you may think of disagreement when you hear the word *argument*, not all people who write arguments are trying to win a dispute. Instead, they may want to persuade people to *support a cause* or *make a commitment*. Political leaders and ministers frequently write for these purposes. Writers may also argue in order to get people to *take action* or to try to *change a situation*. Editorial writers, reformers, and political activists often have these purposes in mind.

Sometimes writers persuade in order to *change behavior or attitudes*. Someone advocating a new approach to child rearing would have such a purpose, as would a person arguing against racial or sexual prejudice. Other writers argue to *refute a theory*. For example, feminist writers continually seek to disprove the belief that women are less talented and creative than men. Writers also use persuasive strategies to *arouse sympathies, to stimulate concern, to win agreement,* and *to provoke anger.* They may incorporate several of these purposes into one piece of writing.

AUDIENCE

More than any other kind of writing, persuasion and argument require you to think about your audience. To choose effective rhetorical strategies, you must have a clear sense of who may read your writing, what kinds of attitudes and biases those persons will bring to the reading, and what readers expect to get from an essay. Making such analysis of an audience may be difficult, and sometimes you have to work by instinct rather than information. Usually, however, you can assume that readers will fit into one of the following classes:

1. *Readers who already agree with your ideas and are reading mainly for reinforcement or encouragement.* These readers do not expect a tightly reasoned and carefully structured argument; rather, they want to see their position stated with vigor and conviction.
2. *Readers who are interested in and are inclined to agree with the issue you are discussing but want to know more.* Although they are interested in evidence that will help them make a decision, they do not expect a completely rational argument and will not object if you use slanted language or emotional examples to strengthen a point.
3. *Readers who are neutral on an issue and want explanations and arguments based on evidence and logical reasoning before they make up their minds.* For these readers, you must make a carefully developed and factual argument, although you can also reinforce facts with opinions.
4. *Readers who are skeptical about an issue and will not take a stand until they hear both sides of an argument explained*

in complete detail. They expect you to provide appropriate data and documentation and provide the impression that you are knowledgeable, capable, and balanced.

STRATEGIES

Collecting Evidence

To construct an argument you need to collect one or more of the following kinds of evidence: *facts, judgments,* and *testimony.*

Facts are a valuable ally in building an argument because they cannot be debated. It is a fact that the stock market crashed on October 29, 1929. It is a fact that on September 11, 2001, terrorists crashed two airplanes into the twin towers of the World Trade Center, killing nearly 3,000 people. But not all facts are so clear-cut, and some statements that look like facts may not be facts. A stock analyst who announces a company's projected earnings for the next five years is making an estimate, not a statement of fact.

Judgments are conclusions inferred from facts. Unlike opinions, judgments lend credibility to an argument because they result from careful reasoning. A doctor considering a patient's symptoms reaches a tentative diagnosis of either tuberculosis or a tumor. If the laboratory test eliminates tuberculosis, then the patient probably has a tumor that is either malignant or benign, a question that can be settled by surgery and further testing.

Testimony affirms or asserts facts. A person who has had direct experience (an *eyewitness*) or who has developed expertise in a subject (an *expert witness*) can provide testimony based on facts, judgment, or both. An eyewitness is asked to report facts, as when an observer reports seeing a man drown in a strong current. An expert witness is asked to study facts and render a judgment, as when a coroner reports that an autopsy has shown that the victim did not drown but died of a heart attack.

Both kinds of testimony can constitute powerful evidence. Eyewitness testimony provides authenticity. Expert testimony provides authority. Each has its limitations, however. An eyewitness is not always trustworthy; eyewitness testimony can be distorted by faulty observation or biased opinion. An expert witness is not infallible or always unbiased; expert testimony, though often difficult for the nonexpert to challenge, can be disputed by other experts employing a different method of investigation. Each type of testimony can be abused. An eyewitness account of an event may be convincing, but it should not be used to draw parallels to unrelated events. And an expert's credentials in one field, whatever eminence they convey, do not automatically carry over to other fields.

The best way to evaluate evidence in an argument is to determine whether it is *pertinent, verifiable,* and *reliable.* A stock analyst who uses the success of the polio vaccine as a reason for investing in a drug company researching a vaccine for the common cold is not presenting evidence that is *pertinent* to the argument. A historian who claims that Amelia Earhart's flying ability was impaired by Alzheimer's disease is using an argument that is not *verifiable.* And an attorney who builds a case on the eyewitness testimony of a person who has been arrested several times for public intoxication is not using the most *reliable* evidence.

Arranging Evidence

After you have collected your evidence, you need to determine how to *arrange* it. Because every argument creates its own problems and possibilities, no one method of arrangement will always work best. Sometimes you may have to combine methods to make your case. To make an informed decision, you need to consider how you might adapt your evidence to one of the four common strategies: **induction, deduction, claims and warrants,** and **accommodation.**

Induction Often called the *scientific method, induction* begins by presenting specific evidence and then moves to a general conclusion. This arrangement reflects the history of your investigation. You begin your research with a question you want to answer. You then collect a cross-section of evidence until a pattern emerges, and you arrange your individual pieces of evidence in a way that helps your readers see the pattern you have discovered. You need not list all the false leads or blind alleys you encountered along the way unless they changed your perspective or confirmed your judgment. At this point, you make what scientists call an *inductive leap:* you determine that although you have not collected every example, you have examined enough to risk proposing a probable conclusion.

For example:

Research question: Why is our company losing so many valuable data processors to other companies?

Evidence:
1. Most data processors are women who have preschool children. (Provide facts.)
2. A nearby day-care center used by employees has closed because it lost federal funding. (Provide facts.)
3. Other day-care centers in the area are inconvenient and understaffed. (Provide testimony.)
4. Other companies provide on-site day care for children of employees. (Provide facts.)
5. On-site day care is beneficial to the emotional well-being of both preschool children and their mothers because of the possibility of contact during the workday.

Conclusion: Therefore, our company needs to provide on-site day care to retain valuable employees.

Deduction   Usually identified with classical reasoning, *deduction* begins with a general statement or *major premise* that when restricted by a *minor premise* leads to a specific conclusion. Unlike induction, which in theory makes an assertion only in its conclusion, deduction does make initial assertions (based on evidence) from which a conclusion is derived. This strategy is called a *three-step syllogism:*

> <u>Major premise</u>: Retention of data processors who have preschool children is promoted by on-site day care.
> <u>Minor premise</u>: Our company wants to retain data processors who have preschool children.
> <u>Conclusion</u>: Our company should establish on-site day-care centers.

To gain your audience's acceptance of your major and minor premises, you must support each assertion with specific evidence. Demonstrate that retaining data processors who have preschool children is promoted by on-site day-care centers and that "our company" wants to retain computer operators who have preschool children. If your readers accept your premises, then they are logically committed to accepting your conclusion.

Claims and Warrants Often called the *Toulmin argument* after Stephen Toulmin, the legal philosopher who analyzed the process and defined its terminology, *claims and warrants* argues from a general principle to a specific example, but it presents a more complex arrangement than a syllogism.

You begin by asserting a *claim* (or a general assertion about the argument you intend to make), then provide evidence to support your claim. The statement that links the claim to the evidence is called a *warrant.* In some arguments, the warrant is implied; in others, you need to state it directly. Additional parts of the claims and warrants strategy include *support* to strengthen your argument, *qualifiers* to modify or limit your claim, and *reservations* to point out instances in which your claim may not apply.

For example:

Claim: Retention of data processors who have preschool children is promoted by on-site day-care centers.

Evidence:
1. Many of our data processors have preschool children.
2. These employees have difficulties arranging and paying for day-care services.
3. Mothers are more effective employees when they don't have to worry about their children.

Warrant: Our company should establish on-site day-care centers.

Support:
1. Competitors who provide on-site day care for their employees have a high retention rate.
2. Data processors at such companies have a lower absentee rate.
3. The cost of training new data processors is expensive.

Qualification: Some of our data processors do not have pre-school children.

Reservation: Because our company wants to retain a qualified workforce, we don't want to add expenses to the workplace that will penalize data processors who do not have children.

Claims and warrants is an effective arrangement because, like induction, it enables you to present evidence systematically; and, like induction, the inclusion of qualifiers and reservations suggests that you are considering your evidence objectively. But, like deduction, claims and warrants enables you to provide a clear and cogent link (warrant) between your general assertion (claim) and the data you have collected (evidence).

Accommodation Sometimes called *nonthreatening argument,* *accommodation* arranges evidence so that all parties believe their position has received a fair hearing. Induction reveals how a chain of evidence leads to a conclusion. Deduction demonstrates why certain premises demand a single conclusion. Although both procedures work effectively in specific situations, they occasionally defeat your purpose. Readers may feel trapped by the relentless march of your argument; though unable to refute your logic, they are still unwilling to listen to reason. Accommodation takes your audience's hesitations into account. Instead of trying to win the argument, you try to improve communication and increase understanding.

To employ this strategy, begin by composing an objective description of the controversy:

> *Women data processors who have preschool children are leaving the company.*

Then draft a complete and accurate statement of the contending positions, supplying evidence that makes each position credible:

Corporation board: We need a qualified workforce, but we are not in business to provide social services. (Provide evidence.)

Fellow workers (single, male, etc.): We understand their problem, but providing an on-site day-care center is giving expensive, preferential treatment to a small segment of the workforce. (Provide evidence.)

Competitors: We need better data processors if we are going to compete, and we will provide what is necessary to hire them. (Provide evidence.)

Next, show where and why you and the various parties agree:

> *The corporation should not be in the day-care business; women data processors have the right to market their skills in a competitive market.*

Then present your own argument explaining where it differs from other positions and why it deserves serious consideration:

> *We have invested a large amount of money in training our workforce; child care is an appropriate investment in view of the long-term contribution these people will make to the corporation.*

Finally, present a proposal that might resolve the issue in a way that recognizes the interests of all concerned:

> *The corporation might help to fund the nearby day-care center that was previously supported by government money.*

Monitoring the Appeals

In developing an argument, you must keep track of how you are using the three basic appeals of argument: the ***emotional appeal,*** the ***ethical appeal,*** and the ***logical appeal.*** These three appeals are rarely separate; they all weave in and out of virtually every argument. But to control their effects to your advantage, you must know when and why you are using them.

The Emotional Appeal Readers feel as well as think, and to be thoroughly convinced, they must be emotionally as well as intellectually engaged by your argument. Some people think that the *emotional appeal* is suspect because it relies on the feelings, instincts, and opinions of readers. They connect it to the devious manipulations of advertising or politics. The emotional appeal is often used to stampede an audience into thoughtless action, but such abuses do not negate its value. The emotional appeal should never replace more rational appeal, but it can be an effective strategy for convincing your readers that they need to pay attention to your argument.

The greatest strength of the emotional appeal is also its greatest weakness. Dramatic examples, presented in concrete images and connotative language, personalize a problem and produce powerful emotions. Some examples produce predictable emotions: an abandoned puppy or a lonely old woman evokes pity; a senseless accident or recurring incompetence evokes anger; a smiling face or a heroic deed evokes delight. Some examples, however, produce unpredictable results, and their dramatic presentation often works against your purpose. It would be difficult to predict, for instance, how your readers would respond to the plight of an undocumented immigrant working mother's need for health insurance. Some might pity her; others might disdain her illegal status and her desire for federal funding from taxpaying citizens. Because controversial issues attract a range of passions, use the emotional appeal with care.

All the writers in this chapter use emotional appeals, but those who rely on it most heavily are Brigid Brophy's argument for animal rights and Anna Quindlen's argument against the death penality.

The Ethical Appeal The character (or *ethos*) of the writer— not the writer's morality—is the basis of the *ethical appeal*. It suggests that the writer is someone to be trusted, a claim that emerges from a demonstration of competence as an authority on the subject under discussion. Readers trust a writer who has established a reputation for informed, reasonable, and reliable writing about controversial subjects.

You can use the ethical appeal in your argument either by citing authorities who have conducted thorough investigations of your subject or by following the example of authorities in your competent treatment of evidence. There are two potential dangers with the ethical appeal. First, you cannot win the trust of your readers by citing as an authority in one field someone who is best known to be an authority in another field. Second, you cannot convince your readers that you are knowledgeable if you present your argument exclusively in personal terms. Your own experience may allow you to assemble detailed and powerful evidence. But to establish your ethical appeal, you need to balance such evidence with the experience of other authorities.

All the writers in this chapter rely on their ethical appeal, but it works most effectively for writers such as Martin Luther King Jr., who has established himself as a symbolic authority on racism and Vicki Hearne, who has established herself as an authority on animals by her work as a dog trainer.

The Logical Appeal The rational strategies used to develop an argument constitute a *logical appeal.* Some people think that the forceful use of logic makes an argument absolutely true. But controversies contain many truths, no one of which can be graded simply true or false. By using the logical appeal, you acknowledge that arguments are conducted in a world of probability, not certainty. By offering a series of reasonable observations and conclusions, you establish the most reliable case.

The logical appeal is widely used and accepted in argument. Establishing the relationships that bind your evidence to your assertion engages your readers' reasoning power, and an appeal to their intelligence and common sense is likely to win their assent. But the logical appeal is not infallible. Its limit is in acknowledging limits: How much evidence is enough? There is no simple answer to this question. For example, the amount of evidence required to convince fellow workers that your company should provide on-site day care may not be sufficient to persuade the company's board of directors. On the other hand, too much evidence, however methodically analyzed, may win the argument but lose your audience. Without emotional or ethical appeal, your "reasonable" presentation may be put aside in favor of more urgent issues. Accurate and cogent reasoning is the basis for any sound argument, but the logical appeal, like the emotional and ethical appeals, must be monitored carefully to accomplish your purpose.

The essays in this chapter use a variety of evidence. Vicki Hearne relies on personal experience to make her case against animal rights advocates; Eric Liu also relies on personal experience to argue his case about racism; and H. L. Mencken creates what might be considered a "logical appeal" by citing what appears to be fact, judgment, and eyewitness and expert testimony.

PERSUASION AND ARGUMENT

Points to Remember

1. To argue well, you have to know your audience and your purpose. Do you understand your audience's interests, their backgrounds, and what questions they might have? Do you know what you want to accomplish with this particular group of readers? It's useful to write out the answers to both of these questions before you start.

2. Understand the three principal kinds of persuasive appeals.

   - *Appeal to reason.* Emphasizes logic, evidence, authority, cause and effect, precedent, and comparison and analogy.
   - *Appeal to emotion.* Emphasizes feelings, the senses, personal biases, connotative language, and images and metaphor.
   - *Appeal from integrity and character.* Emphasizes the writer's (ethos)—competence, experience, and reputation.

   The most persuasive writers usually combine elements from all three kinds of appeals.

3. Construct your arguments as a lawyer would construct a case to present to a jury: state your claim and back it up with evidence and reason, but, when appropriate, also use metaphor and connotation.

4. Always assume that your audience is intelligent, if perhaps uninformed about some particulars. Be respectful; avoid a superior tone.

5. Argue responsibly.
   - Don't overstate your claim.
   - Don't oversimplify complex issues.
   - Support your claims with specific details and evidence.

© *Courtesy of the Center for International Rehabilitation.*

In this public service advertisement created by the Leo Burnett advertising company, PALM, or Physicians Against Land Mines, presents its argument about the death, dismemberment, and disability caused by land mines. The text below Emina Uzicanin's missing leg describes how, as a child playing on the outskirts of Sarajevo, she stepped on a land mine. In addition to this emotional story, the text offers other compelling evidence: "every 22 minutes another civilian is killed or maimed by a land mine"; "there are over 60 million unexploded land mines in nearly 70 countries." Select another public service advertisement campaign—such as those sponsored by MADD (Mothers Against Drunk Driving) or ADL (Anti-Defamation League)—and analyze the visual and textual features that make it a persuasive argument.

MARTIN LUTHER KING JR.

Martin Luther King Jr. (1929–1968), was born
in Atlanta, Georgia, and was educated at More-
house College, Crozer Theological Seminary, and
Boston University. Ordained a Baptist minister
in his father's church in 1947, King soon became
involved in civil rights activities in the South. In
1957, he founded the Southern Christian Leadership Conference and established himself as America's most prominent spokesman for nonviolent
racial integration. In 1963, he was named *Time*
magazine's Man of the Year; in 1964, he received
the Nobel Peace Prize. In 1968, he was assassinated
in Memphis, Tennessee. His writing includes *Letter from Birmingham Jail* (1963), *Why We Can't
Wait* (1964), and *Where Do We Go from Here:
Chaos or Community?* (1967). "I Have a Dream"
is the famous speech King delivered at the Lincoln
Memorial at the end of the March on Washington
in 1963 to commemorate the one hundredth anniversary of the Emancipation Proclamation. King
argues that realization of the dream of freedom for
all American citizens is long overdue.

I Have a Dream[1]

FIVE SCORE YEARS ago, a great American, in whose sym-   1
bolic shadow we stand, signed the Emancipation Proclamation. This momentous decree came as a great beacon light

---

[1] Martin Luther King Jr., Reprinted by arrangement with The Heirs to
the Estate of Martin Luther King Jr., c/o Writers House as agent for the
proprietor, New York, NY. Copyright 1963 Dr. Martin Luther King Jr.;
copyright renewed 1991 Coretta Scott King.

of hope to millions of Negro slaves who had been seared in the flames of withering injustice. It came as a joyous daybreak to end the long night of captivity.

But one hundred years later, we must face the tragic fact 2 that the Negro is still not free. One hundred years later, the life of the Negro is still sadly crippled by the manacles of segregation and the chains of discrimination. One hundred years later, the Negro lives on a lonely island of poverty in the midst of a vast ocean of material prosperity. One hundred years later, the Negro is still languishing in the corners of American society and finds himself an exile in his own land. So we have come here today to dramatize an appalling condition.

> *There will be neither rest nor tranquility in America until the Negro is granted his citizenship rights.*

In a sense we have come to our nation's capital to cash a 3 check. When the architects of our republic wrote the magnificent words of the Constitution and the Declaration of Independence, they were signing a promissory note to which every American was to fall heir. This note was a promise that all men would be guaranteed the unalienable rights of life, liberty, and the pursuit of happiness.

It is obvious today that America has defaulted on this 4 promissory note insofar as her citizens of color are concerned. Instead of honoring this sacred obligation, America has given the Negro people a bad check; a check which has come back marked "insufficient funds." But we refuse to believe that the bank of justice is bankrupt. We refuse to believe that there are insufficient funds in the great vaults of opportunity of this nation. So we have come to cash this check—a check that will give us upon demand the riches of freedom and the security of justice. We have also come to this hallowed spot to remind

America of the fierce urgency of *now*. This is no time to engage in the luxury of cooling off or to take the tranquilizing drug of gradualism. *Now* is the time to make real the promises of Democracy. *Now* is the time to rise from the dark and desolate valley of segregation to the sunlit path of racial justice. *Now* is the time to open the doors of opportunity to all of God's children. *Now* is the time to lift our nation from the quicksands of racial injustice to the solid rock of brotherhood.

It would be fatal for the nation to overlook the urgency 5 of the moment and to underestimate the determination of the Negro. This sweltering summer of the Negro's legitimate discontent will not pass until there is an invigorating autumn of freedom and equality. 1963 is not an end, but a beginning. Those who hope that the Negro needed to blow off steam and will now be content will have a rude awakening if the nation returns to business as usual. There will be neither rest nor tranquility in America until the Negro is granted his citizenship rights. The whirlwinds of revolt will continue to shake the foundations of our nation until the bright day of justice emerges.

But there is something I must say to my people who stand 6 on the warm threshold which leads into the palace of justice. In the process of gaining our rightful place we must not be guilty of wrongful deeds. Let us not seek to satisfy our thirst for freedom by drinking from the cup of bitterness and hatred. We must forever conduct our struggle on the high plane of dignity and discipline. We must not allow our creative protest to degenerate into physical violence. Again and again we must rise to the majestic heights of meeting physical force with soul force. The marvelous new militancy which has engulfed the Negro community must not lead us to a distrust of all white people, for many of our white brothers, as evidenced by their presence here today, have come to realize that their destiny is tied up with our destiny and their freedom is inextricably bound to our freedom. We cannot walk alone.

And as we walk, we must make the pledge that we shall 7 march ahead. We cannot turn back. There are those who are asking the devotees of civil rights, "When will you be satisfied?" We can never be satisfied as long as the Negro is the victim of the unspeakable horrors of police brutality. We can never be satisfied as long as our bodies, heavy with the fatigue of travel, cannot gain lodging in the motels of the highways and the hotels of the cities. We cannot be satisfied as long as the Negro's basic mobility is from a smaller ghetto to a larger one. We can never be satisfied as long as a Negro in Mississippi cannot vote and a Negro in New York believes he has nothing for which to vote. No, no, we are not satisfied, and we will not be satisfied until justice rolls down like waters and righteousness like a mighty stream.

I am not unmindful that some of you have come here out of great trials and tribulations. Some of you have come fresh from narrow jail cells. Some of you have come from areas where your quest for freedom left you battered by the storms of persecution and staggered by the winds of police brutality. You have been the veterans of creative suffering. Continue to work with the faith that unearned suffering is redemptive. 8

Go back to Mississippi, go back to Alabama, go back to South Carolina, go back to Georgia, go back to Louisiana, go back to the slums and ghettoes of our northern cities, knowing that somehow this situation can and will be changed. Let us not wallow in the valley of despair. 9

I say to you today, my friends, that in spite of the difficulties and frustrations of the moment I still have a dream. It is a dream deeply rooted in the American dream. 10

I have a dream that one day this nation will rise up and live out the true meaning of its creed: "We hold these truths to be self-evident; that all men are created equal." 11

I have a dream that one day on the red hills of Georgia the sons of former slaves and the sons of former slaveowners will be able to sit down together at the table of brotherhood. 12

I have a dream that the state of Mississippi, a desert state sweltering with the heat of injustice and oppression, will be transformed into an oasis of freedom and justice. 13

I have a dream that my four little children will one day live in a nation where they will not be judged by the color of their skin but by the content of their character. 14

I have a dream today.   15

I have a dream that the state of Alabama, whose gover-   16
nor's lips are presently dripping with the words of interpo-
sition and nullification, will be transformed into a situation
where little black boys and black girls will be able to join
hands with little white boys and white girls and walk together
as sisters and brothers.

I have a dream today.   17

I have a dream that one day every valley shall be exalted,   18
every hill and mountain shall be made low, the rough places
will be made plain, and the crooked places will be made
straight, and the glory of the Lord shall be revealed, and all
flesh shall see it together.

This is our hope. This is the faith with which I return to   19
the South. With this faith we will be able to hew out of the
mountain of despair a stone of hope. With this faith we will
be able to transform the jangling discords of our nation into
a beautiful symphony of brotherhood. With this faith we
will be able to work together, to pray together, to struggle
together, to go to jail together, to stand up for freedom
together, knowing that we will be free one day.

This will be the day when all of God's children will be able   20
to sing with new meaning.

> *My country, 'tis of thee*
> *Sweet land of liberty,*
> *Of thee I sing:*
> *Land where my fathers died,*
> *Land of the pilgrims' pride,*
> *From every mountainside*
> *Let freedom ring.*

And if America is to be a great nation this must become   21
true. So let freedom ring from the prodigious hilltops of New
Hampshire. Let freedom ring from the mighty mountains of
New York. Let freedom ring from the heightening Alleghenies
of Pennsylvania!

Let freedom ring from the snowcapped Rockies of   22
Colorado!

Let freedom ring from the curvaceous peaks of California!   23

But not only that; let freedom ring from Stone Mountain   24
of Georgia!

Let freedom ring from Lookout Mountain of Tennessee!   25

Let freedom ring from every hill and molehill of Missis-   26
sippi. From every mountainside, let freedom ring.

When we let freedom ring, when we let it ring from every   27
village and every hamlet, from every state and every city, we
will be able to speed up that day when all of God's children,
black men and white men, Jews and Gentiles, Protestants and
Catholics, will be able to join hands and sing in the words of
the old Negro spiritual, "Free at last! free at last! thank God
almighty, we are free at last!"

For Study and Discussion

QUESTIONS ABOUT PURPOSE

1. King has at least two strong messages. One message is local and
   immediate; the other one is national and long range. How would
   you summarize those two messages?
2. How does King use his speech to reinforce his belief in nonvio-
   lence as the appropriate tool in the struggle for civil rights?

QUESTIONS ABOUT AUDIENCE

1. King gave this speech to a huge live audience that had come to
   Washington for a march for freedom and civil rights. How much
   larger is the national audience he is addressing, and why is that
   audience also important?
2. This speech is one of the most widely anthologized of modern speeches. What audiences does it continue to appeal to and
   why?

QUESTIONS ABOUT STRATEGIES

1. How does King draw on metaphor to engage his listeners' feelings of injustice and give them hope for a new day?
2. In what way do King's talents as a minister serve his purposes in
   the speech?

For Writing and Research

1. *Analyze* the economic metaphors King uses throughout his speech.
2. *Practice* by persuading a group of your fellow students that it is the "content of their character" that is the measure of their success.
3. *Argue* that much of King's dream has or has not come true since he gave this speech more than forty years ago.
4. *Synthesize* the arguments about race in Booker T. Washington's "Atlanta Exhibition Address" and W. E. B. Dubois's "The Niagara Movement Manifesto." Then trace the development of race relations in the United States.

ERIC LIU

Eric Liu was born in Poughkeepsie, New York, in 1968 and was educated at Yale University. He worked as a legislative aide for Senator David Boren of Oklahoma and then as a speechwriter for Secretary of State Warren Christopher and President Bill Clinton. He is currently the publisher and editor of *The Next Progressive,* a journal of opinion; the editor of *NEXT: Young American Writers on the New Generation* (1994); and the author of *The Accidental Asian: Notes of a Native Speaker* (1998) and *The True Patriot* (2007). In "A Chinaman's Chance: Reflections on the American Dream," reprinted from *NEXT,* Liu argues that the American Dream is more about seizing opportunity than about claiming prosperity.

A Chinaman's Chance [2]
Reflections on the American Dream

A LOT OF people my age seem to think that the American Dream is dead. I think they're dead wrong. 1

Or at least only partly right. It is true that for those of us 2 in our twenties and early thirties, job opportunities are scarce. There looms a real threat that we will be the first American generation to have a lower standard of living than our parents.

But what is it that we mean when we invoke the American 3 Dream?

In the past, the American Dream was something that 4 held people of all races, religions, and identities together. As

---

James Comer has written, it represented a shared aspiration among all Americans—black, white, or any other color—"to provide well for themselves and their families as valued members of a democratic society." Now, all too often, it seems the American Dream means merely some guarantee of affluence, a birthright of wealth.

At a basic level, of course, the American Dream is about   5
prosperity and the pursuit of material happiness. But to me, its meaning extends beyond such concerns. To me, the dream is not just about buying a bigger house than the one I grew up in or having shinier stuff now than I had as a kid. It also represents a sense of opportunity that binds generations together in commitment, so that the young inherit not only property but also perseverance, not only money but also a mission to make good on the strivings of their parents and grandparents.

---

*I want to prove . . . that a Chinaman's
chance is as good as anyone else's.*

The poet Robert Browning once wrote that "a man's reach   6
must exceed his grasp—else what's a heaven for?" So it is in America. Every generation will strive, and often fail. Every generation will reach for success, and often miss the mark. But Americans rely as much on the next generation as on the next life to prove that such struggles and frustrations are not in vain. There may be temporary setbacks, cutbacks, recessions, depressions. But this is a nation of second chances. So long as there are young Americans who do not take what they have—or what they can do—for granted, progress is always possible.

My conception of the American Dream does not take   7
progress for granted. But it does demand the *opportunity* to achieve progress—and values the opportunity as much as the achievement. I come at this question as the son of immigrants. I see just as clearly as anyone else the cracks in the idealist

vision of fulfillment for all. But because my parents came here with virtually nothing, because they did build something, I see the enormous potential inherent in the ideal.

I happen still to believe in our national creed: freedom 8
and opportunity, and our common responsibility to uphold them. This creed is what makes America unique. More than any demographic statistic or economic indicator, it animates the American Dream. It infuses our mundane struggles—to plan a career, do good work, get ahead—with purpose and possibility. It makes America the only country that could produce heroes like Colin Powell—heroes who rise from nothing, who overcome the odds.

I think of the sacrifices made by my own parents. I appreci- 9
ate the hardship of the long road traveled by my father—one of whose first jobs in America was painting the yellow line down a South Dakota interstate—and by my mother—whose first job here was filing pay stubs for a New York restaurant. From such beginnings, they were able to build a comfortable life and provide me with a breadth of resources—through arts, travel, and an Ivy League education. It was an unspoken obligation for them to do so.

I think of my boss in my first job after college, on Capitol 10
Hill. George is a smart, feisty, cigar-chomping, take-no-shit Greek-American. He is about fifteen years older than I, has different interests, a very different personality. But like me, he is the son of immigrants, and he would joke with me that the Greek-Chinese mafia was going to take over one day. He was only half joking. We'd worked harder, our parents doubly harder, than almost anyone else we knew. To people like George, talk of the withering of the American Dream seems foreign.

It's undeniable that principles like freedom and opportu- 11
nity, no matter how dearly held, are not enough. They can inspire a multiracial March on Washington, but they can not bring black salaries in alignment with white salaries. They can draw wave after wave of immigrants here, but they can not provide them the means to get out of our ghettos and barrios and Chinatowns. They are not sufficient for fulfillment of the American Dream.

But they are necessary. They are vital. And not just to the 12
children of immigrants. These ideals form the durable thread
that weaves us all in union. Put another way, they are one of
the few things that keep America from disintegrating into a
loose confederation of zip codes and walled-in communities.

What alarms me is how many people my age look at our 13
nation's ideals with a rising sense of irony. What good is such
a creed if you are working for hourly wages in a dead-end job?
What value do such platitudes have if you live in an urban war
zone? When the only apparent link between homeboys and
housepainters and bike messengers and investment bankers
is pop culture—MTV, the NBA, movies, dance music—then
the social fabric is flimsy indeed.

My generation has come of age at a time when the country 14
is fighting off bouts of defeatism and self-doubt, at a time
when racism and social inequities seem not only persistent
but intractable. At a time like this, the retreat to one's own
kind is seen by more and more of my peers as an advance.
And that retreat has given rise again to the notion that there
are essential and irreconcilable differences among the races—a
notion that was supposed to have disappeared from American
discourse by the time my peers and I were born in the sixties.

Not long ago, for instance, my sister called me a "banana." 15

I was needling her about her passion for rap and hip-hop 16
music. Every time I saw her, it seemed, she was jumping and
twisting to Arrested Development or Chubb Rock or some
other funky group. She joked that despite being the daughter
of Chinese immigrants, she was indeed "black at heart." And
then she added, lightheartedly, "You, on the other hand—
well, you're basically a banana." Yellow on the outside, but
white inside.

I protested, denied her charge vehemently. But it was too 17
late. She was back to dancing. And I stood accused.

Ever since then, I have wondered what it means to be black, 18
or white, or Asian "at heart"—particularly for my generation.
Growing up, when other kids would ask whether I was Chinese or Korean or Japanese, I would reply, a little petulantly,
"American." Assimilation can still be a sensitive subject. I
recall reading about a Korean-born Congressman who had

gone out of his way to say that Asian-Americans should expect nothing special from him. He added that he was taking speech lessons "to get rid of this accent." I winced at his palpable self-hate. But then it hit me: Is this how my sister sees me?

There is no doubt that minorities like me can draw strength 19 from our communities. But in today's environment, anything other than ostentatious tribal fealty is taken in some communities as a sign of moral weakness, a disappointing dilution of character. In times that demand ever-clearer thinking, it has become too easy for people to shut off their brains: "It's a black/Asian/Latino/white thing," says the variable T-shirt. "You wouldn't understand." Increasingly, we don't.

The civil-rights triumphs of the sixties and the cultural rev- 20 olutions that followed made it possible for minorities to celebrate our diverse heritages. I can appreciate that. But I know, too, that the sixties—or at least, my generation's grainy, hazy vision of the decade—also bequeathed to young Americans a legacy of near-pathological race consciousness.

Today's culture of entitlement—and of race entitlement in 21 particular—tells us plenty about what we get if we are black or white or female or male or old or young.

It is silent, though, on some other important issues. For 22 instance: What do we "get" for being American? And just as importantly, What do we owe? These are questions around which young people like myself must tread carefully, since talk of common interests, civic culture, responsibility, and integration sounds a little too "white" for some people. To the new segregationists, the "American Dream" is like the old myth of the "Melting Pot": an oppressive fiction, an opiate for the unhappy colored masses.

How have we allowed our thinking about race to become 23 so twisted? The formal obstacles and the hateful opposition to civil rights have long faded into memory. By most external measures, life for minorities is better than it was a quarter century ago. It would seem that the opportunities for tolerance and cooperation are commonplace. Why, then, are so many of my peers so cynical about our ability to get along with one another?

The reasons are frustratingly ambiguous. I got a glimpse   24
of this when I was in college. It was late in my junior year,
and as the editor of a campus magazine, I was sitting on a
panel to discuss "The White Press at Yale: What Is to Be
Done?" The assembly hall was packed, a diverse and noisy
crowd. The air was heavy, nervously electric.

Why weren't there more stories about "minority issues"   25
in the Yale *Daily News?* Why weren't there more stories on
Africa in my magazine, the foreign affairs journal? How many
"editors of color" served on the boards of each of the major
publications? The questions were volleyed like artillery, one
round after another, punctuated only by the applause of an
audience spoiling for a fight. The questions were not at all
unfair. But it seemed that no one—not even those of us on
the panel who *were* people of color—could provide, in this
context, satisfactory answers.

Toward the end of the discussion, I made a brief appeal   26
for reason and moderation. And afterward, as students milled
around restlessly, I was attacked: for my narrowminded-
ness—How dare you suggest that Yale is not a fundamentally
prejudiced place!—for my simplemindedness—Have you,
too, been co-opted?

And for my betrayal—Are you just white inside?   27

My eyes were opened that uncomfortably warm early   28
summer evening. Not only to the cynical posturing and the
combustible opportunism of campus racial politics. But more
importantly, to the larger question of identity—my identity—
in America. Never mind that the aim of many of the loudest
critics was to generate headlines in the very publications they
denounced. In spite of themselves—against, it would seem,
their true intentions—they got me to think about who I am.

In our society today, and especially among people of my   29
generation, we are congealing into clots of narrow com-
monality. We stick with racial and religious comrades. This
tribal consciousness-raising can be empowering for some.
But while America was conceived in liberty—the liberty, for
instance, to associate with whomever we like—it was never
designed to be a mere collection of subcultures. We forget

that there is in fact such a thing as a unique American identity
that transcends our sundry tribes, sets, gangs, and cliques.

I have grappled, wittingly or not, with these questions of 30
identity and allegiance all my life. When I was in my early
teens, I would invite my buddies overnight to watch movies,
play video games, and beat one another up. Before too long,
my dad would come downstairs and start hamming it up—
telling stories, asking gently nosy questions, making corny
jokes, all with his distinct Chinese accent. I would stand back,
quietly gauging everyone's reaction. Of course, the guys
loved it. But I would feel uneasy.

What was then cause for discomfort is now a source of 31
strength. Looking back on such episodes, I take pride in my
father's accented English; I feel awe at his courage to laugh
loudly in a language not really his own.

It was around the same time that I decided that continued 32
attendance at the community Chinese school on Sundays was
uncool. There was no fanfare; I simply stopped going. As
a child, I'd been too blissfully unaware to think of Chinese
school as anything more than a weekly chore, with an annual
festival (dumplings and spring rolls, games and prizes). But
by the time I was a peer-pressured adolescent, Chinese school
seemed like a badge of the woefully unassimilated. I turned
my back on it.

Even as I write these words now, it feels as though I am 33
revealing a long-held secret. I am proud that my ancestors—
scholars, soldiers, farmers—came from one of the world's
great civilizations. I am proud that my grandfather served in
the Chinese Air Force. I am proud to speak even my clumsy
brand of Mandarin, and I feel blessed to be able to think idi-
omatically in Chinese, a language so much richer in nuance
and subtle poetry than English.

Belatedly, I appreciate the good fortune I've had to be the 34
son of immigrants. As a kid, I could play Thomas Jefferson in
the bicentennial school play one week and the next week play
the poet Li Bai at the Chinese school festival. I could come
home from an afternoon of teen slang at the mall and sit
down to dinner for a rollicking conversation in our family's
hybrid of Chinese and English. I understood, when I went

over to visit friends, that my life was different. At the time, I just never fully appreciated how rich it was.

Yet I know that this pride in my heritage does not cross 35 into prejudice against others. What it reflects is pride in what my country represents. That became clear to me when I went through Marine Corps Officer Candidates' School. During the summers after my sophomore and junior years of college, I volunteered for OCS, a grueling boot camp for potential officers in the swamps and foothills of Quantico, Virginia.

And once I arrived—standing 5′4″, 135 pounds, bespec- 36 tacled, a Chinese Ivy League Democrat—I was a target straight out of central casting. The wiry, raspy-voiced drill sergeant, though he was perhaps only an inch or two taller than I, called me "Little One" with as much venom as can be squeezed into such a moniker. He heaped verbal abuse on me, he laughed when I stumbled, he screamed when I hesitated. But he also never failed to remind me that just because I was a little shit didn't mean I shouldn't run farther, climb higher, think faster, hit harder than anyone else.

That was the funny thing about the Marine Corps. It is, 37 ostensibly, one of the most conservative institutions in the United States. And yet, for those twelve weeks, it represented the kind of color-blind equality of opportunity that the rest of society struggles to match. I did not feel uncomfortable at OCS to be of Chinese descent. Indeed, I drew strength from it. My platoon was a veritable cross-section of America: forty young men of all backgrounds, all regions, all races, all levels of intelligence and ability, displaced from our lives (if only for a few weeks) with nowhere else to go.

Going down the list of names—Courtemanche, Dou- 38 gherty, Grella, Hunt, Liu, Reeves, Schwarzman, and so on— brought to mind a line from a World War II documentary I once saw, which went something like this: The reason why it seemed during the war that America was as good as the rest of the world put together was that America *was* the rest of the world put together.

Ultimately, I decided that the Marines was not what I 39 wanted to do for four years and I did not accept the second lieutenant's commission. But I will never forget the day of the graduation parade: bright sunshine, brisk winds, the band playing Sousa as my company passed in review. As my mom and dad watched and photographed the parade from the rafters, I thought to myself: this is the American Dream in all its cheesy earnestness. I felt the thrill of truly being part of something larger and greater than myself.

I do know that American life is not all Sousa marches and 40 flag-waving. I know that those with reactionary agendas often find it convenient to cloak their motives in the language of Americanism. The "American Party" was the name of a major nativist organization in the nineteenth century. "America First" is the siren song of the isolationists who would withdraw this country from the world and expel the world from this country. I know that our national immigration laws were once designed explicitly to cut off the influx from Asia.

I also know that discrimination is real. I am reminded of 41 a gentle old man who, after Pearl Harbor, was stripped of his possessions without warning, taken from his home, and thrown into a Japanese internment camp. He survived, and by many measures has thrived, serving as a community leader and political activist. But I am reluctant to share with him my wide-eyed patriotism.

I know the bittersweet irony that my own father—a strong 42 and optimistic man—would sometimes feel when he was alive. When he came across a comically lost cause—if the Yankees were behind 14–0 in the ninth, or if Dukakis was down ten points in the polls with a week left—he would often joke that the doomed party had "a Chinaman's chance" of success. It was one of those insensitive idioms of a generation ago, and it must have lodged in his impressionable young mind when he first came to America. It spoke of a perceived stacked deck.

I know, too, that for many other immigrants, the dream 43 simply does not work out. Fae Myenne Ng, the author of *Bone,* writes about how her father ventured here from China under a false identity and arrived at Angel Island, the detention center outside the "Gold Mountain" of San Francisco. He got out, he labored, he struggled, and he suffered "a bitter no-luck life" in America. There was no glory. For him, Ng suggests, the journey was not worth it.

But it is precisely because I know these things that I want   44
to prove that in the long run, over generations and across ethnicities, it *is* worth it. For the second-generation American, opportunity is obligation. I have seen and faced racism. I understand the dull pain of dreams deferred or unmet. But I believe still that there is so little stopping me from building the life that I want. I was given, through my parents' labors, the chance to bridge that gap between ideals and reality. Who am I to throw away that chance?

Plainly, I am subject to the criticism that I speak too much   45
from my own experience. Not everyone can relate to the second-generation American story. When I have spoken like this with some friends, the issue has been my perspective. *What you say is fine for you. But unless you grew up where I did, unless you've had people avoid you because of the color of your skin, don't talk to me about common dreams.*

But are we then to be paralyzed? Is respect for different   46
experiences supposed to obviate the possibility of shared aspirations? Does the diversity of life in America doom us to a fractured understanding of one another? The question is basic: Should the failure of this nation thus far to fulfill its stated ideals incapacitate its young people, or motivate us?

Our country was built on, and remains glued by, the idea   47
that everybody deserves a fair shot and that we must work together to guarantee that opportunity—the original American Dream. It was this idea, in some inchoate form, that drew every immigrant here. It was this idea, however sullied by slavery and racism, that motivated the civil-rights movement. To write this idea off—even when its execution is spotty— to let American life descend into squabbles among separatist tribes would not just be sad. It would be a total mishandling of a legacy, the squandering of a great historical inheritance.

Mine must not be the first generation of Americans to lose   48
America. Just as so many of our parents journeyed here to find their version of the American Dream, so must young Americans today journey across boundaries of race and class to

rediscover one another. We are the first American generation to be born into an integrated society, and we are accustomed to more race mixing than any generation before us. We started open-minded, and it's not too late for us to stay that way.

Time is of the essence. For in our national political culture today, the watchwords seem to be *decline* and *end*. Apocalyptic visions and dark millennial predictions abound. The end of history. The end of progress. The end of equality. Even something as ostensibly positive as the end of the Cold War has a bittersweet tinge, because for the life of us, no one in America can get a handle on the big question, "What Next?" 49

For my generation, this fixation on endings is particularly enervating. One's twenties are supposed to be a time of widening horizons, of bright possibilities. Instead, America seems to have entered an era of limits. Whether it is the difficulty of finding jobs from some place other than a temp agency, or the mountains of debt that darken our future, the message to my peers is often that this nation's time has come and gone; let's bow out with grace and dignity. 50

A friend once observed that while the Chinese seek to adapt to nature and yield to circumstance, Americans seek to conquer both. She meant that as a criticism of America. But I interpreted her remark differently. I *do* believe that America is exceptional. And I believe it is up to my generation to revive that spirit, that sense that we do in fact have control over our own destiny—as individuals and as a nation. 51

If we are to reclaim a common destiny, we must also reach out to other generations for help. It was Franklin Roosevelt who said that while America can't always build the future for its youth, it can—and must—build its youth for the future. That commitment across generations is as central to the American Dream as any I have enunciated. We are linked, black and white, old and young, one and inseparable. 52

I know how my words sound. I am old enough to perceive my own naïveté but young enough still to cherish it. I realize that I am coming of age just as the American Dream is showing its age. Yet I still have faith in this country's unique destiny—to create generation after generation of hyphenates like me, to channel this new blood, this resilience and energy into an ever more vibrant future for *all* Americans. 53

And I want to prove—for my sake, for my father's sake,   54
and for my country's sake—that a Chinaman's chance is as
good as anyone else's.

For Study and Discussion

QUESTIONS ABOUT PURPOSE

1. To what criticisms *about* his generation is Liu responding? To
   what criticisms *from* his generation is he responding?
2. What specific attitudes among young people does Liu challenge?

QUESTIONS ABOUT AUDIENCE

1. Liu wrote this essay for a 1994 book titled *NEXT: Young American Writers on the New Generation,* a book he edited. What kind
   of readers do you think he envisioned for this book?
2. What do you think Liu's appeal might be to generations younger
   and older than his?

QUESTIONS ABOUT STRATEGIES

1. How does Liu's description of his parents' experience advance
   his argument?
2. Liu was one of President Clinton's speechwriters. How does he
   use the strategies of political argument to make his case?

For Writing and Research

1. *Analyze* how Liu presents his evidence about *racism.*
2. *Practice* by arguing that students on your campus do or do
   not express racism by splitting into separate groups.
3. *Argue* that events such as the election of President Barack
   Obama indicate that America's young people are increasingly tolerant of people from different races and cultures.
4. *Synthesize:* Research the treatment of Chinese immigrants in
   the United States. Then research the contributions Chinese
   Americans have made to our culture in the last decade. Then
   use this information to argue that Liu's faith in the American
   Dream is justified.

A Debate About Animal Rights

BRIGID BROPHY

Brigid Brophy was born in London, England, in 1929 and attended St. Paul's Girls' School and St. Hugh's College, Oxford University, where she read classics on a Jubilee Scholarship. Quick-witted, sharp-tongued, and keenly intelligent, she soon became a writer, following the family tradition established by her father, novelist John Brophy. Her first novel, *Hackenfeller's Ape* (1954), won the Cheltenham Literary Festival prize for the best first novel, and her subsequent works such as *The King of a Rainy County* (1957), *Flesh* (1962), and *Palace Without Chairs* (1978) have established her reputation as a gracefully witty novelist. Her nonfiction includes works as diverse as *Mozart the Dramatist: A New View of Mozart's Operas and His Age* (1964), *Black Ship to Hell* (1962), a meditation on the human impulse for self-destruction, and *Black and White: A Portrait of Aubrey Beardsley* (1970), a sketch of the famous Art Nouveau figure. Brophy is an astute literary critic and an impassioned defender of her moral and political opinions. In "The Rights of Animals," reprinted from *Don't Never Forget: Collected Views and Reviews* (1966), she argues one of her favorite causes—the responsibility of the superior species (human beings) to behave decently toward the inferior species (animals).

The Rights of Animals[3]

W ERE IT ANNOUNCED tomorrow that anyone who fancied it might, without risk of reprisals or recriminations, stand at a fourth-storey window, dangle out of it a length of string with a meal (labelled "Free") on the end, wait till a chance passer-by took a bite and then, having entangled his cheek or gullet on a hook hidden in the food, haul him up to the fourth floor and there batter him to death with a knobkerry, I do not think there would be many takers.   1

Most sane adults would, I imagine, sicken at the mere thought. Yet sane adults do the equivalent to fish every day: not in panic, sexual jealousy, ideological frenzy or even greed—many of our freshwater fish are virtually inedible, and not one of them constitutes a threat to the life, love or ideology of a human on the bank—but for amusement. Civilisation is not outraged at their behaviour. On the contrary: that a person's hobby is fishing is often read as a guarantee of his sterling and innocent character.   2

The relationship of Homo sapiens *to other animals is one of unremitting exploitation.*

The relationship of *Homo sapiens* to the other animals is one of unremitting exploitation. We employ their work; we eat and wear them. We exploit them to serve our superstitions: whereas we used to sacrifice them to our gods and tear out their entrails in order to foresee the future, we now sacrifice them to Science and experiment on their entrails in the hope—or on the mere off chance—that we might thereby see a little more clearly into the   3 present. When we can think of no pretext for causing their death and no profit to turn it to, we often cause it nonetheless, wantonly, the only gain being a brief pleasure for ourselves, which is usually only marginally bigger than the pleasure we could have had without killing anything; we could quite well enjoy our marksmanship or crosscountry galloping without requiring a real dead wild animal to shew for it at the end.

It is rare for us to leave wild animals alive; when we do, we often do not leave them wild. Some we put on display in a prison just large enough for them to survive, but not in any full sense to live, in. Others we trundle about the country in their prisons, pausing every now and then to put them on public exhibition performing, like clockwork, "tricks" we have "trained" into them. However, animals are not clockwork but instinctual beings. Circus "tricks" are spectacular or risible as the case may be precisely *because* they violate the animals' instinctual nature—which is precisely why they ought to violate both our moral and our aesthetic sense. 4

But where animals are concerned humanity seems to have switched off its morals and aesthetics—indeed, its very imagination. Goodness knows those faculties function erratically enough in our dealings with one another. But at least we recognise their faultiness. We spend an increasing number of our cooler moments trying to forestall the moral and aesthetic breakdowns which are liable, in a crisis, to precipitate us into atrocities against each other. We have bitter demarcation disputes about where the rights of one man end and those of the next man begin, but most men now acknowledge that there are such things as the rights of the next man. Only in relation to the next animal can civilised humans persuade themselves that they have absolute and arbitrary rights—that they may do anything whatever that they can get away with. 5

The reader will have guessed in some detail by now what sort of person he confronts in me: a sentimentalist; probably a killjoy; a person with no grasp on economic realities; a twee anthropomorphist, who attributes human feelings (and no doubt human names and clothes as well) to animals, and yet actually prefers animals to humans and would sooner succour a stray cat than an orphan child; a latter-day version of those folklore English 6 spinsters who in the nineteenth century excited the ridicule of the natives by walking round Florence requesting them not to ill-treat their donkeys; and *par excellence*, of course, a crank.

Well. To take the last item first: if by "crank" you mean 7 "abnormal," yes. My views are shared by only a smallish (but probably not so small as you think) part of the citizenry—as yet. Still, that proves nothing either way about the validity of our views. It is abnormal to be a lunatic convinced you are Napoleon, but equally (indeed, numerically considered, probably even more) abnormal to be a genius. The test of a view is its rationality, not the number of people who endorse it. It would have been cranky indeed in the ancient world to raise the question of the rights of slaves—so cranky that scarcely a voice went on record as doing so. To us it seems incredible that the Greek philosophers should have scanned so deep into right and wrong and yet never *noticed* the immorality of slavery. Perhaps three thousand years from now it will seem equally incredible that we do not notice the immorality of our oppression of animals.

Slavery was the ancient world's patch of moral and aes- 8 thetic insensitivity. Indeed, it was not until the eighteenth and nineteenth centuries of our own era that the human conscience was effectively and universally switched on in that respect. Even then, we went on with economic and social exploitations which stopped short of slavery only in constitutional status, and people were found to justify them. But by then the exploiters had at least been forced onto the defensive and felt obliged to produce the feeble arguments that had never even been called for in the ancient world. Perhaps it is a sign that our conscience is about to be switched on in relation to animals that some animal-exploiters are now seeking to justify themselves. When factory farmers tell us that animals kept in "intensive" (i.e. concentration) camps are being kindly spared the inclemency of a winter outdoors, and that calves do not mind being tethered for life on slats because they have never known anything else, an echo should start in our historical consciousness: do you remember how the childlike blackamoors were kindly spared the harsh responsibilities of freedom, how the skivvy didn't feel the hardship of scrubbing all day because she was used to it, how the poor didn't mind their slums because they had never known anything else?

The first of the factory farmers' arguments is, of course, 9 an argument for ordinary farms to make better provision for animals in winter, not for ordinary farms to be replaced by torture chambers. As for the one about the animals' never having known anything else, I still shan't believe it valid but I shall accept that the factory farmers genuinely believe it themselves when they follow out its logic by using their profits to finance the repatriation of every circus and zoo animal that was caught in the wild, on the grounds that those *have* known something else.

Undismayed by being a crank, I will make you a free gift of 10 another stick to beat me with, by informing you that I am a vegetarian. Now, surely, you have me. Not only am I a more extreme crank, a member of an even smaller minority, than you had realised; surely I *must*, now, be a killjoy. Yet which, in fact, kills more joy: the killjoy who would deprive you of your joy in eating steak, which is just one of the joys open to you, or the kill-animal who puts an end to all the animal's joys along with its life?

Beware, however (if we may now take up the first item in 11 your Identikit portrait of me), how you call me a sentimentalist in this matter. I may be less of one than you are. I won't kill an animal in order to eat it, but I am no respecter of dead bodies as such. If our chemists discovered (as I'm sure they quickly would were there a demand) how to give tenderness and hygiene to the body of an animal which had died of old age, I would willingly eat it; and in principle that goes for human animals, too. In practice I suspect I should choke on a rissole which I knew might contain bits of Great-Aunt Emily (whether through love for or repulsion from her I am not quite sure), and I admit I might have to leave rational cannibalism to future generations brought up without my irrational prejudice (which is equally irrational whether prompted by love or by repulsion for the old lady). But you were accusing me, weren't you, of sentimentality and ignorance of economic realities. Have you thought how much of the world's potential food supply *you* unrealistically let go waste because of your sentimental compunction about eating your fellow citizens after they have lived out their natural lives?

If we are going to rear and kill animals for our food, I think we have a moral obligation to spare them pain and terror in both processes, simply because they are sentient. I can't *prove* they are sentient; but then I have no proof *you* are. Even though you are articulate, whereas an animal can only scream or struggle, I have no assurance that your "It hurts" expresses anything like the intolerable sensations I experience in pain. I know, however, that when I visit my dentist and say "It hurts," I am grateful that he gives me the benefit of the doubt. 12

I don't myself believe that, even when we fulfill our minimum obligation not to cause pain, we have the right to kill animals. I know I would have no right to kill you, however painlessly, just because I liked your flavour, and I am not in a position to judge that your life is worth more to you than the animal's to it. If anything, you probably value yours less; unlike the animal, you are capable of acting on an impulse to suicide. Christian tradition would permit me to kill the animal but not you, on the grounds that you have, and it hasn't, an immortal soul. I am not a Christian and do not avail myself of this licence; but if I were, I should in elementary justice see the soul theory as all the more reason to let the animal live out the one mortal life it has. 13

The only genuine moral problem is where there is a direct clash between an animal's life and a human one. Our diet proposes no such clash, meat not being essential to a human life; I have sustained a very healthy one for ten years without. And in fact such clashes are much rarer in reality than in exam papers, where we are always being asked to rescue either our grandmother or a Rubens from a blazing house. . . . 14

The most genuine and painful clash is, of course, on the subject of vivisection. To hold vivisection never justified is a hard belief. But so is its opposite. I believe it is never justified because I can see nothing (except our being able to get away with it) which lets us pick on animal that would not equally let us pick on idiot humans (who would be more useful) or, for the matter of that, on a few humans of any sort whom we might sacrifice for the good of the many. If we do permit 15 vivsection, here if anywhere we are under the most stringent minimum obligations. The very least we must make sure of is that no experiment is ever duplicated, or careless, or done for mere teaching's sake or as a substitute for thinking. Knowing how often, in every other sphere, pseudowork proliferates in order to fill time and jobs, and how often activity substitutes for thought, and then reading the official statistics about vivisection, do you truly believe we *do* make sure? . . .

Our whole relation to animals is tinted by a fantasy—and   16
a fallacy—about our toughness. We feel obliged to demonstrate we can take it; in fact, it is the animals who take it. So shy are we of seeming sentimental that we often disguise our humane impulses under "realistic" arguments: foxhunting is snobbish: factory-farmed food doesn't taste so nice. But foxhunting would still be an atrocity if it were done by authenticated, pedigreed proletarians, and so would factory-farming even if a way were found of making its corpses tasty. So, incidentally, would slavery, even if it were proved a hundred times more economically realistic than freedom.

The saddest and silliest of the superstitions to which we   17
sacrifice animals is our belief that by killing them we ourselves somehow live more fully. We might live more fully by entering imaginatively into their lives. But shedding their blood makes us no more full-blooded. It is a mere myth, often connected with our myth about the *savoir vivre* and sexiness of the sunny south (which is how you managed to transform me into a frustrated British virgin in Florence). There is no law of nature which makes *savoir vivre* incompatible with "live and let live." The bullfighter who torments a bull to death and then castrates it of an ear has neither proved nor increased his own virility; he has merely demonstrated that he is a butcher with balletic tendencies.

Superstition and dread of sentimentality weight all our   18
questions against the animals. We *don't* scrutinise vivisection rigorously—we somehow think it would be soft of us to do so, which we apparently think a worse thing to be than cruel. When, in February of this year, the House of Lords voted against a Bill banning animal acts from circuses, it was pointed

out that animal-trainers would lose their jobs. (Come to think of it, many human-trainers must have lost theirs when it was decided to ban gladiator acts from circuses.) No one pointed out how many unemployed acrobats and jugglers would *get* jobs to replace the animals. (I'm not, you see by the way, the sort of killjoy who wants to abolish the circus as such.) Similarly with the anthropomorphism argument, which works in both directions but is always wielded in one only. In the same House of Lords debate, Lady Summerskill, who had taken the humane side, was mocked by a noble lord on the grounds that were *she* shut up in a cage she would indeed suffer from mortification and the loss of her freedom, but an animal, not being human, wouldn't. Why did no one point out that a human, in such circumstances, dreadful as they are, would have every consolation of the human intellect and imagination, from reading books to analysing his circumstances and writing to the Home Secretary about them, whereas the animal suffers the raw terror of not comprehending what is being done to it?

In point of fact, I am the very opposite of an anthropomorphist. I don't hold animals superior or even equal to humans. The whole case for behaving decently to animals rests on the fact that we are the superior species. We are the species uniquely capable of imagination, rationality and moral choice—and that is precisely why we are under the obligation to recognise and respect the rights of animals. 19

For Study and Discussion

QUESTIONS ABOUT PURPOSE

1. What practices would Brophy like to see outlawed in England?
2. What emotional reactions does she hope to evoke in her readers?

QUESTIONS ABOUT AUDIENCE

1. How does Brophy address her readers?
2. What does she hope to accomplish by identifying herself as crank, a killjoy, and a sentimentalist to her readers?

QUESTIONS ABOUT STRATEGIES

1. How does Brophy go about getting her readers to put themselves in the place of animals?
2. Throughout this essay, what is Brophy's chief strategy for refuting arguments in favor of hunting, raising animals for food, using them for entertainment, and experimenting with them in laboratories?

For Writing and Research

1. *Analyze* the various methods Brophy uses to disarm her readers' objections to her argument.
2. *Practice* by describing an experience in which you witnessed cruelty to animals.
3. *Argue* that Brophy's argument to protect the rights of animals would have severe economic consequences.
4. *Synthesize:* Research the legislation that has been enacted by the National Institutes of Health about animals in laboratory experiments. Then argue that such experiments with animals help save human lives.

VICKI HEARNE

Vicki Hearne (1946–2001) was born in Austin, Texas, and was educated at the University of California at Riverside and Stanford University. She has taught creative writing at the University of California at Davis and Yale University. Her own writing includes two volumes of poetry, *Nervous Horses* (1980) and *In Absence of Horses* (1984); a novel, *The White German Shepherd* (1988); and two extraordinary books of nonfiction, *Adam's Task: Calling Animals by Name* (1986) and *Bandit: Dossier of a Dangerous Dog* (1991)—all of which focus on the complicated relationship between humans and animals. An expert animal trainer, Hearne established the National Pit Bull Terrier Defense Association and Literary Society. In "What's Wrong with Animal Rights?" reprinted from *Harper's*, Hearne argues that animal rights activists have "got it all wrong" because they are preoccupied with the problems of animal suffering rather than the possibility of animal happiness.

What's Wrong with Animal Rights?[4]

NOT ALL HAPPY animals are alike. A Doberman going over a hurdle after a small wooden dumbbell is sleek, all arcs of harmonious power. A basset hound cheerfully performing the same exercise exhibits harmonies of a more lugubrious nature. There are chimpanzees who love precision the way musicians or fanatical housekeepers or accomplished

---

hypochondriacs do; others for whom happiness is a matter of invention and variation—chimp vaudevillians. There is a rhinoceros whose happiness, as near as I can make out, is in needing to be trained every morning, all over again, or else he "forgets" his circus routine, and in this you find a clue to the slow, deep, quiet chuckle of his happiness and to the glory of the beast. Happiness for Secretariat is in his ebullient bound, that joyful length of stride. For the draft horse or the weight-pull dog, happiness is of a different shape, more awesome and less obviously intelligent. When the pulling horse is at its most intense, the animal goes into himself, allocating all of the educated power that organizes his desire to dwell in fierce and delicate intimacy with that power, leans into the harness, and MAKES THAT SUCKER *MOVE.*

Work is the foundation of the happiness a trainer and an animal discover together.

If we are speaking of human beings and use the phrase "animal happiness," we tend to mean something like "creature comforts." The emblems of this are the golden retriever rolling in the grass, the horse with his nose deep in the oats, the kitty by the fire. Creature comforts are important to animals—"Grub first, then ethics" is a motto that would describe many a wise Labrador retriever, and I have a pit bull named Annie whose continual quest for the perfect pillow inspires her to awesome feats. But there is something more to animals, a capacity for satisfactions that come from work in the fullest sense—what is known in philosophy and in this country's Declaration of Independence as "happiness." This is a sense of personal achievement, like the satisfaction felt by a good wood-carver or a dancer or a poet or an accomplished dressage horse. It is a happiness that, like the artist's, must come from something within the animal, something trainers call "talent." Hence, it cannot be imposed on the animal. But it is also something that does not come *ex nihilo.* If it had not been a fairly ordinary   2 thing, in one part of the world, to teach young children to play the pianoforte, it is doubtful that Mozart's music would exist.

Happiness is often misunderstood as a synonym for plea- 3
sure or as an antonym for suffering. But Aristotle associated happiness with ethics—codes of behavior that urge us toward the sensation of getting it right, a kind of work that yields the "click" of satisfaction upon solving a problem or surmounting an obstacle. In his *Ethics,* Aristotle wrote, "If happiness is activity in accordance with excellence, it is reasonable that it should be in accordance with the highest excellence." Thomas Jefferson identified the capacity for happiness as one of the three fundamental rights on which all others are based: "life, liberty, and the pursuit of happiness."

I bring up this idea of happiness as a form of work because 4
I am an animal trainer, and work is the foundation of the happiness a trainer and an animal discover together. I bring up these words also because they cannot be found in the lexicon of the animal-rights movement. This absence accounts for the uneasiness toward the movement of most people, who sense that rights advocates have a point but take it too far when they liberate snails or charge that goldfish at the county fair are suffering. But the problem with the animal-rights advocates is not that they take it too far, it's that they've got it all wrong.

Animal rights are built upon the
misconceived premise that rights were created
to prevent us from unnecessary suffering.

Animal rights are built upon a misconceived premise that 5
rights were created to prevent us from unnecessary suffering. You can't find an animal-rights book, video, pamphlet, or rock concert in which someone doesn't mention the Great Sentence, written by Jeremy Bentham in 1789. Arguing in favor of such rights, Bentham wrote: "The question is not, Can they *reason*? nor, can they *talk*? but, can they suffer?"

The logic of the animal-rights movement places suffer- 6
ing at the iconographic center of a skewed value system.
The thinking of its proponents—given eerie expression in a
virtually sado-pornographic sculpture of a tortured monkey
that won a prize for its compassionate vision—has collapsed
into a perverse conundrum. Today the loudest voices calling
for—demanding—the destruction of animals are the humane
organizations. This is an inevitable consequence of the apo-
theosis of the drive to relieve suffering: Death is the ultimate
release. To compensate for their contradictions, the humane
movement has demonized, in this century and the last, those
who made animal happiness their business: veterinarians,
trainers, and the like. We think of Louis Pasteur as the man
whose work saved you and me and your dog and cat from
rabies, but antivivisectionists of the time claimed that rabies
increased in areas where there were Pasteur Institutes.

An anti-rabies public-relations campaign mounted in England 7
in the 1880s by the Royal Society for the Prevention of Cruelty
to Animals and other organizations led to orders being issued to
club any dog found not wearing a muzzle. England still has her
cruel and unnecessary law that requires an animal to spend six
months in quarantine before being allowed loose in the country.
Most of the recent propaganda about pit bulls—the crazy claim
that they "take hold with their front teeth while they chew away
with their rear teeth" (which would imply, incorrectly, that they
have double jaws)—can be traced to literature published by the
Humane Society of the United States during the fall of 1987 and
earlier. If your neighbors want your dog or horse impounded
and destroyed because he is a nuisance—say the dog barks, or
the horse attracts flies—it will be the local Humane Society to
whom your neighbors turn for action.

In a way, everyone has the opportunity to know that the 8
history of the humane movement is largely a history of miser-
ies, arrests, prosecutions, and death. The Humane Society is
the pound, the place with the decompression chamber or the
lethal injections. You occasionally find worried letters about
this in Ann Landers's column.

Animal-rights publications are illustrated largely with photo- 9
graphs of two kinds of animals—"Helpless Fluff" and "Agonized

Fluff," the two conditions in which some people seem to prefer their animals, because any other version of an animal is too complicated for propaganda. In the introduction to his book *Animal Liberation*, Peter Singer says somewhat smugly that he and his wife have no animals and, in fact, don't much care for them. This is offered as evidence of his objectivity and ethical probity. But it strikes me as an odd, perhaps obscene, underpinning for an ethical project that encourages university and high school students to cherish their ignorance of, say, great bird dogs as proof of their devotion to animals.

I would like to leave these philosophers behind, for they are inept connoisseurs of suffering who might revere my Airedale for his capacity to scream when subjected to a blowtorch but not for his wit and courage, not for his natural good manners that are a gentle rebuke to ours. I want to celebrate the moment not long ago when, at his first dog show, my Airedale, Drummer, learned that there can be a public place where his work is respected. I want to celebrate his meticulousness, his happiness upon realizing at the dog show that no one would swoop down upon him and swamp him with the goo-goo excesses known as the "teddy-bear complex" but that people actually got out of his way, gave him room to work. I want to say, "There can be a six-and-a-half-month-old puppy who can care about accuracy, who can be fastidious, and whose fastidiousness will be a foundation for courage later." I want to say, "Leave my puppy alone!" 10

I want to leave the philosophers behind, but I cannot, in part because the philosophical problems that plague academicians of the animal-rights movement are illuminating. They wonder, do animals have rights or do they have interests? Or, if these rightists lead particularly unexamined lives, they dismiss that question as obvious (yes, of course, animals have rights, prima facie) and proceed to enumerate them, James Madison style. This leads to the issuance of bills of rights— the right to an environment, the right not to be used in medical experiments—and other forms of trivialization. 11

The calculus of suffering can be turned against the philosophers of festering flesh, even in the case of food animals, or exotic animals who perform in movies and circuses. It is true 12 that it hurts to be slaughtered by man, but it doesn't hurt nearly as much as some of the cunningly cruel arrangements meted out by "Mother Nature." In Africa, 75 percent of the lions cubbed do not survive to the age of two. For those who make it to two, the average age at death is ten years. Asali, the movie and TV lioness, was still working at age twenty-one. There are fates worse than death, but twenty-one years of a close working relationship with Hubert Wells, Asali's trainer, is not one of them. Dorset sheep and polled Herefords would not exist at all were they not in a symbiotic relationship with human beings.

A human being living in the "wild"—somewhere, say,   13
without the benefits of medicine and advanced social organizations—would probably have a life expectancy of from thirty to thirty-five years. A human being living in "captivity"—in, say, a middle-class neighborhood of what the Centers for Disease Control call a Metropolitan Statistical Area—has a life expectancy of seventy or more years. For orangutans in the wild in Borneo and Malaysia, the life expectancy is thirty-five years; in captivity, fifty years. The wild is not a suffering-free zone or all that frolicsome a location.

The questions asked by animal-rights activists are flawed,   14
because they are built on the concept that the origin of rights is in the avoidance of suffering rather than in the pursuit of happiness. The question that needs to be asked—and that will put us in closer proximity to the truth—is not, do they have rights? or, what are those rights? but rather, what is a right?

Rights originate in committed relationships and can be   15
found, both intact and violated, wherever one finds such relationships—in social compacts, within families, between animals, and between people and nonhuman animals. This is as true when the nonhuman animals in question are lions or parakeets as when they are dogs. It is my Airedale whose excellencies have my attention at the moment, so it is with reference to him that I will consider the question, what is a right?

When I imagine situations in which it naturally arises that   16
A defends or honors or respects B's rights, I imagine situations in which the relationship between A and B can be indicated with a possessive pronoun. I might say, "Leave her

alone, she's my daughter" or, "That's what she wants, and she is my daughter. I think I am bound to honor her wants." Similarly, "Leave her alone, she's my mother." I am more tender of the happiness of my mother, my father, my child, that I am of other people's family members; more tender of my friends' happiness than your friends' happinesses, unless you and I have a mutual friend.

Possession of a being by another has come into more and more disrepute, so that the common understanding of one person possessing another is slavery. But the important detail about the kind of possessive pronoun that I have in mind is reciprocity: If I have a friend, she has a friend. If I have a daughter, she has a mother. The possessive does not bind one of us while freeing the other; it cannot do that. Moreover, should the mother reject the daughter, the word that applies is "disown." The form of disowning that most often appears in the news is domestic violence. Parents abuse children; husbands batter wives.

Some cases of reciprocal possessives have built-in limitations such as "my patient / my doctor" or "my student / my teacher" or "my agent / my client." Other possessive relations are extremely limited but still remarkably binding: "my neighbor" and "my country" and "my president."

The responsibilities and the ties signaled by reciprocal possession typically are hard to dissolve. It can be as difficult to give up an enemy as to give up a friend, and often the one becomes the other, as though the logic of the possessive pronoun outlasts the forms it chanced to take at a given moment, as though we were stuck with one another. In these bindings, nearly inextricable, are found the origin of our rights. They imply a possessiveness but also recognize an acknowledgment by each side of the other's existence.

The idea of democracy is dependent on the citizens' having knowledge of the government; that is, realizing that the government exists and knowing how to claim rights against it. I know this much because I get mail from the government and see its "representatives" running about in uniforms. Whether I actually have any rights in relationship to the government is less clear, but the idea that I do is symbolized by the right to vote. I obey the government, and, in theory, it obeys me, by counting my ballot, reading the *Miranda* warning to me, agreeing to be bound by the Constitution. My friend obeys me as I obey her; the government "obeys" me to some extent, and, to a different extent, I obey it.

What kind of thing can my Airedale, Drummer, have   21 knowledge of? He can know that I exist and through that knowledge can claim his happiness, with varying degrees of success, both with me and against me. Drummer can also know about larger human or dog communities than the one that consists only of him and me. There is my household— the other dogs, the cats, my husband. I have had enough dogs on campuses to know that he can learn that Yale exists as a neighborhood or village. My older dog, Annie, not only knows that Yale exists but can tell Yalies from townies, as I learned while teaching there during labor troubles.

Dogs can have elaborate conceptions of human social struc-   22 tures, and even of something like their rights and responsibilities within them, but these conceptions are never elaborate enough to construct a rights relationship between a dog and the state, or a dog and the Humane Society. Both of these are concepts that depend on writing and memoranda, officers in uniform, plaques and seals of authority. All of these are literary constructs, and all of them are beyond a dog's ken, which is why the mail carrier who doesn't also happen to be a dog's friend is forever an intruder—this is why dogs bark at mailmen.

It is clear enough that natural rights relations can arise   23 between people and animals. Drummer, for example, can insist, "Hey, let's go outside and do something!" if I have been at my computer several days on end. He can both refuse to accept various of my suggestions and tell me when he fears for his life—such as the time when the huge, white flapping flag appeared out of nowhere, as it seemed to him, on the town green one evening when we were working. I can (and do) say to him either, "Oh, you don't have to worry about that" or, "Uh oh, you're right, Drum, that guy looks dangerous." Just as the government and I—two different species of organism—have developed improvised ways of communicating, such as the vote, so Drummer and I have worked out a number of ways to make our expressions known. Largely through obedience, I have taught him a fair amount about how to get responses from me. Obedience is reciprocal; you cannot get responses from a dog to whom you do not respond accurately. I have enfranchised him in a relationship to me by educating him, creating the conditions by which he can achieve a certain happiness specific to a dog, maybe even specific to an Airedale, inasmuch as this same relationship has allowed me to plumb the happiness of being a trainer and writing this article.

Instructions in this happiness are given terms that are alien   24
to a culture in which liver treats, fluffy windup toys, and miniature sweaters are confused with respect and work. Jack Knox, a sheepdog trainer originally from Scotland, will shake his crook at a novice handler who makes a promiscuous move to praise a dog, and will call out in his Scottish accent, "Eh! Eh! Get back, get BACK! Ye'll no be abusin' the dogs like that in my clinic." America is a nation of abused animals, Knox says, because we are always swooping at them with praise, "no gi'ing them their freedom." I am reminded of Rainer Maria Rilke's account in which the Prodigal Son leaves—has to leave—because everyone loves him, even the dogs love him, and he has no path to the delicate and fierce truth of himself. Unconditional praise and love, in Rilke's story, disenfranchise us, distract us from what truly excites our interest.

In the minds of some trainers and handlers, praise is dis-   25
honesty. Paradoxically, it is a kind of contempt for animals that masquerades as a reverence for helplessness and suffering. The idea of freedom means that you do not, at least not while Jack Knox is nearby, helpfully guide your dog through the motions of, say, herding over and over—what one trainer calls "explainy-wainy." This is rote learning. It works tolerably well on some handlers, because people have vast unconscious minds and can store complex preprogrammed behaviors. Dogs, on the other hand, have almost no unconscious minds, so they can learn only by thinking. Many children are like this until educated out of it.

If I tell my Airedale to sit and stay on the town green, and   26
someone comes up and burbles, "What a pretty thing you
are," he may break his stay to go for a caress. I pull him back
and correct him for breaking. Now he holds his stay because
I have blocked his way to movement but not because I have
punished him. (A correction blocks one path as it opens
another for desire to work; punishment blocks desire and
opens nothing.) He holds his stay now, and—because the stay
opens this possibility of work, new to a heedless young dog—
he watches. If the person goes on talking, and isn't going
to gush with praise, I may heel Drummer out of his stay
and give him an "Okay" to make friends. Sometimes something about the person makes Drummer feel that reserve is
in order. He responds to an insincere approach by sitting
still, going down into himself, and thinking, "This person
has no business pawing me. I'll sit very still, and he will go
away." If the person doesn't take the hint from Drummer,
I'll give the pup a little backup by saying, "Please don't
pet him, he's working," even though he was not under any
command.

The pup reads this, and there is a flicker of a working   27
trust now stirring in the dog. Is the pup grateful? When the
stranger leaves, does he lick my hand, full of submissive blandishments? This one doesn't. This one says nothing at all,
and I say nothing much to him. This is a working trust we are
developing, not a mutual-congratulation society. My backup
is praise enough for him; the use he makes of my support is
praise enough for me.

Listening to a dog is often praise enough. Suppose it is   28
just after dark and we are outside. Suddenly there is a shout
from the house. The pup and I both look toward the shout
and then toward each other: "What do you think?" I don't so
much as cock my head, because Drummer is growing up, and
I want to know what he thinks. He takes a few steps toward
the house, and I follow. He listens again and comprehends
that it's just Holly, who at fourteen is much given to alarm-
ing cries and shouts. He shrugs at me and goes about his
business. I say nothing. To praise him for this performance

would make about as much sense as praising a human being for the same thing. Thus:

A. *What's that?*
B. *I don't know. [Listens] Oh, it's just Holly.*
C. *What a goooooood human being!*
B. *Huh?*

This is one small moment in a series of like moments that will culminate in an Airedale who on a Friday will have the discrimination and confidence required to take down a man who is attacking me with a knife and on Saturday clown and play with the children at the annual Orange Empire Dog Club Christmas party. 29

People who claim to speak for animal rights are increasingly devoted to the idea that the very keeping of a dog or a horse or a gerbil or a lion is in and of itself an offense. The more loudly they speak, the less likely they are to be in a rights relation to any given animal, because they are spending so much time in airplanes or transmitting fax announcements of the latest Sylvester Stallone anti-fur rally. In a 1988 *Harper's* forum, for example, Ingrid Newkirk, the national director of People for the Ethical Treatment of Animals, urged that domestic pets be spayed and neutered and ultimately phased out. She prefers, it appears, wolves—and wolves someplace else—to Airedales and, by a logic whose interior structure is both emotionally and intellectually forever closed to Drummer, claims thereby to be speaking for "animal rights." 30

She is wrong. I am the only one who can own up to my Airedale's inalienable rights. Whether or not I do it perfectly at any given moment is no more refutation of this point than whether I am perfectly my husband's mate at any given moment refutes the fact of marriage. Only people who know Drummer, and whom he can know, are capable of this relationship. PETA and the Humane Society and the ASPCA and the Congress and NOW—as institutions—do have the power to affect my ability to grant rights to Drummer but are otherwise incapable of creating conditions or laws or rights that would increase his happiness. 31

Only Drummer's owner has the power to obey him—to obey who he is and what he is capable of—deeply enough to grant him his rights and open up the possibility of happiness.

For Study and Discussion

QUESTIONS ABOUT PURPOSE

1. What kind of relationship between animals and their owners would Hearne like to see?
2. How does that ideal relationship fit in with her ideas about animal rights?

QUESTIONS ABOUT AUDIENCE

1. What groups of people do you think are likely to respond positively to Hearne's essay? To what extent do you fit into that group?
2. How does her work as an animal trainer establish her authority with her readers?

QUESTIONS ABOUT STRATEGIES

1. How does Hearne's comparison between the life expectancy of animals and humans in the wild and captivity advance her argument?
2. How does her description of her relationship with her Airedale, Drummer, support her argument?

For Writing and Research

1. *Analyze* the way Hearne explains the difference between the avoidance of suffering and the pursuit of happiness.
2. *Practice* by describing your experience training or caring for an animal.
3. *Argue* that Hearne undercuts her argument by using highly anthropomorphic images.
4. *Synthesize:* Reread Brigid Brophy's "The Rights of Animals." Then write an essay in which you explain the major difference between her argument and the argument Hearne is making in her essay. You may also want to consider what guidelines for dealing with animals the two authors would be likely to agree on.

A Debate About the Death Penalty

H . L . M E N C K E N

H(enry) L(ouis) Mencken (1880–1956) was born in Baltimore, Maryland. After graduating from Brooklyn Polytechnic Institute at the age of sixteen, he decided to forgo a college education for a plan of private study and a career in journalism. He joined the *Baltimore Morning Herald* as a reporter and later worked for the Sun Syndicate. Although he maintained his contact with these Baltimore papers throughout his career, he became engaged in many other publishing projects—as literary adviser to Alfred A. Knopf; as coeditor with George Jean Nathan of *The Smart Set;* and then, several years later, as cofounder (with Nathan) of *The American Mercury.* Mencken's own writing ranges from informative cultural history (*The American Language,* 1919) to outrageous iconoclasm (the essays that filled six volumes aptly titled *Prejudices,* 1919–1927) to several volumes of engaging autobiography. Although critics in his time considered him a radical, contemporary readers find most of his opinions conservative. In "The Penalty of Death," taken from the anthology *A Mencken Chrestomathy* (1949), Mencken tries to refute the two common arguments against capital punishment by arguing that the execution of criminals satisfies the basic human need for revenge.

The Penalty of Death[5]

O F THE ARGUMENTS against capital punishment that issue   1
from uplifters, two are commonly heard most often,
to wit:

1. That hanging a man (or frying him or gassing him) is a
   dreadful business, degrading to those who have to do it
   and revolting to those who have to witness it.
2. That it is useless, for it does not deter others from the
   same crime.

The first of these arguments, it seems to me, is plainly too   2
weak to need serious refutation. All it says, in brief, is that the
work of the hangman is unpleasant. Granted. But suppose
it is? It may be quite necessary to society for all that. There
are, indeed, many other jobs that are unpleasant, and yet no
one thinks of abolishing them—that of the plumber, that of
the soldier, that of the garbage-man, that of the priest hearing confessions, that of the sand-hog, and so on. Moreover,
what evidence is there that any actual hangman complains of
his work? I have heard none. On the contrary, I have known
many who delighted in their ancient art, and practiced it
proudly.

In the second argument of the abolitionists there is rather   3
more force, but even here, I believe, the ground under
them is shaky. Their fundamental error consists in assuming
that the whole aim of punishing criminals is to deter other
(potential) criminals—that we hang or electrocute A simply
in order to so alarm B that he will not kill C. This, I believe, is
an assumption which confuses a part with the whole. Deterrence, obviously, is *one* of the aims of punishment, but it is

---

surely not the only one. On the contrary, there are at least half a dozen, and some are probably quite as important. At least one of them, practically considered, is *more* important. Commonly, it is described as revenge, but revenge is really not the word for it. I borrow a better term from the late Aristotle: *katharsis. Katharsis,* so used, means a salubrious discharge of emotions, a healthy letting off of steam. A school-boy, disliking his teacher, deposits a tack upon the pedagogical chair; the teacher jumps and the boy laughs. This is *katharsis.* What I contend is that one of the prime objects of all judicial punishments is to afford the same grateful relief (*a*) to the immediate victims of the criminal punished, and (*b*) to the general body of moral and timorous men.

The thing they crave primarily is the satisfaction of seeing the criminal actually before them suffer as he made them suffer.

These persons, and particularly the first group, are concerned only indirectly with deterring other criminals. The thing they crave primarily is the satisfaction of seeing the criminal actually before them suffer as he made them suffer. What they want is the peace of mind that goes with the feeling that accounts are squared. Until they get that satisfaction they are in a state of emotional tension, and hence unhappy. The instant they get it they are comfortable. I do not argue that this yearning is noble; I simply argue that it is almost universal among human beings. In the face of injuries that are unimportant and can be borne without damage it may yield to higher impulses; that is to say, it may yield to what is called Christian charity. But when the injury is serious Christianity is adjourned, and even saints reach for their sidearms. It is plainly asking too much of human nature to expect it to conquer so natural an impulse. A keeps a store and has a

bookkeeper, B. B steals $700, employs it in playing at dice
or bingo, and is cleaned out. What is A to do? Let B go? If
he does so he will be unable to sleep at night. The sense of
injury, of injustice, of frustration will haunt him like pruri-
tus. So he turns B over to the police, and they hustle B to
prison. Thereafter A can sleep. More, he has pleasant dreams.
He pictures B chained to the wall of a dungeon a hundred
feet underground, devoured by rats and scorpions. It is so
agreeable that it makes him forget his $700. He has got his
katharsis.

    The same thing precisely takes place on a larger scale when 5
there is a crime which destroys a whole community's sense
of security. Every law-abiding citizen feels menaced and frustrated until the criminals have been struck down—until the
communal capacity to get even with them, and more than
even, has been dramatically demonstrated. Here, manifestly,
the business of deterring others is no more than an after-
thought. The main thing is to destroy the concrete scoundrels
whose act has alarmed everyone, and thus made everyone
unhappy. Until they are brought to book that unhappiness
continues; when the law has been executed upon them there
is a sigh of relief. In other words, there is *katharsis.*

    I know of no public demand for the death penalty for ordi- 6
nary crimes, even for ordinary homicides. Its infliction would
shock all men of normal decency of feeling. But for crimes
involving the deliberate and inexcusable taking of human life,
by men openly defiant of all civilized order—for such crimes
it seems, to nine men out of ten, a just and proper punishment. Any lesser penalty leaves them feeling that the criminal
has got the better of society—that he is free to add insult to
injury by laughing. That feeling can be dissipated only by a
recourse to *katharsis,* the invention of the aforesaid Aristotle.
It is more effectively and economically achieved, as human
nature now is, by wafting the criminal to realms of bliss.

    The real objection to capital punishment doesn't lie against 7
the actual extermination of the condemned, but against our
brutal American habit of putting it off so long. After all, every
one of us must die soon or late, and a murderer, it must be

assumed, is one who makes that sad fact the cornerstone of his metaphysic. But it is one thing to die, and quite another thing to lie for long months and even years under the shadow of death. No sane man would choose such a finish. All of us, despite the Prayer Book, long for a swift and unexpected end. Unhappily, a murderer, under the irrational American system, is tortured for what, to him, must seem a whole series of eternities. For months on end he sits in prison while his lawyers carry on their idiotic buffoonery with writs, injunctions, mandamuses, and appeals. In order to get his money (or that of his friends) they have to feed him with hope. Now and then, by the imbecility of a judge or some trick of juridic science, they actually justify it. But let us say that, his money all gone, they finally throw up their hands. Their client is now ready for the rope or the chair. But he must still wait for months before it fetches him.

That wait, I believe, is horribly cruel. I have seen more 8 than one man sitting in the death-house, and I don't want to see any more. Worse, it is wholly useless. Why should he wait at all? Why not hang him the day after the last court dissipates his last hope? Why torture him as not even cannibals would torture their victims? The common answer is that he must have time to make his peace with God. But how long does that take? It may be accomplished, I believe, in two hours quite as comfortably as in two years. There are, indeed, no temporal limitations upon God. He could forgive a whole herd of murderers in a millionth of a second. More, it has been done.

For Study and Discussion

QUESTIONS ABOUT PURPOSE

1. What statements in Mencken's essay are probably meant to shock some of his readers?
2. Does Mencken intend to make a logical appeal? If so, in what ways?

QUESTIONS ABOUT AUDIENCE

1. In what ways do you think contemporary readers' attitudes about the death penalty might be different from those of readers in the 1920s, when this essay was first published? In what ways might they not have changed?
2. To what emotions in his audience is Mencken trying to appeal?

QUESTIONS ABOUT STRATEGIES

1. Why does Mencken start by giving two arguments *against* his thesis?
2. Why does Mencken start paragraph 6 with three qualifying sentences?

For Writing and Research

1. *Analyze* what is fact, judgment, and eyewitness and expert testimony in Mencken's essay.
2. *Practice* by citing the facts, judgments, and testimony that lead you to support or reject capital punishment.
3. *Argue* that Mencken's tone and language encourage you to accept or reject his argument.
4. *Synthesize* the impact of DNA research on several capital punishment cases. Then argue that this new scientific research supports or undercuts public opinion on execution.

ANNA QUINDLEN

Anna Quindlen was born in 1953 in Philadelphia, Pennsylvania, and was educated at Barnard College. She began her career as a reporter for the *New York Post* and then as a reporter and columnist for the *New York Times*. Her columns are collected in *Living Out Loud* (1988) and *Thinking Out Loud* (1993). Quindlen wrote the "Last Word" column for *Newsweek* from 2000 to 2009. She devotes much of her time to writing the kind of novels she describes in *How Reading Changed My Life* (1998). Those best-selling novels include *Object Lessons* (1991), *One True Thing* (1994), *Black and Blue* (1998), *Blessings* (2002) and *Every Last One* (2010). *One True Thing* was adapted for the screen and starred Renée Zellweger and Meryl Streep. In "Execution," reprinted from *Living Out Loud*, Quindlen argues that the death penalty does not accomplish what it was designed for.

Execution[6]

ED BUNDY AND I go back a long way, to a time when there was a series of unsolved murders in Washington State known only as the Ted murders. Like a lot of reporters, I'm something of a crime buff. But the Washington Ted murders—and the ones that followed in Utah, Colorado, and finally in Florida, where Ted Bundy was convicted and sentenced to die—fascinated me because I could see myself as one of the victims. I looked at the studio photographs of young women with long hair, pierced ears, easy smiles, and I

1

---

read the descriptions: polite, friendly, quick to help, eager to please. I thought about being approached by a handsome young man asking for help, and I knew if I had been in the wrong place at the wrong time I would have been a goner. By the time Ted finished up in Florida, law enforcement authorities suspected he had murdered dozens of young women. He and the death penalty seemed made for each other.

The death penalty and I, on the other hand, seem to have nothing in common. But Ted Bundy has made me think about it all over again, now that the outlines of my sixties liberalism have been filled in with a decade as a reporter covering some of the worst back alleys in New York City and three years as a mother who, like most, would lay down her life for her kids. Simply put, I am opposed to the death penalty. I would tell that to any judge or lawyer undertaking the voir dire of jury candidates in a state in which the death penalty can be imposed. That is why I would be excused from such a jury. In a rational, completely cerebral way, I think the killing of one human being as punishment for the killing of another makes no sense and is inherently immoral. 2

> *The death penalty and I . . . have nothing in common.*

But whenever my response to an important subject is rational and completely cerebral, I know there is something wrong with it—and so it is here. I have always been governed by my gut, and my gut says I am hypocritical about the death penalty. That is, I do not in theory think that Ted Bundy, or others like him, should be put to death. But if my daughter had been the one clubbed to death as she slept in a Tallahassee sorority house, and if the bite mark left in her buttocks had been one of the prime pieces of evidence against the young man charged with her murder, I would with the greatest pleasure kill him myself. 3

The State of Florida will not permit the parents of Bundy's   4
victims to do that, and, in a way, that is the problem with an
emotional response to capital punishment. The only reason
for a death penalty is to exact retribution. Is there anyone
who really thinks that it is a deterrent, that there are considerable numbers of criminals out there who think twice about
committing crimes because of the sentence involved? The
ones I have met in my professional duties have either sneered
at the justice system, where they can exchange one charge
for another with more ease than they could return a shirt to
a clothing store, or they have simply believed that it is the
other guy who will get caught, get convicted, get the stiffest
sentence. Of course, the death penalty would act as a deterrent by eliminating recidivism, but then so would life without
parole, albeit at greater taxpayer expense.

I don't believe deterrence is what most proponents seek   5
from the death penalty anyhow. Our most profound emotional response is to want criminals to suffer as their victims
did. When a man is accused of throwing a child from a high-
rise terrace, my emotional—some might say hysterical—
response is that he should be given an opportunity to see
how endless the seconds are from the thirty-first story to the
ground. In a civilized society that will never happen. And
so what many people want from the death penalty, they will
never get.

Death is death, you may say, and you would be right. But   6
anyone who has seen someone die suddenly of a heart attack
and someone else slip slowly into the clutches of cancer
knows that there are gradations of dying.

I watched a television reenactment one night of an execu-   7
tion by lethal injection. It was well done; it was horrible. The
methodical approach, people standing around the gurney
waiting, made it more awful. One moment there was a man
in a prone position; the next moment that man was gone.
On another night I watched a television movie about a little
boy named Adam Walsh, who disappeared from a shopping
center in Florida. There was a reenactment of Adam's parents
coming to New York, where they appeared on morning talk

shows begging for their son's return, and in their hotel room, where they received a call from the police saying that Adam had just been found: not all of Adam, actually, just his severed head, discovered in the waters of a Florida canal. There is nothing anyone could do that is bad enough for an adult who took a six-year-old boy away from his parents, perhaps tortured, then murdered him and cut off his head. Nothing at all. Lethal injection? The electric chair? Bah.

And so I come back to the position that the death penalty   8
is wrong, not only because it consists of stooping to the level of the killers, but also because it is not what it seems. Just before one of Ted Bundy's execution dates was postponed pending further appeals, the father of his last known victim, a twelve-year-old girl, said what almost every father in his situation must feel. "I wish they'd bring him back to Lake City," said Tom Leach of the town where Kimberly Leach lived and died, "and let us all have at him." But the death penalty does not let us all have at him in the way Mr. Leach seems to mean. What he wants is for something as horrifying as what happened to his child to happen to Ted Bundy. And that is impossible.

For Study and Discussion

QUESTIONS ABOUT PURPOSE

1. What does Quindlen mean when she argues that "whenever my response to an important subject is rational and completely cerebral, I know something is wrong"?
2. What does she demonstrate about the "problem with the emotional response to the death penalty"?

QUESTIONS ABOUT AUDIENCE

1. How do Quindlen's references to her family help her connect with her readers?
2. How does she anticipate some of her readers' responses when she discusses "deterrence"?

QUESTIONS ABOUT STRATEGIES

1. How does Quindlen demonstrate that what "many want from the death penalty, they will never get"?
2. How does she use television reenactments to support this assertion?

For Writing and Research

1. *Analyze* Quindlen's opening and concluding paragraphs to assess the effectiveness of her argument.
2. *Practice* by describing the difficulty you had balancing your logical and emotional responses to an event.
3. *Argue* by presenting evidence that supports the assertion that "the punishment should fit the crime."
4. *Synthesize:* Reread Mencken's and Quindlen's arguments about the death penalty. Then write an essay that proposes an accommodation between their two positions.

KURT VONNEGUT JR.

Kurt Vonnegut Jr. (1922–2007) was born in Indianapolis, Indiana, and attended Cornell University, where he studied biochemistry before being drafted into the infantry in World War II. Vonnegut was captured by the Germans at the Battle of the Bulge and sent to Dresden, where he worked in the underground meat locker of a slaughterhouse. He miraculously survived the Allied firebombing of Dresden and, following the war, returned to the United States to study anthropology at the University of Chicago and to work for a local news bureau. In 1947, Vonnegut accepted a position writing publicity for the General Electric Research Laboratory in Schenectady, New York, but left the company in 1950 to work on his own writing. His first three novels—*Player Piano* (1952), a satire on the tyrannies of corporate automation; *The Sirens of Titan* (1959), a science fiction comedy on the themes of free will and determination; and *Cat's Cradle* (1963), a science fantasy on the amorality of atomic scientists—established Vonnegut's reputation as a writer who could blend humor with serious insights into the human experience. His most successful novel, *Slaughterhouse-Five, or the Children's Crusade* (1969), is based on his wartime experiences in Dresden. His other works include *God Bless You, Mr. Rosewater* (1966), *Breakfast of Champions* (1973), *Jailbird* (1979), *Palm Sunday* (1981), *Galápagos* (1985), *Hocus Pocus* (1990), and *Timequake* (1997). His best-known short stories are collected in *Canary in the Cat House* (1961) and *Welcome to the Monkey House* (1968). "Harrison Bergeron," reprinted from the latter collection, is the story of the apparatus that a future society must create to make everyone equal.

Harrison Bergeron[7]

T HE YEAR WAS 2081, and everybody was finally equal. 1
They weren't only equal before God and the law. They
were equal every which way. Nobody was smarter than anybody else. Nobody was better looking than anybody else.
Nobody was stronger or quicker than anybody else. All this
equality was due to the 211th, 212th, and 213th Amend-
ments to the Constitution, and to the unceasing vigilance of
agents of the United States Handicapper General.

Some things about living still weren't quite right, though. 2
April, for instance, still drove people crazy by not being
springtime. And it was in that clammy month that the H-G
men took George and Hazel Bergeron's fourteen-year-old
son, Harrison, away.

It was tragic, all right, but George and Hazel couldn't 3
think about it very hard. Hazel had a perfectly average intelligence, which meant she couldn't think about anything except
in short bursts. And George, while his intelligence was way
above normal, had a little mental handicap radio in his ear.
He was required by law to wear it at all times. It was tuned
to a government transmitter. Every twenty seconds or so, the
transmitter would send out some sharp noise to keep people
like George from taking unfair advantage of their brains.

George and Hazel were watching television. There were 4
tears on Hazel's cheeks, but she'd forgotten for the moment
what they were about.

On the television screen were ballerinas. 5

A buzzer sounded in George's head. His thoughts fled in 6
panic, like bandits from a burglar alarm.

"That was a real pretty dance, that dance they just did," 7
said Hazel.

"Huh?" said George. 8

"That dance—it was nice," said Hazel. 9

[7]Kurt Vonnegut Jr., "Harrison Bergeron" from *Welcome to the Monkey House* by Kurt Vonnegut, Jr., copyright © 1961 by Kurt Vonnegut Jr. Used by permission of Dell Publishing, a division of Random House, Inc.

"Yup," said George. He tried to think a little about the   10
ballerinas. They weren't really very good—no better than
anybody else would have been, anyway. They were burdened
with sashweights and bags of birdshot, and their faces were
masked, so that no one, seeing a free and graceful gesture
or a pretty face, would feel like something the cat drug in.
George was toying with the vague notion that maybe dancers
shouldn't be handicapped. But he didn't get very far with it
before another noise in his ear radio scattered his thoughts.

George winced. So did two of the eight ballerinas.   11

Hazel saw him wince. Having no mental handicap herself,   12
she had to ask George what the latest sound had been.

"Sounded like somebody hitting a milk bottle with a ball   13
peen hammer," said George.

"I'd think it would be real interesting, hearing all the dif-   14
ferent sounds," said Hazel, a little envious. "All the things
they think up."

"Um," said George.   15

"Only, if I was Handicapper General, you know what I   16
would do?" said Hazel. Hazel, as a matter of fact, bore a
strong resemblance to the Handicapper General, a woman
named Diana Moon Glampers. "If I was Diana Moon Glampers," said Hazel, "I'd have chimes on Sunday—just chimes.
Kind of in honor of religion."

"I could think, if it was just chimes," said George.   17

"Well—maybe make 'em real loud," said Hazel. "I think   18
I'd make a good Handicapper General."

"Good as anybody else," said George.   19

"Who knows better'n I do what normal is?" said Hazel.   20

"Right," said George. He began to think glimmeringly   21
about his abnormal son who was now in jail, about Harrison,
but a twenty-one-gun salute in his head stopped that.

"Boy!" said Hazel, "that was a doozy, wasn't it?"   22

It was such a doozy that George was white and trembling,   23
and tears stood on the rims of his red eyes. Two of the eight
ballerinas had collapsed on the studio floor, were holding
their temples.

"All of a sudden you look so tired," said Hazel. "Why   24
don't you stretch out on the sofa, so's you can rest your

handicap bag on the pillows, honeybunch." She was referring to the forty-seven pounds of birdshot in a canvas bag,
which was padlocked around George's neck. "Go on and rest
the bag for a little while," she said. "I don't care if you're not
equal to me for a while."

George weighed the bag with his hands. "I don't mind it," 25
he said. "I don't notice it any more. It's just a part of me."

"You been so tired lately—kind of wore out," said Hazel. 26
"If there was just some way we could make a little hole in the
bottom of the bag, and just take out a few of them lead balls.
Just a few."

"Two years in prison and two thousand dollars fine for every 27
ball I took out," said George. "I don't call that a bargain."

"If you could just take a few out when you came home 28
from work," said Hazel. "I mean—you don't compete with
anybody around here. You just set around."

"If I tried to get away with it," said George, "then other 29
people'd get away with it—and pretty soon we'd be right
back to the dark ages again, with everybody competing
against everybody else. You wouldn't like that, would you?"

"I'd hate it," said Hazel. 30

"There you are," said George. "The minute people start 31
cheating on laws, what do you think happens to society?"

If Hazel hadn't been able to come up with an answer to 32
this question, George couldn't have supplied one. A siren
was going off in his head.

"Reckon it'd fall all apart," said Hazel. 33

"What would?" said George blankly. 34

"Society," said Hazel uncertainly. "Wasn't that what you 35
just said?"

"Who knows?" said George. 36

The television program was suddenly interrupted for a 37
news bulletin. It wasn't clear at first as to what the bulletin
was about, since the announcer, like all announcers, had a
serious speech impediment. For about half a minute, and in a
state of high excitement, the announcer tried to say, "Ladies
and gentlemen—"

He finally gave up, handed the bulletin to a ballerina 38
to read.

"That's all right—" Hazel said to the announcer, "he 39 tried. That's the big thing. He tried to do the best he could with what God gave him. He should get a nice raise for trying so hard."

"Ladies and gentlemen—" said the ballerina, reading 40 the bulletin. She must have been extraordinarily beautiful, because the mask she wore was hideous. And it was easy to see that she was the strongest and most graceful of all the dancers, for her handicap bags were as big as those worn by two-hundred-pound men.

And she had to apologize at once for her voice, which was 41 a very unfair voice for a woman to use. Her voice was a warm, luminous, timeless melody. "Excuse me—" she said, and she began again, making her voice absolutely uncompetitive.

"Harrison Bergeron, age fourteen," she said in a grackle 42 squawk, "has just escaped from jail, where he was held on suspicion of plotting to overthrow the government. He is a genius and an athlete, is under-handicapped, and should be regarded as extremely dangerous."

A police photograph of Harrison Bergeron was flashed on 43 the screen upside down, then sideways, upside down again, then right side up. The picture showed the full length of Harrison against a background calibrated in feet and inches. He was exactly seven feet tall.

The rest of Harrison's appearance was Halloween and 44 hardware. Nobody had ever borne heavier handicaps. He had outgrown hindrances faster than the H-G men could think them up. Instead of a little ear radio for a mental handicap, he wore a tremendous pair of earphones, and spectacles with thick wavy lenses. The spectacles were intended to make him not only half blind, but to give him whanging headaches besides.

Scrap metal was hung all over him. Ordinarily, there was 45 a certain symmetry, a military neatness to the handicaps issued to strong people, but Harrison looked like a walking junkyard. In the race of life, Harrison carried three hundred pounds.

And to offset his good looks, the H-G men required that 46 he wear at all times a red rubber ball for a nose, keep his eyebrows shaved off, and cover his even white teeth with black caps at snaggle-tooth random.

"If you see this boy," said the ballerina, "do not—I repeat, do not—try to reason with him." 47

There was the shriek of a door being torn from its hinges. 48

Screams and barking cries of consternation came from the television set. The photograph of Harrison Bergeron on the screen jumped again and again, as though dancing to the tune of an earthquake. 49

George Bergeron correctly identified the earthquake, and well he might have—for many was the time his own home had danced to the same crashing tune. "My God—" said George, "that must be Harrison!" 50

The realization was blasted from his mind instantly by the sound of an automobile collision in his head. 51

When George could open his eyes again, the photograph of Harrison was gone. A living, breathing Harrison filled the screen. 52

Clanking, clownish, and huge, Harrison stood in the center of the studio. The knob of the uprooted studio door was still in his hand. Ballerinas, technicians, musicians, and announcers cowered on their knees before him, expecting to die. 53

"I am the Emperor!" cried Harrison. "Do you hear? I am the Emperor! Everybody must do what I say at once!" He stamped his foot and the studio shook. 54

"Even as I stand here—" he bellowed, "crippled, hobbled, sickened—I am a greater ruler than any man who ever lived! Now watch me become what I *can* become!" 55

Harrison tore the straps of his handicap harness like wet tissue paper, tore straps guaranteed to support five thousand pounds. 56

Harrison's scrap-iron handicaps crashed to the floor. 57

Harrison thrust his thumbs under the bars of the padlock that secured his head harness. The bar snapped like celery. Harrison smashed his headphones and spectacles against the wall. 58

He flung away his rubber-ball nose, revealed a man that would have awed Thor, the god of thunder. 59

"I shall now select my Empress!" he said, looking down 60
on the cowering people. "Let the first woman who dares rise
to her feet claim her mate and her throne!"

A moment passed, and then a ballerina arose, swaying like 61
a willow.

Harrison plucked the mental handicap from her ear, 62
snapped off her physical handicaps with marvelous delicacy.
Last of all, he removed her mask.

She was blindingly beautiful. 63

"Now—" said Harrison, taking her hand, "shall we show 64
the people the meaning of the word dance? Music!" he
commanded.

The musicians scrambled back into their chairs, and 65
Harrison stripped them of their handicaps, too. "Play your
best," he told them, "and I'll make you barons and dukes
and earls."

The music began. It was normal at first—cheap, silly, 66
false. But Harrison snatched two musicians from their chairs,
waved them like batons as he sang the music as he wanted it
played. He slammed them back into their chairs.

The music began again and was much improved. 67

Harrison and his Empress merely listened to the music 68
for a while—listened gravely, as though synchronizing their
heartbeats with it.

They shifted their weights to their toes. 69

Harrison placed his big hands on the girl's tiny waist, let- 70
ting her sense the weightlessness that would soon be hers.

And then, in an explosion of joy and grace, into the air 71
they sprang!

Not only were the laws of the land abandoned, but the law 72
of gravity and the laws of motion as well.

They reeled, whirled, swiveled, flounced, capered, gam- 73
boled, and spun.

They leaped like deer on the moon. 74

The studio ceiling was thirty feet high, but each leap 75
brought the dancers nearer to it.

It became their obvious intention to kiss the ceiling. 76

They kissed it. 77

And then, neutralizing gravity with love and pure will,   78
they remained suspended in air inches below the ceiling, and
they kissed each other for a long, long time.

It was then that Diana Moon Glampers, the Handicapper   79
General, came into the studio with a double-barreled ten-
gauge shotgun. She fired twice, and the Emperor and the
Empress were dead before they hit the floor.

Diana Moon Glampers loaded the gun again. She aimed   80
it at the musicians and told them they had ten seconds to get
their handicaps back on.

It was then that the Bergerons' television tube burned out.   81

Hazel turned to comment about the blackout to George.   82
But George had gone out into the kitchen for a can of beer.

George came back in with the beer, paused while a handi-   83
cap signal shook him up. And then he sat down again. "You
been crying?" he said to Hazel.

"Yup," she said.   84

"What about?" he said.   85

"I forgot," she said. "Something real sad on television."   86

"What was it?" he said.   87

"It's all kind of mixed up in my mind," said Hazel.   88

"Forget sad things," said George.   89

"I always do," said Hazel.   90

"That's my girl," said George. He winced. There was the   91
sound of a rivetting gun in his head.

"Gee—I could tell that one was a doozy," said Hazel.   92

"You can say that again," said George.   93

"Gee—" said Hazel, "I could tell that one was a doozy."   94

COMMENT ON "HARRISON BERGERON"

Known for his offbeat and sometimes bizarre vision of reality, Vonnegut has created in "Harrison Bergeron" a science
fiction story full of black humor and grotesque details. The
society he creates in the story is reminiscent of the society
pictured in Orwell's *1984,* totally controlled by a government that invades and interferes in every facet of its citizens'
lives. In a travesty of the famous declaration that "All men

are created equal," the government has set out to legislate equality. Vonnegut portrays the results of such legislation in macabre images of people forced to carry weighted bags to reduce their strength, wear grotesque masks to conceal their beauty, and suffer implants in their brain to disrupt their thinking. When a fourteen-year-old boy, Harrison Bergeron, shows signs of excellence, he is first arrested and then ruthlessly destroyed when he throws off his restraints and literally rises to the top.

Underneath the farce, Vonnegut has created a tragic picture of a culture so obsessed with equality that people must be leveled by decree. Mediocrity reigns; any sign of excellence or superiority threatens law and order and must be suppressed immediately. Ultimately, of course, such a society will perish because it will kill its talent and stagnate.

Vonnegut wrote this story in 1961, after the repressive Stalinist regime that wiped out thousands of leaders and intellectuals in Russia; it precedes by a few years the disastrous era of Mao's Red Guards in China, when hundreds of thousands of intellectuals and artists were killed or imprisoned in the name of equality. Is Vonnegut commenting on the leveling tendencies of these totalitarian societies? Or does he see such excesses reflected in our own society? No one knows, but it's the genius of artists to prod us to think about such concerns.

CHAPTER 8

RESOURCES FOR WRITING THE FAMILY: A CASEBOOK

As you have worked your way through this book, you have discovered that you already possess many resources for reading and writing. You read essays on a wide variety of themes. You encountered new and complicated information shaped by unusual and unsettling assertions. But you discovered experiences and feelings that you recognize—the challenge of learning, the ordeal of disappointment, and the cost of achievement. As you examined these essays, you realized that you had something to say about your reading, something to contribute to the themes explored by the writers.

Your work with this book has also enabled you to identify and practice strategies that at each stage of the writing process helped you transform your ideas about a theme into writing. In the beginning, these strategies give rise to certain questions you might ask to explain any topic. (See "Selecting Your Strategy," pages 24 to 27.)

Suppose you want to write an essay on the theme of green technology. You might begin by asking what kinds of green technology are currently available to save energy and protect the environment. You might continue asking questions: What historical forces have created the need for green technology (cause and effect)? How do scientists recommend that our culture convert to green technology (process analysis)? How do they distinguish between the way we currently use energy and the way we would use energy if we were to convert to green technology (comparison and contrast)? How can we convince advocates of traditional technology to convert to green technology (persuasion and argument)? Such questions work like the different lenses you attach to your camera: each lens gives you a different perspective on a subject, a variation on a theme.

If your initial questions enable you to envision your theme from a different perspective, then answering one of these questions encourages you to develop your theme according to a purpose associated with one of the common patterns of organization. For instance, if you decide to write about why you traded your gas guzzler for a hybrid, your choice of purpose seems obvious: to answer the question "Why did it happen?" You would write a cause-and-effect essay. In drafting the essay, however, you may discover questions that you had not anticipated: What caused carmakers to develop hybrid cars? What other types of energy-saving vehicles are currently available? What are the limitations of hybrid cars? How are hybrid cars similar to or different from electric cars?

Responding to these new questions forces you to decide whether your new information develops or distorts your draft. The history of why carmakers decided to develop hybrids may help your readers see a context for your analysis. On the other hand, such information may confuse them, distracting them from your original purpose—to explain why you decided to trade for a hybrid.

As you struggle with your new themes, you may decide that your original purpose no longer drives your writing. You may decide to change your purpose and write a comparison-and-contrast essay. Instead of explaining why you traded for a hybrid, you might decide to use your personal experience, together with some reading, to write a more technical essay explaining how hybrid cars compare with electric cars.

This book has helped you make such decisions by showing how the common patterns of organization evoke different purposes, audiences, and strategies. In this thematic unit, you will have the opportunity to make decisions about a little anthology of writing on the theme of *The Family*.

Before reading these selections, take an initial inventory:

- *What kind of direct experiences have you had with family?*
  What are the most important memories you have of your family?
  What problems did you face growing up in your family?
  How did you overcome these problems?
- *What kind of indirect experiences have you had with families?*
  What have you observed about the relationships in other families?
  What kind of stories have you read about families in newspapers or literature?
  What have you learned by watching stories about families on television or in film?
- *What do you know—or suspect you could learn—about the history and significance of families in our culture?*
  Who have been the great families in our history?
  How have the different ideas about family defined our history?
  How have the revolutions in technology changed the family structure?
  Why are we so fascinated by stories about happy or dysfunctional families?

Thinking about such questions will remind you of the extensive resources you bring to the theme of *The Family*. It is a subject that touches all our lives in some way. And it affects our behavior in countless other ways—what we do with our time, with whom we associate, how we spend our money, what skills we wish to acquire, and what we think of ourselves and our culture.

After you have made a preliminary inventory of your knowledge of and attitudes toward family, read the writings in this chapter. You will notice that each selection asks you to think about the family from a different perspective.

1. *What happened? (Narration and Description)* Amy Tan recounts her the reason she decides to devote her stories to her mother.
2. *How do you do it? How is it done? (Process Analysis)* Serena Nanda analyzes the process of arranging a marriage in India
3. *How is it similar to or different from something else? (Comparison and Contrast)* Anne Roiphe compares two marriages, one that should have ended in divorce, and one that did.
4. *What kind of subdivisions does it contain? (Division and Classification)* Jane Howard classifies the various roles that are typical of good families
5. *How would you characterize it? (Definition)* Howard Moody considers the various definitions that have led to the current debate about the nature of marriage.
6. *How did it happen? (Cause and Effect)* Scott Russell Sanders analyzes the effect of his father's addiction to alcohol on his own life.
7. *How do you prove it? (Persuasion and Argument)* Barbara Kingsolver and Barbara Defoe Whitehead present opposing arguments about the structure of the family

This collection also includes a *photo essay* that presents various "visual texts"—images and photographs—that evoke questions about the way we *see* family. Each visual text is also followed by a writing assignment that asks you to interpret the significance of what you are looking at.

The collection ends with Alice Walker's story "Everyday Use," an engaging story about the nature of family heritage.

As you examine these selections, keep track of how your reading and seeing expand the theme of family—provoking memories, adding information, and suggesting questions you had not considered when you made your initial inventory about family. Because this information will give you new ways to think about your original questions, you will want to explore your thinking in writing.

AMY TAN

Amy Tan was born in 1952 in Oakland, California, and educated at San Jose State University and the University of California, Berkeley. After visiting China for the first time in 1987, Tan began writing a collection of interconnected stories about Chinese-American mothers and daughters, *The Joy Luck Club* (1989). Her subsequent fiction includes *The Kitchen God's Wife* (1991), *The Hundred Secret Senses* (1995), *The Bonesetter's Daughter* (2001), and *Saving Fish from Drowning* (2005). Some of her nonfiction is collected in *The Opposite of Fate: A Book of Musings* (2003). In "Mother Tongue," reprinted from the *Threepenny Review*, Tan recounts how she decided to address her stories to her mother.

Mother Tongue[1]

I AM NOT A SCHOLAR OF ENGLISH or literature. I cannot give   1
you much more than personal opinions on the English language and its variations in this country or others.

I am a writer. And by that definition, I am someone who   2
has always loved language. I am fascinated by language in daily life. I spend a great deal of my time thinking about the power of language—the way it can evoke an emotion, a visual image, a complex idea, or a simple truth. Language is the tool of my trade. And I use them all—all the Englishes I grew up with.

Recently, I was made keenly aware of the different   3
Englishes I do use. I was giving a talk to a large group of

---

[1] Amy Tan, Copyright © 1990 by Amy Tan. First appeared in THE THREE-PENNY REVIEW. Reprinted by permission of the author and the Sandra Dijkstra Literary Agency.

people, the same talk I had already given to half a dozen other groups. The nature of the talk was about my writing, my life, and my book, *The Joy Luck Club*. The talk was going along well enough, until I remembered one major difference that made the whole talk sound wrong. My mother was in the room. And it was perhaps the first time she had heard me give a lengthy speech, using the kind of English I have never used with her. I was saying things like, "The intersection of memory upon imagination" and "There is an aspect of my fiction that relates to thus-and-thus"—a speech filled with carefully wrought grammatical phrases, burdened, it suddenly seemed to me, with nominalized forms, past perfect tenses, conditional phrases, all the forms of standard English that I had learned in school and through books, the forms of English I did not use at home with my mother.

Just last week, I was walking down the street with my 4 mother, and I again found myself conscious of the English I was using, the English I do use with her. We were talking about the price of new and used furniture and I heard myself saying this: "Not waste money that way." My husband was with us as well, and he didn't notice any switch in my English. And then I realized why. It's because over the twenty years we've been together I've often used the same kind of English with him, and sometimes he even uses it with me. It has become our language of intimacy, a different sort of English that relates to family talk, the language I grew up with.

Language is the tool of my trade. And I use all of them—all the Englishes I grew up with.

So you'll have some idea of what this family talk I heard 5 sounds like, I'll quote what my mother said during a recent conversation which I videotaped and then transcribed. During this conversation, my mother was talking about a political

gangster in Shanghai who had the same last name as her family's, Du, and how the gangster in his early years wanted to
be adopted by her family, which was rich by comparison.
Later, the gangster became more powerful, far richer than
my mother's family, and one day showed up at my mother's
wedding to pay his respects. Here's what she said in part:

"Du Yusong having business like fruit stand. Like off the   6
street kind. He is Du like Du Zong—but not Tsung-ming
Island people. The local people call putong, the river east
side, he belong to that side local people. That man want to
ask Du Zong father take him in like become own family. Du
Zong father wasn't look down on him, but didn't take seriously, until that man big like become a mafia. Now important
person, very hard to inviting him. Chinese way, came only to
show respect, don't stay for dinner. Respect for making big
celebration, he shows up. Mean gives lots of respect. Chinese
custom. Chinese social life that way. If too important won't
have to stay too long. He come to my wedding. I didn't see,
I heard it. I gone to boy's side, they have YMCA dinner.
Chinese age I was nineteen."

You should know that my mother's expressive command   7
of English belies how much she actually understands. She
reads the *Forbes* report, listens to *Wall Street Week,* converses
daily with her stockbroker, reads all of Shirley MacLaine's
books with ease—all kinds of things I can't begin to understand. Yet some of my friends tell me they understand 50 percent of what my mother says. Some say they understand 80
to 90 percent. Some say they understand none of it, as if
she were speaking pure Chinese. But to me, my mother's
English is perfectly clear, perfectly natural. It's my mother
tongue. Her language, as I hear it, is vivid, direct, full of
observation and imagery. That was the language that helped
shape the way I saw things, expressed things, made sense of
the world.

Lately, I've been giving more thought to the kind of English   8
my mother speaks. Like others, I have described it to people

as "broken" or "fractured" English. But I wince when I say that. It has always bothered me that I can think of no way to describe it other than "broken," as if it were damaged and needed to be fixed, as if it lacked a certain wholeness and soundness. I've heard other terms used, "limited English," for example. But they seem just as bad, as if everything is limited, including people's perceptions of the limited English speaker.

I know this for a fact, because when I was growing up, my 9
mother's "limited" English limited *my* perception of her. I was ashamed of her English. I believed that her English reflected the quality of what she had to say. That is, because she expressed them imperfectly her thoughts were imperfect. And I had plenty of empirical evidence to support me: the fact that people in department stores, at banks, and at restaurants did not take her seriously, did not give her good service, pretended not to understand her, or even acted as if they did not hear her.

My mother has long realized the limitations of her English 10
as well. When I was fifteen, she used to have me call people on the phone to pretend I was she. In this guise, I was forced to ask for information or even to complain and yell at people who had been rude to her. One time it was a call to her stock-broker in New York. She had cashed out her small portfolio and it just so happened we were going to go to New York the next week, our very first trip outside California. I had to get on the phone and say in an adolescent voice that was not very convincing, "This is Mrs. Tan."

And my mother was standing in the back whispering 11
loudly, "Why he don't send me check, already two weeks late. So mad he lie to me, losing me money."

And then I said in perfect English, "Yes, I'm getting rather 12
concerned. You had agreed to send the check two weeks ago, but it hasn't arrived."

Then she began to talk more loudly. "What he want, I 13
come to New York tell him front of his boss, you cheating me?" And I was trying to calm her down, make her be quiet, while telling the stockbroker, "I can't tolerate any more

excuses. If I don't receive the check immediately, I am going to have to speak to your manager when I'm in New York next week." And sure enough, the following week there we were in front of this astonished stockbroker, and I was sitting there red-faced and quiet, and my mother, the real Mrs. Tan, was shouting at his boss in her impeccable broken English.

We used a similar routine just five days ago, for a situation that was far less humorous. My mother had gone to the hospital for an appointment, to find out about a benign brain tumor a CAT scan had revealed a month ago. She said she had spoken very good English, her best English, no mistakes. Still, she said, the hospital did not apologize when they said they had lost the CAT scan and she had come for nothing. She said they did not seem to have any sympathy when she told them she was anxious to know the exact diagnosis, since her husband and son had both died of brain tumors. She said they would not give her any more information until the next time and she would have to make another appointment for that. So she said she would not leave until the doctor called her daughter. She wouldn't budge. And when the doctor finally called her daughter, me, who spoke in perfect English—lo and behold—we had assurances the CAT scan would be found, promises that a conference call on Monday would be held, and apologies for any suffering my mother had gone through for a most regrettable mistake. 14

I think my mother's English almost had an effect on limiting my possibilities in life as well. Sociologists and linguists probably will tell you that a person's developing language skills are more influenced by peers. But I do think that the language spoken in the family, especially in immigrant families which are more insular, plays a large role in shaping the language of the child. And I believe that it affected my results on achievement tests, IQ tests, and the SAT. While my English skills were never judged as poor, compared to math, English could not be considered my strong suit. In grade school I did moderately well, getting perhaps B's, sometimes B-pluses, in English and scoring perhaps in the sixtieth or seventieth percentile on achievement tests. But those scores were not good 15 enough to override the opinion that my true abilities lay in math and science, because in those areas I achieved A's and scored in the ninetieth percentile or higher.

This was understandable. Math is precise; there is only one correct answer. Whereas, for me at least, the answers on English tests were always a judgment call, a matter of opinion and personal experience. Those tests were constructed around items like fill-in-the-blank sentence completion, such as, "Even though Tom was _____, Mary thought he was _____." And the correct answer always seemed to be the most bland combinations of thoughts, for example, "Even though Tom was shy, Mary thought he was charming," with the grammatical structure "even though" limiting the correct answer to some sort of semantic opposites, so you wouldn't get answers like, "Even though Tom was foolish, Mary thought he was ridiculous." Well, according to my mother, there were very few limitations as to what Tom could have been and what Mary might have thought of him. So I never did well on tests like that. 16

The same was true with word analogies, pairs of words in which you were supposed to find some sort of logical, semantic relationship—for example, "*Sunset* is to *nightfall* as _____ is to _____." And here you would be presented with a list of four possible pairs, one of which showed the same kind of relationship: *red* is to *stoplight, bus* is to *arrival, chills* is to *fever, yawn* is to *boring.* Well, I could never think that way. I knew what the tests were asking, but I could not block out of my mind the images already created by the first pair, "*sunset* is to *nightfall*"—and I would see a burst of colors against a darkening sky, the moon rising, the lowering of a curtain of stars. And all the other pairs of words—red, bus, stoplight, boring—just threw up a mass of confusing images, making it impossible for me to sort out something as logical as saying: "A sunset precedes nightfall" is the same as "a chill precedes a fever." The only way I would have gotten that answer right would have been to imagine an associative situation, for example, my being disobedient and staying out past sunset, catching a chill at night, which turns into 17 feverish pneumonia as punishment, which indeed did happen to me.

I have been thinking about all this lately, about my mother's   18
English, about achievement tests. Because lately I've been
asked, as a writer, why there are not more Asian Americans
represented in American literature. Why are there few Asian
Americans enrolled in creative writing programs? Why do so
many Chinese students go into engineering? Well, these are
broad sociological questions I can't begin to answer. But I
have noticed in surveys—in fact, just last week—that Asian
students, as a whole, always do significantly better on math
achievement tests than in English. And this makes me think
that there are other Asian-American students whose English
spoken in the home might also be described as "broken"
or "limited." And perhaps they also have teachers who are
steering them away from writing and into math and science,
which is what happened to me.

Fortunately, I happen to be rebellious in nature and enjoy   19
the challenge of disproving assumptions made about me. I
became an English major my first year in college, after being
enrolled as pre-med. I started writing nonfiction as a free-
lancer the week after I was told by my former boss that writing was my worst skill and I should hone my talents toward
account management.

But it wasn't until 1985 that I finally began to write fic-   20
tion. And at first I wrote using what I thought to be wittily
crafted sentences, sentences that would finally prove I had
mastery over the English language. Here's an example from
the first draft of a story that later made its way into *The Joy
Luck Club,* but without this line: "That was my mental quandary in its nascent state." A terrible line, which I can barely
pronounce.

Fortunately, for reasons I won't get into today, I later   21
decided I should envision a reader for the stories I would
write. And the reader I decided upon was my mother,
because these were stories about mothers. So with this reader

in mind—and in fact she did read my early drafts—I began to write stories using all the Englishes I grew up with: the English I spoke to my mother, which for lack of a better term might be described as "simple"; the English she used with me, which for lack of a better term might be described as "broken"; my translation of her Chinese, which could certainly be described as "watered down"; and what I imagined to be her translation of her Chinese if she could speak in perfect English, her internal language, and for that I sought to preserve the essence, but neither an English nor a Chinese structure. I wanted to capture what language ability tests can never reveal: her intent, her passion, her imagery, the rhythms of her speech and the nature of her thoughts.

Apart from what any critic had to say about my writing,   22
I knew I had succeeded where it counted when my mother finished reading my book and gave me her verdict: "So easy to read."

For Study and Discussion

QUESTIONS ABOUT PURPOSE

1. In what way does Tan's title, "Mother Tongue", reveal the purpose of her essay?
2. Why do the words *fractured* and *limited* relate to Tan's reflections on thinking and speaking?

QUESTIONS ABOUT AUDIENCE

1. Who is the *you* Tan addresses throughout her essay?
2. How does Tan use quotations from her mother to help her readers understand her mother's English?

QUESTIONS ABOUT STRATEGIES

1. How does Tan use the telephone conversation with the stockbroker to distinguish between *limited* and *standard* English?
2. Why does Tan wait until the end of her essay (paragraph 21) to explain why she decides to devote her stories to her mother?

For Writing and Research

1. *Analyze* the many different types of English Tan learned from talking to her mother.
2. *Practice* by classifying the different types of English, or other languages, you use at home, at school, and among your friends.
3. *Argue* that language is more subtle and sophisticated than math as a way to measure intelligence.
4. *Synthesize:* Research the controversy about the effects of cultural and language diversity on IQ and SAT test scores. Then use this information to argue that such standardized tests do not provide a fair measure of intelligence.

Process Analysis

SERENA NANDA

Serena Nanda was educated at New York University and taught cultural anthropology at John Jay College of Criminal Justice at City University of New York. Her books include *Cultural Anthropology* (1998), *American Cultural Pluralism and Law* (1996), *Neither Man nor Woman: The Hijras of India* (1999), *Gender Diversity: Cross-Cultured Variations* (2000) and *The Gift of the Bride* (2009). Nanda's current research focuses on non-European representations of Europeans in art and performance. In "Arranging a Marriage in India," reprinted from *The Naked Anthropologist: Tales from Around the World* (1992), Nanda contrasts the Indian and American processes of getting married.

Arranging a Marriage in India[2]

Sister and doctor brother-in-law invite correspondence from North Indian professionals only, for a beautiful, talented, sophisticated, intelligent sister, 5'3", slim, M.A. in textile design, father a senior civil officer. Would prefer immigrant doctors, between 26–29 years. Reply with full details and returnable photo.

A well-settled uncle invites matrimonial correspondence from slim, fair, educated South Indian girl, for his nephew, 25 years, smart, M.B.A., green card holder, 5'6". Full particulars with returnable photo appreciated.
—*MATRIMONIAL ADVERTISEMENTS*, INDIA ABROAD

---

[2]Serena Nanda, From "Arranging a Marriage in India" by Serena Nanda. Reprinted by permission of the author.

I N INDIA, ALMOST all marriages are arranged. Even among   1
the educated middle classes in modern, urban India, marriage is as much a concern of the families as it is of the individuals. So customary is the practice of arranged marriage
that there is a special name for a marriage which is not
arranged: It is called a "love match."

On my first field trip to India, I met many young men and   2
women whose parents were in the process of "getting them
married." In many cases, the bride and groom would not
meet each other before the marriage. At most they might
meet for a brief conversation, and this meeting would take
place only after their parents had decided that the match was
suitable. Parents do not compel their children to marry a
person who either marriage partner finds objectionable. But
only after one match is refused will another be sought.

I found it difficult to accept the docile
manner in which this well-educated young
woman awaited the outcome of a process that
would result in her spending the rest of her
life with a man she hardly knew, a virtual
stranger, picked out by her parents.

As a young American woman in India for the first time,   3
I found this custom of arranged marriage oppressive. How
could any intelligent young person agree to such a marriage
without great reluctance? It was contrary to everything I
believed about the importance of romantic love as the only
basis of a happy marriage. It also clashed with my strongly
held notions that the choice of such an intimate and permanent relationship could be made only by the individuals
involved. Had anyone tried to arrange my marriage, I would
have been defiant and rebellious!

At the first opportunity, I began, with more curiosity than   4
tact, to question the young people I met on how they felt

about this practice. Sita, one of my young informants, was a college graduate with a degree in political science. She had been waiting for over a year while her parents were arranging a match for her. I found it difficult to accept the docile manner in which this well-educated young woman awaited the outcome of a process that would result in her spending the rest of her life with a man she hardly knew, a virtual stranger, picked out by her parents.

"How can you go along with this?" I asked her, in frustration and distress. "Don't you care who you marry?"

"Of course I care," she answered. "This is why I must let my parents choose a boy for me. My marriage is too important to be arranged by such an inexperienced person as myself. In such matters, it is better to have my parents' guidance."

I had learned that young men and women in India do not date and have very little social life involving members of the opposite sex. Although I could not disagree with Sita's reasoning, I continued to pursue the subject.

"But how can you marry the first man you have ever met? Not only have you missed the fun of meeting a lot of different people, but you have not given yourself the chance to know who is the right man for you."

"Meeting with a lot of different people doesn't sound like any fun at all," Sita answered. "One hears that in America the girls are spending all their time worrying about whether they will meet a man and get married. Here we have the chance to enjoy our life and let our parents do this work and worrying for us."

She had me there. The high anxiety of the competition to "be popular" with the opposite sex certainly was the most prominent feature of life as an American teenager in the late fifties. The endless worrying about the rules that governed our behavior and about our popularity ratings sapped both our self-esteem and our enjoyment of adolescence. I reflected that absence of this competition in India most certainly may have contributed to the self-confidence and natural charm of so many of the young women I met.

And yet, the idea of marrying a perfect stranger, whom one did not know and did not "love," so offended my American ideas of individualism and romanticism, that I persisted with my objections.

"I still can't imagine it," I said. "How can you agree to   12
marry a man you hardly know?"

"But of course he will be known. My parents would never   13
arrange a marriage for me without knowing all about the boy's family background. Naturally we will not rely only on what the family tells us. We will check the particulars out ourselves. No one will want their daughter to marry into a family that is not good. All these things we will know beforehand."

Impatiently, I responded, "Sita, I don't mean know the   14
family, I mean, know the man. How can you marry someone you don't know personally and don't love? How can you think of spending your life with someone you may not even like?"

"If he is a good man, why should I not like him?" she   15
said. "With you people, you know the boy so well before you marry, where will be the fun to get married? There will be no mystery and no romance. Here we have the whole of our married life to get to know and love our husband. This way is better, is it not?"

Her response made further sense, and I began to have   16
second thoughts on the matter. Indeed, during months of meeting many intelligent young Indian people, both male and female, who had the same ideas as Sita, I saw arranged marriages in a different light. I also saw the importance of the family in Indian life and realized that a couple who took their marriage into their own hands was taking a big risk, particularly if their families were irreconcilably opposed to the match. In a country where every important resource in life—a job, a house, a social circle—is gained through family connections, it seemed foolhardy to cut oneself off from a supportive social network and depend solely on one person for happiness and success.

Six years later I returned to India to again do fieldwork, this   17
time among the middle class in Bombay, a modern, sophisticated city. From the experience of my earlier visit, I decided to include a study of arranged marriages in my project. By

this time I had met many Indian couples whose marriages had been arranged and who seemed very happy. Particularly in contrast to the fate of many of my married friends in the United States who were already in the process of divorce, the positive aspects of arranged marriages appeared to me to outweigh the negatives. In fact, I thought I might even participate in arranging a marriage myself. I had been fairly successful in the United States in "fixing up" many of my friends, and I was confident that my matchmaking skills could be easily applied to this new situation, once I learned the basic rules. "After all," I thought, "how complicated can it be? People want pretty much the same things in a marriage whether it is in India or America."

An opportunity presented itself almost immediately. A 18 friend from my previous Indian trip was in the process of arranging for the marriage of her eldest son. In India there is a perceived shortage of "good boys," and since my friend's family was eminently respectable and the boy himself personable, well educated, and nice looking, I was sure that by the end of my year's fieldwork, we would have found a match.

The basic rule seems to be that a family's reputation is 19 most important. It is understood that matches would be arranged only within the same caste and general social class, although some crossing of subcastes is permissible if the class positions of the bride's and groom's families are similar. Although dowry is now prohibited by law in India, extensive gift exchanges took place with every marriage. Even when the boy's family do not "make demands," every girl's family nevertheless feels the obligation to give the traditional gifts, to the girl, to the boy, and to the boy's family. Particularly when the couple would be living in the joint family—that is, with the boy's parents and his married brothers and their families, as well as with unmarried siblings—which is still very common even among the urban, upper-middle class in India, the girl's parents are anxious to establish smooth relations between their family and that of the boy. Offering the proper gifts, even when not called "dowry," is often an important factor in influencing the relationship between the bride's and groom's families and perhaps, also, the treatment of the bride in her new home.

In a society where divorce is still a scandal and where, in [20] fact, the divorce rate is exceedingly low, an arranged marriage is the beginning of a lifetime relationship not just between the bride and groom but between their families as well. Thus, while a girl's looks are important, her character is even more so, for she is being judged as a prospective daughter-in-law as much as a prospective bride. Where she would be living in a joint family, as was the case with my friend, the girl's ability to get along harmoniously in a family is perhaps the single most important quality in assessing her suitability.

My friend is a highly esteemed wife, mother, and daughter- [21] in-law. She is religious, soft-spoken, modest, and deferential. She rarely gossips and never quarrels, two qualities highly desirable in a woman. A family that has the reputation for gossip and conflict among its womenfolk will not find it easy to get good wives for their sons. Parents will not want to send their daughter to a house in which there is conflict.

My friend's family were originally from North India. [22] They had lived in Bombay, where her husband owned a business, for forty years. The family had delayed in seeking a match for their eldest son because he had been an Air Force pilot for several years, stationed in such remote places that it had seemed fruitless to try to find a girl who would be willing to accompany him. In their social class, a military career, despite its economic security, has little prestige and is considered a drawback in finding a suitable bride. Many families would not allow their daughters to marry a man in an occupation so potentially dangerous and which requires so much moving around.

The son had recently left the military and joined his father's [23] business. Since he was a college graduate, modern, and well traveled, from such a good family, and, I thought, quite handsome, it seemed to me that he, or rather his family, was in a position to pick and choose. I said as much to my friend.

While she agreed that there were many advantages on their [24] side, she also said, "We must keep in mind that my son is both short and dark; these are drawbacks in finding the right match." While the boy's height had not escaped my notice, "dark" seemed to me inaccurate; I would have called him "wheat" colored perhaps, and in any case, I did not realize that color would be a consideration. I discovered, however, that while a boy's skin color is a less important consideration than a girl's, it is still a factor.

An important source of contacts in trying to arrange her son's marriage was my friend's social club in Bombay. Many of the women had daughters of the right age, and some had already expressed an interest in my friend's son. I was most enthusiastic about the possibilities of one particular family who had five daughters, all of whom were pretty, demure, and well educated. Their mother had told my friend, "You can have your pick for your son, whichever one of my daughters appeals to you most."

I saw a match in sight. "Surely," I said to my friend, "we will find one there. Let's go visit and make our choice." But my friend held back; she did not seem to share my enthusiasm, for reasons I could not then fathom.

When I kept pressing for an explanation of her reluctance, she admitted, "See, Serena, here is the problem. The family has so many daughters, how will they be able to provide nicely for any of them? We are not making any demands, but still, with so many daughters to marry off, one wonders whether she will even be able to make a proper wedding. Since this is our eldest son, it's best if we marry him to a girl who is the only daughter, then the wedding will truly be a gala affair." I argued that surely the quality of the girls themselves made up for any deficiency in the elaborateness of the wedding. My friend admitted this point but still seemed reluctant to proceed.

"Is there something else," I asked her, "some factor I have missed?" "Well," she finally said, "there is one other thing. They have one daughter already married and living in Bombay. The mother is always complaining to me that the girl's in-laws don't let her visit her own family often enough. So it makes me wonder, will she be that kind of mother who always wants her daughter at her own home? This will prevent the girl from adjusting to our house. It is not a good thing." And so, this family of five daughters was dropped as a possibility.

Somewhat disappointed, I nevertheless respected my   29
friend's reasoning and geared up for the next prospect. This was also the daughter of a woman in my friend's social club. There was clear interest in this family and I could see why. The family's reputation was excellent; in fact, they came from a subcaste slightly higher than my friend's own. The girl, who was an only daughter, was pretty and well educated and had a brother studying in the United States. Yet, after expressing an interest to me in this family, all talk of them suddenly died down and the search began elsewhere.

"What happened to that girl as a prospect?" I asked one   30
day. "You never mention her any more. She is so pretty and so educated, what did you find wrong?"

"She is too educated. We've decided against it. My hus-   31
band's father saw the girl on the bus the other day and thought her forward. A girl who 'roams about' the city by herself is not the girl for our family." My disappointment this time was even greater, as I thought the son would have liked the girl very much. But then I thought, my friend is right, a girl who is going to live in a joint family cannot be too independent or she will make life miserable for everyone. I also learned that if the family of the girl has even a slightly higher social status than the family of the boy, the bride may think herself too good for them, and this too will cause problems. Later my friend admitted to me that this had been an important factor in her decision not to pursue the match.

The next candidate was the daughter of a client of my   32
friend's husband. When the client learned that the family was looking for a match for their son, he said, "Look no further, we have a daughter." This man then invited my friends to dinner to see the girl. He had already seen their son at the office and decided that "he liked the boy." We all went together for tea, rather than dinner—it was less of a commitment—and while we were there, the girl's mother showed us around the house. The girl was studying for her exams and was briefly introduced to us.

After we left, I was anxious to hear my friend's opin-   33
ion. While her husband liked the family very much and was
impressed with his client's business accomplishments and
reputation, the wife didn't like the girl's looks. "She is short,
no doubt, which is an important plus point, but she is also fat
and wears glasses." My friend obviously thought she could
do better for her son and asked her husband to make his
excuses to his client by saying that they had decided to postpone the boy's marriage indefinitely.

By this time almost six months had passed and I was   34
becoming impatient. What I had thought would be an easy
matter to arrange was turning out to be quite complicated.
I began to believe that between my friend's desire for a girl
who was modest enough to fit into her joint family, yet attractive and educated enough to be an acceptable partner for her
son, she would not find anyone suitable. My friend laughed
at my impatience: "Don't be so much in a hurry," she said.
"You Americans want everything done so quickly. You get
married quickly and then just as quickly get divorced. Here
we take marriage more seriously. We must take all the factors
into account. It is not enough for us to learn by our mistakes.
This is too serious a business. If a mistake is made we have
not only ruined the life of our son or daughter, but we have
spoiled the reputation of our family as well. And that will
make it much harder for their brothers and sisters to get married. So we must be very careful."

What she said was true and I promised myself to be more   35
patient, though it was not easy. I had really hoped and
expected that the match would be made before my year in
India was up. But it was not to be. When I left India my
friend seemed no further along in finding a suitable match for
her son than when I had arrived.

Two years later, I returned to India and still my friend had   36
not found a girl for her son. By this time, he was close to
thirty, and I think she was a little worried. Since she knew I
had friends all over India, and I was going to be there for a
year, she asked me to "help her in this work" and keep an eye
out for someone suitable. I was flattered that my judgment

was respected, but knowing now how complicated the process was, I had lost my earlier confidence as a matchmaker. Nevertheless, I promised that I would try.

It was almost at the end of my year's stay in India that I met a family with a marriageable daughter whom I felt might be a good possibility for my friend's son. The girl's father was related to a good friend of mine and by coincidence came from the same village as my friend's husband. This new family had a successful business in a medium-sized city in central India and were from the same subcaste as my friend. The daughter was pretty and chic; in fact, she had studied fashion design in college. Her parents would not allow her to go off by herself to any of the major cities in India where she could make a career, but they had compromised with her wish to work by allowing her to run a small dressmaking boutique from their home. In spite of her desire to have a career, the daughter was both modest and home-loving and had had a traditional, sheltered upbringing. She had only one other sister, already married, and a brother who was in his father's business.

I mentioned the possibility of a match with my friend's son. The girl's parents were most interested. Although their daughter was not eager to marry just yet, the idea of living in Bombay—a sophisticated, extremely fashion-conscious city where she could continue her education in clothing design— was a great inducement. I gave the girl's father my friend's address and suggested that when they went to Bombay on some business or whatever, they look up the boy's family.

Returning to Bombay on my way to New York, I told my friend of this newly discovered possibility. She seemed to feel there was potential but, in spite of my urging, would not make any moves herself. She rather preferred to wait for the girl's family to call upon them. I hoped something would come of this introduction, though by now I had learned to rein in my optimism.

A year later I received a letter from my friend. The family had indeed come to visit Bombay, and their daughter and my friend's daughter, who were near in age, had become very good friends. During that year, the two girls had frequently visited each other. I thought things looked promising.

Last week I received an invitation to a wedding: My 41
friend's son and the girl were getting married. Since I had
found the match, my presence was particularly requested at
the wedding. I was thrilled. Success at last! As I prepared to
leave for India, I began thinking, "Now, my friend's younger
son, who do I know who has a nice girl for him. . . ?"

FURTHER REFLECTIONS ON ARRANGED MARRIAGE

The previous essay was written from the point of view of a
family seeking a daughter-in-law. Arranged marriage looks
somewhat different from the point of view of the bride and
her family. Arranged marriage continues to be preferred, even
among the more educated, Westernized sections of the Indian
population. Many young women from these families still go
along, more or less willingly, with the practice, and also with
the specific choices of their families. Young women do get
excited about the prospects of their marriage, but there is also
ambivalence and increasing uncertainty, as the bride contem-
plates leaving the comfort and familiarity of her own home,
where as a "temporary guest" she has often been indulged,
to live among strangers. Even in the best situation, she will
now come under the close scrutiny of her husband's family.
How she dresses, how she behaves, how she gets along with
others, where she goes, how she spends her time, her domestic abilities—all of this and much more will be observed and
commented on by a whole new set of relations. Her interaction with her family of birth will be monitored and curtailed
considerably. Not only will she leave their home, but with
increasing geographic mobility, she may also live very far from
them, perhaps even on another continent. Too much expression of her fondness for her own family, or her desire to visit
them, may be interpreted as an inability to adjust to her new
family, and may become a source of conflict. In an arranged
marriage, the burden of adjustment is clearly heavier for a
woman than for a man. And that is in the best of situations.

In less happy circumstances, the bride may be a target of resentment and hostility from her husband's family,

particularly her mother-in-law or her husband's unmarried sisters, for whom she is now a source of competition for the affection, loyalty, and economic resources of a son or brother. If she is psychologically or even physically abused, her options are limited, as returning to her parents' home or getting a divorce is still very stigmatized. For most Indians, marriage and motherhood are still considered the only suitable roles for a woman, even for those who have careers, and few women can comfortably contemplate remaining unmarried. Most families still consider "marrying off" their daughters as a compelling religious duty and social necessity. This increases a bride's sense of obligation to make the marriage a success, at whatever cost to her own personal happiness.

The vulnerability of a new bride may also be intensified by the issue of dowry that, although illegal, has become a more pressing issue in the consumer-conscious society of contemporary urban India. In many cases, where a groom's family is not satisfied with the amount of dowry a bride brings to her marriage, the young bride will be harassed constantly to get her parents to give more. In extreme cases, the bride may even be murdered and the murder disguised as an accident or a suicide. This also offers the husband's family an opportunity to arrange another match for him, thus bringing in another dowry. This phenomenon, called "dowry death," calls attention not just to the "evils of dowry" but also to larger issues of the powerlessness of women as well.

For Study and Discussion

QUESTIONS ABOUT PURPOSE

1. How does Nanda's conversation with Sita help her illustrate her thesis that in India marriage is a family, not an individual decision?
2. How does Sita's criticism of American marriages help Nanda clarify her purpose?

QUESTIONS ABOUT AUDIENCE

1. In what ways does Nanda address her essay to American rather than Indian readers?
2. How does Nanda serve as a substitute for her readers? For example, how does she, and thus her readers, learn about the criteria for a good marriage?

QUESTIONS ABOUT STRATEGIES

1. How does Nanda use the example of the family with five daughters to illustrate the importance of social caste and financial status in Indian marriages?
2. How does she use the example of the well-educated girl to illustrate the importance of finding a good daughter-in-law—as opposed to a good wife?

For Writing and Research

1. *Analyze* how Nanda uses issues such as "dowry death" to present the arranged marriage from the point of view of the bride and her family.
2. *Practice* by describing your experiences on a blind date or arranging a blind date for friends.
3. *Argue* that "love matches" are better than "arranged marriages."
4. *Synthesize:* Research the divorce rate in American culture. See Anne Roiphe's "A Tale of Two Divorces" on pages 490 to 499. Reply to Roiphe's assertion that "We are the only animal species that cannot seem to figure out how to pair off and raise children without maiming ourselves in the process."

ANNE ROIPHE

Anne Roiphe was born in New York City in 1935 and was educated at Sarah Lawrence College. Perhaps best known for the novel *Up the Sandbox!* (1970), her works explore a woman's search for identity in the wake of marriage and divorce in some of her fiction—*The Pursuit of Happiness* (1991)—and nonfiction—*Generation Without Memory: A Jewish Journey in Christian America* (1981), *A Season for Healing: Reflections on the Holocaust* (1988), *1185 Park Avenue: A Memoir* (1999), and *An Imperfect Lens* (2006). Roiphe's 1996 memoir *Fruitful: Living the Contradictions: A Memoir of Modern Motherhood* was nominated for the National Book Award. Her memoir *Epilogue* was published in 2008, and another memoir, *Art and Madness*, in 2011. Roiphe explores the special issues confronted by Jewish women in "A Tale of Two Divorces," reprinted from *Women on Divorce* (1995), where she compares two marriages, one that should have ended in divorce and one that did.

A Tale of Two Divorces[3]

E VERY DIVORCE IS a story, and while they can begin to   1
sound the same—sad and cautionary—each one is as unique as a human face. My divorce is the tale of two divorces, one that never was and one that was. The first is the story of my parents' marriage.

[3]Anne Roiphe, Reprinted by permission of International Creative Management, Inc. Copyright © 1995 by Anne Roiphe.

IMAGES
OF
THE FAMILY
A VISUAL ESSAY

PHOTO 1

Norman Rockwell's *Freedom from Want* (1943) depicts a nostalgic view of the traditional extended family. Research other Rockwell illustrations of the family. Then write an essay using some of these illustrations to argue that Rockwell's view of the family was an accurate portrait or a sentimental distortion. Additional source: consult Barbara Kingsolver's "Stone Soup."

PHOTO 2

This photo features the cast from the ABC television series *Modern Family*. Research the three different families depicted in this illustration and in the televisions series. Then explain how these families change the traditional definition of family. Additional source: consult Howard Moody's "Sacred Rite or Civil Right?"

PHOTO 3

This photograph presents the First Family in an informal pose. What are they doing? How are they dressed? Research photographs of other First Families. Then analyze why this photograph has changed or enriched the way we think about the First Family. Additional Source: consult Jane Howard's "In Search of the Good Family."

PHOTO 4

This photograph portrays a mother and a daughter in a friendly domestic scene. Research the status of single-parent families. Then argue that single-parent families represent a problem or just another variation in our culture. Additional sources: consult Anne Roiphe's "A Tale of Two Divorces" or Barbara Dafoe Whitehead's "Women and the Future of Fatherhood."

PHOTO 5

This photograph illustrates three generations of a family examining a family photo
album or scrapbook. Using this photo as
a source, explain why it is important that
the members of each generation in a family
understand its history and heritage. Additional sources: consult Alex Haley's "My
Furthest Back Person—'The African,'" Serena
Nanda's "Arranging a Marriage in India," or
Alice Walker's "Everyday Use."

PHOTO 6

This photograph demonstrates the impact of technology on family life. Research the number of technological devices purchased by the average American family. Then explain how this picture illustrates the way these devices have changed or erased the traditional roles in a family. Additional source: consult Jane Howard's "In Search of a Good Family."

PHOTO 7

This photograph illustrates how addiction—
in this case, alcohol can lead to domestic
violence. Research the policies and procedures of organizations such as Alcoholics
Anonymous or A Better Way. Then write
an essay explaining how such organizations
attempt to reduce the causes and effects
of domestic violence. Additional source:
consult Scott Russell Sanders's "Under the
Influence."

PHOTO 8

Ariel Skelly's photograph presents the image of a soldier who, after surviving battle, has returned home to his extended family. Research how extended absences—such as war or illness—can change the relationships of among family members. Then write an essay explaining how such experiences may change the character of family reunions. Additional source: Alice Walker's "Everyday Use."

My mother was the late fifth child, raised in a large house   2
on Riverside Drive in New York City. Her father, who came
to America as a boy from a town outside of Suvalki, Poland,
had piled shirts on a pushcart and wandered the streets of the
Lower East Side in the 1880s. His pushcart turned into a loft
with twenty women sewing shirts for him and before he was
twenty-five he owned a small company called Van Heusen
Shirts. He was one of the founding members of Beth Israel
Hospital and I have a photo of him, shovel in hand, black hat
on his head, as the foundation stone is placed in the ground.

My mother grew up, small, plump, nervous, fearful of   3
horses, dogs, cats, cars, water, balls that were hit over nets,
tunnels, and bridges. She was expected to marry brilliantly
into the world of manufacturers of coats, shoes, gowns, store
owners, prosperous bankers whose sons attended the dozens
of teas and charity events where she—always afraid her hair
was wrong, her conversation dull, her dress wrinkled—tried

---

*In twentieth-century America we place so
much emphasis on romance that we barely
notice the other essentials of marriage that
include economics and child rearing.*

---

to obey the instructions of her older sister and sparkle. A girl
after all had to sparkle. She was under five feet. She was near-
sighted. Without her thick glasses she stumbled, recognized
no one, groped the wall for comfort. Her lipstick tended to
smear. She chain-smoked. She lost things. She daydreamed.
Her father died of a sudden heart attack when she was just
thirteen. Her older sisters married millionaires, her brothers
inherited the business. She was herself considered an heiress,
a dangerous state for a tremulous girl, whose soul was perpetually fogged in uncertainty.

At a Z.B.T. Columbia University fraternity party she   4
met my father. He was the Hungarian-born son of a drug

salesman who bet the horses and believed that he had missed his grander destiny. My paternal grandfather was never able to move his family out from the railroad flat under the Third Avenue El. His wife, my grandmother, was a statuesque woman, taller than her husband but overwhelmed by noise, the turmoil of her American days. She never learned English. She stayed home in her nightgown and slippers, sleeping long hours. My father was in law school. He was tall and handsome with black hair slicked down like Valentino and cold eyes set perfectly in an even face. He was an athlete who had earned his college expenses by working summers as a lifeguard in the Catskills. His shoes were perfectly polished. His white shirt gleamed. He loathed poverty. He claimed to speak no other language than English though he had arrived in America at age nine. He told my mother he loved her. Despite the warnings of her siblings, she believed him. If she was not his dream girl, she was his American dream. They went on their honeymoon to Europe and purchased fine china and linen at every stop.

My father became a lawyer for the family shirt company. He was 5 edgy, prone to yell at others; he ground his teeth. He suffered from migraines. He could tolerate nothing out of place, nothing that wasn't spotless. He joined a club where men played squash, steamed in the sauna, and drank at the bar. He stayed long hours at his club. He told his wife she was unbeautiful. She believed him although the pictures of her at the time tell a different story. They show a young woman with soft amused eyes and a long neck, with a shy smile and a brave tilt of the head. My father explained to my mother that he could never admire a short woman, that long legs were the essence of glamour.

My father began to have other ladies. He would meet them 6 under the clock at the Biltmore, at motels in Westchester. He had ice in his heart, but he looked good in his undershirt. He looked good in his monogrammed shirts. He lost his nonfamily clients. They didn't like his temper, his impatience. It didn't matter. He took up golf and was gone all day Saturday and Sunday in the good weather. He made investments in the stock market. He had a genius for bad bets. My mother made up the heavy losses. She had two children and she lived just as she was expected to do, with servants to take care of the details, to wake with the babies, to prepare the food, to mop the floors. She spent her days playing cards and shopping. She went to the hairdresser two, sometimes three times a week. A lady came to the house to wax her legs and do her long red nails. She had ulcers, anxiety attacks, panic attacks. In the evening at about five o'clock she would begin to wait for my father to come home. She could do the crossword puzzle in five minutes. She was a genius at canasta, Oklahoma, bridge, backgammon. She joined a book club. She loved the theater and invested cleverly in Broadway shows. She took lessons in French and flower arranging.

At the dinner table, as the food was being served, my father 7 would comment that he didn't like the way my mother wore the barrette in her hair. She would say bitterly that he never liked anything she wore. He would say that she was stupid. She would say that she was not. Their voices would carry. In the kitchen the maid would clutch the side of the sink until her fingernails were white. My mother would weep. My father would storm out of the house, slamming doors, knocking over lamps. She would shout after him, "You don't love me." He would scream at her, "Who could love you?" She would lie in bed with ice cubes on her swollen eyes, chain-smoking Camel cigarettes. She would call her sister for comfort. Her sister would say, "Don't give him an argument." She would say, "I'll try to do better, I really will."

When I was seven years old, she lay in the bathtub soak- 8 ing and I was sitting on the rim keeping her company. "I could divorce him," she said. "I could do it." Her eyes were puffed. I felt a surge of electricity run through me, adrenaline flowed. "Leave him?" I asked. "Yes," she said. "Should I?" she asked me. "Should I leave him? Would you mind?" I was her friend, her confidante. I did not yet know enough of the world to answer the question. I thought of my home split apart. I thought my father would never see me again. I wondered what I would tell my friends. No one I knew had parents who were divorced. I was afraid. "Who will take care of us?" I asked. My mother let the ashes of her cigarette fall into the tub. "God!" she said. "Help me," she said. But she'd asked the wrong person.

Then she did a brave thing. She went to a psychiatrist. 9 I would wait for her downstairs in the lobby. She would emerge from the elevator after her appointment with her mascara smeared over her cheeks. "When I'm stronger," she said, "I'll leave him." But the years went on. He said she was demanding. He said, "I spend enough time with you. Go to Florida with your sister. Go to Maine with your brother. Stop asking me to talk to you. I've already said everything I want to say." She said, "I need you to admire me. I need you to say you love me." "I do," he said, but then they had a party and I found him in the coat closet with a lady and lipstick all over his face.

He talked about politics. He read history books. He hit 10 on the chin a man who disagreed with him. He yelled at my mother that she had no right to an opinion on anything. He said, "Women with opinions smell like skunks." She said, "He's so smart. He knows so much." She said, "If I leave him no other man will marry me." She said, "I can't leave him."

Week after week, she would say something that irritated 11 him. He would make her cry and then he would scream at her for crying. His screams were howls. If you listened to the sound you would think an animal was trapped and in pain. Dinner after dinner my brother and I would silently try to eat our food as the same old fight began again, built and reached its crescendo.

Finally I was old enough. "Leave him," I said. "I don't 12 know," she said, "maybe." But she couldn't and she wouldn't and the dance between them had turned into a marathon. She quit first. She died at age fifty-two, still married, still thinking, if only I had been taller, different, better. He inherited her money and immediately wed a tall woman, with whom he had been having an affair for many years, whose hands shook when she spoke to him. He called her: "That stupid dame."

"That dumb broad," he would say. He went off to his club. He went for long walks. He had migraines.

This was a story of a divorce that should have been. 13

When I was twenty-seven I found myself checking into a flea- 14 bag hotel in Juárez. My three-year-old daughter was trying to pull the corncob out of the parrot cage and the parrot was try- ing to bite her fingers. I was there, my room squeezed between those of the local drunks and prostitutes, to get a divorce. This was a divorce that should have been and was. I had married a man whom I thought was just the opposite of my father. He was a playwright, a philosopher. He was from an old southern family. He talked to me all the time and let me read and type his manuscripts. I worked as a receptionist to support him. Our friends were poets and painters, beatniks and their group- ies. I had escaped my mother's home or so I thought. What I didn't notice was that my husband was handsome and thought me plain, that my husband was poor and thought me a meal ticket, that my husband—like my father—was dwarfed of spirit and couldn't imagine another soul beside himself. What I didn't know was that I—like my mother—had no faith, no confidence, no sense that I could fly too. I could even write.

My husband had other women and I thought it was an 15 artist's privilege. My husband said, "If Elizabeth Taylor is a woman, then you must be a hamster." I laughed. My hus- band went on binges and used up all our money. I thought it was poetic although I was always frightened; bill collectors called. I was always apologizing. We didn't fight so I thought I had achieved matrimonial heaven, a place where of course certain compromises were necessary.

Then after I had a child I thought of love as oxygen and 16 I felt faint. In the middle of the night when I was nursing the baby and my husband was out at the local bar I discov- ered that loneliness was the name of my condition. I noticed that my husband could not hold his child because he was either too drunk, out of the house, closed into his head, or consumed with nervousness about the applause the outside world was giving or withholding from him. I discovered that

I had married a man more like my father than not and that, more like my mother than not, I had become a creature to be pitied. Like moth to flame I was drawn to repeat. My divorce was related to her undivorce, so the generations unfold back to back handing on their burdens—by contamination, memory, experience, identification, one's failure becomes the other's. The courage it takes to really make things better, to change, is rare and won only at great cost. Yes, we are responsible for ourselves, but nevertheless our family stories course and curse through our veins: our memories are not free.

If my mother had been brave enough to go it alone I might   17
have seen myself differently. I might have been brave enough to let myself be loved the first time around. At least I didn't wait for my entire life to pass before leaping up and away. So this is why I listen with tongue in cheek to all the terrible tales of what divorce has done to the American family. I know that if my mother had left my father not only her life but mine too might have been set on more solid ground. I know that if I had stayed in my marriage my child would have lived forever in the shadow of my perpetual grief and thought of herself as I had, unworthy of the ordinary moments of affection and connection.

In twentieth-century America we place so much emphasis on   18
romance that we barely notice the other essentials of marriage that include economics and child rearing. My mother was undone by the economic equation in her marriage. Money, which we know to be a part of the bitterness of divorce, is in there from the beginning, a thread in the cloak of love, whether we like it or not.

History clunking through our private lives certainly   19
affected my mother's marriage and my bad marriage. Woman's proper role, woman's masochistic stance, immigration, push to rise in social status, the confusion of money damned my mother to a lifetime of tears and almost caught me there too. But history is always present without our always being able to name its nasty work.

The women's movement, which came too late for my   20
mother, sent some women off adventure bound, free of suburb, unwilling to be sole caretakers to find, at the end of

their rainbow isolation, disappointment, bitterness. The sexual revolution, which soon after burned like a laser through our towns and sent wives running in circles in search of multiple pleasures, freedom from convention, and distance from the burdens of domesticity, was a balloon that popped long before the arrival of AIDS. We found we were not, after all, in need of the perfect orgasm. We were in need of a body to spoon with in bed, a story we could tell together as well as sexual equality.

But there is more. Divorce is also the terrible knife that rends family asunder, and for the children it can be the tilting, defining moment that marks them ever after, walking wounded, angry, sad souls akimbo, always prone to being lost in a forest of despair. They can be tough, too tough. They can be helpless, too helpless. They can never trust. They can be too trusting. They can accept a stepparent for a while and then revoke their acceptance. They can protest the stepparent for a while and then change their mind, but either way their own parents' divorce hangs over them, threat, reminder, betrayal always possible. My stepdaughter, now a married woman and a mother herself, speaks of her own parents' breakup, which came when she was only seven, as the most terrible moment in her life. As she says this I have only to listen to the tightness in her voice, watch the slight tremble in her hand to know that the divorce seemed to her like an earthquake. The divorce caused a before and after and everything after is tarnished, diminished by what went before.

I wish this were not so. I wish that we could marry a new mate, repair, go on to undo the worst of our mistakes without leaving ugly deep scars across our children's psyches, but we can't. And furthermore the children will never completely forgive us, never understand how our backs were against the wall: They may try to understand our broken vows but they don't. Of course there are other things our children don't forgive us for. If we die, if we withdraw, if we let ourselves drown in misery, addictions, if we fail at work or lose our courage in the face of economic or other adversity, that too will eat at their hearts and spoil their chances for the gold ring on life's carousel. There are, in other words, many ways to damage children, and divorce is only the most effective and perhaps most common of them.

For a while, in the seventies, divorce was everywhere, a   23 panacea for the heart burdened. We were too excited by the prospects of freedom to see the damage that was done. The wounds are very severe for both partners and children. It may be worth it as it would have been for my mother. It may be necessary, but divorce is never nice. I felt as if the skin had been stripped from my body the first months after my divorce, and I was only twenty-seven years old. I felt as if I had to learn anew how to walk in the streets, how to set my face, how to plot a direction, how to love. I had to admit to failure, take back my proud words, let others help me. It was a relief, but it was a disaster. I had lost confidence in my decisions. It took a long while to gain back what I had lost. I understand why my mother did not have the strength to do it, although she should have.

I cannot imagine a world in which divorce would not   24 sometimes occur. Men and women will always fail each other, miss each others' gestures, change in fatally different ways. There are men who cannot love, who abuse their wives or themselves or some substance. There are women who do the same. There are some disasters that wreck a marriage, a sick or damaged child, an economic calamity, a professional failure. There are marriages that are simply asphyxiated by daily life.

But I can imagine a world in which divorce would be rare,   25 in which the madness, meanness, mess of everyday life were absorbed and managed without social cataclysm. It is per-haps our American obsession with the romantic that leads to so much trouble. If we were able to see marriage as largely an economic, child-rearing institution, as a social encounter involving ambition, class, money, we might be better off. Never mind our very up-to-date goals of personal fitness and fulfillment; we are still characters, all of us, in a nineteenth-century novel.

At the moment, now that my children are of marriageable   26 age I have become a believer in the arranged betrothal. Such marriages could not possibly cause more mischief than those that were created by our free will rushing about in heavy traffic with its eyes closed. Perhaps we should consider love as a product of marriage instead of the other way around. Of course those societies that arrange marriages have other tragic stories of bride burning, lifelong miserable submission experienced by women, sexual nightmares, poor young girls and dirty old men. We are the only animal species that cannot seem to figure out how to pair off and raise children without maiming ourselves in the process.

We can bemoan the social disorder caused by divorce until 27 the moon turns to cream cheese, but we are such fragile souls, so easily cast adrift, wounded, set upon by devils of our own making, that no matter how we twist or turn, no system will protect us from the worst. There is cruelty in divorce. There is cruelty in forced or unfortunate marriage. We will continue to cry at weddings because we know how bittersweet, how fragile is the troth. We will always need legal divorce just as an emergency escape hatch is crucial in every submarine. No sense, however, in denying that after every divorce someone will be running like a cat, tin cans tied to its tail: spooked and slowed down.

For Study and Discussion

QUESTIONS ABOUT PURPOSE

1. In what ways does Roiphe's sentence "My divorce is the tale of two divorces, one that never was and one that was" state the purpose of the essay?
2. How do her stories demonstrate her thesis that marriage requires more than romance?

QUESTIONS ABOUT AUDIENCE

1. How does Roiphe's assertion that all divorce stories sound the same, yet each is as "unique as a human face," help her identify her audience?
2. These two tales focus on women. How does Roiphe anticipate the responses of her male readers?

QUESTIONS ABOUT STRATEGIES

1. How does Roiphe balance her two stories to demonstrate that although they seem different, her husband was like her father and she was like her mother?
2. How does Roiphe use her stepdaughter's experience to make a transition to the final part of her essay?

For Writing and Research

1. *Analyze* what Roiphe means when she says we will always need divorce as an "emergency escape hatch."
2. *Practice* by comparing how your friends or members of your family have reacted to a divorce.
3. *Argue* that divorce is a failure or a liberation. Compare the stories of couples that might support either argument.
4. *Synthesize:* Research the impact the women's movement has had on a divorce. Then use this information to argue that the movement has improved or impaired the quality of marriage in our country.

Division and Classification

JANE HOWARD

Jane Howard (1935–1996) was born in Spring-
field, Illinois, and was educated at the University of
Michigan. Curious about why people do what they
do, Howard specialized in writing profiles of writers such as Truman Capote and John Updike for
magazines such as *Life* and *Smithsonian.* Her books
include *Please Touch: A Guided Tour of the Human
Potential Movement* (1970), *A Different Woman*
(1973), *Families* (1978), and *Margaret Mead: A Life*
(1984). "In Search of the Good Family," adapted
for the *Atlantic Monthly* from *Families,* classifies the
different roles that are characteristic of a good family.

In Search of the Good Family[4]

C ALL IT A clan, call it a network, call it a tribe, call it a   1
family. Whatever you call it, whoever you are, you need
one. You need one because you are human. You didn't come
from nowhere. Before you, around you, and presumably after
you, too, there are others. Some of these others must matter
a lot—to you, and if you are very lucky, to one another. Their
welfare must be nearly as important to you as your own. Even
if you live alone, even if your solitude is elected and ebullient,
you still cannot do without a clan or tribe.

---

*Good families are fortresses with many
windows and doors to the outer world.*

---

[4] Jane Howard, Used with permission of University Press of America, from
"In Search of the Good Family." From *Families* by Jane Howard, 1978;
permission conveyed through Copyright Clearance Center, Inc.

The trouble with the clans and tribes many of us were   2
born into is not that they consist of meddlesome ogres but
that they are too far away. In emergencies we rush across
continents and if need be oceans to their sides, as they do
to ours. Maybe we even make a habit of seeing them, once
or twice a year, for the sheer pleasure of it. But blood ties
seldom dictate our addresses. Our blood kin are often too
remote to ease us from our Tuesdays to our Wednesdays.
For this we must rely on our families of friends. If our relatives are not, do not wish to be, or for whatever reasons
cannot be our friends, then by some complex alchemy we
must try to transform our friends into our relatives. If blood
and roots don't do the job, then we must look to water and
branches, and sort ourselves into new constellations, new
families.

These new families, to borrow the terminology of an   3
African tribe (the Bangwa of the Cameroons), may consist
either of friends of the road, ascribed by chance, or friends of
the heart, achieved by choice. Ascribed friends are those we
happen to go to school with, work with, or live near. They
know where we went last weekend and whether we still have
a cold. Just being around gives them a provisional importance in our lives, and us in theirs. Maybe they will still matter
to us when we or they move away; quite likely they won't. Six
months or two years will probably erase us from each other's
thoughts, unless by some chance they and we have become
friends of the heart.

Wishing to be friends, as Aristotle wrote, is quick work,   4
but friendship is a slowly ripening fruit. An ancient proverb
he quotes in his *Ethics* had it that you cannot know a man
until you and he together have eaten a peck of salt. Now a
peck, a quarter of a bushel, is quite a lot of salt—more, perhaps, than most pairs of people ever have occasion to share.
We must try though. We must sit together at as many tables
as we can. We must steer each other through enough seasons
and weather so that sooner or later it crosses our minds that
one of us, God knows which or with what sorrow, must one
day mourn the other.

We must devise new ways, or revive old ones, to equip 5
ourselves with kinfolk. Maybe such an impulse prompted
whoever ordered the cake I saw in my neighborhood bakery
to have it frosted to say "Happy Birthday Surrogate." I like
to think that this cake was decorated not for a judge but for
someone's surrogate mother or surrogate brother: loathsome
jargon, but admirable sentiment. If you didn't conceive me
or if we didn't grow up in the same house, we can still be
related, if we decide we ought to be. It is never too late, I like
to hope, to augment our families in ways nature neglected to
do. It is never too late to choose new clans.

The best-chosen clans, like the best friendships and the 6
best blood families, endure by accumulating a history solid
enough to suggest a future. But clans that don't last have
merit too. We can lament them but we shouldn't deride
them. Better an ephemeral clan or tribe than none at all. A
few of my life's most tribally joyous times, in fact, have been
spent with people whom I have yet to see again. This saddens
me, as it may them too, but dwelling overlong on such sadness does no good. A more fertile exercise is to think back
on those times and try to figure out what made them, for all
their brevity, so stirring. What can such times teach us about
forming new and more lasting tribes in the future?

New tribes and clans can no more be willed into existence, 7
of course, than any other good thing can. We keep trying,
though. To try, with gritted teeth and girded loins, is after
all American. That is what the two Helens and I were talking
about the day we had lunch in a room way up in a high-rise
motel near the Kansas City airport. We had lunch there at
the end of a two-day conference on families. The two Helens
were social scientists, but I liked them even so, among other
reasons because they both objected to that motel's coffee
shop even more than I did. One of the Helens, from Virginia,
disliked it so much that she had brought along homemade
whole wheat bread, sesame butter, and honey from her parents' farm in South Dakota, where she had visited before the
conference. Her picnic was the best thing that happened, to
me at least, those whole two days.

"If you're voluntarily childless and alone," said the other 8 Helen, who was from Pennsylvania by way of Puerto Rico, "it gets harder and harder with the passage of time. It's stressful. That's why you need support systems." I had been hearing quite a bit of talk about "support systems." The term is not among my favorites, but I can understand its currency. Whatever "support systems" may be the need for them is clearly urgent, and not just in this country. Are there not thriving "mega-families" of as many as three hundred people in Scandinavia? Have not the Japanese for years had an honored, enduring—if perhaps by our standards rather rigid—custom of adopting nonrelatives to fill gaps in their families? Should we not applaud and maybe imitate such ingenuity?

And consider our own Unitarians. From Santa Barbara to 9 Boston they have been earnestly dividing their congregations into arbitrary "extended families" whose members are bound to act like each other's relatives. Kurt Vonnegut, Jr. plays with a similar train of thought in his fictional *Slapstick*. In that book every newborn baby is assigned a randomly chosen middle name, like Uranium or Daffodil or Raspberry. These middle names are connected with hyphens to numbers between one and twenty, and any two people who have the same middle name are automatically related. This is all to the good, the author thinks, because "human beings need all the relatives they can get—as possible donors or receivers not of love but of common decency." He envisions these extended families as "one of the four greatest inventions by Americans," the others being *Robert's Rules of Order*, the Bill of Rights, and the principles of Alcoholics Anonymous.

This charming notion might even work, if it weren't so 10 arbitrary. Already each of us is born into one family not of our choosing. If we're going to devise new ones, we might as well have the luxury of picking the members ourselves. Clever picking might result in new families whose benefits would surpass or at least equal those of the old. As a member in reasonable standing of six or seven tribes in addition to the one I was born to, I have been trying to figure which characteristics are common to both kinds of families.

1. Good families have a chief, or a heroine, or a founder— 11
someone around whom others cluster, whose achievements, as the Yiddish word has it, let them *kvell*, and
whose example spurs them on to like feats. Some blood
dynasties produce such figures regularly; others languish
for as many as five generations between demigods, wondering with each new pregnancy whether this, at last,
might be the messianic baby who will redeem them. Look,
is there not something gubernatorial about her footstep,
or musical about the way he bangs with his spoon on his
cup? All clans, of all kinds, need such a figure now and
then. Sometimes clans based on water rather than blood
harbor several such personages at one time.

2. Good families have a switchboard operator—someone 12
who cannot help but keep track of what all the others are
up to, who plays Houston Mission Control to everyone
else's Apollo. This role is assumed rather than assigned.
The person who volunteers for it often has the instincts
of an archivist, and feels driven to keep scrapbooks and
photograph albums up to date, so that the clan can see
proof of its own continuity.

3. Good families are much to all their members, but every- 13
thing to none. Good families are fortresses with many
windows and doors to the outer world. The blood clans
I feel most drawn to were founded by parents who are
nearly as devoted to what they do outside as they are to
each other and their children. Their curiosity and passion are contagious. Everybody, where they live, is busy.
Paint is spattered on eyeglasses. Mud lurks under fingernails. Person-to-person calls come in the middle of the
night from Tokyo and Brussels. Catcher's mitts, ballet
slippers, overdue library books, and other signs of extra-
familial concerns are everywhere.

4. Good families are hospitable. Knowing that hosts need 14
guests as much as guests need hosts, they are generous
with honorary memberships for friends, whom they urge
to come early and often and to stay late. Such clans exude
a vivid sense of surrounding rings of relatives, neighbors,

teachers, students, and godparents, any of whom at any time might break or slide into the inner circle. Inside that circle a wholesome, tacit emotional feudalism develops: you give me protection, I'll give you fealty. Such pacts begin with, but soon go far beyond, the jolly exchange of pie at Thanksgiving or cake on a birthday. They mean that you can ask me to supervise your children for the fortnight you will be in the hospital, and that however inconvenient this might be for me, I shall manage to do so. It means I can phone you on what for me is a dreary, wretched Sunday afternoon and for you is the eve of a deadline, knowing you will tell me to come right over, if only to watch you type. It means we need not dissemble. ("To yield to seeming," as Martin Buber wrote, "is man's essential cowardice, to resist it is his essential courage . . . one must at times pay dearly for life lived from the being, but it is never too dear.")

5. Good families deal squarely with direness. Pity the tribe 15 that doesn't have, and cherish, at least one flamboyant eccentric. Pity too the one that supposes it can avoid for long the woes to which all flesh is heir. Lunacy, bankruptcy, suicide, and other unthinkable fates sooner or later afflict the noblest of clans with an undertow of gloom. Family life is a set of givens, someone once told me, and it takes courage to see certain givens as blessings rather than as curses. It surely does. Contradictions and inconsistencies are givens, too. So is the battle against what the Oregon patriarch Kenneth Babbs calls malarkey. "There's always malarkey lurking, bubbles in the cesspool, fetid bubbles that pop and smell. But I don't put up with malarkey, between my stepkids and my natural ones or anywhere else in the family."

6. Good families prize their rituals. Nothing welds a family 16 more than these. Rituals are vital especially for clans without histories, because they evoke a past, imply a future, and hint at continuity. No line in the seder service at Passover reassures more than the last: "Next year in Jerusalem!" A clan becomes more of a clan each time it gathers to

observe a fixed ritual (Christmas, birthdays, Thanksgiving, and so on), grieves at a funeral (anyone may come to most funerals; those who do declare their tribalness), and devises a new rite of its own. Equinox breakfasts can be at least as welding as Memorial Day parades. Several of my colleagues and I used to meet for lunch every Pearl Harbor Day, preferably to eat some politically neutral fare like smorgasbord, to "forgive" our only ancestrally Japanese friend, Irene Kubota Neves. For that and other things we became, and remain, a sort of family. . . .

7. Good families are affectionate. This of course is a matter 17
of style. I know clans whose members greet each other with gingerly handshakes or, in what pass for kisses, with hurried brushes of jawbones, as if the object were to touch not the lips but the ears. I don't see how such people manage. "The tribe that does not hug," as someone who has been part of many ad hoc families recently wrote to me, "is no tribe at all. More and more I realize that everybody, regardless of age, needs to be hugged and comforted in a brotherly or sisterly way now and then. Preferably now."

8. Good families have a sense of place, which these days is 18
not achieved easily. As Susanne Langer wrote in 1957, "Most people have no home that is a symbol of their childhood, not even a definite memory of one place to serve that purpose . . . all the old symbols are gone." Once I asked a roomful of supper guests if anyone felt a strong pull to any certain spot on the face of the earth. Everyone was silent, except for a visitor from Bavaria. The rest of us seemed to know all too well what Walker Percy means in *The Moviegoer* when he tells of the "genie-soul of a place, which every place has or else is not a place [and which] wherever you go, you must meet and master or else be met and mastered." All that meeting and mastering saps plenty of strength. It also underscores our need for tribal bases of the sort which soaring real estate taxes and splintering families have made all but obsolete.

So what are we to do, those of us whose habit and 19
pleasure and doom is our tendency, as a Georgia lady put

it, to "fly off at every other whipstitch"? Think in terms of movable feasts, that's what. Live here, wherever here may be, as if we were going to belong here for the rest of our lives. Learn to hallow whatever ground we happen to stand on or land on. Like medieval knights who took their tapestries along on Crusades, like modern Afghanis with their yurts, we must pack such totems and icons as we can to make short-term quarters feel like home. Pillows, small rugs, watercolors can dispel much of the chilling anonymity of a motel room or sublet apartment. When we can, we should live in rooms with stoves or fireplaces or at least candlelight. The ancient saying is still true: Extinguished hearth, extinguished family.

Round tables help too, and as a friend of mine once   20
put it, so do "too many comfortable chairs, with surfaces to put feet on, arranged so as to encourage a maximum of eye contact." Such rooms inspire good talk, of which good clans can never have enough.

9. Good families, not just the blood kind, find some way to   21
connect with posterity. "To forge a link in the humble chain of being, encircling heirs to ancestors," as Michael Novak has written, "is to walk within a circle of magic as primitive as humans knew in caves." He is talking of course about babies, feeling them leap in wombs, giving them suck. Parenthood, however, is a state which some miss by chance and others by design, and a vocation to which not all are called. Some of us, like the novelist Richard R. Brickner, look on as others "name their children and their children in turn name their own lives, devising their own flags from their parents' cloth." What are we who lack children to do? Build houses? Plant trees? Write books or symphonies or laws? Perhaps, but even if we do these things, there should be children on the sidelines if not at the center of our lives.

It is a sadly impoverished tribe that does not allow   22
access to, and make much of, some children. Not too much, of course; it has truly been said that never in history have so many educated people devoted so much attention

to so few children. Attention, in excess, can turn to fawn-
ing, which isn't much better than neglect. Still, if we don't
regularly see and talk to and laugh with people who can
expect to outlive us by twenty years or so, we had better
get busy and find some.

10. Good families also honor their elders. The wider the   23
    age range, the stronger the tribe. Jean-Paul Sartre and
    Margaret Mead, to name two spectacularly confident
    former children, have both remarked on the central
    importance of grandparents in their own early lives.
    Grandparents are now in much more abundant supply
    than they were a generation or two ago, when old age
    was more rare. If actual grandparents are not at hand,
    no family should have too hard a time finding substitute
    ones to whom to pay unfeigned homage. The Soviet
    Union's enchantment with day-care centers, I have
    heard, stems at least in part from the state's eagerness
    to keep children away from their presumably subver-
    sive grandparents. Let that be a lesson to clans based on
    interest as well as to those based on genes.

For Study and Discussion

QUESTIONS ABOUT PURPOSE

1. Why does Howard argue that "you need" a family?
2. How does she define a "new" family?

QUESTIONS ABOUT AUDIENCE

1. How does Howard's use of the pronoun *we* help establish her
   connection to her readers?
2. How does she use the pronouns *you* and *me* to enrich that
   connection?

QUESTIONS ABOUT STRATEGIES

1. How does Howard use images such as a family member "who plays Mission Control to everyone else's Apollo" illustrate the roles she classifies?
2. How does she use quotations from writers and other people to support the categories in her system?

For Writing and Research

1. *Analyze* how Howard uses terms such as *clan, tribe, support system,* and *extended family.*
2. *Practice* by classifying the purpose of the rituals practiced in your family.
3. *Argue* that a "sense of place" is essential to a family concept of "home."
4. *Synthesize:* Examine family documents such as old letters, scrapbooks, and photographs to identify the people in your family that enact the role Howard classifies. Then write an essay sorting those people into a system of subcategories.

HOWARD MOODY

Howard Moody was born in 1921 in Dallas, Texas, and was educated at the University of California and Yale Divinity School. He served as the chaplain at The Ohio State University before becoming the senior minister at the Judson Memorial Church in New York City, where he devoted much of his time to working with the inhabitants of Greenwich Village. A recently published book about his time at this church is entitled *A Voice in the Village: A Journey of a Pastor and a People.* He was also active in many social causes, especially the abortion rights movement. Together with Arlene Carmen, he wrote two books on abortion rights and prostitution. His essays are collected in *The God-Man of Galilee: Studies in Christian Living* (1983). In "Sacred Rite or Civil Right?" Moody examines the various definitions of marriage.

Sacred Rite or Civil Right?[5]

I F MEMBERS OF the church that I served for more than three   1
decades were told I would be writing an article in defense
of marriage, they wouldn't believe it. My reputation was that
when people came to me for counsel about getting married,
I tried to talk them out of it. More about that later.

We are now in the midst of a national debate on the nature   2
of marriage, and it promises to be as emotional and polemical

---

[5] Howard Moody, "Sacred Rite or Civil Right?" Reprinted with permission from the June 5, 2004, issue of *The Nation*. For subscription information, call 1-800-333-8536. Portions of each week's *Nation* magazine can be accessed at http://www.thenation.com.

as the issues of abortion and homosexuality have been over the past century. What all these debates have in common is that they involved both the laws of the state and the theology of the church. The purpose of this writing is to suggest that the gay-marriage debate is less about the legitimacy of the loving relationship of a same-sex couple than about the relationship of church and state and how they define marriage.

In order to fully understand the conflict that has arisen in this debate over the nature of marriage, it is important to understand the difference between the religious definition of marriage and the state's secular and civil definition.

In Western civilization, the faith and beliefs of Christendom played a major role in shaping the laws regarding social relations and moral behavior. Having been nurtured in the Christian faith from childhood and having served a lifetime as an ordained Baptist minister, I feel obligated first to address the religious controversy concerning the nature of marriage. If we look at the history of religious institutions regarding marriage we will find not much unanimity but amazing diversity— it is really a mixed bag. Those who base their position on "tradition" or "what the Bible says" will find anything but clarity. It depends on which "tradition" in what age reading from whose holy scriptures.   3

In the early tradition of the Jewish people, there were multiple wives and not all of them equal. Remember the story of Abraham's wives, Sara and Hagar. Sara couldn't get pregnant, so Hagar presented Abraham with a son. When Sara got angry with Hagar, she forced Abraham to send Hagar and her son Ishmael into the wilderness. In case Christians feel superior about their "tradition" of marriage, I would remind them that their scriptural basis is not as clear about marriage   4 as we might hope. We have Saint Paul's conflicting and condescending words about the institution: "It's better not to marry." Karl Barth called this passage the Magna Carta of the single person. (Maybe we should have taken Saint Paul's advice more seriously. It might have prevented an earlier generation of parents from harassing, cajoling and prodding our young until they were married.) In certain religious branches, the church doesn't recognize the licensed legality of marriage but requires that persons meet certain religious qualifications before the marriage is recognized by the church. For members of the Roman Catholic Church, a "legal divorce" and the right to remarry may not be recognized unless the first marriage has been declared null and void by a decree of the church. It is clear that there is no single religious view of marriage and that history has witnessed some monumental changes in the way "husband and wife" are seen in the relationship of marriage.

In my faith-based understanding, if freedom of choice 5 means anything to individuals (male or female), it means they have several options. They can be single and celibate without being thought of as strange or psychologically unbalanced. They can be single and sexually active without being labeled loose or immoral. Women can be single with child without being thought of as unfit or inadequate. If these choices had been real options, the divorce rate may never have reached nearly 50 percent.

The other, equally significant choice for people to make 6 is that of lifetime commitment to each other and to seal that desire in the vows of a wedding ceremony. That understanding of marriage came out of my community of faith. In my years of ministry I ran a tight ship in regard to the performance of weddings. It wasn't because I didn't believe in marriage (I've been married for sixty years and have two wonderful offspring) but rather my unease about the way marriage was used to force people to marry so they wouldn't be "living in sin."

The failure of the institution can be seen in divorce statis- 7 tics. I wanted people to know how challenging the promise of those vows was and not to feel this was something they had to do. My first question in premarital counseling was, "Why do you want to get married and spoil a beautiful friendship?" That question often elicited a thoughtful and emotional answer. Though I was miserly in the number of weddings I performed, I always made exceptions when there were couples who had difficulty finding clergy who would officiate. Their difficulty was because they weren't of the same religion, or they had made marital mistakes, or what they couldn't believe. Most of them were "ecclesiastical outlaws," barred from certain sacraments in the church of their choice.

The church I served had a number of gay and lesbian couples who had been together for many years, but none of them had asked for public weddings or blessings on their relationship. (There was one commitment ceremony for a gay couple at the end of my tenure.) It was as though they didn't need a piece of paper or a ritual to symbolize their lifelong commitment. They knew if they wanted a religious ceremony, their ministers would officiate and our religious community would joyfully witness. 8

It was my hope that since the institution of marriage had been used to exclude and demean members of the homosexual community, our church, which was open and affirming, would create with gays and lesbians a new kind of ceremony. It would be an occasion that symbolized, between two people of the same gender, a covenant of intimacy of two people to journey together, breaking new ground in human relationships—an alternative to marriage as we have known it. 9

However, I can understand why homosexuals want "to be married" in the old fashioned "heterosexual way." After all, most gays and lesbians were born of married parents, raised in a family of siblings; many were nourished in churches and synagogues, taught about a living God before Whom all Her creatures were equally loved. Why wouldn't they conceive their loving relationships in terms of marriage and family and desire that they be confirmed and understood as such? It follows that if these gays and lesbians see their relationship as faith-based, they would want a religious ceremony that 10 seals their intentions to become lifelong partners, lovers and friends, that they would want to be "married."

Even though most religious denominations deny this cer- 11 emony to homosexual couples, more and more clergy are, silently and publicly, officiating at religious rituals in which gays and lesbians declare their vows before God and a faith community. One Catholic priest who defied his church's ban said: "We can bless a dog, we can bless a boat, but we can't say a prayer over two people who love each other. You don't have to call it marriage, you can call it a deep and abiding friendship, but you can bless it."

We have the right to engage in "religious disobedience" 12 to the regulations of the judicatory that granted us the privilege to officiate at wedding ceremonies, and suffer the consequences. However, when it comes to civil law, it is my contention that the church and its clergy are on much shakier ground in defying the law.

In order to fully understand the conflict that has arisen 13 in this debate over the nature of marriage, it is important to understand the difference between the religious definition of marriage and the state's secular and civil definition. The government's interest is in a legal definition of marriage—a social and voluntary contract between a man and woman in order to protect money, property and children. Marriage is a civil union without benefit of clergy or religious definition. The state is not interested in why two people are "tying the knot," whether it's to gain money, secure a dynasty or raise children. It may be hard for those of us who have a religious or romantic view of marriage to realize that loveless marriages are not that rare. Before the Pill, pregnancy was a frequent motive for getting married. The state doesn't care what the commitment of two people is, whether it's for life or as long as both of you love, whether it's sexually monogamous or an open marriage. There is nothing spiritual, mystical or romantic about the state's license to marry—it's a legal contract.

Thus, George W. Bush is right when he says that "mar- 14 riage is a sacred institution" when speaking as a Christian, as a member of his Methodist church. But as President of the United States and leader of all Americans, believers and unbelievers, he is wrong. What will surface in this debate as litigation and court decisions multiply is the history of the conflict between the church and the state in defining the nature of marriage. That history will become significant as we move toward a decision on who may be married.

After Christianity became the state religion of the Roman   15 Empire in AD 325, the church maintained absolute control over the regulation of marriage for some 1,000 years. Beginning in the sixteenth century, English kings (especially Henry VIII, who found the inability to get rid of a wife extremely oppressive) and other monarchs in Europe began to wrest control from the church over marital regulations. Ever since, kings, presidents and rulers of all kinds have seen how important the control of marriage is to the regulation of social order. In this nation, the government has always been in charge of marriage.

That is why it was not a San Francisco mayor licensing   16 same-sex couples that really threatened the President's religious understanding of marriage but rather the Supreme Judicial Court of Massachusetts; declaring marriage between same-sex couples a constitutional right, that demanded a call for constitutional amendment. I didn't understand how important that was until I read an op-ed piece in the *Boston Globe* by Peter Gomes, professor of Christian morals and the minister of Memorial Church at Harvard University, that reminds us of a seminal piece of our history:

> *The Dutch made civil marriage the law of the land in 1590, and the first marriage in New England, that of Edward Winslow to the widow Susannah White, was performed on May 12, 1621, in Plymouth by Governor William Bradford, in exercise of his office as magistrate.*

There would be no clergyman in Plymouth until the   17 arrival of the Rev. Ralph Smith in 1629, but even then marriage would continue to be a civil affair, as these first Puritans opposed the English custom of clerical marriage as unscriptural. Not until 1692, when Plymouth Colony was merged into that of Massachusetts Bay, were the Clergy authorized by the new province to solemnize marriages. To this day in the Commonwealth the clergy, including those of the archdiocese, solemnize marriage legally as agents of the Commonwealth and by its civil authority. Chapter 207 of the General Laws of Massachusetts tells us who may perform such ceremonies.

Now even though it is the civil authority of the state that 18 defines the rights and responsibilities of marriage and therefore who can be married, the state is no more infallible than the church in its judgments. It wasn't until the mid-twentieth century that the Supreme Court declared anti-miscegenation laws unconstitutional. Even after that decision, many mainline churches, where I started my ministry, unofficially discouraged interracial marriages, and many of my colleagues were forbidden to perform such weddings.

The civil law view of marriage has as much historical diver- 19 sity as the church's own experience because, in part, the church continued to influence the civil law. Although it was the Bible that made "the husband the head of his wife," it was common law that "turned the married pair legally into one person— the husband," as Nancy Cott documents in her book *Public Vows: A History of Marriage and the Nation* (an indispensable resource for anyone seeking to understand the changing nature of marriage in the nation's history). She suggests that "the legal doctrine of marital unity was called coverture . . . [which] meant that the wife could not use legal avenues such as suits or contracts, own assets, or execute legal documents without her husband's collaboration." This view of the wife would not hold water in any court in the land today.

As a matter of fact, even in the religious understanding of 20 President Bush and his followers, allowing same-sex couples the right to marry seems a logical conclusion. If marriage is "the most fundamental institution of civilization" and a major contributor to the social order in our society, why would anyone want to shut out homosexuals from the "glorious attributes" of this "sacred institution"? Obviously, the only reason one can discern is that the opponents believe that gay and lesbian people are not worthy of the benefits and spiritual blessings of "marriage."

At the heart of the controversy raging over sane-sex mar- 21 riage is the religious and constitutional principle of the separation of church and state. All of us can probably agree that there was never a solid wall of separation, riddled as it is with breaches. The evidence of that is seen in the ambiguity of tax-free religious institutions, "in God we trust" printed on our money and "under God" in the Pledge of Allegiance to our country. All of us clergy, who are granted permission by the state to officiate at legal marriage ceremonies, have already compromised the "solid wall" by signing the license issued by the state. I would like to believe that my authority to perform religious ceremonies does not come from the state but derives from the vows of ordination and my commitment to God. I refuse to repeat the words, "by the authority invested in me by the State of New York, I pronounce you husband and wife," but by signing the license, I've become the state's "handmaiden."

It seems fitting therefore that we religious folk should now 22 seek to sharpen the difference between ecclesiastical law and civil law as we beseech the state to clarify who can be married by civil law. Further evidence that the issue of church and state is part of the gay-marriage controversy is that two Unitarian ministers have been arrested for solemnizing unions between same-sex couples when no state licenses were involved. Ecclesiastical law may punish those clergy who disobey marital regulations, but the state has no right to invade church practices and criminalize clergy under civil law. There should have been a noisy outcry from all churches, synagogues and mosques at the government's outrageous contravention of the sacred principle of the "free exercise of religion."

I come from a long line of Protestants who believe in "a 23 free church in a free state." In the issue before this nation, the civil law is the determinant of the regulation of marriage, regardless of our religious views, and the Supreme Court will finally decide what the principle of equality means in our Constitution in the third century of our life together as a people. It is likely that the Commonwealth of Massachusetts will probably lead the nation on this matter, as the State of New York led to the Supreme Court decision to allow women reproductive freedom.

So what is marriage? It depends on whom you ask, in what 24
era, in what culture. Like all words or institutions, human definitions, whether religious or secular, change with time and history. When our beloved Constitution was written, blacks, Native Americans and, to some extent, women were quasi-human beings with no rights or privileges, but today they are recognized as persons with full citizenship rights. The definition of marriage has been changing over the centuries in this nation, and it will change yet again as homosexuals are seen as ordinary human beings.

In time, and I believe that time is now, we Americans will 25
see that all the fears foisted on us by religious zealots were not real. Heterosexual marriage will still flourish with its statistical failures. The only difference will be that some homosexual couples will join them and probably account for about the same number of failed relationships. And we will discover that it did not matter whether the couples were joined in a religious ceremony or a secular and civil occasion for the statement of their intentions.

For Study and Discussion

QUESTIONS ABOUT PURPOSE

1. How does Moody define the purpose of this essay?
2. How does this purpose relate to his attitude toward the debate about gay marriage?

QUESTIONS ABOUT AUDIENCE

1. How does Moody's profession as a minister establish his authority for his readers?
2. How do you think his readers will respond to his "faith-based understanding" of freedom of choice?

QUESTIONS ABOUT STRATEGIES

1. How does Moody illustrate that there is "no single religious view of marriage"?
2. How does he illustrate that "in this nation, the government has always been in charge of marriage"?

For Writing and Research

1. *Analyze* how Moody presents his problems as counseling and officiating minister.
2. *Practice* by describing the changing definitions of *romance* you have applied to your various relationships.
3. *Argue* that the divorce rate is/is not proof that marriage is the eroding cornerstone of our culture.
4. *Synthesize:* Read the definitions of marriage in the Koran; then write an essay assessing whether the Christian or Islamic definition of marriage has the most beneficial impact on culture.

Images of Family: A Visual Essay
Cause and Effect

SCOTT RUSSELL SANDERS

Scott Russell Sanders was born in Memphis, Tennessee, in 1945 and was educated at Brown University and Cambridge University. For many years he taught creative writing at Indiana University. His own writing explores issues such as the family, the environment, and midwestern history and culture. His books include *Wilderness Plots: Tales About the Settlement of the American Land* (1983), *Stone Country* (1985), *Staying Put: Making a Home in a Restless World* (1993), *Hunting for Hope: A Father's Journeys* (1998), and *A Conservational Manifesto* (2009). In "Under the Influence," reprinted from *Secrets of the Universe: Scenes from the Journey Home* (1991), Sanders describes the effects his father's alcoholism had on his own life.

Under the Influence[6]

M Y FATHER DRANK. He drank as a gut-punched boxer gasps for breath, as a starving dog gobbles food—compulsively, secretly, in pain and trembling. I use the past tense not because he ever quit drinking but because he quit living. That is how the story ends for my father, age sixty-four, heart bursting, body cooling and forsaken on the linoleum of my brother's trailer. The story continues for my brother, my sister, my mother, and me, and will continue so long as memory holds.

[6]Scott Russell Sanders, Used with permission of Beacon Press, from Scott Russell Sanders, "Under the Influence" from *Secrets of the Universe: Scenes from the Journey Home* by Scott Russell Sanders, 1992; permission conveyed through Copyright Clearance Center, Inc.

In the perennial present of memory, I slip into the garage 2
or barn to see my father tipping back the flat green bottles of
wine, the brown cylinders of whiskey, the cans of beer disguised in paper bags. His Adam's apple bobs, the liquid gur-
gles, he wipes the sandy-haired back of a hand over his lips,
and then, his bloodshot gaze bumping into me, he stashes
the bottle or can inside his jacket, under the workbench,
between two bales of hay, and we both pretend the moment
has not occurred.

My father drank. . . . The story continues for
my brother, my sister, my mother, and me,
and will continue as long as memory holds.

"What's up, buddy?" he says, thick-tongued and edgy.   3
"Sky's up," I answer, playing along.   4
"And don't forget prices," he grumbles. "Prices are always 5
up. And taxes."
In memory, his white 1951 Pontiac with the stripes down   6
the hood and the Indian head on the snout jounces to a stop
in the driveway; or it is the 1956 Ford station wagon, or the
1963 Rambler shaped like a toad, or the sleek 1969 Bonne-
ville that will do 120 miles per hour on straightaways; or it is
the robin's-egg blue pickup, new in 1980, battered in 1981,
the year of his death. He climbs out, grinning dangerously,
unsteady on his legs, and we children interrupt our game of
catch, our building of snow forts, our picking of plums, to
watch in silence as he weaves past into the house, where he
slumps into his overstuffed chair and falls asleep. Shaking her
head, our mother stubs out the cigarette he has left smoldering in the ashtray. All evening, until our bedtimes, we tiptoe past him, as past a snoring dragon. Then we curl in our
fearful sheets, listening. Eventually he wakes with a grunt,
Mother slings accusations at him, he snarls back, she yells, he
growls, their voices clashing. Before long, she retreats to their
bedroom, sobbing—not from the blows of fists, for he never
strikes her, but from the force of words.

Left alone, our father prowls the house, thumping into fur- 7
niture, rummaging in the kitchen, slamming doors, turning
the pages of the newspaper with a savage crackle, muttering
back at the late-night drivel from television. The roof might
fly off, the walls might buckle from the pressure of his rage.
Whatever my brother and sister and mother may be thinking
on their own rumpled pillows, I lie there hating him, loving
him, fearing him, knowing I have failed him. I tell myself
he drinks to ease an ache that gnaws at his belly, an ache I
must have caused by disappointing him somehow, a murder-
ous ache I should be able to relieve by doing all my chores,
earning A's in school, winning baseball games, fixing the broken washer and the burst pipes, bringing in money to fill his
empty wallet. He would not hide the green bottles in his tool
box, would not sneak off to the barn with a lump under his
coat, would not fall asleep in the daylight, would not roar and
fume, would not drink himself to death, if only I were perfect.

I am forty-two as I write these words, and I know full well 8
now that my father was an alcoholic, a man consumed by disease rather than by disappointment. What had seemed to me
a private grief is in fact a public scourge. In the United States
alone some ten or fifteen million people share his ailment,
and behind the doors they slam in fury or disgrace, countless
other children tremble. I comfort myself with such knowledge, holding it against the throb of memory like an ice pack
against a bruise. There are keener sources of grief: poverty,
racism, rape, war. I do not wish to compete for a trophy in
suffering. I am only trying to understand the corrosive mixture of helplessness, responsibility, and shame that I learned
to feel as the son of an alcoholic. I realize now that I did not
cause my father's illness, nor could I have cured it. Yet for all
this grown-up knowledge, I am still ten years old, my own
son's age, and as that boy I struggle in guilt and confusion to
save my father from pain.

Consider a few of our synonyms for *drunk*: tipsy, tight, pick- 9
led, soused, and plowed; stoned and stewed, lubricated and
inebriated, juiced and sluiced; three sheets to the wind, in
your cups, out of your mind, under the table; lit up, tanked

up, wiped out; besotted, blotto, bombed, and buzzed; plas-
tered, polluted, putrified; loaded or looped, boozy, woozy,
fuddled, or smashed; crocked and shit-faced, corked and
pissed, snockered and sloshed.

It is a mostly humorous lexicon, as the lore that deals   10
with drunks—in jokes and cartoons, in plays, films, and television skits—is largely comic. Aunt Matilda nips elderberry
wine from the sideboard and burps politely during supper.
Uncle Fred slouches to the table glassy-eyed, wearing a lamp
shade for a hat and murmuring, "Candy is dandy bit liquor
is quicker." Inspired by cocktails, Mrs. Somebody recounts
the events of her day in a fuzzy dialect, while Mr. Somebody
nibbles her ear and croons a bawdy song. On the sofa with
Boyfriend, Daughter giggles, licking gin from her lips, and
loosens the bows in her hair. Junior knocks back some brews
with his chums at the Leopard Lounge and stumbles home
to the wrong house, wonders foggily why he cannot locate
his pajamas, and crawls naked into bed with the ugliest girl in
school. The family dog slurps from a neglected martini and
wobbles to the nursery, where he vomits in Baby's shoe.

It is all great fun. But if in the audience you notice a few   11
laughing faces turn grim when the drunk lurches on stage,
don't be surprised, for these are the children of alcoholics.
Over the grinning mask of Dionysus, the leering mask of
Bacchus, these children cannot help seeing the bloated features of their own parents. Instead of laughing, they wince,
they mourn. Instead of celebrating the drunk as one freed
from constraints, they pity him as one enslaved. They refuse
to believe *in vino veritas*, having seen their befuddled parents
skid away from truth toward folly and oblivion. And so these
children bite their lips until the lush staggers into the wings.

My father, when drunk, was neither funny nor honest; he   12
was pathetic, frightening, deceitful. There seemed to be a
leak in him somewhere, and he poured in booze to keep from
draining dry. Like a torture victim who refuses to squeal, he
would never admit that he had touched a drop, not even in his
last year, when he seemed to be dissolving in alcohol before
our very eyes. I never knew him to lie about anything, ever,

except about this one ruinous fact. Drowsy, clumsy, unable to fix a bicycle tire, throw a baseball, balance a grocery sack, or walk across the room, he was stripped of his true self by drink. In a matter of minutes, the contents of a bottle could transform a brave man into a coward, a buddy into a bully, a gifted athlete and skilled carpenter and shrewd businessman into a bumbler. No dictionary of synonyms for *drunk* would soften the anguish of watching our prince turn into a frog.

Father's drinking became the family secret. While growing up, we children never breathed a word of it beyond the four walls of our house. To this day, my brother and sister rarely mention it, and then only when I press them. I did not confess the ugly, bewildering fact to my wife until his wavering walk and slurred speech forced me to. Recently, on the seventh anniversary of my father's death, I asked my mother if she ever spoke of his drinking to friends. "No, no, never," she replied hastily. "I couldn't bear for anyone to know." 13

The secret bores under the skin, gets in the blood, into the bone, and stays there. Long after you have supposedly been cured of malaria, the fever can flare up, the tremors can shake you. So it is with the fevers of shame. You swallow the bitter quinine of knowledge, and you learn to feel pity and compassion toward the drinker. Yet the shame lingers in your marrow, and, because of the shame, anger. 14

For a long stretch of my childhood we lived on a military reservation in Ohio, an arsenal where bombs were stored underground in bunkers, vintage airplanes burst into flames, and unstable artillery shells boomed nightly at the dump. We had the feeling, as children, that we played in a mine field, where a heedless footfall could trigger an explosion. When Father was drinking, the house, too, became a mine field. The least bump could set off either parent. 15

The more he drank, the more obsessed Mother became with stopping him. She hunted for bottles, counted the cash in his wallet, sniffed at his breath. Without meaning to snoop, we children blundered left and right into damning 16 evidence. On afternoons when he came home from work sober, we flung ourselves at him for hugs, and felt against our ribs the telltale lump in his coat. In the barn we tumbled on the hay and heard beneath our sneakers the crunch of buried glass. We tugged open a drawer in his workbench, looking for screwdrivers or crescent wrenches, and spied a gleaming six-pack among the tools. Playing tag, we darted around the house just in time to see him sway on the rear stoop and heave a finished bottle into the woods. In his good night kiss we smelled the cloying sweetness of Clorets, the mints he chewed to camouflage his dragon's breath.

I can summon up that kiss right now by recalling Theodore   17
Roethke's lines about his own father in "My Papa's Waltz":

> *The whiskey on your breath*
> *Could make a small boy dizzy;*
> *But I hung on like death:*
> *Such waltzing was not easy.*

Such waltzing was hard, terribly hard, for with a boy's scrawny   18
arms I was trying to hold my tipsy father upright.

For years, the chief source of those incriminating bottles   19
and cans was a grimy store a mile from us, a cinder block place called Sly's, with two gas pumps outside and a moth-eaten dog asleep in the window. A strip of flypaper, speck-led the year round with black bodies, coiled in the doorway. Inside, on rusty metal shelves or in wheezing coolers, you could find pop and Popsicles, cigarettes, potato chips, canned soup, raunchy postcards, fishing gear, Twinkies, wine, and beer. When Father drove anywhere on errands, Mother would send us kids along as guards, warning us not to let him out of our sight. And so with one or more of us on board, Father would cruise up to Sly's, pump a dollar's worth of gas or plump the tires with air, and then, telling us to wait in the car, he would head for that fly-spangled doorway.

Dutiful and panicky, we cried, "Let us go in with you!"   20
"No," he answered. "I'll be back in two shakes."   21
"Please!"   22

"No!" he roared. "Don't you budge, or I'll jerk a knot in 23
your tails!"

So we stayed put, kicking the seats, while he ducked inside. 24
Often, when he had parked the car at a careless angle, we
gazed in through the window and saw Mr. Sly fetching down
from a shelf behind the cash register two green pints of Gallo
wine. Father swigged one of them right there at the counter,
stuffed the other in his pocket, and then out he came, a bulge
in his coat, a flustered look on his red face.

Because the Mom and Pop who ran the dump were neigh- 25
bors of ours, living just down the tar-blistered road, I hated
them all the more for poisoning my father. I wanted to sneak
in their store and smash the bottles and set fire to the place. I
also hated the Gallo brothers, Ernest and Julio, whose jovial
faces shone from the labels of their wine, labels I would
find, torn and curled, when I burned the trash. I noted the
Gallo brothers' address, in California, and I studied the road
atlas to see how far that was from Ohio, because I meant to
go out there and tell Ernest and Julio what they were doing
to my father, and then, if they showed no mercy, I would
kill them.

While growing up on the back roads and in the country 26
schools and cramped Methodist churches of Ohio and Tennessee, I never heard the word *alcoholism*, never happened
across it in books or magazines. In the nearby towns, there
were no addiction treatment programs, no community mental health centers, no Alcoholics Anonymous chapters, no
therapists. Left alone with our grievous secret, we had no way
of understanding Father's drinking except as an act of will, a
deliberate folly or cruelty, a moral weakness, a sin. He drank
because he chose to, pure and simple. Why our father, so
playful and competent and kind when sober, would choose
to ruin himself and punish his family, we could not fathom.

Our neighborhood was high on the Bible, and the Bible was 27
hard on drunkards. "Woe to those who are heroes at drinking
wine, and valiant men in mixing strong drink," wrote Isaiah.
"The priest and the prophet reel with strong drink, they are

confused with wine, they err in vision, they stumble in giving judgment. For all tables are full of vomit, no place is without filthiness." We children had seen those fouled tables at the local truck stop where the notorious boozers hung out, our father occasionally among them. "Wine and new wine take away the understanding," declared the prophet Hosea. We had also seen evidence of that in our father, who could multiply seven-digit numbers in his head when sober, but when drunk could not help us with fourth-grade math. Proverbs warned: "Do not look at wine when it is red, when it sparkles in the cup and goes down smoothly. At the last it bites like a serpent, and stings like an adder. Your eyes will see strange things, and your mind utter perverse things." Woe, woe.

Dismayingly often, these biblical drunkards stirred up   28
trouble for their own kids. Noah made fresh wine after the flood, drank too much of it, fell asleep without any clothes on, and was glimpsed in the buff by his son Ham, whom Noah promptly cursed. In one passage—it was so shocking we had to read it under our blankets with flashlights—the patriarch Lot fell down drunk and slept with his daughters. The sins of the fathers set their children's teeth on edge.

Our ministers were fond of quoting St. Paul's pronounce-   29
ment that drunkards would not inherit the kingdom of God. These grave preachers assured us that the wine referred to during the Last Supper was in fact grape juice. Bible and sermons and hymns combined to give us the impression that Moses should have brought down from the mountain another stone tablet, bearing the Eleventh Commandment: Thou shalt not drink.

The scariest and most illuminating Bible story apropos   30
of drunkards was the one about the lunatic and the swine. Matthew, Mark, and Luke each told a version of the tale. We knew it by heart: When Jesus climbed out of his boat one day, this lunatic came charging up from the graveyard, stark naked and filthy, frothing at the mouth, so violent that he broke the strongest chains. Nobody would go near him. Night and day for years this madman had been wailing among the tombs and bruising himself with stones. Jesus took one look at him

and said, "Come out of the man, you unclean spirits!" for he could see that the lunatic was possessed by demons. Meanwhile, some hogs were conveniently rooting nearby. "If we have to come out," begged the demons, "at least let us go into those swine." Jesus agreed. The unclean spirits entered the hogs, and the hogs rushed straight off a cliff and plunged into a lake. Hearing the story in Sunday school, my friends thought mainly of the pigs. (How big a splash did they make? Who paid for the lost pork?) But I thought of the redeemed lunatic, who bathed himself and put on clothes and calmly sat at the feet of Jesus, restored—so the Bible said—to "his right mind."

When drunk, our father was clearly in his wrong mind. 31 He became a stranger, as fearful to us as any grave-yard lunatic, not quite frothing at the mouth but fierce enough, quick-tempered, explosive; or else he grew maudlin and weepy, which frightened us nearly as much. In my boyhood despair, I reasoned that maybe he wasn't to blame for turning into an ogre. Maybe, like the lunatic, he was possessed by demons. I found support for my theory when I heard liquor referred to as "spirits," when the newspapers reported that somebody had been arrested for "driving under the influence," and when church ladies railed against that "demon drink."

If my father was indeed possessed, who would exorcise 32 him? If he was a sinner, who would save him? If he was ill, who would cure him? If he suffered, who would ease his pain? Not ministers or doctors, for we could not bring ourselves to confide in them; not the neighbors, for we pretended they had never seen him drunk; not Mother, who fussed and pleaded but could not budge him; not my brother and sister, who were only kids. That left me. It did not matter that I, too, was only a child, and a bewildered one at that. I could not excuse myself.

On first reading a description of delirium tremens—in a 33 book on alcoholism I smuggled from the library—I thought immediately of the frothing lunatic and the frenzied swine.

When I read stories or watched films about grisly metamorphoses—Dr. Jekyll becoming Mr. Hyde, the mild husband changing into a werewolf, the kindly neighbor taken over by a brutal alien—I could not help seeing my own father's mutation from sober to drunk. Even today, knowing better, I am attracted by the demonic theory of drink, for when I recall my father's transformation, the emergence of his ugly second self, I find it easy to believe in possession by unclean spirits. We never knew which version of Father would come home from work, the true or the tainted, nor could we guess how far down the slope toward cruelty he would slide.

How far a man *could* slide we gauged by observing our   34
back-road neighbors—the out-of-work miners who had dragged their families to our corner of Ohio from the desolate hollows of Appalachia, the tightfisted farmers, the surly mechanics, the balked and broken men. There was, for example, whiskey-soaked Mr. Jenkins, who beat his wife and kids so hard we could hear their screams from the road. There was Mr. Lavo the wino, who fell asleep smoking time and again, until one night his disgusted wife bundled up the children and went outside and left him in his easy chair to burn; he awoke on his own, staggered out coughing into the yard, and pounded her flat while the children looked on and the shack turned to ash. There was the truck driver, Mr. Sampson, who tripped over his son's tricycle one night while drunk and got so mad that he jumped into his semi and drove away, shifting through the dozen gears, and never came back. We saw the bruised children of these fathers clump onto our school bus, we saw the abandoned children huddle in the pews at church, we saw the stunned and battered mothers begging for help at our doors.

Our own father never beat us, and I don't think he ever   35
beat Mother, but he threatened often. The Old Testament Yahweh was not more terrible in his wrath. Eyes blazing, voice booming, Father would pull out his belt and swear to give us a whipping, but he never followed through, never needed to, because we could imagine it so vividly. He shoved us, pawed us with the back of his hand, as an irked bear might smack a cub, not to injure, just to clear a space. I can see him grabbing Mother by the hair as she cowers on a chair during

a nightly quarrel. He twists her neck back until she gapes up at him, and then he lifts over her skull a glass quart bottle of milk, the milk running down his forearm, and he yells at her, "Say just one more word, one goddamn word, and I'll shut you up!" I fear she will prick him with her sharp tongue, but she is terrified into silence, and so am I, and the leaking bottle quivers in the air, and milk slithers through the red hair of my father's uplifted arm, and the entire scene is there to this moment, the head jerked back, the club raised.

When the drink made him weepy, Father would pack a bag and kiss each of us children on the head, and announce from the front door that he was moving out. "Where to?" we demanded, fearful each time that he would leave for good, as Mr. Sampson had roared away for good in his diesel truck. "Someplace where I won't get hounded every minute," Father would answer, his jaw quivering. He stabbed a look at Mother, who might say, "Don't run into the ditch before you get there," or, "Good riddance," and then he would slink away. Mother watched him go with arms crossed over her chest, her face closed like the lid on a box of snakes. We children bawled. Where could he go? To the truck stop, that den of iniquity? To one of those dark, ratty flophouses in town? Would he wind up sleeping under a railroad bridge or on a park bench or in a cardboard box, mummied in rags, like the bums we had seen on our trips to Cleveland and Chicago? We bawled and bawled, wondering if he would ever come back.

He always did come back, a day or a week later, but each time there was a sliver less of him.

In Kafka's *The Metamorphosis*, which opens famously with Gregor Samsa waking up from uneasy dreams to find himself transformed into an insect, Gregor's family keep reassuring themselves that things will be just fine again, "When he comes back to us." Each time alcohol transformed our father, we held out the same hope, that he would really and truly come back to us, our authentic father, the tender and playful and competent man, and then all things would be fine. We had grounds for such hope. After his weepy departures and chap-fallen returns, he would sometimes go weeks, even months without drinking. Those were glad times. Joy banged inside my ribs. Every day without the furtive glint of bottles, every meal without a fight, every bedtime without sobs encouraged us to believe that such bliss might go on forever.

Mother was fooled by just such a hope all during the forty-odd years she knew this Greeley Ray Sanders. Soon after she met him in a Chicago delicatessen on the eve of World War II, and fell for his butter-melting Mississippi drawl and his wavy red hair, she learned that he drank heavily. But then so did a lot of men. She would soon coax or scold him into breaking the nasty habit. She would point out to him how ugly and foolish it was, this bleary drinking, and then he would quit. He refused to quit during their engagement, however, still refused during the first years of marriage, refused until my sister came along. The shock of fatherhood sobered him, and he remained sober through my birth at the end of the war and right on through until we moved in 1951 to the Ohio arsenal, that paradise of bombs. Like all places that make a business of death, the arsenal had more than its share of alcoholics and drug addicts and other varieties of escape artists. There I turned six and started school and woke into a child's flickering awareness, just in time to see my father begin sneaking swigs in the garage. 39

He sobered up again for most of a year at the height of the Korean War, to celebrate the birth of my brother. But aside from that dry spell, his only breaks from drinking before I graduated from high school were just long enough to raise and then dash our hopes. Then during the fall of my senior year—the time of the Cuban missile crisis, when it seemed that the nightly explosions at the munitions dump and the nightly rages in our household might spread to engulf the globe—Father collapsed. His liver, kidneys, and heart all conked out. The doctors saved him, but only by a hair. He stayed in the hospital for weeks, going through a withdrawal so terrible that Mother would not let us visit him. If he wanted to kill himself, the doctors solemnly warned him, all he had to do was hit the bottle again. One binge would finish him. 40

Father must have believed them, for he stayed dry the next   41
fifteen years. It was an answer to prayer, Mother said, it was
a miracle. I believe it was a reflex of fear, which he sustained
over the years through courage and pride. He knew a man
could die from drink, for his brother Roscoe had. We children never laid eyes on doomed Uncle Roscoe, but in the
stories Mother told us he became a fairy-tale figure, like a boy
who took the wrong turning in the woods and was gobbled
up by the wolf.

The fifteen-year dry spell came to an end with Father's   42
retirement in the spring of 1978. Like many men, he gave
up his identity along with his job. One day he was a boss at
the factory, with a brass plate on his door and a reputation
to uphold; the next day he was a nobody at home. He and
Mother were leaving Ontario, the last of the many places to
which his job had carried them, and they were moving to a
new house in Mississippi, his childhood stomping grounds.
As a boy in Mississippi, Father sold Coca-Cola during dances
while the moonshiners peddled their brew in the parking lot;
as a young blade, he fought in bars and in the ring, seeking
a state Golden Gloves championship; he gambled at poker,
hunted pheasants, raced motorcycles and cars, played semi-
professional baseball, and, along with all his buddies—in the
Black Cat Saloon, behind the cotton gin, in the woods—he
drank. It was a perilous youth to dream of recovering.

After his final day of work, Mother drove on ahead with   43
a car full of begonias and violets, while Father stayed behind
to oversee the packing. When the van was loaded, the sweaty
movers broke open a six-pack and offered him a beer.

"Let's drink to retirement!" they crowed. "Let's drink to   44
freedom! to fishing! hunting! loafing! Let's drink to a guy
who's going home!"

At least I imagine some such words, for that is all I can   45
do, imagine, and I see Father's hand trembling in midair as
he thinks about the fifteen sober years and about the doctors' warning, and he tells himself *Goddamnit, I am a free
man*, and *Why can't a free man drink one beer after a lifetime
of hard work?* and I see his arm reaching, his fingers closing,

the can tilting to his lips. I even supply a label for the beer, a swaggering brand that promises on television to deliver the essence of life. I watch the amber liquid pour down his throat, the alcohol steal into his blood, the key turn in his brain.

Soon after my parents moved back to Father's treach- 46
erous stomping ground, my wife and I visited them in Mississippi with our five-year-old daughter. Mother had been too distraught to warn me about the return of the demons. So when I climbed out of the car that bright July morning and saw my father napping in the hammock, I felt uneasy, for in all his sober years I had never known him to sleep in daylight. Then he lurched upright, blinked his bloodshot eyes, and greeted us in a syrupy voice. I was hurled back helpless into childhood.

    "What's the matter with Papaw?" our daughter asked.   47

    "Nothing," I said. "Nothing!"   48

    Like a child again, I pretended not to see him in his stupor, 49
and behind my phony smile I grieved. On that visit and on the few that remained before his death, once again I found bottles in the workbench, bottles in the woods. Again his hand shook too much for him to run a saw, to make his precious miniature furniture, to drive straight down back roads. Again he wound up in the ditch, in the hospital, in jail, in treatment centers. Again he shouted and wept. Again he lied. "I never touched a drop," he swore. "Your mother's making it up."

    I no longer fancied I could reason with the men whose 50
names I found on the bottles—Jim Beam, Jack Daniels— nor did I hope to save my father by burning down a store. I was able now to press the cold statistics about alcoholism against the ache of memory: ten million victims, fifteen million, twenty. And yet, in spite of my age, I reacted in the same blind way as I had in childhood, ignoring biology, forgetting numbers, vainly seeking to erase through my efforts whatever drove him to drink. I worked on their place twelve and sixteen hours a day, in the swelter of Mississippi summer, digging ditches, running electrical wire, planting trees,

mowing grass, building sheds, as though what nagged at him was some list of chores, as though by taking his worries on my shoulders I could redeem him. I was flung back into boy-hood, acting as though my father would not drink himself to death if only I were perfect.

I failed of perfection; he succeeded in dying. To the end, he considered himself not sick but sinful. "Do you want to kill yourself?" I asked him. "Why not?" he answered. "Why the hell not? What's there to save?" To the end, he would not speak about his feelings, would not or could not give a name to the beast that was devouring him. 51

In silence, he went rushing off the cliff. Unlike the biblical swine, however, he left behind a few of the demons to haunt his children. Life with him and the loss of him twisted us into shapes that will be familiar to other sons and daughters of alcoholics. My brother became a rebel, my sister retreated into shyness, I played the stalwart and dutiful son who would hold the family together. If my father was unstable, I would be a rock. If he squandered money on drink, I would pinch every penny. If he wept when drunk—and only when drunk—I would not let myself weep at all. If he roared at the Little League umpire for calling my pitches balls, I would throw nothing but strikes. Watching him flounder and rage, I came to dread the loss of control. I would go through life without making anyone mad. I vowed never to put in my mouth or veins any chemical that would banish my every-day self. I would never make a scene, never lash out at the ones I loved, never hurt a soul. Through hard work, relent-less work, I would achieve something dazzling—in the class-room, on the basketball floor, in the science lab, in the pages of books—and my achievement would distract the world's eyes from his humiliation. I would become a worthy sacrifice, and the smoke of my burning would please God. 52

It is far easier to recognize these twists in my character than to undo them. Work has become an addiction for me, as drink was an addiction for my father. Knowing this, my daughter gave me a placard for the wall: WORKAHOLIC. The labor is endless and futile, for I can no more redeem myself 53 through work than I could redeem my father. I still panic in the face of other people's anger, because his drunken temper was so terrible. I shrink from causing sadness or disappointment even to strangers, as though I were still concealing the family shame. I still notice every twitch of emotion in the faces around me, having learned as a child to read the weather in faces, and I blame myself for their least pang of unhappiness or anger. In certain moods I blame myself for everything. Guilt burns like acid in my veins.

I am moved to write these pages now because my own son, at the age of ten, is taking on himself the griefs of the world, and in particular the griefs of his father. He tells me that when I am gripped by sadness he feels responsible; he feels there must be something he can do to spring me from depression, to fix my life. And that crushing sense of responsibility is exactly what I felt at the age of ten in the face of my father's drinking. My son wonders if I, too, am possessed. I write, therefore, to drag into the light what eats at me—the fear, the guilt, the shame—so that my own children may be spared.   54

    I still shy away from nightclubs, from bars, from parties where the solvent is alcohol. My friends puzzle over this, but it is no more peculiar than for a man to shy away from the lions' den after seeing his father torn apart. I took my own first drink at the age of twenty-one, half a glass of burgundy. I knew the odds of my becoming an alcoholic were four times higher than for the sons of nonalcoholic fathers. So I sipped warily.   55

    I still do—once a week, perhaps, a glass of wine, a can of beer, nothing stronger, nothing more. I listen for the turning of a key in my brain.   56

For Study and Discussion

QUESTIONS ABOUT PURPOSE

1. Why does Sanders describe the effects of his father's drinking on "my brother, my sister, my mother and me"?
2. Why does he write this essay for his ten-year-old son?

QUESTIONS ABOUT AUDIENCE

1. How does Sanders's concern that he has "failed his father" establish an emotional relationship with his readers?
2. What does he mean when he says he does not want "to compete for a trophy in suffering"?

QUESTIONS ABOUT STRATEGIES

1. How does Sanders illustrate the response of children of alcoholics to the humorous depiction of drunks?
2. How does he describe his family's reaction to the "mine field" created by his father's drinking?

For Writing and Research

1. *Analyze* how Sanders uses the Bible to present the problem of drunkenness.
2. *Practice* by analyzing the effects a "family secret" has had on you and other members of your family.
3. *Argue* that a "workaholic" has a destructive effect on friends and family.
4. *Synthesize:* Read medical descriptions about the causes and effects of alcoholism. Then write an essay analyzing the most effective treatments and cures.

A *Debate About Family*
Persuasion and Argument

BARBARA KINGSOLVER

Barbara Kingsolver was born in Annapolis, Maryland, in 1955 and was educated at DePauw University and the University of Arizona. She began her writing career as a technical writer in the office of arid studies, and then began working as a freelance journalist before publishing her first novel, *The Bean Trees* (1988). Her other novels include *Animal Dreams* (1990), *The Poisonwood Bible* (1998), *Prodigal Summer* (2000), and *Lacuna* (2009). She has published short stories in *Homeland and Other Stories* (1989); essays in *High Tide in Tucson: Essays from Now or Never* (1995) and *Small Wonder* (2002); and a nonfiction narrative, *Animal, Vegetable, Miracle: A Year of Food Life* (2007). In "Stone Soup," reprinted from *High Tide in Tucson*, Kingsolver argues that there is not necessarily one best model for a successful family.

Stone Soup[7]

IN THE CATALOG of family values, where do we rank an 1
occasion like this? A curly-haired boy who wanted to run before he walked, age seven now, a soccer player scoring a winning goal. He turns to the bleachers with his fists in the air and a smile wide as a gap-toothed galaxy. His own cheering section of grown-ups and kids all leap to their feet and

---

hug each other, delirious with love for this boy. He's Andy, my best friend's son. The cheering section includes his mother and her friends, his brother, his father and stepmother, a stepbrother and stepsister, and a grandparent. Lucky is the child with this many relatives on hand to hail a proud accomplishment. I'm there too, witnessing a family fortune. But in spite of myself, defensive words take shape in my head. I am thinking: I dare *anybody* to call this a broken home.

Families change, and remain the same. Why are our names 2 for home so slow to catch up to the truth of where we live?

When I was a child, I had two parents who loved me with- 3 out cease. One of them attended every excuse for attention I ever contrived, and the other made it to the ones with higher production values, like piano recitals and appendicitis. So I was a lucky child too. I played with a set of paper dolls called "The Family of Dolls," four in number, who came with the factory-assigned names of Dad, Mom, Sis, and Junior. I think you know what they looked like, at least before I loved them to death and their heads fell off.

Arguing about whether nontraditional families deserve pity or tolerance is a little like the medieval debate about left-handedness as a mark of the devil.

Now I've replaced the dolls with a life. I knit my days 4 around my daughter's survival and happiness, and am proud to say her head is still on. But we aren't the Family of Dolls. Maybe you're not, either. And if not, even though you are statistically no oddity, it's probably been suggested to you in a hundred ways that yours isn't exactly a real family, but an impostor family, a harbinger of cultural ruin, a slapdash substitute—something like counterfeit money. Here at the tail end of our century, most of us are up to our ears in the noisy business of trying to support and love a thing called family.

But there's a current in the air with ferocious moral force that finds its way even into political campaigns, claiming there is only one right way to do it, the Way It Has Always Been.

In the face of a thriving, particolored world, this narrow   5
view is so pickled and absurd I'm astonished that it gets airplay. And I'm astonished that it still stings.

Every parent has endured the arrogance of a child-   6
unfriendly grump sitting in judgment, explaining what those kids of ours really need (for example, "a good licking"). If we're polite, we move our crew to another bench in the park. If we're forthright (as I am in my mind, only, for the rest of the day), we fix them with a sweet imperious stare and say, "Come back and let's talk about it after you've changed a thousand diapers."

But it's harder somehow to shrug off the Family-of-Dolls   7
Family Values crew when they judge (from their safe distance) that divorced people, blended families, gay families, and single parents are failures. That our children are at risk, and the whole arrangement is messy and embarrassing. A marriage that ends is not called "finished," it's called *failed*. The children of this family may have been born to a happy union, but now they are called *the children of divorce*.

I had no idea how thoroughly these assumptions overlaid   8
my culture until I went through divorce myself. I wrote to a friend: "This might be worse than being widowed. Overnight I've suffered the same losses—companionship, financial and practical support, my identity as a wife and partner, the future I'd taken for granted. I am lonely, grieving, and hard-pressed to take care of my household alone. But instead of bringing casseroles, people are acting like I had a fit and broke up the family china."

Once upon a time I held these beliefs about divorce: that   9
everyone who does it could have chosen not to do it. That it's a lazy way out of marital problems. That it selfishly puts personal happiness ahead of family integrity. Now I tremble for my ignorance. It's easy, in fortunate times, to forget about the ambush that could leave your head reeling: serious

mental or physical illness, death in the family, abandonment, financial calamity, humiliation, violence, despair.

I started out like any child, intent on being the Family of 10 Dolls. I set upon young womanhood believing in most of the doctrines of my generation: I wore my skirts four inches above the knee. I had the Barbie with her zebra-striped swimsuit and a figure unlike anything found in nature. And I understood the Prince Charming Theory of Marriage, a quest for Mr. Right that ends smack dab where you find him. I did not completely understand that another whole story *begins* there, and no fairy tale prepared me for the combination of bad luck and persistent hope that would interrupt my dream and lead me to other arrangements. Like a cancer diagnosis, a dying marriage is a thing to fight, to deny, and finally, when there's no choice left, to dig in and survive. Casseroles would help. Likewise, I imagine it must be a painful reckoning in adolescence (or later on) to realize one's own true love will never look like the soft-focus fragrance ads because Prince Charming (surprise!) is a princess. Or vice versa. Or has skin the color your parents didn't want you messing with, except in the Crayola box.

It's awfully easy to hold in contempt the straw broken 11 home, and that mythical category of persons who toss away nuclear family for the sheer fun of it. Even the legal terms we use have a suggestion of caprice. I resent the phrase "irreconcilable differences," which suggests a stubborn refusal to accept a spouse's little quirks. This is specious. Every happily married couple I know has loads of irreconcilable differences. Negotiating where to set the thermostat is not the point. A nonfunctioning marriage is a slow asphyxiation. It is waking up despised each morning, listening to the pulse of your own loneliness before the radio begins to blare its raucous gospel that you're nothing if you aren't loved. It is sharing your airless house with the threat of suicide or other kinds of violence, while the ghost that whispers, "Leave here and destroy your children," has passed over every door and nailed it shut. Disassembling a marriage in these circumstances is as much *fun* as amputating your own gangrenous leg. You do it, if you can, to save a life—or two, or more.

I know of no one who really went looking to hoe the harder row, especially the daunting one of single parenthood. Yet it seems to be the most American of customs to blame the burdened for their destiny. We'd like so desperately to believe in freedom and justice for all, we can hardly name that rogue bad luck, even when he's a close enough snake to bite us. In the wake of my divorce, some friends (even a few close ones) chose to vanish, rather than linger within striking distance of misfortune. 12

But most stuck around, bless their hearts, and if I'm any the wiser for my trials, it's from having learned the worth of steadfast friendship. And also, what not to say. The least helpful question is: "Did you want the divorce, or didn't you?" Did I want to keep that gangrenous leg, or not? How to explain, in a culture that venerates choice: two terrifying options are much worse than none at all. Give me any day the quick hand of cruel fate that will leave me scarred but blameless. As it was, I kept thinking of that wicked third-grade joke in which some boy comes up behind you and grabs your ear, starts in with a prolonged tug, and asks, "Do you want this ear any longer?" 13

Still, the friend who holds your hand and says the wrong thing is made of dearer stuff than the one who stays away. And generally, through all of it, you live. My favorite fictional character, Kate Vaiden (in the novel by Reynolds Price), advises: "Strength just comes in one brand—you stand up at sunrise and meet what they send you and keep your hair combed." 14

Once you've weathered the straits, you get to cross the tricky juncture from casualty to survivor. If you're on your feet at the end of a year or two, and have begun putting together a happy new existence, those friends who were kind enough to feel sorry for you when you needed it must now accept you back to the ranks of the living. If you're truly blessed, they will dance at your second wedding. Everybody else, for heaven's sake, should stop throwing stones. 15

Arguing about whether nontraditional families deserve   16
pity or tolerance is a little like the medieval debate about
left-handedness as a mark of the devil. Divorce, remarriage,
single parenthood, gay parents, and blended families simply
are. They're facts of our time. Some of the reasons listed by
sociologists for these family reconstructions are: the idea of
marriage as a romantic partnership rather than a pragmatic
one; a shift in women's expectations, from servility to self-
respect and independence; and longevity (prior to antibiotics
no marriage was expected to last many decades—in Colonial
days the average couple lived to be married less than twelve
years). Add to all this, our growing sense of entitlement to
happiness and safety from abuse. Most would agree these are
all good things. Yet their result—a culture in which serial
monogamy and the consequent reshaping of families are the
norm—gets diagnosed as "failing."

For many of us, once we have put ourselves Humpty-   17
Dumpty-wise back together again, the main problem with
our reorganized family is that other people think we have a
problem. My daughter tells me the only time she's uncomfortable about being the child of divorced parents is when
her friends say they feel sorry for her. It's a bizarre sympathy,
given that half the kids in her school and nation are in the
same boat, pursuing childish happiness with the same energy
as their married-parent peers. When anyone asks how *she* feels
about it, she spontaneously lists the benefits: our house is in
the country and we have a dog, but she can go to her dad's
neighborhood for the urban thrills of a pool and sidewalks
for roller-skating. What's more, she has three sets of grandparents!

Why is it surprising that a child would revel in a widened   18
family and the right to feel at home in more than one house?
Isn't it the opposite that should worry us—a child with no
home at all, or too few resources to feel safe? The child at
risk is the one whose parents are too immature themselves to
guide wisely; too diminished by poverty to nurture; too far
from opportunity to offer hope. The number of children in the
U.S. living in poverty at this moment is almost unfathomably

large: twenty percent. There are families among us that need help all right, and by no means are they new on the landscape. The rate at which teenage girls had babies in 1957 (ninety-six per thousand) was twice what it is now. That remarkable statistic is ignored by the religious right—probably because the teen birth rate was cut in half mainly by legalized abortion. In fact, the policy gatekeepers who coined the phrase "family values" have steadfastly ignored the desperation of too-small families, and since 1979 have steadily reduced the amount of financial support available to a single parent. But, this camp's most outspoken attacks seem aimed at the notion of families getting too complex, with add-ons and extras such as a gay parent's partner, or a remarried mother's new husband and his children.

To judge a family's value by its tidy symmetry is to purchase a book for its cover. There's no moral authority there. The famous family comprised of Dad, Mom, Sis, and Junior living as an isolated economic unit is not built on historical bedrock. In *The Way We Never Were,* Stephanie Coontz writes, "Whenever people propose that we go back to the traditional family, I always suggest that they pick a ballpark date for the family they have in mind." Colonial families were tidily disciplined, but their members (meaning everyone but infants) labored incessantly and died young. Then the Victorian family adopted a new division of labor, in which women's role was domestic and children were allowed time for study and play, but this was an upper-class construct supported by myriad slaves. Coontz writes, "For every nineteenth-century middle-class family that protected its wife and child within the family circle, there was an Irish or German girl scrubbing floors . . . a Welsh boy mining coal to keep the home-baked goodies warm, a black girl doing the family laundry, a black mother and child picking cotton to be made into clothes for the family, and a Jewish or an Italian daughter in a sweatshop making 'ladies' dresses or artificial flowers for the family to purchase." 19

The abolition of slavery brought slightly more democratic arrangements, in which extended families were harnessed together in cottage industries; at the turn of the century came 20 a steep rise in child labor in mines and sweatshops. Twenty percent of American children lived in orphanages at the time; their parents were not necessarily dead, but couldn't afford to keep them.

During the Depression and up to the end of World War 21 II, many millions of U.S. households were more multigenerational than nuclear. Women my grandmother's age were likely to live with a fluid assortment of elderly relatives, in-laws, siblings, and children. In many cases they spent virtually every waking hour working in the company of other women—a companionable scenario in which it would be easier, I imagine, to tolerate an estranged or difficult spouse. I'm reluctant to idealize a life of so much hard work and so little spousal intimacy, but its advantage may have been resilience. A family so large and varied would not easily be brought down by a single blow: it could absorb a death, long illness, an abandonment here or there, and any number of irreconcilable differences.

The Family of Dolls came along midcentury as a great 22 American experiment. A booming economy required a mobile labor force and demanded that women surrender jobs to returning soldiers. Families came to be defined by a single breadwinner. They struck out for single-family homes at an earlier age than ever before, and in unprecedented numbers they raised children in suburban isolation. The nuclear family was launched to sink or swim.

More than a few sank. Social historians corroborate that 23 the suburban family of the postwar economic boom, which we have recently selected as our definition of "traditional," was no panacea. Twenty-five percent of Americans were poor in the mid-1950s, and as yet there were no food stamps. Sixty percent of the elderly lived on less than $1,000 a year, and most had no medical insurance. In the sequestered suburbs, alcoholism and sexual abuse of children were far more widespread than anyone imagined.

Expectations soared, and the economy sagged. It's hard 24 to depend on one other adult for everything, come what may. In the last three decades, that amorphous, adaptable structure we call "family" has been reshaped once more by economic tides. Compared with fifties families, mothers are far more likely now to be employed. We are statistically more likely to divorce, and to live in blended families or other extranuclear arrangements. We are also more likely to plan and space our children, and to rate our marriages as "happy." We are less likely to suffer abuse without recourse, or to stare out at our lives through a glaze of prescription tranquilizers. Our aged parents are less likely to be destitute, and we're half as likely to have a teenage daughter turn up a mother herself. All in all, I would say that if "intact" in modern family-values jargon means living quietly desperate in the bell jar, then hip-hip-hooray for "broken." A neat family model constructed to service the Baby Boom economy seems to be returning gradually to a grand, lumpy shape that human families apparently have tended toward since they first took root in the Olduvai Gorge. We're social animals, deeply fond of companionship, and children love best to run in packs. If there is a *normal* for humans, at all, I expect it looks like two or three Families of Dolls, connected variously by kinship and passion, shuffled like cards and strewn over several shoeboxes.

The sooner we can let go of the fairy tale of families functioning perfectly in isolation, the better we might embrace the relief of community. Even the admirable parents who've stayed married through thick and thin are very likely, at present, to incorporate other adults into their families—household help and baby-sitters if they can afford them, or neighbors and grandparents if they can't. For single parents, this support is the rock-bottom definition of family. And most parents who have split apart, however painfully, still manage to maintain family continuity for their children, creating in many cases a boisterous phenomenon that Constance Ahrons in her book *The Good Divorce* calls the "binuclear family." Call it what you will—when ex-spouses beat swords into plowshares and jump up and down at a soccer game together, it makes for happy kids.

Cinderella, look, who needs her? All those evil stepsisters? That story always seemed like too much cotton-picking fuss over clothes. A childhood tale that fascinated me more was the one called "Stone Soup," and the gist of it is this: Once upon a time, a pair of beleaguered soldiers straggled home to a village empty-handed, in a land ruined by war. They were famished, but the villagers had so little they shouted evil words and slammed their doors. So the soldiers dragged out a big kettle, filled it with water, and put it on a fire to boil. They rolled a clean round stone into the pot, while the villagers peered through their curtains in amazement.

"What kind of soup is that?" they hooted.   27

"Stone soup," the soldiers replied. "Everybody can have   28
some when it's done."

"Well, thanks," one matron grumbled, coming out with   29
a shriveled carrot. "But it'd be better if you threw this in."

And so on, of course, a vegetable at a time, until the whole   30
suspicious village managed to feed itself grandly.

Any family is a big empty pot, save for what gets thrown   31
in. Each stew turns out different. Generosity, a resolve to turn bad luck into good, and respect for variety—these things will nourish a nation of children. Name-calling and suspicion will not. My soup contains a rock or two of hard times, and maybe yours does too. I expect it's a heck of a bouillabaisse.

For Study and Discussion

QUESTIONS ABOUT PURPOSE

1. In paragraphs 19 through 23, Kingsolver gives several snapshots of what so-called traditional families have actually looked like for the past several decades. What do you think she hopes to accomplish with these accounts?
2. What new insights do you think Kingsolver wants her readers to have about the divorce process?

QUESTIONS ABOUT AUDIENCE

1. What experience with divorce, single parenthood, and the step-families created by second marriages do you think today's readers

under forty are likely to have? How do those experiences affect the way they are likely to respond to an essay like this?

2. What details in the essay suggest that Kingsolver feels she is writing more for women than for men?

QUESTIONS ABOUT STRATEGIES

1. Kingsolver has published several successful novels, two of which—*The Bean Trees* and *Pigs in Heaven*—tell the story of a single mother who adopts and raises a child. What strategies do you see in this essay that you think might have come from her talent for writing fiction?
2. Kingsolver draws examples from two sources: from her own experience and observations and from historical examples from previous eras. What are the strengths of examples from each of these sources?

For Writing and Research

1. *Analyze* how Kingsolver uses historical evidence to challenge the myth of the "traditional family."
2. *Practice* by demonstrating how reconstructed families—like Kingsolver's—offer children more advantages than disadvantages.
3. *Argue* that the ideas of romantic love presented in the movies provide a distorted view of family values.
4. *Synthesize* some of the data presented in Stephanie Coontz's *The Way We Never Were* (1992). Then use this evidence to support the argument that the idea of a traditional family is a "nostalgia trap."

BARBARA DAFOE WHITEHEAD

Barbara Dafoe Whitehead was born in Rochester, Minnesota, in 1944 and was educated at the University of Wisconsin and the University of Chicago. She has contributed articles to *Commonweal,* the *New York Times,* and the *Wall Street Journal.* Her most controversial article, "Dan Quayle Was Right," published in *The Atlantic,* refers to former vice president Dan Quayle's criticism of the television show *Murphy Brown* because its title character chose to have a baby without being married. Whitehead has also written another controversial article for *the Atlantic,* "The Failure of Sex Education." These articles have led to books such as *The Divorce Culture* (1997), *Goodbye to Girlhood: What's Troubling Girls and What We Can Do About It* (1999), and *Why There Are No Good Men Left: The Romantic Plight of the New Single Woman* (2003). In "Women and the Future of Fatherhood," reprinted from *The Wilson Quarterly* (1996), Whitehead argues that even the best mothers cannot be good fathers.

Women and the Future of Fatherhood[8]

MUCH OF OUR contemporary debate over fatherhood is governed by the assumption that men can solve the fatherhood problem on their own. The organizers of last   1

---

[8]Barbara Dafoe Whitehead, "Women and the Future of Fatherhood" from *The Divorce Culture* by Barbara Dafoe Whitehead, copyright © 1996 by Barbara Dafoe Whitehead. Used by permission of Alfred A. Knopf, a division of Random House, Inc.

year's Million Man March asked women to stay home, and the leaders of Promise Keepers and other grass-roots fatherhood movements whose members gather with considerably less fanfare simply do not admit women.

There is a cultural rationale for the exclusion of women. 2 The fatherhood movement sees the task of reinstating responsible fatherhood as an effort to alter today's norms of masculinity and correctly believes that such an effort cannot succeed unless it is voluntarily undertaken and supported by men. There is also a political rationale in defining fatherlessness as a men's issue. In the debate about marriage and parenthood, which women have dominated for at least 30 years, the fatherhood movement gives men a powerful collective voice and presence.

> *[This] notion of marriage as a union of two sovereign selves may be inadequate to define a relationship that carries with it the obligations, duties, and sacrifices of parenthood.*

Yet however effective the grass-roots movement is at stir- 3 ring men's consciences and raising their consciousness, the fatherhood problem will not be solved by men alone. To be sure, by signaling their commitment to accepting responsibility for the rearing of their children, men have taken the essential first step. But what has not yet been acknowledged is that the success of any effort to renew fatherhood as a social fact and a cultural norm also hinges on the attitudes and behavior of women. Men can't be fathers unless the mothers of their children allow it.

Merely to say this is to point to how thoroughly marital 4 disruption has weakened the bond between fathers and children. More than half of all American children are likely to spend at least part of their lives in one-parent homes. Since the vast majority of children in disrupted families live with their mothers, fathers do not share a home or a daily life with their children. It is much more difficult for men to make the kinds of small, routine, instrumental investments in their children that help forge a good relationship. It is hard to fix a flat bike tire or run a bath when you live in another neighborhood or another town. Many a father's instrumental contribution is reduced to the postal or electronic transmission of money, or, all too commonly, to nothing at all. Without regular contact with their children, men often make reduced emotional contributions as well. Fathers must struggle to sustain close emotional ties across time and space, to "be there" emotionally without being there physically. Some may pick up the phone, send a birthday card, or buy a present, but for many fathers, physical absence also becomes emotional absence.

Without marriage, men also lose access to the social and 5 emotional intelligence of women in building relationships. Wives teach men how to care for young children, and they also encourage children to love their fathers. Mothers who do not live with the father of their children are not as likely as married mothers to represent him in positive ways to the children; nor are the relatives who are most likely to have greatest contact with the children—the mother's parents, brothers, and sisters—likely to have a high opinion of the children's father. Many men are able to overcome such obstacles, but only with difficulty. In general, men need marriage in order to be good fathers.

If the future of fatherhood depends on marriage, however, 6 its future is uncertain. Marriage depends on women as well as men, and women are less committed to marriage than ever before in the nation's history. In the past, women were economically dependent on marriage and assumed a disproportionately heavy responsibility for maintaining the bond, even if the underlying relationship was seriously or irretrievably damaged. In the last third of the 20th century, however, as women have gained more opportunities for paid work and the availability of child care has increased, they have become less dependent on marriage as an economic arrangement. Though it is not easy, it is possible for women to raise children on their own. This has made divorce far more attractive as a remedy for an unsatisfying marriage, and a growing number of women have availed themselves of the option.

Today, marriage and motherhood are coming apart. 7 Remarriage and marriage rates are declining even as the rates of divorce remain stuck at historic highs and childbearing outside marriage becomes more common. Many women see single motherhood as a choice and a right to be exercised if a suitable husband does not come along in time.

The vision of the "first stage" feminism of the 1960s and 8 '70s, which held out the model of the career woman unfettered by husband or children, has been accepted by women only in part. Women want to be fettered by children, even to the point of going through grueling infertility treatments or artificial insemination to achieve motherhood. But they are increasingly ambivalent about the ties that bind them to a husband and about the necessity of marriage as a condition of parenthood. In 1994, a National Opinion Research survey asked a group of Americans. "Do you agree or disagree: one parent can bring up a child as well as two parents together." Women split 50/50 on the question; men disagreed by more than two to one.

And indeed, women enjoy certain advantages over men 9 in a society marked by high and sustained levels of family breakup. Women do not need marriage to maintain a close bond to their children, and thus to experience the larger sense of social and moral purpose that comes with raising children. As the bearers and nurturers of children and (increasingly) as the sole breadwinners for families, women continue to be engaged in personally rewarding and socially valuable pursuits. They are able to demonstrate their feminine virtues outside marriage.

Men, by contrast, have no positive identity as fathers out- 10 side marriage. Indeed, the emblematic absent father today is the infamous "deadbeat dad." In part, this is the result of efforts to stigmatize irresponsible fathers who fail to pay alimony and child support. But this image also reflects the fact that men are heavily dependent on the marriage partnership to fulfill their role as fathers. Even those who keep up their child support payments are deprived of the social importance and sense of larger purpose that comes from providing for children and raising a family. And it is the rare father who can develop the qualities needed to meet the new cultural ideal of the involved and "nurturing" father without the help of a spouse.

These differences are reflected in a growing virtue gap. 11 American popular culture today routinely recognizes and praises the achievements of single motherhood, while the widespread failure of men as fathers has resulted in a growing sense of cynicism and despair about men's capacity for virtuous conduct in family life. The enormously popular movie *Waiting to Exhale* captures the essence of this virtue gap with its portrait of steadfast mothers and deadbeat fathers, morally sleazy men and morally unassailable women. And women feel free to vent their anger and frustration with men in ways that would seem outrageous to women if the shoe were on the other foot. In *Operating Instructions* (1993), her memoir of single motherhood, Anne Lamott mordantly observes, "On bad days, I think straight white men are so poorly wired, so emotionally unenlightened and unconscious that you must approach each one as if he were some weird cross between a white supremacist and an incredibly depressing T. S. Eliot poem."

Women's weakening attachment to marriage should not 12 be taken as a lack of interest in marriage or in a husband-wife partnership in child rearing. Rather, it is a sign of women's more exacting emotional standards for husbands and their growing insistence that men play a bigger part in caring for children and the household. Given their double responsibilities as breadwinners and mothers, many working wives find men's need for ego reinforcement and other forms of emotional and physical upkeep irksome and their failure to share housework and child care absolutely infuriating. (Surveys show that husbands perform only one-third of all household tasks even if their wives are working full-time.) Why should men be treated like babies? women complain. If men fail to meet their standards, many women are willing to do without them. Poet and polemicist Katha Pollitt captures the prevailing sentiment: "If single women can have sex, their own homes, the respect of friends and interesting work, they don't need to tell themselves that any marriage is better than none. Why not have a child on one's own? Children are a joy. Many men are not."

For all these reasons, it is important to see the father-   13
hood problem as part of the larger cultural problem of the decline of marriage as a lasting relationship between men and women. The traditional bargain between men and women has broken down, and a new bargain has not yet been struck. It is impossible to predict what that bargain will look like—or whether there will even be one. However, it is possible to speculate about the talking points that might bring women to the bargaining table. First, a crucial proviso: there must be recognition of the changed social and economic status of women. Rightly or wrongly, many women fear that the fatherhood movement represents an effort to reinstate the status quo ante, to repeal the gains and achievements women have made over the past 30 years and return to the "separate spheres" domestic ideology that put men in the workplace and women in the home. Any effort to rethink marriage must accept the fact that women will continue to work outside the home.

Therefore, a new bargain must be struck over the division   14
of paid work and family work. This does not necessarily mean a 50/50 split in the work load every single day, but it does mean that men must make a more determined and conscientious effort to do more than one-third of the household chores. How each couple arrives at a sense of what is fair will vary, of course, but the goal is to establish some mutual understanding and commitment to an equitable division of tasks.

Another talking point may focus on the differences in   15
the expectations men and women have for marriage and

intimacy. Americans have a "best friends" ideal for marriage that includes some desires that might in fact be more easily met by a best friend—someone who doesn't come with all the complicated entanglements of sharing a bed, a bank account, and a bathroom. Nonetheless, high expectations for emotional intimacy in marriage often are confounded by the very different understandings men and women have of intimacy. Much more than men, women seek intimacy and affection through talking and emotional disclosure. Men often prefer sex to talking, and physical disrobing to emotional disclosing. They tend to be less than fully committed to (their own) sexual fidelity, while women view fidelity as a crucial sign of commitment. These are differences that the sexes need to engage with mutual recognition and tolerance.

In renegotiating the marital bargain, it may also be use- 16 ful to acknowledge the biosocial differences between mothers and fathers rather than to assume an androgynous model for the parental partnership. There can be a high degree of flexibility in parental roles, but men and women are not interchangeable "parental units," particularly in their children's early years. Rather than struggle to establish identical tracks in career and family lives, it may be more realistic to consider how children's needs and well-being might require patterns of paid work and child rearing that are different for mothers and fathers but are nevertheless equitable over the course of a lifetime.

Finally, it may be important to think and talk about mar- 17 riage in another kind of language than the one that suffuses our current discourse on relationships. The secular language of "intimate relationships" is the language of politics and psychotherapy, and it focuses on individual rights and individual needs. It can be heard most clearly in the personal-ad columns, a kind of masked ball where optimists go in search of partners who respect their rights and meet their emotional needs. These are not unimportant in the achievement of the contemporary ideal of marriage, which emphasizes egalitarianism and emotional fulfillment. But this notion of marriage as a union of two sovereign selves may be inadequate to define a relationship that carries with it the obligations, duties, and sacrifices of parenthood. There has always been a tension between marriage as an intimate relationship between a man and a woman and marriage as an institutional arrangement for raising children, and though the language of individual rights plays a part in defining the former, it cannot fully describe the latter. The parental partnership requires some language that acknowledges differences, mutuality, complementarity, and, more than anything else, altruism.

There is a potentially powerful incentive for women to 18 respond to an effort to renegotiate the marriage bargain, and that has to do with their children. Women can be good mothers without being married. But especially with weakened communities that provide little support, children need levels of parental investment that cannot be supplied solely by a good mother, even if she has the best resources at her disposal. These needs are more likely to be met if the child has a father as well as a mother under the same roof. Simply put, even the best mothers cannot be good fathers.

For Study and Discussion

QUESTIONS ABOUT PURPOSE

1. What changes in women's behaviors and attitudes would Whitehead like to bring about?
2. What changes in men's behaviors and attitudes would Whitehead like to bring about?

QUESTIONS ABOUT AUDIENCE

1. Whom do you see as the principal audience that Whitehead hopes to reach with this essay, men or women? On what evidence do you base your answer?
2. How might readers over forty and those under forty respond differently to this essay?

QUESTIONS ABOUT STRATEGIES

1. Whitehead's argument is built on strong statements like these: "Today, marriage and motherhood are coming apart," and "Men . . . have no positive identity as fathers outside marriage." In light of your own observations about today's families, how credible do you find these statements? Why?
2. Although Whitehead is writing about a topic that often generates a great deal of emotion, she is careful not to sound angry or to blame anyone. How does her argument benefit from her maintaining this moderate tone?

For Writing and Research

1. *Analyze* the evidence Whitehead presents for why "men need marriage in order to be good fathers."
2. *Practice* by demonstrating why men and women need to "renegotiate the marriage bargain."
3. *Argue* that the media have stereotyped "steadfast mothers" and "deadbeat dads."
4. *Synthesize* the research that supports the argument that women don't need marriage to have children.

ALICE WALKER

Alice Walker was born in 1944 in Eatonton, Georgia, and attended Spellman College and Sarah Lawrence College. She then became active in the civil rights movement, helping to register voters in Georgia, teaching in the Head Start program in Mississippi, and working on the staff of the New York City welfare department. In subsequent years, she began her own writing career while teaching at Wellesley College, the University of California at Berkeley, and Brandeis University. Her writing reveals her interest in the themes of sexism and racism, themes she embodies in her widely acclaimed novels: *The Third Life of Grange Copeland* (1970, *Meridian* (1976), *The Color Purple* (1982), *Possessing the Secret of Joy* (1992), *Now Is the Time to Open Your Heart* (2005), and *Devil's My Enemy* (2008). Her stories, collected in *In Love and Trouble: Stories of Black Women* (1973) and *You Can't Keep a Good Woman Down* (1981), and essays found in *Living by the Word* (1988), *The Same River Twice* (1996), and *Overcoming Speechlessness* (2010), examine the complex experiences of black women. "Everyday Use" reprinted from *In Love and Trouble,* focuses on a reunion that reveals two contrasting attitudes toward the meaning of family heritage.

Everyday Use[9]
For Your Grandmama

I WILL WAIT for her in the yard that Maggie and I made so clean and wavy yesterday afternoon. A yard like this is more comfortable than most people know. It is not just a   1

---

yard. It is like an extended living room. When the hard clay is swept clean as a floor and the fine sand around the edges lined with tiny, irregular grooves anyone can come and sit and look up into the elm tree and wait for the breezes that never come inside the house.

Maggie will be nervous until after her sister goes: she will 2
stand hopelessly in corners homely and ashamed of the burn scars down her arms and legs, eyeing her sister with a mixture of envy and awe. She thinks her sister has held life always in the palm of one hand, that "no" is a word the world never learned to say to her.

You've no doubt seen those TV shows where the child 3
who has "made it" is confronted, as a surprise, by her own mother and father, tottering in weakly from backstage. (A pleasant surprise, of course: What would they do if parent and child came on the show only to curse out and insult each other?) On TV mother and child embrace and smile into each other's faces. Sometimes the mother and father weep, the child wraps them in her arms and leans across the table to tell how she would not have made it without their help. I have seen these programs.

Sometimes I dream a dream in which Dee and I are sud- 4
denly brought together on a TV program of this sort. Out of a dark and soft-seated limousine I am ushered into a bright room filled with many people. There I meet a smiling, gray, sporty man like Johnny Carson who shakes my hand and tells me what a fine girl I have. Then we are on the stage and Dee is embracing me with tears in her eyes. She pins on my dress a large orchid, even though she has told me once that she thinks orchids are tacky flowers.

In real life I am a large, big-boned woman with rough, 5
man-working hands. In the winter I wear flannel nightgowns to bed and overalls during the day. I can kill and clean a hog as mercilessly as a man. My fat keeps me hot in zero weather. I can work all day, breaking ice to get water for washing. I can eat pork liver cooked over the open fire minutes after it comes steaming from the hog. One winter I knocked a bull calf straight in the brain between the eyes with a sledge

hammer and had the meat hung up to chill before nightfall. But of course all this does not show on television. I am the way my daughter would want me to be: a hundred pounds lighter, my skin like an uncooked barley pancake. My hair glistens in the hot bright lights. Johnny Carson has much to do to keep up with my quick and witty tongue.

But that is a mistake. I know even before I wake up. Who 6 ever knew a Johnson with a quick tongue? Who can even imagine me looking a strange white man in the eye? It seems to me I have talked to them always with one foot raised in flight, with my head turned in whichever way is farthest from them. Dee, though. She would always look anyone in the eye. Hesitation was no part of her nature.

"How do I look, Mama?" Maggie says, showing just enough 7 of her thin body enveloped in pink skirt and red blouse for me to know she's there, almost hidden by the door.

"Come out into the yard," I say. 8

Have you ever seen a lame animal, perhaps a dog run over 9 by some careless person rich enough to own a car, sidle up to someone who is ignorant enough to be kind to him? That is the way my Maggie walks. She has been like this, chin on chest, eyes on ground, feet in shuffle, ever since the fire that burned the other house to the ground.

Dee is lighter than Maggie, with nicer hair and a fuller 10 figure. She's a woman now, though sometimes I forget. How long ago was it that the other house burned? Ten, twelve years? Sometimes I can still hear the flames and feel Maggie's arm sticking to me, her hair smoking and her dress falling off her in little black papery flakes. Her eyes seemed stretched open, blazed open by the flames reflected in them. And Dee. I see her standing off under the sweet gum tree she used to dig gum out of; a look of concentration on her face as she watched the last dingy gray board of the house fall in toward the red-hot brick chimney. Why don't you do a dance around the ashes? I'd wanted to ask her. She had hated the house that much.

I used to think she hated Maggie, too. But that was 11 before we raised the money, the church and me, to send her to Augusta to school. She used to read to us without pity; forcing words, lies, other folks' habits, whole lives upon us two, sitting trapped and ignorant underneath her voice. She washed us in a river of make-believe, burned us with a lot of knowledge we didn't necessarily need to know. Pressed us to her with the serious way she read, to shove us away at just the moment, like dimwits, we seemed about to understand.

Dee wanted nice things. A yellow organdy dress to wear   12 to her graduation from high school; black pumps to match a green suit she'd made from an old suit somebody gave me. She was determined to stare down any disaster in her efforts. Her eyelids would not flicker for minutes at a time. Often I fought off the temptation to shake her. At sixteen she had a style of her own: and knew what style was.

I never had an education myself. After second grade the   13 school was closed down. Don't ask me why: in 1927 colored asked fewer questions than they do now. Sometimes Maggie reads to me. She stumbles along good-naturedly but can't see well. She knows she is not bright. Like good looks and money, quickness passed her by. She will marry John Thomas (who has mossy teeth in an earnest face) and then I'll be free to sit here and I guess just sing church songs to myself. Although I never was a good singer. Never could carry a tune. I was always better at a man's job. I used to love to milk till I was hoofed in the side in '49. Cows are soothing and slow and don't bother you, unless you try to milk them the wrong way.

I have deliberately turned my back on the house. It is three   14 rooms, just like the one that burned, except the roof is tin; they don't make shingle roofs any more. There are no real windows, just some holes cut in the sides, like the portholes in a ship, but not round and not square, with rawhide holding the shutters up on the outside. This house is in a pasture, too, like the other one. No doubt when Dee sees it she will want to tear it down. She wrote me once that no matter where we "choose" to live, she will manage to come see us. But she will never bring her friends. Maggie and I thought about this and Maggie asked me, "Mama, when did Dee ever *have* any friends?"

She had a few. Furtive boys in pink shirts hanging about   15
on washday after school. Nervous girls who never laughed.
Impressed with her they worshiped the well-turned phrase,
the cute shape, the scalding humor that erupted like bubbles
in lye. She read to them.

When she was courting Jimmy T she didn't have much   16
time to pay to us, but turned all her faultfinding power on
him. He *flew* to marry a cheap gal from a family of ignorant
flashy people. She hardly had time to recompose herself.

When she comes I will meet—but there they are!   17

Maggie attempts to make a dash for the house, in her shuf-   18
fling way, but I stay her with my hand. "Come back here,"
I say. And she stops and tries to dig a well in the sand with
her toe.

It is hard to see them clearly through the strong sun. But   19
even the first glimpse of leg out of the car tells me it is Dee.
Her feet were always neat-looking, as if God himself had
shaped them with a certain style. From the other side of the
car comes a short, stocky man. Hair is all over his head a foot
long and hanging from his chin like a kinky mule tail. I hear
Maggie suck in her breath. "Uhnnnh," is what it sounds like.
Like when you see the wriggling end of a snake just in front
of your foot on the road. "Uhnnnh."

Dee next. A dress down to the ground, in this hot weather.   20
A dress so loud it hurts my eyes. There are yellows and oranges
enough to throw back the light of the sun. I feel my whole
face warming from the heat waves it throws out. Earrings,
too, gold and hanging down to her shoulders. Bracelets dangling and making noises when she moves her arm up to shake
the folds of the dress out of her armpits. The dress is loose
and flows, and as she walks closer, I like it. I hear Maggie go
"Uhnnnh" again. It is her sister's hair. It stands straight up
like the wool on a sheep. It is black as night and around the
edges are two long pigtails that rope about like small lizards
disappearing behind her ears.

"Wa-su-zo-Tean-o!" she says, coming on in that gliding   21
way the dress makes her move. The short stocky fellow with
the hair to his navel is all grinning and he follows up with

"Asalamalakim, my mother and sister!" He moves to hug Maggie but she falls back, right up against the back of my chair. I feel her trembling there and when I look up I see the perspiration falling off her chin.

"Don't get up," says Dee. Since I am stout it takes some- 22
thing of a push. You can see me trying to move a second or two before I make it. She turns, showing white heels through her sandals, and goes back to the car. Out she peeks next with a Polaroid. She stoops down quickly and lines up picture after picture of me sitting there in front of the house with Maggie cowering behind me. She never takes a shot without making sure the house is included. When a cow comes nibbling around the edge of the yard she snaps it and me and Maggie *and* the house. Then she puts the Polaroid in the back seat of the car, and comes up and kisses me on the forehead.

Meanwhile Asalamalakim is going through the motions 23
with Maggie's hand. Maggie's hand is limp as a fish, and probably as cold, despite the sweat, and she keeps trying to pull it back. It looks like Asalamalakim wants to shake hands but wants to do it fancy. Or maybe he don't know how people shake hands. Anyhow, he soon gives up on Maggie.

"Well," I say. "Dee."   24

"No, Mama," she says. "Not 'Dee,' Wangero Leewanika 25
Kemanjo!"

"What happened to 'Dee'?" I wanted to know.   26

"She's dead," Wangero said. "I couldn't bear it any longer 27
being named after the people who oppress me."

"You know as well as me you was named after your aunt 28
Dicie," I said. Dicie is my sister. She named Dee. We called her "Big Dee" after Dee was born.

"But who was *she* named after?" asked Wangero.   29

"I guess after Grandma Dee," I said.   30

"And who was she named after?" asked Wangero.   31

"Her mother," I said, and saw Wangero getting tired.   32
"That's about as far back as I can trace it," I said. Though, in fact, I probably could have carried it back beyond the Civil War through the branches.

"Well," said Asalamalakim, "there you are."   33

"Uhnnnh," I heard Maggie say.   34

"There I was not," I said, "before 'Dicie' cropped up in   35
our family, so why should I try to trace it that far back?"

He just stood there grinning, looking down on me like   36
somebody inspecting a Model A car. Every once in a while he
and Wangero sent eye signals over my head.

"How do you pronounce this name?" I asked.   37

"You don't have to call me by it if you don't want to,"   38
said Wangero.

"Why shouldn't I?" I asked. "If that's what you want us to   39
call you, we'll call you."

"I know it might sound awkward at first," said Wangero.   40

"I'll get used to it," I said. "Ream it out again."   41

Well, soon we got the name out of the way. Asalamalakim   42
had a name twice as long and three times as hard. After I
tripped over it two or three times he told me to just call him
Hakim-a-barber. I wanted to ask him was he a barber, but I
didn't really think he was, so I didn't ask.

"You must belong to those beef-cattle peoples down the   43
road," I said. They said "Asalamalakim" when they met you,
too, but they didn't shake hands. Always too busy: feeding the cattle, fixing the fences, putting up salt-lick shelters,
throwing down hay. When the white folks poisoned some of
the herd the men stayed up all night with rifles in their hands,
I walked a mile and half just to see the sight.

Hakim-a-barber said, "I accept some of their doctrines,   44
but farming and raising cattle is not my style." (They didn't
tell me, and I didn't ask, whether Wangero [Dee] had really
gone and married him.)

We sat down to eat and right away he said he didn't eat   45
collards and pork was unclean. Wangero, though, went on
through the chitlins and corn bread, the greens and everything else. She talked a blue streak over the sweet potatoes.
Everything delighted her. Even the fact that we still used
the benches her daddy made for the table when we couldn't
afford to buy chairs.

"Oh, Mama!" she cried. Then turned to Hakim-a-barber.   46
"I never knew how lovely these benches are. You can feel

the rump prints," she said, running her hands underneath her and along the bench. Then she gave a sigh and her hand closed over Grandma Dee's butter dish. "That's it!" she said. "I knew there was something I wanted to ask you if I could have." She jumped up from the table and went over in the corner where the churn stood, the milk in its clabber by now. She looked at the churn and looked at it.

"This churn top is what I need," she said. "Didn't Uncle 47 Buddy whittle it out of a tree you all used to have?"

"Yes," I said. 48

"Uh huh," she said happily. "And I want the dasher, too." 49

"Uncle Buddy whittle that, too?" asked the barber. 50

Dee (Wangero) looked up at me. 51

"Aunt Dee's first husband whittled the dash," said Maggie 52 so low you almost couldn't hear her. "His name was Henry, but they called him Stash."

"Maggie's brain is like an elephant's," Wangero said, 53 laughing. "I can use the churn top as a centerpiece for the alcove table," she said, sliding a plate over the churn, "and I'll think of something artistic to do with the dasher."

When she finished wrapping the dasher the handle stuck 54 out. I took it for a moment in my hands. You didn't even have to look close to see where hands pushing the dasher up and down to make butter had left a kind of sink in the wood. In fact, there were a lot of small sinks; you could see where thumbs and fingers had sunk into the wood. It was beautiful light yellow wood, from a tree that grew in the yard where Big Dee and Stash had lived.

After dinner Dee (Wangero) went to the trunk at the foot 55 of my bed and started rifling through it. Maggie hung back in the kitchen over the dishpan. Out came Wangero with two quilts. They had been pieced by Grandma Dee and then Big Dee and me had hung them on the quilt frames on the front porch and quilted them. One was in the Lone Star pattern. The other was Walk Around the Mountain. In both of them were scraps of dresses Grandma Dee had worn fifty and more years ago. Bits and pieces of Grandpa Jarrell's Paisley shirts. And one teeny faded blue piece, about the size of a penny matchbox, that was from Great Grandpa Ezra's uniform that he wore in the Civil War.

"Mama," Wangero said sweet as a bird. "Can I have these   56
old quilts?"

I heard something fall in the kitchen, and a minute later   57
the kitchen door slammed.

"Why don't you take one or two of the others?" I asked.   58
"These old things was just done by me and Big Dee from
some tops your grandma pieced before she died."

"No," said Wangero. "I don't want those. They are   59
stitched around the borders by machine."

"That'll make them last better," I said.   60

"That's not the point," said Wangero. "These are all pieces   61
of dresses Grandma used to wear. She did all this stitching
by hand. Imagine!" She held the quilts securely in her arms,
stroking them.

"Some of the pieces, like those lavender ones, come from   62
old clothes her mother handed down to her," I said, moving up to touch the quilts. Dee (Wangero) moved back just
enough so that I couldn't reach the quilts. They already
belonged to her.

"Imagine!" she breathed again, clutching them closely to   63
her bosom.

"The truth is," I said, "I promised to give them quilts to   64
Maggie, for when she marries John Thomas."

She gasped like a bee had stung her.   65

"Maggie can't appreciate these quilts!" she said. "She'd   66
probably be backward enough to put them to everyday use."

"I reckon she would," I said. "God knows I been sav-   67
ing 'em for long enough with nobody using 'em. I hope
she will!" I didn't want to bring up how I had offered Dee
(Wangero) a quilt when she went away to college. Then she
had told me they were old fashioned, out of style.

"But they're *priceless!*" she was saying now, furiously; for   68
she has a temper. "Maggie would put them on the bed and
in five years they'd be in rags. Less than that!"

"She can always make some more," I said. "Maggie knows   69
how to quilt."

Dee (Wangero) looked at me with hatred. "You just will 70
not understand. The point is these quilts, *these* quilts!"

"Well," I said, stumped. "What would *you* do with them?" 71

"Hang them," she said. As if that was the only thing you 72
could do with quilts.

Maggie by now was standing in the door. I could almost 73
hear the sound her feet made as they scraped over each
other.

"She can have them, Mama," she said, like somebody used 74
to never winning anything, or having anything reserved for
her. "I can 'member Grandma Dee without the quilts."

I looked at her hard. She had filled her bottom lip with 75
checkerberry snuff and it gave her face a kind of dopey, hang-
dog look. It was Grandma Dee and Big Dee who taught her
how to quilt herself. She stood there with her scarred hands
hidden in the folds of her skirt. She looked at her sister with
something like fear but she wasn't mad at her. This was Maggie's portion. This was the way she knew God to work.

When I looked at her like that something hit me in the 76
top of my head and ran down to the soles of my feet. Just
like when I'm in church and the spirit of God touches me
and I get happy and shout. I did something I never had done
before: hugged Maggie to me, then dragged her on into the
room, snatched the quilts out of Miss Wangero's hands and
dumped them into Maggie's lap. Maggie just sat there on my
bed with her mouth open.

"Take one or two of the others," I said to Dee. 77

But she turned without a word and went out to Hakim- 78
a-barber.

"You just don't understand," she said, as Maggie and I 79
came out to the car.

"What don't I understand?" I wanted to know. 80

"Your heritage," she said. And then she turned to Maggie, 81
kissed her and said, "You ought to try to make something of
yourself, too, Maggie. It's really a new day for us. But from
the way you and Mama still live you'd never know it."

She put on some sunglasses that hid everything above the 82
tip of her nose and her chin.

Maggie smiled; maybe at the sunglasses. But a real smile,   83
not scared. After we watched the car dust settle I asked Maggie to bring me a dip of snuff. And then the two of us sat
there just enjoying, until it was time to go in the house and
go to bed.

COMMENT ON "EVERYDAY USE"

Walker's "Everyday Use" describes a difference between a
mother's and her visiting daughter's understandings of the
word *heritage*. For Mama and her daughter Maggie, heritage is a matter of everyday living, of "everyday use." For
Mama's other daughter, Dee (Wangero), however, heritage
is a matter of style, a fashionable obsession with one's roots.
These comparisons are revealed first in Walker's description
of the physical appearance of the characters. Mama is fat and
manly, and Maggie bears the scars from a fire. By contrast,
Dee (Wangero) is beautiful and striking in her brightly colored African dress, earrings, sunglasses, and Afro hairstyle.
Next, Walker compares the characters' skills. Mama can
butcher a hog or break ice to get water, and Maggie is able
to make beautiful quilts. Dee (Wangero), on the other hand,
thinks of herself as outside this domestic world, educated by
books to understand the cultural significance of her heritage.
The problem posed by the debate over family possessions is
whether heritage is an object to be preserved, like a priceless
painting, or a process to be learned, like the creation of a
quilt.

CHAPTER 9

USING
AND
DOCUMENTING
SOURCES

The essays in *The River Reader* are sources. Many of the writing assignments ask you to *analyze* these sources or to use them to support your own ideas. Most academic writing asks you to use sources—from books, journals, magazines, newspapers, and the Internet—to augment and advance the ideas in your writing. Every time you cite a source, or use it in some way, you must *document* it. The student research paper at the end of this chapter uses MLA style to cite print and Web sources.

This chapter explains the style recommended by the Modern Language Association (MLA) for documenting sources in research papers. It also analyzes some of the implications of MLA style for your research and composing. More detailed information is given in the *MLA Handbook* and the *MLA Style Manual.**

*Modern Language Association, *MLA Handbook for Writers of Research Papers,* 7th ed. (New York: MLA, 2009); Modern Language Association, *MLA Style Manual and Guide to Scholarly Publishing,* 3rd ed. (New York: MLA, 2008).

MLA style has three major features:

- All sources cited in a paper are listed in a section entitled **Works Cited,** which is located at the end of the paper.
- Material borrowed from another source is documented within the text by a brief parenthetical reference that directs readers to the full citation in the list of works cited.
- Numbered footnotes or endnotes are used to present two types of supplementary information: (1) commentary or explanation that the text cannot accommodate and (2) bibliographical notes that contain several source citations.

IMPLICATIONS FOR YOUR RESEARCH AND COMPOSING

Evaluating Resources

As you begin collecting sources to advance your research, evaluate them according to the following criteria:

1. **A source should be relevant.** Ask yourself, Does the content of this source apply directly to the topic of the paper? Whether the source is relevant is not always apparent. When you begin your research, your lack of perspective on your subject may make every source seem potentially relevant. Titles of sources may be misleading or vague, prompting you to examine a source unrelated to your subject or dismiss a source as too theoretical or general when it could actually give you vital perspectives on your subject. The status of your sources may also change as you restrict or redefine your subject. A source that seemed irrelevant yesterday may appear more pertinent today. For example, a source that discusses waste management may seem irrelevant today when the topic of your paper is global warming; but when you decide to focus your paper on alternate sources of fuel, the source may suddenly seem essential to your argument.

2. **A source should be authoritative.** Ask yourself, Does the author of a particular source have the necessary expertise or experience to speak authoritatively about the subject of your paper? Most print sources enable you to judge the credentials and bias of the author. You can usually judge the authority of a book or an article because the book has been reviewed by knowledgeable persons or the article has been evaluated by peer reviewers or the journal's editorial board. But you have no way to evaluate the authority of many electronic sources. A source you assume is authoritative may have been posted by a hacker or someone who wishes to further his or her own agenda. For example, the information contained on a Wikipedia site is posted by all sorts of unidentifiable writers who may or may not be reliable authorities.

3. **A source should be current.** Ask yourself, Is this source current? You don't want to cite a fifty-year-old source if you are writing about the latest cures for cancer. However, you may want to use that same fifty-year-old source if you are writing about changes in the history of cancer therapy. Writers often cite standard print sources to establish the reliability of their arguments. Then they will cite recent electronic sources to address issues that have arisen since the print sources were originally published. Keep in mind that electronic sources are not necessarily the most current, since many print sources—old and new—are now posted on the Web. To make sure that your sources are reliable and current, you may need to mix print and electronic sources.

4. **A source should be comprehensive.** Ask yourself, Does this source cover the major issues I need to discuss in my paper? Some sources focus on an extremely narrow aspect of your subject; others will cover every feature and many related, or unrelated, topics as well. Begin reading the most comprehensive first because it will cover the essential information in the more specialized sources and give you related subtopics within your subject. Most books, for example, are comprehensive sources, whereas most Web sites provide only "bits" of information.

5. **A source should be stable.** Ask yourself, If I use this source, will my readers be able to locate it if they want to read more about the topic of my paper? You will want to cite sources that provide the best and most stable information on your topic. There is nothing more stable than a book. Even if a library does not own a book or if a book goes out of print, librarians can find a copy for your readers through interlibrary loan. This is also true for most articles. But electronic sources are not stable. The source you stumble on today may not be there tomorrow. Your readers will not be able to find it because it may be renamed, reclassified, or simply deleted. If your readers want to check your sources, you should cite sources they can find.

6. **A source should provide links.** Ask yourself, Does this source help me locate other sources? The best sources lead to other sources, which can enrich your research. The subject headings on a source provide an excellent system for linking up with other sources. Annotated bibliographies not only link you to other sources but also provide you with an assessment of their value. Of course, the chief advantage of the Web and its various search engines is that they allow you to link up with thousands of sources by simply pointing and clicking. If your source provides such links, your readers can use them to trace the research that informs the source and the way you have used it to broaden and deepen the research in your paper.

Compiling Source Information

Once you have located sources you suspect will prove useful, create a computer file for each item. List the source in the appropriate format. (Use the formats shown in the guidelines for "Preparing the List of Works Cited," pages 580–593.) To guarantee that each file is complete and accurate, take your information directly from the source rather than from an online catalog or a bibliographical index. Your file will help you keep track of your sources throughout your research. Alphabetizing the files will enable you to prepare a provisional list of Works Cited.

The provisional list must be in place *before* you begin writing your paper. You may expand or refine the list as you write, but to document each source in your text, you first need to know its correct citation. Thus, although Works Cited will be the last section of your paper, you must prepare a provisional version of it first.

Taking Notes

Note taking demands that you read, select, interpret, and evaluate the information that will form the substance of your paper. After you have returned material to the library or turned off your computer, your notes will be the only record of your research. If you have taken notes carelessly, you will be in trouble when you try to use them in your paper. Many students inadvertently plagiarize because they are working from inaccurate notes. (See "Avoiding Plagiarism," pages 576–579.)

If you are relying on your computer to create your source files, you may also commit plagiarism by falling into the "copy-paste trap." The most efficient way to work with electronic sources is to **copy** important passages from online sources and then **paste** them into your research files. But this quick and easy way of saving information can also get you into a lot of trouble. If you simply copy the material you have found without marking it as a quotation and identifying its source, you may later assume that you composed the material that you see pasted in your file and present it as your own writing. (See "Avoiding Plagiarism," pages 576–579.)

As you select information from a source, use one of three methods to record it: **quoting, summarizing,** or **paraphrasing.**

Quoting Sources

Although quoting an author's text word for word is the easiest way to record information, use this method selectively and quote only those passages that deal directly with your subject in memorable language. When you copy and paste a passage into a file, place quotation marks at the beginning and end of the passage. If you decide to omit part of the passage, use ellipsis points to indicate that you have omitted words from the original source. To indicate an omission from the middle of a sentence, use three periods (. . .) and leave a space before and after each period. To indicate the omission of the end of a sentence or of more than one sentence, use three spaced periods following the sentence period (. . . .).

To move a quotation from your notes to your paper, making it fit smoothly into the flow of your text, use one of the following methods.

1. **Work the quoted passage into the syntax of your sentence.**

    Morrison points out that "the history of perse-cuted writers is as long as the history of literature itself" (2).

2. **Introduce the quoted passage with a sentence and a colon.**

    Literary critics have commented on how the per-secution of writers signals a change in a culture: "[it] is the earliest harbinger of the steady peeling away of additional rights and liberties that will fol-low" (Morrison 2).

3. **Set off a long quoted passage with an introductory sentence followed by a colon.**

    This method is reserved for long quotations (four or more lines of prose; three or more lines of poetry). Double-space the quotation, and indent it one inch (ten spaces) from the left margin. Because this special placement identifies the passage as a quotation, do not enclose it within quotation marks. Notice that the final period goes *before* rather than *after* the parenthetical reference. Leave one space after the final period. If the long quotation extends to two or more paragraphs, then indent the first line of these additional paragraphs one-quarter inch (three spaces).

In "Peril," Toni Morrison explains why dictators need to suppress writers:

> We all know nations that can be identified by the flight of writers from their shores. . . .
>
> Unpersecuted, unjailed, unharassed writers are trouble for the ignorant bully, the sly racist, and the predators feeding off the world's resources. The alarm, the disquiet, writers raise is instructive because it is open and vulnerable, because if unpoliced it is threatening. Therefore, the historical suppression of writers is the earliest harbinger of the steady peeling away of additional rights and liberties that will follow. The history of persecuted writers is as long as the history of literature itself. (2)

Summarizing and Paraphrasing Sources

Summarizing and paraphrasing an author's text are the most efficient ways to record information. The terms *summary* and *paraphrase* are often used interchangeably to describe a brief restatement of the author's ideas in your own words, but they may be used more precisely to designate different procedures.

A *summary* condenses the content of a lengthy passage. When you write a summary, you formulate the main idea and outline the main points that support it. A *paraphrase* restates the content of a short passage. When you paraphrase, you reconstruct the passage phrase by phrase, recasting the author's words as your own.

A summary or a paraphrase is intended as a complete and objective presentation of the author's ideas, so be careful not to distort the original passage by omitting major points or by adding your own opinion. Because the words of a summary or a paraphrase are yours, they are not enclosed by quotation marks. But because the ideas you are restating came from someone else, you need to cite the source in your notes and in your text. (See "Avoiding Plagiarism," pages 576–579.)

The following examples illustrate two common methods of introducing a summary or a paraphrase into your paper.

1. **Summary of a long quotation** (See the Morrison quotation on page 575.)

   Often the best way to proceed is to name the author of a source in the body of your sentence and to place the page numbers in parentheses. This procedure informs your reader that you are about to quote or paraphrase. It also gives you an opportunity to state the credentials of the authority you are citing.

   Award-winning novelist Toni Morrison argues that dictators need to persecute writers to control what is said in and about their countries (2).

2. **Paraphrase of a short quotation** (See the last sentence of the Morrison quotation on page 575.)

   You may decide to vary the pattern of documentation by presenting the information from a source and placing the author's name and page number in parenthesis at the end of the sentence. This method is particularly useful if you have already established the identity of your source in a previous sentence and now want to develop the author's ideas in some detail without having to clutter your sentences with constant references to his or her name.

   Writers have been persecuted throughout literary history (Morrison 2).

Works Cited

Morrison, Toni. "Peril." *Burn This Book*. Ed. Toni Morrison. New York: HarperCollins, 2009. Print.

Avoiding Plagiarism

Plagiarism is theft. It is using someone else's words or ideas without giving proper credit—or without giving any credit at all—to the writer of the original. Whether plagiarism is intentional or unintentional, it is a serious offense that your instructor and school will deal with severely. You can avoid plagiarism by adhering scrupulously to the following advice.

1. **Document your sources whenever you**

   - Use a direct quotation;
   - Copy a table, chart or other diagram;
   - Construct a table from data provided by others;
   - Summarize of paraphrase a passage in your own words;
   - Present examples, figures, or factual information that you have taken from a specific source and used to explain or support your judgments.

2. **Take notes carefully,** making sure that you identify quotations when you copy and paste them into your computer files. Also, be sure to identify a passage in your notes that is a summary or paraphrase. (See "Taking Notes," page 573.)

3. **Formulate and develop your own ideas,** using sources to support rather than replace your own work.

   The following passage is taken from Bill Bryson's *At Home: A Short History of Private Life*. The first two examples (Versions A and B) illustrate how students committed plagiarism by trying to use this source in their text. The last example (Version C) illustrates how a student avoided plagiarism by carefully citing and documenting the source.

   ### Original Passage

   The Eiffel Tower wasn't just the largest thing that anyone had ever proposed to build, it was the largest completely useless thing. It wasn't a palace or burial chamber or place of worship. It didn't even commemorate a fallen hero.

Version A

The Eiffel Tower was the largest thing that anyone had ever proposed to build, it was also the
largest useless thing. It wasn't a palace or a burial
chamber or a place of worship. It didn't even commemorate a fallen hero.

Version A is plagiarism. Because the writer of Version A does
not indicate in the text or in a parenthetical reference that the
words and ideas belong to Bryson, her readers will believe
the words are hers. She has stolen the words and ideas and
has attempted to cover the theft by changing or omitting an
occasional word.

Version B

Bill Bryson points out that the Eiffel Tower wasn't
just the largest thing that anyone had ever proposed to build, it was the largest completely useless thing. It wasn't a palace or a burial chamber or
a place of worship. It didn't even commemorate a
fallen hero (213).

Version B is also plagiarism, even though the writer acknowledges his source and documents the passage with a parenthetical reference. He has worked from careless notes and
misunderstood the difference between quoting and paraphrasing. He has copied the original word for word yet
supplied no quotation marks to indicate the extent of the
borrowing. As written and documented, the passage masquerades as a paraphrase when in fact it is a direct quotation.

Version C

Bryson argues that Eiffel's tower did not serve
any useful purpose: "It wasn't a palace or a burial
chamber or a place of worship. It didn't even commemorate a fallen hero" (213).

Version C is one satisfactory way of handling this source material. The writer has identified her source at the beginning of the sentence, letting her readers know who is being quoted. She then rephrases Bryson's assertion about the tower in her own words and concludes the sentence with a colon. Next she marks the words she is using from Bryson's passage by placing quotation marks at the beginning and end of the passage. Finally, she provides a parenthetical reference to the page number in the source listed in Works Cited.

Works Cited

Bryson, Bill. *At Home: A Short History of Private Life*. New York: Doubleday, 2010. Print.

DOCUMENTING SOURCES

To avoid clutter in sentences, MLA recommends placing the parenthetical reference at the end of the sentence but before the final period. Notice that there is no punctuation mark between the author's name and the page citation.

> In the nineteenth century, the supposed golden age of American education, "college faculties acted as disciplinary tribunals, periodically reviewing violations of rules . . . " (Graff 25).

On some occasions, you may want to place the reference within your sentence to clarify its relationship to the part of the sentence it documents. In such instances, place the reference at the end of the clause but before the comma.

> Graff suggest that though college faculties in the nineteenth century "acted as disciplinary tribunals, periodically reviewing violation of rules" (25), the myth persists that they taught in the golden age of American education.

When the reference documents a long quotation that is set off from the text, place it at the end of the passage but *after* the final period. (See pages 574–575 for a discussion of long quotations.)

Gerald Graff's description of college in the nineteenth century corrects the popular myth about the golden age of American education:

> College faculties acted as disciplinary tribunals, periodically reviewing violations of rules such as those requiring students to attend chapel services early every morning, to remain in their rooms for hours every day, and to avoid the snares of town. Nor were these restrictions relaxed for the many students in their late twenties or older, who lived alongside freshman as young as fourteen. The classes themselves, conducted by the system of daily regulations, were said to have "the fearsome atmosphere of a police station." (25)

Works Cited

Graff, Gerald. *Professing Literature: An Institutional History.* Chicago: U of Chicago P, 1987. Print.

PREPARING THE LIST OF WORKS CITED

In an academic paper that follows MLA style, the list of works cited is the only place where readers will find complete information about the sources you have cited. For that reason, your list must be thorough and accurate.

The list of works cited appears at the end of your paper and, as its title suggests, lists only the works you have cited in your paper. Occasionally, your instructor may ask you to prepare a list of works consulted. That list would include not only the sources you cite but also the sources you consulted as you conducted your research. In either case, MLA prefers Works Cited or Works Consulted to the more limited heading Bibliography (literally, "description of books") because those headings are more likely to accommodate the variety of sources—articles, films, Internet sources—that writers may cite in a research paper.

To prepare the list of works cited, follow these general guidelines:

1. Paginate the Works Cited section as a continuation of your text. If the conclusion of your paper appears on page 8, begin your list on page 9 (unless there is an intervening page of endnotes).
2. Double-space between successive lines of an entry and between entries.
3. Begin the first line of an entry flush left, and indent successive lines one-half inch or five spaces.
4. List entries in alphabetical order according to the last name of the author.
5. If you are listing more than one work by the same author, alphabetize the works according to title (excluding the articles, *a, an,* and *the*). Instead of repeating the author's name, type *three* hyphens and a period, and then give the title.
6. List the medium of publication in every entry in the list of works cited. For example: Rose, Mike. *The Mind at Work. Valuing the Intelligence of the American Worker.* New York: Viking, 2004. Print. Or: Gladwell, Malcolm. "Most Likely to Succeed." *The New Yorker.com.* 15 Dec. 2008 Web. 28 March 2009.
7. List date of access at the end of the citation of a Web source.
8. *Italicize* the titles of works published as independent units: books, plays, long poems, pamphlets, periodicals, films. Do not *italicize* article titles.
9. If you are citing a book whose title includes the title of another book, *italicize* the main title, but do not *italicize* the other title (for example, *A Casebook on Ralph Ellison's* Invisible Man).
10. Use quotation marks to indicate titles of short works, such as articles, that appear in larger works (for example, "Minutes of Glory." *African Short Stories*). Also use quotation marks for song titles and for titles of unpublished works, including dissertations, lectures, and speeches.

11. Use Arabic numerals except with names of monarchs (Elizabeth II) and except for the preliminary pages of a work (ii–xix), which are traditionally numbered with Roman numerals.

12. Use lowercase abbreviations to identify the parts of a work (for example, *vol.* for *volume*), a named translator (*trans.*), and a named editor (*ed.*). However, when these designations follow a period, they should be capitalized (for example, Woolf, Virginia. *A Writer's Diary*. Ed. Leonard Woolf).

13. Whenever possible, use appropriate shortened forms for the publisher's name (Random instead of Random House).

14. Separate author, title, and publication information with a period followed by one space.

15. Use a colon and one space to separate the volume number and year of a periodical from the page numbers (for example, Trimmer, Joseph. "Memoryscape: Jean Shepherd's Midwest." *Old Northwest* 2 [1976]: 357–69).

16. Treat inclusive page numbers in text citations and in the list of works cited as follows: 67–68, 102–03, 237–42, 389–421.

In addition to these guidelines, MLA recommends procedures for documenting an extensive variety of sources, including Web sources and nonprint materials such as films and television programs. The following models illustrate sources most commonly cited.

Sample Entries: Books in Print

When citing books, provide the following general categories of information:

Author's last name, first name. *Book Title*. Additional information. City of publication: Publisher, publication date. (medium) Print.

Entries illustrating variations of this basic format appear below and are numbered to facilitate reference.

1. A BOOK BY ONE AUTHOR

Wilkerson, Isabel. *The Warmth of Other Suns: The Epic Story of America's Great Migration*. New York: Random, 2010. Print.

2. TWO OR MORE BOOKS BY THE SAME AUTHOR

Florida, Richard. *The Rise of the Creative Class: And How It's Transforming Work, Leisure, Community and Everyday Life*. New York: Basic, 2002. Print.

———. *The Flight of the Creative Class: The Global Competition for Talent*. New York: Basic, 2002. Print.

3. A BOOK BY TWO OR THREE AUTHORS

Arum, Richard, and Josipa Roksa. *Academically Adrift: Limited Learning on College Campuses*. Chicago: U of Chicago P, 2011. Print.

Goldberg, Carey, Beth Jones, and Pamela Ferdinand. *Three Wishes: The True Story of Good Friends, Crushing Heart and Astonishing Luck on our Way to Love and Motherhood*. New York: Little Brown, 2010. Print.

4. A BOOK BY FOUR OR MORE AUTHORS

Hoy, Michael, John Livernois, Chris McKenna, Ray Rees, and Thanasis Stengos. *Mathematics for Economics*. 3rd ed. Cambridge: MIT Press, 2011. Print.

5. A BOOK BY A CORPORATE AUTHOR

National Geographic Society. *Cradle and Crucible: History and Faith in the Middle East*. Washington: National Geographic, 2002. Print.

6. A BOOK BY AN ANONYMOUS AUTHOR

Literary Market Place 2012: The Dictionary of the American Book Publishing Industry. Medford, NJ: Bowker, 2011. Print.

7. A BOOK WITH AN EDITOR

Jackson, Kenneth T., ed. The Encyclopedia of New York City. New Haven: Yale UP, 1995. Print.

8. A BOOK WITH AN AUTHOR AND AN EDITOR

Toomer, Jean. Cane. Ed. Darwin T. Turner. New York: Norton, 1988. Print.

9. A BOOK WITH A PUBLISHER'S IMPRINT

Hillenbrand, Laura. Seabiscuit: An American Legend. New York: Ballantine-Random, 2001. Print.

10. AN ANTHOLOGY OR COMPILATION

Smith, Barbara Leigh, and John McCann, eds. Reinventing Ourselves: Interdisciplinary Education, Collaborative Learning, and Experimentation in Higher Education. Bolton, MA: Anker, 2001. Print.

11. A WORK IN AN ANTHOLOGY

Peterson, Rai. "My Tribe Outside the Global Village." Visual Media and the Humanities: A Pedagogy of Representation. Ed. Kecia Driver McBride. Knoxville: U of Tennessee P, 2004. Print.

12. AN INTRODUCTION, PREFACE, FOREWORD, OR AFTERWORD

Shulman, Lee S. Foreword. Disciplinary Styles in the Scholarship of Teaching and Learning. Eds. Mary Taylor Huber and Sherwyn P. Morreale. Washington: American Assn. of Higher Educ., 2002. Print.

13. A MULTIVOLUME WORK

Burlingame, Michael. *Abraham Lincoln: A Life.* 2 vols. Baltimore: The Johns Hopkins U, 2008. Print.

14. AN EDITION OTHER THAN THE FIRST

Murray, Donald. *The Craft of Revision.* 5th ed. Boston: Wadsworth, 2004. Print.

15. A BOOK IN A SERIES

Eggers, Dave, ed. *The Best American Nonrequired Reading, 2011.* Boston: Houghton, 2011. Print. The Best American Series.

16. A REPUBLISHED BOOK

Malamud, Bernard. *The Natural.* 1952. New York: Avon, 1980. Print.

17. A SIGNED ARTICLE IN A REFERENCE BOOK

Tobias, Richard. "Thurber, James." *Encyclopedia Americana.* 2002 ed. Print.

18. AN UNSIGNED ARTICLE IN A REFERENCE BOOK

"Tharp, Twyla." *Who's Who of American Women.* 27th ed. 2008–2009. Print.

19. A GOVERNMENT DOCUMENT

National Commission on Terrorist Attacks upon the United States. *The 9/11 Commission Report: Final Report of the National Commission on Terrorist Attacks on the United States.* Washington: GPO, 2004. Print.

20. PUBLISHED PROCEEDINGS OF A CONFERENCE

Sass, Steven A., and Robert K. Triest. *Social Security Reform: Conference Proceedings: Links to Saving, Investment and Growth.* Boston: Fed. Reserve Bank of Boston, 1997. Print.

21. A TRANSLATION

Giroud, Françoise. *Marie Curie: A Life*. Trans. Lydia Davis. New York: Holmes, 1986. Print.

22. A SACRED TEXT

The Oxford Annotated Bible with the Apocrypha. Ed. Herbert G. May and Bruce M. Metzger. New York: Oxford University UP, 1965. Print. Rev. Standard Vers.

Qur'an: The Final Testament (Authorized English Version) with Arabic Text. Trans. Rashad Khalifa. Fremont: Universal Unity, 2000. Print.

23. A BOOK WITH A TITLE IN ITS TITLE

Habich, Robert D. *Transcendentalism and the* Western Messenger: *A History of the Magazine and Its Contributors, 1835–1841*. Rutherford, NJ: Fairleigh Dickinson UP, 1985. Print.

24. A BOOK PUBLISHED BEFORE 1900

Field, Kate. *The History of Bell's Telephone*. London, 1878. Print.

25. AN UNPUBLISHED DISSERTATION

Beins, Agatha. *Free Our Sisters, Free Ourselves: Feminism through Feminist Periodicals, 1970–1983*. Diss. Rutgers University, 2011. Print.

26. A PUBLISHED DISSERTATION

Schottler, Beverly A. *A Handbook for Dealing with Plagiarism in Public Schools*. Diss. Kansas State U, 2003. Ann Arbor: UMI, 2004. Print.

Sample Entries: Articles in Periodicals

When citing articles in periodicals, provide the following general categories of information:

Author's last name, first name. "Article title."
Periodical Title Volume (Date): Inclusive pages.
Print.

Entries illustrating variations on this basic format appear
below and are numbered to facilitate reference.

27. A SIGNED ARTICLE FROM A DAILY NEWSPAPER

Green, Penelope. "The Slow Life Picks Up Speed." *New York
Times* 31 Jan. 2008. Natl. ed.: D+, Print.

28. AN UNSIGNED ARTICLE FROM A DAILY NEWSPAPER

"Sunnis Worry of Future in New Shiite-run Iraq." *Chicago Tri-
bune* 13 Feb. 2005, sec. 1: 16. Print.

29. AN ARTICLE FROM A MONTHLY OR BIMONTHLY MAGAZINE

Fallows, James. "Dirty Coal, Clean Future." *Atlantic Monthly*
Dec. 2010: 64–78. Print.

30. AN ARTICLE FROM A WEEKLY OR BIWEEKLY MAGAZINE

Als, Hilton. "Queen Jane, Approximately." *The New Yorker*
9 May 2011: 54–63. Print.

31. AN ARTICLE IN A JOURNAL WITH CONTINUOUS PAGINATION

Flower, Linda. "Intercultural Inquiry and the Transformation
of Service." *College English* 65 (2002): 181–201. Print.

32. AN ARTICLE IN A JOURNAL THAT NUMBERS PAGES IN EACH ISSUE SEPARATELY

Madden, Thomas F. "Revisiting the Crusades." *Wilson Quarterly* 26.4 (2002): 100–03. Print.

33. AN EDITORIAL

"Poverty and Health." Editorial. *Washington Post* 31 Aug. 2004: A20. Print.

34. A REVIEW

Kolbert, Elizabeth. "America's Top Parent." Rev. of *Battle Hymn of the Tiger Mother*, by Amy Chua. *The New Yorker* 31 Jan. 2011: 70–73. Print.

35. AN ARTICLE WHOSE TITLE CONTAINS A QUOTATION OR A TITLE WITHIN QUOTATION MARKS

DeCuir, Andre L. "Italy, England and the Female Artist in George Eliot's 'Mr. Gilfil's Love-Story.'" *Studies in Short Fiction* 29 (1992): 67–75. Print.

36. AN ABSTRACT FROM *DISSERTATION ABSTRACTS OR DISSERTATION ABSTRACTS INTERNATIONAL*

Creek, Mardena Bridges. "Myth, Wound, Accommodation: American Literary Responses to the War in Vietnam." *DAI* 43 (1982): 3539A. Print.

Sample Entries: Miscellaneous Print and Nonprint Sources

37. FILMS; RADIO AND TELEVISION PROGRAMS

The King's Speech. Dir. Tom Hooper. Perf. Colin Firth, Geoffrey Rush, and Helena Bonham Carter. Momentum, 2010. Film.

"New York, New York (1944–1951)." *Leonard Bernstein—An American Life.* Prods. Steve Rowland and Larry Abrams. NPR. WBST, Muncie. 18 Jan. 2005. Radio.

"Seeds of Destruction." *Slavery and the Making of America.*
Prod. Clara Gazit. PBS. WNET, New York. 16 Feb. 2005.
Television.

38. PERFORMANCES

The Producers. By Mel Brooks. Dir. Susan Stroman. Perf.
Nathan Lane and Matthew Broderick. St. James Theater,
New York. 8 Oct. 2002. Performance.

Spano, Robert, cond. *Wagner, Mendelssohn, Wyner and Haydn.*
Concert. Boston Symphony Orch. Symphony Hall, Boston.
17 Feb. 2005. Performance.

39. RECORDINGS

Mozart, Wolfgang A. *Cosi Fan Tutte.* Perf. Kiri Te Kanawa,
Frederica von Stade, David Rendall, and Philippe Huttenlo-
chen. Cond. Alain Lombard. Strasbourg Philharmonic Orch.
LP. RCA, 1978.

McKenna, Lori. *Lorraine.* Signature Sounds, 2011. CD.

40. WORKS OF ART

Botticelli, Sandro. *Giuliano de' Medici.* 1478–1480. Tempera
on panel. Samuel H. Kress Collection. Natl. Gallery of Art,
Washington.

Rodin, Auguste. *The Gates of Hell.* 1880–1917. Sculpture.
Rodin Museum, Paris.

41. INTERVIEWS

Obama, Barack. "Obama in Command: The Rolling Stone
Interview." By Jann Wenner. *Rolling Stone* 28 Sep, 2010:
36–46. Print.

Martone, Michael. Telephone interview. 6 Jan. 2005.

Patterson, Annette. E-mail interview. 16 Feb. 2005.

42. MAPS AND CHARTS

Wine Country Map. Map. Napa Valley: Wine Zone, 2004. Print.

43. CARTOONS AND ADVERTISEMENTS

Lynch, Mike. Cartoon. *Chronicle Review* 18 Feb. 2005: B17. Print.

Lufthansa. Advertisement. *New Yorker* 11 Oct. 2004: 27. Print.

44. LECTURES, SPEECHES, AND ADDRESSES

Greenfield, Jeff. "In the News with Jeff Greenfield: A Political Analysis." 92nd Street Y. New York. 12 April 2009. Lecture.

Scholes, Robert. "The Presidential Address." MLA Convention. Philadelphia. 29 Dec. 2004. Address.

45. PUBLISHED AND UNPUBLISHED LETTERS

Fitzgerald, F. Scott. "To Ernest Hemingway." 1 June 1934. *The Letters of F. Scott Fitzgerald*. Ed. Andrew Turnbull. New York: Scribner's, 1963, 308–10. Print.

Stowe, Harriet Beecher. Letter to George Eliot. 25 May 1869. Berg Collection. New York Public Lib., New York. Print.

Sample Entries: Web Publications

MLA style for Web publications resembles the MLA format for print publications in most respects except for

(1) marking the medium of publication (for example, Web) and (2) including the user's date of access. In the past, MLA has required the inclusion of the URL (uniform resource locator) in each citation. But a URL may have more information than readers need and may be so long and complex that it invites transcription errors. Readers are more likely to find sources on the Web by searching for titles, authors' names, or key words. For that reason, MLA no longer requires the inclusion of the URLs in entries of Works Cited. But because Web documents are periodically updated, MLA requires that you supply the date of access—that is, the date you viewed the document. The date of access should be placed at the end of each entry.

Although MLA no longer requires URLs, you may decide to include them because you suspect your readers will have difficulty finding some of your sources or your instructor requires them. If you include a URL, place it directly after the date of access. Enclose the URL in angle brackets: <and>. For lengthy and complex URLs, give enough information about the path so that your readers can locate the exact page to which you are referring from the search page of the site or database. If you need to break the URL, at the end of a line, do so only after a slash, and do not add punctuation or hyphens that are not in the original URL.

When citing information from a Web publication, provide the following general categories of information:

> **Author's last name, first name. "Article title"** or *Book Title.* **Publication information for any printed version. Or subject line of forum or discussion group.** *Title of overall Web site.* **Version or edition used. Publisher or sponsor of site; if not available, use N.p. Date of publication; if nothing is available, use n.d. Medium of publication (Web). Date of Access.**

CHAPTER 9 USING AND DOCUMENTING SOURCES

46. A PROFESSIONAL HOME PAGE

Council on Undergraduate Research. Web. 26 Jan. 2012.

47. AN ACADEMIC DEPARTMENT HOME PAGE

Department of English. Ball State U. Web. 3 April 2011.

48. A PERSONAL HOME PAGE

Neville, Susan. Home page. Web. 1 April 2012.

49. AN ONLINE BOOK (AVAILABLE IN PRINT)

Anderson, Sherwood. *Winesburg, Ohio.* New York: Huebsch, 1919. *Google Book Search.* Web. 17 Mar. 2012.

50. AN ONLINE POEM

Dickinson, Emily. "success is counted sweetest." *The Complete Poems.* Boston: Little, Brown, 1924. *Bartelby.com.* Web. 31 Mar. 2012.

51. AN ARTICLE IN A SCHOLARLY JOURNAL

Bloom, Lynn Z. "Consuming Prose: The Delectable Rhetoric of Food Writing." *College English* 70.4 (2008): 346–61. *National Council of Teachers of English.org.* Web. 17 Feb. 2012.

52. AN ARTICLE IN A REFERENCE DATABASE

"Jasper Johns." *Encyclopædia Britannica Online.* Encyclopædia Britannica. 2008. Web. 9 Mar. 2012.

53. AN ARTICLE IN A MAGAZINE

Davison, Peter. "Robert Frost and 'The Road Not Taken.'" *The Atlantic.com.* Atlantic Monthly Group. 26 Mar. 2009. Web. 28 Mar. 2012.

54. A POSTING TO A DISCUSSION GROUP (WITH URL)

Inman, James. "Re: Technologist." Online posting. 24 Sept. 1997. *Alliance for Computers in Writing.* 27 Feb. 2005 <acw-l@unicorn.acs.ttu.edu>.

55. A PERSONAL E-MAIL MESSAGE

Johnson, Alfred B. "Audio Interactive Awards." Message to James W. Miles. 14 Feb. 2005. E-mail.

USING NOTES

In MLA style, notes (preferably endnotes) are reserved for two specific purposes.

1. **To supply additional commentary on the information in the text**

   Thurber's reputation continued to grow until the 1950s, when he was forced to give up drawing because of his blindness.[1]

   Note

   [1]Thurber's older brother accidently shot him in the eye with an arrow when they were children, causing the immediate loss of that eye. He gradually lost the sight of the other eye because of complications from the accident and a cataract.

2. **To list (and perhaps evaluate) several sources or to refer readers to additional sources**

   The argument that American policy in Vietnam was on the whole morally justified has come under attack from many quarters.[1]

   Note

   [1] For a useful sampling of opinion, see Draper 32 and Nardin and Slater 437.

Notice that the sources cited in this note are documented like parenthetical references, and the note itself directs readers to the complete citation in the list of works cited.

Works Cited

Draper, Theodore. "Ghosts of Vietnam." *Dissent* 26 (1979): 30–41. Print

Nardin, Terry, and Jerome Slater. "Vietnam Revisited." *World Politics* 33 (1981): 436–48. Print

As illustrated above, a note is signaled with a superscript numeral (a numeral raised above the line) typed at an appropriate place in the text (most often at the end of a sentence, after the period). The note itself, identified by a matching number followed by a space, appears at the end of the text (an endnote) or at the bottom of the page (a footnote). MLA recommends that you keep notes to a minimum so your readers are not distracted from your main point.

ANNOTATED STUDENT RESEARCH PAPER

The author of the following research paper uses many features of MLA style to document her paper. At her instructor's request, she submitted a final version of her thesis and outline. Adhering to MLA style, she did not include a title page with her outline or paper. Instead, she typed her name, her instructor's name, the course title and the date on separate lines (double spacing between lines) at the upper left margin. Then after double-spacing again, she typed the title of her paper, double-spaced, and started the first line of her text. On page 1 and successive pages, she typed her last name and the page number in the upper right-hand corner, as recommended by MLA.

Tricia Johnson[1]

Mr. Smith

English 104

6 May 2011

Pixel or Pages: The Textbook Debate

Thesis: Although there has been much discussion
about how digital media may affect the future of
books, educators see many possibilities for the marriage of print and digital texts in the classroom.

   I. Digital textbooks are flexible

     A. Digital textbooks are easy to use

     B. Digital textbooks can transmit content on
       multiple platforms

     C. Digital textbooks can be customized for use
       in individual classrooms

  II. Digital textbooks are inexpensive

     A. Digital textbooks are cheaper than tradi-
       tional textbooks

     B. Digital databases contain free material

 III. Digital textbooks encourage the development
    of real world skills

     A. Digital media is the common medium in
       corporate culture

     B. Educators need to close the gap between
       academic and corporate culture

[1] "Pixels or Pages: The Textbook Debate" from Trimmer MLA Guide.
Reprinted with permission.

IV. Digital media is unstable

  A. Students must continually upgrade their technology

  B. Instructors question the reliability of digital sources

V. Traditional print textbooks have significant advantages

  A. Students read faster when reading on a page

  B. Students read with more comprehension when reading on a page

  C. Students read with less engagement when reading online

  D. Students form sentimental attachments to books.

VI. The marriage of traditional print textbooks and digital textbooks enriches the educational experience

  A. Students can still obtain print copies of books

  B. Students can read old print manuscripts in digital format

  C. Students use digital and print texts for different purposes.

  D. Students find value in the inclusion of both mediums in the classroom.

  E. Students need to focus on the content of the text rather than its format

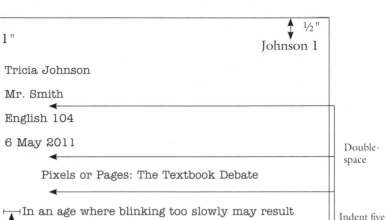

½"

1"

Johnson 1

Tricia Johnson

Mr. Smith

English 104

6 May 2011

Double-
space

Pixels or Pages: The Textbook Debate

In an age where blinking too slowly may result

Indent five
spaces or
one-half inch

in missing the new generation of iPhone, methods

for understanding and communicating information

are rapidly changing to accommodate and utilize

new technologies. While 'text' is used to mean

words on a page, the onset of the Internet has

created new ways to communicate through digi-

tal texts like e-books and online articles, newspa-

pers, and blogs. Multimodal texts, or media which

combines multiple sensory elements, also begin to

play a larger role as video, games, and social net-

working become part of how people connect and

converse. For students, teachers, and universi-

ties, the increasing importance of electronic media

presents a new range of problems and promises.

Although there has been much discussion about

how digital media may affect the future of books,

educators see many possibilities for the marriage

of print and digital texts in the classroom.

    One of the types of digital text most interest-

ing to students is the e-textbook, whose flexibility

1"

1 "

½ "

Johnson 2

makes it a favorite for individual and classroom use. When asked why he enjoys reading digital

Documentation: Personal interview.

texts, student Chris Dibble pointed to how easy his e-textbooks are to use: "I enjoy being able to access my texts anywhere without carrying extra materials with me. . . . It's too much hassle to find and rent print sources when everything available in print is available online." This adaptability to student needs and classroom situations makes e-textbooks a smart choice for teachers. They can transmit content to students via multiple mediums, such as wireless connections, e-mail, websites, flash drives, and CD-ROMS and in most classroom settings, even with a limited number of e-readers or computers (Cavanaugh 5). In fact, some publishers are beginning to offer "custom textbooks," or digital texts suited exactly to an instructor's individual course; custom textbooks draw from many separate sources, including relevant book chapters, scholarly articles, lecture notes, or data

Documentation: Paraphrasing of electronic source.

and research (Acker). Because they can compile large amounts of information in one place, one computer loaded with e-textbooks can do the work of a heavy, cumbersome backpack full of traditional books, enabling students to avoid strained muscles, and helping instructors avoid the hassle of requesting multiple textbooks in order to teach only a few specific chapters.

1"   ½"

Johnson 3

E-books also often list at prices competitive with or much below print textbooks. Because e-texts are so inexpensive, many students find them an appealing alternative to print. This year, the Grossmont College Library reported students often save forty to fifty percent off the list price of a new print book when buying a new e-book ("Traditional Textbooks vs. eTextbooks—Which Is Right for You?"). Some digital texts may even be available for much less through the internet. Thanks to online text repositories like Project Gutenberg, digital copies of more than 10,000 works of public domain literature are available for free (Cavanaugh 15).

Since electronic texts are so easy to attain, many instructors have jumped on new media as a way to engage students and pioneer learning techniques relevant to the real world. Researchers Eric Klopfer, Scot Osterweil, Jennifer Groff, and Jason Haas of the Massachusetts Institute for Technology advocate use of the electronic media they see in corporate settings—such as PricewaterhouseCoopers' use of a game featuring an outer space mining company to teach its employees about derivatives—in the classroom. They believe that using real world technologies like games,

Documentation: Citing a college website.

Documentation: Citing names of authors to introduce quotation.

Johnson 4

simulations, and social networking will help to make instruction relevant in ways it hasn't been before:

> Undoubtedly, without these recent technologies (i.e. digital games, Web 2.0, etc.) in the classroom, strong lessons can still be achieved, but there's a sharp disconnect between the way students are taught in school and the way the outside world approaches socialization, meaning-making, and accomplishment. It is critical that education not only seek to mitigate this disconnect in order to make these two 'worlds' more seamless, but of course also to leverage the power of these emerging technologies for instructional gain. (3)

They share the social networking experiment of high school literature teacher John as an example of the power of new media in the classroom. John set up an account on the networking site Ning to post files for assigned readings, relevant hyperlinks and videos, and a discussion board to talk about assignments. After only a short period of use, John was thrilled by the results, reporting that the literature discussions were "so popular that many of his students would check into them to see if anything what was happening, even though

Marginal notes:

Quotation: Long quotation of more than four lines set off from text and *not* placed with quotation marks.

Quotation: Incorporating short quotation into writer's own sentence.

1"

½"

Johnson 5

John hadn't specifically posted an assignment or activity" (12). As society becomes increasingly tech-savvy, digital media and the e-textbook are increasingly relevant new resources for students and instructors.

Although electronic media provides many benefits impossible with traditional print text, it also suffers from instability. While users are often asked to invest a substantial amount of money for an e-reading platform, many e-readers rapidly upgrade their technology. For example, Amazon has released four versions of the Kindle e-reader since its initial release four years ago, not to mention the updated Kindle 2 international version, Kindle DX, Kindle DX international version, and Kindle DX Graphite ("Kindle Facts and Figures (History & Specs)"; "Kindle Store"). While these rapid improvements mean better products for consumers, they also result in products that soon become obsolete and need to be replaced at additional cost.

Documentation: Citing two sources.

While e-readers and other technology continue to change at a break-neck pace, books in print require only one purchase and can be kept for years, even a lifetime, without becoming outdated. The relatively recent medium of digital publishing also suffers from a lack of authority and credibility necessary for scholarly acceptance. Student Rachel Brickley articulates the perception of many

½"

1"

Johnson 6

Quotation:
Using sentence
and colon to
introduce short
quotation.

students in regards to online information: "Books
are much safer for research, even if they aren't
as easy to get. I feel that I don't have to verify as
much whether the text is legitimate with books."

In his article, "Temptation, Trash, and Trust:
The Authorship and Authority of Digital Texts,"

Documentation:
Using both
paraphrase and
quotation to cite
same source.

Sian Bayne conducted many similar student interviews and found digital texts carry a stigma of
untruthfulness: "The tendency in digital text for
the speaker, or author, to be displaced from his
or her central position—to be ambiguous, marginal,
collective or anonymous - translated for inter-
viewees into a general distrust of the veracity of
text on the Internet" (20). When discussing online
sources, the students Bayne interviewed referred
to much of the information available as "trash"
and "rubbish" (21) and, rather than being granted
authorship, creators of digital content are "just
publishing their ideas up" (22). Because it is often
not apparent whether digital information has been
thoroughly screened for value in the same way the
print publishing system ensures, readers tend to
be guarded about endowing online sources, sometimes even legitimate ones, with the same automatic trust they give to books (Bayne 24).

Traditional textbooks also provide significant
advantages in reading speed, comprehension,
engagement, and student connection to text.

½"

1"

Johnson 7

A 2008 Stanford Center for Teaching and Learn-

ing report compiled research findings about the

difference between reading print and online texts,

demonstrating that print reading has many unique

benefits for students. For example, the report

found that research participants in a Nielsen 2008

study read ten to thirty percent slower when read-

ing online as opposed to reading from a page (1).

The document also reports the findings of O'Hara

and Sellin's 1997 study, demonstrating that print

readers followed the text's format seamlessly,

often using their finger as a guide or making out-

lines, while text navigation for online readers was

"slow, laborious, and detracted from reading" (2).

Edward Walton's 2007 study of reactions to digi-

tal text found that students often read e-texts with

less engagement than they might have with print

because of the inherent searchability of electronic

content: " . . . since the e-book system facilitates

locating desired terms in a collection of e-books,

and the reader can bypass the author's structured

arguments to read only a sentence or two of the

'pertinent' section, little if any critical thinking

has occurred" (95). Though digital text may seem

convenient to students, Walton wonders whether

the ease with which students can keyword search

might make the caliber of their work suffer rather

than improve: "how much does the reader read

1"

½"

Johnson 8

before quoting an author as supporting their position, and does the author actually support the reader's argument?" (95) Many readers also form a sentimental connection to books in print, feeling that the experience of holding a book carries special value. Student Samantha Roderick finds a physical connection to print that she doesn't with digital texts: "I like the smell of books, and I know it's not related to how the text is read, but I just do. Books have a certain feel, a warmth to them; I feel more wrapped up in the warmth of the book when I'm reading it. The computer seems cold."

Although some researchers and scholars believe that electronic media is a detriment to print culture, others believe that it can enrich, rather than harm, the educational experience. In his article on the changing format of university libraries, Timothy W. Luke urges librarians to measure the benefits of digital text against the prospect of a world without print texts: "One is left . . . to judge between the possibilities of profound loss and immeasurable gain as e-textuality spreads" (209). However, the debate about whether to adopt digital or print texts may actually be best solved by instituting a combination of both. Prominent book historian Robert Darnton does not see a conflict between print and digital texts. In his book *The Case for Books: Past, Present, and Future,* he reassures those worried about the end of print that books

Documentation: Personal interview.

Documentation: Citing book title to identify source.

1"

and electronic media can coexist peacefully, and even benefit each other:

> . . . its [the book's] past bodes well for its future, because libraries were never warehouses of books. They have always been and always will be centers of learning. Their central position in the world of learning makes them ideally suited to mediate between the printed and the digital modes of communication. (xvi)

The combined use of print and digital texts allows university libraries to offer more options to student patrons than ever before. These "cybraries" can include many electronic copies of a single print document, and make old manuscripts available to the public in digital form, along with preserving the print text (Luke 202). Walton's 2007 study also suggests both mediums should be employed in university libraries; his research shows that students utilize e-books for research and are receptive to e-textbooks, but they still prefer print books as the main format for extended reading (97). Walton concludes that both mediums must be retained to serve student needs: "For academic libraries evaluating the possibility of adding e-books to their collections, they must face the reality that e-books will not replace the need for purchasing books" (98).

Just as students find merit in both electronic and print texts in the library, they also benefit from instructors who employ both mediums in the

Documentation: Summarizing main argument of sources.

1"

½"

Johnson 10

classroom. Student Ethan Johnson believes electronic interaction augments his learning experience: "We do an online discussion where every day you have to write about the topic online even before you get in class, so the instructor can shape the discussion in the next class in response to the online discussion." Andrew Arnett, another student, says the electronic supplement that came with his textbook helps him understand and retain information when used in conjunction with his reading: "I use the games and lesson reviews on the textbook CD after I read the book. I guess you could just read the book or just look at the CD, but it's better together. I get all the info best from the text, and then I feel like I remember it better when I do the extra exercises on the CD."

Ultimately, the importance of books and digital media lies not in its format, but in the text itself. Text, when reduced to its barest form, is simply information. Whether read in a book, viewed on a screen, or watched in a video, it facilitates discussion and the sharing of knowledge and ideas between people—ideas with the potential to change the world. Combined use of print and electronic media offers opportunities for vital, dynamic discourse connecting people around the globe in a way unprecedented to this point in history. Presented with the gift of knowledge, text, in its many forms, provides students, teachers, and society at large with an abundance of resources.

Johnson 11

Works Cited

Acker, Stephen R. "Will Digital Texts Succeed?"

Campus Technology 21.7 (2008): 54-56.

ERIC. EBSCO. Web. 1 May 2011.

Arnett, Andrew, Personal interview. 17 April

2011.

Bayne, Sian. "Temptation, Trash and Trust: The

Authorship and Authority of Digital Texts."

E-Learning 3.1 (2006): 16–26. ERIC. EBSCO.

Web. 1 May 2011.

Brickley, Rachel. Personal interview. 21 April

2011.

Cavanaugh, Terence W. *The Digital Reader: Using

E-Books in K-12 Education.* Eugene, OR:

International Society for Technology in Edu-

cation, 2006. Print.

Center for Teaching and Learning. "Brief Sum-

mary of Online Reading vs. Print Reading."

Senate of the Academic Council. Stanford

University. Fall 2008. Web. 17 April 2011.

Darnton, Robert. *The Case for Books: Past, Pres-

ent, and Future.* New York: PublicAffairs,

2009 Print.

Dibble, Christopher. Personal interview. 25 April

2011.

Johnson, Ethan. Personal interview. 22 April

2011.

Double space

Indent five spaces

Sample entry: A book by one author

Medium of publication

1 "   ↕ ½ "
                                              Johnson 12

"Kindle Facts and Figures (History & Specs)."
    Website Monitoring Blog. Siteimpulse, 4
    Nov. 2010. Web. 5 May 2011.

Medium of
publication ——— "Kindle Store." *Amazon, com.* Amazon.com, 2011.
    Web. 5 May 2011.

Klopfer, Eric, Scot Osterweil, Jennifer Groff, and
    Jason Haas. "The Instructional Power of Dig-
    ital Games, Social Networking, Simulations,
    and How Teachers Can Leverage Them."
    The Education Arcade. Massachusetts Insti-
    tute of Technology. 2009. Web. 3 May 2011.

Date of Access ———
Luke, Timothy W. "The Politics and Philosophy of
    E-text: Use Value, Sign Value, and Exchange
    Value in the Transition from Print to Digi-
    tal Media." *Libr@ries: Changing Information
    Space and Practice.* Ed. Cushla Kapitzke and
    Bertram C. Bruce. Mahwah, NJ: Lawrence,
    2006. 197-210. Print.

Roderick, Samantha. Personal interview. 17 April
    2011.

"Traditional Textbooks vs. eTextbooks—Which Is
    Right for You?" *Grossmont College Library.*
    Grossmont College. n.d. Web. 3 May 2011.

Sample entry:
An article on ——— Walton, Edward W. "Faculty and Student Percep-
a website
    tions of Using E-Books in a Small, Academic
    Institution." American Libraries. American
    Library Association. April 2007. Web. 3
    May 2011.

RHETORICAL GLOSSARY

abstract terms Terms that refer to qualities or characteristics we can conceive of mentally but cannot see, touch, or hear—for example, *bravery, laziness, perseverance*. Writers often illustrate such terms with examples to help readers grasp their significance. See also **concrete terms**.

accommodation Sometimes called "nonthreatening argument." The arrangement of evidence in such a way that all parties believe their position has received a fair hearing.

active reading A manner of reading in which one reads intently and consciously, simultaneously reading for meaning and being aware of one's responses to content and style. An active reader often reads with a pencil, underlining important phrases or sentences and writing notes in the margin.

allusion A reference to a person, event, or story familiar to the reader and that will enrich the writer's meaning because it draws on shared knowledge with the reader.

analogy A comparison between two things or concepts that share certain characteristics although in most ways they are not similar.

analysis The process that divides something into its parts to understand the whole more clearly.

annotate To make notes or comments about a piece of writing.

appeals Strategies used in persuasion and argument. Although most arguments combine different kinds of appeals, many rely on one dominant appeal to make a compelling case.

    emotional appeal A strategy that appeals to feelings, relying heavily on figurative language and provocative imagery to persuade readers.

    ethical appeal A strategy that appeals to the character (or *ethos*) of the writer, relying on the writer's reputation and competence to persuade readers.

    logical appeal A strategy that appeals to reason, relying on factual evidence, expert testimony, and logic to persuade readers.

argument A piece of writing or an oral presentation in which an author or speaker seeks to persuade an audience to accept a proposition or an opinion by giving reasons and evidence. An argument does not necessarily involve

609

controversy or anger; often it is simply a statement that presents a claim or a particular point of view.

assumption Something taken for granted, presumed to be true without need for further explanation or proof. Writers usually make the assumption that their readers have certain knowledge and experiences that they can count on as they present their arguments.

audience The readers for whom a piece of writing is intended. That audience may be close or distant, a small group or a large number, popular or specialized. Professional writers nearly always tailor their writing toward a particular audience about whom they know a good deal—for example, the readers of the *New York Times* or *Parade*—and they adapt their vocabulary and style to suit that audience.

audience analysis Questions that help identify the writer's audience: (1) Who am I writing for? (2) What do they expect of me? (3) What knowledge do they already have? (4) What kind of evidence and strategies are they most likely to respond to?

brainstorming A way of generating ideas and material for writing by thinking about a topic intently and jotting down random thoughts as they occur to you without regard to whether they seem immediately useful and relevant.

cause and effect A mode of writing that explains or persuades by analyzing cause-and-effect relationships.

central pattern The dominant mode of exposition in an essay. Most writers use more than one expository pattern when they construct an essay.

ceremonial discourse An argument, usually presented orally on special occasions, that appeals to the audience's pride, loyalty, and compassion.

claims and warrants Often called the Toulmin argument after Stephen Toulmin, the legal philosopher who analyzed and defined its terminology. A method of arranging evidence in an argument that begins by asserting a *claim* (or general assertion), then presents evidence to support that claim, and provides a *warrant* (or justification) that links the claim to the evidence.

classification and division A method of organizing an explanation or argument by dividing a topic into distinct parts or classes and discussing the characteristics of those classes.

comparison and contrast A popular and convenient way of organizing an essay or article to highlight important ways in which two things or processes can be similar yet different.

concept A broad intellectual notion that captures the essential nature of an idea, system, or process—for example, the concept of affirmative action or the concept of intellectual property.

conclusion The final paragraph or section of an essay that brings the argument or explanation to appropriate closure and leaves the reader feeling that the author has dealt with all the issues or questions he or she has raised.

concrete terms Terms that refer to something specific and tangible that can be perceived through the senses—for example, *rocky, sizzling, bright yellow*. See also **abstract terms**.

connotation The added psychological and emotional associations that certain words and phrases carry in addition to their simple meaning. For instance, words like *liberty* and *individualism* carry heavily positive connotations in our culture; they may carry negative connotations in a culture that puts great value on tradition and discipline.

critical reading Questioning and analyzing content while reading in order to judge the truth, merit, and general quality of an essay or article. A critical reader might ask, What is the source of the author's information? What evidence does he cite in support of his claim? or, What organization or special interest might she be affiliated with?

deduction Usually identified with classical reasoning, or the *syllogism*. A method of arranging evidence that begins with a *major premise*, is restricted by a *minor premise*, and ends with a *conclusion*.

definition A type of essay that identifies and gives the qualities of a person, object, institution, pattern of behavior, or political theory in a way that highlights its special characteristics.

denotation The specific, exact meaning of a word, independent of its emotional associations.

description A kind of factual writing that aims to help the reader visualize and grasp the essential nature of an object, an action, a scene, or a person by giving details that reveal the special characteristics of that person or scene.

diction The selection of words to form a desired effect. To achieve this effect, writers consider words from various levels of usage—*popular, learned, colloquial,* and *slang*—and vary words that have appropriate *denotations* and *connotations.*

discovery draft The first draft of an essay. In a discovery draft, writers expect to discover something new about their purpose, audience, and strategies.

division and classification See **classification and division**.

documentation A system used for giving readers information about where the writer found the sources he or she used in an academic or research paper or a technical report. Writers document their sources by inserting footnotes, endnotes, or in-text citations so a reader who wants to know more about the topic can easily find the article or book the author is citing or track down other related articles by the same author. The most common system writers use for documentation in academic papers in writing classes is Modern Language Association (MLA) style.

draft A preliminary version of a piece of writing that enables the author to get started and develop an idea as he or she writes. Authors often write and revise several drafts before they are satisfied with a piece of writing.

editing Small-scale changes in a piece of writing that is close to being complete. Editing may involve changing some word choices, checking for correct spelling and punctuation, eliminating repetition, rearranging sentences or paragraphs, and generally polishing a manuscript into final form before submitting it to an instructor or editor.

essay An article or short nonfiction composition that focuses on a specific topic or theme. An essay is generally analytical, speculative, or interpretive. Thus a news story would not be an essay, but an opinion piece could be.

evidence Specific kinds of information that support the claims of an argument. The most common forms of evidence are:

facts Specific, detailed evidence—often reported in numbers—that is difficult to refute.

judgments Conclusions that are inferred from facts. Judgments lend credibility to an argument because they result from careful reasoning.

testimony Statements that affirm or assert facts. *Eyewitness testimony* enables a person who has had direct experience with an event to report what he or she saw. *Expert witness testimony* enables a recognized authority on a subject to present facts and judgments.

example A specific incident, object, or anecdote used to illustrate and support a claim or expand on an assertion or generalization. Skillful writers know that readers expect and need examples to clarify a statement, develop a thesis sentence, or support an opening assertion.

figurative language Language that uses vivid and sometimes fanciful comparisons to enliven and enrich prose. Such language often takes the form of metaphors that explain an unfamiliar thing or process by comparing it to a familiar thing.

focus As a verb, to concentrate or emphasize; as a noun, the point of concentration or emphasis. Skillful writers know how to focus their writing on a single central idea or point; they have learned to "write more about less," to narrow their topic down to one that they can explore fully and enrich with details.

free-writing A way to generate ideas for an essay or article by writing down whatever comes to mind about a topic, without concern for organization or style. In free-writing, work quickly to capture ideas. Don't stop to consider whether a phrase or sentence is pertinent or useful—just get it down. After you accumulate a substantial amount of material, you can comb through it to find a starting point for your first draft.

generalization A broad statement that makes a general claim or an assertion without giving specific details or supporting evidence. Writers often begin an essay with a generalization and then use the next sentences and paragraphs to give details and information that expand on and support the generalization.

headnote A short introductory note before a piece of writing. For example, before each essay in *The River Reader* is a headnote about its author. Its purpose is to give you enough information about the author's age, cultural heritage, and education to put him or her in some cultural context and to give you a few other pertinent facts, such as what else he has written or where she has published other articles.

hypothesis A statement, created during *planning*, of a possible or working purpose for your writing.

image In writing, an impression or visual effect created by an author through the skillful use of language that appeals to the senses of sight and sound.

logic An intellectual system or process that uses reason and evidence to arrive at conclusions. Often writers not only construct a logical framework for their arguments, setting up cause-and-effect relationships or establishing a chain of reasoning, but also embellish the logic with some figurative and emotional language.

metaphor See **figurative language**.

mode A style or pattern of writing or discourse that has certain features that characterize it and make it distinctive. The essays in *The River Reader* are classified according to their mode: narration and description, process analysis, division and classification, definition, cause and effect, persuasion and argument, and so on. Often a writer combines two or three modes in an essay or article but emphasizes one dominant mode.

narration A mode of nonfiction writing that develops an idea or makes a point by telling a story or anecdote. The major strategy for fiction.

pace The rate at which an essay or article moves. Writers can create different paces through word choice, sentence length, and the selection of verbs.

paraphrase A passage that briefly restates in the writer's own words the content of a passage written by someone else, in such a way that it retains the original meaning.

persuasion The process of using language to get readers to accept opinions, beliefs, or points of view. The essays in the Persuasion and Argument chapter of *The River Reader* are the most strongly persuasive, but in an important sense, most essays tend to be persuasive.

plagiarism Using someone else's words or ideas without giving proper credit to the original author. Having another person write something that you turn in for credit—for instance, a term paper taken from the Internet or a commercial source—also constitutes plagiarism and can bring serious consequences.

planning The first stage in the writing purpose. A series of strategies designed to find and formulate information in writing. See **brainstorming** and **free-writing**.

plot The chain of events that develops a story, enabling a writer to put characters into a set of circumstances, describe their behavior, and show the consequences that ensue.

point of view The angle or perspective from which a story or account is told. An account in which the narrator uses "I" and gives an account of an event as it appeared to him or her is called *first-person* point of view. When the narrator recounts an incident as a detached but fully informed observer, he or she is using the *third-person omniscient* point of view.

purpose The goal of an author in a piece of writing. An author may wish to inform, to persuade, to explain, to support an assertion, or to entertain. Sometimes an author combines two or more of these purposes, but usually the author has a primary goal, one that should be evident to the reader.

quotation A passage that gives the actual words a speaker or writer has used in an article, book, speech, or conversation. Authors often use quotations to support their arguments. Such passages must always appear in quotation marks in academic papers or, indeed, in any writing done by a responsible author. Writers who fail to give proper credit for a quotation risk losing the respect of their readers or, in college, getting disciplined for plagiarism. You'll find the proper format for citing quotations in Chapter 9, "Using and Documenting Sources."

refute To counteract an argument or seek to disprove a claim or proposition.

response A reader's reaction to what he or she reads. Readers can respond in different ways—analytically, critically, emotionally, or approvingly—but in nearly every case, that response will come from their own experiences and background: what they know, where they grew up, what kind of culture they lived in, and so on. Readers look at an essay through the lens shaped by their own lives, and that lens affects what they see.

revising Making substantial changes in a written draft, changes that may involve narrowing the topic, adding or deleting material, rearranging sections, or rewriting the introduction or conclusion. Don't look at revising as a process of correcting a draft; rather, you develop your essay by the process of revising and often can clarify and strengthen your ideas by the process. Many writers revise an essay through three or four drafts.

strategy The means or tactic a writer uses to achieve his or her purpose. In the essays in *The River Reader,* authors use various strategies: narration and description, comparison and contrast, process analysis, cause and effect, and so on.

summary A passage that condenses the ideas and content of a long passage in a few sentences or paragraphs; a summary should be objective and accurate.

synthesis An essay that requires writers to incorporate sources, including images, to support an argument. Synthesis essays require the writer to synthesize or integrate these varied sources, particularly to evaluate, cite, and utilize the source material effectively. These researched synthesis essays help writers formulate informed arguments, as well as remind them that they must consider various interpretations to analyze, reflect on, and write about a given topic.

testimony Evidence offered in support of a claim or assertion. The term suggests factual statements given by experts or taken from sources such as historical or government records or from statistical data. Eyewitness accounts are frequently used as testimony.

thesis sentence A comprehensive sentence, usually coming in the first paragraph or so of an essay, that summarizes and previews the main idea the author is going to develop in the essay.

tone The emotional attitude toward their topic that authors convey in their writing. They create tone through the choices they make of words—particularly verbs—of sentence and paragraph length, of styles—formal or informal—and with the kinds of images and figurative language they use.

visual texts Texts that provide a pictorial method for displaying information. These representational graphics can add visual interest to your subject, illustrate complicated ideas with shapes and images, and provide powerful and dramatic evidence to support your purpose. The most common types of visual texts are as follows:

bar graphs The comparison of numerical data through vertical or horizontal bars.

diagrams The use of line drawings to outline, label, and identify various parts of an object, structure, or process.

flow charts The use of line drawings and text to illustrate the interaction and movement among various parts of an object, structure, or process.

line graphs The comparison of numerical data through lines that portray trends over time.

maps The representation of the features of an area by illustrating their form, size, and relationships.

pie charts The representation of the subdivisions of a subject as pieces of a pie designed to represent percentages. Taken together, these individual percentages add up to 100 percent.

works cited The list of references and sources that appears at the end of an academic paper or report that uses Modern Language Association (MLA) style; this list gives enough information about those sources to enable readers to evaluate them or use them for further research.

writing process The steps used in creating a piece of writing. While there is no single writing process that works for every writer or every writing task, writing specialists have found certain patterns when they analyze how most writers seem to work. They agree that productive writers tend to work through a series of steps in the process of creating an essay or article.

Stage 1: Planning. The process of discovering one's topic and generating material. Typical activities are reading and researching, brainstorming, free-writing, talking with fellow writers, and making rough preliminary outlines.

Stage 2: Drafting. Writing a first version of the paper that puts down ideas in some organized form. Many writers continue to generate ideas as they write and often write two or three drafts before they complete one they think is fairly satisfactory.

Stage 3: Revising and rewriting. Reviewing the completed first draft and making substantial changes, perhaps by narrowing the focus, reorganizing, adding and deleting material, or writing a new introduction or conclusion.

Stage 4: Editing, polishing, and proofreading. Making minor word changes, polishing style, and checking for spelling and typographical errors.

writing situation The context in which a piece of writing is created. Every piece of writing, from business memos to inaugural speeches, is created within some context. Its components are (1) the writer, (2) the topic, (3) the purpose, (4) the audience, and (5) the strategy. To figure out what your writing situation is for any particular assignment, ask yourself,

- What is my persona or role in this situation?
- What do I want to say?
- What is my purpose?
- Whom am I writing to or for?
- What strategy, or organization pattern, clarifies my purpose?

By working out an answer to each of these questions before you begin to write, you'll have a good start on turning out a focused and effective product.

CREDITS

617

618 CREDITS

620

CREDITS

renewed 1978 by Sonia Pitt-Rivers, reprinted by permission of Houghton Mifflin Harcourt Publishing Company and Bill Hamilton as the Literary Executor of the Estate of the Late Sonia Brownell Orwell and Secker & Warburg Ltd. All rights reserved.

ANNA QUINDLEN "Execution" from *Living Out Loud* by Anna Quindlen, copyright © 1987 by Anna Quindlen. Used by permission of Random House, Inc.

ANNE ROIPHE Reprinted by permission of International Creative Management, Inc. Copyright © 1995 by Anne Roiphe.

KRISTIE FERGUSON "The Scenic Route"—© Cengage Learning

SCOTT RUSSELL SANDERS Used with permission of Beacon Press, from Scott Russell Sanders, "Under the Influence" from *Secrets of the Universe: Scenes from the Journey Home* by Scott Russell Sanders, 1992; permission conveyed through Copyright Clearance Center, Inc.

DAVID SEDARIS From *Me Talk Pretty One Day* by David Sedaris. Copyright © 2000 by David Sedaris. By permission of Little, Brown and Company. All rights reserved.

AMY TAN Copyright © 1990 by Amy Tan. First appeared in THE THREEPENNY REVIEW. Reprinted by permission of the author and the Sandra Dijkstra Literary Agency.

JUDITH VIORST "The Truth About Lying" by Judith Viorst. Copyright © 1981 by Judith Viorst. Originally appeared in *Redbook*. Used by permission of The Choate Agency, LLC. All rights reserved.

LEWIS THOMAS "The Technology of Medicine," copyright © 1971 by The Massachusetts Medical Society, from *The Lives Of A Cell* by Lewis Thomas. Used by permission of Viking Penguin, a division of Penguin Group (USA), Inc.

JAMES THURBER The Art of Fiction No. 10. Interviewed by George Plimpton & Max Steele, *Writers at Work: The Paris Review Interviews.*

CALVIN TRILLIN "Comforting Thoughts" by Calvin Trillin. From *Enough's Enough*. Published by Ticknor & Fields. Copyright © 1988, 1990 by Calvin Trillin. Reprinted with permission of Lescher & Lescher, Ltd. All rights reserved.

PERSONAL INTERVIEW WITH CALVIN TRILLIN Reprinted with permission of the author and Lescher & Lescher, Ltd. All rights reserved.

MARK TWAIN "Two Views of the River" by Mark Twain.

KURT VONNEGUT JR. "Harrison Bergeron" from *Welcome to the Monkey House* by Kurt Vonnegut, Jr., copyright © 1961 by Kurt Vonnegut Jr. Used by permission of Dell Publishing, a division of Random House, Inc.

SARAH VOWELL Reprinted with the permission of Simon & Schuster, Inc., from *Partly Cloudy Patriot* by Sarah Vowell. Copyright © 2002 by Sarah Vowell. All rights reserved.

ALICE WALKER "Everyday Use" from *In Love & Trouble: Stories Of Black Women*, copyright © 1973 by Alice Walker, reprinted by permission of Houghton Mifflin Harcourt Publishing Company. All rights reserved.

SUBJECT INDEX

NAME INDEX